MATHEWS COUNTY, VIRGINIA

Lost Landscapes, Untold Stories

Martha W. McCartney

Published by the Mathews County Historical Society, Inc.
Hard cover ISBN: 978-0-692-55457-9
Soft cover ISBN: 978-0-692-55458-6
Library of Congress Control Number: 2015955019
Printed in the United States of America
The Dietz Press

Index compiled by Gregory J. Brown and Joe Brown

Dedicated to the people of Mathews County, especially my grandchildren, Madeleine, Laurel, and Nicholas Hobert

MATHEWS COUNTY, VIRGINIA

Map courtesy of Elizabeth O. Whitley.

TABLE OF CONTENTS

INTRODUCTION

Captain John Smith, who astutely observed that, "Geography without History seemeth as carkasse without motion," added that, "History without Geography wandereth as [a] vagrant without a certaine habitation." Smith's statement, though quaintly phrased, means that whenever a link is forged between history and geography, everything we know becomes much more meaningful. With that thought in mind, whenever possible the people and events described in this volume have been linked to the geographic settings with which they were associated.

Initially, major collections of historical maps were examined in an attempt to identify public roads, ferries, mills, churches, military sites, and other culturally-sensitive areas. The facsimiles and original maps utilized are in the collections maintained by the Colonial Williamsburg Foundation, the Library of Congress, the National Archives, the Virginia Historical Society, the Library of Virginia, the National Oceanic and Atmospheric Administration, the Virginia Department of Historic Resources, the University of North Carolina, and the Mathews Memorial Library. Maps in private collections also were consulted.

The names of some of Mathews County's more important tidal estuaries have changed over the centuries and in many instances, small streams that bore names in the seventeenth, eighteenth, and nineteenth centuries are now nameless. For example, the names of Isle of Wight, Ducking Pond, and Bennetts Creeks are now obsolete. Although some of the names by which various parts of Mathews County are known (for instance, Bandy Ridge and Crab Neck) are deeply rooted in the past, the location of Bear Mountain is less familiar. Therefore, for the sake of discussion, whenever possible the names of historic waterways and geographic features have been linked with their modern equivalents the first time the historic name appears. Some of the place names used in the twentieth and twenty-first centuries also have been subject to change. For example, in 1917 when the United States Geological Survey made a map of Mathews County, what we know as Burke Mill Branch, which forms part of the boundary line between Mathews and Gloucester Counties, was known as the North End Branch and what's now known as the North End Branch was identified as Morgan's Branch.

Mathews County sustained massive record losses in 1865 when Richmond burned, as did most of the other counties on the Middle and James-York peninsulas. However, the quantity and quality of Mathews County's surviving antebellum records tend to be underestimated, as do those of its antecedent, Gloucester County. Much useful information about Mathews County has been gleaned from the surviving records of Gloucester County. For example, Gloucester County Surveyors Plat Book A, which embraces the years 1733-1810, includes more than a dozen plats and sketches of land in Kingston Parish, acreage that lies within the boundaries of today's Mathews County. Of unique interest is a plat dating to 1733, which includes the boundary lines of a land patent that was issued in 1652. Quite remarkably, Surveyors Plat Book A also contains sketches of buildings that were in existence during the mid-eighteenth century, structures that have disappeared from Mathews County's cultural landscape. Adding to this body of knowledge are seventeenth and eighteenth century plats depicting land in Mathews County, drawings that are preserved in collections of private papers. Many of the plats drawn by Mathews County surveyors during the nineteenth century contain handsome sketches of the buildings that stood on local properties.

Land patents and grants provide us with the names of the European colonists who first acquired acreage in what became Mathews County. When patents are analyzed, it is often possible to track the spread of early European settlement and the gradual development of Mathews County's cultural landscape. This process also provides us with information on the Chiskiack Indians' landholdings and the tribe's movements within Mathews County. Patents for land on the upper side of the Piankatank River, in what is now Middlesex County, were examined because some of them make reference to properties located on the lower side of the river. The court records of Middlesex County, which are remarkably intact, also provided useful information on Mathews. Supplementary research was carried out in the court records of Old Rappahannock, York, Richmond, Westmoreland, and Elizabeth City Counties.

Because surnames often were spelled phonically and variations were common, especially during the seventeenth and eighteenth centuries when formal education was a rarity, the most frequently used version of a person's first and last names is listed first and less commonly used variations appear in parentheses. Whenever fathers and sons or mothers and daughters were known to share identical first and last names, a Roman numeral has been used to distinguish between the generations. The titles of clergy, royalty, and military officers have been provided the first time they are used.

Kingston Parish's colonial vestry books and the parish's register of vital records include information that most of us would consider secular. These ecclesiastical records, compiled while the Church of England was Virginia's State Church and enjoyed quasigovernmental status, provide us with many useful insights. For instance, the Kingston Parish register reveals that John Gwyn, the 15-year-old son of Humphrey and Frances Gwyn, perished in a boating accident on September 12, 1770. Other personal insights, such as the identification of children who were considered illegitimate, can be gleaned from the records compiled by parish officials. Unexpectedly, a microfilm of the Kingston Parish register was found to contain the names of almost 1,860 enslaved men, women, and children who were born, baptized, or died between 1746 and 1827. Moreover, it was discovered that several slaveholders who were members of Ware Parish and one family from Middlesex County, had their slaves baptized in Kingston Parish, probably because one of Kingston Parish's churches was more convenient. Conversely, the vestry book of Middlesex County's Christ Church Parish was found to yield information on certain residents of Kingston Parish. Interestingly, some blank pages in the back of a book in which Kingston Parish vestry records were kept from 1774 through 1798, contain notations by someone associated with the Billups family, who recorded his own business transactions and miscellaneous information. Included are some pages of Billups birth records and two pages on which are recorded the births of slaves during the 1820s and 1830s, plus a notation that Humphrey Cook, who was black, was born on March 6, 1790, at 10 p.m. Kingston Parish's vestry records that date from 1850 to 1938 were once preserved in Richmond at the headquarters of the Diocese of Virginia, but are not currently available.

Genealogist Ethel Watson White Legg Mason, better known as Polly Cary Mason, collected information on colonial Gloucester County and its descendant, Mathews County. Her research, which took her into the courthouses of counties throughout eastern Virginia and into numerous collections of private papers and overseas sources, culminated in publication of a remarkable two-volume set of abstracts that comprise an invaluable finding aid. Mrs. Mason completed the first volume of abstracts but died while working on the second volume. Her husband, George Carrington Mason, a noted church historian, completed her work and saw that it was published. However, on account of his involvement, the Richard Billups Papers that Polly Cary Mason utilized were split into two collections. The largest of these, preserved at the College of William and Mary in the Swem Library's Department of Special Collections, was given to the College by Mrs. W.R. Stoakes in 1941. It includes maps, plats, patents, and deeds that are intimately associated with Mathews County, along with merchants' accounts, and records of shipbuilding. Also in the collection at Swem are Mathews records associated with the War of 1812, records on the sale of the Kingston Parish glebe, a recipe for a purge, and directions for how to sharpen a file. The other set of Richard Billups Papers, given to the Virginia Historical Society by George Carrington Mason's executor, contains receipts, numerous plats, and other documents that were in his possession at the time of his death. Included are most of the records that Mr. Mason used when completing the second volume of his late wife's abstracts. There is a third collection of Billups Papers, those of John Billups, which is preserved at the Library of Virginia; it includes a list of Kingston Parish tithables in 1774.

Overseas records, particularly those of the British Archives, have been accessed through the use of online survey reports and microfilms available at the Colonial Williamsburg Foundation's Rockefeller Library. For example, records of the Naval Office were found to provide detailed information of the mercantile activities of Mathews' maritime community. Also useful were overseas documentary sources associated with Bacon's Rebellion and with the men and women who remained loyal to the British government during the American Revolution.

Records generated by the High Court of the Admiralty and the Naval Office led to the discovery that shipbuilding as an industry had commenced in Mathews by the late seventeenth century, whereas the *Journals of the Executive Council of Colonial Virginia* provide us with useful information on issues involving maritime law. Advertisements that appeared in the *Virginia Gazette* and other newspapers during the eighteenth and nineteenth centuries were used as a means of gathering information on local shipbuilding during the eighteenth and nineteenth centuries. Peter J. Wrike's master's thesis, available in the Mathews County Historical Society Archives and at the Old Dominion University Library, was useful in identifying Mathews County shipbuilders. The account books of the British firm, John Norton and Sons, provide us with detailed information on the goods that were imported by certain Mathews County families and the agricultural commodities they exported. The writings of the Rev. Thomas Feilde of Kingston Parish and those of the renowned botanist, John Clayton, describe local flora and fauna, whereas the letter book of Francis Hargrave, a young teacher, provides many insights on local life.

Official records associated with the Revolutionary War were examined as were applications for veterans' pensions. Contemporary issues of the *Virginia Gazette* were found to contain detailed information on the Battle of Cricket Hill and on Gwynn's Island. Documentation was found on Mathews men and women who remained loyal to the British government and enslaved men, women, and children who fled to the British as a means of seeking freedom. Similarly, the Executive Papers (documents generated by Virginia governors) were found to contain useful information on the War of 1812's impact on Mathews County. Alan Taylor's carefully researched book, which describes the tightly forged connection between war and slavery in Virginia, was an invaluable guide to useful items in the Executive Papers and other manuscript collections.

One primary source that sheds a great deal of light on how densely Mathews County was developed and populated is the state enumeration for Kingston Parish, compiled in 1784. That document not only lists the names of household heads and the number of whites and blacks living in each household, it also includes the number of dwellings on each household head's property along with the number of other buildings. For example, thanks to the state enumeration, we know that most middling planter households in the region had a dwelling and three or four outbuildings or dependencies. However, the estate of the late William Armistead of Hesse included 3,000 acres of land, a main dwelling, and a remarkable 33 other buildings.

Real estate tax rolls, commonly known as land tax lists, commenced being filed with the State Auditor's Office in 1782 and were organized by parish or tax district. Tax officials specified the quantity of land and number of parcels owned by each taxpayer and they often included references to contiguous properties. As time went on, the information tax assessors compiled became more comprehensive. For example, from the early nineteenth century on, they typically indicated when and by what means acreage was transferred from one person to another. Then, in 1814 they began including rudimentary locational information. Therefore, through the study of land tax lists, it is possible to bridge some of the gaps in Mathews County's antebellum court records. Real estate tax rolls shed a great deal of light upon how Mathews County was developed and when specific properties changed hands. They also provide us with insight into broad developmental trends that occurred in the county during the eighteenth, nineteenth, and twentieth centuries.

Commencing in 1820, Virginia's tax commissioners were supposed to record the collective value of the habitable buildings that stood upon the parcels they assessed. Often, assessors made note in their "Comments" column the estimated worth of any new buildings that had been constructed since their last visit and conversely, they reduced a landowner's assessment if a previously existing building or buildings had been razed or destroyed. Assessors tended to omit from their estimates uninhabitable man-made features such as ruinous buildings, fence lines, roads and wells, and they almost always excluded slave quarters. Thanks to Mathews County tax commissioner Francis Armistead's imperfect understanding of a legal change that took effect in 1820, it is possible to identify inexpensive but *habitable* buildings that were in existence at that time. From 1850-1851 on, Virginia's tax assessors often began recording the name by which properties were commonly known.

Personal property tax rolls, which commenced being cor
provide us with many useful insights for they shed light on the s
nomic status of specific households, including those headed by member
the African-American community who were free. Personal property tax rolls yield a wealth of information on the number of slaves under a specific slaveholder's control, along with the quantity of livestock, wheeled vehicles, household furnishings, and other taxable personal property that taxpayers owned at specific points in time. These data, like real estate tax rolls, are extremely useful in gauging socioeconomic status and individual wealth. Tax assessors' records compiled in 1815 include a tabulation of specific types of household furnishings (for instance, walnut and mahogany furniture, mirrors and paintings in gilt frames, and tableware made of cut glass or precious metals, or perhaps a large musical instrument) then considered taxable luxury items. These records provide us with insight into the household furnishings of Mathews County's elite. Tax officials annually made note of the locality in which property owners resided, thereby making it possible to identify absentee landowners. Mathews County's personal property tax rolls also contain the names of those who purchased licenses as merchants, tavern keepers, and millers. Because enslaved African Americans were considered taxable personal property, tax rolls for certain years include slaves' names. Sometimes when slaves were manumitted, the tax assessor noted by whom they were set free.

The official records of the Civil War and documents generated by the Union and Confederate navies were utilized extensively. Also examined were the musters and duty rosters of the Mathews County men who saw military service. Pension and service records were used to gather and consolidate information on the number of men captured, killed, wounded, or incapacitated due to wartime activities, those who were assigned to military units on the basis of their skill sets (for example, boat-builders and house carpenters who were put to work constructing gunboats), and those detained as prisoners-of-war. Data from demographic records were used as a means of determining men's age and occupations at the time of enlistment and whether there was a correlation between social status and the rank achieved. Almost all of the actions initiated by the Union military by land and by sea were geared toward stopping the smuggling of arms and other upplies to Richmond and capturing blockade runners, especially Captain John Yates Beall and the Confederate Volunteer Coast Guard. Information was gathered on runaway slaves who joined the Union military and on military activity that occurred in Mathews County during the Civil War. Postwar interviews with former slaves also were found to provide useful insights.

Harvard University's digital archives, which include an abundance of legislative records, encompass those of the Confederate government, providing us with rare insight into the laws under which Virginia officials were operating. Other volumes of nineteenth and early twentieth century legal records are available at the College of William and Mary's Swem Library and the Marshall-Wythe School of Law. Court records maintained in the office of the Mathews County Clerk of Court include deeds and wills from 1865 to the present, along with real estate tax rolls dating to 1850 and 1860s and from 1870, on. There also is a fee book which dates to 1795 and includes a list of the fees local citizens paid for legal transactions such as recording deeds and wills and court costs. Mathews County's well preserved Land Books 1 and 2 contain surveys that date from 1817, on. Also available are books containing the names of the men and women who received marriage licenses between 1827 and 1835 and between 1839 and 1850, and a register of marriages, commencing in 1857. These records were succeeded by a marriage register, which opens in 1861 and lists the names and ages of the brides and grooms along with their place of birth, current residence, names of their parents, the groom's occupation, and the name of the person performing the marriage ceremony. Commencing in 1865 the county clerk's office commenced maintaining a record of the births that occurred in Mathews County; each child's date of birth is accompanied by his or her parents' names, occupations, and race.

Mathews County's chancery decrees begin in 1870 and its Circuit Court minutes in 1868, whereas the county's oyster plat books commence in 1892. Records of the Board of Supervisors are available from 1900 on, as are induction and discharge records for those who served in the military during World War II, the Clerk of Court's Order Books, fiduciary records, and a volume that contains the names of people who were identified as epileptic, alcoholic, or mentally impaired. Also available is a medical register that contains the names of local doctors and when they were licensed and a book of criminal indictments. The first 401 pages of the book containing the Mathews County Board of Supervisors' earliest dated minutes have been lost or destroyed. Therefore, it is uncertain when the Board convened for the first time or who was elected Board chair. However, the surviving pages of the minute book that commences on page 402 and continues thereafter in uninterrupted sequence, contain the minutes of the Board meeting that occurred on June 18, 1887.

One of the most remarkable sets of records that has come to light during the course of my research are two volumes of processioners records, which were compiled in 1866 and 1867 in an attempt to offset the loss of Mathews County's antebellum court records. These records, which include properties in Militia Districts 1 and 2 but not District 3, provide invaluable information about land ownership patterns in two-thirds of Mathews County. An abundance of fragmentary or incomplete groups of records, dating to the 1860s, 1870s, and 1880s, have been preserved at the Library of Virginia and are available on microfilm. Also included are some antebellum court documents.

The records of Virginia's overarching branches of government, both before and after the Civil War, contain a wealth of information on people, places, and events directly associated with Mathews County and its antecedent, Gloucester County. For example, personal matters such as estate settlements, divorces, the freeing of slaves, and petitions of various sorts can be found in paperwork generated by the legislature and in the Executive Papers of Virginia's governors. Demographic or population census records which commenced being compiled in 1790 and became increasingly detailed as time went on, yield a great deal of information on local citizens' household size, family composition, ethnicity, school attendance, levels of literacy, and relative wealth. It should be noted that prior to 1850, census-takers recorded the names of household heads but failed to identify other household members. Slave schedules, compiled by census-takers in 1850 and 1860, provide the gender, age, and racial classification of a household's slaves.

Agricultural census records, compiled every decade between 1850 and 1880, are a good source of information on land use patterns, farm productivity, and the types of livestock a household owned. They also disclose whether a farmer had made a significant investment in agricultural equipment, perhaps taking advantage of advances in scientific farming, and whether the household produced saleable crops, such as fruits and vegetables that could be sold in urban markets, or other types of marketable commodities, such as smoked hams or other saleable goods. Industrial census records, which identify certain Mathews County residents who were engaged in manufacturing, and social statistics, which reveal the number of schools, churches, and libraries that were in the county during the mid-nineteenth centuries, give us a snapshot of local life. Diaries and letters kept by people who visited the county or lived there also provide detailed insights.

When the legal documents described above are used in conjunction with information drawn from land patents, historical maps, old photographs, quitrent rolls, military records, demographic records, agricultural and industrial census records and social statistics, Mutual Assurance Society policies, personal narratives and correspondence, accounts in historical newspapers, business records, and collections of private papers, we get much more than a fleeting glimpse of past life. Historic newspapers, made available by means of online subscriptions at the Mathews Memorial Library, the Colonial Williamsburg Foundation's Rockefeller Library, and the Library of Virginia, provide access to an abundance of useful articles, advertisements, and opinion pieces. Because newspaper data bases are highly searchable and often include the same sources, whenever a specific edition of a newspaper is cited, the reader is invited to search for that item in a subscription data base to which he or she has convenient access.

Records compiled by the Freedmen's Bureau during the late 1860s were helpful in understanding life in Mathews County right after the Civil War, whereas the narratives recorded by employees of the Works Progress Administration's Federal Writers Project during the 1930s were insightful. WPA interviews with two ex-slaves from Mathews County, conducted in 1937 by Claude W. Anderson, can be found online at the Library of Virginia's web site and in a book of interviews with former slaves, *Weevils in the Wheat*. Nearly a dozen WPA interviews with the county's white residents, conducted by Harriet G. Miller in 1939, can be found in the University of Virginia's Albert and Shirley Small Special Collections Library, part of the

Alderman Library. All of these interviews, which cover a broad variety of subjects, provide a unique perspective on everyday life during the late nineteenth and early twentieth centuries.

The Mathews County Historical Society's archives, preserved in the Mathews Memorial Library, contain a wealth of information on local families and the properties with which they were associated. This remarkable and growing collection is comprised of primary and secondary sources, transcriptions of oral history interviews, church histories, personal correspondence, artifacts, and ephemera. The library's electronic catalog is a searchable finding aid, which makes it possible to locate specific items within the historical society's boxed archival materials. Within this text, whenever the historical society's archival material is cited, reference is made to the numbered box in which that material may be found. The Mathews Memorial Library's web site, which provides patrons access to a wealth of additional useful web sites, also is an extremely important source. The reference works in the Chesapeake Room are invaluable.

Local newspapers—specifically, the *Gloucester-Mathews Gazette-Journal* and its predecessors—provide many useful insights into community life. Microfilms are available at the Mathews Memorial Library in the Chesapeake Room. Information on Mathews County and its inhabitants is available at numerous record repositories throughout the United States, including the Colonial Williamsburg Foundation's Rockefeller Library and the College of William and Mary's Swem Library in Williamsburg; the Library of Congress and National Archives in Washington, D.C., and College Park, Maryland; the Library of Virginia; the Virginia Historical Society, the Museum of the Confederacy, the Valentine Museum, and the Virginia Department of Historic Resources in Richmond; the Mariner's Museum in Newport News; the National Park Service archives in Yorktown; the U.S. Army Corps of Engineers Archives in Norfolk; and the Huntington Library in San Marino, California. Oral history interviews conducted by Jessica Taylor as part of the Tidewater Management Project, Samuel Proctor Oral History Program, at the University of Florida in Gainesville, Florida, provided useful insights and important supplementary information.

Readers are encouraged to consult the endnotes that appear at the end of each chapter. They contain annotation, which has been provided for the sake of scholarly credibility and to lend future researchers a helping hand. Sometimes, they contain supplementary information that couldn't be accommodated in the body of the text. The annotation that accompanies each chapter includes occasional references to institutional web sites, along with links to specific material. However, because web sites are constantly being modified, links often become obsolete. Therefore, it is recommended that researchers pursuing a specific line of inquiry consult the host site and then search for the topic of interest. During 2014 the Mathews County Historical Society underwrote publication of a book entitled *New Point Comfort Lighthouse, Its History and Preservation*. Because the authors, Mary Louise and J. Candace Clifford, made abundant use of documents that are preserved in the National Archives, their work, which is annotated, has been cited freely.

ACKNOWLEDGMENTS

The Mathews County Historical Society's book committee, chaired by Reed Lawson, who served with Forrest Morgan, Graham Hood, and Earl Soles, guided the production of this comprehensive history of Mathews County. Mrs. Lawson, as the historical society's archivist, provided outstanding support and made unaccessioned materials accessible. Becky Foster Barnhardt of the Mathew Memorial Library generously shared her abundant knowledge of local history and primary sources. Moreover, she was selflessly forthcoming with information that otherwise might have escaped notice, and also agreed to review the book manuscript. Mathews County Clerk of Court, the Honorable Angela Ingram and her predecessor, Dr. E. Eugene Callis, graciously provided work space and unfettered access to the materials in the clerk's office. Archivist Quatro Hubbard and archaeologist David K. Hazzard of the Virginia Department of Historic Resources assisted by providing ready access to architectural and archaeological site files, whereas David Brown and Thane Harpole provided access to electronic site reports and the recent architectural survey of Mathews County. Longtime colleagues Susan Shames, George Yetter, Douglas Mayo, Marianne Martin, and Carl Lounsbury of the Colonial Williamsburg Foundation were readily available to offer assistance or answer questions whenever needed. Susan Riggs of Swem Library's Department of Special Collections and Frances Pollard of the Virginia Historical Society were extremely helpful, especially when making their institutions' sets of the Billups Family Papers readily accessible for efficient examination. Underwater archaeologist John Broadwater graciously answered pesky questions about all things maritime and David Riggs of the National Park Service shared his extensive knowledge of Revolutionary War and Civil War military features.

Holly J.M. Horton of the Middlesex County Museum and Historical Society responded to a query about a historic site in her county. Brian Palmer and his wife, Erin Hollaway, provided research support by obtaining a copy of an obscure document that is preserved at the Huntington Library in San Marino, California. Archaeologist Gregory J. Brown of the Maryland Historical Trust, with the assistance of Joe Brown, edited this book. He also produced the maps that depict the boundaries of Virginia's original counties. Elizabeth O. Whitley of the Mathews County Planning and Zoning Office produced the modern map of Mathews County. The Honorable Margaret Walker, Gloucester County's Clerk of Court, permitted a photograph to be taken of a plat in Gloucester's earliest dated survey book. Archivist Minor Weisinger of the Library of Virginia, a longtime friend, patiently fielded questions about obscure documentary sources deeply buried in the library's web site. Avery Hicks of the Williamsburg Regional Library processed countless requests for interlibrary loans and Tiffany W. Cole of the University of Virginia's Alderman Library also rendered invaluable assistance. Professional forester Paul Verbyla shared his knowledge of the types of vegetation that would have been present in Mathews County at the time the early colonists arrived. Sanford B. Wanner, former James City County administrator, provided web addresses and contact information that provide many useful insights into the organization of Virginia's county governments as a whole. Elsa Cooke Verbyla of the *Gloucester-Mathews Gazette-Journal* provided access to digitized finding aids that she has compiled and occasionally fielded my pesky questions.

Time and again, the people of Mathews County have demonstrated their deep appreciation of local history. Some citizens have shared personal narratives or perhaps objects accumulated by their forebears. Others have shown their love for the county by donating historical documents to the Mathews County Historical Society archives and the Mathews Memorial Library or by diligently working to preserve the county's abundance of historic buildings and cultural resources. The Mathews County Historical Society is deeply grateful for the financial support provided by the Mathews Community Foundation, the William F. and Catherine K. Owens Foundation, and the J. Edwin Treakle Foundation. It is with great respect and affection that this comprehensive history is presented to the people of Mathews County.

Martha Waldrop McCartney
July 2015

1

Through A Glass, Darkly

Prehistory to 1633

Mathews County's Geological Setting: A Cultural Determinant

The Chesapeake Bay, which borders Mathews County on the east, was formed some 35 million years ago when a mile-wide meteorite, traveling at a great rate of speed, plunged into the ocean near North America's eastern shore and struck the earth's crust. The impact blasted a crater literally thousands of feet deep and more than fifty miles in diameter, displacing many million tons of water, sediment, and debris. The cavity created, known to geologists as the Chesapeake Bay Impact Crater, is the largest such chasm in the United States and is located approximately five miles west of the town of Cape Charles, Virginia. Over eons, the existence of the Chesapeake Bay has had an immeasurable impact upon the natural environment and therefore, humankind. Significantly, navigable tributaries of the Chesapeake Bay define virtually all of Mathews County's borders.

Mathews, which is part of the Middle Peninsula, envelops approximately 87 square miles of land, has an estimated 214 miles of shoreline, and is Virginia's second smallest county. According to soil scientists, Mathews County largely consists of shallow, poorly drained Fallsington soils (particularly those of the Dragston series) that are nearly level and wooded. Tidal marshes and coastal beach dunes are found in the eastern and southern coastal sections of the county, whereas Mathews' westernmost territory consists of uplands characterized by steep, undulating terrain. These uplands, defined by a marine terrace, are thought to represent an ancient shoreline. When Captain John Smith arrived in Virginia in April 1607, he aptly commented that the countryside bordering the Chesapeake Bay was "a plain wilderness as God first made it."

Joseph Martin, who traveled about Virginia in 1835, documenting each county's natural attributes, described Mathews County's soil as a sandy loam with a substratum of clay. He said that marl could be found in some parts of the county by digging to a sufficient depth. He indicated that springs of water were relatively rare in Mathews and that when wells were dug to a depth of 20 feet or more, one could find "cockle shells, oyster shells, and the shells of many testaceous [hard-shelled] animals not known at the present day." He said that around the time of his visit, the "leg bone of an animal, supposed to be an ox, although much larger than that animal now exists," was found at a great depth. Martin noted the somewhat elevated banks of the Piankatank River and said that from that point the terrain descended in an almost uninterrupted plain. He surmised that the land "at some period [was] covered by the sea, or bay, as the whole face of the country incontestably proves."[1]

Virginia's First Inhabitants: The Native Americans

Thousands of years before the first European colonists arrived in Virginia, an indigenous population inhabited the Coastal Plain, leaving a faint imprint upon the land. The early history of the Indians, or Native Americans, though largely unrecorded, is an integral part of our heritage. Knowledge of these very early people comes to us through archaeology and the analysis of cultural materials. Between 15,000 and 8000 BC, when North America's earliest inhabitants, the Paleoindians, were alive, the climate and environment were vastly different than they are today, for there were enormous continental glaciers. The sea level was much lower and what we know as the Chesapeake Bay was a narrow river. Winters were long and hard and summers were short, cool, and moist. Streams flowed through tundra-like grasslands and hardwood forests of spruce, fir, hickory, beech, hemlock, oak, and pine covered much of Virginia. Large portions of the continental shelf, currently underwater, were exposed and many of today's slow-moving rivers were much more active. Freshwater marsh vegetation developed on the clays being deposited in streams.

Paleoindians lived in small, mobile groups that anthropologists call bands, which can be likened to an extended family. They roamed across a large but somewhat limited area, establishing small, temporary encampments wherever food was available. They derived much of their nourishment from plant foods and made use of small game, fish, and large mammals like deer, elk, bear, and moose. Hunters developed stone tools that enabled them to kill animals that were attracted to rivers, lakes, and salt licks. Fluted projectile points have been found throughout Virginia, mostly in the southeast, to the east of the fall line. These bifaces often are found in association with specialized tools fabricated from relatively scarce cherts and jaspers. An archaeological survey of Mathews County's coastal shoreline, conducted in 2007, and artifacts collected by local residents suggest that the Paleoindians favored this region. Like other shoreline areas of the Chesapeake Bay, Paleoindian sites seem to be concentrated around upland interfluves: long, narrow landforms that once separated stream valleys. A large and remarkably well-preserved stone knife, found on Gwynn's Island by Mark Small and displayed at the Gwynn's Island Museum, attests to the Paleoindian presence around 12,000 years ago.

During the Early Archaic period (8000–6000 BC), significant environmental changes occurred, as the cold, moist climate of the Pleistocene Age became drier and more temperate. Warmer winds melted glaciers hundreds of miles to the north and the ocean's temperature rose. The sea level rose too, and spread water across Virginia's Coastal Plain, creating the Chesapeake Bay. The rising water also covered or eroded most of the places frequented by the early hunters. Open grasslands were gradually replaced by forests of pine, cypress, sweet gum, and oak; and elk, deer, and bear were prolific. The rise of fresh water marshes was part of this change. In some locales, there was an intermediate phase of transitional hardwood species, such as beech, birch, and hemlock. As vegetation became more profuse, Early Archaic people, who were nomadic hunter-gatherers, collected more plant foods, such as fruits and nuts, and made abundant use of animal skins, especially deer. They also began to vary the size and shape of their stone tools, making side or corner notches that were useful in attach-

Paleoindian knife found in Mathews County, Virginia.
Courtesy of the Virginia Department of Historic Resources and the Gwynn's Island Museum.

ing points to spears. During the Early Archaic period, the native population grew, thanks to a more hospitable environment. Corner-notched projectile points, a diagnostic artifact associated with these early people, have been found in Mathews County.

By the time of the Middle Archaic period (6000–2500 BC), Virginia's Indians had become adjusted to their new woodland environment. Long winters and short summers had been replaced by seasons much like we have today; and large amounts of rain caused rivers to overflow their banks, depositing rich topsoil on the floodplain. The Indians commenced exploiting marine foods, such as oysters, after the stabilization of sea level around 4000 BC. They continued to go about their seasonal hunting and gathering, utilizing tools and weapons that were more functional and sophisticated. Women began using mortars and pestles to crush nuts and seeds from which they could prepare food. Using their stone axes, Middle Archaic people cut wood to build houses and make fires. Settlements of up to fifty people began appearing along the floodplains. Game animals became more accessible to the Indians, which made hunting easier. Archaeologists have discovered bifurcated and stemmed projectile points in the eroded coastal areas of Mathews County.

By the Late Archaic period (2500–1200 BC), there were perhaps tens of thousands of Indians in Virginia. Because the floodplain, which was forested, contained an abundance of plant and animal life, Late Archaic Indians enjoyed a wide variety of foods, greatly enhancing their diet. Small bands of people were attracted to the floodplain, where they merged to form small settlements or hamlets. The natives also began nurturing plant species, such as gourds and squash, and they learned how to preserve foodstuffs for leaner times, making use of storage pits they dug in or near their homes. This transition resulted in the establishment of substantial, possibly semi-sedentary base camps along major streams, where fish and shellfish could be gathered. Within the Coastal Plain, saltwater oysters were an important food source. The Indians' discarded oyster shells formed middens or refuse heaps. When examining Mathews County's shoreline, archaeologists have found stemmed projectile points, as well as shards of steatite bowls, evidence of Late Archaic period people.

Between 2000 BC and 1000 AD, the Indians became more sedentary and began making and firing clay vessels, which they used for cooking and storage. First, they dug good clay from a riverbank or bluff. Then, they blended it with water and added crushed rock or shell, for they had learned through experience that this process (called *tempering*) reduced shrinking and cracking. The clay pot, fabricated by hand, was allowed to air dry before it was baked in an open fire. Once the vessel cooled, it could be used for cooking or storage. Differences in the size, shape, body, surface treatment, and decoration of the natives' clay pots provide archaeologists with ways to date the sites they discover. By the Early Woodland Period (1200–500 BC), the eastern United States was densely forested. Again, the indigenous people responded to the changing environment by modifying their mode of subsistence. As the population grew, diverse groups of natives who lived in scattered but settled hamlets began to make the transition to tribal-level organization. Subsistence patterns evolved that eventually culminated in sedentary horticultural practices.

Middle Woodland people, who lived between 500 BC and 900 AD, planted maize (commonly known now as corn), a domesticated species that was brought into the eastern United States from Mexico. The introduction of corn provided the Indians with better nutrition that enabled their population to increase. Archaeologists believe that religious ceremonies linked to the harvesting and planting of corn may have led to the development of societies in which rank and status were important.

Middle Woodland people experimented with specialized crafts and increased their trading activities. This enabled native leaders to share information about farming and to spread their cultural traditions and beliefs. The Indians began living in hamlets and small villages scattered along Virginia's major streams. They hunted wild game by using the bow and arrow instead of spears, and they modified the grooved axe. They also developed the celt, a specialized stone tool for woodworking. Crafts became increasingly refined and distinctive cultural traditions emerged. As a result, the Indians established trade networks that allowed them to exchange goods. Exotic Woodland-period artifacts found along Gwynn's Island's southern shoreline included a fragment of a stone platform pipe and a slate-expanded center bar gorget. The presence of these artifacts suggests that trade goods were exchanged with native people as far away as the Ohio Valley. In time, the rank or status of some families was enhanced within their tribal group. Archaeologists have found evidence of Early, Middle, and Late Woodland period occupation in Mathews County.

Indians in the Late Woodland Period (900 to 1600 AD), though more sedentary than their forebears, followed a seasonal pattern of hunting and gathering. They lived in villages that sometimes included hundreds of people, who worked toward their community's support and followed the direction of tribal leaders. They preferred to inhabit the banks of tidal waterways during the warm months; and in winter, when their gardens were dormant and fishing was less productive, they moved inland and relied upon stored food and whatever game they could procure. Beans, squash, and corn were Late Woodland Indians' principal food crops and in time, they began cultivating tobacco. The women and elderly men of an Indian village usually planted crops using the slash-and-burn method of clearing the ground they used for agriculture. The vegetable crops they grew helped to fulfill their nutritional needs. This allowed them to linger in one location for longer periods of time, and enabled them to thrive and become more populous.

The Coastal Plain offered the Indians an abundance of fresh and saltwater fish (such as shad and sturgeon) and shellfish (such as oysters and crabs). However, archaeologists have found fewer shell middens in Mathews County than might be expected in light of the region's wealth of seafood. Numerous species of game were available in eastern Virginia. Undoubtedly, the

The Way they Broyle their Fish, *an engraving by Theodor de Bry. Courtesy of the Jamestown-Yorktown Foundation.*

most important was the white-tailed deer, which provided the natives with food and deerskin garments. Indian men and women spent a lot of time away from their villages, hunting, fishing, and gathering wild plants, but they returned home by fall, when corn was ready to be harvested. During the fall and winter months, large groups of Indian men sometimes joined in communal hunts, but they also hunted throughout the year, alone or in small groups.

Waterways not only provided the Indians with a source of food, they also served as a conduit of transportation. The natives hewed and burned dugout canoes so that they could harvest seafood and transport people and goods. Sometimes, the natives would build their villages on both sides of a relatively narrow stream. Their houses were usually situated close to the shore, and sometimes Indian towns extended along the waterfront for a considerable distance. Within Late Woodland villages, houses were clustered close together or interspersed with fields that were used for gardens. Sometimes, Indian towns were surrounded by a palisade. The villages of Late Woodland Indians, organized around a complex economic, social, and political structure, provided them with security, companionship, and an opportunity to accumulate wealth. The Indians fabricated a wide variety of pottery forms and wrought objects of stone, copper, and shell that reflected their belief systems. Ceremonial life was important and creativity flourished.

Archaeologists believe that control of the food supply led to the development of native societies in which there were differences in the rank or status of certain individuals. In chiefdoms, which had begun to develop by the late 1500s, leaders accepted tribute, which they retained or redistributed to others. In time, the literally hundreds of Indian villages that existed in Tidewater Virginia began to compete for territory and economic supremacy. Weaker tribes were forced to pay tribute to stronger ones that guaranteed them protection in times of war. Prehistorians and anthropologists believe that by the mid-to-late sixteenth century a paramount or dominant chiefdom had begun to emerge. Virginia's Algonquians shared a common linguistic bond with some of the native peoples to the north and south, a distinct dialect that set them apart from those communicating in the Iroquoian, Siouan, and other tongues. Prior to the time the first colonists arrived, the Indians' way of life became well established.[2]

Early European Encounters

Scholars believe that European explorers visited the Western Hemisphere nearly five hundred years before Christopher Columbus set sail. Despite Spanish and Portuguese claims, by the 1520s other European countries began taking an interest in the newly-discovered continent. In 1531, Bristol merchant Robert Thorne urged King Henry VIII of England to seek a northern route to Cathay, and others took up the cry. Spain, meanwhile, laid claim to much of North America. In 1546, an English ship, forced into the Chesapeake Bay by stormy weather, encountered natives who were willing to trade. Then, around 1560 a party of Spanish explorers visited the Chesapeake and took aboard an Indian boy, reputedly a chief's son, and spirited him away. In 1570, a small group of Spanish Jesuits attempted to establish a mission in coastal Virginia, intending to use the captured—and presumably converted—Indian youth as an intermediary in spreading their message. The Jesuits' attempts went awry, and they were killed. In 1572, their deaths were avenged by men that Cuba's governor sent to the Chesapeake. The Spaniards killed a large number of Indians and then weighed anchor, undoubtedly leaving in their wake a legacy of dread and suspicion.[3]

Captain Christopher Newport, commander of the small fleet that brought the Virginia Company of London's first colonists across the Atlantic, set sail from England on December 20, 1606. Captain John Smith and others in the group had a working knowledge of the Algonquian language and were undoubtedly familiar with the narratives produced by the men who attempted to establish a colony on Roanoke Island during the 1580s. Thus, some of the first colonists had an idea of what to expect once they touched land. When Captain Newport reached Virginia in the spring of 1607, he opened a sealed box that contained the names of the seven men who were to serve as the colony's first council. As the highest ranking officials in Virginia, they had the right to elect their own president. Importantly, the Virginia Company's instructions to its colonists brought to the New World the rudiments of English common law.

Replicas of the Discovery, Godspeed, *and* Susan Constant, *which brought the first colonists to Virginia. Courtesy of the Jamestown-Yorktown Foundation.*

After a tiny outpost had been planted on Jamestown Island, Captain Newport and his fellow explorers ventured up the York River and viewed the shore line, making note of the sites at which native villages were located. The map made by Robert Tindall (Tyndall), a mariner who had crossed the ocean with Newport, included the York's major tributaries, which eventually became known as the Pamunkey and Mattaponi Rivers. Captain John Smith and other early visitors observed that the neck of land defined by the junction of the Pamunkey and Mattaponi Rivers was home to the Pamunkey Indians, then at the core of the Powhatan Chiefdom, whose territory covered all of Virginia's coastal plain. This enormous expanse of land extended from the Potomac River to a point well below the Blackwater River. Hardwoods probably dominated local forests, which would have included some chestnut trees and a scattering of pine. Forestation in the western part of today's Mathews County, which includes white and red oaks, gums, maples and other hardwoods plus occasional pines, is thought to mimic the region's appearance when the first colonists arrived.[4]

In late 1607 or early 1608, Captain John Smith crossed the head of the Piankatank (Payankatank, Pyankatank) River. In his narratives, "A True Relation and A Map of Virginia," he commented that the river was navigable for about 30 miles and was home to around forty Indian fighting men.[5] Smith later described how Powhatan's warriors had driven the Kecoughtan Indians from their village on the upper side of the James River's mouth in 1608. He said that Powhatan sent some of his men to Kecoughtan and that after everyone had gotten settled for the night, they ambushed their hosts, killing 24 men. Powhatan's warriors spared the lives of the Kecoughtan village's leader and the community's women and children but took them prisoner. Then, Powhatan sent some of his own people to the mouth of the James River, where they repopulated Kecoughtan. Toward the end of the colonists' first year in Virginia, Smith and his men embarked on a second voyage of exploration. It was then that they sailed up the Piankatank River and encountered some of the region's native inhabitants. On his famous map of Virginia, Smith identified the village of the Piankatank Indians who lived on the upper side of the Piankatank River in the immediate vicinity of the Middlesex County community known as Piankatank Shores. Smith learned that the Piankatank were the natives Powhatan had routed from Kecoughtan and replaced with his own people.

On Captain John Smith's second voyage of exploration, he was injured by a stingray whose barbs inflicted a painful flesh wound. Fortunately, one of his companions, Dr. Walter Russell, applied healing oil that eased his discomfort and Smith, with his usual braggadocio, claimed that he ate the fish for dinner. He gave the name "Stingray Isle" to what we know as Stingray Point, a large promontory on the lower side of the Rappahannock River's mouth, a relatively short distance from the Piankatank River. That name has endured, as has that of Gosnolls or Gosnold Bay, near the mouth of the Piankatank, where Captain John Smith and his men anchored for the night and encountered a sudden storm.[6]

Native Life at the Time of Colonization

Captain John Smith observed that Indian men spent most of their time hunting, fishing, and engaging in wars, whereas the women and children made mats, baskets, and pottery and raised the crops upon which their villages depended. He described the Powhatans as generally tall and straight, with black hair and dusky complexions, and noted that the men rarely had beards. He said that the natives were exceptionally strong and agile and tolerated even the worst weather. Although early explorers' accounts describe how Virginia's native inhabitants lived, it is important to remember that their narratives reflect the writers' *perception* of Indian culture. Subtle differences between the two cultures almost certainly escaped notice and European writers probably misunderstood or misinterpreted many larger issues. For example, the Powhatans considered land a part of the earth, like the sky, water, and the air, and therefore available to all for subsistence. Thus, the European concept of *owning* land was foreign to them. The two cultures also had vastly different views of religion. The Powhatans, while open to the idea of a Christian deity, were reluctant to renounce their own gods. Although both cultures viewed accumulated wealth as an emblem of social status, they had a much different concept of inheritance: with the Powhatan, it passed through the female line rather than the male. In light of the vast cultural differences between the two peoples and their mutual lack of understanding, they were destined to collide.

When the English established their first permanent settlement in May 1607, Tidewater Virginia's natives were under the sway of Powhatan, or Wahunsonacock, a paramount chief. He reigned over 32 districts that encompassed more than 150 villages, whose inhabitants paid him tribute and supported him in times of war. John Smith described Powhatan as a monarch to whom many lesser kings (or *werowances*) were subservient. Thus, the people of the Powhatan Chiefdom were members of a society in which rank and status were important. Anthropologists believe that the Powhatan

Chiefdom took form during the 1570s, when Powhatan inherited the right to lead six or more small chiefdoms within a vast territory that extended from the falls of the James River, northward to the York. In 1607, when the first colonists arrived, Powhatan was trying to seize control of the Chickahominy, a strong native group governed by a council of elders, not a solitary, all-powerful leader. He had already replaced the Kecoughtan Indians with his own people and had asserted his supremacy over some of the lesser chiefdoms between the Rappahannock and Potomac Rivers. By the close of 1608 Powhatan controlled almost all of the sub-chiefdoms or districts located in Virginia's Coastal Plain. He died in 1617, a year after the death of his daughter, Pocahontas, who had married John Rolfe, a European colonist.[7]

Climatic Conditions at the Time of European Contact

The University of Arkansas's study of tree-ring data from a bald cypress near Jamestown Island reveals that the first European colonists arrived during a period of severe drought that lasted from 1606 to 1612, the driest period in 770 years. Conditions were particularly severe in eastern Virginia. Drought conditions would have created a crisis for both natives and colonists, because plant materials would not have been readily available for subsistence. That, in turn, would have affected the availability of game animals and fish, and water quality would have been at its poorest. Regional drought would have increased the salinity of Virginia's tidal waterways, especially near Jamestown Island, which lies squarely within the James River's oligohaline zone, where the exchange between fresh and salt water is minimal. Thus, when the first Virginia colonists arrived, the natives they encountered would have experienced a bad crop year and were probably dealing with food shortages.[8]

Becoming Established

The first colonists came ashore in a richly forested region. Therefore, when they erected insubstantial houses and the other structures they needed to shield themselves from the elements, they availed themselves of the abundance of timber that was close at hand. However, they adapted Old World building techniques to the new setting in which they lived. The early colonists' buildings were earth-fast, that is, they were constructed on posts that were driven into the ground or set into shallow holes. After upright corner posts had been erected to form a pen or framework, irregularly spaced and crudely aligned perpendicular posts were placed along the sides. These secondary posts, set into a trench, created sidewalls to which clay was applied, forming walls. The roof of these insubstantial and slightly framed buildings was most likely covered with a thatch of reeds.[9]

Tobacco, Virginia's Money Crop

Between 1611 and 1614, John Rolfe, through experimentation, developed a strain of sweet-scented tobacco that quickly became such a lucrative money crop that it attained acceptance as currency. Through experience, Virginia Company officials learned that the colony critically needed farmers and laborers, to produce a dependable and adequate food supply as well as women to establish homes. Many colonists, lured by the prospect of wealth, planted tobacco instead of food crops and then complained bitterly about hunger while awaiting supplies from England. They also bartered with the Indians for corn and other food and sometimes took it by force, making enemies in the process. In 1619 Secretary of the Colony John Pory declared that Virginia was ideal for agriculture but he admitted that the colony's riches lay in tobacco. The boom in tobacco prices continued until around 1630, when overproduction glutted the market. Even so, tobacco remained the staple crop of the Chesapeake colonies and by 1639 the quantity exported annually was between one and two million pounds.[10] In fact, tobacco was still an important money crop when European settlement reached what became Mathews County.

Tobacco was a highly labor intensive crop. Virginia colonists and their servants (male and female alike) used the hill-and-hoe form of agriculture, a concept they borrowed from the Indians but modernized and adapted to their own means. After they cut down trees or girdled them so that they would die, they pulverized the soil with their hoes and then mounded it into a hill. It was into these hills that they transplanted tiny tobacco seedlings, grown in specially prepared seed beds. During the growing season, the colonists topped each tobacco plant to channel growth into the leaves and they removed excess leaves and suckers, secondary growth that would sap strength from the plant. The colonists weeded their tobacco hills throughout the growing season and plucked off worms that attacked the plant. At harvest time, they cut the leaves, hung them up to dry, and then packed them into large wooden casks called hogsheads. As time went on, the colonists learned how to maximize the amount of tobacco they could raise on their cleared ground. Although the price of tobacco declined as production increased, it remained saleable and therefore was considered a reliable means of making money. The timing of planting, topping, suckering, worming, and cutting were critical to the crop's success but it did not require investment in a plow and oxen, nor extensive clearing and soil preparation.[11]

Establishment of the Headright System

The Virginia Company's Great Charter, adopted in November 1618, made private land ownership possible, for it introduced the *headright system*, a policy that lured prospective immigrants to Virginia. Under the headright system, those who immigrated to Virginia at their own expense sometime prior to May 1616 and lived in the colony for at least three years were eligible for 100 acres of land. People who came later on, paid for their own passage, and stayed in Virginia for three or more years were entitled to 50 acres. Anyone who underwrote the cost of another's transportation became eligible for 50 acres on that person's behalf. The Great Charter prompted groups of investors to pool their resources and send large groups of indentured servants or contract workers to Virginia. Also, successful planters could use their disposable income to bring indentured servants to Virginia. This enabled them to amass substantial amounts of land while fulfilling their need for labor. Also, by placing their servants upon newly acquired property, they could claim that it was occupied or "seated." Headright certificates could be bought and sold and therefore had monetary value.[12] The opportunity to reap substantial profits by growing tobacco while simultaneously accumulating land fueled the spread of settlement.

The Nascence of Representative Government

In the spring of 1619 Virginia's new governor, Sir George Yeardley, arrived and assumed the reins of government. In accord with his instructions, which were based upon the Virginia Company's Great Charter, the colony was subdivided into four corporations or boroughs, each of which was vast in size and spanned both sides of the James River. The settlements within those corporations were invited to send delegates or burgesses to Jamestown to convene in an assembly that would formulate the colony's laws. On July 30, 1619, Governor Yeardley, his six councilors, and two delegates or burgesses from eleven of the colony's small settlements gathered in the church as members of New World's first legislative assembly. After the Reverend Richard Buck of Jamestown offered a prayer for guidance, the assembly's speaker, John Pory, read aloud excerpts from the Virginia Company's Great Charter and reviewed two of the four books of laws that had been sent to the colony. Then, the burgesses formed two committees to study the remaining books of laws. Their prerogative wasn't challenging the rules set down for governing the colony, but to petition for any changes they felt were necessary. Any laws the burgesses drafted were subject to the monarch's approval.

At the assembly's 1619 session, laws were enacted stipulating that trade with the Indians was to be regulated by the colony's governing officials and the number of natives allowed to live and work within the settlements was to be restricted. The colonists were required to provide their households with a year's supply of corn or maize, storing some for use in times of need, and to plant vineyards, mulberry trees, and silk flax. Tobacco growers had to follow certain procedures when preparing their crop for market. No one was allowed to venture further than 20 miles from home, visit Indian towns, or undertake a voyage longer than seven days without obtaining permission from the governing officials. Household heads were required to furnish the Secretary of the Colony with a list of those under their care.

According to Captain John Smith, by 1622 courts had been set up "in convenient places," perhaps a reference to the right of private plantations' leaders to arbitrate disputes among their own people. At Jamestown the governor and his council began to convene regularly as a court. By 1625 there were local courts in at least two of the colony's corporations and there was one on the Eastern Shore.[13]

The Link between Church and State

When the Virginia colony's burgesses convened at Jamestown in the summer of 1619, twelve of the thirty-four laws the burgesses enacted dealt with religion, morality, or other forms of personal discipline. Each of the colony's four corporations was to have "a godly and learned minister," who was provided with a 100-acre glebe, or home farm, and six servants to work the land. Two churchwardens chosen by the corporation's clergyman were responsible for maintaining the church, reporting wrongdoers, and collecting church taxes or dues. Those who persisted in "skandulous offences" could be excommunicated, which brought certain arrest and confiscation of all personal property. Clergy were to report to the authorities anyone suspected of committing moral offenses such as intoxication, fornication, or swearing. These policies reflect the close link between church and state while Virginia had an Established Church. In addition to the enforcement of moral law, the clergy were obliged to make note of the christenings, marriages and burials they performed.

Government records for the years 1622–32 reveal that local churchwardens routinely reported people who got drunk, swore, or committed other acts deemed immoral or socially unacceptable. Public officials in turn meted out what they considered appropriate punishment, often resorting to whipping or another form of public humiliation. Sometimes slanderers were obliged to kneel and offer a public apology, but gossipy or combative women were sometimes dunked in the nearest river. When county courts were established in 1634, some of the church's responsibilities for maintaining public morality were transferred to the local judiciary, to whom churchwardens reported directly. During the early seventeenth century, writers often used Biblical metaphors (particularly those of the Old Testament) to describe their sufferings. Days in the church calendar were used to identify secular dates upon which rent and taxes were due and public events occurred.[14] Thus, the State Church had quasi-governmental status and religious law permeated daily life throughout the colonial period.

Population Growth and the Burgeoning Need for Workers

The rapidly expanding market for tobacco created substantial opportunities for those who immigrated to Virginia and became planters. Also, the relatively high price of tobacco during the 1620s led to a search for ways to increase productivity. Between 1620 and 1670 the annual rate of productivity per worker more than doubled. Simultaneously, shipping costs were halved. Although tobacco prices had begun to decline sharply by 1630 and dwindled for another 50 years, tobacco production remained profitable because planters were able to produce more of the crop with fewer hands. When tobacco consumption rose in response to lower prices and planters rushed to meet that demand, they quickly discovered that additional laborers increased production significantly.

It is estimated that 75,000 whites emigrated from the British Isles to the Chesapeake colonies between 1630 and 1680 when tobacco consumption was on the rise. Approximately half to three-quarters of these people were indentured servants, many of whom were poor, unskilled youths. At first the labor shortage was so critical that employers often worked alongside their servants. Planters were especially eager to procure males to toil in the tobacco fields, and during the 1630s six times as many men as women became indentured servants. Between 1640 and 1680, only one out of every four servants was female. This sex ratio, which left many men without an opportunity to marry and rear a family, perpetuated the need for immigrant labor. So did the fact that many servants died before they became "seasoned"—that is, adjusted to the climate and to the hardships of living in a wilderness environment.[15]

In the beginning, many of Virginia's indentured servants were from the English middle class and were respectable citizens who simply lacked the means to pay for their own transportation or to outfit themselves for life in the colony. These men and women represented a broad cross-section of society and ranged from the younger sons of prominent families, yeoman farmers, husbandmen, artisans, and laborers, to former prison inmates.[16] Often, they were young males in their late teens or early twenties. Men and women interested in becoming indentured servants, and sometimes minors' legal guardians, signed a contract agreeing to exchange a certain number of years' work for transportation to Virginia. These contracts could be marketed to planters in need of laborers. Indentured servants' contracts, considered personal property, could be resold or passed along by means of a bequest. People who acquired indentured servants were supposed to provide them with food, clothing, and shelter. They could also discipline their servants, but only within the limits of the law. Indentured servants (especially men and boys) usually worked as field hands from dawn to dusk, six days a week, throughout the growing season.

The 1640s brought changes in the laws regulating indentured servitude. Adult servants (those who were age 20 or older) usually served for four years, whereas those under the age of 12 were sometimes bound out for seven or more years. Skilled or literate servants could often negotiate shorter terms because they were capable of performing tasks considered more valuable. Indentured servants were entitled to "freedom dues," an allotment of corn and clothing, as soon as their contract expired. Servants were forbidden to marry without their master's consent. If they did so, or engaged in unsanctioned sexual liaisons, they could be punished, usually by having their time of service extended. Anyone absconding more than once could be branded upon the cheek with an "R." People sometimes harbored runaways instead of returning them to their rightful owners.

Indentured servants gained a few legal rights as time went on and a labor shortage developed. They could file formal complaints against masters who failed to provide them with food and clothing or treated them "in an unchristian manner." Legal records reveal that a few indentured servants did indeed take their masters to court, but it is likely that they were at a distinct disadvantage. Former servants, upon being freed, often leased land until they could acquire some acreage of their own. New immigrants did likewise while fulfilling the headright system's residency requirements.[17]

The Introduction of African Workers

In August 1619, an event occurred that irrevocably changed the course of Virginia history. It was then that a Dutch frigate, the *White Lion*, fresh from a plundering expedition in the West Indies, sailed into Hampton Roads with 20-some Africans aboard. Shortly thereafter, most, if not all, of the newly-arrived African men and women were brought up to Jamestown and sold into servitude. It is uncertain whether they set foot on land at Old Point Comfort (Kecoughtan), where the Dutch ship arrived, or were kept aboard until they were transferred to the vessel that brought them up to Jamestown. Similarly, whether or not they were treated as slaves after they arrived in Virginia is still open to scholarly debate. According to John Rolfe, three or four days after the Dutch man-of-war left Virginia, the ship *Treasurer* came in, but left hastily because Kecoughtan's inhabitants refused to supply its master and crew with victuals they desperately needed. Approximately 30 or 40 Africans were aboard the *Treasurer* and some are known to have stayed in Virginia. The *Treasurer* continued to Bermuda, where the remaining Africans were off-loaded. Some were acquired by the islands' governor, Nathaniel Butler, who referred to them as "slaves." His use of that term suggests that he did not consider them servants who had a prospect of freedom.[18]

In recent years scholars have learned much about the origin of Virginia's first Africans. Research suggests that they were captured in Angola, on the West Coast of Africa, having been removed from a Portuguese slave ship, the *San Juan Batista*, which was taken by English corsairs. There is evidence that in accord with Portuguese law, some of these Africans, who came from São Paulo de Loanda, were baptized as Christians before they were brought to the New World. Even so, the Dutch and Portuguese seem to have considered them slaves. Some of the African people aboard the *San Juan Batista* may have been enslaved in the Kingdom of Kongo, to the north of Angola, or in the territory to Angola's east or south. However, it is more likely that they came from the Kingdom of Ndongo, against which the local Portuguese military had been waging large campaigns since 1618. During that conflict thousands of Kimbundo-speaking people were captured and enslaved. It is estimated that between 1617 and 1621 approximately 50,000 slaves were exported from Angola, including approximately 4,000 baptized Christians. Many of these people came from the royal district of Ndongo, between the Lukala and Lutete rivers. If the Africans who came to Virginia in 1619 were indeed from the Lukala-Lutete river area, they probably spoke a common language and shared a complex ethnic identity.

Taking Slaves to Market.
Courtesy of the Colonial Williamsburg Foundation,
Department of Archaeological Research.

Although slavery in Virginia was not fully institutionalized until the very early eighteenth century, the Africans' distinctive appearance, unfamiliar language, and exotic cultural background surely set them apart from the European colonists and placed them at a decided disadvantage. Slavery, though not legalized in England, was not an unfamiliar concept because the English were well aware of the Spaniards' use of slave labor in their mines in the Americas. In fact, as early as 1611, Virginia's deputy-governor, Sir Thomas Dale, spoke of enslaving Native Americans and compelling them to work on government-sponsored projects.

Today it is impossible for us to fully appreciate the pain, anguish, humiliation, and brutality Africans endured when they were captured, branded with a hot iron, and taken from their homeland. Surviving accounts indicate that African rulers who lived in the interior of the continent sometimes had their agents ensnare other blacks, whom they sold to slavers. These people, who were tied together by the neck with leather thongs, were marched overland to the coast. There, they were sold to traders and then imprisoned and branded with the mark of the slaver who bought them. Next, they were loaded aboard the ships that brought them to the New World. It is not surprising that some Africans committed suicide by leaping into the sea. During the Middle Passage from West Africa to America, shipboard conditions were cramped and unsanitary, producing an alarming death rate. The number of dead varied greatly from ship to ship and from voyage to voyage. It has been estimated that just over half of the Africans captured and sold to slavers lived to reach the New World. Once these survivors reached the Americas, the "seasoning" or acclimatization process took a toll. Despite these massive losses, especially in the beginning, the slave trade was profitable, yielding investors a return of approximately twenty-five to fifty percent.[19]

African Contributions to Agricultural Practices

Many of the Africans brought to Virginia during the seventeenth century had a specialized knowledge of agriculture and other practical skills that made a significant contribution to the developing colony. Those from agrarian tribes, who had been servants or agriculturists in their homeland, probably found it somewhat easier to adjust to the New World, because they would have had some preparation for working in agricultural fields. But those who were accustomed to a higher position in the social order would have found life especially difficult. Of immediate use was the Africans' familiarity with the cultivation of tobacco.

Senegambian farmers and those in Sierra Leone were familiar with the cultivation of tobacco, which had been brought to West Africa by the Portuguese in the 1500s. Africans readily took to the habit of smoking tobacco for recreation. In 1607 one English visitor remarked that tobacco was planted near most of the houses in Sierra Leone; in 1620 another Englishman encountered people near the Gambia River, who offered to trade tobacco and pipes for English goods. Some African farmers cultivated tobacco especially for trade. John Barbot, who visited the area between the Senegal River and the Windward Coast between 1678 and 1682, commented that farmers and others were "never without a pipe [of tobacco] in their mouths." It is likely that the West Africans' knowledge and experience in tobacco cultivation maximized production and contributed heavily to its success as a money crop in Virginia. Significantly, in Africa both men and women were involved in the cultivation of tobacco. Senegambian women typically raised it in small family plots, whereas the men probably were responsible for growing large crops intended for commercial use. Tobacco was planted on the floodplain after corn was harvested, and Africans were aware that the characteristics and palatability of tobacco depended upon the soil in which it was grown. All of this specialized knowledge would have been invaluable to Virginia colonists dependent upon an agrarian economy.[20]

Another attribute of African agriculture that was readily transferred to Virginia was the method of tilling the ground. In West Africa, farmers practiced the same hoe-and-hill method of growing corn and tobacco that the early colonists had learned from the Indians. John Barbot noted that "two [African] men will dig as much land in a day as one plow can turn over in England." Although tobacco and corn weren't staple crops in West Africa, most African immigrants knew how to raise them. Therefore, their knowledge and skills were extremely important to Virginia planters. Africans also had a working knowledge of animal husbandry, for many of the people who inhabited the northern part of Senegambia were nomads who tended wandering herds of foraging livestock, usually cattle, sheep and goats. Those who were pastoralists lived near the river. Further south, where rain was more abundant, settled people grew agricultural crops, such as peas, beans, peanuts, rice, millet, sweet potatoes, cotton, and indigo. Poultry were also raised as a food source. Among Africans with specialized skills were fishermen, potters, weavers, blacksmiths, and leather-dressers. In their homeland, local markets and urban centers facilitated the exchange (or bartering) of commodities and agricultural products.[21]

European Intrusion into Native Land

During the first quarter of the seventeenth century, when the Virginia colonists discovered that enormous profits could be reaped from cultivating tobacco, they established plantations along the banks of the James River inland to the fall line, and across the Chesapeake Bay, on the Eastern Shore. This rapid encroachment upon native territory culminated in a major Indian attack that occurred on March 22, 1622, and claimed more than a third of the European settlers' lives. By then, Powhatan's brother, Opechancanough, a charismatic warrior, had become paramount chief.

The Chiskiack Indians, whose territory extended along the lower side of the York River in the vicinity of Indian Field Creek, were subjected to the retaliatory raids the colonists undertook in the wake of the 1622 attack. Undoubtedly the natives' presence made the settlers uneasy. In 1624 and again in 1627 Virginia officials considered building a palisade from Martin's Hundred to Chiskiack, but no action was taken. However, by 1629–30 settlement along the banks of James River was so well established that the colonists decided to move into the countryside along the lower side of the York. In 1633 work commenced on the construction of a palisade that ran between the heads of Archer's Hope (College) and Queens Creeks, cordoning off an area for the colonists' exclusive use. Land was offered to those willing to seat within the Chiskiack Indians' territory. Among the York River frontier's first settlers was Christopher Wormeley I, who in 1639 patented land in what became Mathews County. Wormeley was the governor of Tortuga from 1632 to 1635 and Virginia's Secretary of State from 1635 to 1649.[22]

The Chiskiack Indians Move to Middle Peninsula

During the mid-1630s, when European settlers began clearing and seating land along the lower side of the York River, the Chiskiack Indians vacated their homeland and moved to the Middle Peninsula. By 1642 they were living along the lower side of the Piankatank River, just west of Hugh Gwyn's 1,700-acre patent. The riverine environment in which the Indians established new homes would have provided them with game, fish, and plant materials: the natural resources they would have needed for subsistence. Interestingly, the Chiskiack settled in territory that lay directly across the Piankatank River from the site to which the Kecoughtan Indians reportedly withdrew after Powhatan routed them from their village at the mouth of the James River. With the exception of the Piankatank River, original Indian place names in Mathews County have faded into oblivion. However, seventeenth-century land patents reveal that Wadinger Creek was known as Tankes or Tanx (Little) Chiskiack Creek during the 1640s and that the Chiskiack Indians' old and new towns were used as reference points in several early patents.[23]

Notes

1 http://web.com.wm.edu/geology/virginia/provinces/coastalplain/cbis.html; John Smith, *Travels and Works of Captain John Smith, President of Virginia and Admiral of New England, 1580–1631,* Edward Arber, ed. (Edinburgh, 1910), II, 102; Darrin L. Lowery, *Archaeological Survey of the Coastal Shorelines Associated with Mathews County, Virginia: An Erosion Threat Study* (Easton, Maryland, 2008), 17; http://pubs.usgs.gov/pp/2006/1731/PP1731.pdf; United States Department of Agriculture (USDA), *Soil Survey, Mathews County, Virginia,* "Mathews County, Virginia" (Richmond, 1958–1962), 22; Joseph Martin, *A New and Comprehensive Gazetteer of Virginia and the District of Columbia* (Charlottesville, 1836), 227–228.

2 Keith T. Egloff et al., *First People: The Early Indians of Virginia* (Richmond, 1992), 10–15, 17–20, 23–27, 29–33, 42–45; Lowery, *Survey*, 5–6, 165–166; William and Mary Center for Archaeological Research (WMCAR), *Integrated Management Plan, Mathews County Courthouse Square Historic District (057-0002; 44MT0073), Mathews, Virginia* (Williamsburg, 2007), 5– 6, 112–113; Helen C. Rountree, *Pocahontas's People: The Powhatan Indians of Virginia* (Norman, Oklahoma, 1990), 6; Gerald Johnson et al., *Geological Development and Environmental Reconstruction of Jamestown Island* (Williamsburg, 2001), 157–158.

3 Egloff et al., *First People,* 47–48; David B. Quinn, *North America from Earliest Discovery to First Settlement, the Norse Voyages to 1612* (New York, 1977), 239; Clifford M. Lewis et al., *The Spanish Jesuit Mission* (Chapel Hill, 1953), 38, 89–92, 107–109, 118–121, 133–137.

4 John Smith, "Virginia Discovered and Discribed [*sic*]," 1610; *Travels and Works* , 49–51; Conway Sams, *The Conquest of Virginia, The Second Attempt* (Norfolk, 1929), 807–810; Quinn, *North America*, 202; Robert Tindall, "Draughte of Virginia," 1608; Lyon G. Tyler, comp., *Narratives of Early Virginia* (New York, 1907), 49–51; Thomas E. Davidson, "The People of Tsenacommachah: Powhatan Indians in the Williamsburg Area," in *Williamsburg, Virginia: A City Before the State* (Charlottesville, 2000), 7, 9; USDA, *Soil Survey,* 22.

5 In his "General History," Smith said that at the time of his visit, the Piankatank Indians had fifty to sixty warriors (Smith, *Travels and Works*, II, 104).

6 Smith, *Travels and Works*, I, 53, 147, 175, 187, 229, 232; II, 55, 104, 128, 168–169, 178.

7 Smith, "Discovered," 1610; *Travels and Works*, 49–51, 375; Tyler, *Narratives*, 49–51; Rountree, *Pocahontas's People,* 10–11; Stephen R. Potter, "Early English Effects on Virginia Algonquin Exchange and Tribute in the Tidewater Potomac," in Peter H. Wood et al., *Powhatan's Mantle* (Lincoln, Nebraska, 1989), 152–154; Christian F. Feest, "Virginia Algonquins," in *Handbook of North American Indians: Northeast* (Washington, D.C., 1978), Vol. XV, 255; Susan M. Kingsbury, comp., *Records of the Virginia Company of London* (Washington, D. C., 1906–1935), III, 73; Egloff et al., *First People,* 48–54.

8 David W. Stahl et al., "The Lost Colony and Jamestown Droughts," *Science* 280 (April 1998), 566. The Spanish Jesuits who attempted to establish a mission on the York River

between 1566 and 1569 arrived in a period of extreme drought, as did the "Lost Colonists," who reached Roanoke Island during a drought that extended from 1587 to 1589 (Dennis B. Blanton, "The Climatic Factor in Late Prehistoric and Post-Contact Human Affairs," in *Indian and European Contact in Context: The Mid-Atlantic Region* [Gainesville, 2004], 17).

9 Cary Carson et al., "Impermanent Architecture in the Southern American Colonies," *Winterthur Portfolio*, Vol. 16, No. 2/3, (Summer–Autumn, 1981), 141–144, 153–154, 158; Willie Graham et al., "Adaptation and Innovation: Archaeological and Architectural Perspectives on the Seventeenth Century Chesapeake," *William and Mary Quarterly* 3rd Ser., 64 (2007):461–465.

10 Lyman Carrier, *Agriculture in Virginia, 1607–1699* (Charlottesville, 1957), 20.

11 Darrett B. Rutman and Anita H. Rutman, *A Place in Time, Middlesex County, Virginia, 1650–1750* (New York, 1984), 40–43.

12 Wesley F. Craven, *The Virginia Company of London, 1606–1624* (Charlottesville, 1957), 45; W. Stitt Robinson, *Mother Earth, Land Grants in Virginia, 1607–1699* (Charlottesville, 1957), 21–22; Thad Tate et al., eds., *The Chesapeake in the Seventeenth Century* (Williamsburg, 1965), 93.

13 Kingsbury, *Virginia Company*, III, 153–177.

14 For example, Michaelmas or St. Michael's Day, September 29th, was the date on which one planter's annual rent came due (Patent Book I, 599).

15 Allan Kulikoff, *Tobacco and Slaves: The Development of Southern Cultures in the Chesapeake, 1680–1800* (Chapel Hill, 1986), 31–33.

16 The doubling of England's population between 1520 and 1630 led to widespread poverty and vagrancy.

17 Tate et al., *Chesapeake,* 93; William W. Hening, comp., *The Statutes At Large: Being a Collection of All the Laws of Virginia* (Richmond, 1809–1823), I, 252–253.

18 In March 1620, a little over six months after the first Africans arrived, there were 32 African men and women in Virginia (Ferrar Papers, Pepys Library, Magdalen College, Cambridge University, Manuscripts 138, 139, 159, 178).

19 Engel Sluiter, "New Light on the '20 and Odd Negroes' Arriving in Virginia," *William and Mary Quarterly* 3rd Ser., 54 (1997):395–398.

20 Scholars estimate that nearly half of the approximately five thousand African men and women who were brought to Virginia by the Royal African Company between 1683 and 1721 came from Senegambia, a region whose location fostered the development of economic and cultural exchanges among neighbors. Smaller shipments originated in Sierra Leone, the Gold Coast, the Niger Delta, and Angola (John Thornton, "The African Experience of the '20 and Odd Negroes' Arriving in Virginia," *William and Mary Quarterly* 3rd Ser., 55 [1998]:421–434).

21 Thornton, "The African Experience," 421–434; Ira Berlin and Philip D. Morgan, *Cultivation and Culture: Labor and the Shaping of Slave Life in the Americas* (Charlottesville, 1983), 30; Martha W. McCartney with Lorena S. Walsh et al., *A Study of the Africans and African Americans on Jamestown Island and at Green Spring, 1619–1803* (Yorktown, 2003), 32–33.

22 Martha W. McCartney, "Last Refuge: Tribal Preserves in Eastern Virginia," in *Indian and European Contact* (Gainesville, 2004), 223–228; *Virginia Immigrants and Adventurers, 1607–1635* (Baltimore, 2007), 52–54; William L. Shea, *The Virginia Militia in the Seventeenth Century* (Baton Rouge, 1983), 46–62; Smith, "Discovered," 1610; *Travels and Works*, II, 104; Hening, *Statutes,* I, 205, 208–209; Patent Book V, 416.

23 Hening, *Statutes*, I, 208–209; Patent Book I, 798; II, 165; V, 192; VI, 60, 438.

2

Land and Sea, Indefinitely Wild
1634–1660

Mathews County's Origin

In 1634, when Virginia was subdivided into eight shires or counties, Mathews County's "grandparent," Charles River County, was formed. Its territory, which was vast and vaguely defined, extended along the lower side of the York River, encompassing what later became New Kent, Hanover, and Louisa Counties, and on the Middle Peninsula, Gloucester, King and Queen, Mathews, and Middlesex Counties. Charles River County also gave rise to Caroline, Essex, King George, King William, Lancaster, Orange, Richmond, and Spotsylvania Counties. In 1634 Charles River County had 510 inhabitants—men, women, and children who lived in the loosely defined lower York River settlements known as Chiskiack (Kiskyacke), York, and New Poquoson. At that time there were 4,914 settlers in the Virginia colony.[1]

According to law, each Virginia county had a local court with justices or commissioners of the peace, a sheriff, a clerk, and other lesser functionaries. County justices could take depositions, settle petty disputes and minor criminal cases, and try civil cases involving less than ten pounds sterling. The establishment of county courts, whose authority increased over time, relieved the governor and his council of handling routine matters, allowing them to focus on important cases and function as an appellate body.[2] Besides court officials, each county had a lieutenant, the local military leader responsible for seeing that the militia was armed properly and drilled regularly. Burgesses were elected at the county seat, which was at the hub of local life. By 1643, Charles River County had been renamed York County, and European colonists had begun claiming land in today's Mathews County.[3]

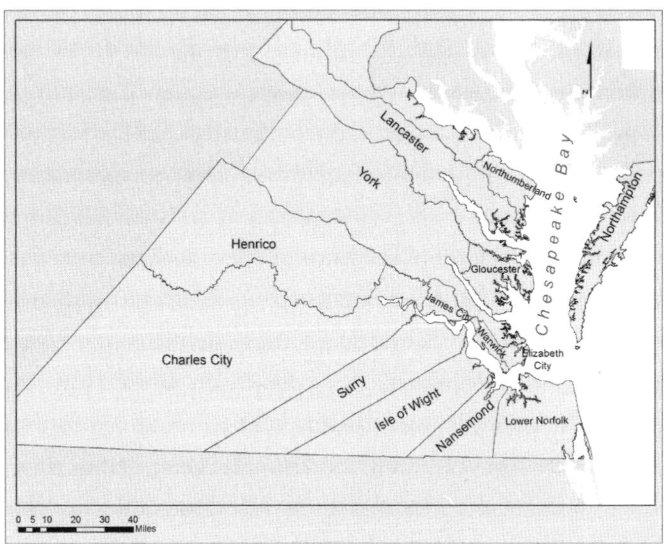

In 1634, when Virginia was subdivided into eight shires or counties, the territory that became Mathews County was part of Charles River (later, York) County. Map by Gregory Brown.

Staking a Claim

Seventeenth-century surveyors typically laid out a patent for waterfront land by projecting an arbitrary straight line that paralleled the river bank. Then, from a specific reference point on that baseline, they would measure a distance in poles that was equal to half of the patent's total acreage. They would then define each of the patent's side lines by running a perpendicular line inland for a distance of one mile. This simple method was in common use throughout much of the seventeenth century, when very few of Virginia's surveyors had formal training and there was an abundance of unclaimed land.[4] Evidence of this surveying technique can be seen on a fragmentary plat for some acreage on the upper side of the North River, which shows the boundaries of a patent issued to Thomas Curtis in 1642 that later belonged to Hugh Nevitt (Nevett). Another example is a survey of the acreage Robert Lendall patented in 1652.[5] Interestingly, County Routes 617 and 660 in Whites Neck, County Route 611 (the extension of Church Street), and portions of State Routes 198 and 14 are roughly a mile from the major rivers they parallel, raising the possibility that these roads follow the back lines of very early waterfront patents. Throughout the colonial period, the land that settlers patented and seated could be transferred from hand-to-hand as if it were owned outright. However, under the law, virtually all Virginia land was owned by the monarchy. Consequently, those who patented acreage in the colony were supposed to pay annual land rent, or quitrent, to the Crown.

Virginia planters and their servants, when seating new land, usually constructed crude huts that they occupied while erecting insubstantial but weatherproof frame houses. Building a simple dwelling or "Virginia house" allowed a patentee to legitimatize his land claim while fulfilling the basic need for shelter. As prospective planters had to make a substantial investment in the workers they needed to cultivate their land, they tended to skimp on housing costs and channel their resources into purchasing labor. Many people placed their undeveloped property in the hands of their indentured servants or tenants, often landless freemen, who agreed to build a dwelling and other essential structures, leaving all in good repair.[6]

Architectural historians surmise that by the second half of the seventeenth century the riven clapboard carpentry of the "Virginia house" had become the dominant way of building, replacing the insubstantial dwellings the early colonists erected when they vacated the fort at Jamestown. The frame of a new house was fabricated from timber that was hewn into posts or split from straight trees. When these posts were seated in the ground in strategically placed holes, they formed an earth-fast frame that gave the structure stability and eliminated the need for braces. As time went on and more of these post-supported houses were erected, experienced builders learned to assemble sidewalls that accommodated the vertical framing members. This made the proper alignment of corner posts easier to achieve and it also provided the building with a framework to which wooden siding could be affixed. Overhead, a roof made of clapboard replaced thatching and was attached to a square timber called a false plate. By the middle of the seventeenth century, many dwellings had end chimneys instead of a central one. Thanks to this added support, the ordinary "Virginia house" erected during the third quarter of the seventeenth century was more sturdily built than its predecessors. When colonists wanted houses that were two rooms deep, they began constructing buildings on continuous ground-laid sills and used roofs that had a greater span and required more complex carpentry. In time, buildings with continuous sills were set upon masonry foundations.[7]

Opening the Frontier to Settlement

Early on, Virginia planters learned that the soil best suited to producing sweet-scented tobacco, the most marketable variety, occurred along the banks of the colony's rivers. As this type of soil was of limited distribution, planters rushed to stake claims to land they knew would yield substantial crops. One such area was the Middle Peninsula, with its abundance of navigable waterways which "afforded a commodious Road for Shipping at every Man's Door." Virginia Land Office records, though incomplete, reveal that between April 1635 and January 1637, acting-governor John West issued a number of patents for acreage on the fringes of the colony's frontier. On December 19, 1635, West and the members of his council awarded Hugh Gwyn (Gwynn), a member of the Grand Assembly, a patent for 1,000 acres of land at the Piankatank River's mouth, acreage that included much of Gwynn's Island and some land on the lower side of Milford Haven.[8] Whether Gwyn, a resident of York County, attempted to seat his land during the 1630s is open to conjecture, but a severe drought that occurred in 1638 would have presented many challenges. However, when he re-patented his acreage in January 1642, he enlarged his holdings by 700 acres, raising the possibility that he had seated at least part of his first patent and was entitled to claim more land. In 1640 and 1646, Gwyn represented York County in the assembly and served as a county justice. Sometime prior to June 4, 1640, three of his servants (a Dutchman, a Scot, and a black man) fled to Maryland. Although he asked the Quarter Court's permission to sell them or put them to hire in Maryland, the justices decided that all three runaways had to be returned to their master in Virginia. Both white men were sentenced to a whipping, but John Punch, a black man, was ordered to serve Gwyn for the rest of his life. This is a classic example of how an indentured servant's race made a difference, legally. Hugh Gwyn was returned to the assembly in 1652, this time representing newly-formed Gloucester County.[9]

In 1641 the territory on the north side of the York River was officially opened to settlement. Prospective patentees had access to land that extended in a northerly direction and included the countryside abutting the Chesapeake Bay, Mobjack Bay and its tributaries, and the Piankatank River. Those intending to establish homesteads within what was then native-held territory were ordered to settle in groups of 100 or more "able men" and to provide their names to the justices of York County. The burgesses decided to offer the Indians' elderly paramount chief, Opechancanough, 50 barrels of corn a year for the territory the colonists seated; they also agreed that if he refused to accept it, settlement could proceed anyhow. Thus, the burgesses acknowledged that the colonists were preparing to enter land the natives considered theirs. Most of the men who claimed thousands of acres of land on the frontier were members of the planter elite who were heavily involved in the colony's political affairs. Many were land speculators, who made abundant use of the headright system and managed to accumulate thousands of acres on which they could grow tobacco. These well-to-do planters rarely occupied the outlying property they patented. Instead, they placed their indentured servants or tenants on their acreage in order to legitimatize their land claim.[10]

The Plantation System: A Way of Life

Scholars generally agree that between 1640 and 1660 the status of Africans and African Americans in Virginia society began to erode, with the result that black and white servants were treated differently. When indentured servants were unhappy with lengthy and sometimes nebulous terms of service, they could take legal action against their masters.[11] But blacks brought to the colony involuntarily had a limited opportunity to become fluent in the English language and even less of a chance to gain an understanding of the law. Thus, they were at a considerable disadvantage when trying to bargain for better treatment or for their freedom. The length of a white servant's term of indenture was specified in his/her contract or was set by law if no contract existed. Blacks in servitude gradually came to be regarded as "servants for life," a custom that was eventually codified into law.

Other legal differences emerged as time went on. In March 1643 all males, whether black or white, and all black females, were subject to a capitation tax, that is, they were taxable if they were age 16 or older. But significantly, white females were not. When the law was revised again in February 1645, "all negro men and women, and all other men from the age of sixteen to sixty" were deemed taxable. This legislation was purportedly enacted because some people had no scruples about claiming who was—and wasn't—taxable. In October 1649, the burgesses, who felt that many settlers were circumventing the law, decided that "all male servants imported hereafter into the collony of what age soever they be, shall be brought into the lists and shall be liable to pay country levys." Exempt from the law were those imported "by theire parents or otherwise," who were free and under the age of 16. Some Virginia planters had Indian servants or slaves living in their household or employed natives to hunt and fish. An act passed by the Grand Assembly in March 1658 declared that all blacks and Indians of both sexes who were age 16 or older were to be considered tithable. During the month of June, household heads were required to provide a list of all tithables to the clerk of their county court.[12]

A Time of Change

Tobacco continued to be the colony's main money crop, but as time went on, grains became increasingly important. When Dutch mariner David DeVries cruised Virginia's waters in 1643, he commented that plantations once "exhausted by tobacco planting were now sown with fine wheat, and some of them with flax." Several years later, another writer spoke of the abundance and variety of domestic livestock and the agricultural prosperity that was seen everywhere. Thanks to growth in the tobacco industry, the demand for cheap labor increased. This led to a surge in immigration and in the importation of indentured servants and Africans from abroad.

A tobacco plant, Virginia's money crop.
Courtesy of the Jamestown-Yorktown Foundation.

Another change that occurred during the early 1640s was the rise of representative government. This change occurred gradually, in part because the Crown failed to interfere in its evolution. In 1643, Virginia's assembly became bicameral, for the burgesses began meeting apart from the governor and council. Virginia's legal system was based upon English law, and the assembly enacted legislation from time to time to meet the colony's changing needs. By the mid-seventeenth century, colonists' homesteads were sparsely scattered throughout eastern Virginia, and some settlers had moved west as far as the fall line.

In 1646, a man queried about conditions in Virginia said that there were 19,000 English and 500 Africans in the colony. He estimated that the settlers had 20,000 cattle, 1,500 sheep, 190 horses, 150 asses, and more hogs and goats than could be counted. He said that there were ten watermills, two windmills and thirty horse-mills. In 1647, another writer reported that the Africans in the colony "remain in Christian mens hands and are so dispersed that I can make no narrative of them." He indicated that good brick and tile were being made in Virginia, as were earthenware vessels. He added that there was a shortage of artisans and proffered that a tinkerer or tin-worker could earn an exceptionally good living. He said, "Our houses are built of wood except it be some particular men of worth," and claimed that they were "very warm and dry with good conveniency and handsome, of a good pitch and will endure the weather well." He noted that most buildings had earthen floors, and closed by saying that "our housing is both board walled and daubed and covered with boards."[13]

Mathews County's First Patentees

As soon as the eastern part of Middle Peninsula was thrown open to settlement, planters rushed in. During 1642 and 1643 at least 23 patents were issued for acreage in what became Mathews County. Virtually all of these patents were on the waterfront and were issued by Sir William Berkeley shortly after he took office as governor.[14] It was then that Richard Bennett, Christopher Boyce, John Condon, Thomas Curtis, Edmund Dawber, Abraham and William English, Thomas Glasscock, Hugh Gwyn, William Hockaday, John Holder, John Lilly (Lily, Lylley), Arthur Price, Peter Rigby, Abraham Turner, Thomas Symons, William Tyman, Thomas Say, and William Worlich (Worleigh) claimed land bordering the Chesapeake and Mobjack Bays, the North and East Rivers, New Point Comfort, Winter Harbor and its tributaries, and in the countryside along the Piankatank River, including Milford Haven. Some of these parcels were "seated," rendering their titles secure. Surviving land records suggest that the most sought-after land bordered the North and Piankatank Rivers, Blackwater Creek, and Mobjack Bay, where there were eight patents for 1,000 acres or more. A handful of the land transactions that occurred during the 1640s and very early 1650s were recorded in York County, the jurisdiction in which the newly patented acreage lay.[15] There are relatively few surviving patents for land on the west side of the East River except for the acreage near its mouth, perhaps because those records have been lost or destroyed.

North River Patentees

Along the upper side of the North River's mouth was a 1,600-acre tract that Edmund (Edmond) Dawber claimed in 1642, property that bordered Seasand Creek[16] and abutted Thomas Curtis's patent.[17] Dawber, who by 1638 had married Virginia governor Sir Thomas Gates' daughter, Margaret, failed to seat his acreage within the obligatory seven years' time and renewed his land claim in 1649. In 1652, when he tried to renew his patent for a second time, his request was denied, for almost half of his acreage already had been assigned to Peter Ransone and William ap Thomas. Their 700 acres was contiguous to the property of Thomas Preston, whose land overlooked Mobjack Bay and abutted east upon what is now known as Whites Creek. William Whitby, a Warwick County burgess and speaker of the assembly, also tried to claim part of Edward Dawber's acreage, as did William Holder, John Hewlett, and William Daynes (Daines). William ap Thomas's land overlooked Mobjack Bay and extended in a westerly direction as far as Isle of Wight (Diggs) Creek. Thomas's land eventually came into the hands of Captain Thomas Todd of Lower Norfolk County. Todd assigned it to Robert Bristow (Bristowe), who came to Virginia in 1660 and married Avarilla (Averilla), the daughter of Major Thomas Curtis, a burgess. Bristow, who returned to England during the late 1670s and became an important merchant and London alderman, owned property on both sides of the North River. He added 230 acres to the Todd acreage by means of headrights, amassing 930 acres that he patented in 1673. Robert Bristow's acreage, which became known as the North River Plantation, spanned the waterfront between Diggs Creek and a nameless inlet just west of Minter Point and Whites Neck's tip. The Bristow plantation also abutted the acreage of Peter Ransone, Thomas Ryland, and Thomas Preston. Robert Bristow's descendants retained possession of the North River Plantation until the close of the American Revolution.

On the upper side of Diggs Creek and extending upstream along the North River was a 1,100-acre plantation established by Peter Ransone, an Elizabeth City County burgess whose 1652 patent extended across Broad Neck (Raymond) Creek. Ransone had an adjacent 300-acre parcel that extended from Raymond Creek to Bald Eagle Neck Creek, now a nameless stream near Snow Hill. Peter Ransone's 1,100 acres descended to his sons George, James, and William in 1658.[18] Their descendants, who had the property surveyed during the mid-eighteenth century, acknowledged that the easternmost part of their acreage had become part of Robert Bristow's plantation. To the Ransone patent's west was land belonging to Richard Dudley, who patented 200 acres on the lower side of Blackwater Creek in 1652; Dudley enhanced his holdings in 1659 and 1684 by acquiring the 639 acres that Thomas Curtis had claimed in 1642. At the mouth of Blackwater Creek was a patent that belonged to Thomas Says, whose name was applied to Says (later Roys) Point; by 1651 Says's land had come into the possession of Edmond Welch. On the upper side of Blackwater Creek and straddling its head, was a 1,150-acre tract that Thomas Curtis first claimed in 1652. By 1667 that acreage had descended to George Curtis, who in 1671 conveyed it to Hugh Nevitt. When Nevitt had the Curtis patent surveyed, he found that it enveloped 1,170 acres. Two of the Nevitt patent's boundary lines and part of a third are shown on a survey that was made in 1733. When Hugh Nevitt made his will on July 27, 1673, he left his Blackwater Creek plantation to his kinsman, William Nevitt, along with all of the goods, servants, and cattle that were on the property. Nevitt's land later descended to a nephew, John Nevitt.

To the west of Blackwater Creek's mouth was a patent that belonged to Colonel Richard Dudley, land that formerly belonged to Ralph Green. By 1680 Dudley had sold his property to Robert Peyton, whose son mortgaged it to Edmund Berkeley of Middlesex County. Upstream from Dudley's patent was some acreage near Green Plains that Abraham Turner patented in 1642. Turner's land, which abutted the property on which Auburn was built, escheated to the Crown and came into the hands of Hannah Tompkins of York County and her descendants. To Turner's west was land to which Richard Creedle had staked a claim by 1642. Part of Creedle's acreage, a promontory that protruded into the North River, became known as Creedle (Cradle) Point.

Land near the head of the North River, whose branches are now known as Burke Mill Stream and North End Branch, was considered prime real estate. Edmund Dawber patented 2,400 acres there in 1642, land that already had been claimed by George Levitt and Thomas Symons. The Dawber acreage at the head of the North River eventually came into the hands of Richard Young, who in 1682 sold it to John Buckner and Henry Whiting; they determined that their patent contained an additional 273 acres. By 1650, Anthony Elliott, an Elizabeth City County burgess who by 1650 had begun investing in real estate in the Middle Peninsula and Northern Neck, laid claim to a 1,150-acre tract situated between the head of the North River and the swamp associated with the North River mill. Elliott was named to the Council of State in 1657 and a year later, became a Gloucester County burgess. By 1656 Elliott's North River acreage had come into the hands of Abraham Iverson, whose patent mentioned a horse path, probably the forerunner of Route 14. In 1659 William Snelling patented some acreage a mile and a half west of Iverson's land; Snelling's property was adjacent to a stream that by 1670 had become known as Snellings Creek and later, Dancing Creek. In 1653 Joan Callis (Careless) patented 450 acres on the east side of the North River dams, near Abraham Iverson's land, and renewed her patent in 1661. By 1684 her property had escheated to the Crown and was reassigned to Charles Jones. Also at the head of the North River was the land of George Burge (Burgh), whose acreage was on Gwyn's Ridge. His heirs, who resided in England, authorized Peter Beverley to sell their property. Also situated at the head of the North River was the North River Quarter, which Robert Beverley I owned in partnership with his brother-in-law Colonel John Armistead.[19]

The East River

In 1643 Lieutenant William Worlich (Worleigh) secured a patent for 550 acres of land on the west side of the East River's mouth, overlooking Mobjack Bay. His acreage, which encompassed the tip of Whites Neck, extended up the East River and abutted Repulse (Whites) and Chestnut Creeks. Worlich, who arrived in Virginia in 1622 as a young indentured servant, went on to become a successful merchant. He rose in prominence and served several terms in the assembly representing Elizabeth City County. He also did business on the Eastern Shore, where John Neal, formerly of Elizabeth City, served as his attorney. By 1652 much of Worlich's patent on the East River had come into the hands of Thomas Preston, who had acquired it from Thomas Conyer (Conniers). Preston's land adjoined Thomas Todd's property, portions of which escheated to the Crown and came into the hands of Thomas Falkener and Robert Bristow. Todd's patent on the East River abutted Chestnut Creek and was reportedly a mile from the North River. His near-neighbors on the East River were John White, William Holder, and Richard Normansell, whose land extended up the west side of the river. As time went on, members of the White family expanded their holdings in the area, with the result that the territory between the East and North Rivers became known as Whites Neck. Further upstream were the landholdings of the Curtises, the Carys, the Dudleys, and Hugh Nevitt, whose properties on the North River extended inland for a considerable distance.[20]

In 1652, Thomas Todd patented 150 acres on the east side of the East River's mouth-acreage that abutted that of Philip Hunley and William Hampton. He also laid claim to some land on Winter Harbor near John Smith's patent, and a neighboring tract near Horn Harbor. John Mann had acquired Todd's acreage by the late 1650s, amassing a total of 600 acres. His property ran inland and abutted that of William Holder and William Worlich, who had land at the head of Horn Harbor. Robert Cully acquired Mann's property sometime prior to 1682, when he and Ralph Armistead patented an additional 63½ acres. In time, the acreage that Cully amassed came into the hands of the Armistead family, from whom it passed to the Smiths. By 1683, Peter Starling or Sterling was in possession of some land near the head of Horn Harbor Creek.[21]

By the early 1650s planters began claiming land on both sides of Pudding (Put In) and Lendalls (Woodas) Creeks. In October 1652, Robert Lendall of York County, a middling planter, used the headright system to patent 150 acres on the upper side of Woodas Creek and bordering the East River. He renewed his patent in 1661, after the monarchy was restored, and his family seems to have retained possession of the property for many years after. Among the legal papers accumulated by the Billups family is a plat showing the parameters of Robert Lendall's 1652 patent, which extended inland for a mile and lay across Woodas Creek from what became the Kingston Parish glebe. When Lendall confirmed his patent in 1661, Mr. Armistead's land was described as adjacent and further up the East River.[22]

By 1653 George Collins had acquired 350 acres that abutted the East River and lay between Put In and Woodas Creeks. Inland, at the head of Collins' property, was a 613-acre tract that Philip Hunley patented in 1651 and gradually enlarged. By 1665, the Collins parcel, which escheated to the Crown, was patented by Richard Dudley. When he had his newly acquired patent surveyed, it was found to contain 455 acres, not 350. By 1684, Colonel Richard Dudley's property on Put In Creek had become Kingston Parish's glebe. Closer to the head of Put In Creek were several parcels that Mark Foster Sr. and his son, Mark Jr. claimed during the mid-to-late 1650s. By the mid-1670s much of the Foster property had come into the hands of Philip Hunley, whose descendants retained it for many years.[23]

In 1667, Adam Bennett patented 330 acres of land on the east side of the East River, adjacent to a small creek near the end of Landing Lane. After Bennett's death, Captain John Armistead patented the property, but he was obliged to relinquish it in 1675 when Robert Bennett, the decedent's son and heir, filed a legal claim that was upheld. Robert Bennett was told that if he failed to produce legal heirs, the property would revert to Armistead. By 1679, the Bennett or Armistead property had come into the possession of Humphrey Toy, whose land abutted Bennett's Creek. Toy's land adjoined that of Christopher Dickens, whose patent was contiguous to Philip Hunley's expansive holdings. Henry Prouse and Roger Leonard also owned 300 acres near Adam Bennett's land. When Francis Jarvis acquired part of Prouse's land, it was said to abut Lendall's corner.[24]

In 1651, William Armistead of Elizabeth City County secured a patent for more than 1,800 acres of land at the head of the East River. His acreage straddled Upright Creek, the northernmost extension of the East River's head, and it encompassed several hundred acres that lay between Upright Creek and the river's westerly branch, which leads toward Route 14 and the site on which Trinity Church eventually was built. Armistead's land at the East River's head abutted a small tract owned by John White, but also extended down the east side of the East River to a point below Bennett's Creek, adjoining Robert Lendall's land. William Armistead's land descended to his son, Anthony, and ultimately, to Anthony's son, John, who re-patented it during the mid-to-late 1670s. When John Armistead moved to Kingston Parish, he settled on his late grandfather's land on the Piankatank River, but retained his acreage on the East River. Armistead's land was near that of Duncan Bohannon and John Machen, who also owned property near the East River's head, abutting Adam Bennett's patent, a short distance downstream.[25]

Patents Bordering the Mobjack and Chesapeake Bays

By 1650, merchant and burgess William Worlich, who had land on the west side of the East River's mouth, had patented 650 acres in the lower part of New Point Comfort Neck, a peninsula that was bordered by the Chesapeake Bay and extended in a southerly direction toward Mobjack Bay's entrance.[26] Worlich's land was east of some acreage that belonged to John Gundry of Elizabeth City, who also owned some land on the upper side of New Point Comfort (Dyers) Creek. Gundry's patent was directly across from Thomas Dyer's land, which abutted west on some acreage owned by Ralph Armistead. By 1684 Worlich's 650 acres in the southerly part of New Point Comfort Neck had been assigned to John Banister and John Corbett had claimed 300 acres in the northerly end of the neck, across from Dyers Creek's mouth. Corbett's land escheated to the Crown and was claimed by Edward Davis in 1700. He, too, allowed his land to lapse and in 1713 it was patented by surveyor Thomas Cooke.[27]

To the northwest of New Point Comfort Neck and abutting Mobjack Bay was a two-pronged stream known as Ducking Pond Creek.[28] Christopher Wormeley I, Tortuga's governor from 1632 to 1635 and Virginia's Secretary of State from 1635 to 1649, patented 4,000 acres in that vicinity on October 25, 1639.[29] By 1650, William Plummer, William Holder, and John Watts had come into possession of portions of the Wormeley patent; so had John Gundry, who owned 100 acres on Ducking Pond Creek. Later in the century Edward Davis patented a large tract at the head of the creek, which became known as Davis Creek. Part of the land he claimed had been patented by John Corbett in 1684 but abandoned.[30]

In 1651, Richard Grigson patented 450 acres on the east side of Pepper Creek's mouth. By 1666, his original patent plus an additional 45 acres had come into the hands of the Rev. Justinian Aylemer, minister of the James City Parish church at Jamestown. After Aylemer's death sometime prior to 1671, his widow, the former Frances Armistead, married Christopher Wormeley II. In 1650, William Worlich patented some land on Mobjack Bay that adjoined William Morgan's 300 acres on the west side of Pepper Creek's mouth. Morgan's acreage extended up Mobjack's shoreline as far as Sloop Creek and ran inland to a gut separating it from the acreage of Richard Hull, who during 1650 and 1651 laid claim to 550 acres on the west side of Pepper Creek. In 1655 Hull added to the size of his holdings by purchasing 300 acres from Winifred Morrison. Her acreage at the head of Pepper Creek abutted the lower side of Horn Harbor. In time, Walter Morgan acquired William Morgan's property, which was eventually developed as Belleview.[31] Near William Morgan's acreage on the west side of Pepper Creek was land that Henry Singleton patented in 1651. Singleton's patent bordered the property of a Mr. Hampton, probably William Hampton, a gentleman whose land was in the same vicinity. By 1661, Singleton had acquired a 400-acre tract that William Leithermore and John Thomas had gotten from John Walker in 1652. That acreage, near the head of Garden Creek, extended toward the East River. Henry Singleton gradually expanded his holdings in the vicinity of the East River's mouth and West Landing Creek, where his land adjoined that of Robert Cully and Ralph Armistead.[32]

By 1651 Winifred, the widow of Major Richard Morrison of Elizabeth City County, had patented 400 acres on the lower side of Horn Harbor and near the head of Pepper Creek. In 1655 her property was assigned to her neighbor, Richard Hull, from whom it passed to John Borum. John Banister, Thomas Foote, and John Borum eventually patented part of Richard Hull's acreage and sold it to Mark Thomas. John Needles also owned land near Mrs. Morrison's. By 1689, his patent had come into the possession of Thomas Todd. During the early 1650s, William Worlich, who already had secured other patents in Kingston Parish, claimed some land on the upper side of Horn Harbor, acreage adjacent to that of William Holder and John Smithey, whose property was near Winter Harbor. Francis Hale and William Bedlam also claimed land in that area during the early 1650s. On the upper side of Horn Harbor and bordering the Chesapeake Bay was a marsh-rimmed tract that Giles Vandercastle and John Tullitt patented in 1678. Tullitt, a skillful builder who owned a brick row house in urban Jamestown and sometimes hosted assembly meetings, was authorized to supply the brick used in the construction of the colony's new capitol building in Williamsburg in 1700. In 1709, he was hired to build the College of William and Mary's main building.[33]

In 1653, John Pead (Peade) patented 150 acres between Horn and Winter Harbors, in what eventually became known as Potato Neck. His acreage, which abutted the Chesapeake Bay, was on the lower side of Winter Harbor Creek. Pead's descendants inherited his property and settled permanently in Kingston Parish. His land was near that of Richard Reyley (Riply), who acquired 400 acres in 1652, using headright certificates he purchased from John Walker. Archibald Bromley (Brownley) later laid claim to 900 acres within Potato Neck. In 1652, Thomas Todd acquired a 450-acre tract on the lower side of Winter Harbor. In 1661, he conveyed his parcel to William Smart, who assigned it to Robert Griggs. Griggs, upon obtaining Smart's acreage, patented 252 acres that Walter Pritchard had secured in 1652, land that abutted the Chesapeake Bay and Charles Sallace's property. Griggs also came into possession of Richard Reyley's patent. In 1689, when Robert Griggs' daughter, Ruth, and her husband, Mottram Wright, decided to have her late father's Winter Harbor plantation surveyed, it was found to contain 1,200 acres. The Wrights exchanged their acreage for a like amount in Old Rappahannock County, which straddled the Rappahannock River.[34]

By the mid-seventeenth century, land speculators had begun acquiring acreage along the south side of Garden Creek. Among the first were Edward Lucas and John Hampton, who in 1655 claimed 150 acres apiece. Their patents, which came into the hands of Charles Hill in 1658, were near the head of Garden Creek and extended toward the East River, perhaps reaching the heads of Weston and Tabbs Creeks. Hill sold his property to Samuel Hathaway and George Moseley, who by 1662 had conveyed the 300-acre parcel to Rowland Williams. Finally, in 1673, Secretary of the Colony Robert Beverley I patented both men's properties. By 1678, John Digges had acquired the Beverley property and some contiguous acreage, amassing a total of 1,800 acres that included the headwaters of the streams that flow into Garden Creek, Horn Harbor, and Winter Harbor. Robert Griggs, whose plantation was on the lower side of Winter Harbor, also owed land on Winter Harbor's upper side, toward Garden Creek. In 1662 he and Edward Wyatt patented 370 acres that abutted the land of John

Smithey and extended toward the Chesapeake Bay. By 1683 Smithey owned nearly 1,200 acres between Garden Creek, Winter Harbor, and the bay.[35]

In 1642, Peter Rigby of York County, a real estate speculator, patented 450 acres on the upper side of Garden Creek, abutting Lillys (now Stokes) and Rigby's Creeks and including Rigby Point, later known as Rigby Island.[36] As time went on, Rigby's acreage was acquired by Edmund Cheesman I, who in 1650 patented 50 acres of marshland and woods on the north side of Garden (Garden Patch) Creek, close to the Chesapeake Bay. Cheesman, a resident of Elizabeth City during the mid-1620s, moved to York County, where he settled permanently and became a county justice. He married John Lilly's widow, Mary, who became a member of the Quaker faith. After it became illegal for groups of Quakers to assemble, the Cheesman couple received a stern rebuke from York County's court justices. In 1662, Edmund Cheesman I leased all of his land in eastern York County to his brother, John, and established a plantation near Chisman (Cheesman) Creek. When Edmund Cheesman I died in the early 1670s, his landholdings descended to his son, Thomas, who in 1680 re-patented his 530 acres on the upper side of Garden Creek. The Cheesman land abutted Henry Forrest's property, Garden Creek and its marsh, Rigby Point, the Chesapeake Bay, and Stokes Creek's head.[37]

In 1642, John Lilly (Lylley), whose widow married Edmund Cheesman I, patented the 350 acre peninsula that became known as Lilleys Neck, adjacent to the acreage owned by Peter Rigby and Edward Peirsifull. In 1682 when Lilly's son laid claim to an adjacent 234 acres, his property was said to abut the holdings of Henry Forrest and George Billups. In 1658 Forrest patented 700 acres, part of which already had passed through the hands of real estate speculator Abraham Moone, Thomas Bourne, and George Billups. Forrest and his descendants retained their property for several generations. George Billups patented 750 acres just west of Lilleys Neck in 1653. As time went on, Billups and his descendants extended their holdings into the countryside bordering Billups Creek and toward the head of Garden Creek. The Billups family's landholdings also ran in an easterly direction, approaching the acreage that Peter Rigby had sold to Edmund Cheesman I. In 1682, Morris Mackashannock patented 140 acres on the lower side of

Peach Point (Sluts, later Stutts) Creek, land he purchased from George Billups. Mackashannock's neighbor was Edward Lassells, Mathews County's earliest known shipbuilder.[38]

The Piankatank River Countryside

Hugh Gwyn, who in December 1635 secured a patent for 1,000 acres that included part of an island and land on the lower side of the Piankatank River's mouth, re-patented his acreage in August 1642. This raises the possibility that he had failed to develop his property within the required seven years, or that he wanted to have his original patent confirmed by the colony's newly-arrived governor, Sir William Berkeley. Gwyn's 1642 patent encompassed much of Gwynn's Island and extended along the lower bank of Milford Haven, enveloping the northeastern part of Crab Neck between Point Breeze and Lanes Creek. In July 1642, John Conden (Connydon) and William and Abraham English tried to secure patents for land in Crab Neck, but both men's claims were overridden by Hugh Gwyn's.[39] In January 1643, Gwyn enhanced the size of his original patent by claiming an additional 700 acres, 200 acres of which was marshland. His new patent, which encompassed his previous land claim, extended in a westerly direction along Milford Haven as far as the Narrows and Hills (Stingray) Bay and took in a little more than a mile and a half of shoreline.[40] Like other early waterfront patents, Gwyn's grant ran inland for one mile; therefore, its back line would have terminated near portions of modern-day County Routes 223 and 639 and Route 198. During the 1650s, when Virginia was under the sway of the Commonwealth government, Gwyn, who was then a colonel, laid claim to 300 acres of surplus land that was on the southwestern end of Gwynn's Island and bordered Deep (Edwards) Creek. He also added 165 acres on the lower side of Milford Haven, which extended his holdings across Queens Creek and into Cow Neck. In 1657, Gwyn consolidated all of these land claims into a patent for 2,000 acres, which enveloped more than 2.6 miles of the Piankatank's shoreline.

Three miles up the Piankatank River, in the vicinity of Plumtree (Burton) Point, was a second 2,000-acre tract that Hugh Gwyn patented in

1642. Although Christopher Boyce tried to claim the same riverfront acreage, when the men's dispute was aired before the Grand Assembly in 1652, Gwyn's patent was upheld. This acquisition engulfed more than 3.1 miles of shoreline, extending Gwyn's holdings across Gwyn's (Chapel) Creek and approaching Iron Point and Warehouse Cove. In 1642, Richard Bennett, a wealthy merchant with Puritan leanings, patented 100 acres on the east side of Queens Creek, inland and directly behind Hugh Gwyn's acreage. By 1652, Richard Cary (Carey) had come into possession of part of the Gwyn acreage on the east side of Queens Creek, and to the west, William Armistead acquired a portion of the Gwyn land that Armistead's descendants developed as the plantation called Hesse. Others who claimed land to the west of Hugh Gwyn's massive holdings in 1642 included William Hockaday, who patented 1,100 acres on the west side of Hockadays (Cobbs) Creek, where a dramatic curve in the river forms a natural harbor. To Hockaday's west and abutting east upon Wadinger (Tankes Chiskiack) Creek was the 1,000-acre tract claimed by Arthur Price, a merchant, York County burgess, and real estate speculator.[41]

Surviving patents, though incomplete, suggest that during the early 1640s relatively few patentees claimed land along the upper side of the Piankatank River. However, many early patents have been lost or destroyed, leaving major gaps in surviving records. In 1642, Peregrin Bland, a York County burgess, patented 1,000 acres near what became known as Healy (Bland) Creek, and John Mottram of York County, who ultimately settled in the Northern Neck, patented 1,900 acres to Bland's west, encompassing Wilton Point.[42] Between the patents secured by Mottram and Bland was a 200-acre riverfront parcel that belonged to Hugh Gwyn. An official transcription of Mottram's 1642 patent for what he called Mottram's Mount makes reference to Glebe (Wilton) Creek, which suggests that there were enough settlers in the region to justify the presence of a clergyman. It is likely that other patentees claimed land along the Piankatank's upper side during the early 1640s, particularly near the river's mouth, where Thomas Bourne was in possession of riverfront acreage later in the decade. Bourne's landholdings encompassed Store Point (Stove Point Neck), Bourne (Jackson) Creek, and extended west as far as Barbeque (Moore) Creek.[43]

Native Resistance to Expansion

The Indians of the Powhatan Chiefdom probably watched uneasily as increasing numbers of European colonists ventured into their remaining territory. Despite an April 1642 reference in minutes of the colony's assembly to a treaty "of peace with friendship with the Indians," the natives made a second attempt to drive the colonists from their land. This attack, which occurred on April 18, 1644, claimed the lives of an estimated four to five hundred settlers. Again, Opechancanough was credited with leading the assault. Especially hard hit were those who lived in the upper reaches of the York River and on the lower side of the James River near Hampton Roads. Retaliatory marches were undertaken against specific native groups, and the inhabitants of relatively remote areas were ordered to withdraw to positions of greater safety. Captain William Claiborne, who was convinced that the Indians of the Northern Neck were not involved in the attack, led a large and well-equipped army against the Pamunkey Indians' stronghold in Pamunkey Neck, destroying their villages and cornfields. Afterward, the Indians withdrew into the forest and disappeared from view.

In October 1644, legislation was enacted that authorized all but those who lived in "places of danger" to go back to their homes. Settlers whose return would place them at risk were allowed to reoccupy their patents as long as they had the local military commander's approval and there were at least ten able-bodied men in the group equipped with arms and ammunition. Some people were reluctant to return to their property, and after a few months the colony's governing officials declared that those who failed to reoccupy their patents would be presumed to have abandoned them. This may have impelled some settlers to return to their homesteads despite their fear of being attacked. In February 1645, while Governor William Berkeley was in England procuring much needed military supplies, the colonists continued to press their offensive. Because so few military supplies were on hand and the colonists were unable to procure more, members of the assembly decided to build forts or garrisons in strategic locations along the frontier. These outposts, located near Indian towns, were built for the purpose of maintaining surveillance over the natives. A search party was sent out to capture the paramount chief, Opechancanough, dead or alive; when they sighted him, Governor Berkeley rallied a party of horsemen and set out in pursuit. The aged Indian leader was captured and brought back to Jamestown, where he was jailed. According to early eighteenth century historian Robert Beverley II, while Opechancanough was incarcerated, he was shot in the back by a soldier whose family had perished at the hands of the Indians. It was an inglorious end for a native emperor whose people accorded him a godlike status, but it also was an important turning point in the colonists' relationship with the Indians.[44]

The 1646 Indian Treaty

On October 5, 1646, Necotowance, the late Opechancanough's immediate successor and a comparatively weak leader, concluded a formal peace agreement with the Virginia government, whose officials promised to protect his people from their enemies. The Indians, in return, agreed to pay an annual tribute to the Crown's representatives, thereby acknowledging their subservience. They also indicated their willingness to allow the colony's governor to appoint or confirm their leaders. This was an especially significant policy change, one that hastened the disintegration of the Powhatan Chiefdom, for it was designed to scatter the native groups formerly unified under a powerful paramount chief. Under the terms of the 1646 treaty the tributary natives agreed to withdraw from the James-York Peninsula, inland as far as the fall line, and to abandon their territory on the lower side of the James, down to the Blackwater River. Indians entering the territory ceded to the Virginia government could be lawfully slain, unless they were garbed in "a coate of striped stuff" that official messengers were to wear as a badge of safe conduct. All trade with the Indians was to be conducted at specific "checkpoints." The one closest to Mathews County was on the lower side of the York River at Captain William Tayloe's house, adjacent to Kings Creek. Colonists who had seated land on the north side of the York prior to the signing of the treaty had to withdraw from that area. However, they were given until March 1, 1647, to remove or slaughter their cattle and hogs, to fell trees, or to cut sedge.[45] The 1646 treaty specified that if Virginia's governing officials decided to allow colonists to move into the territory east of Poropotank Creek, the Indians' leaders would to be notified. Settlers who moved to the north side of the York River without official permission were to be deemed guilty of a felony.

It is likely that colonists holding patents for land on the north side of the York River were angered by the order to abandon their property. In 1648, a group of planters, who claimed that many people were being forced to expend their labor "upon barren and overwrought ground" instead of new and fertile soil, asked the Grand Assembly to allow settlement to expand into the vast territory north of the York River. The burgesses acquiesced to political pressure and on September 1, 1649, the burgesses officially opened the Middle Peninsula and Northern Neck to settlement. Colonists swarmed into the territory that the 1646 treaty reserved for the natives. This policy change occurred in synch with official abandonment of the military outposts established in 1645 and 1646. Seating requirements were extremely lax and with the exception of those patenting lots in urban Jamestown, only one acre had to be placed under cultivation and only one house built to substantiate a claim to new land. At first, patentees were given three years in which to seat their land, but after a short while, that time frame was extended to seven years.[46]

The Chiskiack or "North" Indians' Land

In October 1649, Virginia's governing officials decided to allocate 5,000 acres to each of three Indian groups whose territory was surrounded by colonized land: the Pamunkey, the Weyanoke, and the "Northern Indians" or Chiskiack, whose leader was named Ossakican (Wassatickon). It was then that the Chiskiack Indians were assigned acreage along the south side of the Piankatank River, within what became Gloucester and Mathews Counties. The Chiskiack Indians' preserve or reservation, which included the land on which they were living, was to be laid out by a qualified surveyor. In accord with the surveying conventions then used for riverfront patents, the Indians' property, which traced the shoreline of the Piankatank River, would have extended inland for one mile. On the east, the Chiskiack Indians' boundary line commenced at the "land of mr. Heugh [Hugh] Gwinn," the 2,000 acres he had patented in 1642, and a small creek, most likely Chapel or Gwynn's Creek. From that point, the Indians' land extended upstream in a straight line for 7.8 miles along the waterfront, crossing Chiskiack (Ferry) Creek, encompassing Hell Neck, and reaching Harper Creek.[47] Assembly members knew that colonists had patented some of the acreage being allocated to the Indians and agreed that those patentees would be paid a thousand pounds of tobacco for every 500 acres confiscated and that they would be allowed to claim a comparable amount of land elsewhere.[48] Among those affected were William Hockaday, whose 1,100 acres of land lay between Cobbs and Wadinger Creeks, and Arthur Price, whose 1,000-acre patent lay to the west of Hockaday's land and abutted east on Wadinger Creek. Hockaday, who like Price was a merchant, attorney, land speculator, and York County justice and burgess, was obliged to relinquish his 1,000-acre patent, but he was allowed to retain his 900-acre tract that lay inland and directly behind the Chiskiack Indians' preserve.[49]

In March 1652, Colonel George Ludlow, a burgess and York County resident who came to Virginia sometime prior to 1641 and was named to the Governor's Council in 1642, patented 2,000 acres on the lower side of the Piankatank River. His property, which lay on the west side of Chapel Creek, was situated within the eastern part of the 5,000 acres assigned to the Chiskiack Indians in October 1649. Ludlow's patent stated that he had acquired his acreage from the King of the Chiskiack in exchange for some land on the upper side of the Piankatank and that the bargain had been acknowledged before the governor and his council. When George Ludlow made his will in 1655, he left his real and personal estate in Virginia to his nephew, Thomas, whose widow, Mary, had inherited the property by 1662. When assembly members chided Mrs. Mary Ludlow for encroaching upon the Chiskiack Indians' land, they referred to an existing survey of the natives' property.[50]

Besides the Ludlow acreage, the Chiskiack Indians divested themselves of another large piece of their tribal land. On October 29, 1655, Pindavako, guardian of the young king of the Chiskiack, confirmed a gift of land that Wassatickon, the Chiskiacks' late king, had made to Edward Wyatt, nephew of former Virginia governor, Sir Francis Wyatt. The agreement, endorsed at Major William Wyatt's home in front of witnesses, stated that the Indians were giving Edward Wyatt all of their land between Hugh Gwyn's boundary line and Uttamarke or Dancing Creek, a small stream just east of Ferry

Creek. Moreover, the Indians agreed not to sell the rest of their land without his consent. The 1,230 acres of Indian land that Edward Wyatt patented in 1662 extended in an easterly direction from Wadinger Creek's mouth.[51]

The Chiskiack Indians, by transferring more than 2,000 acres to George Ludlow and 1,230 acres to Edward Wyatt, relinquished their rights to all but 1,770 acres of the tribal land they had been assigned by the colonial government. As the natives' concept of land ownership was vastly different than that of the colonists, they probably didn't realize that when they conveyed acreage to others, they were relinquishing all claims to it. In November 1656, the Council of State decided to assign the Chiskiack Indians' remaining land to what they called the "glebes of Gloucester" and church officials were authorized to take possession of the acreage as soon as the Indians deserted it. However, in March 1661, the Chiskiack Indians' land title was confirmed and they were allowed to hunt and to retain any guns currently in their possession.[52]

In October 1652, Captain Augustine Warner, who came to Virginia in 1628 and served as a burgess, patented 2,500 acres on the west side of Wadinger Creek, directly behind the Chiskiack Indians' land and contiguous to the "old branches of the *old* Cheescake [Chiskiack] town." That statement, when viewed in light of Augustine Moore's June 1652 claim for acreage on the north side of the Piankatank, across from the Chiskiack Indians' *new* town, suggests that the natives had abandoned their old village on the west side of Wadinger Creek, in the western part of their territory, and had moved east, establishing a new town near Cobbs Creek.[53] In October 1669 when a census was made of eastern Virginia's native population, there were only 15 Chiskiack (Chiskoyack) Indian warriors, all of them were residing in Gloucester County. In 1670 cartographer Augustine Herrman identified the site of the old Chiskiack town on the west side of Ferry Creek in the vicinity of Hell Neck. By 1686 Robert Beverley I had come into possession of acreage between Wadinger (Cheesecake) Creek and Hockadays (Baylys, Cobbs) Creek, which he bequeathed to his son, Peter. Beverley indicated that his acreage on the Piankatank River abutted that of John Mann.[54]

Ramifications of the English Civil War

Even before England became embroiled in a bloody civil war, tensions between the royalists and the supporters of Parliament, dubbed the Roundheads, had spilled over to the colonies. Virginians, by and large, were sympathetic to the monarchy, and after they learned that King Charles I had been beheaded, the burgesses proclaimed his son's right to the throne and declared that anyone questioning Charles II's right of succession would be considered treasonous. Governor William Berkeley, who was fiercely loyal to the Crown, invited exiled royalists to seek refuge in Virginia and freely granted them land.

As soon as England's civil war ended and Oliver Cromwell's government came into power, a Parliamentary fleet set sail for Virginia to proclaim the Commonwealth government's supremacy. When Cromwell's representatives arrived at Jamestown, they discovered that Sir William Berkeley's troops were prepared to defend the capital city; however, Berkeley surrendered peacefully and relinquished his governorship. The articles of surrender Berkeley signed in March 1652 acknowledged that Virginia was under the purview of the Commonwealth's laws, which had not been imposed through the use of force. The burgesses were allowed to conduct business as usual but could not enact legislation contradicting the laws of the Commonwealth. Virginia's charter was to be confirmed by Parliament, and the legality of the colony's land patents was to be upheld. Virginians, like all English citizens, were entitled to free trade, and no taxes could be imposed upon them without their assembly's consent. All publicly-owned arms and ammunition had to be surrendered, and anyone refusing to subscribe to the articles of surrender had to leave Virginia within a year. During 1659, the Commonwealth government strengthened the Navigation Acts, which were intended to restrict Virginia's trade with foreign nations. This prompted Governor Berkeley to remind his superiors that the articles of surrender granted Virginians the right of "free trade with all nations in amity with the people of England."[55] Many important changes occurred in Virginia while the Commonwealth government was in power.

The Status of Native Land

Legislation passed in 1652 specified that "all the Indians of the collonye shall hold and keep those seats of land that they now have." The burgesses, aware of the wrongs being done to the Indians, admitted that they were barely able to subsist and declared that acreage would be assigned to native groups who requested it. They also decided that no one could purchase Indian land without the approval of the Quarter Court, then the colony's highest ranking judicial body. There was a legal loophole, however, whereby county court justices were allowed to make peace agreements with neighboring Indian tribes and approve their land transactions. Indian land was considered desirable, and as the Rev. Hugh Jones astutely noted, "Whenever we meet with an old Indian field, or place where they have lived, we are sure of the best ground." In 1656, the burgesses authorized Tributary Indian tribes to hunt and gather outside of the territory they had ceded to the government in 1646, except for land the colonists had enclosed with fences. Later, natives were permitted to hunt, fish, and gather plant materials within the colonized area as long as they were unarmed and carried a license issued by a county court. Very little was done to protect the Indians or their tribal land; in fact, court documents reveal that high-ranking officials often were unscrupulous about taking part of the Indians' tribal land. Finally, in 1662, the assembly decided to assign each Indian group 50 acres per warrior, land that was to be taken as an aggregate. This acreage allowance was generalized as a three-mile ring or buffer zone around each Indian town. Encouraging the natives to settle in groups was advantageous to the colonists, for it left open spaces into which settlement could expand.[56]

The Establishment of Gloucester County

The Middle Peninsula was declared open to settlement in 1649 and within two years' time, the territory north of the York River was so populous that Gloucester County was formed. A May 21, 1651, patent for land in "Gloster" County was issued approximately eight months before Sir William Berkeley had to surrender the colony to representatives of England's Commonwealth government. Gloucester County extended from the north side of the York River to the south side of the Piankatank River. Its easternmost limits were delimited by the Chesapeake Bay, but its westerly boundary was undefined until King and Queen County was formed in 1691. In late April 1652 Gloucester County's electorate sent Hugh Gwyn and Francis Willis as delegates to the assembly. The location of Gloucester County's first seat of government is uncertain, although it probably was near the center of the county and on a main road. The justices of newly-formed counties usually convened in a private home or a tavern until a courthouse could be built.[57]

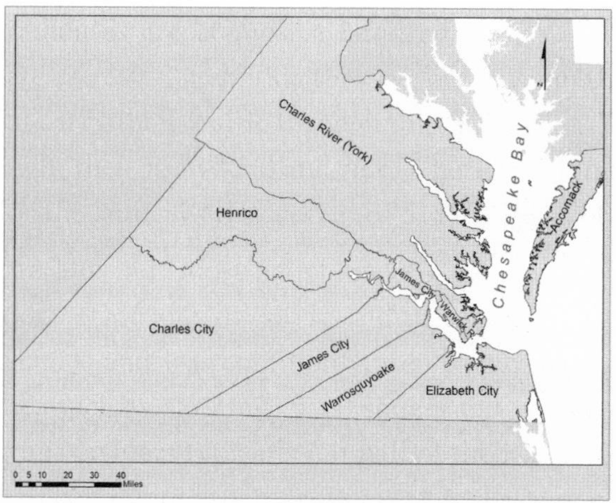

In 1651 Gloucester County was formed from part of York County. In 1791 part of Gloucester became Mathews County. Map by Gregory Brown.

The Colony at Midcentury

A description of Virginia published in 1649 indicates that approximately 15,000 English people were in the colony, along with 300 blacks, who were described as good servants. The writer reported that Governor Berkeley had successfully grown rice at Green Spring and said that "the ground and Climate [in Virginia] is very proper for it as our Negroes affirme." He added that "in their own Country [it] is most of their food, and very healthful for our bodies." In 1650, another writer sent word to England that in Virginia, a good cow was worth 500 to 600 pounds of tobacco in the summer, or 300 pounds in the winter. He said that swine and poultry were abundant and that most people did their own slaughtering and butchering. He added that coopers and tailors could make a good living in Virginia, as could carpenters, joiners, and smiths, if equipped with the tools of their trade. The writer estimated that fully 30 to 40 ships visited the colony every year, supplying the settlers' necessities. Governor Berkeley, who constantly sought new ways to enhance Virginia's economic potential, supported inland exploration in search of minerals, precious metals, and other natural resources, and to increase Indian trade. Thanks to his efforts, new trade routes were opened and the groundwork was laid for Virginia's claim to the Ohio River Valley.

Settlement continued to fan out in every direction and forestlands were converted to cleared fields used for agriculture. Eastern Virginia was dotted with small and middling farmsteads that were interspersed with the larger plantations of the more prosperous. Generally, when colonists moved into new territory, they vied for waterfront property that had good soil and convenient access to shipping. Successful planters usually managed to acquire several small tracts, which they consolidated into relatively large holdings, and they used them to raise tobacco and other crops. Some visitors commented that Virginia's plantations, when seen from a distance, resembled small villages. One man said that most homes were built of wood and consisted of "but one story besides the loft." He described them as "contrived so delightfull, that your ordinary houses in England are not so handsome" and said that "usually the rooms are large, daubed and whitelimed, glazed and flowered [floored], and if not glazed windows, shutters which are made very pritty [*sic*] and convenient." He spoke of seeing free-ranging cattle, hogs, and poultry, and said that Virginians had "all things of their own, growing or breeding without drawing the peny [penny] to send for this or that."[58]

The Formation of Kingston Parish

In March 1652, when the Commonwealth government came into power in Virginia, ecclesiastical law was suspended, but the clergy were allowed to continue using the Book of Common Prayer as long as they omitted all references to the monarchy. Parish vestries were authorized to collect church dues for only one more year. By 1656, however, the burgesses had become concerned about colonists' failure to seek religious instruction, and ordained ministers hesitated to move to Virginia because they couldn't depend on being paid. Moreover, some of the civil duties relegated to parish officials were being neglected or omitted altogether. For example, since 1632, the clergy had maintained a register of the baptisms, marriages, and funerals they had performed and submitted those records annually to the colony's governing officials. In 1657, the assembly started requiring vestries to maintain a register in which parishioners' births, baptisms, marriages, and deaths were recorded, and to present those registries to the county court each March. Vestries were also supposed to "procession" the land in their parishes every four years. That is, two or more vestrymen were to meet with the owners of contiguous properties to verify their common boundaries or resolve boundary disputes. Parish vestries were responsible for seeing that the poor, the widowed, the orphaned, and the illegitimate children received care. At the parish church, people gathered not only to worship, but also to mingle and socialize. In Virginia, as in England, christenings, marriages, and funerals were public rites that brought together the members of a community. The door of a parish church served as a bulletin board of sorts, where public notices and other announcements were posted.

When the assembly convened in March 1656, its members enacted legislation that required the justices of newly-formed counties that had not been "laid off into parishes" to do so at once. Colonists categorized as tithable were supposed to contribute toward building their parish's church, and any surplus funds were to go toward purchasing a glebe and livestock for the incumbent minister. It may have been in response to this legislative act that Gloucester County was carved into four parishes—Abingdon, Kingston, Petsworth, and Ware—and that what remained of the Chiskiack Indians' tribal land was offered to church officials. Legislation enacted in March 1661 specified that natural boundaries be used to define the parameters of parishes and counties whenever possible. Kingston Parish already met those criteria, for it was bound on the north by the Piankatank River; on the south by Mobjack Bay; on the east by the Chesapeake Bay; and on the west by the North River's easternmost branch and headwaters and Wadinger Creek. In 1791, when Mathews County was carved out of Gloucester County's northernmost territory, its boundaries embraced virtually all of Kingston Parish, but also included some acreage within neighboring Ware Parish.[59]

Other Important Changes

In March 1655, the Grand Assembly authorized the establishment of one or two markets or trading zones in each of the colony's counties. Each market could extend for a mile-and-a-half to two miles along both sides of a navigable waterway. Although Gloucester County's earliest records have been lost or destroyed we know that in nearby Middlesex County, which was formed from Lancaster County in 1669, there was an official market on the Piankatank River on Richard Perrott's property at Doctor Point. This market, which extended for two miles along the river, would have provided Kingston Parish's settlers with ready access to imported goods.

By the mid-to-late 1650s, England's excess population had been siphoned off and the flow of indentured servants had slowed to a trickle. This occurred at a time when a growing numbers of laborers were needed to toil in the tobacco fields. Meanwhile, the number of workers of African descent grew rapidly, thanks to importation and natural increase. This fueled development of the plantation system, which in turn created an even greater demand for labor. It is not surprising that large landowners, who typically served as Virginia's lawmakers, tended to fashion legislation that furthered their own interests. In March 1655, the assembly modified the laws that regulated indentured servants' contracts. They lengthened the terms of newly-arrived servants and specified that Irish servants, who came to Virginia without indentures, had to serve for six years if they were age 16 or older, or until age 24 if they were younger. Those terms were somewhat longer than the ones assigned to other Europeans. This legislative change occurred while the Commonwealth government was in power, and Oliver Cromwell's men were pressing the cause of Protestantism in Ireland. In 1658, the 1655 law extending Irish servants' terms was expanded to include "all aliens." However, as soon as the monarchy was restored, the assembly repealed the new laws, noting that they were full of "rigour and inconvenience" and might discourage servant immigration. The burgesses also declared that no servant from a Christian nation who came to Virginia without an indenture would be required to serve longer than those of comparable age. The life of most indentured servants was hard. Although artisans and people of specialized skills might be able to negotiate for better treatment, most servants worked from sunup to sundown and slept in sheds or lofts. Their diet, according to one European traveler, was "an excellent but somewhat indigestible soup" made of corn that was sometimes augmented with cornbread or meat. Servants often became ill during their first few months in Virginia and many did not live long enough to gain their freedom. As a group, those of higher status often viewed them disdainfully, terming them "poor miserable Wretches," and sometimes, servants encountered inhumane or sadistic masters.[60]

NOTES

1 Charles Cocke, *Diocese of Southern Virginia* (Richmond, 1964), 164; British Public Records Office (BPRO), Colonial Office (CO) 8/55 f 155; Hening, *Statutes*, I, 249; Emily J. Salmon and Edward D. C. Campbell, *The Hornbook of Virginia History* (Richmond, 1994), 16–17, 165, 167.

2 By the early 1620s, the Governor's Council had begun convening monthly as a judicial body. In 1658 they started meeting only four times a year, but their sessions were lengthy. By 1662, the Quarter Court had become known as the General Court (Henry Hartwell et al., *The Present State of Virginia and the College [1697] by Henry Hartwell, James Blair and Edward Chilton* [Princeton, 1940], 19; Hening, Statutes, II, 17–32, 58–59, 244).

3 Cocke, *Southern Virginia*, 164; CO 8/55 ff 155; Hening, *Statutes*, I, 249; Patent Book I, 174, 183, 798–799.

4 The linear measurement that seventeenth-century surveyors used was the pole, which was 16.5 feet in length. The linear pole that modern surveyors use is 33 feet.

5 Gloucester Surveyors Plat Book A (1733–1810), 4–5; Untitled plat of Robert Lendall's patent, Billups Papers, Swem, Box 9 folder 31; Box 10 folder 3; Robinson, *Mother Earth*, 21–22; Thad Tate et al., *Chesapeake*, 93; William Maxwell, ed., *Virginia Historical Register II* (1849), 190–193.

6 Through the analysis of faunal remains, zooarchaeologists have learned that wild resources, such as game, waterfowl, and fish, were a critical component in the early settlers' diet. The same most likely was true when Mathews County was part of the Virginia frontier (Graham et al., "Adaptation," 473–474). However, when the native population moved further inland and domestic livestock was brought into the region, dietary patterns changed.

7 Graham, et al., "Adaptation," 467–470, 505.

8 Milford Haven may have been named after a deep-water port in southern Wales.

9 Patent Book I, 806, 865; III, 120; H. R. McIlwaine, *Minutes of the Council and General Court of Colonial Virginia* (Richmond, 1924), 466; Martha W. McCartney, *Jamestown People to 1800: Landowners, Public Officials, Minorities, and Native Leaders* (Baltimore, 2012), 143–144;

Robert Beverley (II), *History of the Present State of Virginia* (1705), L.B. Wright, ed. (Chapel Hill, 1947), 57; Blanton, "Climate Factor," 17.

10 William G. Stanard, ed., "Virginia Assembly of 1641: A List of Members and Some of the Acts," *Virginia Magazine of History and Biography* 9 (1901–1902): 52–53; Hening, *Statutes*, I, 237. In 1935 a local resident WPA worker Harriet G. Miller interviewed said that according to local lore, a man on the Piankatank River brought a number of convict servants to the colony. After they had worked off their indebtedness, he freed them and reportedly allowed them to take his name. The informant proffered that that "is why there are so many people of that name in the county." However, he failed to mention the surname to which he referred (Harriet G. Miller, University of Virginia, Alderman Library, Albert and Shirley Small Special Collections Library, "Interviews," Box 11).

11 Servants also could sue if they believed that the terms of their contracts were being violated.

12 Hening, *Statutes*, I, 242, 292, 361, 411, 454–455, 471, 538–539; II, 289–290, 464–465; Nell M. Nugent, *Cavaliers and Pioneers: Abstracts of Virginia Land Patents and Grants* (Baltimore, 1969), I, 326; Thad W. Tate, *The Negro in Eighteenth Century Williamsburg* (Williamsburg, 1965), 3, 5–6; William P. Palmer, comp., *Calendar of Virginia State Papers* (New York, 1968), I, 10; McIlwaine, *Minutes*, 411. The term "tithable," which appears in the seventeenth- and eighteenth-century Virginia records, refers to a person who is considered taxable on account of age or racial classification. Those taxes, imposed by the colony's assembly, went toward the support of the civil government but also the Established Church, which also had taxing authority.

13 Peter Force, comp., *Tracts and Other Papers, Relating to the Origin, Settlement and Progress of the Colonies in North America* (Gloucester, Mass., 1963), Vol II, Book 8: 3, 14–15; III, Book 14:18; Ferrar Papers, Manuscripts 1106, 1121, 1149, 1152, 1182.

14 In June 1642 the colony's assembly gave Governor William Berkeley some property in urban Jamestown and said that it was in appreciation for his "many worthy favours manifested toward the colony" (Hening, *Statutes*, I, 267; McIlwaine, *Minutes*, 498). As many of the men who received patents in 1642 were high-ranking officials, such as councilors and burgesses, Berkeley was probably currying their favor.

15 Patent Book I, 500, 798–799, 801, 804, 806, 808, 811, 825–826, 828, 830, 865, 867, 870, 919–920, 918, 930.

16 Probably Diggs Creek.

17 According to the minutes of the Governor's Council and records in the British Archives that date to the late 1630s and early 1640s, Edmund Dawber, as Margaret Gates' husband, was entitled to 8,000 acres of Virginia land, half of which was to be free of quitrents (William G. Stanard, ed., "Notes from Council and General Court Records," *Virginia Magazine of History and Biography* 13 [1906]: 394; Virginia Colonial Records Project Survey Reports [SR] 4545, 12509). Margaret Gates set sail for Virginia in early 1611 with her parents and two sisters. However, Sir Thomas's wife died at sea and so he sent his daughters home a few months later (McCartney, *Jamestown People*, 169–170).

18 George Ransone in 1674 bequeathed to his daughter, Elizabeth, 500 acres at the mouth of Diggs Creek, acreage that abutted the land of his brother, James. He also left her some livestock, a silver cup, and a gold seal ring. George Ransone's widow, Margaret, married John Aschough of Middlesex County (Polly Cary Mason, comp. *Records of Colonial Gloucester County* [Newport News, 1946–1948], II, 126–127).

19 Patent Book I, 804, 808, 828, 830, 866–867, 930; II, 325, 327; III, 2, 94, 107–108, 128, 146, 204, 270; IV, 97, 377, 525, 535; V, 410; VI, 97, 383, 479, 515, 562; VII, 1, 212, 371, 513; VIII, 352; York County Deeds, Orders, Wills 5 (1672–1676):66; Norfolk County Deed Book 4 (1675–1686):216a; Hening, *Statutes*, I, 376–377; William G. Stanard, ed., "Historical and Genealogical Note and Queries," *Virginia Magazine of History and Biography* 14 (1906):208; Gloucester County Surveyors Plat Book A (1733–1810), 13, 23; SR 3725; Augustine Herrman, "Virginia and Maryland as it is planted and inhabited this present year 1670," 1673; Peter W. Coldham, *American Migrations 1765–1799* (Baltimore, 2000), 536–538; Mathews County Land Tax Lists 1782; Mason, *Gloucester*, II, 45, 104, 108, 112. During the 1970s Hannah Tompkins' plantation, located in Poquoson, was identified by state archaeologists, who conducted excavations there.

20 McCartney, *Jamestown People*, 456; Patent Book I, 918; III, 5, 14, 70, 128, 204, 270; IV, 531; V, 410; VI, 374; XXXIII, 366.

21 Patent Book II, 228, 233, 311; III, 182–183; IV, 531; VI, 660; VII, 62, 219, 288; VIII, 18; IX9, 138; Gloucester County Surveyors Plat Book A (1733–1810):3.

22 Patent Book III, 173; IV, 66; VI, 661.

23 Patent Book III, 232, 268; IV, 355; V, 479; VI, 100, 102, 660; VII, 62–63; Billups Papers, Swem, Box 9 folder 31; Box 10 folder 3; McIlwaine, *Minutes*, 393.

24 Patent Book VI, 554, 659, 666, 681; VII, 15; Mason, *Gloucester*, I, 7.

25 Patent Book II, 331; III, 1; IV, 661; VI, 102, 536, 548, 657, 666; McCartney, *Jamestown People*, 40–41.

26 In patents, New Point Comfort sometimes was referred to as an island, probably because its low-lying attachment to the mainland could be inundated by tidal waters.

27 Patent Book II, 233; VI, 660; VII, 62, 353, 357, 359; IX, 282; X, 122.

28 The creek probably attracted large flocks of waterfowl. No documentary evidence has come to light suggesting that a ducking stool was located near or in the immediate vicinity of Ducking Pond Creek. The ducking stool, like stocks and the pillory, was a punishment device used for public shaming and could be found close to many county courthouses during the seventeenth century.

29 Christopher Wormeley I used Thomas Dyer's headright when patenting 500 acres in 1638 (Patent Book I, 691). The Secretary's office was responsible for issuing patents. Therefore, unless Wormeley recused himself, he would have issued his own patent. Wormeley's patent for 4,000 acres has been lost or destroyed.

30 Patent Book II, 223, 229, 256; VII, 357, 359; VIII, 262; X, 324; McCartney, *Jamestown People*, 456–457. Holder and Watts patented 200 acres apiece.

31 Patent Book II, 232, 255, 270, 336, 356; III, 10; V, 598; VII, 220; McCartney, *Jamestown People*, 45.

32 Patent Book II, 233, 311; III, 138; IV, 532; VI, 103; V, 588; IX, 126.

33 Patent Book II, 128, 227–228, 233, 356; III, 34, 117, 190, 243; IV, 528; VI, 658; VII, 161; VIII, 18; McCartney, *Jamestown People*, 416.

34 Patent Book II, 400; III, 127, 182, 268; IV, 532; VI, 231; VII, 215; Old Rappahannock County Deed Book 8 (1688–1692):130–133, 144. The Wrights were not unique in exchanging one parcel of land for another. They may have traded it for property they felt would be more suitable for growing tobacco (Mason, *Gloucester*, II, 96–99).

35 Patent Book III, 168, 353; IV, 347, 369–370, 439, 524; V, 326; VI, 493–494, 658–659; VII, 279.

36 Rigby may have been Peter Ridley, a vagrant and former inmate of Bridewell Prison, who was sent to Virginia during the mid-to-late 1620s (McCartney, *Jamestown People*, 600).

37 Patent Book I, 811; II, 262; VII, 62; McCartney, *Jamestown People*, 109–110, 345.

38 Patent Book I, 800; II, 2; IV,314; V, 250; VI, 514; VII, 213, 220, 222, 275, 283, 287, 351, 358; IX, 283; Mason, *Gloucester,* II, 124. Morris Creek's name may be derived from that of Morris Mackashannock, whose patent was in that vicinity.

39 English owned other acreage in the area, property that descended to his daughters, Sarah Long and Mary Shipley.

40 Gwyn's 1635 and 1642 patents for 1,000 acres ran along the Piankatank for 1.56 miles.

41 Patent Book I, 798, 800–801, 806, 811, 825, 830, 865, 870; III, 120; IV, 161, 530; Mason, *Gloucester*, II, 45; Hening, *Statutes*, I, 375. Arthur Price was the son-in-law of patentee Robert Bristow of the North River plantation.

42 Later, much of Mottram's land came into the hands of Richard Perrott (Patent Book VI, 196).

43 Patent Book I, 803, 805; III:5.

44 McIlwaine, *Minutes*, 227, 296, 501; Hening, *Statutes*, I, 285–286, 291–294.

45 That is, marsh grass that could be used for thatching roofs or perhaps weaving baskets or mats.

46 Hening, *Statutes*, I, 322–327.

47 In 1670 cartographer Augustine Herrman, who visited Virginia and Maryland and carefully mapped both colonies' shorelines, identified Ferry Creek as Chiskiack Creek. Just east was Snellings Creek, a small stream now known as Dancing Creek (Herrman, "Virginia and Maryland," 1673).

48 Warren M. Billings, "Some Acts Not in Hening's Statutes: The Acts of Assembly April 1652, November 1652, and July 1653," *Virginia Magazine of History and Biography* 83 (1975):65–66.

49 Patent Book II, 169; McCartney, *Jamestown People*, 303.

50 Patent Book III, 23, 32, 116; Hening, *Statutes*, II, 153. On October 23, 1655, George Ludlow of York County added a codicil to his will, stipulating that if his nephew, Thomas Ludlow, who stood to inherit all of his Virginia property, were to marry Mrs. Rebecca Hurst, his inheritance would go to another heir (McCartney, *Jamestown People*, 265).

51 Patent Book IV, 419; McCartney, *Jamestown People*, 322. The agreement the Chiskiack Indians made with Edward Wyatt is preserved in the archives of the Huntington Library in San Marino, California (Mason, *Gloucester*, I, frontispiece).

52 Beverley Fleet, *Colonial Virginia Abstracts* (Baltimore, 1988), III, 41, 104; McIlwaine, *Minutes*, 227, 296, 506; Hening, *Statutes*, I, 285–286, 291–294; II, 36; Nugent, *Cavaliers*, I, xxi–xxii.

53 Patent Book III, 122, 302; McCartney, *Jamestown People*, 424. Interestingly, the Chiskiack Indians' old town was across the Piankatank River from the village in which the Piankatank (former Kecoughtan) Indians had been living in 1608 when Captain John Smith sailed up the Piankatank.

54 Hening, *Statutes*, II, 275; Mason, *Gloucester*, II, 108, 126.

55 Hening, *Statutes*, I, 359–361, 457, 468; II, 139; Force, *Tracts*, II, Book 8, 13–14; III, Book 10, 49–50; Salmon and Campbell, *Hornbook*, 19.

56 Hening, *Statutes*, II, 138–140; Billings, "Some Acts," 65–66; Hugh Jones, *The Present State of Virginia* (Charlottesville, 1956), 55.

57 Patent Book II, 320, 324; III, 8; Hening, *Statutes*, I, 363, 371.

58 Force, *Tracts*, II, 8, 3, 14–15; III, 14, 18; Ferrar Papers, Manuscripts 1106, 1121, 1149, 1152, 1182. Scientists have found that eastern Virginia experienced very dry conditions from 1650 to 1653 and again during 1660 (Blanton, "Climate Factor," 17).

59 Hening, *Statutes*, I, 183, 364, 399–400, 542; II, 18, 30, 39, 102, 469; McIlwaine, *Minutes*, 506; Bishop William Meade, *Old Churches, Ministers And Families Of Virginia* (Baltimore, 1966), I, 325; Cocke, *Diocese of Virginia*, 95–98; Rutman and Rutman, *A Place in Time*, 53.

60 Rutman and Rutman, *A Place in Time*, 130–131, 210; Hening, *Statutes*, I, 412–414, 476; Lancaster County Deed Book 1 ([1652–1657): 201; Middlesex County Order Book 1673–1680:131; Patent Book VI, 196.

3

A Wilderness of Milk and Honey
1661–1699

Stimulating Virginia's Economy

In 1660, when Governor William Berkeley, a steadfast royalist, proclaimed that the monarchy had been restored, celebrants at Jamestown marked the occasion by sounding trumpets, firing guns, and drinking. A few months later, Berkeley set sail for England to urge the newly-formed Restoration government to consider Virginia's economic interests in policy-making decisions. He lobbied against the Navigation Acts and asked for the Crown's support in maximizing the colony's productivity. When Berkeley returned to Virginia, he tried to showcase the colony's economic potential. He had his servants and slaves produce glass, earthenware, salt, and wine at his plantation, Green Spring, where they also undertook trials of potash, flax, hemp, and silk. Nonetheless, King Charles II ignored Berkeley's recommendations and often pursued public policies contrary to the colony's best interests.

In response, the Berkeley government instituted some economic initiatives that were intended to stimulate the colony's productivity. For example, in 1662 flax seed was given to county officials so that they could supply it to local inhabitants. Those who raised flax, spun its fibers into yarn, and wove cloth a yard wide were eligible for a bounty. Likewise, those who planted mulberry trees and made silk were to be rewarded. Each county's officials were supposed to have a tan-house built, where tanners, curriers, and shoemakers could process hides into leather goods; and they were to have a loom set up so that a weaver could produce fabric for the manufacture of clothing. Any county that failed to comply with the new legislative mandates was subject to a fine. Although it is uncertain how Middle Peninsula officials responded to these directives, in 1665 the Rev. Alexander Moray, who lived near the mouth of the Ware River, wrote his kinsman that he had planted 10,000 mulberry trees and was hoping to reap good silk within the next two or three years. He commented that common white salt was extremely expensive and asked how the people of La Rochelle, in western France, made it from bay water.[1] The legislation enacted in 1662 also offered significant rewards to those who constructed watercraft, incentives that may well have given rise to Mathews County's long-lived shipbuilding industry. Anyone who constructed a small vessel that was between 20 and 50 tons burthen and had a deck stood to receive a bounty of 50 pounds of tobacco per ton. Those who built a ship that was between 50 and 100 tons burthen would receive a reward of 100 pounds of tobacco per ton, and those who built one that exceeded 100 tons burthen would receive 200 pounds of tobacco per ton.[2]

Updating the Colony's Laws

Virginia's legal code was revised extensively in 1661 and took effect in 1662. For the first time, each county could send only two burgesses to the assembly. Jamestown, as the capital city, retained its ancient right to representation and any hundred-acre tract on which a hundred tithable (that is, taxable) citizens took up residence was entitled to the same privilege. Each county court was to have eight justices, and the first man appointed to office was to serve as sheriff. Vestries could have no more than 12 members. Tax rates were established by the colony's burgesses, but county courts were authorized to issue marriage licenses. When the assembly formally adopted English common law in 1662, legislation was enacted that regulated local elections and set public officials' fees. Procedures were established for the probate process, determining land ownership, formalizing land transfers, and setting the prices that tavern-keepers, millers, and ferrymen could charge. Not unexpectedly, these responsibilities added to the county court's workload, but they also gave officials an opportunity to earn more lucrative fees from performing public duties.

To discourage the "idleness and debaucheryes" attributable to drunkenness, local court justices were ordered to see that their county seat had no more than one or two taverns. A limited number were permissible at ports, ferry landings, and major roads, where they were necessary "for the accommodation of travelers." Among the other issues the burgesses addressed in 1662 were: relations with the Indians, the treatment of indentured servants, controlling the quality of tobacco, and the proper observance of the Sabbath. Only escaped prisoners, accused felons, or those suspected of insurrection could be arrested on Sundays, because the burgesses felt that the prospect of being taken into custody at church would discourage attendance. Quakers and other non-conformists could be fined for failing to attend or support the Established Church, and informants were rewarded for turning them in. Three or four sites in every parish were to be set aside as public burial grounds where the dead were to be interred unless prior arrangements had been made. This law was intended to prevent the concealment of wrongful deaths. Vestrymen had to procession the boundaries of land within their parish every four years and see that disputed property lines were surveyed. From 1691 on, processioning was to be done between September and March. A procedure was established for appointing the surveyors of public highways, whose duties were defined by law. Every county seat was supposed to have a pillory, stocks, whipping post, and ducking-stool near the courthouse, and local courts' meeting dates were established. Half of each county's eight justices were "of the quorum," that is, one or more of them had to be present at every court session. Plaintiffs and defendants were supposed to summarize their cases in writing and were guaranteed the right to a jury trial. The Quarter Court, renamed the General Court, continued to serve as an appellate body for the county judiciary, but it reserved the right to return cases to county courts.

In 1666, a new law spelled out what was required of new patentees. Specifically, anyone who built a house, kept livestock on his property for a year, or cleared an acre of ground and planted crops could secure his patent. Patentees were given three years in which to seat their land. One late seventeenth-century account indicates that people tended to take advantage of the loosely defined seating requirements. For example, construction of any building, no matter how small or humble, even a shed for hogs, counted as a house; likewise, an acre of ground was considered planted, no matter how poorly it was tended.[3] It is likely that such insubstantial development was scattered throughout what was then Gloucester County.

Class Differences Emerge

As the seventeenth century wore on and the colony's population increased, social and political distinctions between the classes became more apparent. The gap widened between those with greater and lesser opportunities for economic advancement, with the result that Virginia became a distinctly stratified society. As Darrett H. and Anita Rutman noted in their seminal study of Middlesex County, Mathews County's near neighbor, "[L]aw, custom, and even public architecture acknowledged social differentiation." Status determined whether someone was whipped or fined for an offense and where people sat in church. At the pinnacle of society were the governor and his councilors, who shared some of their power with members of the assembly. Below the burgesses were county justices and other local officials, all of whom were appointed by the governor and his council. Virtually all of these men derived fees and privileges from performing their official duties. Assembly members, though elected, were drawn from the upper ranks of society and often were able to use their official positions to further their own economic interests and political aspirations. Moreover, familial, political, and social connections among the colony's leaders enabled them to enhance and perpetuate their role in the governmental establishment. These connections also extended into the affairs of the church, to which official interest was linked, and often the same men who held office as burgesses, naval officers, or county officials served as parish vestrymen. The plantations of the wealthiest and most powerful families were massive in size and relatively self-sufficient.

Virginians at the lower end of the socio-economic scale interacted with their own peers and had a much more limited opportunity to enhance their personal fortunes. Female servants were sometimes able to find a home or improve their lot by marrying; male servants, having fulfilled their terms of indenture, usually sought to acquire land of their own, though they often lacked the means to do so. Some landless freedmen rented acreage from larger planters, but others simply became paupers or transients who wandered from place to place. They ranked just above ethnic minorities such as blacks and Indians, whose legal rights and opportunities for advancement were very limited. Somewhere between the top and bottom rungs of the socioeconomic ladder were numerous Virginians whose landholdings were of modest size. They were middling farmers, skilled workers, and others with a limited but adequate amount of disposable income. Scholars have found that most middling planters and their wives rarely ventured very far from their own neighborhoods except to attend church or to barter for the goods and services they needed. The spheres of social interaction were very limited for women; on the other hand, most men attended militia musters and upon occasion made a trip to the county seat or perhaps the colony's capital.

During the 1660s, the burgesses authorized parishes, which were responsible for public welfare, to build workhouses where poor children (not necessarily orphans) could be educated and trained to spin, weave, and perform other useful tasks. In December 1662, the burgesses decided that all female servants who worked as crop hands were to be considered tithable. Moreover, for the first time, black females were subjected to a poll or capitation tax, whether or not they were categorized as servants or free. It was around this time that some members of Virginia's planter elite began referring to their black servants as slaves.[4] Although English law and colonial custom acknowledged that slavery and Christianity were incompatible, Virginia's assembly passed a law in 1667 specifying that "the conferring of baptism does not alter the condition of freedom."

Researchers have found that, over time, there was a significant change in the way the domestic landscape was organized. During the first few decades of the seventeenth century, masters and servants usually shared living accommodations. However, by the latter part of the century, most farmsteads included a main house and one or more outbuildings, such as detached kitchens, living quarters for workers, and tobacco houses. This arrangement, which by mid-century became a permanent feature of the Virginia plantation, removed workers and the services they provided from the main house and segregated them from the family. Archaeologists have found that throughout the seventeenth and early eighteenth centuries, buildings with only two rooms were the most common type.[5]

The 1663 Plot by Indentured Servants

In late August 1663, a group of male indentured servants in Gloucester County decided to demand that their masters release them from a year of their time. If that failed, they intended to murder anyone who opposed them and then leave Virginia. The instigators, former soldiers in Oliver Cromwell's army, included laborers William Ball, William Bell, William Bendell (Budell), Thomas Collins, Richard Darbishire, John Gunter, John Hayte, Thomas Jones, William Poultney, and a man named Birkinhead (Berkenhead). In early September, they met "at a little house of Mr. Peter Knight's in ye woods neere unto Mrs. Cooke's quarter," where they swore an oath of secrecy, and agreed to meet at Poplar Spring a week later to set their plan in motion. They intended to go to the plantations of Colonel Francis Willis and Mrs. Katharine Cooke, a widow, where they would seize enough guns, ammunition, and other weapons to arm thirty men.[6] But before the men's plan got very far, Birkinhead disclosed the plot. Word was sent to the governor, who took immediate action. When the perpetrators were rounded up and interrogated by Colonel Willis, Abraham Iverson, and Major John Smith, they were deemed treasonous and guilty of conspiracy. Four of them were hanged, but Birkinhead was freed and rewarded handsomely. The memory of the would-be servant uprising endured, and in April 1670, people from Gloucester, Middlesex, and York Counties asked the Council of State to prohibit the importation of convicts as servants. The Council responded by forbidding mariners to bring ashore "any Jaile bird or such others who for notorious offenses have deserved to dye in England." The reprieve was brief, however, for in early 1718 Parliament passed an act "for the Further Preventing Robbery, Burglary and other Felonies, and for the More Effectual Transportation of Felons." Afterward, all but those convicted of the most heinous or trivial crimes could be sentenced to "transportation" (exile) for a period of seven or fourteen years.[7]

The Dutch Threaten Virginia

In early June 1665, Governor Berkeley was notified that England was at war with the Dutch; he was ordered to see that the colony's defenses were readied and that all trading ships were protected. Ships with ordnance, then lying at Old Point Comfort, were sent to Tindall's (Gloucester) Point and three other locations. In September 1667, nearly four months after Dutch ships attacked the tobacco fleet anchored in the James River, the colony's governing officials decided to build an earthen-walled fort at Gloucester Point and four other locations. By November 1667, construction had gotten underway on the fort at Gloucester Point. Taxpayers in Gloucester, York, and New Kent Counties shared the cost of materials and men. Five months after the forts were completed, peace was restored and defensive fortifications were no longer needed. By 1671, however, hostilities with the Dutch had resumed. This time, the burgesses decided to have a brick fort built on each of the colony's major rivers. It was then that Fort James was erected at Gloucester Point. Although the Dutch attacked the tobacco fleet near Old Point Comfort in July 1673, capturing or burning nineteen ships, there is no evidence that Fort James ever saw military action. That was fortunate, for in February 1672 a Virginia official sent word to England that there wasn't enough powder there "to charge a piece of ordnance." In early 1690, Governor Francis Nicholson reminded the burgesses that whenever there was a threat of an enemy attack, ships were supposed to withdraw to positions of greater safety. Those in the Piankatank River were to move as far upstream as they could go, and those near Mobjack Bay were to proceed up its tributaries. Nicholson reiterated his plan in 1692 and the same strategy was proposed in 1702 and 1703.[8]

A Plethora of Challenges

The late 1660s brought a chain of events that must have proved daunting for Governor Berkeley, who was then sixty-two years old. While he struggled to understand Charles II's dismissive attitude toward the colony and attempted to promote economic development, the Dutch attacked. Then came a spate of severe weather that wrought massive destruction. In April

1667, a storm that produced hail "as big as Turkey Eggs" destroyed spring crops, broke "all the glass windowes and beat holes through the tiles of our houses," and "killed many young hogs and cattle." Mid-summer brought a forty-day rainy spell that drowned the season's crops, and in August, a killer hurricane struck that lasted for twenty-four hours and destroyed an estimated ten thousand houses. Strong winds, accompanied by heavy rain, caused severe flooding and forced many families to flee from their homes. Wave action ripped vessels from their moorings. Fences were blown down and escaped livestock roamed freely, damaging what was left of the year's corn, tobacco, and field crops. The disasters of 1667, taken as a whole, must have been demoralizing for the colonists and their aging governor. When the burgesses convened in 1668, August 27 was declared a day of annual fasting and atonement, for many people felt that the recent hurricane was attributable to "the anger of God Almighty against us."

Tax revenue was in short supply. Back in 1660 the assembly divided each county into four precincts, each of which had its own commissioner. It was the duty of the county sheriff to see that his jurisdiction's inhabitants gave an accurate list of tithables to their precinct's commissioner. When the law was amended in 1662, court-appointed county tax commissioners were required to post a notice on the doors of parish churches to remind everyone to report his/her household's tithables before the end of June. Tax commissioners had to deliver an account of the tithables within their precincts to the August session of their county court, whose clerk had to send his list to the clerk of the assembly. Fraud was a common problem, for some people purposefully failed to accurately account for the tithables in their households. Therefore, in 1663, the burgesses decided to require household heads to identify each tithable person by name. Informants who reported those suspected of concealing tithables could be awarded one of the accused person's servants or 1,000 pounds of tobacco if the accusation proved to be true. Finally, in 1670, the burgesses began requiring county clerks to post lists of tithables on the courthouse door and to leave it there for a full day. This allowed people to discover whether their neighbors were evading taxation and were therefore guilty of fraud.

In September 1672, the assembly enacted legislation that required court-appointed officials to compile a list of all tithables who had been born in the colony, including all black and Indian children. Those who failed to register children paid a fine every year the youngsters remained unregistered. All African-American women born in Virginia were accounted tithable at age 16. The law was expanded in 1680, and all black children imported into the colony had to be brought to court to have their ages adjudged and recorded. They became tithable at age 12, whereas white servants brought into the colony became tithable at age 14. Two years later, the burgesses decided that all Indian women, like black women, were tithable. Surviving court records from Tidewater counties reveal that each of these laws was put to use soon after being passed.[9]

Expanding the Frontier

As time went on, planters, especially high-ranking officials, began demanding the right to patent portions of the large and desirable tracts that had been assigned to the visibly dwindling native population. In 1667, the burgesses asked the governor to allow settlers to move into the Indians' tribal territory, contending that the availability of good land would encourage more people to immigrate to Virginia. That, they insisted, would relieve the current population of the "tyranny exerted by the colony's Indians." Ironically, in October 1669, when a census was made of the colony's native population, only 15 Chiskiack Indian warriors then resided within Gloucester County, and the other tribes living in eastern Virginia were very small.

Around 1669, Middlesex County was formed from the southernmost portion of Lancaster County's territory, which in 1664 was called the Pyankatank Parish. Middlesex County's boundaries were defined on the north by the Rappahannock River, on the south by the Piankatank River, on the east by the Chesapeake Bay, and on the west by Essex County. Historical records demonstrate that those living along both sides of the Piankatank did not consider the waterway an impediment, and well-to-do planters often owned land on both sides of the river. In 1670, when Augustine Herrman toured Tidewater Virginia and Maryland by boat and prepared a topographically sensitive map, natives and European settlers were living in relatively close proximity throughout eastern Virginia and on the Eastern

Shore. Herrman labeled the sites of major plantations, but omitted those belonging to people of middling and lesser means. Within the boundaries of what became Mathews County, he identified the North, East, and Piankatank Rivers, along with Mobjack Bay. He also labeled New Point Comfort and Cheesecake (Chiskiack), Garden, Queens, Blackwater, and Snelling Creeks. He attributed an area to the Cheesecake (Chiskiack) Indians and indicated that nearby was a ferry across the Piankatank. Herrman labeled Dragon Swamp and indicated that Indians were living in its upper reaches. His map reveals that plantations then lined the banks of the Piankatank River and other tributaries of the Chesapeake Bay.[10]

The map that Augustine Herrman made in 1670 showed the territory along the lower side of the Piankatank River that was inhabited by the Chiskiack Indians. Courtesy of the Library of Congress.

Kingston Parish

The records of colonial Kingston Parish, established during the 1650s, are incomplete, and the bulk of the parish's seventeenth- and early eighteenth-century records have been lost or destroyed. Even so, there are vestry minutes that date to November 15, 1679, and some of the parish's other late seventeenth-century records have survived. Kingston Parish's earliest vestry minutes describe meetings that were held in "the North River Precinct," territory that was on the east side of the North River's main branch and extended toward the western branch of the East River. Bishop William Meade, who during the mid-nineteenth century chronicled the history of Virginia's parishes, observed that the vestry of colonial Kingston Parish, unlike many of its contemporaries, included men of middling means.

Land patents and surviving vestry records indicate that the North River Precinct's chapel was on the North River in the immediate vicinity of Richard Creedle's patent, which encompassed what became known as Creedle or Cradle Point.[11] In time, the land between the east side of the North River and the Blackwater Creek became known as Chapel Neck. In 1680, Kingston Parish's vestry and parishioners were responsible for the support of a second chapel, one that was located on Chapel Creek, a tributary of the Piankatank River. During the mid-1850s Bishop William Meade noted that according to local tradition, the house of worship on Chapel Creek was "a private chapel of the 'family of Hesse'"—that is, the Armisteads.[12] Both of these houses of worship were most likely small wooden buildings.[13] They were served by one clergyman, the Rev. Michael (Mychaell) Zyperus, a man of unsavory reputation,[14] and one vestry, although each chapel had a sexton. Vestry records reveal that each of Kingston Parish's chapels was provided with a large Bible and a copy of the Book of Common Prayer.

Sometime prior to 1684, probably during Mr. Zyperus's ministry, the vestry acquired the property that was developed as the parish glebe. That 455-acre tract lay between the mouths of Put In and Woodas Creeks and was land that Colonel Richard Dudley, a vestryman from at least 1679 to 1687, had patented in 1662. Colonel Lawrence Smith surveyed the glebe in 1684, and the vestry enlarged it a decade later by obtaining an additional 40 acres of contiguous land. When the glebe was resurveyed in 1712, official county surveyor Thomas Cooke determined that it encompassed 533 acres, and that in 1684 when Colonel Lawrence Smith laid out the property's westernmost boundary line, he had unwittingly encroached upon the upper limits of Robert Lendall's patent. The glebe house depicted on Cooke's plat, the earliest known image of its kind, had two chimneys and was situated at a site overlooking Put In Creek.[15] Virginia vestries were legally required to provide their clergy with a good glebe and decent housing. Also, vestrymen were keenly aware that ministers were in short supply and expected housing worthy of their rank and status. Therefore, most vestries provided glebe houses that were comparable to, or better than, those of middling planters.

By October 1687, Kingston Parish's vestry had begun gathering the funds they needed to build a new chapel for the North Precinct. Unlike the building being replaced, the new chapel was to be fabricated of brick. Parish records reveal that by early October 9, 1690, construction had gotten underway and that the vestry had agreed to pay Daniel Hunter for building a bridge across the North River. This raises the possibility that Kingston Parish's new North Precinct chapel was being built further inland, rather than in Chapel Neck. In fact, it was probably around this time that the first house of worship was built on the parcel that eventually was occupied by Trinity Church.[16]

A Colonial Parish's Responsibilities

Although Kingston Parish's vestry records include occasional references to children born out of wedlock and in need of parish support, rarely did the parish clerk note more than one parent's name. However, Middlesex County court records that date to August 16, 1695, provide us with more detail. According to court testimony, one little girl's mother, Elizabeth Byrd Eddington, resided in Christ Church Parish and her reputed father lived in Kingston Parish. Therefore, Middlesex County's justices were obliged to determine which parish should be held responsible for the child's support. Three witnesses testified that about ten years earlier, Elizabeth, whose husband was out of the country, conceived a child with the son of John Banister, a gentleman, who resided on the southerly part of New Point

Comfort. One person said that when Elizabeth had brought the little girl to the entrance of the Banister home, "old Mr. Banister" told one of his servants to take her to Ralph Armistead, then Kingston Parish's churchwarden. According to the witnesses, when Elizabeth found out, she retrieved the child from Armistead and took her to her own home.[17] Precisely why this youngster was at risk for becoming a ward of the parish is unclear, unless her mother was impoverished or seriously ill.

In 1683, Lieutenant Governor Francis Lord Howard authorized Colonel Thomas Pate to issue marriage licenses to people in Gloucester and Middlesex Counties and to collect the fees associated with doing so. Clergy were not supposed to perform marriages unless the couple had obtained a marriage license and posted bans in their parish church—that is, publicly announced their intention to wed. Colonel Pate was authorized to appoint one or two other men to grant marriage licenses.[18]

Bacon's Rebellion

During the mid-1670s, Virginia colonists began chafing under the Navigation Acts' restraints and they continued to resent the king for having given the Northern Neck to some of his favorites. Taxes soared and there were rumors of Indian troubles in the New England colonies. On the fringes of Virginia's frontiers, strong, warlike natives who lived above the fall line sometimes raided outlying homesteads and attacked the colony's Tributary Indians, who were entitled to government protection. Governor William Berkeley, who was nearing 70 and had been in office for nearly 30 years, was perceived as being complacent and unresponsive. Furthermore, because the planter elite had solidified their political power during his administration, most public officials were viewed as opportunists who profited handsomely from performing duties considered a public trust.

When Virginia's governing officials convened in March 1676, they decided to have defensive forts built at nine strategically important locations. Men were pressed into service to garrison the forts, while supplies and military equipment were procured through public levies. As it turned out, these fortifications, built at public expense, were extremely unpopular, for they were utterly useless against highly mobile bands of natives who launched surprise attacks. In fact, many colonists, who grumbled about paying for the forts, likened them to expensive "mousetraps." This frustration and other factors prompted Nathaniel Bacon, whose Henrico County plantation was attacked by Indians, to lead an unauthorized march against the natives. Thus began the popular uprising known as Bacon's Rebellion, which spread throughout Tidewater Virginia.

In late June 1676, Bacon and his followers converged on Jamestown, where he demanded—and received—a commission that allowed him to pursue the Indians. Later, he and his men returned and forced the assembly at gunpoint to enact a group of new laws. One made it legal to patent Indian land as soon as it was abandoned. This gave unethical planters the right to drive the Tributary natives from their acreage and take it for themselves. When Bacon left Jamestown, he began roaming the countryside, trying to rally supporters. Governor Berkeley, meanwhile, received a petition from some people in Gloucester County questioning the validity of Bacon's commission. If it was illegitimate, they wanted protection from his men, who were said to be confiscating loyalists' horses, arms, and ammunition, leaving them defenseless. Berkeley set out for Gloucester, whose citizens, though loyal, were unwilling to oppose Bacon. Berkeley grew uneasy about the lack of support and withdrew to Arlington, Colonel John Custis's plantation on the Eastern Shore. Bacon, on the other hand, marched to Middle Plantation, where he drafted a "Declaration of the People," leveling charges against Governor Berkeley. He also produced a "Manifesto" that justified his own actions. Afterward, he had his men seize three ships anchored in the James River and dispatched them to the Eastern Shore to confront Berkeley in his place of refuge.

Sir William Berkeley, Virginia's longest serving royal governor. Courtesy of the Jamestown-Yorktown Foundation.

When Governor Berkeley returned to Jamestown on September 7, 1676, he discovered that the capital city was in the hands of Bacon's men. He offered to pardon Bacon's common soldiers if they would lay down their arms, but many of them feared repercussions and fled. Meanwhile, Bacon, who had been unable to muster enough men to undertake a march against the natives on the colony's frontier, attacked a convenient target, the Pamunkey Indians, who had recently signed a peace agreement with the Berkeley government. Bacon and his followers pursued the Pamunkeys into Dragon Swamp, where they killed men, women and children indiscriminately, took captives, and plundered the natives' goods. Bacon then set out for Jamestown, displaying his Pamunkey prisoners along the way as evidence of his prowess as an Indian fighter. Upon reaching the isthmus that connected Jamestown Island to the mainland, he had his men dig a defensive trench and commence shelling the capital city. Governor Berkeley, who realized that he was badly outnumbered, returned to the Eastern Shore. As soon as he departed, Bacon and his men entered Jamestown and on September 19, 1676, set the capital city ablaze. The fierce fire destroyed the colony's statehouse, the parish church, and most of the community's other buildings.[19] Afterward, Bacon and many of his followers withdrew to Gloucester Point, where his followers pledged their loyalty to their leader. While in Gloucester County, Bacon made his headquarters at Colonel Augustine Warner's home. He drafted a document denouncing the Berkeley government and then demanded that the county's men sign it. Many of them chose to remain neutral, which angered Bacon's men, who began looting and plundering the property of those they perceived as Berkeley supporters.

On October 26, 1676, the popular uprising was literally dealt a mortal blow. Nathaniel Bacon reportedly succumbed to the bloody flux and a "lousey disease" while he was at the Gloucester County residence of Colonel Thomas Pate. Berkeley, upon learning of Bacon's demise, proffered that he had been felled by the hand of Providence and cited Bacon's often blasphemous language. He also quoted "an honest Minister," who proposed the following epitaph: "Bacon is Dead I am sorry at my hart That lice and flux should take the hangmans part."[20] Nathaniel Bacon's successor, Joseph Ingram, was an uninspiring and more cautious leader who lacked charisma and a sense of purpose. In the words of one eyewitness to Bacon's Rebellion, "The Lion had no sooner made his exitt, but the Ape (by indubitable right) steps upon the stage." Another equally unflattering writer said that "the Titmouse … was becom an Elliphant." Ingram divided his men into small groups and had them withdraw into the countryside at the head of the York River, where they braced themselves for an attack they considered inevitable. One of the places in which Ingram's men holed up was Colonel Pate's residence, where Bacon had died.[21]

The Rebellion Subsides

When Governor Berkeley returned to Jamestown in January 1677, he discovered that the capital city lay in ruins. When he withdrew to Green Spring, he found his plantation "much spoilt and plundered." His revenge was swift and sweet; his men seized the opportunity to quell the uprising, and many of the rebel leaders were hunted down and captured. When the king's Special Commissioners arrived in Virginia in late January 1677 with troops sent to quell the popular uprising, they learned that Governor Berkeley and his supporters had gained the upper hand, Bacon was dead, and there was widespread destruction. When the commissioners launched an official inquiry into the causes of Bacon's Rebellion, they invited each county's freeholders to submit a petition in which they explained why they were dissatisfied with the Berkeley government. The list of grievances compiled by Gloucester County freeholders included complaints about taxes and the costliness and ineffectiveness of the forts built to defend the colonists against the Indians. They also claimed that assembly meetings, which were costly, were being held too frequently; and that Major Robert Beverley I, one of Governor Berkeley's most ardent supporters, had abused his power by conscripting soldiers and then using them to cut down trees on his own property. The petitioners stressed the importance of seeing that the colony's arms and ammunition were kept in a secure place.

Sands Knowles of Kingston Parish was among those who submitted a formal complaint to the king. He claimed that he had never taken up arms against the government and was forced to take Bacon's oath. He said that on October 20, 1676, he was taken into custody by Governor Berkeley's men and transported to the Eastern Shore, where he was held prisoner at

Colonel Custis's house until March 15, 1677. Knowles said that while he was being detained, Robert Beverley I and his men raided his plantation at the head of the East River near the horse path, and carried off provisions, slaves, servants, and goods worth £400. On February 10, 1677, when Governor Berkeley made a list of those exempt from the king's pardon, he included Sands Knowles. However, on March 15, Berkeley and his council decided that Knowles would be pardoned if he took the oath of obedience, posted bail, and relinquished all claims to whatever personal belongings had been seized. Knowles availed himself of the general pardon but after Berkeley left Virginia, he sent a petition to England asking for the return of his confiscated property: a shallop, three black slaves, five English servants, and goods of considerable value. James Bridgeforth, John Bond, and Thomas Whittinoll, as witnesses, attested to the Knowles claim's validity. Sands Knowles may not have been completely innocent of crimes against the Berkeley government, for in 1678 he was accused of counterfeiting the orders of the king's commissioners who were sent to investigate the underlying causes of Bacon's Rebellion. As time went on, Knowles seems to have regained his standing in the community. In February 1691, when the ship *Bristol* overtook a small French barque in Mobjack Bay, its captain and crew removed two of its pedreroes, or small guns, and three muskets, and at the governor's instructions put them ashore at Sands Knowles' plantation in Gloucester County. In 1702, Knowles was one of Gloucester's justices of the peace, and in 1704 he paid quitrent on 575 acres of land in the county.

George Seaton of Kingston Parish, a county justice whose land was on the west side of Queens Creek and approximately a mile from the Piankatank River, was captured by Robert Beverley I in November 1676. Like Sands Knowles, he was detained on the Eastern Shore and his personal property was seized. Later, he was brought to Green Spring plantation and put on trial. When Seaton begged for clemency, Berkeley and his council agreed that he could receive the king's pardon if he relinquished all claims to the property that had been confiscated by Beverley's men, with the exception of four hogsheads of tobacco. After Seaton was pardoned and released, he submitted a petition to the king's commissioners, asking for the return of his goods, valued at £150. The commissioners determined that Seaton's only crime was taking an oath of loyalty to Bacon under duress. The plantation of Major Robert Bristow of Ware Neck, a wealthy merchant who owned land in Kingston Parish, on the east side of the North River's mouth, was plundered by Bacon's followers. On October 15, 1677, Sir John Berry, one of the king's commissioners, reported that Bristow had lost provisions, livestock, arms and ammunition, merchants' goods, and large quantities of strong liquor. Berry testified that Bristow was kept prisoner until Bacon's death and was knowledgeable about the events that had transpired in Virginia. Bristow returned to England permanently, but he retained his real estate in Virginia.[22]

The Treaty of 1677

On May 29, 1677, Virginia's governing officials executed a formal peace agreement with the colony's Tributary Indians. At a site that in 1699 became Williamsburg, the colony's new capital city, native leaders affixed their signature marks to what became known as the Treaty of Middle Plantation. Under the terms of the agreement, they acknowledged their allegiance to the Crown and conceded that their land rights were derived from the monarch. The Treaty of Middle Plantation, as initially written, consisted of twenty-one articles and was signed by five Indian leaders: the queen of the Pamunkey and her son, called Captain John West;[23] the king of the Nottoways; the queen of the Weyanoke; and the king of the Nansemond. Conspicuously absent were the leaders of the Chiskiack, who lived on the Piankatank River in what was then Gloucester County, and the leaders of the Rappahannock, Chickahominy, Mattapony, and Totachus (Totosky) Indians, who in 1669 were residing in territory that later became King William and King and Queen Counties. It is likely that these native groups were the "Severall Nations" whom the treaty reunited under the queen of the Pamunkey, "as anciently." From the natives' perspectives, one of the 1677 treaty's most important provisions was the prohibition against colonists' seating land within three miles of an Indian town. Moreover, all of the signatory tribes, like other English subjects, were entitled to receive protection from their enemies and had the right to make use of the colony's judicial system. In October 1677, the assembly made provisions for the establishment of trade marts where Indian goods could be bought and sold. The Chiskiack Indians in Gloucester County and the Wicomico Indians in Northumblerland were told to work with both counties' justices when deciding where a trade mart would be set up. In 1680 the Treaty of Middle Plantation was expanded somewhat.

In time, some government officials contended that the 1677 treaty created more problems than it had solved, for the Tributary tribes often quarreled among themselves and when they took their disagreements to court, the justices made enemies of whomever they sided against. Also, the Virginia government was obligated to protect the Tributary tribes from attacks by aggressive natives who lived above the fall line and raided frontier settlements.[24]

The Tobacco Economy

During Thomas Lord Culpeper's governorship (1677–83), tobacco prices plummeted thanks to a glut on the market. Although Virginia's economy deteriorated, Culpeper ignored the situation and went to England, leaving Sir Henry Chicheley in charge as deputy-governor. During the winter of 1681–2, impoverished planters in upper New Kent County and on the Middle Peninsula circulated petitions urging the passage of legislation that stinted, or limited, tobacco production. Chicheley summoned the burgesses to Jamestown to discuss the matter, but before they could meet, instructions from Governor Culpeper arrived, specifying that the assembly was not to convene until the following November. When the burgesses learned that the assembly session had been postponed, they became angry. Within a week, gangs of planters, frustrated with the government's inaction, began going from plantation to plantation, destroying tobacco plants. Chicheley ordered local militia commanders to have their men prevent further trouble, but plant cutting began anew in August and by the time it ceased, much of the year's crop lay in ruins. In New Kent County alone, half of the year's tobacco crop was destroyed. An improvement in the price of tobacco after 1682 alleviated the planters' distress.[25]

Mathews County's First Known Shipbuilder

Sometime prior to 1675 Edward Lassells (Lassel) of Kingston Parish began building seagoing vessels, perhaps in response to the legislative incentives put into place by Governor William Berkeley and the colony's assembly in 1662. Lassells constructed a sloop for Thomas Rabley, a Dutchman and influential Jamestown resident, but Rabley was so dissatisfied with Lassells' work that on June 17, 1675, he sued him in the General Court. By 1682 Lassells had secured a patent for 330 acres on the lower side of Milford Haven, on the southeast side of Peach Point (Stutts) Creek's head. On February 2, 1693, he sent a letter to England in which he proposed using Virginia's cypress trees as masts in vessels built for the Royal Navy. English officials decided that before an agreement could be made, the Naval Board had to consult the owners of merchant ships and others involved in the Virginia trade. Ultimately, the Lords of the Admiralty decided to give Lassells' idea a trial run. They told him outfit two royal navy ships, the *Foresight* and the *Archangel,* with topmasts and crossjack yards of Virginia cypress, which they would use on their return to England. However, for safety's sake, both vessels were supposed to retain their own English spars as reserve. Historic records fail to disclose whether the Naval Board hired Lassells to provide additional masts to the Royal Navy.[26]

Gloucester Point Becomes an Urban Community

In 1680, when an act was passed to encourage the establishment of ports and towns, land surrounding the cove on the east side of Gloucester Point was selected as the site of Gloucester Town, one of 20 planned urban communities. John Williams, whose acreage flanked the cove on the east, and Lawrence Smith, whose plantation bordered it on the west, were paid 10,000 pounds of tobacco apiece for their land. Each of the new planned communities was to be fifty acres in size, and surveyors were hired to lay out each town into half-acre lots. A tobacco storage warehouse was to be built at Gloucester Point "att Tindall [Sarah's] Creek side on John Williams' land." All imports, including slaves, indentured servants, and merchandise, were to be landed and sold at one of the new port towns. Likewise, all goods exported from Virginia were to pass through one of the ports. Presumably, people who lived within what became Mathews County would have procured their workers and imported goods at Gloucester Town, unless they decided to go to Urbanna, another official port. Most Virginia planters took a dim view of the town-founding legislation, for they felt that it would prove to be a hardship. However, the new legislation had some benefits, for a half-acre lot was offered very cheaply to anyone willing to build a dwelling or warehouse within a year. Also, tradesmen who settled in the port towns were immune to prosecution for bad debt for a period of five years. In 1682, the assembly authorized payment to the surveyor who laid out Gloucester Town, but the plat he prepared seems to have been lost or destroyed. A plat made in 1707 reportedly replicates the planned town's original layout and reveals that several Kingston Parish residents owned lots there. They included shipbuilder Edward Lassells or his son Edward Jr., James Ransone, merchant Robert Bristow, Francis Willis, John Gwyn, and perhaps others.

In 1691, when a second town act was passed, Yorktown was established on the lower side of the York River, directly across from Gloucester Town. Throughout the late seventeenth century and much of the eighteenth century, Yorktown and Gloucester Town were important centers of commerce and trade. A ferry plied the river between the two towns, and tobacco inspection warehouses brought a steady stream of planters to the area. Forts faced each other across the river, controlling waterborne access to the inland countryside. Gloucester Town's and Yorktown's commercial facilities were in use throughout much of the eighteenth century and Yorktown was an official port of entry for international trade. Although the 1691 town act was suspended in April 1693, the assembly partially reinstated it in 1699 and appointed town trustees, who were authorized to sell lots and confirm land titles within the port towns; the planned towns' exclusive trading privileges were not restored.[27]

A Mariner's Nightmare: The Wolf Trap and New Point Comfort

When cartographer Augustine Herrman made a map of Virginia and Maryland in 1670, he omitted a group of treacherous shoals off the eastern cost of the Middle Peninsula. On March 17, 1691, the H.M.S. *Wolfe*, a hired ship under the command of Captain George Purvis and part of the king's convoy, reportedly ran aground near "Point Noo Point" on some shoals that were located approximately halfway between New Point Comfort and Gwynn's Island. Men from Gloucester and Middlesex Counties, who were pressed into service, brought their boats alongside the *Wolfe* and managed to salvage its cargo, which included guns and ammunition. They also refloated the ship. Although Captain Purvis readily admitted that the men had saved the *Wolfe* and its cargo, he refused to compensate them or the owners of the boats involved in the rescue. Therefore, the men, convinced that they had been treated unjustly, sent a petition to the Governor's Council, asking to be paid. Their plea was successful, and Captain Purvis was ordered to compensate them for their work, including the time it took them to reach his ship. Although the *Wolfe* was still anchored in Milford Haven on December 15, 1692, Captain Purvis left Virginia without paying the men. When the ship returned in 1693, members of the Governor's Council, angered by the fact that Captain Purvis had ignored their orders, stipulated that the ship's owners were not to be paid until the men had been compensated. In time, the shoals on which the *Wolfe* had run aground were dubbed as the Wolf Trap. When John Thornton and Walter Hoxton made charts of the Chesapeake Bay in the early eighteenth centuries, they identified the Wolf Trap as a known hazard to mariners.[28] The shoals may have been marked with a beacon during much of the eighteenth century.

A Courthouse for Gloucester County

On February 26, 1680, Edmund Gwyn (Gwynn) of Ware Parish, a reputed descendant of Hugh Gwyn, conveyed to the justices of Gloucester County a six-acre tract of land on the forerunner of Route 17, part of the acreage on which he was living. He specified that the parcel was to be used for the construction of a county courthouse "and other necessary buildings," and stated that if the property ever ceased being used for that purpose, it was to revert to his heirs. He also noted that his acreage was entailed land. When the justices of Gloucester County's court convened on February 27, they agreed to give Gwyn the exclusive right "to keep ordinary for the accommodation of all people" at the county seat as long as he "behaves himselfe civilly according to the laws provided for Ordinary Keepers." In March 1684, when the justices of nearby Middlesex County decided to build a new courthouse, they indicated that they wanted it to be "at least of equall goodness and dimentions wth ye Brick Courte house lately built in Gloucester County."[29] From this, we know that the Gloucester County courthouse built in the early 1680s was fabricated of brick.

On April 19, 1684, the assembly decided that every county was to have a seal that its clerk of court could use to authenticate official documents. A surviving impression of Gloucester County's seal was affixed to the Revolutionary War pension application of Lieutenant Joshua Singleton, a document preserved in the National Archives. The courthouse complex that stood upon Edmund Gwyn's entailed land served Gloucester County for more than eighty years. A plat prepared in 1736 shows the site at which it was located, along with the county's old and new prisons. A map made in 1774 suggests that the old courthouse was located 700 to 800 feet southeast of the new one built in 1766.[30]

Durand du Dauphine's Visit

In 1686, when Durand de Dauphine, a French Huguenot, arrived in Virginia, he came ashore on New Point Comfort. Later, he commented that the area was "one of the most beautiful in all Virginia," but "it is not the most healthful or inhabited by the most honest people." He said that "everywhere we were required to drink so freely that even if there were twenty, all would drink to a stranger and he must pledge [toast] them all." He also concluded that the area's drinking water made him ill and said that "the inhabitants of the neighborhood looked so sickly that I judged the country to be unhealthy." He said that "those honest people forced me to drink their cider willy-nilly but had I wished to buy some, they would have charged me six sols a jug, while charging each other but two." Durand, despite his negative comments, went on to say that:

> Nature had delighted in giving to this land many useful charms, one of them being that at various points the sea extends into the land small inlets of a hundred and fifty to two hundred feet wide. Some extend in half a league, others less. The Indians have settled on these Inlets which they call Criks. On some there is only one plantation on each shore of the creek but the larger ones, which go farther inland have as many as five or six, their houses are at most a hundred or fifty feet distant from these creeks—at ebbtide they not only visit in their small boats, but carry their traffic through this channel. …When the wind's high, they go by land and ride. There are so many little havens for the launches that come to load the casks of tobacco.

According to Durand, most people were scattered about the countryside on plantations of various sizes. He said that tobacco was an acceptable medium of exchange and was commonly used to purchase land, livestock, and commodities such as clothing, hats, shoes, and wooden furniture. He noted that Virginia farmers typically left half of their land forested and cultivated the rest. They rotated their crops every four years, converting tilled ground to pasture and pasture to tilled ground. Durand added that local farmers "do not know what it is to plough the land with cattle, but just make holes into which they drop the seeds." He noted that they planted their tobacco amidst the stumps of felled trees, which resulted in a bleak landscape.[31]

Durand commented that farmers' houses were usually wooden buildings roofed over with narrow chestnut planking. The more affluent coated the interior walls of their dwellings with mortar, but Virginians, "whatever their rank," tended to build "only two rooms with some closets on the ground floor" and two rooms overhead in an attic. He said that many plantations had a detached kitchen, a tobacco house, and separate dwellings for servants and black slaves. As a consequence, Durand said that "when you come to the home of a person of some means, you think you are entering a fairly large village." Tobacco houses were ubiquitous, as were farmers' small frame houses, unpainted and often crudely made, and constructed on ground-set posts or puncheons. Often, rural families constructed rail fences by laying logs lengthwise to form a base. Then, they pounded stakes into the ground on either side of the logs to secure them in place, and laid rails within those stakes. Farmers allowed their cattle and hogs to roam in the woods, where wolves were kept at bay by faithful dogs. Durand spoke warmly of Virginia hospitality and said that most people freely shared what they had with travelers. He described a wedding he had attended, where the guests dined sumptuously upon meats of all kinds and quenched their thirst with beer, cider, and punch. The merrymakers smoked, sang, and danced the night away, until overtaken by a combination of drunkenness and fatigue.[32]

Closing Out the Century

As time went on, settlement continued to spread. An official report prepared during the 1690s indicated that most of the Virginia colony's land east of the fall line had been patented. The writers claimed that the ancient headright system was much abused, thanks to the submission of fraudulent documents to county courts. They also said that dishonest surveyors sometimes produced drawings of property they hadn't visited or included more—or perhaps different—acreage than had been patented. Although patentees were supposed to build improvements on their land within three years or place an acre or more under cultivation, many people took advantage of the loosely worded legal requirements. As a result, planters often owned large tracts they never developed, thereby preventing others from acquiring it.

Gloucester County, like other parts of the Middle Peninsula, remained predominantly rural throughout the colonial period. Major plantation seats, the homes of the elite and more successful, were scattered along the banks of the York River and its tributaries, and along the Severn, Ware, North, East, and Piankatank Rivers and Mobjack Bay, where there was convenient access to commercial shipping. In time, development occurred in the interior, for inland transportation routes opened the region to more widely dispersed settlement. By 1691, a main road, portions of which became part of modern Route 17, extended beyond Dragon Swamp; the forerunners of Routes 14 and 198 had long been in existence. The improvement of these main thoroughfares would have accelerated the development of land throughout all four of Gloucester County's parishes.

Although officials in England continued to complain about what they called a straggling mode of settlement, Virginians, hungry for new land on which to grow tobacco, kept expanding the colony's frontier. However, the number of indentured servants coming to the Chesapeake failed to keep pace with the need for labor, with the result that the price of servants began to rise. Often, as soon as indentured servants were free, they would rent land on which they could raise tobacco or would hire themselves out as sharecroppers while they accumulated the funds they needed to acquire land. This strategy was a good one while tobacco prices were high, but between 1680 and 1720, when the tobacco market was unstable and the crop was often unprofitable, there were fewer opportunities for ex-servants to improve their lot. This put a damper upon white servants' desire to immigrate to Virginia. As a result, by the 1680s the small planter's dominance in the Chesapeake had begun to dwindle.

Another change occurred that affected socioeconomic conditions. As living conditions improved and fecundity increased, patentees' large holdings often were distributed among a growing number of family members. Social historians Darrett and Anita Rutman, who studied Middlesex County's inhabitants, found that while almost all couples married for life, most people were relatively short-lived. As a result, there were many widows and widowers, especially widows of childbearing age. In fact, the Rutmans found that relatively few children lived to adulthood without experiencing the loss of one or both parents. Living with a step-parent was commonplace, for widows and widowers usually remarried. Often, children were named after their parents and grandparents, thereby preserving a family connection.[33]

Other factors affected daily life. Although servants and slaves usually performed similar tasks and may have enjoyed many of the same privileges, as the seventeenth century drew to a close, increasing numbers of Africans were imported into Virginia: men, women, and children who were unaccustomed to plantation life. It was probably was very difficult for experienced black workers, who had been in the colony for a long time, to adjust to the increased regimentation that many Virginia planters deemed necessary to control the newcomers. On the other hand, some people seem to have continued leaving their servants and slaves to fend for themselves. In October 1696, a group of Gloucester County citizens presented a petition to the Assembly asking that a law be passed that would prohibit blacks from living in a quarter that did not have a Christian overseer. The proposal was rejected, perhaps because this practice was fairly common throughout Tidewater.[34]

At the end of the seventeenth century, the assembly enacted legislation that affected land acquisition by means of the headright system. By the mid-seventeenth century, prospective patentees had begun using Africans as headrights and some people claimed headrights on behalf of Indians imported into Virginia from other colonies. Because both trends accelerated as time went on, especially after the slave trade opened up, in April 1699 the General Assembly disallowed the use of Africans as headrights. Records of the Virginia Land Office demonstrate clearly that Virginia officials implemented the new policy just as soon as it became law.[35]

Another important change occurred in late October 1687. It was then that the king's "Declaration for Liberty of Conscience" was read aloud in Jamestown. This so-called act of toleration, which gave non-Anglicans the right to assemble for worship, was announced "with the beat of the drum and the firing of two great guns and with all the joyfulness this collony is capable to express." Even so, the State Church's authority over the colony's citizens remained intact. People had to pay taxes to support the Established Church regardless of their beliefs, and religious dissenters, for example, Quakers, often were harassed or otherwise ill-treated. In 1704 historian Robert Beverley II noted that there were few dissenters in Virginia: only three small meetings of Quakers and two of Presbyterians. There is no documentary evidence suggesting that Kingston Parish was home to an organized group of religious dissenters.[36]

NOTES

1 As early as 1614 men were sent to the tip of the Eastern Shore to make salt from seawater by boiling it in kettles.

2 J.A.C. Chandler and E.G. Swem, eds., "Letters Written by Mr. Moray, A Minister, to Sr. R. Moray, from Ware River in Mockjack Bay, Virginia, Feb. 1, 1665." *William and Mary Quarterly* 2nd Ser., 2 (1893–1894):157–161.

3 Hartwell et al., *Present State*, 19; Hening, *Statutes*, II, 17–32, 82, 244.

4 The Rev. John Clayton claimed that Governor William Berkeley, who referred to some of his bond workers as slaves, bribed three Turkish servants with offers of manumission and plantations if they would cast off their heathenism and convert to Christianity. In fact, Clayton said that two of the men converted but the third held out until he was age 80. He added that while he was rector of the church at Jamestown, the elderly convert became very devout and regularly attended church at Jamestown (Edward L. Bond, *Spreading the Gospel in Colonial Virginia: Sermons and Devotional Writings* [Lanham, Maryland, 2004], 415–416, 475–476).

5 Warren M. Billings et al., *Colonial Virginia: A History* (White Plains, New York), 55, 66–68, 122; Rutman and Rutman, *A Place in Time*, 128–129; Carr et al., *Colonial Chesapeake Society*, 226–227; Graham et al., "Adaptation," 506–508, 517.

6 One man was a drummer so they planned to procure a drum from the Willis plantation.

7 Hening, *Statutes*, II, 191, 204; Beverley, *History*, 68–69; McIlwaine, *Minutes*, 209–210, 511; Peter W. Coldham, ed., *British Emigrants in Bondage, 1614–1788* (Baltimore, 2005), i–iv; *The King's Passengers to Maryland and Virginia* (Westminster, Maryland, 2006), ii; Lyon G. Tyler, ed., "Virginia Colonial Records," *William and Mary Quarterly* 1st Ser., 15 (1907):39–43.

8 Hening, *Statutes*, II, 256–257, 291–292; H. R. McIlwaine, ed., *Journals of the House of Burgesses, 1619–1776* (Richmond, 1905–1915), 1660–1693:47; *Minutes*, 458; *Executive Journals Of The Council Of Colonial Virginia* (Richmond, 1925–1945), I, 154, 256, 533; II, 239, 324; John Clayton, "Map of Jamestown," 1688; BPRO, CO 1/29 ff 72–75; 1/30 ff 169–170; Force, *Tracts*, I, Book 11:24–25.

9 Hening, *Statutes*, II, 19, 83–84, 170, 260, 280, 296, 479–480, 497; Bond, *Spreading the Gospel*, 415–416, Lorena S. Walsh, *Motives of Honor, Pleasure and Profit: Plantation Management in the Colonial Chesapeake, 1607–1763* (Chapel Hill, 2010), 379–382. Official records from Virginia's Eastern Shore and those of Henrico, Surry, Isle of Wight, and York Counties, which are relatively complete, contain numerous references to young Indians who were brought before local court justices so that their age could be decided. This would have determined when the youngsters would be considered taxable. During the 1680s and 1690s most, if not all, Indian children in the households of Virginia planters were considered servants, not slaves. However, like African servants and slaves and white indentured servants, Indians' time of service could be bought and sold and conveyed from hand to hand by bequest. Court records reveal that many of these Indian children had been captured by

Tributary natives and sold to the colonists. Therefore, under the law, they did not have the same legal status that the Tributaries did.

10 Hening, Statutes, II, 274, 329; Herrman, "Virginia," 1673; Chamberlayne, *The Parish Register of Christ Church, Middlesex County, Virginia, from 1653–1812* (Easley, South Carolina, 1988), x.

11 In 1935 when WPA worker Harriet G. Miller interviewed some of Mathews County's residents, one informant said that Isleham, the home of Sir John Peyton, could be found an "old Episcopal graveyard." The interviewee said that "on a portion of this land stood several hundred years ago North River Precinct Chapel and from this 'Chapel Neck' has derived its name." Ms. Miller noted the presence of "old stones or slabs," an indication that the graveyard was visible in 1935 (Miller, "Interviews," Box 11).

12 This statement is not supported by the documentary evidence currently available.

13 During the mid-1970s one writer stated that Kingston Parish's seventeenth-century chapels were fabricated of logs. This is unlikely. Archaeological and architectural research indicates that during the seventeenth century, almost all churches and chapels were constructed with timber framing, sawn boards, and other riven timbers, then the most commonly used building material in Virginia. Exceptions were the church at Jamestown, the colony's original capital city, and the brick church that John Page built at Middle Plantation in 1683 (Graham et al., "Adaptation," 481–483).

14 Secondary sources indicate that Mr. Zyperus (Zyperius, Ziperius), a licensed minister of the Dutch Reformed church, lived in Curaçao for a while. He moved to New York and served a congregation in Harlem until the early 1660s, when he moved to Virginia, where Anglican clergy were in short supply and ministers from other Protestant denominations were sometimes hired. In August 1664, the Rev. Samuel Drisius, who knew Zyperus, informed church officials in the Netherlands that the young clergyman had "left for Virginia long ago. He behaved most shamefully here, drinking, cheating and forging other people's writings, so that he was forbidden not only to preach, but even to keep school." In 1680 Michael Zyperus was identified by Virginia officials as Kingston Parish's minister (J. Franklin Jamison, ed., *Narratives of New Netherland, 1609–1664* [New York, 1909], 413; Meade, *Old Churches*, I, 325–326).

15 Charles G. Chamberlayne, *The Vestry Book of Kingston Parish, Mathews County, Virginia, 1679–1796* (Bowie, Maryland, 1999), 1–2; Patent Book III, 232; 5, 479; VII, 1, 532; VIII, 390; Billups Papers, Swem, Box 9 Folder 31; Box 10 Folder 3.

16 Chamberlayne, *Kingston Parish*, 6–8, 19. Whenever a church was abandoned or replaced, the old building and its yard were marked with a ditch, probably as a means of preserving what had been a burial ground.

17 Chamberlayne, *Kingston Parish*, 24–26, passim; Middlesex County Deed Book 2 [1694–1703):62–63; Patent Book VII, 357. Traditionally, an illegitimate child's father was responsible for at least part of its support.

18 Chamberlayne, *Christ Church*, 41.

19 In 1680 when Virginia's burgesses had to address the need of erecting a new statehouse, Gloucester Point was strongly favored but lost in a two-to-one vote.

20 Where Nathaniel Bacon's corpse was buried remains a mystery. According to one contemporary account, "his bones were never found to be exposed on a gibbet as was purpos'd, stones being laid in his coffin" by Richard Lawrence, one of his most loyal supporters.

21 Wilcomb E. Washburn, *The Governor And The Rebel: A History of Bacon's Rebellion in Virginia* (New York, 1972), 18–19, 32–33, 69–71, 79–81, 84–85, 153–166; Force, *Tracts*, I, Book 8:23–24; Book 11:13, 26–27; Charles Andrews, comp., *Narratives of the Insurrections, 1665–1690* (New York, 1967), 87, 92; John D. Neville, *Bacon's Rebellion* (Richmond, 1976), 313, 323.

22 Hening, *Statutes*, II, 545–548, 552; III, 569; Washburn, *Rebel*, 84–91, 223, 225, 233; Neville, *Rebellion*, 83–84, 313, 323, 362–363; York County Deeds, Orders, Wills Book 6:5; McIlwaine, *House, 1660–1693*, 70; McIlwaine, *Minutes*, 458–459, 531; *Executive Journals*, I, 157; Patent Book IV, 191; VI, 139; VII, 223, 553; Louis Des Cognets Jr., ed., *English Duplicates Of Lost Virginia Records* (Baltimore, 1981), 233–234; SR 749, 4561, 5386, 6618, 7444, 66186; BPRO, CO 1/41 ff 294–297;1/42 f 35ro; 5/1371 ff 171–178; 391/2 170–172; Privy Council (PC) 2/66 ff 212–213; State Papers (SP) 44/28 f 222; Mason, *Gloucester*, I, 84, 121.

23 Young West, described in the narrative of T.M. (Thomas Mathew) as the son of an English colonel, was likely the offspring of Captain John West, who by 1656 owned land in Pamunkey Neck, near the Pamunkey queen's village. She had been widowed in 1656 when her husband, Totopotomoy, was slain while fighting alongside the English. According to a descendant of the elder Captain West, his English wife, Unity, deserted him because of his liaison with the queen of Pamunkey (Force, Tracts, I, Book 8:14–15; John F. Dorman, ed., *Adventurers of Purse and Person, Virginia 1607–1624/25* [Baltimore, 2004–2007], I, 773; III, 490; Martha W. McCartney, "Cockacoeske, Queen of Pamunkey: Diplomat and Suzeraine" in *Powhatan's Mantle: Indians in the Colonial Southeast*, ed. Peter H. Wood et al., eds. [Lincoln, Nebraska, 2006], 263).

24 Hening, *Statutes*, II, 275–277, 405; McIlwaine, *House, 1660–1693*:135.

25 Arthur P. Middleton, *Tobacco Coast: A Maritime History of the Chesapeake Bay in the Colonial Era* (Newport News, 1953), 40, 109–113, 119, 122, 127. Rolling roads were the well-defined pathways along which planters and their servants rolled hogsheads of tobacco to inspection and storage warehouses.

26 McIlwaine, *Minutes*, 412; Patent Book VII, 222; SR 6324; McCartney, *Jamestown People*, 250).

27 H.R. McIlwaine, ed., *Legislative Journals of the Council of Colonial Virginia* (Richmond, 1981), 436; *House, 1660–1693*, 171, 180; *Executive Journals*, I, 26; Hening, *Statutes*, II, 473; III, 59; John W. Reps, *Tidewater Towns In Colonial Virginia* (Princeton, 1972), 86–88.

28 Mathews Archives, Box 18 R; McIlwaine, *Executive Journals*, I, 175–176, 194–195, 297; BPRO, Admiralty (ADM) 2/173 f 115; 52/122 ff 1–52, 117;CO 5/1306 ff 312–313; 5/1307 ff 4–5; SR 6324, 9208; Herrman, "Virginia," 1673; Walter Hoxton, "This Map

of the Peninsula between Delaware & Chesapeak[e] Bays," 1735; John Thornton, "A New Map of Virginia, Maryland, Pennsilvania [*sic*], New Jersey, Part of New York and Carolina,: [ca. 1700]; Alexander C. Brown, "Wolf Trap: The Baptism of a Chesapeake Bay Shoal," *Virginia Magazine of History and Biography* 59 (1951):176–183. According to Brown, the British Museum's Harley Manuscripts contain the journals kept by two men who were aboard the *Wolfe* when it ran aground.

29 On May 14, 1774, when a surveyor prepared a plat for John Fox, depicting "Part of the Town of Botetourt," a small square tract labeled with the letter "D" was identified as "the Place where the Old Courthouse stood & supposed to be on the six acres given by Gwyn to build a courthouse & prison on" (Francis Tomkies, "Town of Botetourt," 1774).

30 Members of the Read family had owned land in this vicinity since the third quarter of the seventeenth century (Patent Book V, 280, 586; VI, 331; X, 173). John Throckmorton, [untitled plat of the prison bounds], June 31, 1754; Purdie and Dixon, *Virginia Gazette*, April 4 and July 26, 1766; September 28, 1769; McIlwaine, *Legislative Journals*, 1423; [Francis Tomkies], "Pt. of an Acre of Land on which Gloucester Courthouse now stands," August 9, 1769; "Town of Botetourt," 1774.

31 By the late seventeenth century, Virginia farmers had begun producing fodder crops that would support more livestock. They sowed wheat in late October or early November, planted corn in April, and transplanted tobacco in May.

32 Durand de Dauphine, *A Brief Description of America with a Longer One of Virginia And Maryland*, Gilbert Chinard, trans. (New York, 1934), 30, 107–111, 117–120, 128–133, 136–138; Warren M. Billings, ed., *The Papers of Francis Howard, Baron Howard of Effingham, 1643–1695* (Richmond, 1989), 51, 82, 115, 192, 198, 229.

33 This tradition also was followed by the enslaved.

34 Kulikoff, *Tobacco*, 35–38; Nugent, *Cavaliers*, II, 369; Walsh, *Carter's Grove*, 25, 31–32, 85; McIlwaine, *House, 1695–1702*, 72.

35 Rutman and Rutman, *A Place in Time*, 57–58, 65–66, 75, 79; Hartwell et al., *Present State*, 16–2–; Hening, *Statutes*, III, 304–329; IV, 81; V, 424–425; Nugent, *Cavaliers*, III, viii; McIlwaine, *Executive Journals*, I, 347.

36 McIlwaine, *Executive Journals*, I, 517; William G. Stanard, "Genealogy," *Virginia Magazine of History and Biography* 36 (1928):100; York County Deeds, Orders, Wills 1687–1691:70–73; Beverley, *History*, 261.

4

Among the Fields, Above the Sea
1700–1750

Advent of a New Century

In July 1702, Virginia's governing officials informed their superiors that Gloucester County had 2,626 tithables: that is, taxable white males and blacks of both sexes age 16 or older. At least eight of the 13 men then serving as county court justices owned land in Kingston Parish: Ambrose Dudley, John Gwyn, Anthony Gregory, Peter Kemp, Sands Knowles, James Ransone, Thomas Todd, and Conquest Wyatt. Peter Beverley was Gloucester's clerk of court, and Miles Cary was the county's official surveyor. Gloucester County had a population of 5,834, including 3,206 women and children, and the county militia had 594 members, 121 of whom were horse soldiers or dragoons. According to Robert Beverley II, the governor normally chose a wealthy planter to serve as commander of the county militia. He and the county's other militia officers were usually men of substance. Middling landowners typically formed a troop of horse soldiers, but less affluent white males were likely to be in a company of foot soldiers. Free black men, legally unable to bear arms, served in supportive roles.

Virginia's 1704 quitrent roll reveals that more people paid taxes on land in Kingston Parish than in any other Gloucester County locality. In Kingston Parish, 117 men and women paid quitrent on an aggregate of 46,537 acres.[1] Roughly a third of this acreage (15,582 acres) was part of estates that enveloped 1,000 acres or more; these properties were owned or leased by eleven individuals. Another 16 people had tracts that ranged from 600 to

990 acres. Therefore, more than half of the land in Kingston Parish was controlled by only 27 people. Kingston Parish's largest plantation belonged to a Captain Armistead, probably John Armistead, who was credited with 3,675 acres. It is likely that some of the men and women who had vast tracts of land in Kingston Parish were absentee owners whose properties were in the hands of servants or tenants. Three Kingston Parish widows paid quitrent in 1704. A total of 41 people had control of between 100 and 300 acres, whereas 19 others had use of less than 100 acres. Because quitrent rolls include the names of leaseholders as well as landowners, we cannot safely assume that everyone credited with acreage actually owned it or conversely, that someone whose name was omitted from the list did not own land.

Many of the people who paid quitrent on their Kingston Parish land in 1704 were the heirs of people who had patented their property during the second half of the seventeenth century. One such example was John Banister of New Point Comfort Island; another was Richard Dudley. The Billupses, Callises, Elliotts, Hunleys, Lillys, Plummers, Pressons, Ransones, and Singletons had also owned land in the parish since the mid-to-late seventeenth century. Humphrey Toy, who patented 550 acres in 1679, by 1704 had doubled the amount of acreage under his control, exercising his legal right to do so when his original patent was seated. Although it is tempting to assume that those credited with very little acreage were in the lower ranks of society, there were exceptions. Henry Bolton, who paid quitrent on only 50 acres, served as a Kingston Parish churchwarden and clerk of the vestry, positions requiring literacy and usually reserved for men of means. Likewise, Edward Sadler, who paid quitrent on only 20 acres, was considered a gentleman and served on Kingston Parish's vestry in 1687.[2]

Patenting Criteria Change

In 1705, the House of Burgesses made seating requirements more explicit. Anyone staking a legal claim to unpatented acreage was obliged to clear and plant at least one acre of ground and build a frame house that was at least 12 feet long and 12 feet wide. This law was amended in 1713, and henceforth would-be patentees had three years in which to build a "good dwelling house" at least 20 feet long and 16 feet wide. Moreover, they had to improve the soil of the acreage they were acquiring and place some livestock upon their property. Another way prospective patentees could secure their land titles was by draining or clearing three acres of marsh or swamp out of every 50 acres they sought to acquire. By 1720 anyone who cleared and enclosed three out of every 50 acres as pasturage or expended ten pounds current money on constructing buildings or planting trees and hedges fulfilled the minimum planting and seating requirements. How conscientiously these laws were obeyed or enforced is uncertain; however, they were reaffirmed in 1748.[3]

Around 1722, when the Rev. Hugh Jones described agricultural practices in Tidewater Virginia, he noted that when land was exhausted from the cultivation of tobacco, planters amended the soil by using the ground as a pen for their cattle. He added that "cow pen tobacco tastes strong" and that tobacco planted in wet, marshy ground "smoaks in the pipe like leather" unless well aged. He said that corn or maize, which thrived in Virginia, was planted in hills and weeded much like tobacco. He noted that marshes, woods, and old fields provided good pasturage for livestock, and that hogs could be fattened on the various types of roots and reeds found in marshes. According to Jones, most plantations had some peach and apple trees, and often, a few cherry trees. He said that seafood was excellent in the Tidewater, especially oysters, crabs, sheepsheads, rocks, drums, sturgeons, and trout. Also available were wild geese and ducks of various types. He closed by mentioning that deer and wild turkeys had become less plentiful than they previously had been.[4]

The Ordinary Workings of Local Government

On monthly court days, county justices heard civil suits, held preliminary hearings in criminal cases, issued tavern licenses, naturalized new citizens, and decided whether freed slaves should be allowed to remain in the county. They were empowered to try all cases except capital crimes and outlawry, with one major exception. A group of county justices of the peace, under a commission of *oyer and terminer*—that is, with the right to hear and determine—could try the enslaved without the benefit of a jury.[5]

A solitary justice of the peace could hear civil cases that involved less than twenty shillings and could investigate white people who were suspected of committing a crime. Local court justices were also responsible for seeing that their jurisdiction's public roads were kept in usable condition. According to legislation enacted during early eighteenth century, the men who served as county justices were required to take an oath of office in which they promised to "do equal right to the poor and to the rich" and to use their "cunning, wit and power" in accord with the law.[6]

The Development of Transportation Networks

By 1702, the Virginia assembly had begun licensing and regulating ferry-keepers. The locations of ferries and the fees that ferrymen could charge became a prerogative of the legislature, and the types of watercraft that could be used varied according to the width and depth of the body of water being traversed. The proprietors of ferries that crossed broad expanses of open water had to use a flat-bottomed boat that was at least 15 feet long, if transporting horses. A foot-boat at least 12 feet long, with a three-man crew, was required when conveying human passengers.[7] Scows, which could be used to cross shallow water, had to be long enough to carry a wagon and four horses. Their ferrymen used poles long enough to reach the river bed so that they could push their crafts along. A ferry boat that crossed a very narrow stream could be powered by oars or ropes.

In 1705, Virginia's legislature enacted some laws that regulated the construction and maintenance of public roads. Highways that provided access to the county seat and the capital city had to be properly maintained, and existing public roads had to be kept passable—that is, clear of debris, such as brush and fallen trees. County courts had the authority to appoint surveyors to lay out new public roads as the need arose, and freeholders were obliged to provide the labor that was required to build and maintain them. If a road crossed a mill dam, the mill's owner had to keep both in usable condition. A 1738 law called for the placement of a sturdy post or stone marker at major intersections, pointing the way to the most important destination to which each road led.[8]

More Labor for the Land

More than 70,500 slaves were brought into Virginia between 1699 and 1775. Many of these men, women, and children passed through customs at Yorktown, the official port of entry for all imports then entering Gloucester County. The York River Customs District included not only shipping that entered and left the York River but also vessels that arrived and departed from the Severn, Ware, North, East, and Piankatank Rivers. Customs records indicate that during the 1770s, approximately 60 percent of the slaves imported into Virginia came from Africa and 40 percent from the West Indies. The direct importation of Africans into the colony during the 1730s resulted in the Africanization of slavery—that is, men and women with "country markings" such as ritual scarring, filed teeth, and plaited hair. They would have been conspicuous among the population of creolized African-Americans, who had adopted some of the ways of white society. Many whites probably found the unfamiliar languages, religious practices, music, and material culture of Africans somewhat disturbing because of their "differentness." Transplanted Africans would have been vulnerable to New World diseases, and only after the sex ratio became more evenly balanced were there opportunities for newly arrived Africans to establish families. During this formative period, planters made increased demands upon their slaves, such as making them work longer hours and more days, and paid little heed to their nutritional and medical needs, clothing, and shelter. These changes occurred as the number of white servants declined and those of African descent became more numerous. Successful planters, who placed their slaves under the supervision of overseers or farm managers, distanced themselves physically and psychologically from those who toiled on their behalf.

Scholars have concluded that by 1730, the number of days slaves were required to work had increased. There were only three holidays a year—Christmas, Easter, and Whitsuntide—and for almost all slaves, Saturday became a full workday. Moreover, slaves were obliged to respond to any situation their master considered urgent, and a slave's workday often extended into the night. Enslaved women and girls age 12 or over typically performed the same field labor as male slaves, often as part of the same work group or "gang." When slave owners classified workers as "full" or "partial" hands, they were referring to allowances for youth, disability or advanced age. Customs gradually evolved concerning the amount of work expected, weekly food rations, and the type and quantity of new clothing that was issued each year. Slaveholders or their overseers who tried to deviate from these traditions often met with resistance manifested as work slowdowns, feigned illness, or running away.

The sweet-scented tobacco raised on the Middle Peninsula's plantations during the late seventeenth and early eighteenth centuries was marketable and brought high prices, but production per laborer dropped during the 1720s and 1730s, a period characterized by unfavorable weather patterns. The tobacco inspection acts, followed by an increase in tobacco prices, encouraged Middle Peninsula planters to grow larger crops. They also began to plant more grain, especially corn, since some of the region's soils were unfavorable for wheat. The addition of grains was not easily achieved because a supply of livestock forage was important for the draft animals needed to pull a plow. Also, if planters intended to raise more grain, they had to make greater use of plows and many farmers were slow to substitute plows for hoes.[9]

The Slave Code and Its Implications

In October 1705, the House of Burgesses updated the legal code to address the colony's changing needs. By that date, Virginia's black population had increased markedly, slavery had gained widespread acceptance, and large numbers of Africans were being imported specifically as slaves. Several of the laws enacted in 1705 by burgesses, who were also slaveholders, dramatically affected the lives of all non-whites. They also made an unmistakable distinction between the way white servants and blacks, whether enslaved or free, were treated under the law. The "act concerning Servants and Slaves" summarized and codified earlier laws that had been passed in piecemeal fashion. This body of legislation was to govern the lives of Africans and their descendants for generations to come. In time, the statutes applicable to people of African descent became known as the "slave code."

From 1705 on, enslaved blacks, Indians, and racially-mixed people were relegated to the status of personal property that could be bought and sold, passed along by means of a bequest, and used as collateral to secure debts.[10] Those who bought or sold slaves did not have to report their transactions to the clerk of the county court. The slave code reiterated the fact that non-Christians who immigrated to Virginia couldn't obtain their freedom through religious conversion. All non-whites, whether enslaved or free, were ineligible to hold any public office whatsoever, and they couldn't serve in the militia. Neither blacks nor Indians were allowed to testify in court. Therefore, they couldn't sue to collect debts, and if they were indentured servants, they couldn't sue for their freedom if their masters detained them after their contracts expired. One new statute took a strong stand against interracial marriage. The definition of a tithable was also expanded in 1723.

Slaves accused of a capital crime could be tried by a panel of local court justices without the benefit of a jury. Disobedient slaves could receive corporal punishment, and if they fought back, they could receive up to thirty lashes at the county whipping post. Slaves weren't allowed to possess guns, swords, clubs, or any other weapons; and they couldn't leave their home property without written permission from their owner or overseer. They were denied the right to own livestock and if they had some, local churchwardens could seize the animals, sell them, and use the proceeds toward support of the poor. The legal statute stating that the "baptism of slaves doth not exempt them from bondage" also declared that "all children shall be bond or free, according to the condition of their mothers." A colony-wide patrol system intended to control slaves' movement was authorized in 1738. Each county had an officer and four men who had the authority to visit "places suspected of entertaining unlawful assemblies of slaves, servants, or disorderly persons" and arrest any slave found away from home without a pass.

The Native American population, like enslaved blacks, was also subjected to new restrictions. A 1711 law required them to wear special badges whenever they ventured into colonized areas.[11] Three years later a new statute prohibited use of the titles "king" and "queen" in reference to native leaders. Thus, as Virginia's Indians assumed a less forceful role in society and declined in population and strength, they were subjected to some of the same discriminatory practices to which blacks and other minorities were subjected.[12]

During the first quarter of the eighteenth century, slaves were concentrated in Tidewater Virginia, where tobacco was of prime importance. Therefore, slave ships typically stopped at places like Yorktown, where wealthy planters could purchase their human "merchandize." Edward Kimber, an English traveler who visited Maryland and Virginia in 1745–6, said that when newly imported slaves were sold, buyers examined them "as the Butchers do Beasts in Smithfield, to see if they are proof in Cod, Flank and Shoulders." He said that a newly imported African, "if he must be broke, either from Obstinacy or, which I am more apt to suppose, from Greatness of Soul, [he] will require more hard Discipline than a young Spaniel." He added that if such newcomers were shown how to hoe or to push a wheelbarrow, they'd often "take the one by the Bottom, and the other by the Wheel; and they often die before they can be conquer'd." Kimber spoke of slaves being whipped until they were unconscious and declared that slavery was "the worst and greatest of Evils." Among imported slaves, men outnumbered women by roughly two to one. This would have prevented many men from finding wives and forming families. Only the wealthy could purchase large numbers of slaves at one time but most planters could afford to buy one or two a year. By mid-century, however, most successful Tidewater planters didn't need to purchase additional workers, for natural increase usually supplied the extra hands they needed.[13]

Indentured Servants and Transported Convicts

White indentured servants of both sexes came from all over Great Britain and some were even paid a salary. A servant whose contract expired received his freedom dues and was allowed to leave his master's plantation. Until that time, a servant was considered his master's personal property and his contract could be sold or passed down through inheritance. Shiploads of indentured servants came to Virginia and were auctioned off at dockside to the highest bidder. Prices for indentured servants varied and usually depended on their skills. A servant with specialized knowledge usually could bargain for a shorter or more favorable term. Like a slave, an indentured servant needed his/her master's permission to leave his plantation, to perform work for anyone else, to marry, or to keep money for personal use. An unruly servant could be whipped or otherwise punished for improper behavior. Due to poor living conditions, hard labor, the need to adjust to a new climate, and susceptibility to native diseases, many servants didn't live long enough to attain their freedom. They often ran away; because they usually spoke English and were white, they were more difficult to recapture than enslaved blacks. Runaway servants, if captured, were usually punished by extending their contracts. Much of what we know about indentured servants has been gleaned from county court records and advertisements for runaways. Some male indentured servants were highly skilled workers who found employment as bricklayers, joiners, shoemakers, blacksmiths, clerks, coachmen, and gardeners. Female indentured servants usually performed domestic chores like laundry, sewing, and housekeeping.

Transported convicts of both sexes, though considered far less desirable, were also sold to plantation owners. Most of these jailbirds were male, young, unskilled, and poor; but some had useful skills, like carpentry, blacksmithing, and husbandry. Many of those sentenced to transportation were people judges felt could be rehabilitated. Convict servants performed the same type of work as indentured servants but usually served longer terms and were considered untrustworthy. Like indentured servants and slaves, convict servants frequently ran away. For example, in April 1755, Colonel Francis Tompkies (Tomkies) of Gloucester County, a surveyor who sometimes worked in Kingston Parish, placed an advertisement in the *Virginia Gazette* in an attempt to recover John Linley, a convict servant. He said that Linley's traveling companion was another convict servant, a malt-maker who had been employed by Warner Lewis. Sometimes, political prisoners were shipped to the colonies. Advertisements for runaway servants and slaves reveal that upon reaching Virginia, they often tried to slip away from the ship.[14]

Attempted Flights to Freedom

In March 1710, some enslaved blacks and Indians, and possibly some indentured servants, decided to make a break for freedom on Easter Sunday, vowing to overcome all opposition. However, one slave disclosed the plan and the escape attempt was foiled before it got underway. All of the accused insurgents, each of whom lived on the James-York Peninsula or on the lower side of the James River, were rounded up and interrogated. Finally, on April 19, 1710, two men, an African or African-American named Scipio, and an Indian named Salvadore, were tried before the General Court, found guilty of high treason, and sentenced to death. Both men were executed, probably by hanging, and then quartered. Salvadore was put to death in Surry County, but Scipio was sent to Gloucester and executed at the courthouse. Afterward, his head and quarters were put on display in Gloucester, Middlesex, King and Queen, and Lancaster Counties. Lieutenant Governor Edmund Jennings later commented that the two slaves had been executed so that "their fate will strike such a terror" that others would not attempt an uprising. Lieutenant Governor Alexander Spotswood later made reference to the trials of Salvadore and Scipio, astutely noting that, "We are not to depend on Either their Stupidity, or that Babel of Languages among 'em; freedom Wears a Cap which Can without a Tongue, Call Together all Those who Long to Shake of[f] The fetters of Slavery."[15]

Another attempted insurrection occurred in 1723, when some Middle Peninsula slaves decided to rebel. Slaves in Middlesex County seemed to have been at the core of the uprising. After deliberation on the part of the governor, his council, and the House of Burgesses, it was decided that the ringleaders would be transported from the colony. Bambo Tom, one of Thomas Smith's slaves, and Sanon or Sanco, Isaac, and Jeffery, Armistead Churchill's slaves, were among those implicated. As the law allowed, they were to be taken to Barbados, Jamaica, or another island in the West Indies, where they would be sold as slaves. In accord with the law, the government compensated the owners of the exiled slaves for their value.[16]

Life in the Countryside

When William Hugh Grove toured Virginia in 1732, he noted that along the banks of the colony's rivers were "pleasant Seats" that "Shew Like little villages, for having Kitchens, Dairy houses, Barns, Stables, Store houses, and some of them 2 or 3 Negro Quarters all Separate from Each other but

Many planters' wives tended gardens. Courtesy of the Colonial Williamsburg Foundation, Department of Archaeological Research.

near the mansion houses make a shew to the river of 7 or 8 distinct Tenements tho' all belong to one family." Historical maps support Grove's description, for they reveal that during the mid-eighteenth century, plantations owned by Virginia's elite lined the banks of the colony's major rivers, including the Piankatank.

Real estate advertisements that appeared in the *Virginia Gazette* during the 1730s and 1740s suggest that 90 percent or more of the dwellings in eastern Virginia were of frame construction. The smallest house that was advertised measured only 12 feet by 16 feet and was situated upon an 890-acre plantation, whereas the largest measured 25 feet by 30 feet, had a brick chimney and a bricked cellar, and was on a 600-acre tract. The average house enclosed only 420 square feet. The domestic complexes on most of the farms offered for sale included a main house and outbuildings, such as kitchens, tobacco houses, hen houses, dairies, smokehouses, barns, and slave quarters. This pattern of development seems to have been prevalent on Middle Peninsula and throughout the rest of eastern Virginia. For example, in November 1766, when Joseph Gayle of Kingston Parish offered to sell his 337-acre plantation, which was only half a mile from the East River warehouse, he said that his property contained a good dwelling-house with two brick chimneys and four fireplaces, plus the usual outbuildings and two orchards. Only about a quarter of a mile away was another dwelling that measured 16 feet by 20 feet and had a brick chimney, perhaps a residence suitable for the occupancy of a tenant or farm manager. Also present was a slave quarter. When Abraham Iverson, who owned land in Ware and Kingston Parishes, tried to sell some of his land in 1777, he informed the public that his acreage was on the North River, within half a mile of a good mill, and six miles from a church.

Men and women of means almost always employed a white male to oversee the agricultural operations on their property. The contractual agreement that a landowner made with overseer made usually described the duties he was expected to perform. For example, in 1707, when Sarah Allaman of Kingston Parish hired Charles Degge, a local man, as her plantation's overseer, she specified that he was to take charge of her slaves and livestock, to see that certain crops were planted, that tobacco was readied for shipment, and to make sure that her fences were maintained. In exchange, Degge was to receive room and board, a horse to ride, and a share of the crops that were planted. In addition, his laundry was to be done. Likewise, when Robert Peyton hired Francis Singleton as his overseer, the terms of the contract were very similar; however, Singleton was also to be paid £13 a year.

Slaves occupied a wide variety of accommodations. Sometimes they lived in a loft over a kitchen or another dependency, or found shelter in a tobacco house. By the mid-eighteenth century, however, most slaves inhabited small frame structures that had one or two rooms. Some slave houses were built of logs or covered with riven clapboard, but others were miserable hovels. Slave quarters usually had dirt floors, wattle-and-daub chimneys, unfinished interior walls, small doors, and windows that were equipped with sliding wooden shutters. One English visitor, who spent the night in a shelter shared by an overseer and six slaves, said that it was a small building that stood upon blocks about a foot from the ground and was neither lathed nor plastered. The little house, which was covered with thin boards, had two doors and a window without glass. It had no ceiling, loft, or brick chimney. Research by architectural historian Camille Wells suggests that slave housing was similar to the buildings occupied by many of the Chesapeake region's common planters and landless laborers, who were poor and had few material resources.

Historian Robert Beverley II described the type of houses constructed by some of the more affluent members of Virginia society. He said that several gentlemen had "built themselves large Brick Houses of many Rooms on a Floor and several Stories high, as also some Stone Houses." He added that these dwellings often had large glass windows and were much taller than the houses formerly built by the gentry. He indicated that the "Drudgeries

A plat made in 1734 to settle a lawsuit contains a picture of a little schoolhouse located on Thomas Peyton's property at the head of Blackwater Creek. This image is the earliest known rendering of a Virginia schoolhouse. Gloucester County Surveyors Plat Book 1, pages 4-5.

of Cookery, Washing, Dairies &c. are perform'd in Offices detacht from the Dwelling-Houses," which kept them "cool and Sweet." Beverley said that most of these finer homes had roofs of cypress or pine shingles and that very few houses in the colony had tiled roofs. He indicated that some plantations had a small schoolhouse in which a tutor provided rudimentary education to the planter's children and perhaps to neighborhood youngsters whose families paid a modest amount of tuition. A plat made in 1734 to settle a lawsuit contains a picture of a little schoolhouse that was located on Thomas Peyton's property, which straddled the head of Blackwater Creek and crossed part of the North River's North End Branch. The image on the Peyton plat may well be the earliest dated sketch of a Virginia schoolhouse.

Men of privilege whose forebears were born in the Chesapeake often assumed control of well-established plantations, a few undeveloped parcels, and numerous slaves. Sometimes they attached an entail to their real and personal estate, ensuring that it would descend almost intact to their eldest son. This strategy led to the creation of great estates throughout Tidewater Virginia, but sometimes created legal complications for the heirs, issues that only could be resolved by an act of assembly. Sometimes, the owners of entailed property who wanted to provide an inheritance for their younger sons or a respectable dowry for their daughters had to purchase undeveloped tracts on the frontier. By 1760 the practice of entailing property began to lose favor.

As time went on, slaveholding became increasingly common among middling planters, who purchased or inherited slaves, and by the mid-eighteenth century, 50 to 60 percent of Tidewater households owned one or more slaves. Slaves were offered for sale when funds were needed to settle an estate or pay off a planter's debts. When sales were local, buyers often were allowed to purchase slaves on credit by giving a bond backed by good security. This made slaves affordable to those with assets to mortgage or who could find someone to serve as guarantor for the debt. Through the acquisition of slaves, ordinary planters were able to increase their income by expanding their agricultural operations.[17]

Privateers and Pirates

Although King William's War ended in 1697, by 1702 England was embroiled in Queen Anne's War, otherwise known as the War of the Spanish Succession. The French were considered a serious threat and governing officials, wary of an attack, mapped out a defensive strategy. Because emboldened French privateers had begun venturing into Virginia waters, sometimes coming within view of the king's warships, in March 1708, the governor and his council decided to have lookouts posted at regular intervals along the seacoast. Two men were stationed on New Point Comfort and two more on Gwynn's Island. Large cannon were also placed in strategic locations to signal an enemy's approach. One of these weapons, which could be heard for miles, was at New Point Comfort.

During the early eighteenth century, piracy also posed problems. On May 12, 1729, at 1 AM, five men and a woman quietly slipped aboard the sloop *John and Elizabeth*, anchored at the Piankatank River's mouth. They seized the vessel's tackle and quickly overpowered the sloop's master, John Grymes of King George County, and his servant, Alexander Abbott, who were sound asleep below deck. Grymes later said that he was forcibly placed in his cabin and that the sloop's hatch was secured. Edmund Williams, the self-proclaimed pirates' leader, and his accomplices George Caves, George Cole alias Sanders, Edward Edwards, Jeremiah Smith, and Mary Critchett stole Grymes's and Abbott's clothing and other personal belongings. They tried to persuade Abbott to join them, but he declined. At daybreak, the would-be pirates weighed anchor, but because they were unfamiliar with the Piankatank's channel, the sloop ran aground. When a high tide put the vessel afloat, currents carried it across the Chesapeake Bay to the Tangier Islands. Some of the men went ashore on Watts Island to obtain drinking water, but left hastily because the island's inhabitants seemed suspicious of their motives.

Over the next few days the *John and Elizabeth* drifted up and down the bay, at the mercy of the tides and the sloop's inexperienced crew. Finally, when a strong wind blew the sloop toward the mouth of the York River, the pirates allowed Grymes and Abbott to go ashore in a small flat. Because both men had been stripped of their clothing, the pirates let them cover their nakedness with some raw hides that were aboard, animal skins that belonged to Mann Page, Esquire. Later, the pirates were caught and hauled before the Court of Admiralty on August 14, 1729. This tribunal included five members of the governor's council, two of the Crown's tax officials, and Attorney General John Clayton, a judge of the Court of Vice Admiralty.[18] Grymes and Abbott testified against their captors and identified them as convict servants. All of six of the accused were found guilty and sentenced to death. Passenger manifests for vessels that brought convicts to Virginia in 1727 and 1728 included the names of George Cole, Mary Critchett, and Jeremiah Smith, convicted felons who came to Virginia aboard ships registered in the Rappahannock River. An Edward Edwards, a convict who arrived in early 1725, may have been the pirates' ringleader.

Episodes of piracy were usually mentioned in the newspapers published along the Atlantic seaboard. For example, in 1745 the snow *Flying-Fish*, which was transporting cargo from Barbados to Maryland, encountered a well-armed French privateer. Although the snow's captain was able to ransom his vessel and cargo with 3,000 pieces of eight and again set out for Maryland, he ran afoul of a storm and was driven shore at New Point Comfort, where his vessel was destroyed.[19]

Regulating Maritime Commerce

Whenever seagoing vessels entered or exited from Virginia's main rivers or the Eastern Shore, their captains or masters were obliged to stop at the nearest port of entry or custom house. The James River, which had more commercial traffic than Virginia's other rivers, had two ports of entry or Naval Districts. The York, Rappahannock, and Potomac Rivers, and the Eastern Shore had one district apiece. When a ship arrived at a port of entry, a representative of that district's naval officer would record its name and the names of its master and owner, examine the vessel's manifest, and inspect its cargo. He would usually make note of the vessel's type, when and where it was built and registered, and its point of embarkation. The ships that passed through Virginia's naval offices were engaged in transatlantic or coastal trade, depending on their type and size. Ship returns reveal that relatively few of these vessels had been built in the colony. The goods imported into Virginia on these ships usually consisted of large quantities of British manufactures of various types. Imports also could include "plantation goods" such as rum, salt, sugar, and molasses that were brought in from Bermuda, Jamaica, or Barbados, or perhaps agricultural products, naval stores, or other commodities produced by the mainland colonies. This trading pattern, which became known as "triangular trade," was established during the seventeenth century and persisted until the time of the American Revolution. Occasionally, manufactured goods of British origin entered Virginia through Maryland, North Carolina, or other mainland colonies. Transatlantic imports often included human cargo, such as indentured servants and transported convicts from Great Britain or Africans destined to become slaves. Frequently exported from Virginia were large quantities of tobacco, staves, plank, corn, pork, beef, wheat, buck skins, ship masts and yards, and various forest products.

Records that Virginia's naval officers transmitted to England between 1699 and 1781, which are relatively complete, reveal that the goods imported and exported from Kingston Parish and other parts of Gloucester County passed through the custom house at Yorktown, the York River District's official port of entry. Shipping returns compiled at Yorktown suggest that relatively few of the Kingston Parish men engaged in maritime commerce actually built the vessels in which they went to sea. Nearly three-quarters of these people, who showed a partiality for square-sterned sloops or schooners, were involved in trade that was limited to other mainland colonies or the Caribbean. Two men had brigantines, and three others owned three or more ships, probably because their trading ventures were so lucrative.

Shipping returns reveal that in March 1700, Robert Peyton Sr., whose plantation was on Blackwater Creek, owned the sloop *Blackwater*, a 20-ton vessel built in Virginia in 1697. When the *Blackwater* passed through customs, it was carrying "English goods legally imported" from North Carolina. A month later, the *Blackwater,* which had made another trip to North

Carolina, passed through customs again, this time transporting provisions. Peyton's neighbor, Thomas Todd, took his sloop to Maryland in 1701 and returned with apparel for indentured servants and slaves. Naval office records for 1725 reveal that when the *Grenock,* a 130-ton ship, landed at Yorktown, aboard were British goods and thousands of yards of linen. The *Grenock*, built on Mobjack Bay in 1713, was registered in Glasgow, Scotland, and was owned by William Andrew; her master was James Watson. Thomas Seal's ship, the *William*, built on Mobjack Bay in 1715, was registered in Liverpool in 1722. In 1729 the *William* arrived at Yorktown with hogsheads of rum, three Africans, and a substantial quantity of European goods. Walter Keeble, the owner and master of the *Catherine*, a 50-ton sloop built in 1727, left Virginia in 1728 with 500 hogsheads of tobacco. Later, Keeble went to sea as master of Gwyn Read's schooner, the *Adventure,* which transported a large cargo from Virginia to London. John Hayes was the master of the *Freewill*, a Virginia-built vessel that was owned by Thomas Hayes; in 1725 when the *Freewill* passed through customs, she was carrying rum, sugar, and molasses imported from Barbados.

During the late 1720s, Henry Armistead, owner of the *Lucy,* a brigantine built on the Piankatank River, made at least two trips to the Caribbean and brought in rum, sugar, and molasses from Jamaica. He also had the *Prince Frederick*, which was built in 1729 and between March 1730 and March 1731 brought in a cargo of animal skins and beeswax from North Carolina, plus barrels of whale oil. During the same period, Armistead sent containers of flour, bread, fish, beef, and tongues to Barbados. He also owned the *Pretty Patsy*, which was built in 1730 and carried a crew of 14. Between June 1731 and June 1732, she went to London with a large quantity of tobacco; and a few months later, Armistead sent her to Bristol with another large shipment of tobacco, sassafras roots, tons of iron, and thousands of staves for barrels and hogsheads. Shipping returns reveal that each time the *Pretty Patsy* returned to Yorktown, she had aboard large cargoes of European goods. By 1736, Armistead had sold her to the infamous Jonathan Forward, who became wealthy by transporting convicts to Virginia and Maryland.

Francis Willis, who had land in Kingston and Ware Parishes, and his business partner, John Jarvis, owned the *Stanton,* an 80-ton brigantine with a crew of eight. In 1730–1, the *Stanton* brought in cotton and sugar from

Jamaica and then headed to Surinam with large quantities of flour, bread, agricultural products, and some European goods. On another occasion, Willis sent the *Stanton* to Barbados with candles, beef, flour, and butter. Besides the *Stanton*, Willis owned the *Gloucester*, a vessel built in 1728. By 1738, he had acquired the *Molly*. Willis was engaged in commerce for at least one more decade and added the *Mobjack* to his fleet. He sometimes used George Read as master of the *Gloucester*, but by 1731 Read had acquired his own three-ton schooner, the *Experiment*, and had begun making trips to Maryland with a three-man crew. On one occasion he transported a load of apothecary's wares, a still, two trunks, a desk, and other household goods from Virginia to Maryland. By 1731, John Lewis, who owned land in at least two of Gloucester County's parishes, had purchased the *Stanton* from Willis and Jarvis and sent it to sea with a cargo of flour, bread, lard, beeswax, pork, and plank. Lewis also owned the brigantine *Priscilla*, which made at least two trips to Madeira with large quantities of wheat, corn, legumes, bales of woolens, barrel hoops, and casks. On another voyage he brought in rum, molasses, and sugar from Barbados. In 1737, Lewis's crew set sail for Bristol with a cargo of iron, shingles, barrels of turpentine, lumber, and wool. By 1738, he had acquired Henry Armistead's *Pretty Patsy*, and within four years' time he bought the *Success*, the *Grampus*, and the *Penguin*. By the early 1740s, John King had come into possession of the *Pratt*, a prize ship, and John Thompson had acquired the *Baniff*, also condemned and made a prize.

During the mid-eighteenth century, the *Virginia Gazette* started publishing the names of ships before or after they cleared customs. For example, the *Virginia Gazette* indicated that in August 1767 Humphrey Keeble, captain of the *Julia and Betsy*, intended to set sail for Antigua with a supply of corn, flour, staves, and timber. A year later, the *Gazette* reported that Keeble had just arrived from New York with loaf sugar and sail cloth. Storekeepers often announced the arrival of imported goods. For instance, in 1777 a shipment of St. Croix rum, sugar, and Hyson tea was offered for sale at The Battery, a store or tavern near North, where slave auctions also were held.[20]

Virginia's Tobacco Inspection System

By the eighteenth century, most small farmers sold their tobacco to a British merchant's representative or to larger planters, who resold it. Merchants' representatives usually settled in a strategic location, such as a riverfront town, and exchanged imported goods for hogsheads of tobacco. During the colonial period the York River was straight and deep for about forty miles above its mouth and could accommodate the largest sailing vessels. It was the main conduit by which Kingston Parish planters exported their tobacco overseas and procured European goods.

In 1713, the House of Burgesses established a tobacco inspection system in an attempt to improve the quality, uniformity, and reputation of Virginia tobacco, thereby enhancing its price. The owners of tobacco warehouses, usually called "rolling-houses," could charge a flat fee for storage, and they received an annual salary for performing inspections. Gloucester Town was selected as the site of a tobacco inspection warehouse, and in October 1714, the two men designated tobacco inspectors were issued scales and weights, equipment used in performing their official duties. This very early inspection system was short-lived. It was unpopular with Virginia planters *and* British merchants because hogsheads of tobacco often were intermixed during the inspection process. Therefore, no one could be assured that the tobacco he received after inspection was as good as what was brought to the warehouse.

In May 1730, a new tobacco inspection system was instituted, one that was considered convenient and reliable. All hogsheads of tobacco that were to be sold were brought to public warehouses and examined by officials, who saw that any trash was removed and destroyed. Inspected tobacco was then repacked and stored until it was exported. Thanks to regulation of the quality and uniformity of the tobacco changing hands, buyers and sellers were able to exchange tobacco notes instead of trying to bargain with a sample of their crop. The tobacco inspection procedure introduced in 1730 stimulated tobacco sales and was still in use at the close of the Revolutionary War.

Tobacco inspectors were paid an annual salary, whereas warehouse owners received rent for the facilities they provided. Both were accountable to government officials. Each tobacco inspection warehouse was equipped with a large balancing beam, scales, ropes, hooks, and weights of various sizes. Because the warehouses were enlarged according to need, they often were asymmetrical. Therefore, when the assembly decided to require tobacco warehouse owners to enclose them with a fence, many protested because their buildings were in a "crowded and irregular situation." They offered instead to "surround all the Houses ... with one sufficient Pallisade of Posts and Plank" and to see that "Doors [were] well secured by Locks." Security was especially important in an era when tobacco was a medium of exchange that was equivalent to currency. The hogsheads of tobacco examined at an inspection warehouse would pass through a custom house before being shipped overseas.[21]

The East River Warehouse

In November 1738, the House of Burgesses decided that an official tobacco inspection warehouse should be built on the east side of the East (Easternmost) River on land that had belonged to the late Mr. Thomas Hayes, a Gloucester County justice, merchant, and owner of the ship *Freewill*.[22] His estate, which enveloped what is now known as Williams Wharf, was to be paid £10 a year for use of the warehouse and each of the warehouse's tobacco inspectors was to receive an annual salary of £30. The new tobacco inspection warehouse, a public facility, was to be constructed at a site that was convenient to shipping but far enough from the water to escape tidal flooding. When the burgesses convened in May 1742, they decided that the warehouse on the East River would continue to serve as a tobacco inspection station. They also agreed that each of the East River warehouse's inspectors would be paid an annual salary of £25 and that the warehouse's owner would continue to be compensated at £10 a year.

Over the years, the assembly continued to enact legislation that created new tobacco inspectorates, authorized existing ones to continue functioning, or temporarily or permanently discontinued inspectorates whose business was waning. Under the law, planters could take their tobacco to the nearest inspection warehouse. Those living in Kingston Parish could transport their tobacco to the East River warehouse or to an inspectorate located on the upper side of the Piankatank River at Major Mathew Kemp's landing, a facility that had been in existence since at least 1734.[23] In 1748, the inspector at the East River warehouse was paid £30 per year, whereas the one at Kemp's warehouse was paid £35, an indication that a somewhat larger quantity of tobacco was processed there. In June 1750, James and Thomas Hayes were identified as the official inspectors at the East River warehouse, which suggests that the Hayes family still owned the warehouse property.[24]

A devastating hurricane that struck the Mid-Atlantic coast in mid-October 1749 was reportedly even worse than the "Great Gust of 1724." According to one account, the waters of the Chesapeake Bay rose as much as 15 feet, wreaking havoc and depositing small watercraft nearly a mile further inland than normal high tide. Therefore, it is likely that the East River warehouse and the tobacco stored there sustained damage. Then, in 1751, southeastern Virginia was hit by another severe storm that brought torrential rain, strong winds and high tide, affecting eight tobacco inspection warehouses. One was the East River warehouse, where the rising tide damaged stored tobacco. Afterward, the planters and merchants who had sustained losses petitioned the government for reimbursement because the ruined tobacco had been stored in public warehouses. In February 1752, Virginia officials agreed to compensate them and authorized the colony's treasurer to reimburse each man or woman who could produce a valid claim for tobacco that had been inspected and was stored in the warehouse at the time of the storm. The owners of transfer tobacco—leaves that had been inspected, repacked, and readied for use as a medium of exchange—were also eligible for compensation. More than a third of the 14,563 pounds of tobacco damaged at the East River warehouse belonged to botanist and clerk of court John Clayton.[25] Others who had produced substantial quantities of the crop included Robert Banks, William Elliott, William Garrot (Garrett), John Machen, and Thomas Williams, all of whom had had between 500 and 600 pounds of tobacco stored in the warehouse when the storm struck. Ann Collins, Sarah White, Catherine Spencer, Elizabeth Longest, and Elizabeth Noldes also filed compensatory claims. Some of the transfer tobacco that was damaged in the flood belonged to Anna Armistead, Ann Cary, and the estate of Captain John Armistead. The East River warehouse was repaired or rebuilt, and in 1765 it was among the inspection facilities that continued their official duties; the warehouse's inspectors continued to be paid £30 a year. By the late 1760s, the East River warehouse ceased functioning as a tobacco inspectorate, for its name disappeared from official records. Nonetheless, the warehouse at what became known as Williams Wharf was at the hub of commercial activity for nearly 200 years.[26]

Life in Kingston Parish

Kingston Parish's population, like the rest of Tidewater Virginia, continued to grow, and sometime prior to September 1715, a house of worship was built on the East River's east side, below Put In Creek's mouth.[27] The vestry identified it as the "Easternmost River church," not a chapel, implying that it was a more noteworthy building. The Easternmost River church was in the southerly or lower part of Kingston Parish, and was convenient to parishioners living in the vicinity of the Mobjack and Chesapeake Bays. Those living in the northerly or upper part of the parish would have been able to attend services in the North River Precinct's brick chapel, built around 1690 on the acreage now occupied by Trinity Church.

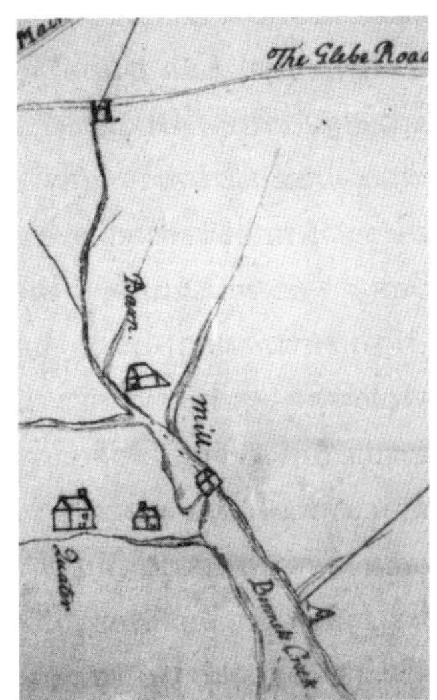

On December 5, 1754, a plat was made of the Rev. Thomas Hughes' land on Bennett's Creek. Hughes had a tide mill. Gloucester County Surveyors Plat Book 1, page 34.

In 1724, when the Bishop of London queried Virginia clergy about conditions in their parishes, Kingston Parish's pulpit was either vacant or the incumbent clergyman failed to respond. However, the Rev. Thomas Hughes of Abingdon Parish, who owned a plantation in Kingston Parish, said that his parish had an endowed free school, whose master was George Ransone, and that in Abingdon, slaves were often allowed to attend worship services. The area's population continued to grow, and in 1726, when Lieutenant Governor Hugh Drysdale compiled a report on Virginia's counties, he indicated that Gloucester County had 3,421 tithable persons and produced sweet-scented tobacco. John Clayton was Gloucester's clerk of court and Thomas Cook (Cooke) was the official land surveyor. Henry Armistead, Thomas Booth, Giles Cooke, Thomas Hayes, George Nicholas, Thomas Read Jr., Gabriel Throckmorton, Charles Tomkies, and Francis and Henry Willis were county justices and Francis Willis was sheriff. Giles Cook and Henry Willis, Gloucester's coroners, represented the county in the House of Burgesses. Mann Page I, the county lieutenant, was in command of 290 horse soldiers and 721 foot soldiers. Gloucester County had four parishes and Emanuel Jones, Thomas Hughes, John Richards, and a Mr. Wye were the incumbent clergymen. Wye, whose first name is uncertain, was at Kingston Parish. Three years later, when an updated report was sent to England, the Rev. John Blacknall was Kingston Parish's minister.

Sometime prior to September 1740, while Mr. Blacknall was at Kingston Parish, the vestry decided to replace the North River Precinct's chapel with a new brick building, which parishioners called the Upper Church. They also agreed to replace the Easternmost River church, or Lower Church, with a brick house of worship located on the same plot of ground as its predecessor. One or both new churches seem to have been completed by October 1742. Parish records reveal that in 1741, while both buildings were under construction, the vestry decided to make extensive repairs to the parish's "chapel," probably the relatively small house of worship on Chapel Creek that served as a chapel-of-ease for parishioners living along the lower side of the Piankatank.

The Easternmost River church's congregation seems to have grown steadily during the Rev. John Blacknall's ministry because within two years' time, the vestry decided to expand the building by adding a north transept. The Easternmost River church was close to a focal point of commercial activity for it was on the road that led to the East River warehouse. After Mr. Blacknall's death in the late 1740s, his widow stayed on in Kingston Parish, as did his son, Charles.[28] The Easternmost River Church was still serving the parish in the 1770s, at which time it was known as the "old church."

A Parish Responsibility: Providing for the Poor

By the late seventeenth century, Virginia's parish vestries were struggling with the need to provide food, shelter, clothing, and medical care to the poor, often landless transients. Because this legal obligation had become extremely burdensome, they sought the assembly's help and received permission to build workhouses for the poor. In 1755, the House of Burgesses again authorized parish vestries to construct or rent houses or other buildings that could be used for the maintenance of the poor. They also acknowledged that the number of paupers had greatly increased in recent years. Poor children could be bound out at an early age and adults could be hired out or put to work, generating income to offset the cost of their support. Kingston Parish's vestry records suggest that there was little or no interest in building a poorhouse. However, by 1751, substantial quantities of corn were purchased for distribution to the poor, and on at least one occasion, Kingston's vestry gave an indigent woman the funds she needed to build a home for herself. Over the years, the vestry gave widows and their children enough income to subsist and sometimes provided the poor with shoes and clothing. Often, the aged and the infirm were given shelter in private homes.

Parishioners occasionally took orphaned or illegitimate children into their homes as indentured servants or apprentices and agreed to provide them with food, clothing, and shelter, an arrangement that relieved the parish of expense. Parishioners sometimes gave poor children, as wards of the parish, food and shelter but were reimbursed from parish revenues. Colonial Kingston Parish's baptismal registers, though fragmentary, reveal that at least fifteen illegitimate children were baptized in the parish during the second half of the eighteenth century. Almost all of these youngsters were the offspring of single white females. One child was the son of a white woman and a black man; in accord with the law, the youngster assumed the status of his mother, who was free.[29]

The Great Awakening Reaches the Middle Peninsula

During the 1730s and 1740s there was a groundswell of dissent from the Church of England, the official state church. It was then that a religious revival known as the Great Awakening swept through the colonies from New England to Georgia and permeated rural Virginia. Powerful preaching awakened in many believers the need for salvation and redemption, and by downplaying ritual, ceremony, and hierarchy, the Great Awakening made Christianity intensely personal. Like-minded people in some localities began gathering to hear readings of the Bible, religious tracts, and sermons. Evangelists, sometimes known as "New Light" preachers, usually called upon their followers to renounce dancing, horseracing, and card-playing, which they deemed sinful, in favor of prayer and repentance; at emotionally-charged revival meetings, they threatened the unrepentant with hellfire and eternal damnation. During the 1760s, 70s, and 80s, the Baptists, Methodists, and Presbyterians attracted a large and loyal following in Virginia. These religious stirrings brought about a revolution in Southern religious life that coincided with growing resentment of the Mother Country and erosion of interest in the Church of England. When evangelical preachers began attracting large crowds, some Anglican clergy asked high-ranking government officials to control itinerant ministers' activities. They responded by exercising the Act of Toleration's requirement that dissenting ministers be licensed. Anglican clergy and many members of the gentry class found the Great Awakening unappealing, and declared that the so-called "New Light" and "New Side" ministers and their followers had "turn'd the World upside down."[30] The Great Awakening invigorated not only those eager to Christianize the enslaved, it also heightened slaves' interest in a faith that provided them with comfort and hope in an otherwise oppressive world. Consequently, the revivalist movement increased the number of slaves and free blacks who converted to Christianity. In Methodist—and especially Baptist—churches, blacks adapted Psalms, hymns, and sermons to the repetitive call and response and bodily movements of their African heritage. Scholars believe that as early as the 1780s the contours of a distinctive African-American religion had already begun to take shape.[31] The Great Awakening's growing appeal to blacks, together with prompting from the Bishop of London, may have impelled Kingston Parish's clergy to commence baptizing slaves during the 1740s.

John Clayton, Mathews County's "Exalted Genius"

One of Mathews County's most fascinating citizens was the renowned botanist John Clayton, son and namesake of Virginia Governor Edward

Nott's secretary and attorney general.[32] Young Clayton, who came to Virginia in 1715 when he was around 19 or 20, became Gloucester County clerk Peter Beverley's assistant, and by October 20, 1720, had succeeded him in office. In 1723 Clayton married Elizabeth (Betty), the daughter of Major Henry Whiting of Elmington plantation, Beverley's son-in-law and a former member of the Governor's Council. Years later, Clayton noted that he had purchased 450 acres from Peter Kemp, Thomas Boswell, and Joseph Amiss, and developed it into a family estate.[33] The Clayton plantation, eventually known as Windsor, lay between the Page family's North End Plantation in the upper reaches of the North River and the head of Wadinger Creek. Insurance policies and a marriage contract signed by John and Betty Clayton's grandson Jasper S. Clayton in 1806 reveal that Windsor was bordered on two sides by land that belonged to one of his Whiting kinsmen. John and Betty Clayton were communicants of Ware Parish, but in 1771 John had one of their slaves baptized in Kingston Parish, probably at the Upper Church, a mile or so closer to their home.[34]

Clayton was keenly interested in botany and by the 1730s, had begun collecting native plant specimens which he sent to colleagues overseas and in other American colonies. He had time to explore the countryside and collect plants because he only had to be in the clerk's office on court days; routine tasks were performed by his deputy clerk. Clayton began compiling his "Catalogue of Plants, Fruits and Trees Native to Virginia," using Swedish botanist Linnaeus's classificatory system. He sent a copy of his manuscript to Dutch botanist Jan Frederik Gronovius, who published it as *Flora Virginica*. As a botanist and plant taxonomist, Clayton was greatly respected by his peers, and he corresponded with Linnaeus and other greats. Over the years, he carefully collected, identified, and then dried plant specimens that he preserved in his herbarium but also sent to colleagues. He also maintained a garden with native plants and cultivars he obtained from contacts in Europe. Although Clayton was preoccupied with native plants, he was also interested in agricultural crops, such as varieties of wheat that would thrive in Virginia. Official records reveal that he was a highly successful planter who sent his hogsheads of tobacco to the East River warehouse so that they could be inspected and readied for an overseas market. In 1751 storm waters and high tides damaged more than 5,000 pounds of Clayton's tobacco, stored in the East River warehouse, awaiting shipment.[35]

John Clayton could be fractious, and in 1754 he sued his neighbor, Captain Thomas Boswell, whose cornfield at the head of Wadinger Creek had encroached on his land. A September 1754 plat for the northernmost portion of the Clayton property shows its border with Boswell's land on the east. The two men clashed again when Boswell, who in 1762 secured a £250 debt to Clayton by posting four slaves as collateral, in 1768 offered the same slaves as a lottery prize. That impelled Clayton to put an item in the *Virginia Gazette*, notifying would-be lottery ticket purchasers that the slaves had been mortgaged to him. Within a month's time, Clayton used the *Virginia Gazette* to inform the public that Captain Boswell had taken steps to secure his debt and that the lottery could proceed as planned.

Courtesy of the Virginia Native Plant Society.

The letters that John Clayton exchanged with London merchant John Norton and his representatives between 1768 and 1773 provide a great deal of insight into the Clayton couple's personal tastes and life on their plantation. At the end of each summer, John sent a letter to Norton, enclosing a lengthy list of items he wanted to order, always asking to have them cleared through the custom house at Yorktown. Clayton's lists reveal that he, and perhaps wife Betty, were fond of Queen's china, a popular type of earthenware, and on one occasion they ordered a dozen plates, a couple bowls, and some one-pint drinking vessels.[36] The Claytons also ordered a dozen blue and white china teacups, saucers, and dishes; a dozen tortoiseshell plates; a dozen wineglasses; and some cut glass. The couple's flatware included a dozen buckhorn knives and forks and they made abundant use of pewter plates and dishes. Their household furnishings included one or more corner cupboards; two mahogany tables, one of which had a drawer; six sturdy mahogany chairs with Spanish leather bottoms; a sealskin trunk with a brass lock; and two Scotch (Scottish) wool carpets, one that measured 12 feet by 15 feet and another that was 9 feet by 14 feet.

John Clayton's sartorial needs were simple but dignified.[37] In 1770, he ordered two pairs of shoes, two pairs of large stockings, two pairs of men's pinchback shoe buckles, and a wig that was "grizzle" (gray) and "fashionable." He also requested an amber-headed walking cane with a black silk string. Most of the items Clayton ordered for himself were geared toward fueling his intellectual pursuits. On one occasion, he asked for two sturdy garden spades—one small and one large—and a large tin watering pot for his garden. He wanted six green glass case bottles that were 6 inches square and 12½ inches tall; each one was to hold two gallons and to have a good cork.[38] He asked for seeds and expressed his annoyance whenever withered or dead plant specimens arrived. Clayton regularly ordered books, magazines, and journals, reams of paper, quill pens, ink, and ink bottles; and on one occasion requested a mahogany ruler that was 18 inches long. A book of sermons and a volume of Biblical literature suggest an interest in religion. In 1770, he asked for a pair of spectacles, but when they arrived, he informed John Norton that they were utterly useless, for he had sent ones much better suited to a younger man. He told Norton that he needed spectacles that were appropriate for a 77-year-old man who couldn't distinguish one object from another at a distance or read a book unless it was close to his face.[39] Clayton seems to have been especially fond of Weston's Snuff, usually ordering six bottles a year.

The orders John Clayton placed on behalf of his wife reveal that she was fashion-conscious and elegantly but conservatively attired. Substantial quantities of fine fabric—such as taffeta, shalloon, and brocade—were requested along with black silk millinery, some of which was adorned with black egret feathers. He also procured on her behalf a black velvet hood with strings, a blue satin bonnet, and a black Brussels lace petticoat that was 45 inches long. Betty Clayton's fondness for fine footwear is reflected in orders for at least ten pairs of shoes a year. Some of her size-5 pumps were made of blue or green leather and some of satin or calfskin. Gloves of various types and an assortment of brightly hued handkerchiefs complimented many of her outfits. Two tortoiseshell combs "to keep up the hair" and two brushes were ordered for Mrs. Clayton, who had also requested a cloak with a fur-trimmed hood, a French wax necklace and earrings, and an ivory stick-fan in a case.

Many of the items that John Clayton ordered from England were utilitarian. For example, he tried to procure four large clamps for horse brushes, two dozen broad hoes, half a dozen narrow hoes, and a like number of felling axes. He also wanted hundreds of yards of specific types of fabric, large quantities of sewing thread and tape, and thousands of needles and pins, all of which were intended to address his household's clothing needs. He usually asked for a firkin of Crown soap, some medicinal substances, refined sugar, spices, and favorite foods, such as chocolate, raisins, currants, and capers. He also seems to have enjoyed Madeira wine, coffee, and green tea. On one occasion he ordered six pewter chamber pots. Almost annually, he asked for dozens of fishhooks and line suitable for catching drum, sheepshead, and trout. Clayton ordered a cap for his postilion and asked for large quantities of white cotton fabric for his slaves' clothing. Every year, he ordered train or whale oil, perhaps for use in an iron lamp, and in 1773, he asked for a large quantity of rush candles that were lengthy and "suited to burn in chambers to keep light the whole night."

In May 1773, John Clayton's selection as president of the Society for the Advancement of Useful Knowledge, a significant honor, was announced in the *Virginia Gazette*. Perhaps on account of failing health or a keen awareness of his advancing age, he made his will on October 25, 1773. He left his property in England to his eldest sons, John and William, and he bequeathed the plantation on which he lived to his son, Jasper.[40] Jasper also stood to receive 21 slaves, who were mentioned by name. John Clayton, who had outlived his wife, died in late 1773, having served as Gloucester's clerk of court for 53 years. On January 6, 1774, his will was proved, and his death was announced in the *Virginia Gazette*. Jasper Clayton served for a time as Gloucester's deputy clerk, and his brother William became clerk of the New Kent County court. In 1787, while William Clayton held office in New Kent, arsonists set his office ablaze, perhaps destroying an expanded version of John Clayton's original manuscript that was published as *Flora Virginica*. In 1794, the hundreds of plant specimens that John Clayton sent to

Gronovius became the John Clayton Herbarium, part of London's Natural History Museum.[41]

John Clayton's Garden

By 1738, John Clayton had begun mentioning his garden in correspondence with his peers. John Bartram told fellow botanist Peter Collinson that he had crossed the Piankatank River and "rode to John Clatons where the river was prety wide." Although Clayton was away from home, Bartram toured his garden, which he described as "best furnished with variety of plants but falls short of ours in pensilvania" which had species from European countries. When Bartram returned to Virginia in 1760, he found Clayton at home. The two men became friends and corresponded frequently. In 1765 Clayton told Bartram that his garden was "intirely ruined with the cold piercing winds and frosts." On one occasion he sent Bartram a box of rooted plants, delivered by Clayton's friend and neighbor, Richard Blacknall.[42]

Over the years, doubts have arisen about the location of John Clayton's house and garden and whether he resided at Windsor, traditionally considered his home. Dr. John Dunn (1862–1934), a Clayton enthusiast, quoted the botanist as saying that he had found *Zannichellia*, or horned pond weed, a plant that flourishes in the Chesapeake Bay's tributaries but also survives in fresh water, "in litore fluminis Piankitank dicti juxta hortum meum," that is, "on the shore of the Piankatank River near my garden." This statement has given rise to speculation that Clayton's garden, and perhaps his dwelling, were situated at a site traditionally known as the Old Office, which overlooks the Piankatank River. However, primary sources combine to refute that hypothesis. On October 25, 1773, when John Clayton prepared his will, he stated that he was leaving the 450-acre plantation in Ware Parish "whereon I now live" to his son, Jasper, noting that he had purchased his land from Peter Kemp, Thomas Boswell, and Joseph Amiss (Ames).[43] A September 1754 plat that depicts a portion of Boswell's and Clayton's land places the Clayton plantation between the heads of the North River and Wadinger Creek. On November 26, 1755, Boswell tried to sell a 350-

acre plantation in Gloucester County, perhaps some of the property that was contiguous to Clayton's acreage.[44] During the early twentieth century Dr. John Dunn stated that he saw "Winsor Road on which stood this garden, marked now by traces of a brick wall, and I see the trees in the river's swamp where grew the famous Chelone 'flore alba.'"[45]

In 1782 Jasper Clayton, who inherited his late father's plantation, paid taxes on 400 acres of land, but in 1791, when Mathews County was formed, he was credited with 548 acres. By 1802 the botanist's grandson Jasper S. Clayton, as residual heir, was in possession of the 548 acres. In 1802 when he purchased an insurance policy on his home, Windsor, it was described as a two-story dwelling whose central block measured 24 feet by 16 feet and had an English basement. Attached to each end was a wing that measured 12 feet by 16 feet. The overall dimensions of Clayton's rooms would have accommodated the large Scottish carpets that his grandfather, John Clayton, ordered in 1772.[46]

Between 2002 and 2004, avocational archaeologists Robert and Lisa Harper, with the assistance of some volunteers, excavated the remains of what they presumed was the Clayton home, Windsor. Near Soles, they unearthed brick foundations that corresponded to the dimensions of the house described on Jasper S. Clayton's 1802 and 1806 insurance policies. One of the artifacts unearthed at the site was an octagonal cufflink with an *I* (often the way a *J* was written) superimposed upon a *C*, a design reminiscent of a well-preserved red wax seal that botanist John Clayton affixed to a letter he sent to British merchant John Norton in 1773. The Harpers also reported finding shards of Astbury ware, a ceramic manufactured during the 1740s, wine bottle glass, buttons, corroded iron fragments (perhaps the remains of tools), and pieces of green glass that they surmised came from a bell jar or cloche.[47] Interestingly, during the early twentieth century, when a topographic quadrangle sheet was made that showed the northwestern part of Mathews County, a farm lane linked the archaeological site the Harper couple tested with Burkes Pond Road, that is, County Route 602. That road and Route 14's forerunner would have enabled clerk of court John Clayton and his successor, son Jasper, to reach Gloucester Courthouse by making a journey of only seven or eight miles.

The County Seat

On May 27, 1736, while John Clayton was clerk of court, the justices of Gloucester County ordered a survey to be made of the prison bounds, i.e., the exercise yard to which non-criminals were allowed access. Gloucester County surveyor John Throckmorton cited the 1736 court order on June 31, 1754, when he prepared a plat on which he delimited the prison bounds. Throckmorton depicted the county courthouse that stood upon the six-acre lot that Edmund Gwyn had given to the county in 1680, and he also showed some of the other buildings that were nearby. When preparing his plat, Throckmorton reversed north and south, perhaps so that he could depict the front elevation of the north-facing courthouse. He indicated that six structures were located within the prison bounds, an 18½-acre parcel that straddled "The Main Road." On the south side of the road, but at the top of the plat, were the courthouse and the county's old and new prisons. On the north side of the road, but depicted at the bottom of the plat, were shown an ordinary, William Kemp's house, and another little building.[48]

Concern for Public Wellbeing

In 1745, when Virginia's burgesses convened, they enacted legislation that authorized county justices to appoint inspectors for pork, beef, flour, tar, pitch, and turpentine. The law specified that each barrel's contents had to contain a full measure and meet specified standards. For instance, salted meat was to be packed a certain way and barrels of flour were not to contain Indian corn. Colonial officials' attempt to regulate these commodities and control their quality endured, and after the Revolutionary War, became a responsibility of the state. A 1748 law made it illegal to "cast corpses in the rivers and creeks," legislation that was necessary because mariners and the masters of slave ships frequently threw the dead overboard "to the annoyance of the adjacent inhabitants." How frequently a corpse washed ashore is open to conjecture. A law that reeks of cruelty made it legal to dismember slaves going abroad at night or running away and staying out" unless they already had been disciplined by another authority.[49]

NOTES

1 In 1704 quitrent was paid on 31,603 acres in Ware Parish; 28,426 acres in Abingdon Parish; and 41,123 acres in Petsworth or Petso Parish.

2 Des Cognet, *Lost Virginia Records*, 13, 143–144; Kathleen M. Brown, *Good Wives, Nasty Wenches, and Anxious Patriarchs: Gender, Race, and Power in Colonial Virginia* (Chapel Hill, 1996), 179; Beverley, *History*, 253; Patent Book II, 312; III, 34, 94, 108, 128, 204; IV, 337, 532; V, 479; VI, 103–104, 374, 428, 475; VII, 357, 588; Chamberlayne, *Kingston Parish*, 6, 13–14.

3 Hartwell et al., *Present State*, 16–20; Hening, *Statutes*, III, 304–329; IV, 81; V, 424–425; McIlwaine, *Executive Journals*, I, 347; Nugent, *Cavaliers*, III, viii.

4 Jones, *Present State*, 77–79.

5 This is another example of how the enslaved were denied the protection of common law.

6 Billings et al., *Colonial Virginia*, 55, 122; Hening, *Statutes*, III, 503–511.

7 A large canoe also was deemed sufficient for those traveling without horses (Joan Charles, comp., *Gloucester and Mathews Newspaper Articles*, 1770–1922 [Gloucester, 2014], 7).

8 Hening, *Statutes*, III, 218–221, 472–474; IV, 93–94, 438–439; V, 16, 33.

9 Berlin and Morgan, *Cultivation and Culture*, 110–112, 116–117, 177–178, 181–182.

10 Official records from Henrico, Isle of Wight, Surry, and York Counties, and Virginia's Eastern Shore, which are relatively complete, contain numerous references to young Indians being brought before local court justices so that their ages could be determined. This would have established when the youngsters would be considered taxable. Prior to 1705, most, if not all, Indian children in the households of Virginia planters were considered servants, not slaves. However, like African servants and slaves and white servants, Indians' time of service could be bought and sold or conveyed by means of a bequest. Court records reveal that many of the Indian children sold into servitude had been captured by members of Virginia's Tributary tribes. Therefore, they did not have the same legal status as members of the Tributary Indians.

11 This law applied to all Indians, including members of Tributary tribes. One of these badges is preserved at the Virginia Historical Society.

12 Hening, Statutes, III, 51, 276–277, 298, 333–336, 447–463; IV, 137; V, 35–36; VI, 31–35, 109–110, 121–124, 362–369; VII, 518; Waverley K. Winfree, ed., *The Laws of Virginia; Being A Supplement To Hening's The Statutes At Large, 1700–1750* (Richmond, 1971), 251; McIlwaine, Executive Journals, II, 286, 365.

13 Walter Minchinton et al., eds., *Virginia Slave-Trade Statistics*, 1698–1775 (Richmond, 1984), xiv–xv, 20–52; Elizabeth Donnan, *Documents Illustrative of the History of the Slave Trade to America* (New York, 1965), II, 299–300; Ira Berlin, *Many Thousands Gone: The First Two Centuries of Slavery in North America*, 110–112, 116–117; Parks, *Virginia Gazette*, April

22, 1737; Kimber, "Observations," 150–151; Berlin and Morgan, *Cultivation and Culture*, 171.

14 Gary B. Nash, *Red, White, and Black: The Peoples of Early America* (Englewood, New Jersey, 1974), 53–54, 217–220; Hunter, *Virginia Gazette*, July 17, 1752; April 11, 1755.

15 William N. Sainsbury et al., comp., *Calendar of State Papers, Colonial Series, America and the West Indies* (Valduz, 1964), XXV, 83; McIlwaine, *Executive Journals*, III, 234–236, 242–243; *House, 1702–1710*:240; Palmer, *Calendar*, I, 129–130.

16 Waverly K. Winfree, *Supplement*, 257–259.

17 Beverley, *History*, 289–290; Purdie, *Virginia Gazette*, October 31, 1777; Hunter, *Virginia Gazette*, November 13, 1766; Mason, *Gloucester*, II, 42–43; Gloucester County Surveyors Plat Book A (1733–1810), 4–5; Walsh, *Motives*, 401–404; John Henry, "Map of Virginia," 1770; Fry and Jefferson, "Virginia," 1751–1775; Billings et al., *Colonial Virginia*, 55, 122.

18 Clayton was the father of botanist John Clayton.

19 SR 4829; BPRO, High Court of Admiralty (HCA) 1/99 ff 8–9; Peter W. Coldham, comp., *The King's Passengers to Maryland and Virginia* (Westminster, Maryland, 2006), 23, 36, 38, 40; McIlwaine, *Executive Journals*, III, 205–206, 208–209; Charles, *Newspapers*, 6.

20 Colonial Office 5/1442–1444; Rind, *Virginia Gazette*, August 11, 1768; September 21, 1769; Purdie and Dixon, *Virginia Gazette*, August 27, 1767; January 10, 1777; Dixon, *Virginia Gazette*, October 3, 1777.

21 McIlwaine, *Executive Journals*, III, 381; V, 328, 331; *House, 1752–1755*:13, 73, 75; *1758–1761*:240; *1761–1765*:132, 141; *1773–1776*:89; Hening, *Statutes*, IV, 262–267, 335, 383, 387; V, 144; V, 136, 142, 144; VI, 169, 173, 176–177, 236, 242; VIII, 78, 80, 98, 100–101, 323; X, 273; XI, 448; XIII, 480, 503; Walsh, *Motives*, 405, 424–425; Gloucester County Records, Huntington Library, Brock Box 40. Tobacco imports to Great Britain rose from 41 million pounds in 1730 to 85 million pounds in 1753; by 1763, 98 million pounds were being exported.

22 One of Hayes's sons may have been the Thomas Hayes or Haynes who in 1747 purchased and patented 168 acres on the east side of the East River, adjoining the property of James Callis, Mathew Gayle, Alexander Cray, Joseph Billups, Henry Knight, and someone named Poole (Patent Book XXVIII, 240). The Hayeses of Kingston Parish may have been related to merchant Herbert Hayes of Abingdon Parish in Gloucester County (VCRP SR 4634).

23 Mathew Kemp inherited 1,100 acres from his uncle, Edmund Kemp, and re-patented his Middlesex County acreage in 1661. It was located on the east side of Healy Creek. Kemp's property extended in an easterly direction along the upper side of the Piankatank River to Moore Creek. The tobacco inspectorate at Kemp's landing was still operational in 1742 (Patent Book IV, 528; SR 3514; Hening, *Statutes*, IV, 142; Middlesex County Order Book 1732–1737:37; 1740–1745:148, 170, 176, 200).

24 Hening, *Statutes*, VI, 172–173, 176; McIlwaine, *Executive Journals*, V, 328.

25 Clayton's accounts with a London merchant attest to his success as a planter, but he also would have acquired some saleable tobacco as fees for his duties as clerk.

26 Hening, *Statutes*, IV, 14; V, 14, 142–146; VI, 236–238, 242–243; VIII, 78, 97; Parks, *Virginia Gazette*, December 29, 1738; David M. Ludlum, *Early American Hurricanes, 1492–1870* (Boston, 1963), 20–21, 23–24. The House of Burgesses sometimes consolidated the work of two or three tobacco inspection warehouses under one set of inspectors but didn't eliminate the inspectorates themselves. There was a disciplinary procedure for tobacco inspectors who were derelict in their duties (Hening, *Statutes*, VIII, 79, 98–100).

27 The Easternmost River church was on the parcel currently occupied by Christ Church and its cemetery.

28 Jones, *Present State*, 97–99; William S. Perry, comp., *Historical Collections Relating to the American Colonial Church*, I, 286–288, 308– 309; Des Cognet, *Lost Virginia Records*, 33, 46; Parks, *Virginia Gazette*, January 21, 1737. In December 1770, after Charles Blacknall's death, his goods and slaves were offered for sale at the Kingston Parish glebe, which suggests that he had been living on the property. The Rev. John Dixon's son, John Jr., was then identified as Blacknall's executor. In April 1771 some of the decedent's slaves were taken to Williamsburg and offered to the highest bidder in an auction held in front of the Raleigh Tavern (Purdie and Dixon, *Virginia Gazette*, December 13, 1770; April 11, 1771).

29 Hening, *Statutes*, II, 44; VI, 31–32, 475–478; Billings et al., *Colonial Virginia*, 58–59; McIlwaine et al., *House of Burgesses*, 1695–1702, 158; Chamberlayne, *Kingston Parish*, 24–26, 28–29, 44–45, 63–64, 66–68, 70, 72, 77, 79–81, 83, 97, 99, 107, 121; Emma R. Matheny and Helen Yates, comp. *Kingston Parish Register, Gloucester and Mathews Counties*, 1749–1827 (Richmond, 1963), 28, 30–31, 46, 48, 62, 78, 81, 88, 91, 96, 102, 106, 108.

30 In 1809 the renowned architect Benjamin Latrobe attended a Methodist camp meeting at which a blacksmith-turned-preacher warned his listeners about "the burning billows of hell" that would "wash up against the Soul of the glutton and the miser." He cried out "When hell gape and the fire roars, Oh poor sinful damned souls ... all of ye, will ye be damned? Will ye? Will ye?" Latrobe reported that "a general groaning and shrieking was now heard from all quarters" (Benjamin H. Latrobe, *The Journal of Latrobe* [New York, 1905], 111).

31 Isaacs, *Worlds*, 37–38; Bond, *Spreading the Gospel*, 416.

32 Botanist John Clayton should not be confused with his kinsman, the Rev. John Clayton, onetime rector of James City Parish and also a gifted naturalist.

33 The 638 acres that Peter Kemp patented in 1687 bordered the east side of Wadinger Creek and lay one mile inland, behind the acreage that had been assigned to the Chiskiack Indians (Patent Book VII, 638). Thomas Boswell seems to have acquired some of the Kemp property. Joseph Amiss (Amee or Ames) may have been a descendent of Thomas Amies, who had some land in Gloucester County on Dragon Swamp, an extension of the Piankatank River (Patent Book VI, 666).

34 John Clayton's son, Jasper, also had some of his slaves baptized in Kingston Parish between 1771 and 1777.

35 This is the equivalent of five fully packed hogsheads. Had Clayton been in possession of the "Old Office," as some have presumed, his land would have bordered the Piankatank River and would have been much closer to the tobacco inspectorate located at Kemp's Landing. Clayton's plantation and that of Kemp are identified on the map made by Joshua Fry and Peter Jefferson in 1751.

36 In his diary, Landon Carter of Sabine Hall in Richmond County described the botanist John Clayton as a learned man but "as vain of it as you please." He went on to say that Clayton was "a good companion but a desperate drinker." In another entry, Carter described an argument he and Clayton had had about the meaning of a Greek word (Landon Carter, *The Diary of Colonel Landon Carter*, Jack P. Green, ed. [Charlottesville, 1962], II, 729, 731).

37 A local tailor probably fabricated his dressier clothing.

38 The specificity of John Clayton's request raises the possibility that he was using the bottles as terraria or containers in which to nurture plants.

39 Clayton's cramped handwriting toward the end of his life may be a reflection of his poor vision.

40 When the state enumeration was compiled in 1784, Jasper Clayton of Ware Parish, who had possession of his late father's property, was credited with a dwelling and five dependencies (U.S. Bureau of the Census, comp., *Heads of Families at the First Census of the United States Taken in the Year 1790* [Baltimore, 2002], 69).

41 Edmund and Dorothy S Berkeley, *John Clayton, Pioneer of American Botany* (Chapel Hill, 1963), 23–25, 27, 152–153, 171–172; Joanne Young, "The Clerk of Gloucester," *Colonial Williamsburg Journal* Vol. XX No. 4 (1998), 57–59; Leonard, *General Assembly*, xxi; Palmer, *Calendar* , IV, 321, 329–330, 376; Hening, *Statutes*, VI, 242; XII, 692; Gloucester Surveyors Plat Book A (1733–1810), 28–29, 35; Marriage contract between Mary Berkeley and Jasper S. Clayton, 1806, Mason, *Gloucester*, II, 49; John Clayton, October 25, 1773, will, Mathews Archives, Box 18 R, folder 45–5; Johann F. Gronovius, "Virginia," 1762; Martha W. McCartney, comp., *Kingston Parish Register: Mathews, Gloucester, and Middlesex Counties, Virginia, Slaves and Slaveholders, 1746–1827* (Baltimore, 2014), 10, 23, 26, 31, 59, 64; Purdie and Dixon, *Virginia Gazette*, June 9, 1768; June 16, 1768; May 13, 1773; January 6, 1774; John Norton and Sons Papers, folders 12–13, 20–21, 28–29, 32, 34, 37, 72, 80, 89, 95; www.encyclopediavirginia.org.

42 Berkeley and Berkeley, *Clayton*, 90, 146, 167; William Darlington, *Memorials of John Bartram and Humphry Marshall with Notices of their Botanical Contemporaries* (Philadelphia, 1849), 409, 412.

43 This was the same amount of land on which Clayton had paid taxes in 1770; it was the only land he owned in Gloucester County.

44 Hunter, *Virginia Gazette*, November 26, 1755. Boswell's 350 acres contained a good dwelling and outbuildings and was home to 13 slaves and 30 cattle. At least part of Thomas Boswell's property came into the hands of his son, Dr. Machen Boswell, who had it in 1793 when he made his will. The Boswell acreage passed sequentially through the hands

of Daniel Fitchett, John Fitchett, and Sands Smith before it came into the possession of Alfred Billups. In 1845 when Billups mortgaged his land, he referred to his property as the "Old Office," perhaps because Dr. Boswell's office had been located there. In time, some people assumed that the "Old Office" was associated with Gloucester clerk John Clayton (Gloucester County Land Tax Lists 1787–1790; Mathews County Land Tax Lists 1791–1845; Deed Book 4:79; Library of Virginia, Lost Records Localities Collection 1674-2014, record number 000013117; Lyon G. Tyler, ed., "Seawell Family," *William and Mary Quarterly*, 1st Ser., 8 (1899–1900):55; *Gloucester-Mathews Gazette-Journal*, March 23, 1967; Becky Foster Barnhardt, personal communication, December 13, 2013).

45 Clarence R. Williams, "Dr. John Dunn as a Virginia Botanist," *William and Mary Quarterly* 2nd Ser., 15 (1935):114–115. Route 3, built sometime after the Civil War but before 1916, is now known as Windsor Road.

46 Mason, *Gloucester*, II, 34; Gloucester County Land Tax Lists 1782; Mathews County Land Tax Lists 1791–1802; Mutual Assurance Society Policy Numbers 787 (1802) and 1150 (1806). In 1802 when Jasper S. Clayton insured Windsor, it was described as being situated between the properties of Francis Whiting and James Sparks.

47 *Gloucester-Mathews Gazette-Journal*, August 5, 2004.

48 Members of the Read family had owned land in this vicinity since the third quarter of the seventeenth century (Patent Book V, 280, 586; VI, 331; X, 173; John Throckmorton, [untitled plat of the prison bounds], June 31, 1754).

49 Hening, *Statutes*, V, 352–353; VI, 75, 101, 111.

5

Labour Spread Her Wholesome Store
1751–1775

Economic Expansion

When Virginia farmers commenced growing fodder crops to support more livestock, they discovered that crop rotation and manuring had significant benefits. Expanding overseas grain markets during the 1740s prompted many Virginians to abandon hill-and-hoe agriculture in favor of more progressive techniques. Throughout the Chesapeake, successful planters who utilized their numerous slaves to till the soil took advantage of the rising market for grain and meat. In 1772, John Hobday of Kingston Parish announced that he had invented a horse-drawn machine that would separate wheat from straw. He claimed that his wheat machine would yield 120 bushels of wheat per day if three horses were used. Four prominent planters, who examined a model of Hobday's machine, determined that it was fully functional. Over time, much of Gloucester County was cleared for cultivation and drainage ditches were dug to remove excessive moisture from the soil.

Successful planters sometimes constructed gristmills that served their own plantations and those of their neighbors. Others built large merchant mills that ground grain and corn for local consumption. For example, during the mid-eighteenth century Dr. John Symmer (Symmons), a Gloucester County physician who owned several pieces of property, including one in Kingston Parish at the head of the North River, had a gristmill.[1] Kingston Parish vestry records reveal that between 1756 and 1763 Dr. Symmer attended to the medical needs of numerous parishioners. Sometime prior to 1754 the Rev. Thomas Hughes of Abingdon Parish, who invested in 518 acres of land that straddled Bennett's Creek, owned a tide mill that would have served families at the head of the East River. A plat of the Hughes property, partitioned after his death, contains sketches of the deceased clergyman's tide mill, a house, a quarter, and a barn. At Hughes's death his sons Gabriel and Edward each received half of the plantation and may have shared the mill.

During the eighteenth century most families ate meals cooked in a single pot and in skillets placed over coals on a hearth. Courtesy of the Colonial Williamsburg Foundation, Department of Archaeological Research.

During the mid-eighteenth century, when the British and French were at war, the colony experienced shortages of manufactured goods. Small to middling households started raising fiber-producing crops like flax that could be spun into yarn, and more successful planters had their slaves spin yarn and weave cloth that could be made into clothing. Coastal trade became increasingly important and Virginia planters began speculating in West Indian goods, such as sugar, wine, molasses, and salt, which they acquired in the Caribbean in exchange for tobacco, grains, and forest products. When international conditions improved, some enterprising Virginia planters began importing saleable merchandise. They usually placed their business establishments in a village or near a busy intersection, tavern, ferry-landing, or warehouse. Alternatively, those who lived on navigable waterways sometimes had stores at their own landings. For example, during the 1750s and 60s Robert Dalgleish operated a mercantile establishment in Kingston Parish and sometimes provided goods to the parish poor. Later on, Matthew Anderson, whose property, The Exchange, was located on the lower side of the North River, informed the public that he had for sale everything from farming equipment to hats, fine fabric, medicinal products, and imported china. His merchandise would have been readily available to the households living along the North and East Rivers or to those traveling overland along Route 14's forerunner. Sometimes, merchants' ships dropped anchor at popular wharves and sold their wares directly from their vessels. That may account for the name given to a long, narrow promontory on the upper side of the Piankatank River's mouth, which by 1653 had become known as Store (later, Stove) Point. Like stores and taverns, the establishments of blacksmiths, wheelwrights, shoemakers, and tailors were usually located where they were readily accessible to the traveling public. During the 1760s, William Carney, a shoemaker, made footwear for members of George Hunley's household, whereas Henry Harris attended to Hunley's blacksmithing needs, and James Cray, a weaver, provided him with cloth. Hunley also bought goods from James Mills. When Hunley became ill, Dr. George Johnston provided him with snakeroot, an herb that probably contributed to his death.

Throughout the prerevolutionary period, indentured servants and slaves continued to flow into the colony. An indentured servant named John Harrower, a Scot who came to Virginia in 1773, kept a journal in which he described his time in the colony. He said that after almost seventeen weeks at sea, he arrived in Fredericksburg, where his contract was sold to a wealthy planter in need of a tutor. Harrower mentioned a fellow servant who became drunk and verbally abused the ship's officers. For his offenses, he was horsewhipped, put in irons, and thumb-screwed. Then, he was gagged and put into handcuffs. A list of the names and occupations of a group of indentured servants who left London in February 1774 reveals that many of them had useful skills that would have been in great demand.[2]

The East River Warehouse

The East River warehouse, a well-known local landmark, continued to be a focal point of commerce and trade even after it ceased functioning as an official tobacco inspectorate in the late 1760s. On November 13, 1766, Robert Tompkins announced that on December 3 he intended to sell a 40-acre clear and level tract located within 60 yards of the warehouse, and said that his property was a good location for a merchant. Tompkins indicated that he also was willing to sell 251 acres of woodland adjacent to his 40 acres. Three years later, in the wake of a hurricane that struck in early September 1769, John Hughes tried to sell 230 acres that were within a mile of the East River warehouse and near a branch of the river. Joseph Gayle, Caleb and Ransone Hunley, and John Lucas, when disposing of some of their land, mentioned its proximity to the East River warehouse, and when William Lucas decided to sell off some slaves, livestock, and household furniture, he held the sale at the warehouse. Thieves broke into the East River warehouse in 1773 and stole some tobacco notes. A year later, Thomas Dixon, a mariner and storekeeper, who indicated that he was located at the East River warehouse, placed an advertisement in the *Virginia Gazette*, trying to recover a lost mare that belonged to his brother, the Rev. John Dixon, and had strayed or been stolen from the College of William and Mary's pasture.[3] A hurricane that affected eastern Virginia in September 1775 and passed up the Chesapeake Bay undoubtedly caused some concern for planters whose tobacco and merchandize was in the immediate vicinity of the East River warehouse.[4]

Tobacco being loaded for shipment. Courtesy of the Library of Congress.

Turbulent Weather

Earlier, in mid-September 1769, a severe hurricane cut a broad swath through eastern Virginia, destroying houses and field crops. Fallen trees blocked local roads, impeding transportation, and the torrential rain created floodwaters that broke through mill dams. Surging waters destroyed wharves and drove small vessels ashore, and according to eyewitness accounts, numerous sailing vessels ran aground or were cast onto dry land. Among the beached watercraft was Captain Thomas Lilly's ship, the *Friendship.* Another vessel, the *Fortune,* which was on its way from London to Virginia and Maryland with 59 indentured servants, dropped anchor to the north of New Point Comfort, where its captain and crew hoped to ride out the storm. However, the ship's anchor failed and the *Fortune*, a snow, was driven ashore on Gwynn's Island. Many of the *Fortune's* passengers, who were skilled tradesmen, reached land and fled. George Brown of Kingston Parish was among the several men to whom some of the escaped servants were to be returned. On September 21, the owner of the *Fortune* announced that the vessel's hull would be sold at an auction held at the plantation of Henry Knight.[5]

Shipbuilding in Kingston Parish

In November 1766, Robert Tompkins of Kingston Parish, whose land was close to the East River warehouse, announced that he had two seagoing vessels that were under construction and almost ready to sell. Shortly thereafter, Thomas Smith of Kingston Parish informed the public that he wanted to sell a new ship of 236 tons burthen that was made of seasoned timber and was well suited for the tobacco trade. Another shipbuilder actively working in Kingston Parish was Robert Billups, whose shipyard on Queens Creek had a new workhouse and a blacksmith shop. In 1771, when he announced that he was going to sell his home tract and another piece of property, he indicated that his plantation was well timbered and had an excellent landing for a ship's carpenter or merchant. Billups also offered to sell a large schooner and a schooner-boat and said that both vessels would be finished by December 1. His decision to sell was involuntary, for he had used his landholdings as collateral when agreeing to serve as high sheriff Gwyn Read's *security*, thereby guaranteeing that Read would faithfully perform his official duties.

In 1768, Edward Hughes, who inherited part of the Rev. Thomas Hughes's property at the head of the East River, announced that he was prepared to sell a new schooner of 71 tons burthen that was built of the best quality white oak and would hold nearly 3,000 bushels of grain. He also offered for sale a three-year-old sloop of 29 tons burthen that was outfitted with sails, anchors, and other equipment. In 1772, Hughes announced that he was building a flat that would hold 25 hogsheads of tobacco and expected to have it ready to sell by May. He said that he was willing to undertake the construction of small buildings and that he had for sale heart pine shingles and good pine and cypress lumber suitable for a variety of projects.[6] James Davis also had a shipyard in Kingston Parish, and in May 1775 announced that he had a newly built 23-ton vessel that was ready for launching. Collectively, these advertisements demonstrate that shipbuilding had become an important part of the local economy. Other local shipbuilders included William Bohannon, Christopher Cully (Culley), Josiah Foster, Christopher Gayle, Ambrose Hunley, and Mathias (Matthias) James.[7]

Destabilizing Factors in the Lives of Slaves

By the 1750s the majority of Virginia slaves were native born and quite naturally emotionally attached to their immediate and extended families. Often, the slaves on one plantation were related to those who lived elsewhere in the community. Because the enslaved were considered property, their marriages were not recognized by law. As a result, relatively few eighteenth-century slaveholders made an earnest effort to keep families together. Even so, slaves took their own weddings very seriously, whether they were married in a special ceremony or simply moved in together. This contrasted sharply with customs in Africa, where marriage was a religious rite, often accompanied by weeks of celebration. According to oral tradition, owners usually insisted that their slaves obtain their consent before marrying. Once approval was received, the bride and groom participated in a ceremony generally known as "jumping the broomstick"—i.e., with friends and family looking on, they solemnly stepped across a broomstick that was placed on the floor, usually in the bride's home. Sometimes, this rite of passage included a scriptural reading. Occasionally, owners saw to it that their slaves were united in a conventional religious ceremony. When slaves from neighboring plantations married, the husband usually obtained a pass from his master to visit his wife on Saturday nights.

One of a slave's greatest fears was the prospect of permanent separation from close kin. Because slaves could be used as collateral when their owners were securing a loan, they could be sold if the debt wasn't repaid. Census records and personal property tax rolls reveal that during the eighteenth century, middling planters' households sometimes included 30 or more members, black and white, who required food, clothing, shelter and medical care, whether or not they were able to work. This responsibility sometimes proved to be financially overwhelming and could force an owner to sell one or more of his slaves. Another set of circumstances that could lead to the disruption of black families was the settling of estates, which often required the sale or distribution of the decedent's slaves among several heirs.[8]

Slave auctions were usually held at the county seat or in another location that was well known to the public. For instance, in January 1771, 25 of the late John Armistead's slaves were auctioned off at the tavern and store known as The Battery. Sometimes, slaves were sold directly from their owner's plantation. Contemporary descriptions of slave auctions recount their dehumanizing aspects, where slaves were examined physically like livestock. Many planters realized that threatening to sell or separate family members was an even more effective means of control than corporal punishment. Slaves sometimes ran away to visit family members from whom they had been separated. For example, in 1755, a young slave named Ben, who was said to be a very good plowman, fled from Francis Willis Jr.'s plantation in Gloucester and was thought to be heading for Colonel John Willis's home in Brunswick County. Advertisements that appeared in the *Virginia Gazette* throughout the eighteenth century reveal that slaves and indentured servants frequently absconded from their owners. Undoubtedly, some left home on account of ill treatment.[9]

Kingston Parish's Clergy

The Rev. John Dixon (Dickson), the eldest son of the John Dixon of Bristol, England, came to Virginia and attended the College of William and Mary. He went to England for his ordination, and then returned to serve as faculty usher at the college. He arrived in Kingston Parish sometime prior to October 1748 and acquired many thousands of acres of land through his marriage to a Gloucester County woman. For reasons that are unclear, by October 1749, the vestry had released Dixon from his position and hired the Rev. Richard Locke, who remained in Kingston Parish for a little over a year. Afterward, Dixon returned and stayed until 1770.[10] One of Dixon's first acts, upon settling in Kingston Parish, was baptizing the slaves who lived on the parish glebe, adults named Lewis and Frances and boys named Judah and Simon.[11] He also baptized his own slaves, perhaps hoping to lead his parishioners by example. Vestry records reveal that shortly after Dixon moved to Kingston Parish, the dwelling on the glebe was refurbished, its outbuildings were repaired, and a stable was built. These amenities brought the parish into conformance with a 1748 law that required vestries to provide their clergy with "a convenient mansion house, kitchen, barn, stable, dairy, meat house, corn house, and garden well paled or enclosed."[12]

The Rev. John Dixon received a substantial infusion of funds around 1758 when his father died. He inherited a half-acre lot in the town of Falmouth on which stood Dixon's Warehouse, a newly-built tobacco inspectorate, and a tract of land in Stafford County, adjoining Falmouth. He also received a share of his late father's livestock, slaves, and other personal property. Collectively, these bequests and the wealth provided by a good marriage would have provided the clergyman with an abundance of disposable income. In 1759, a slave quarter was erected on the Kingston Parish glebe, and in 1767, a house was built for the glebe's farm manager. It was during Dixon's almost 21-year ministry that the vestry of Kingston Parish decided to replace its Upper Church, built between 1740 and 1742, with a newer one and to order new furnishings for its altar. From that time on, the vestry commenced referring to the newly-constructed Upper Church as the "New Church," and the Lower or Easternmost River church was dubbed the "Old Church." A plat of Churchill Armistead's Old Town plantation at the head of the East River shows one of the river's tributaries leading in a westerly direction toward what was identified as the "New Church."[13]

Dixon and his wife, Lucy, added to the size of their family while they lived in Kingston Parish. When she died on November 26, 1769, she was buried on the grounds of the Upper Church.[14] In autumn 1770, Dixon resigned from his position as Kingston Parish's minister and became a Professor of Divinity and Moral Philosophy at the College of William and Mary. In April 1777, he and two other faculty members were accused of neglect and misconduct. Dixon died a month later, and according to the Kingston Parish register, was buried on May 9, 1777, at "the new Church." When his estate was settled, his warehouse in Falmouth was sold as was some of his personal property.

By January 1771, Kingston Parish's vestry had hired the Rev. Thomas Feilde, another respected clergyman. He was so favorably impressed with the region's "natural curiosities" that he described them in a letter he sent to a colleague in England. He said that he was occupying a house on a 500-acre plantation—that is, the Kingston Parish glebe—which was situated on "a beautiful River & not far from the great Bay of Chesapeake." He added that his parish was one of the most populous in Virginia and that he had found employment only eleven weeks after arriving in the colony. Interestingly, in a statement that preceded Edmund Ruffin's famous agricultural experiments by almost a half-century, Feilde proffered that the deposits of marl or pulverized shells that could be found throughout the Tidewater probably could be used as "a rich manure for the Land, especially if burnt." Feilde stayed at Kingston Parish for six years.[15]

Samuel Williams: Williams Wharf's Namesake

During the early 1770s, Samuel Williams of Northampton County began purchasing land along the upper side of the East River. In time, he amassed almost 640 acres that extended from the lower side of Put In Creek's mouth to the vicinity of Weston Creek and from the East River to the "Old Church," the Lower Church of Kingston Parish. Williams initially bought more than half of a 500-acre riverfront tract from Caleb Hunley and his son, Ransone. An advertisement the Hunleys placed in the *Virginia Gazette* in October 1770 indicated that their property, located "in the middle of the parish," extended for at least two miles along the banks of the East River, and contained warehouses and a storehouse "well calculated for public business", perhaps a reference to the East River warehouse, by then a disused tobacco inspectorate. Besides commercial facilities, the Hunleys' property had a good dwelling, some outbuildings, slave quarters, and an apple orchard capable of producing 3,000 gallons of cider a year.[16] The Rev. John Dixon, the wealthy and financially savvy former minister of Kingston Parish, bought the rest of the Hunley tract and quickly resold it to Williams.[17]

Williams went on to buy part of a contiguous 341-acre tract that surrounded the lot on which Kingston Parish's Lower Church stood. That acreage, which also belonged to Caleb Hunley and his son, was surveyed by Francis Tomkies in September 1770. It straddled the forerunner of County Route 614, which terminated at the East River warehouse, and touched upon the banks of the East River and Put In Creek. The plat that Tomkies prepared reveals that in 1770, the Hunleys' 341 acres were leased to John Gayle and John Davis. Davis, who had been clerk of the Lower Church since 1751, occupied a house on the property, which abutted southeast upon Joshua Gayle's estate and southwest upon James Peed's acreage. Samuel Williams continued to expand his holdings, perhaps trying to provide for

Downstream view from Williams Wharf.
Courtesy of Becky Foster Barnhardt, Mathews County Historical Society.

his numerous heirs, who included his third wife, Margaret; sons William and Thomas; and several daughters. Samuel and Margaret Williams were living on the Eastern Shore in 1773 when he conveyed some Northampton County land to his eldest son, John. However, they moved to Kingston Parish sometime prior to June 1775 when Samuel had the first of four infant slaves baptized. Thus, the Williams' were residing on their Kingston Parish plantation when the Revolutionary War began. Their daughter, Peggy, was baptized in the parish church on January 9, 1776.[18]

The County Court as Seat of Government

Except during the Interregnum, the appointment of Virginia's county justices was the prerogative of the governor and his council. The county court's responsibilities continued to grow, and by 1757 its justices could decide all cases under common law and chancery except those involving loss of life or limb. They could also prosecute outlawry and cases involving less than 25 shillings or two hundred pounds of tobacco. The county court compiled lists of tithables, laid out the county levy, recorded land conveyances, bound out poor children to trades, and combined the functions of the orphans, probate, and claims courts. The chief functionary of the county court was the sheriff, who also was a justice. Although he was a gubernatorial appointee, he was chosen from three justices nominated by the court. The sheriff was to serve a one-year term unless otherwise specified. A solitary justice of the peace could issue a warrant for the arrest of a traitor, felon, pirate, disturber of the peace, or any other criminal who could be made to appear before him or the court as a whole.

By 1766, Gloucester County's justices had decided to have a new courthouse built and had selected the site on which it was to be erected. Court justice Lewis Burwell placed an advertisement in the *Virginia Gazette* on April 4, 1766, announcing that "the building of Gloucester County courthouse is to be let to the lowest bidder" and said that he and his fellow justices intended to be present at the county seat on April 22 to make an agreement with the successful bidder. Two and a half years later, Gloucester County's justices sought to hire a contractor willing to undertake "the building of two brick prisons" at the county seat. A plat that surveyor Francis Tomkies made on May 14, 1774, indicates that the new county courthouse stood upon some acreage formerly belonging to the Read family, who had owned it outright, whereas the old courthouse was located on some entailed land vested in Edmund Gwyn's descendants. Tomkies' 1774 plat indicated that there were two new prisons: one across from the courthouse and the other opposite the "Clubhouse." He also identified "the Place where the old Courthouse stood" and noted that it was located "on the six acres given by Gwyn, to build a courthouse & prison on," that is, the acreage Gwyn had provided in 1680. Members of the Read family, which intermarried with the Gwyns, had owned land in that vicinity since the third quarter of the seventeenth century.[19]

Kingston Parish in 1774

In 1774 and 1775, Gloucester County officials made a parish-by-parish list of household heads and the number of tithable persons in each household. Such lists, and the one compiled in 1770, were used by the county government for tax purposes but also by parish vestries who could collect the tax money needed to support the State Church. In November 1774, Kingston Parish's vestry paid Gloucester's clerk of court for a copy of the parish's list of tithables. That list, among the Billups Papers at the Library of Virginia, includes an incomplete list for 1775. Vestry records reveal that people sometimes tried to conceal the actual number of tithable individuals in their households in order to reduce their taxes. The 1774 list of Kingston Parish tithables included 306 household heads, only ten of whom were women. Almost 78 percent of Kingston Parish households included between one and five taxable people. Another 12 percent had between 6 and 10 tithables, and almost 6 percent had between 11 and 15 tithables. Only 4 percent headed households with 16 to 20 tithables: Jane Carter, James Davis, John Elliott Sr., Humphrey Gwyn, William Plummer, John Robinson, Edward Tabb, and Toy Tabb's estate. Rarer still were the five people whose households included 21 or more tithables: William Armistead, Robert Billups, John Dixon, John Peyton, and Thomas Smith.[20]

Lost Landscapes: Gone But Not Forgotten

Eighteenth- and nineteenth-century surveys reveal that a multitude of Mathews County's early buildings have been lost or destroyed. Today, their remains are archaeological sites, many of which await discovery. For example, six houses are shown on a plat that was made in November 1736 during an attempt to settle a boundary dispute between Thomas Leithmore (Leitmore) and the Singleton family. The Singleton property, which consisted of Henry Singleton's 400-acre patent, extended along Mobjack Bay from the lower side of Pepper Creek to the lower side of Sloop Creek and contained houses attributed to various members of the Singleton family. Also shown were the dwellings of the plaintiff, Thomas Leithmore; Mrs. Armistead, whose home was on the west side of Horn Harbor's head; and Robert Cully, whose house was situated on the upper side of Sloop Creek. William Morgan's 500-acre patent and Richard Ripley's acreage were also in the immediate vicinity of the Singleton property. All of these families' forebears came into possession of their property during the 1650s and 60s.[21]

Peter Ransone owned a 1,100-acre plantation, which was situated between Diggs and Raymond Creeks, on the east side of the North River's mouth.[22] After his death, the plantation was carved into three parcels that went to his sons George I, James I, and William. When George Ransone died, his share of his late father's property went to his daughter, Elizabeth, who in 1694 conveyed it to her uncle, James I. At his death, his acreage descended to his sons Robert, Peter II, and George II. In 1744 George Ransone II had a survey made of his grandfather's 1,100-acre plantation and the three pieces into which it had been carved. James Ransone I's widow was credited with a 400-acre parcel that contained a house; James I's son, George II, had 350 acres that contained the home of his late grandfather, Peter Ransone I; and James I's uncle William had 350 acres that were vacant. Surveyor John French's primitive sketches of the Ransones' houses suggest that each dwelling had a pair of end chimneys. French executed a second survey of the Ransone property in 1745, likely because his 1744 plat was found to be inaccurate. This time he indicated that Robert Bristow's plantation had engulfed 201 acres of George Ransone II's 350 acres, but he included an additional 300 acres on the upper end of Peter Ransone I's original patent, extending it from Raymond Creek upstream to Bald Eagle Neck Creek, now a nameless stream. The Ransone plantation, as a whole, was resurveyed in 1750 when Richard Ransone sued his cousins. In 1774, when patentee Peter Ransone I's grandson, James II, died, his widow, Letitia, received a dower share of his 373-acre plantation. In 1775, when she tried to sell the property, she said that it had a good dwelling house with two rooms on each floor, some outbuildings, and an orchard. Also available for purchase were several Virginia-born slaves. William Hayes bought the acreage and sometime prior to 1816 sold it to Houlder Hudgins, who had it at the time of his death. The Ransone acreage was then known as the Isle of Wight plantation.[23]

At the head of Blackwater Creek, a tributary of the North River, was Thomas Peyton's plantation. In 1733, Peyton and his lessee, William Tabb, sued George Dudley, who had allegedly encroached upon Peyton's property. When a survey was done in 1734, the parameters of a 1652 patent were identified, as were three streams whose names are now obsolete: White Marsh and Dividing Creeks, tributaries of Blackwater Creek, and the Spirit Branch at Blackwater Creek's head. Route 14's forerunner was identified as the North River Mill road. John Tompkins's property was contiguous to Peyton's, as were neighbors named Hills and Bolton. Also shown on the plat were dwellings occupied by Thomas Peyton or his tenant, Peyton's orchard, two old houses, a small dwelling attributed to someone named Bridges or Bridger, and a schoolhouse located in Dudley's cornfield. The schoolhouse may have been used by a teacher who lived with a host family and provided instruction in exchange for room, board, a modest salary, and perhaps a few acres on which to plant crops.[24]

On the east side of Whites Neck, overlooking the mouth of the East River and Mobjack Bay, were 94 acres that belonged to Richard White. In 1751, his home stood at a site close to the mouth of Hatters (now Whites) Creek. To the west, but also adjacent to Mobjack Bay and the creek, was a 125-acre tract that contained the homes of William White and a Mrs. White. Virginia Land Office records indicate that William White had received a patent for those 125 acres in 1748, acreage that had escheated to the Crown, having formerly belonged to Henry Preston and his predecessor, Thomas Preston.[25] Contiguous to the Whites' property and extending up the west side of the East River to the lower side of Thomas Creek was another tract of escheat land attributed to Henry Preston. In 1748, when John Machen acquired Preston's property, which purportedly consisted of 645 acres, it was surveyed and found to contain only 606 acres; Machen received a patent for the property in 1755. To Machen's north, across Thomas Creek, was the acreage of John Cary. In 1786, Cary's property, which had previously belonged to Richard Cary, was partitioned and divided between John Elliott's heirs and James Booker's wife, Dorothy. Mrs. Booker received the southerly part of the property, which bordered Thomas Creek.[26]

In 1747, a 1,047-acre tract on the lower side of Queens Creek's head was surveyed in order to settle a dispute between John Webb and Robert Read. The plat that was made reveals that there were three houses on the property. One, located close to Queens Creek, belonged to the defendant, Robert Read, and a short distance away was the home of the Widow Longest. To the south and set back from the creek was Henry Gwyn's dwelling and in the westernmost part of the tract was a home occupied by the Widow Palister. At the time of the survey, the southwesterly branch of Queens Creek was identified as the Beaver Dam.

Some land on the east side of Queens Creek's mouth and fronting on Hills Bay and the Narrows was partitioned in 1753. At that time, Mildred Brooks received three houses and 238 acres that bordered Queens Creek, whereas Gregory Iverson's wife Joanna was given 239 acres near Queens Creek, plus a tract of land on the lower side of Horn Harbor. In 1753, Winder Creek was known as the Home House Creek and its uppermost branches defined the acreage on which Mildred Brooks's houses stood. In 1754, when a plat was made for Joseph Brooks, who was in possession of nearly 301 acres on the upper side of Queens Creek, his dwelling was shown prominently. The first branch on the upper side of Queens Creek, called the Dirty Branch, formed the westerly boundary of John Mathews's property, which bordered directly upon the Piankatank River.[27]

In 1774, John Willis tried to sell his 300-acre plantation between the East and North Rivers bordering Mobjack Bay, property that purportedly had a good dwelling and other necessities and included 15 acres of marshland. Less than a month after Willis placed his advertisement in the *Virginia Gazette*, an anonymous person inquired about the lowest price he would take and his terms of credit. The property was still for sale in October 1776. Around the same time Willis placed his ad, George W. Plummer announced that he had for sale an 800-acre plantation near New Point Comfort that had a dwelling house with two brick chimneys, outbuildings, and four orchards. Plummer also intended to sell 30 Virginia-born slaves.[28]

One particularly intriguing feature in Mathews County's lost landscape is a location near the head of Blackwater Creek and North that during the eighteenth and nineteenth centuries was known as "The Battery," the site of a tavern and store.[29] In 1771 an auction was to be held there to dispose of the late John Armistead's slaves and a year later, plans were made to hold "a Great Cock Match" at the Battery. Then in 1777, someone announced that a large quantity of St. Croix rum and sugar would be sold there along with a few pounds of Hyson tea.[30] John Hudgins Sr. was in possession of the 60-acre Battery tract from at least 1782 to 1793, and throughout that period he purchased licenses as a tavern-keeper. In 1793, Hudgins' acreage, then reduced to only 40 acres, came into the hands of William Dudley, who retained it until his death just prior to 1802. From 1793 through 1798 Dudley was a licensed tavern-keeper whose business was known as "The Battery." In December 1804 George E. Dudley, who combined William Dudley's 40 acres with some land he already owned, offered to sell the Battery tract, then defined as 630 acres on Blackwater Creek, adjoining the plantations of John Peyton, Philip Tabb, and Hunley Gayle. According to Dudley, there were three tenements on his property, which was located halfway between Gloucester and Mathews courthouses. He added that his plantation was a prime location for a store and tavern, and said that a Captain James Gibson was then in residence. In 1826, when cartographer Herman Böye made a map of Virginia, he identified the location known as The Battery. Eventually, that acreage became part of Isleham, a plantation that passed through the hands of the Peytons and the Taliaferros. In 1855 when a plat was made of Isleham, then the property of Warner T. Taliaferro, a 129-acre parcel on the lower side of Route 14's forerunner was identified as the "Battery Field" and the surveyor utilized "the battery" as a marker. A Union Army map, made between 1861 and 1865, identified a site at the head of Blackwater Creek as the "Battery." It suggests that the trajectory of Route 14 may have shifted somewhat.[31]

Another important feature in Mathews County's lost landscape is the plantation known as North End or North River. On January 24, 1730, when Mann Page I of Rosewell made his will, he bequeathed to his second oldest son, John I, who was born on February 20, 1725, a tract of land in Ware Parish that he "lately purchased of Col. Francis Willis."[32] That acreage lay between the North River's widely splayed western branch, now known as Burke Mill Stream, and the northeastern or main branch of the North River, now called the North End Branch. Page also left to his son, John I, "all the slaves and stock of Cattle and Hogs belonging to the land hereby devised to him" and £500 at age 21.[33] Around the time John Page I attained his majority, he married Jane (Jenny), the daughter of the late William Byrd II of Westover and his wife, the former Maria Taylor. The money John I inherited in 1746, the year his eldest son, Mann Jr., was born, and the £1,500 Jane received for marrying with her mother's consent most likely enabled the young couple to build a substantial home on the plantation he called North River or North End, where archaeologists have identified the remains of a large brick dwelling. Datable artifacts recovered from the site strongly suggest that it was the dwelling built by John I and Jane, which descended to their son, Mann Jr., and grandson, John III. Although the Page couple had another fourteen children while living at North End, only eleven survived. A plat made in November 1752 reveals that John Page I's North End acreage lay just south of Windsor, botanist John Clayton's home tract, and it abutted west upon 229 acres that belonged to John Armistead, whose land lay on the east side of the Burke Mill Stream and directly below the Clayton property. Page enhanced the size of his holdings by purchasing the Armistead tract and an adjoining 63 acres (what eventually became known as the Burke's Mill property) from Francis Willis around 1754. The mill tract contained a gristmill and mill dam, two houses, and an elongated building, a probable storehouse. Then, in 1768 Page acquired half of a 637-acre tract at the head of the North River that the late Dr. John Symmers' executors sold.[34]

An attorney and member of the Council of State, John Page I was a county justice and served on the College of William and Mary's Board of Visitors. The affectionate letters he received from his mother-in-law, Maria Taylor Byrd, during the 1750s and 60s while he was living at North End reveal that she held him in high regard. In accordance with the will John Page I made on May 25, 1771, his eldest son, Mann Jr., who was then age 28, stood to inherit the North End plantation and 30 slaves of all ages, excluding those at the Bridge Quarter.[35] He appointed his sons Mann Jr. and John II, his brother Mann, and Council president William Nelson as executors. On May 12, 1771, when John Page I added a codicil to his will, he asked his executors to see that the residue of his estate was divided among his wife and children after his other bequests had been made and his just debts were paid. Jane Byrd Page died at North End in August 1774 and John I passed away on October 1, 1774, while visiting the home of his brother, Mann, at Mannfield plantation near Fredericksburg.[36] When a list of Kingston Parish's taxable parishioners was compiled in 1774, Mann Page Jr. was credited with 14 tithable slaves, roughly half of the enslaved people he would have had under his control. In early November, the late John Page I's executors placed an advertisement in the *Virginia Gazette*, asking his creditors to present their claims. His debts must have been enormous, because on December 8, 1774, the executors announced that they planned to sell 150 of his choice Virginia-born slaves at Gloucester Courthouse on January 10. Three days later, they intended to hold an auction at Page's home at which time his valuable household and kitchen furniture, cattle, sheep, hogs, and horses would be sold.

It is unclear how much of the late John Page I's personal estate at North End was left after these two sales. However, in March 1776 his eldest son, Mann Page Jr., who was residing there, placed an advertisement in the *Virginia Gazette*, offering his thoroughbred race horse, "Damon," for stud service. Two years later, he informed the public that his pedigreed horse, "Shakespeare," was available at his plantation, as was excellent pasturage. On August 29, 1778, Mann Page Jr. of North End, who was only 32 years old, made his will. He left to his wife, the former Mary Mason Selden, the daughter of Samuel Selden of Stafford County, life rights in his land, slaves, and livestock in Gloucester County for the duration of her widowhood and named their eldest son, John Page III, as his primary heir. When Mann Jr. died in October 1778, he was survived by his widow, Mary, and their three underage children. He bequeathed £200 to Philip Edward Jones and £300 to John Iveson, perhaps his farm managers or overseers at North End.[37]

Complex litigation undertaken in 1831 and 1843 reveals that the widowed Mary Mason Selden Page, who was widowed at age 24, remarried in 1782, taking as her second husband a cousin, Dr. Wilson Cary Selden of Buckroe in Elizabeth City County. Dr. Selden, a surgeon and Revolutionary War veteran, became his stepchildren's guardian and managed their property. According to court documents, Dr. Selden and his wife Mary "had their permanent dwelling in the county of Gloucester" until they relocated to Elizabeth City County between late 1784 and early 1785.[38] Although the Seldens and the Page children resided in Elizabeth City in 1785 and 1786, an adult white male, perhaps a farm manager or tenant, and a substantial number of slaves continued to live at North End. Mrs. Mary Mason Selden Page Selden died on September 17, 1787, while she and her husband were visiting Winchester. Although the real estate taxes on the late Mann Page Jr.'s 2,800-acre North End plantation were paid through 1788, after Mary's death, they fell into arrears and taxes were paid on only 1,200 acres.[39] Between 1792 and 1794 Mathews County's tax officials began making note of the back taxes owed on the Page estate and the interest that was due. Personal property tax rolls indicate that Dr. William Byrd Page, the late Mann Page Jr.'s brother, who had been living in England and joined the British Army, had returned to Mathews County by 1791 and may have resided at North End. The late Mann Page Jr.'s eldest son, John III, came of age in 1793, and during 1794 sold North End to Andrew Van Bibber,[40] a Baltimore merchant and arms dealer whose descendants retained the property for another generation. A plat made in 1822 when the Van Bibbers disposed of the lower part of the original North End tract indicated that the 321 acres they were selling was the one "containing the old buildings." The 1822 plat also showed the massive North River mill, situated where Route 14's forerunner crossed the Burke Mill Stream bridge, then known as the North River bridge. In 1848, the Van Bibbers conveyed the mill and 1,180 acres to William R. Smart, who still owned it at the time of the Civil War.[41]

Another component of Mathews County's lost landscape is the plantation called the Old Town. During the early 1650s, William Armistead patented thousands of acres of land in Kingston Parish. One of the tracts he owned, known as the Old Town, encompassed the East River's northernmost extension, Upright Creek, and a branch of the river that extended in a northwesterly direction. Although the origin of the Old Town tract's name is uncertain, its fields may have contained obvious signs of Native American occupation, such as projectile points and pot sherds, or perhaps evidence of early European settlement. As time went on, William Armistead's landholdings on the East River descended to his son, John, who married Mary Churchill and produced a son, Churchill. On July 7, 1775, the *Virginia Gazette* announced that Churchill Armistead of Gloucester County had married Miss Betsy Boswell, also of Gloucester. He was appointed the county militia's lieutenant and sometime prior to 1782 came into possession of the Old Town tract. An undated plat, made by surveyor James Booker and preserved at the Virginia Historical Society, delimits the 884½-acre plantation's boundaries, which commenced at "the crossing place" to the south of the "New Church"—that is, the northwesterly branch of the East River that extended toward Kingston Parish's Upper Church.[42] The boundary line then passed by Dr. Livingston's orchard before reaching a tree at the corner of Mr. Christopher Brown's land. From that point, it ran along the road and crossed Beal's (Bell's) Bridge before turning southward, following the East River downstream. Booker indicated that a house, occupied by Mr. Robert Green, was situated near the river's junction with the nameless stream that extended toward the new church. Green, a member of Kingston Parish, married Elizabeth Respess in 1764 and was still living in the parish in 1771, perhaps on the Old Town tract.[43]

In 1782 Churchill Armistead owned 16 slaves of taxable age, a large herd of livestock, and 856 acres that in 1784 contained a dwelling and three outbuildings. By 1787 he was credited with an additional 392 acres, also considered part of the Old Town. In 1788 Armistead paid taxes on only 392 acres, for he had sold the bulk of his property to Dr. John Lewis Fulwell (Fullwell) of Northampton County. From 1791 through 1795, Armistead was credited with 342 acres called the Old Town and in 1796 he was in possession of Old Town Point, the southernmost part of the property, which was delimited by the East River and its westerly branch. By 1797, Armistead, who was near the end of his life, had disposed of his Old Town property.

On February 27, 1793, Dr. Fulwell, still a resident of Northampton County, bequeathed the Old Town tract to his son, Victor Augustus Fulwell, to whom he also left all of his medicines, medical books, and equipment. Dr. Fulwell asked his widow to live in his son's household at the Old Town unless she preferred to continue residing on the Eastern Shore. He noted that although the plantation had formerly been known as Old Town, he had renamed it Oldendorp. Dr. Fulwell died sometime prior to January 14, 1795, at which time his will was proved. His son, Victor Augustus Fulwell, also a physician, continued to live in Mathews County and was residing there at the time of his death in 1796; his only child and heir was Maria A. Fulwell. A partition suit undertaken between 1816 and 1822 reveals that after the younger Dr. Fulwell's death, his sister, Margaret F. Lane, and her children tried to claim a share of his estate and that of Victor's and Margaret's brother, George Lewis Fulwell.[44]

Prelude to Independence

In 1763 the House of Burgesses, in an attempt to cope with the enormous debt accumulated during the French and Indian War, issued treasury notes secured by future taxes and released £500,000 in paper currency. Lieutenant Governor Francis Fauquier responded by lecturing the burgesses on the need to place British merchants on a more favorable footing. Meanwhile, George Grenville, King George III's Lord of the Treasury, sought ways to force the American colonies to retire their war debt and shoulder the cost of their own defense. He decided to enforce existing laws, such as the Navigation Acts, and encouraged Parliament to pass legislation that was designed to generate new tax revenues. British merchants, uneasy about being paid in currency that had little real value outside of Virginia, persuaded Parliament to pass the Currency Act, which forbade the colonies to issue paper money. Parliament also enacted other pieces of legislation that the colonists found offensive. One required them to purchase stamps for numerous types of documents. When word of the Stamp Act's passage reached Virginia, members of the House of Burgesses opposed it, for they felt that taxes were being imposed without the colonists' consent. Some county justices resigned instead of enforcing the Stamp Act, and others simply ignored it. Parliament repealed the Stamp Act in February 1766, but preserved the Quartering Act, which required the colonists to provide accommodations to British soldiers. Even more offensive was the Declaratory Act, which asserted Parliament's right to pass laws that were binding upon the colonies. Then, in May 1767, legislation was introduced in Parliament, imposing duties on imported goods and slaves; some of those funds were to go toward the support of colonial governors and judges. Virginia's court justices, and those of several other colonies, flatly refused to cooperate.

Virginia Governor Norborne Berkeley, Baron de Botetourt, called the House of Burgesses into session in May 1769 and tried to dissuade its members from the "erroneous and dangerous Principles" they had adopted. The burgesses, in turn, asserted their exclusive right to levy taxes upon Virginia's inhabitants, and called for an annual meeting of "a general congress" comprised of delegates from all of the colonies. They also decided not to import any goods or manufactures (except paper) that would be taxed in America. Tensions increased, and Parliament threatened to prosecute anyone who disrupted trade with Great Britain. Then, they undertook a series of political maneuvers designed to assert their authority over the American colonies. They allowed the duties on all imported goods *except tea* to expire, along with the Fee Bill, which authorized county officials to charge fees for the duties they performed. County courts closed because local officials had no source of funding. This angered Virginians, who made plans to hold a general meeting, the Virginia Convention, to discuss ceasing all trade with Great Britain.

When Gloucester County's freeholders convened at the county courthouse on July 14, 1774, they approved 12 resolutions or "resolves." Although they professed their loyalty to the Crown, they insisted that "taxation and representation are inseparable," and added that since the colonies could not be represented in the British Parliament, Parliament had no right to impose internal taxes upon America. Gloucester's freeholders also voiced their disapproval of the restrictions placed upon the port of Boston, Massachusetts. The men who signed the Gloucester Resolves pledged to neither import nor purchase goods from Great Britain and declared that they would curtail exports to the Mother Country until the Boston embargo was repealed. They agreed to cease doing business with anyone in the county who hadn't signed the resolves and asked attorneys not to prosecute cases involving debts owed to the British. Gloucester County's clerk of court, Jasper Clayton, was clerk of the freeholders meeting.

On July 28, 1774, the *Virginia Gazette* published the text of the Gloucester Resolves, which prompted meetings throughout the colony. Some Virginia ports, upon learning of the situation in Massachusetts, immediately banned British trade. When the Virginia Convention met in Williamsburg in early August, Thomas Whiting and Lewis Burwell represented Gloucester County. The resolutions the Convention endorsed were in essence a blueprint for ones the first Continental Congress adopted. In November 1774, when Captain Howard Esten arrived in the York River with a shipment of tea, members of Gloucester's Committee of Safety expected to join their counterparts from York County in hosting a "tea party" like the one held in Boston. However, by the time Esten's ship reached Gloucester Town, the tea had already "met with its deserved fate" at the hands of people in Yorktown. In February 1775, Virginia Governor John Murray, Lord Dunmore, received word of a ban on exporting gunpowder and arms to the colonies. He was also ordered to secure all of the military stores that were on hand and to prevent the election of delegates to a second Continental Congress. During this period the British Parliament naïvely assumed that a relatively small number of American colonists were resisting their policies. On April 3, when the Gloucester Committee of Safety met, its members endorsed the Resolves generated by the March 20 meeting of the Virginia Convention.[45]

The Call to Arms

The Gunpowder Incident, which occurred in Williamsburg on April 21, 1775, made it abundantly clear that the relationship between Great Britain and her American colonies had deteriorated dramatically. When the Gloucester County Committee's members convened on April 25, they passed resolutions encouraging the payment of bounties to those who would manufacture gunpowder and make cards for processing wool and cotton. A week later, the Committee resolved not to ship any hogsheads of tobacco to Great Britain until the Continental Congress's sentiments were known. During late July and much of August 1775, when the Third Virginia Convention convened at St. John's Church in Richmond, county committees and delegates were chosen, along with a Committee of Safety that was empowered to make and enforce rules to maintain social order. An ordinance was passed encouraging the manufacture of saltpeter, gunpowder, refined sulfur, and arms for the use of Virginia troops. Virginia was divided into 16 military districts, each of which was required to recruit 500 militiamen. The Military District of Gloucester included Essex, Gloucester, King and Queen, King William, and Middlesex Counties. Each district had a Committee of Safety, comprised of three members from each county's Committee of Safety. Community-based minutemen were subject to immediate call.

The Articles of Confederation did not allow the Continental Congress to raise an army by means of a draft or to collect the funds needed to pay a standing army. However, men could enlist in the Continental Army or Line, which was expected to work closely with the state-controlled militia units called out for short periods of time. Continental, state line, and minute men were age 35 or under, whereas men between 16 and 50 could serve in the local militia. Men considered unfit for active duty were organized for the purpose of performing guard duty. The Continental Army's units changed frequently, especially in the first two years of the war, but from 1777 on, the army's organization became increasingly systematic. The result was that by the end of the war, the Continental Army bore very little resemblance to the troops that assembled in 1775.[46]

Lord Dunmore's Proclamation

By late summer 1775, the breach between Great Britain and her American colonies had become irreparable, and on August 23, King George III declared that the colonies were in "open and avowed rebellion." The king's declaration was published in the November 10 edition of the *Virginia Gazette*, which was distributed throughout the colony. During this period Lord Dunmore and his fleet, despite the colonists' resistance, were relatively free to cruise Virginia waters, seize vessels, and touch land almost anywhere. The British were in control of Norfolk, Portsmouth, and Gosport, and Lord Dunmore declared martial law. He also broadened his reach to include neighboring colonies. In mid-November 1775, Lord Dunmore offered freedom to all of the rebelling colonists' slaves and indentured servants and invited them to bear arms on behalf of the king. The assembly responded by publishing the Virginia Declaration, which reviled Dunmore for filling slaves with false hope and striking at the foundations of Virginia society. It is unclear how many slaves and servants left home in support of the British cause, but it is certain that many did so.[47]

Notes

1 Two of the parcels Dr. Symmer owned were on opposite sides of the Piankatank River and included the landings associated with Turk's Ferry. His 700 acres in Kingston Parish, a tract called "Edwards," had an abundance of good timber (Purdie and Dixon, *Virginia Gazette*, October 29, 1767; June 9, 1768; June 16, 1769).

2 Gloucester County Surveyors Plat Book A (1733–1810):37; Chamberlayne, *Kingston Parish*, 29, 31, 53, 56, 77, 85; Walsh, *Motives*, 419–423; Mason, *Gloucester*, II, 69–70; Purdie and Dixon, *Virginia Gazette*, October 29, 1767; March 11, 1770; November 14, 1771; November 19, 1772; Purdie, *Virginia Gazette*, April 19, 1776; Dixon and Hunter, *Virginia Gazette*, August 24, 1776; Patent Book III, 46; Middlesex County Surveys 1735–1807:50; John Harrower, *The Journal of John Harrower, An Indentured Servant in the Colony of Virginia, 1773–1776* (New York, 1963), xiv–xv, 38, 41, 166–168; USDA. *Soil Survey*, 22.

3 The accounts maintained by John Billups as George Hunley's executor reveal that in 1764 the decedent had purchased dry goods from Captain Dixon (Mason, *Gloucester*, II, 69).

4 Purdie and Dixon, *Virginia Gazette*, November 13, 1766; September 21, 1769; September 28, 1769; September 4, 1774; Hunter, *Virginia Gazette*, November 3, 1766; September 21, 1769, September 28, 1769; Rind, *Virginia Gazette*, March 11, 1773; September 14, 1769; August 30, 1770; October 11, 1770; Pinckney, *Virginia Gazette*, September 21, 1775; Ludlum, *Hurricanes,* 26–27.

5 Ludlum, *Hurricanes*, 26–27; Purdie and Dixon, *Virginia Gazette*, September 14, 1769; Rind, *Virginia Gazette*, September 21, 1769; *Pennsylvania Gazette*, September 28, 1769; October 12, 1769.

6 In 1771 Richard Respess was identified as a house builder to whom John Blacknall owed money. When the state enumeration was taken in 1784, Richard Respess Sr., who owned land on Milford Haven, was credited with a dwelling and five outbuildings (Mason, *Gloucester*, II, 70, 81; U.S. Bureau, *Heads of Families,* 68.

7 Purdie and Dixon, *Virginia Gazette*, March 26, 1767; June 9, 1768; November 7, 1771; February 27, 1772; Dixon and Hunter, *Virginia Gazette,* May 27, 1775; Hunter, *Virginia Gazette*, November 13, 1766; Purdie, *Virginia Gazette,* August 15, 1766; November 28, 1777; Dixon and Nicholson, *Virginia Gazette,* October 23, 1778; Richard Billups Papers, Swem, Box 1 folder 13.

8 For example, in 1798 when Edmund Borum of Mathews County made his will, he named family members to whom his slaves would be given (Edmund Borum, will, February 1, 1798, Virginia Lee Hutchinson Davis, comp., *Tidewater Virginia Families*, 10 [August/September 2001]:42).

9 Walsh, *Motives,* 403; Charles, *Newspapers*, 8, 14; Thad W. Tate, *The Negro in Eighteenth Century Williamsburg* (Williamsburg, 1965), 47; Purdie and Dixon, *Virginia Gazette*, March 5, 1767; July 23, 1767; November 26, 1772; Rind, *Virginia Gazette*, January 10, 1771; T.H. Breen et al., *Myne Owne Grounde* (New York, 1980), 10; William L. Katz, *The Negro in Virginia* (New York, 1969), 79–81; Charles L. Perdue Jr., *The Negro in Virginia* (Winston–Salem, 1994), 89.

10 Locke maintained a register of the marriages he performed while Kingston Parish's rector, noting whether the couple had obtained a marriage license and posted bans.

11 Dixon may have been influenced by the Rev. William Dawson of the College of William and Mary, who informed a colleague that he intended to ask the assembly to urge Virginia clergy to convert the enslaved to Christianity.

12 The buildings on glebes, maintained at parish expense, were supposed to be in good repair when a new minister arrived. Conversely, departing clergy were supposed to leave their glebes in good condition.

13 Chamberlayne, *Kingston Parish*, 52. George Carrington Mason mistakenly identified Churchill Armistead as Armistead Churchill, a resident of Middlesex County.

14 Mrs. Dixon's tombstone and gravesite are located on the grounds of Trinity Church (Christine L. Sheridan and Elsie W. Ernst, comp., *Tombstones of Mathews County, Virginia, 1711–1986* [Mathews County, 1988], 112).

15 Chamberlayne, *Kingston Parish*, 19, 24, 27, 31, 39–43, 68–69, 88, 93–94, 98–99; James Booker, "Plat of Churchill Armistead's land, the Old Town tract," n.d., Richard Billups Papers, Virginia Historical Society; Francis Tomkies, [Untitled Plat], September 11, 1770, Williams Family Papers, Library of Virginia; Lothrop Withington, comp., *Virginia Gleanings in England* (Baltimore, 1980), 304–306; SR 4431; Hening, Statutes, VI, 89; Purdie and Dixon, *Virginia Gazette*, January 18, 1770; September 8, 1774; Dixon and Hunter, *Virginia Gazette*, November 14, 1777; Purdie, Virginia Gazette, April 4, 1777; Emma R. Matheny and Helen K. Yates, comp., *Kingston Parish Register, Gloucester and Mathews Counties, Virginia, 1749–1827:* 117; Martha W. McCartney, *Kingston Parish Register, Mathews, Gloucester, and Middlesex Counties, Virginia, Slaves and Slaveholders 1746–1827*, 21, 40, 45, 76; Lyon G. Tyler, ed., "Old Tombstones in Mathews County," *William and Mary Quarterly* 1st Ser. 3 (1895):256. While the Rev. Thomas Feilde was staying in Williamsburg, he visited the Governor's Palace gardens and observed that shells were being excavated from a large pit "opened purposefully for getting this matter which is used for making walks instead of gravel" (The Rev. Thomas Feilde, February 16, 1771, letter to Dr. Makenzie, Huntington Library, Brock Box 117 f 1). Kingston Parish's original parish register reveals that Feilde, like the Rev. John Dixon, was conscientious about baptizing slaves.

16 The Hunleys also tried to sell an adjacent 170–acre parcel that was half–forested.

17 An undated plat in the Williams Family Papers indicates that the land Dixon sold to Williams was on the upper side of the road to the East River warehouse and skirted part of Put In Creek's mouth (Anonymous, "A Plat of the land bought by John Dixon and adjoining the land he [Williams] bought of Davis and Hunley at East warehouse," n.d.)

18 Rind, *Virginia Gazette*, October 11, 1770; Purdie and Dixon, *Virginia Gazette*, October 18, 1770; November 11, 1770; Francis Tomkies, [untitled plat], September 11, 1770; Williams Family Papers plats, receipts; Chamberlayne, *Kingston Parish*, 114–118,123–125; Matheny and Yates, *Register*, 115; Mason, *Gloucester*, II, 72. Four of the Williams' infant slaves were baptized during the Rev. Thomas Feilde's ministry (McCartney, *Register*, 8, 11, 35, 48).

19 Patent Book V, 280, 586; VI, 331; X, 173; John Throckmorton, [untitled plat of the prison bounds], June 31, 1754; Purdie and Dixon, *Virginia Gazette*, April 4, 1776; July 26, 1766; September 28, 1769; McIlwaine, *Legislative Journals*, 1423; H.R. McIlwaine, comp., *Justices of Colonial Virginia* (Richmond, 1922), 50, 52; [Francis Tomkies], "Pt. of an Acre of Land on which Gloucester Courthouse now stands," August 9, 1769; Francis Tomkies, "Town of Botetourt," 1774.

20 Chamberlayne, *Kingston Parish*, 104–105; Billups Papers, Library of Virginia. In May 1774 William Plummer tried to sell his 500-acre plantation on a tributary of the East River. It reportedly had a good overseer's house and an abundance of white oak and pine trees (Rind, *Virginia Gazette*, May 12, 1774).

21 Gloucester County Surveyors Plat Book A (1733–1810): 8–9; Patent Book III, 10, 138; IV, 532; VI, 103.

22 The trajectory of County Route 617 is one mile from the North River's shore and probably delimited the back line of Peter Ransone's original patent.

23 Mathews County Will Book 1, 24–28; Gloucester Surveyors Plat Book A (1733–1810): 12–13, 23; Judith McGhan, comp., *Virginia Will Records* (Baltimore, 1993), 516, 534; Lyon G. Tyler, "Ransone Family," *William and Mary Quarterly* 1st Ser., 10 (April 1902):264–265; Dixon and Hunter, *Virginia Gazette*, March 11, 1775.

24 During the colonial period, plantation schools were typically in session from April to September, and the school day consisted of six to eight hours of instruction per day. Philip Vickers Fithian, a Westmoreland County tutor who provided instruction to Robert Carter III's children, indicated that the schoolhouse in which he taught was comparable to the plantation's kitchen and laundry. John Harrower, a schoolmaster at a Spotsylvania County plantation, described his school as a "neat little house" that was weather-boarded with plank and plastered on the inside with shell lime. It is likely that the little schoolhouse on the Peyton property was similar.

25 In 1784 William White's 125 acres had a dwelling and one outbuilding (U.S. Bureau, *Heads of Families*, 68; Mathews County Land Tax Lists 1784).

26 Gloucester County Surveyors Plat Book A (1733–1810):17, 22, 41; Patent Book XXXII, 645; XXXIII, 366. In 1748, when the Machen property was surveyed, a portion of County Route 606's forerunner was shown.

27 Gloucester Surveyors Plat Book A (1733–1810): 15, 32–33.

28 Rind, *Virginia Gazette*, February 10, 1774; February 24, 1774; Purdie and Dixon, *Virginia Gazette*, February 10, 1774; March 3, 1774; May 5, 1774; Dixon, *Virginia Gazette*, October 11, 1776.

29 These cultural features shouldn't be confused with the nineteenth-century house later known as The Battery.

30 Hyson tea, a Chinese green tea, was highly prized during the eighteenth century.

31 Rind, *Virginia Gazette*, January 10, 1771; Purdie and Dixon, *Virginia Gazette*, May 28, 1772; Purdie, *Virginia Gazette*, October 3, 1777; Charles, *Newspapers*, 46–47; Böye, "Map of Virginia," 1826; Gloucester County Land Tax Lists 1782–1790; Mathews County Land Tax Lists 1791–1803; Personal Property Tax Lists 1791–1798; Land Book 1, 228–229; Anonymous, "York River and Mobajack [*sic*] Bay, Virginia," [1861–1865].

32 Members of the Willis family had been living in Gloucester County since the seventeenth century.

33 The entail on the late Mann Page I's estate was docked in 1732 on account of the decedent's debts to British merchants and to Virginia merchant Robert Carter (Winfree, *Supplement*, 359–361). Once the entail had been "docked" or removed, Page's executors could sell some of his real and personal property to pay his debts.

34 Sir John Peyton, the owner of Isleham, purchased the other half of Dr. Symmons' tract (Gloucester County Surveyors Plat Book A [1733–1810]:37).

35 This suggests that Page had subdivided his plantation into one or more subsidiary farms or quarters. The Bridge Quarter probably was close to the bridges that carried Route 14's forerunner across the Burke Mill Stream and the North End Branch.

36 The obituaries of John and Jane Byrd Page were published in the *Virginia Gazette* (Purdie and Dixon, *Virginia Gazette*, August 11, 1774; Pinkney, *Virginia Gazette*, October 6, 1774).

37 Neither man then owned land in the county.

38 This contradicts a Page family genealogist's claim that North End was destroyed by fire during the Revolutionary War (Richard C.M. Page, *Genealogy of the Page Family in Virginia* [New York, 1893], 87).

39 In 1791 Wilson Cary Seldon and his stepson, John Page II, were living in Elizabeth City County (Elizabeth City County Personal Property Tax Lists 1791).

40 At the close of the Revolutionary War, Andrew Van Bibber and his brother, Isaac, angrily informed Sir John Peyton that the state currency they had received for selling muskets to the Virginia government was unacceptable and they wanted Continental money only. In 1795 Andrew Van Bibber asked George Washington whether he would exchange 400 acres on the lower side of the North River for a piece of property Van Bibber owned in King William County near the Custis property (Palmer, *Calendar*, II, 25; Letter from Andrew Van Bibber, September 28, 1795, The Papers of George Washington, Library of Congress, Washington, D.C.; Gloucester County Land Tax Lists 1795–1798; John C. Fitzpatrick,

ed., *The Writings of George Washington* (Washington, D.C., 1942), XXXIV, 327–328, 428). If Van Bibber had been able to acquire Washington's land, he would have had better access to shipping.

41 John Page III was living at Buckroe when he made his will in May 1800 and named as heirs his brother and sister, stepparents, nieces and nephews, and reputed son, John Page Barron; he died a month later. William G. Stanard, ed., "Mann Page Will," *Virginia Magazine of History and Biography* 32 (1924):39–43; "John Page Will," *Virginia Magazine of History and Biography* 34 (1926): 276–277; Hening, *Statutes*, V, 277–284; Gloucester County Surveyors Plat Book A (1733–1810): 28–29, 37; Marion Tinling, ed., *The Correspondence of the Three William Byrds of Westover*, 600, 622–624, *passim*; Page, *Genealogy*, 85–87; Meade, *Old Churches and Families*, I, 147; Purdie, *Virginia Gazette*, March 15, 1776; March 6, 1778; Purdie and Dixon, *Virginia Gazette*, August 11, 1774; November 10, 1774; December 8, 1774; Pinkney, *Virginia Gazette*, October 6, 1774; Kingston Parish Tithables 1774–1775, Billups Papers, Library of Virginia; Elizabeth City County Personal Property Tax Lists 1782–1790; Mathews County Land Tax Lists 1791–1800; Personal Property Tax Lists 1791–1800; Delinquent Land Tax Lists 1792–1813; Land Book 1, 43; Frederick County Chancery Causes, 1843; Billups Papers, Swem, Box 2 Folder 5; https://bulk.resource.org/courts.gov/c/us/42/42/us.37.html; Mathews County Deed, 1848; Blanche A. Chapman, *Wills and Administrations of Elizabeth City County, Virginia, 1688–1800* (Smithfield, 1941), 66. William R. Smart enhanced the size of the property associated with his mill by acquiring some adjoining acreage that Samuel W. Tilton had used as collateral when borrowing money from John H. Blake in January 1861. Tilton defaulted on his debt and Smart acquired his acreage at a public auction held in spring 1863 (Mathews County Deed Book 1:3–4; Charles, *Newspapers*, 106).

42 Although the parish's Upper Church was built in the early 1740s, it continued to be known colloquially as the New Church.

43 In 1782 Robert Green paid taxes on 250 acres, perhaps the tract that in 1790 was credited to Churchill Armistead's estate (Gloucester County Land Tax Lists 1782–1790).

44 Patent Book II, 331; III, 1; VI, 336, 657; Richard Billups Papers, Virginia Historical Society; Matheny and Yates, *Register,* 10, 57; Gloucester County Land Tax Lists 1782; Minute Book 1822–1825:113; Mathews County Land Tax Lists 1791–1799; Personal Property Tax Lists 1796; Purdie, *Virginia Gazette*, July 7, 1775; October 13, 1775; Purdie and Dixon, *Virginia Gazette*, May 28, 1767; Northampton County Deed Book 26:254; Wills, Etc. Book 29 (1792–1795):325; Deed Book 26:254.

45 Purdie and Dixon, *Virginia Gazette*, July 28, 1774; September 8, 1774; November 24, 1774; Pinckney, *Virginia Gazette,* January 19, 1775; April 28, 1775; Rind, *Virginia Gazette*, July 28, 1774; William J. Van Schreeven et al., *Revolutionary Virginia: The Road to Independence* (Charlottesville, 1973–1979), I, 137–138; II, 175; John E. Selby, *Chronology of Virginia and the War of Independence* (Charlottesville, 1973), 2.

46 Pinkney, *Virginia Gazette*, April 28, 1775; May 4, 1775; Hening, *Statutes*, VIII, 16–17.

47 John E. Selby, *Revolution in Virginia: 1775–1783* (Charlottesville, 1988), 1–5; *Chronology*, 18–19, 23.

6

Times That Try Men's Souls
1776–1795

Local Citizens React

Once it was certain that war was inevitable, able-bodied freemen between the ages of 15 and 50 began enrolling in their county's militia.[1] From Kingston Parish came distinguished military leaders such as Sir John Peyton (a baronet), Thomas Whiting, and Thomas Boswell, as well as militia captains John Billups Sr., Richard Billups, William Buckner, Jasper Clayton, John Dixon, Benjamin Shackleford, William Smith, John Whiting, and John Willis. Churchill Armistead, John Billups Jr., Dudley Cary, John Foster, John Foster Jr., George Green, Hugh Hayes, and Philip Tabb held the rank of lieutenant; and Peter Bernard, Richard Davis, William Davis, Samuel Eddins, Josiah Foster, John Gayle, John Hayes, George Plummer, and Thomas Tabb were ensigns. All of these men were under the command of Gloucester's county lieutenant, Warner Lewis, whose rank and status increased when on the battle field.

On July 24, 1775, the Gloucester County Committee of Safety passed a resolution thanking John and William Degge (Digges), William Hudgins, and shipbuilder John Parsons, all of Kingston Parish, for informing the authorities about imported goods' being ashore in Urbanna, contrary to the non-importation agreement. Others violated the agreement. In April 1776, imported goods were offered for sale at Humphrey Billups's home; and Matthew Anderson, who lived in Ware Parish on the lower side of the North River, regularly advised the public that he was selling imported goods. In early May, Thomas Posey of the 7th Virginia Regiment was ordered to set up camp at New Point Comfort to guard against a surprise attack by the enemy. On May 20 he inspected the guard at Burton's Point and dined with Mr. Armistead, probably at Hesse.

In preparation for war, the Virginia Committee of Safety decided to have salt works and powder mills built at public expense and to undertake other projects in support of the military. The Board of Naval Commissioners was given the responsibility of establishing a small navy. They were to oversee the construction and repair of state navy vessels and were in charge of public ropewalks, dockyards, and shipyards. The Naval Commissioners also had to procure several armed vessels from the merchant fleet's owners and to find suitable locations where state shipyards could be built. By June 1776, construction of a state-owned shipyard on the Chickahominy River had gotten underway, but naval vessels were built on private property in a handful of other Tidewater counties. During the war, several ships were built by the numerous shipbuilders in what became Mathews County.[2]

Smallpox, the Scourge of Lord Dunmore's Army

Virginia experienced smallpox outbreaks from time to time, but when the disease appeared in Lord Dunmore's army in January 1776, it was very virulent and spread quickly. Although most of Dunmore's British troops had been vaccinated, the black men he recruited in Virginia and the women and children who accompanied them were especially susceptible to the disease and died by the hundreds in Norfolk. In late May, Dunmore decided to move his base to Gwynn's Island, where his surgeons could inoculate his recruits *en masse* and the sick could be isolated. He was acquainted with John Randolph Grymes, a British loyalist, and was aware that Grymes had a plantation on the island. Dunmore sent word to Lord George Germain that there were horses on Gwynn's Island, and said that he had asked Grymes to form a small troop that could assist in defending any part of the island. Captain Andrew Snape Hamond of the H.M.S. *Roebuck*, who was familiar with Gwynn's Island, knew that it had plenty of fresh water and a good harbor.

On August 31, 1776, the *Virginia Gazette* published the names of slaves known to be part of Lord Dunmore's Ethiopian Regiment, or to have joined his fleet and gone to Gwynn's Island. The *Gazette's* publisher, who called them "Lord Dunmore's black banditti," commented that most of the slaves could be "distinguished by their owners' surnames." Nearly a hundred men, women, and children were aboard the ships *Dunluce* and *Dunmore*, but on May 29, an almost equal number were encamped on Gwynn's Island. Some had spent time aboard the fleet's hospital brig, *Adonis.* According to eyewitness accounts, hundreds of these people endured the ravages of smallpox while sheltered in small, hastily constructed huts on Gwynn's Island. Dunmore informed his superiors that "there was not a ship in the fleet that did not throw one, two or three more dead overboard every night." While based on Gwynn's Island, Dunmore continued to attract six to eight black recruits each day. Most of them succumbed to smallpox shortly after they arrived.[3]

Engraving of John Murray, Lord Dunmore, by Charles B. Hall. Courtesy of Ohio History Central, August 19, 2015, http://ohiohistorycentral.org/w/John_Murray.

Military Action at Gwynn's Island

On May 26, 1776, a hundred men from Lord Dunmore's 14th Regiment, 100 royal marines, 150 loyalists from Norfolk, 50 seamen, and 300 African-Americans came ashore on Gwynn's Island. Dunmore had his men erect a breastwork and four embrasures on a small point on the western end of the island, overlooking Milford Haven and Hills Bay. On the southeastern tip of the island, Dunmore had his men build two batteries and a stockade fort to keep the Americans from slipping ashore. British ships secured the approach to the island, rendering it inaccessible by sea.[4] Lord Dunmore's decision to land so many men on Gwynn's Island caught Virginia leaders by surprise. In fact, General Andrew Lewis readily admitted that he had "never heard of such a Place before the Enemy reached it." On the mainland, Lewis and four companies of men from his Gloucester County battalion threw up the earthworks eventually known as Fort Cricket Hill.[5] Because the Americans lacked cannon, the British easily kept them at the water's edge. When a few gunshots were exchanged, Captain Dohickey Arundel, a Frenchman fighting on the American side, was mortally wounded. William Barry, an American mariner detained aboard the *Roebuck,* managed to escape in a canoe. When he reached the mainland, he informed Colonel Churchill that the British were planning to come ashore to procure livestock. Thanks to this intelligence, the Americans were able to move the animals to a more secure location. When the British did venture ashore, they reportedly burned some houses.[6]

On June 1, 1776, the *Virginia Gazette* reported that Lord Dunmore had landed 800 men on Gwynn's Island and that the entrenchment the British had thrown up on the landward side was chiefly guarded by the black regiment. The *Gazette* also reported that the Gloucester militia assembled on the opposite shore lacked cannon. The *Pennsylvania Gazette*, quoting a June 3 posting in an Alexandria, Virginia, newspaper, said that the *Roebuck, Fowey, Otter*, and 60 to 80 other vessels were at Gwynn's Island and were going to spend the summer there unless disturbed. Two weeks later, the *Virginia Gazette* reported that Lord Dunmore had erected hospitals on Gwynn's Island and that his old friend Andrew Sprowle was dead. Captain Hamond of the *Roebuck* later informed his superiors that while the British fleet lay

Infantry, Continental Army, by H.A. Ogden. Courtesy of www.ducksters.com.

at Gwynn's Island, carpenters found a flat and outfitted it with a cannon and oars. He said that it proved very useful in making mischief among the enemy when the fleet was at St. George's Island.[7]

Although General Lewis surmised that Dunmore might be trying to lure the Americans away from their capital city of Williamsburg,[8] he set out for Gloucester on July 8 with veteran units of the 1st and 2nd Regiments. He also brought cannon for the American earthworks, and he summoned Colonels William Daingerfield of Gloucester and Hugh Mercer of Fredericksburg to confront Dunmore and his men. When Lewis reached the American position opposite Gwynn's Island, he observed that the British had several hundred men bivouacked in tents at the western end of the island. He also learned that they had erected an artillery battery at The Narrows and that the *Otter* and several tenders were stationed in the channel near Narrows Point. On July 9, Lewis noticed that the *Dunmore,* which had exchanged positions with the *Otter,* was exposed to two 18-pound guns that the Virginians had been able to move into place. Therefore, at ebb tide, he ordered the gunners to open fire. During the battle, in which the *Dunmore* was hit a dozen times, Lord Dunmore was wounded by flying splinters, and the ship's mate was killed. When the *Otter* came to the *Dunmore's* defense, it too was struck by cannon fire and sustained serious damage. After four tenders that were in the channel ran aground, three were burned and the fourth was captured. Two more tenders were burned the next day, along with the ship *Logan*. James Parker's battery, which had a 6-pound cannon, was silenced by the Americans who had use of four 9-pounders. Lord Dunmore, who knew that he wasn't going to receive aid from General Henry Clinton and that the Americans lacked boats, realized that he had about 48 hours to leave Gwynn's Island. While the British fleet was preparing for departure, a great storm swept in. Some of Dunmore's vessels were lost or driven ashore, and many lost their anchors and cables. The British withdrawal from Gwynn's Island, completed by July 13, coincided with an emerging need for American troops in New York, where General Howe was amassing a 25,000-man army and needed reinforcements.

When the Americans went ashore on Gwynn's Island, they found a gruesome sight, for the ground was littered with the bodies of the dead and the dying. They quickly discovered that Dunmore's people were infected with smallpox and other diseases, and that he had erected hospitals on the island. Many of these victims lay unburied "without a shovelful of earth upon them." One eyewitness reported that he had counted at least 130 graves, many of which were large enough for mass burials. Another man commented that nearly 500 people had died on Gwynn's Island and that their bodies were strewn over the ground from the battery to Cherry Point. Dunmore himself described the hasty evacuation as one of "distress and confusion." The Americans, fearful of contamination, set ablaze the flimsy brush huts that sheltered the dead and dying. The departing British left behind Alexander Silver, a little boy related to Captain Squires, and Sarah Lecke, wife of the *Roebuck's* lieutenant.[9]

General Lewis reported that after the British left Gwynn's Island, his men recovered a 6-pound cannon, at least £1,000 worth of cables, anchors, and bars of iron, and 50 head of cattle. He said that Captain Robert Tompkins of the galley *Henry* was sent to the island to look for a sunken flat containing some of Lord Dunmore's cannon. The Americans remained vigilant despite the British navy's departure, and in September 1776 Commodore John Thomas Boucher and Captain Edward Travis of the galley *Manley* were stationed near New Point Comfort. Word of the British defeat at Gwynn's Island reached Boston, where the *Massachusetts Spy* published an eyewitness's account of the military action. News of the defeat also reached Ireland, and on September 23, 1776, the *Leicester Journal* published a letter stating that the Americans (termed "Provincials") had raised a masked battery within point-blank range of Dunmore's ships. The letter went on to say that 30 of those ships were destroyed and that Dunmore had to burn another 30, leaving him with only 11 vessels out of a fleet of 71.

Thomas Jefferson, governor of the Commonwealth of Virginia, made a crude sketch map of Gwynn's Island and identified the position of Dunmore's ships, the earthworks erected by the British and the Americans, and some of the island's topographic features. His map was probably based on intelligence data he had received (perhaps from General Lewis). Jefferson indicated that at the time of combat, three houses overlooked Milford Haven; he attributed two of the dwellings to the Gwynns and one to the Keebles. He also identified the Grymes plantation in the northernmost part of Gwynn's Island. Jefferson commented that Narrows Point was about 200 yards wide and half a mile long and that enemy ships were aligned in Hills Bay. He depicted Deep (Edwards) Creek, which he said ran inland for approximately three-quarters of a mile. He noted that a ditch that was 20 to 30 yards wide had been cut from Hills Creek, which he identified as a pond, to Milford Haven and said that it was large enough to accommodate pilot boats. He estimated the distance between Breeze and Sandy Points as about one-half mile and stated that at high tide the water was about five feet deep. He noted that the water within Milford Haven, which he estimated to be about three miles in length, was 17 or 18 feet deep.[10]

Despite the clash between the British and American forces at Gwynn's Island and its impact on the terrain, Humphrey Gwyn's advertisement in the *Virginia Gazette* in mid-August 1776 implies that his plantation was minimally affected. When he offered to lease his 500-acre Gwynn's Island farm for a year, he said that it had a good dwelling-house and other buildings and that he was willing to sell a good crop of corn that was still in the field. Two years later, Gwyn tried to sell his plantation along with his livestock and field crops. The mainland farms occupied by Daniel and Elisha Marchant, Henry Powell, Philip Peed, and Joseph and John Shipley, located on the lower side of Milford Haven, close to the Narrows, sustained significant damage. On November 7, 1776, all six men asked the Virginia government for compensation, claiming that they were impoverished because their field crops had been destroyed by American troops camped near their property. The claimants said that the men had traipsed through their fields repeatedly when going to and from their battery at Cricket Hill and that they were forced to vacate their homes, which were put to use by the soldiery or razed. Each of the homeowners, in compensation for his losses, was given a substantial quantity of corn.

The men aboard Virginia's naval vessels also dealt with deprivation. In August 1776 the Navy Board sent some supplies to Captain Thomas Lily of the brig *Liberty*, which had spent time at Gwynn's Island. The items included a bolt of osnabrig fabric, two pieces of duck cloth, 12 pounds of twine, and 35 shirts for the use of the *Liberty's* seamen. On the other hand, the Navy Board postponed their review of a petition from the marines aboard the galley *Henry,* Captain Robert Tompkins' ship, who were in dire need of clothing. Finally, in October, they were given a large quantity of supplies from the public store, including shoes, stockings, jackets, breeches, worsted caps, and yard goods. A spyglass, an hour glass, a large speaking-trumpet, ten barrels of bread, and some iron were also sent to the *Henry*.[11]

Salvage Operations

More than 20 years after the Americans confronted the British at Gwynn's Island, Captain Samuel Eddens (Eddins or Eddin), a longtime resident of Kingston Parish, sought payment for the anchors and cables he had recovered in July 1776, shortly after Lord Dunmore's fleet departed. He said that he had been ordered to Gwynn's Island to observe the approach of Lord Dunmore and the British fleet. He indicated that when the British left the island in the midst of a severe storm, they lost a substantial number of anchors and cables, and had abandoned some additional ones when they set out to harass the Americans' inbound merchantmen. Eddens, who claimed that he had fabricated a device that enabled him to sweep the bottom of the Piankatank River, said that he had recovered 17 anchors and cables that British vessels left behind. He indicated that the state took most of the anchors for its own armed vessels and sold the rest for the public's benefit. According to Eddens, one anchor that weighed more than 3,000 pounds was put to use on the continental frigate *Virginia*, built at Baltimore. He said that he had leased a schooner from Stapleton Keebler of Gwynn's Island for 26 days and that while he was using it in salvage operations, it sustained $50 worth of damage. In 1798, Eddens again asked for compensation for his expenses and the salvaged naval gear he had provided to American vessels.[12]

Achieving Independence

In June 1776, when the Virginia Convention adopted a constitution for the Commonwealth of Virginia, some important structural changes occurred in the upper levels of government. The House of Burgesses readily evolved into the House of Delegates, but a number of public offices, positions formerly occupied by royal appointees, had to be filled and the judicial system had to be modified. The fledgling state government was obliged to address needs that ranged from trade and the monetary system to civil defense and public welfare. The structure of county government stayed intact, as did the link between church and state. As a result, county courts and parish vestries, which were appointive bodies, retained their taxing authority.[13] County justices were appointed by the governor, just as they had been before the war; and when a vacancy occurred, the court's surviving justices recommended a replacement. County justices had the right to levy taxes, try cases, and appoint lesser local officials all in a single session; and they rotated the sheriffry among themselves. Many people disliked the traditional arrangement and because local justices had taxing authority, equated it to taxation without representation.

As the summer of 1776 wore on, Gloucester County's Committee of Safety met frequently. Committee members praised militia commander Warner Lewis for protecting the county by positioning men as guards, and they agreed to reimburse Sir John Peyton for the provisions and four guns that he had furnished to the militia. The Committee of Safety's members tried to decide what to do with vessels that had been captured off the coast, including the ship in which Andrew McCann had been taken prisoner. Meanwhile, the Continental Congress adopted Richard Henry Lee's resolution for independence, and on July 4, 1776, the Declaration of Independence was accepted. In late August, James Davis, a Kingston Parish shipbuilder, was paid for blacksmith's work he had done for the schooner *Revenge*, and he agreed to build a row galley and finish it by December 25. Then, on September 26, 1776, Kingston Parish residents Edward Anderson, Christopher Cully, Joshua Foster, Robert Gayle, Houlder Hudgins, Henry Knight, and Peter Smith were authorized to construct large flat-bottomed boats that could be used to transport troops. Each one was to be equipped with oars and built in accordance with certain specifications. In October, the Navy Board ordered Captain William Smith, who headed a company of minutemen, to release any who were ship's carpenters or their apprentices. In late October, when Brigadier General Fielding Lewis rendered an account of the troops at Gloucester Point, the governor and his advisors decided to dismiss the companies under the command of Captains William Smith, Phillip Taliaferro, Mordecai Throckmorton, and William Richards because only 48 men were considered fit for duty.

John Hobday of Kingston Parish, superintendent of the public salt works at Yorktown and Gloucester from 1776 through 1778, had the right to hire workers and to use soldiers in the works located in Robin's Neck. In November 1776, he voiced his objections when he learned that the funds he needed to hire workmen and soldiers and provide them with alcoholic beverages were to be deducted from his pay. In October 1778, John and Bennett Tompkins, whose land was on the west side of Blackwater Creek, asked for compensation for the salt works that had been built on their land; when their claim was rejected, they protested. Perhaps in response to these complaints, on July 10, 1779, the Committee of Safety announced that it would rent the public salt works and its equipment to the highest bidder for a period of 17 months and let the lessee pay his rent in salt. This approach may have generated very little interest, because in late November, Samuel DuVal and Company announced that on December 16 the "great SALT WORKS in Robin's Neck" and "all the apparatus" would be rented to the highest bidder for a two year period. In 1780–1, Gloucester County, which had 850 militia men, had by far the largest military force on the

Middle Peninsula. According to a report Colonel John Peyton sent to one of his superiors on June 19, 1781, from time to time British ships sailed into the mouth of the Piankatank River, and some of their men would come ashore on Gwynn's Island to steal livestock. Peyton also said that the British occasionally ventured up the Piankatank on plundering expeditions. He indicated that slaves continued to flee to the British and sometimes, seamen managed to slip away.[14]

Providing Pensions to Military Veterans

As early as July 1775, the Virginia assembly's delegates decided to provide pensions to men disabled by military service and unable to be self-supporting. Later in the year, they declared veterans exempt from paying "head," or capitation, taxes on themselves as tithables. The state's pension policy became more inclusive in 1777, when veterans' widows became eligible for a pension if their husbands had been in the state militia or the Continental Line. To underwrite the cost of widows' pensions, county officials were authorized to collect the funds they needed from local residents. Finally, in 1778, the General Assembly decided that permanently disabled military men could receive full pay for life and that widows could receive half of their late husbands' pensions. Meanwhile, delegates to the Continental Congress, keenly aware that recruits were needed for the Continental Line, realized that pensions and land bounties were effective incentives to enlist. The first federal pension law, enacted in 1776, extended half-pay benefits to every man who lost a limb during a military engagement or was so disabled that he was unable to earn a living; proportionate relief was offered to the partially disabled.

Despite these pension policies, Congress lacked the right to raise money, so the payment of veterans' pensions was left to the states. Land bounties were offered to officers and enlisted men who agreed to serve until the end of the war, but the amount of acreage awarded depended upon rank. Privates and non-commissioned officers were entitled to 100 acres; ensigns could receive 150 acres; lieutenants could receive 200 acres; and higher-ranking officers could receive proportionately more. General George Washington was so desperate to retain officers in the Continental service that in May 1778 Congress voted to provide them with a pension of seven years of half-pay, and enlisted men who remained in the Continental Line until the end of the war were to receive $80 each. Two years later, Congress extended officers' benefits to their widows and orphans. Finally, in 1780, members of Congress agreed to give half-pay for life to all officers who continued in service until the end of the war. Over the next several years, the pension law was changed several times, always with a focus on the disabled and their dependents.

The state of Virginia's pension policy expanded in 1779 when the legislature decided that deceased veterans' indigent parents could receive a pension and that all officers in the state militia were eligible for a land bounty—that is, 100 acres of unappropriated land. Then, in 1780, the assembly agreed to provide an allowance of corn and pork to the widows and aged parents of military veterans. However, as time went on and tax money became increasingly scarce, the state government decided to reduce the amount of support disabled veterans and their dependents were eligible for and to screen their applications more closely. At that point, county court justices were ordered to verify military veterans' disabilities in order to determine whether they should continue receiving a pension. In October 1782, the assembly enacted legislation that required all pensioners to attend musters of their county's militia. If they failed to do so, they could lose their pension unless they could prove that they were disabled. This policy remained in effect throughout the next several years. In 1792, more than 1,300 disabled Virginia veterans received pensions. All were noncommissioned officers or privates, and none received more than $5 a month. Two years later, the assembly ordered every county court to compile an annual list of qualified pensioners and send it to the governor. [15]

Some of Mathews County's Revolutionary War Veterans

Revolutionary War veterans' service claims, supported by witnesses' sworn statements, describe their military careers and disabilities. For example, when Private Gabriel Hughes of Kingston Parish appeared before Mathews County's justices on August 13, 1832, he used the family Bible to prove that he was born in 1762. Under oath, Hughes stated that he had enlisted in Captain Richard Billups' company at age 16 and had served one tour of duty before being assigned to Captain Philip Tabb, Lieutenant James Gwynn, and Ensign Houlder Hudgins. He added that Colonel John Peyton, Colonel John Page, and Major Throckmorton were his field officers while he was in the Virginia Line. Hughes said that his unit was summoned whenever British river barges ventured into local waters and that he participated in a Gloucester engagement when British Colonel Banastre Tarleton's men brutally attacked French horse soldiers. Hughes indicated that he was one of the 125 Gloucester men sent to King and Queen, New Kent, and James City Counties when General Benedict Arnold began moving up the James River. He was discharged in 1781 after the siege of Yorktown, and was seldom summoned for duty afterward. Hughes' pension application was approved, making him eligible to receive $50.66 a year. After his death, his widow, the former Mary Williams, whom he had married in 1785, continued to receive his service benefits.

George Willis, who was living in Mathews County in 1798, submitted a petition to the state legislature asking for a pension. He said that he had been in one of Colonel George Baylor's regiments of light dragoons and had been assigned to guard the life of General George Washington. He said that he was among the soldiers surrounded by the British while quartered in a barn in old Herringtown and that he received bayonet wounds, was stripped of his clothes, and was left to die. Willis said that he received some medical care and managed to recover from his wounds but was left permanently disabled and unable to be self-supporting. After submitting three applications, he received a half-pension.

Henry Hughes, when applying for a pension in 1825, said that in February 1776, while he was a cadet, he entered Captain Charles Tompkies' infantry company, which was part of the 7th Virginia Regiment. He asked the state to provide him with disability pay for his wartime service, and said that he had been transferred to the Continental command six months after he had enlisted in the Virginia militia and was promoted to ensign. Hughes said that he was discharged from the Continental army by General Washington in October 1777 on account of poor health. After he recovered, he reenlisted as a volunteer in a militia company and rose to the rank of lieutenant. Hughes indicated that he was based at Gloucester Town when the British surrendered in October 1781. His claim, though supported by a witness, was rejected.

William Armistead indicated that he had enrolled in the state militia in late 1776 in response to a summons from Sir John Peyton and said that he was under the command of Captain Robert Gayle. He stated that he had served a month at Point Comfort[16] and was summoned for duty twice in 1777 and once in 1778, each time for two to three months' service. Armistead said that in 1778, when British barges ventured into Pepper Creek, he helped to repel them. He served under Captain Peter Barnet and Colonel Boswell for three months, and said that in 1781 he had been sent to Williamsburg with Captain John Billups, to help drive off the British who were sailing up the James River.

Others presented less complicated service records. George Callis, who was in Billups' militia company, said that he enlisted shortly after Lord Dunmore's arrival at Gwynn's Island. Anthony Hudgins, a local man born in 1759, joined the army in 1776 and served several short tours under Captains John Billups, Josiah and Isaac Foster, and Robert Gayle. Hugh Hudgins, who was born in March 1764, enlisted in the military in early January 1780, and served at New Point Comfort and Gloucester. Like Anthony Hudgins, he served several short tours of duty. With the Hudgins' was George Brooks, who indicated that he had entered the service in 1776 and served at New Point Comfort and Gloucester until the end of the war. When William Callis applied for a pension on May 8, 1834, he indicated that he was age 69 and had entered the military in 1780. He said that in 1782 he had been stationed in the guard house at Cricket Hill. William Buckner, a captain and sailing master who applied for a pension, said that he spent three years in the Virginia Navy. He indicated that he was born in 1750 and had served until the end of the war, commanding both land and naval forces. At one point he became a prisoner-of-war.

Local widows also applied for pensions. In October 1835, Kemp Hudgins' widow, the former Joice Minter, told pension officials that her husband, who had served under Captain Josiah Foster, died in 1797. She said that Kemp had entered the military in 1776 and had married her in 1777. Richard Armistead's 84-year-old widow, the former Elizabeth Jarvis, applied for a pension on October 8, 1836. She said that her husband had enlisted with Captain Josiah Foster in 1778, after they had been married for eight years, and that he had served until the end of the war, mostly as a guard. It is unclear whether either woman's pension was approved.

A number of blacks, both enslaved and free, served on behalf of the American cause, and after the war some slaves were freed on account of their meritorious service. Three African-American men from Gloucester County are known to have served, and undoubtedly there were many others whose names aren't included in the written record. Emanuel Driver, a free black man who was born around 1750, enlisted in the 2nd Virginia Regiment in 1776 and was discharged in 1780 or 1781. George Monghon (Monoggon), who also indicated that he was from Gloucester County, was a seaman in the Virginia Navy.

In 1778 Ephraim Hearn (Hern), an African-American, indicated that he was born around 1745, was free, and made his living as a weaver. When applying for a pension, he said that he had been drafted as a soldier in Gloucester and had marched to Valley Forge with Captain Callohill Mennis. Hearn said that he was there for 18 months, including the infamous winter of 1777–8. On December 10, 1778, he enlisted as a private in the 1st Virginia Regiment, and he was captured by the British in Charleston, South Carolina in May 1780. He was detained for nine months. When military officials decided that he and some other prisoners-of-war would be sent overland to New York, he managed to escape and returned to Gloucester County. On March 23, 1796, he received a warrant for 200 acres of land as a bounty for his years of military service. Ephraim Hearn, who was 84, was living in Gloucester County when he applied for a federal military pension on August 8, 1829. His household included his 60-year-old wife, Molly, and their daughter, Betsy, age 20. The Hearns' possessions at the time of Ephraim's pension application included three chairs, an old table, a spinning wheel, an iron pot, a cow, a yearling, and five hogs. In 1850, a free black household in Mathews County included a 15-year-old boy named Ephraim Hearn, perhaps a descendant.[17]

A Circuitous Path to Freedom

Although documentation is scarce, it is certain that a few enslaved African-American men and women who lived in Kingston Parish fled to the British and received a certificate of freedom. Polly Cary (Carey), who was born around 1757 and belonged to Humphrey Gwyn of Gwynn's Island, said that she joined the British forces in 1776 and obtained a certificate of freedom from British General Samuel Birch. Polly, who was the mother of Jenny and Charlotte Cary, moved to Shelburne, Nova Scotia, in 1783 when the British withdrew from New York. Jenny, born in 1779, and her sister, Charlotte, born in 1782, identified themselves as mulattoes (those of mixed race) and said that they had been born within British lines and had accompanied their mother to Nova Scotia. Henry Gwyn, an African-American slave, said that he was born around 1750 and that his master also was named Henry Gwyn. He said that in 1781 he had run away and joined the British and had obtained a certificate of freedom from General Thomas Musgrave. In 1783, Gwyn, who identified himself as an ex-slave, was working for the Royal Artillery Department when he went to Port Mouton, Nova Scotia, having left New York during the evacuation. Hannah Wallace, who was born around 1761 and was one of William Armistead's slaves, said that she had left home in 1776. She too obtained a certificate of freedom from General Musgrave and went to work for the Royal Artillery Department.

Edward Hughes of Mathews County and his slave, Edward, were captured by one of the three armed frigates in British Commodore William Hotham's fleet, cruising the waters of the Chesapeake. According to Sir John Peyton, Hotham released Hughes but detained Edward, a skillful pilot. Hotham reportedly assured Hughes that he would release Edward as soon as he found a better pilot. How the slave Edward felt about this turn of events is open to speculation. A young American mariner, detained aboard the *Roebuck* while it was anchored near Gwynn's Island, testified that three runaway slaves had arrived by canoe, seeking refuge. The British promised them freedom and sent them ashore to obtain some poultry. When the men returned with the fowls, one of them brought along his wife and two children. According to the mariner, the British promised each of the runaway slaves a plantation, but detained them as rebels and treated them poorly.[18]

Mathews County Loyalists

Some Mathews County residents remained loyal to the Crown. The Rev. Thomas Feilde (Feild) began serving as Kingston Parish's minister in January 1771. Vestry records suggest that Mr. Feilde, a married man with two sons and a daughter, was a respected member of the community. However, when the American colonies broke away from England, he remained loyal to the Crown, a stance that put him at odds with most of his parishioners. On February 2, 1777, Edmund and William H. Feilde, who shared their clergyman father's loyalist views, slipped away from Kingston Parish by canoe and reached the H.M.S. *Richmond's Prize*, which was about 10 miles offshore. After a few weeks aboard the ship, the Feilde brothers found passage to London and joined British military units. On April 28, 1777, Kingston Parish's vestry (which included seven men whose patriotic views are well documented),[19] approved the Rev. Thomas Feilde's annual salary. However, on July 15, 1777, the same group of vestrymen relieved Mr. Feilde of his position and purportedly informed him "that he is no longer considered the minister of the gospel in this parish." When discharging him, they noted that "Nature teaches human beings not to nourish the viper in the bosom." The postwar petitions filed by Mr. Feilde's wife, Elizabeth, and one of his sons told a slightly different story, for they stated that the clergyman alienated the Kingston Parish vestry members by refusing to celebrate a special day of thanksgiving that Congress ordered after British General John Burgoyne's defeat at Saratoga, New York, on October 7, 1777.[20] Feilde and his wife were permitted to retire to British lines and ultimately withdrew to New York. Although she secured passage to England, he remained on Staten Island, where he died in February 1781. In 1784, Mrs. Elizabeth Feilde, then a resident of Chelsea, England, filed a compensatory claim with the British government. She not only asserted a claim to her late husband's annual salary, but also to the income he would have derived from use of the Kingston Parish glebe, part of his stipendiary support. Mrs. Feilde's claim was denied, as were those filed by her sons.[21]

When the Revolutionary War broke out, Robert Bristow, a wealthy London merchant and the great-great-grandson of immigrant Robert Bristow, owned thousands of acres of Virginia land. His 930-acre North River

Plantation, at the tip of Whites Neck, had been in the hands of his forebears since 1673.[22] Robert Bristow also owned the Black Creek plantation in Ware Neck and he was in possession of thousands of acres in Northumberland and Lancaster Counties. His letter book reveals that during much of the eighteenth century Colonel Francis Willis was responsible for managing the Bristow plantations in Kingston and Ware Parishes, as Bristow himself still lived in London. Willis advised Bristow to begin raising surplus corn, wheat, beef, and peas, saleable commodities that would generate enough income to pay the salary of one or more resident farm managers, see that Bristow's slaves were clothed, and pay the taxes that he owed. He also urged Bristow to have his slaves cultivate the land with plows rather than hoes so that his acreage would yield more substantial crops of grain. That approach, Willis proffered, would generate enough income to more than cover Bristow's investment and allow his tobacco crop to be pure profit. During the 1750s and 60s James Pasley and Francis Stubbs, who successively served as resident overseer of the Bristow properties, seem to have ignored Colonel Willis's advice even though it was based upon modern agricultural practices. Willis eventually decided that Bristow's slaves were "of such a Nature" that "if they are allowed to live Lazy, they will not complain."[23]

The Virginia assembly, in an attempt to fund the war, passed the Act of Sequestration in October 1777. It allowed the land, slaves, livestock, crops, and other property belonging to British loyalists to be confiscated and placed in the hands of specially-appointed conservators. All income derived from the loyalists' property was to be sent to the Commonwealth of Virginia's loan office. On August 6, 1779, an inquisition was held in Gloucester County, at which time the late Robert Bristow's family's representatives tried to claim compensation for his real and personal property. Their claim was dismissed and Bristow's property was allowed to escheat to the Commonwealth of Virginia. Two special commissioners sold his Gloucester County property in early October. At the time of his death, Robert Bristow was in possession of 700 acres of land, 22 slaves, 17 black cattle, 39 hogs, and five horses in Kingston and Ware Parishes. In 1789, the widowed Mary Bristow, a resident of Middlesex, England, tried to recover funds equal to the value of her late husband's plantations and slaves. The supportive documentation her legal representatives submitted on behalf of her young son established his legal right to each of the plantations he claimed, all of which had been used for the cultivation of tobacco. Mrs. Bristow's representatives claimed that the Americans had confiscated and then sold 2,000 acres of her late husband's land, along with 111 slaves and a large amount of livestock, raising more than £228,326. On November 4, 1793, Francis Willis submitted a petition to the Virginia government, asking for compensation for his work as executor or conservator of Robert Bristow's estate from 1778–80. He said that in accord with the Act of Sequestration, he was supposed to be compensated for managing Bristow's estate. He added that while he was Gloucester County's escheator, he had sold the Bristow property and conveyed the proceeds, which amounted to more than £55,824, to the state treasurer. It was likely around 1780, when Francis Willis disposed of the Bristow property, that the White family acquired additional acreage in what became known as Whites Neck.[24]

Another British loyalist who owned a plantation in Mathews County was John Randolph Grymes, a wealthy young gentleman. He was the second oldest son of the late Philip Grymes, Virginia's Receiver General and a member of the governor's council. His grandfather was John Grymes of Brandon in Middlesex County, who served as a burgess, councilor, auditor general, and receiver general. John Randolph Grymes, who was educated in England, inherited his late father's land and slaves in Gloucester, King and Queen, and Middlesex Counties, some of which acreage had belonged to his grandfather. Because of Grymes' outspoken loyalty to the king, he found himself the object of public censure in July 1776.[25] In the compensatory claims that he submitted to the British government in 1778, 1780, and 1782, he professed his loyalty to the Crown and said that had served in the military for three years. He indicated that he had attained the rank of major in the Queen's Rangers and had participated in Lord Dunmore's expedition to Virginia. Grymes stated that shortly before war broke out, he bought a 1,160-acre plantation on Gwynn's Island. Although no records associated with his purchase have come to light, Thomas Jefferson's sketch of Gwynn's Island indicates that Grymes' plantation was on the northernmost portion of the island, across from Stove (Store) Point, acreage owned by the Grymes family.[26] John Randolph Grymes, when documenting his loyalty, said that he had raised a company under Lord Dunmore to defend Gwynn's Island, the scene of combat in 1776. He said that when the British left the island, all of his personal property, including his slaves, was considered free booty. He claimed that 25 of his slaves on Gwynn's Island had been captured and sold as plunder, another 12 had died while in the army, and that 30 more had been confiscated. He also said that six of his convict servants had been taken into the army. Grymes does not seem to have been compensated for his losses, although he was paid for his military service.[27]

Dr. William Byrd Page, a younger son of councilor John Page I of North End Plantation, was a loyalist and filed a series of compensatory claims. In one of the petitions he submitted to officials in England, he said that he had gone to Scotland in late 1771 to study medicine at the University of Edinburgh and that while he was there, his father had provided him with an allowance of £100 a year. According to Dr. Page, when his father died in 1774, the family estate came into the hands of his eldest son, Mann Jr., and his financial support ended; the result was that he was eventually imprisoned for indebtedness. Dr. Page insisted that he had remained loyal to the Crown, but admitted that he had enlisted in Lord Dunmore's army in order to be released from jail. During the 1780s he continued to submit claims to British authorities and asked for funds that would enable him to return to his family in Virginia. Local tax records reveal that he eventually reached Mathews County and was living there during the 1790s.[28]

Loyalist and merchant John Wilkie, who lived on Queens Creek, attracted the attention of Gloucester County's Committee of Safety in early spring 1776. He was sent to Williamsburg and detained in the guardhouse, and two of his sailing vessels were seized by the authorities, who noted that one ship, of 1,800-tons burthen, was "particularly calculated for fast sailing." When Wilkie was put on trial in Gloucester County on April 4, 1776, he was found guilty of "giving intelligence to our enemies" and of purposefully going aboard British warships. An inventory of his goods, made during his incarceration, included a few personal items, an outfitted schooner, and a new vessel that was on the stocks and half-built. Also in Wilkie's possession were some dry goods and items that belonged to James Johnson, perhaps merchandise that was in Wilkie's store. On June 11, 1776, Wilkie's schooner and half-finished vessel, which had been advertised in the *Virginia Gazette*, were sold at auction at Robert Matthews' home in Gloucester County. Wilkie was then described as a "condemned Tory."

Wilkie went to Halifax, Nova Scotia, and in 1790 submitted a compensatory claim to British authorities. After professing his loyalty to the Crown, he said that he had lived on Queens Creek in Kingston Parish since 1772 and had owned several ships before war broke out. Wilkie indicated that in 1775, when he returned from a voyage to St. Eustatius, he learned that his brother and business partner, Thomas, had left the colony and enlisted in the military in support of the king. Wilkie stated that he had joined the British navy and become a pilot in Lord Dunmore's fleet and that the disabling wounds he received while in the navy prevented him from being self-supporting. John Wilkie's claim for compensatory damages included wartime loss of a slave, the goods in his Kingston Parish store, a 50-ton schooner, and a 55-ton schooner that was on the stocks and ready to launch.[29]

John Wilkie's brother, Thomas, also submitted a claim for wartime losses and described himself as a Kingston Parish merchant and mariner engaged in trade in the West Indies. He said that when he left Virginia, his business affairs were entrusted to his brother John and another business partner, Robert Wylie. Thomas Wilkie said that when the war began, he and Wylie joined Lord Dunmore's fleet. He claimed that he had lost a schooner and tobacco notes along with a cargo of slaves, tobacco, corn, naval goods, rum, and molasses, which together were worth more than £2,149. The losses sustained by the Wilkie brothers' business partner, Scotsman Robert Wylie, seem to have been much greater than theirs. Wylie said that before the war, he had resided on Queens Creek in Kingston Parish, where he had kept a store in partnership with Andrew Ritchie and was involved in the West Indian trade for several years, using his own vessel. However, in April 1776, he was obliged to take refuge with Lord Dunmore's fleet in Norfolk, at which time he became master or lieutenant on a succession of naval vessels. Wylie said that Dunmore's men had given one of his schooners to some black seamen, who had lost it; and he claimed that his schooner, the *John*, which he had built himself, had been seized and outfitted by the Americans, who renamed her the *Betsy* and put her to use. In 1789, Robert Wylie, then in Ayrshire, Scotland, submitted a claim for more than £365—a sum that included the loss of three schooners, dry goods, Indian corn, sugar, molasses, and some debts, probably tobacco notes. His claim, like those of the Wilkie brothers, was rejected on November 5, 1789.[30]

Other British loyalists, though not Mathews County residents, submitted claims for wartime losses they attributed to the military action on Gwynn's Island in 1776. James Agnew, a Scottish merchant who had lived at Portsmouth, reported that William Forsythe's ship was burned at Gwynn's Island. Hugh Miller of Norfolk, Virginia, said that he had joined the British navy in 1775 and was part of Lord Dunmore's fleet. He claimed that his new 50-ton sloop was destroyed at Gwynn's Island in July 1776 and his sloop, the *John,* also in British service, was lost in a gale on the Chesapeake Bay.[31]

Shipbuilding and Commerce Continue

Advertisements in the *Virginia Gazette* reveal that while the American Revolution was underway, Kingston Parish shipbuilders continued to ply their trade. On July 10, 1778, Henry Forrest, who lived on Milford Haven, announced that within three months' time he would complete construction of a large vessel with a 42-foot-long keel and a 16-foot beam. In the fall, Josiah Fowler offered to sell a slightly larger vessel that was nearing completion. This was followed by Thomas Smith notifying the public that he intended to sell a ship that was on the stocks near his home on the East River. He said that the vessel was designed to sail fast and to stow tobacco. Joseph Smith placed an advertisement in the *Virginia Gazette* in 1779 announcing that he intended to sell a newly constructed brigantine at the East River warehouse. He said that the ship, built by Matthew Gayle at the warehouse, was ready to launch and that it had a 56½-foot keel, was 20 feet in breadth, and had an 8-foot hold. Potential buyers were invited to contact the *Gazette's* publishers or Francis Willis in Gloucester. Sometimes, ships were custom-built. Joseph Billups agreed to build a boat for John Avery if Avery made an advance payment of £300 and 120 gallons of good West Indian rum, and Matthias James, a joiner, agreed to build a sloop for John Fowler.

Daring mariners continued to venture into international waters and sometimes were captured. The 15-ton ship *Whim*, which set out from

Gwynn's Island in 1778, safely reached St. Thomas but when it returned home a few months later with a cargo of wine, rum, sugar, and salt, it was captured off Chincoteague Inlet. In 1778, the High Court of the Admiralty's marshal offered to sell an almost new 40- to 50-ton sloop with a cargo of bread and flour at the East River warehouse. He indicated that Captain Richard Billups, who lived near the warehouse, had recovered the vessel near New Point Comfort. Matthew Gayle and his brother, Hunley, were among Mathews County's most renowned shipbuilders. Both men were involved in building the *Montezum*, which was described as a finely crafted vessel based in Baltimore. Although Matthew died of smallpox in 1794, Hunley, who continued the family tradition of building ships in the East River, produced the copper-clad *Orozimbo* in 1805, an exceptionally fast vessel.[32]

Another member of the Gayle family involved in the shipbuilding business was George Gayle. In 1795, he placed an advertisement in a Norfolk newspaper, trying to recover his apprentice, Richard James, who had run away.[33] Gayle was still building ships on the East River in 1807 when he announced that he had a new schooner ready to sell. An account book maintained by a member of Richard Billups's family indicates that in 1794 and 1795 John Foster and his father purchased timber and built the ship *Brilliant*, seemingly with the assistance of William Hudgins. Later, the Fosters hired shipbuilders Gabriel Miller and Augustus Digges to do some work on the vessel, and Billups's records also show that Digges's slave, Essex, was involved in the project.

After the Revolutionary War, waterborne commerce along the Atlantic Seaboard increased in importance, and news of shipwrecks or vessels that ran aground appeared in newspapers from time to time. In 1784, the *Massachusetts Spy*, published in Worcester, Massachusetts, informed the public that a ship from Ireland had been lost somewhere above New Point Comfort and that some of the vessels passengers and crew had perished. In 1790, a Philadelphia newspaper reported that William Walker and his men, who were taking a family to New Point Comfort, abandoned their passengers and sailed away in their new sloop. New Point Comfort seems to have been a popular landing site and ships often paused there when making their way up or down the Chesapeake Bay.[34]

The War Comes to a Close

In a carefully contrived diversionary stratagem, General George Washington led the British to believe that the French fleet, *en route* to North America, was planning to attack New York. Sir Henry Clinton, who succumbed to the ruse, asked the British Army's Commanding General, Charles Lord Cornwallis, for reinforcements and advised him to secure his position in the harbor at Yorktown. Meanwhile, British Admiral Thomas Graves learned that French naval forces, which had formerly held a position off the coast of Rhode Island and the Jersey Capes, were sailing southward; and he surmised that their destination was the Chesapeake. Cornwallis, convinced that the harbor between Yorktown and Gloucester Point was the only place on the Chesapeake where a line of battleships could be protected against a superior force, began moving his men into the region. Rumors ran rampant, and on August 15, a Philadelphia newspaper reported that Cornwallis's men had landed near the mouth of the York River and that they were planning to erect a strong fortification at New Point Comfort. Two weeks later, the French fleet sailed into the mouth of the Chesapeake Bay, and several ships moved inland to the mouth of the York River, blocking Cornwallis's communications and reinforcements. Although British vessels arrived off the Virginia Capes, the French vessels guarding the York remained at their station. Thus, Cornwallis and his forces were trapped. On September 30, the British abandoned their outermost earthworks and took refuge in Yorktown, which the Continental and French forces began to bombard. On October 16, Cornwallis asked to parley, and shortly thereafter came the moment of capitulation. Articles of Surrender were signed on October 19, 1781, at Yorktown and Gloucester Point with full military ceremony. Although the British proposed that loyalists not be punished "on account of having joined the British Army," the Americans felt that the matter should be decided in court. With the surrender of Cornwallis's army, the American colonies' independence was won, but another seventeen months elapsed before a formal peace treaty was signed.

Despite the surrender at Yorktown, the British occasionally caused problems. On December 9, 1782, Philip Tabb of North River informed Colonel John Page that according to Lieutenant Hudgins, six British barges carrying 300 men ventured into the Thoroughfare, a stream separating Gwynn's Island from the mainland. Some of the British landed at Richard Brooks' house and robbed him. Then, they marched to the home of a Mr. Laine (Lane), where they seized his slaves, household goods, and some wearing apparel. Lieutenant Hudgins said that he gathered 30 men and fired upon a barge that was moving up Stutts (Sluts) Creek,[35] thereby forcing the British to return to Milford Haven. Tabb told Page that his soldiers were in dire need of ammunition.

While some British troops were detained in Gloucester County as prisoners-of-war and Rochambeau and his army wintered over in Gloucester and other parts of Tidewater Virginia, no evidence has come to light suggesting that any of these men spent time in Kingston Parish. In January 1782, some Gloucester residents asked to be compensated for the horses they furnished to French troops during the military operations at Yorktown, but it is uncertain whether payment was forthcoming. At least three Kingston Parish residents requested compensation for goods and services they had furnished to the American and French Allied Army. In 1781, John Hughes asked to be paid £16.19.4 for the 730 pounds of beef and four muttons he had furnished to the army, and Thomas Hughes requested £1.10 for providing 12 days of horse service. The goods and services supplied by Edward Hughes, who requested £152.7.6, were much more valuable than those of his brothers, for he had provided the military with 596 pounds of corn and his boats were repeatedly used to transport brandy, bacon, corn, oats, and shot for the army. He also indicated that his cart and team were used to haul a large quantity of oats.[36]

Changes in Government

In May 1779, the General Assembly noted that county officials were inconsistent when compiling land tax records, for some of them expressed assessed values in currency while others stated the equivalent in gold or silver. There also was concern about tax commissioners failing to assign land its true fair market value. Henceforth, if a county's assessors disagreed about the assigned value of a specific parcel, those values had to be averaged. In 1780, assembly members decided that all land, with the exception of urban lots and property that contained ferry landings, mills, mines, and so on would be assessed on the basis of its fair market value and physical characteristics—that is, whether it was high, low, marshy, hilly, and so on. In November 1781, the General Assembly reminded county officials that land was to be assessed without regard to structural improvements. Thus, it did not matter whether a landowner's acreage contained an upscale dwelling or a small farmhouse; both would pay the same amount of tax. This policy was in effect until the assembly changed the law in 1819. When the General Assembly convened in October 1782, delegates noted that there were vast differences in the values that Virginia's tax assessors were assigning to the types of land in their counties. In an attempt to overcome this inequity, the assembly divided the state into four large tax districts, each of which shared common attributes and soils of similar quality. Then, they assigned a standard monetary value per acre to comparable soil types within each district. Mathews County's predecessor, Gloucester County, was grouped with other Tidewater counties. By law, county clerks of court and the clerk of the General Court had to provide local tax commissioners with a list of the properties that had changed hands during the previous year.[37]

In October 1779, the General Assembly's members decided to apply personal property taxes to all white males who were age 21 or older with the exception of those serving in the military. All slaves were to be taxable except for the aged or infirm. The tax code was modified from time to time and from 1782 on, the owners of wheeled vehicles, such as coaches, riding chairs, wagon stages, and chariots were taxed; this was the forerunner of today's personal property tax.

By May 1780, Virginia's delegates to the assembly realized that the tax code they had adopted hadn't raised the amount of revenue that was needed to pay for the war. Therefore, they decided that in 1781, 1782, 1783, and 1784, they would impose a tax of one shilling per window on those who owned buildings with glass windows. They also agreed that if insufficient revenues were raised, they would sell some public property, specifically the colonial governor's palace and capitol in Williamsburg, some acreage in James City and York Counties, and some property on the Eastern Shore. The legislature decided that ordinaries should be licensed and that the owners of billiard tables or stud horses should pay a special tax. As currency was in short supply, assembly members agreed that taxes could be paid in various types of marketable agricultural commodities, such as wheat, rye, oats, barley, corn, and bacon. Despite this accommodation, many Tidewater Virginia households found it hard to make ends meet and to keep their taxes from falling into arrears during the postwar period.

Kingston Parish's elite do not appear to have had that problem, for in 1783, Sir John Peyton paid taxes on 119 slaves and William Armistead was taxed on 86. Thomas Smith and Mordecai Throckmorton had around 50 slaves. John Armistead's estate; John Billups Sr.; Dudley Cary; James Davis; Joseph Digges; John Elliott Sr.; Hugh, John, and Mary Hayes; Gabriel Hughes; Armistead and John Smith; Thomas Tabb; and Samuel Williams were taxed on 20 to 30 slaves apiece. The majority of Kingston Parish's slaveholders had fewer than ten slaves, and some people owned none at all. Although Virginia's elected officials continued to grapple with paying off war debt, they yielded to public pressure in 1784 and deemed that only slaves who were age 16 or older would be taxable. In 1785 Gloucester County Sheriff John Peyton and sheriffs from other localities asked the assembly not to penalize them for failing to collect taxes, citing the "scarcity of money and the Poverty of the people." However, the delegates apparently weren't sympathetic, for they sued Peyton in the General Court. He, in turn, asked Governor Edmund Randolph to suspend the judgement filed against him until he could undertake proceedings against his deputies.

In April 1787, Gloucester County's inhabitants sent a petition to the General Assembly, stating that at the close of the recent war, paper money had little or no value and that very little tobacco could be raised. They contended that most people's land, cleared for many years, was worn out and unproductive. They said that the winter of 1784 had been especially severe and had reduced the number of cattle and that corn had been in short supply for two or three years. They noted that shipbuilding, which had formerly provided at least 400 people with employment, was at a standstill, and that ship's carpenters, frustrated with the lack of business, had started taking their timber to Norfolk, selling it for a fraction of its worth. The petitioners closed by saying that in light of their current circumstances, they were unable to pay their taxes unless they sold their land or slaves. The legislators ignored their plea and decided that as of October 1787, all slaves who were age 12 or older were to be considered taxable personal property. This change prompted some backlash and in November 1787 a group of Gloucester County citizens submitted a petition objecting to the change. They said that they were willing to pay a tax on adult male slaves, who were income-producing, but they objected to being taxed upon women and children, whose support, they claimed, was more of a burden than a benefit. Instead, they recommended the imposition of a tax on luxury items. The General Assembly finally adopted that strategy in 1814.[38]

Protecting the Homeland: A Need for Military Defense

After the close of the American Revolution, state officials were concerned that the British might return and attack their breakaway colonies. Virginia was still divided into the military districts, established in 1775; and county militia units, which mustered in their home communities, elected their own officers, whose names were submitted to the county court. However, in a holdover from the colonial era, the justices had to seek confirmation from the governor, who actually commissioned the officers. Most county justices served as high-ranking militia officers and held other important government positions. Thus, local political power was concentrated in men who were relatively affluent and influential in their communities, just as it had been before the war. Sometimes, the members of militia companies and county justices wrangled over the names that were be submitted to the governor as officer candidates.[39] In March 1785, Lieutenant Colonel John Page of Rosewell and other community leaders were asked to recommend field officers for the Gloucester militia and to ascertain how many men were members of the militia. Several months later, Page reported that the county lieutenant, Sir John Peyton, had failed to provide militia returns, but he estimated that the militia had "increased to 1000 men." Page indicated that Meacham Boswell held the rank of major and that there was support for designating James Baytop a lieutenant colonel, and Mordecai Throckmorton, Thomas Buckner, and John Hughes as majors. He added that if those promotions were approved, they would have good officers for two battalions.

During the first year or two that Mathews County was in existence, it didn't have as many militia companies as Virginia counties were supposed to have. By June 1794, that situation had been rectified and Mathews had the obligatory eight companies of militia. The Mathews militia included two companies of light infantry, and were comprised 798 free white males who were age 16 or older. All of these men were part of Regiment 61 of the 14th Brigade in Division 4. The Mathews militia was inadequately armed and in 1795, when a suspected privateer entered the East River, Colonel William Lindsay sent word to the governor that his cutter was unfit for duty. A week later, H. Young reported that he would try to prevent the privateer from sailing, although the militias of Gloucester and Mathews Counties lacked arms and ammunition. Upon further investigation, Young informed the governor that the schooner was displaying the French national flag and that its captain lived in Portsmouth. Young said that although schooners from Baltimore had arrived in Mathews with ammunition, his men still lacked weaponry. Maintaining the state's defenses was an ongoing problem, and in 1798, Larkin Smith informed the governor that a troop of cavalry couldn't be raised in Mathews County. Finally, in March 1801, state officials sent 55 stand of arms to Mathews County; they were delivered them to Robert Shields of York County, custodian of his military district's weaponry. In 1807 Henry Lee asked whether the militia of Gloucester and Mathews Counties should be exempt from the draft. This followed close on the heels of Mathews citizens' formally protesting the way the commander of the British ship *Leopold* had treated the crew of the U.S. frigate *Chesapeake*.[40]

Early Postal Service

In 1781, the United States Congress, which anticipated ratification of the Articles of Confederation, set up three departments of government. By that time, the Post Office Department, established in 1775, was already functional. Cartographer Christopher Colles, who in 1789 made maps of the roads between Annapolis and Yorktown, charted the routes that post riders were to follow, utilizing the routes that Rochambeau's Army used in 1781 and 1782. Colles's maps suggest that no overland postal route passed through the Middle Peninsula in 1789. The next decade brought improvement, and on April 9, 1798, a group of Mathews County citizens signed a yearlong contract with Richard Billups, who agreed to furnish a horseback rider who would transport the mail from the post office in Gloucester to Henry Respess's tavern in what was then Mathews Courthouse. The post rider was supposed to arrive in Gloucester around the time the northern mail was delivered and give the mail from Mathews to the northbound rider. By 1809, there was a post office at North End or the crossroads community called North. Not unexpectedly, there were occasional complaints about local mail service. In February 1810, John Patterson placed an advertisement in the Richmond newspaper, *The Enquirer*, asking postmasters to see whether a communication he had sent to two men in Philadelphia had ended up in their offices' cache of "dead letters." He said that the letter he had sent included $610 worth of bank notes. In 1835, there was a post office at Belle Isle, and one was still located at North End.[41]

The 1790 Census and the State Enumeration

Although the original copies of the first census in 1790 for Virginia were burned during the War of 1812, the tax lists that county officials compiled from 1782 to 1785 contain more information than such records usually provide.[42] These documents, commonly known as state enumerations, are available for only 39 Virginia counties, one of which is Gloucester. The state enumeration for 1784, which is comprehensive, sheds a great deal of light on the area's built environment. When Thomas Smith of Kingston Parish, James Hubbard of Petsworth Parish, James Seawell of Abingdon Parish, and Mordecai Throckmorton of Ware Parish gathered information on Gloucester County, they identified household heads by name and noted the number of whites and blacks associated with each household. The state enumeration for 1784 also includes the number of dwellings and other buildings attributed to each household head. Such dependencies would have included kitchens, dairies, schoolhouses, store houses, barns, stables, tobacco houses, workshops, and slave quarters.[43] For example, in 1784, Kingston Parish tax official Thomas Smith noted that there were two dwellings on John Eddens Sr.'s acreage.

The number of buildings on a landowner's property usually reflected socioeconomic status. George Wooden (Wooding), a man of modest means who owned 30 acres on Woodas Creek, had a dwelling and only one dependency. In marked contrast, the 3,000-acre estate of the late William Armistead of Hesse included a main dwelling plus a remarkable 33 other buildings and Thomas Smith Sr. had 19. Thanks to the state enumeration, we know that the majority of Kingston Parish's landowners had a dwelling and three or four outbuildings, although some people had more. For example, the plantations of Robert Armistead, Benjamin Bragg, William Digges Sr., Ambrose Callis, Dorothy and George Dudley, John Elliott Sr., Hugh Gwyn, Humphrey Hudgins Sr., Joseph Knight, Letitia Ransone, and the late John Dixon's estate had between six and eight outbuildings apiece. On the other hand, James Nutall and Thomas Tabb were credited with 10 outbuildings, Gabriel Hughes had 13, and Robert Cary and Ambrose Merchant had 16. Some people were credited with structures even though they were not listed in the tax rolls. This raises the possibility that they were tenants or occupied property owned by a family member. Also, they simply may have failed to pay their taxes, a relatively common occurrence in the wake of the American Revolution. In nearby Ware Parish, the distribution of wealth was much the same.

Although the antebellum court records of Gloucester and Mathews County are fragmentary, a handful of eighteenth-century wills and inventories, preserved in collections of private papers, provide insight into the material culture of some Kingston Parish households. In 1781, when William Lilly's executors made an inventory of his personal property, they noted that he had 22 slaves and a substantial quantity of livestock. Also in Lilly's possession at the time of his death were books on husbandry, a grammar book, three Bibles, four prayer books, and some other reading materials. His modest household furnishings included two tables, a chest, a pair of candle sticks, seven featherbeds, twenty chairs with leather seats, and four that had rush seats. The Lilly family had use of a kettle, a sugar box, dozens of pewter plates, jugs, dishes, and basins; they also had five silver teaspoons, a luxury item. On hand were numerous utilitarian items such as steelyards, a flax wheel, three spinning wheels, cards for processing flax and hemp, iron pots, a spice mortar and pestle, a grindstone, saws, axes, wedges and mawls, cooper's tools, sheep sheers, three plows, a large quantity of salt for preserving meat, 300 pounds of tobacco, a gun, a sword, a pistol, and a riding chair. In contrast, the estate of William Morris, inventoried in 1795, included the usual utilitarian items that were essential to managing a household and running a farm, but the decedent also was credited with two walnut tables, a desk, and a sideboard, eight pictures, eight silver tablespoons, and other items indicating that he was a man of means. In 1784 Morris had a dwelling and four outbuildings at New Point Comfort and by 1791 he was in possession of 343½ acres.[44]

Disestablishment of the State Church and Impact on Kingston Parish

As early as October 16, 1776, when Virginia's General Assembly held its very first session, 10,000 of Virginia's male freeholders presented a 125-page petition, asking for disestablishment of the Church of England and religious equality under the law. This manuscript initiated a lengthy public debate over the relationship between church and state and whether the church should have public support. James Madison, who became our fourth president, circulated his "Memorial and Remonstrance against Religious Assessments," which received widespread support. The act that Virginia's General Assembly passed in October 1784, authorizing the incorporation of the Protestant Episcopal Church, maintained parish vestries' taxing authority and designated them as trustees with the right to hold and manage church-owned property such as glebes and houses of worship. This legislation produced backlash and registered voters in many Virginia counties called for its repeal. Some Kingston Parish members, who were present in 1785 when the Protestant Episcopal Church of Virginia held its first General Convention, filed a petition in July 1786, urging assembly members not to repeal the law. Nonetheless, when the legislature convened in October, the Statute of Religious Freedom became law, abolishing the State Church and denying it the right of general taxation. Separation between church and state was achieved thanks to that legislation. The new law was not applicable to actively used Episcopal churches, and vestries were allowed to retain the parish glebe until the incumbent clergyman died or moved away.

Under the Statute of Religious Freedom, much of the former State Church's real estate reverted to the Commonwealth of Virginia and could be sold as surplus property. Funds yielded by the sale of parish-owned real estate were to be given to county Overseers of the Poor, who had taxing authority and were responsible for providing public welfare.[45]

Kingston Parish vestry minutes, though fragmentary, reveal that church officials leased the parish glebe to the highest bidder at a public auction and allowed the glebe's slaves to be hired out. They were probably allowed to do this because the incumbent clergyman was alive but wasn't occupying the glebe. According to nineteenth-century church historian Bishop William Meade, the Rev. Robert Read became Kingston Parish's minister after the Rev. Thomas Feilde's hasty departure in 1777, and in 1784, the Rev. Thomas Hopkinson replaced Read.[46] The vestry hired the Rev. James McBride in November 1786, a month after the Statute of Religious Freedom was passed, and authorized him to take possession of the glebe on January 1, 1787. During 1787 Kingston Parish's vestry decided to have both of its churches repaired, along with the buildings on the glebe, perhaps using rent money to cover the cost. On August 19, 1792, the Rev. Armistead Smith of Mathews County, who had just been ordained by the Protestant Episcopal Church, was hired by Kingston Parish's vestry, which continued to place the glebe in the hands of tenants. In 1793, it rented for £3 a year; and tenants were allowed to pay with cash, agricultural commodities, labor, or a combination of all three options. For example, John Owen, a cobbler, paid part of his rent by making shoes, probably for the parish poor. Among those who are known to have rented portions of the glebe between 1793 and 1798 were John Owen, John Brownley, James Smith, James Jarvis, Joseph Billups Sr., John Hugget, Joseph Taber Jr., and John Callis. By 1812, when "the old church in Kingston Parish" again was in need of repairs, 28 parishioners pledged their support; and Christopher Tompkins, Sands Smith, Dr. S. Sheppard, Anthony Hudgins, and Armistead Smith agreed to collect the funds.

Receipts preserved in the Billups Papers at the College of William and Mary indicate that during the 1790s, Mathews County's Overseers of the Poor paid local people to provide room and board to orphans, the elderly, and the infirm, just as parish vestries had done in the past. In 1795, they paid John Christian for procuring planks and making a coffin for Elizabeth Peed and they bound out poor orphans and children from impoverished families. The poor had to meet certain residency requirements, just as they did before the war. Despite the Disestablishment, state officials continued to take a role in regulating the clergy and in monitoring public morality. Virginia's first "blue law" was passed in 1792, making it illegal to work on Sunday. The General Assembly also began licensing clergy, who could not be arrested for civil causes if they had taken an oath to the Commonwealth of Virginia and were preaching publicly or performing worship services. It also became illegal to disrupt congregations who had assembled for religious worship, although sometimes those gatherings were fraught with emotion. The legislature, displaying further interest in moral rectitude, took a stand against swearing, public drunkenness, and adultery.[47]

The Ravages of Wind and Weather

During the 1780s, Tidewater Virginia was struck by a series of storms. On October 8, 1783, a hurricane that moved up the coast produced sustained high winds, and in Norfolk the tide reportedly rose as much as 25 feet. Two years later, another storm severely impacted Virginia and North Carolina. Although newspaper accounts fail to describe how these weather incidents affected the countryside bordering the Mobjack Bay and the nearby coastline, in Norfolk almost all of the ships in the harbor were driven from their moorings, numerous warehouses were destroyed, and rising tides seeped into the lower stories of houses near the waterfront. In nearby Portsmouth, the town was flooded and at least 30 vessels were driven ashore. A third hurricane tore through eastern Virginia in late July 1788. This coastal storm, which passed south and west of Bermuda, brought high winds that were accompanied by high tides and struck Portsmouth, Norfolk, Hampton, and Yorktown as it made its way northward. A writer in Norfolk said that the rising tide didn't reach the heights attained in 1785, but strong winds felled trees, destroyed houses and fences, and leveled crops. Sir John Peyton, whose property was in Kingston Parish, sent a letter to the governor, saying that the tide reached a depth of six feet in some local residents' houses and several people were drowned. He added that crops and livestock were lost and that the "damage exceeds anything I ever heard of in this part of the world." He added that tidal floodwaters had impregnated agricultural fields with so much salt that he doubted that "they will produce anything for some years to come."[48]

Broadening the Path to Freedom

During the American Revolution, substantial numbers of Americans came to realize that slavery was inconsistent with the doctrines upon which they based their struggle for independence. In May 1782, Virginia's General Assembly broke new ground by passing a law that enabled slaveholders to emancipate their slaves. A slave's owner could free a slave by bequest or could execute a deed of manumission that was entered into the records of the county court. All slaves freed under the new law were to be given copies of their deeds of emancipation or the wills under which they were freed. This documentation was critically important, for former slaves had to carry it with them whenever they left their home county. Anyone freeing a slave who was over the age of 45 or of unsound body or mind had to provide him or her with support and maintenance. The same rules applied to male ex-slaves who were under the age of 21 or females under age 18. Former slaves who failed to pay their personal property taxes or any other taxes they owed could be hired out until they had satisfied their debt. In October 1783, the General Assembly decided to free slaves who had served in the military, for most delegates agreed that anyone who had faithfully completed his term of enlistment and "contributed towards the establishment of American liberty and independence" was entitled to "enjoy the blessings of freedom." Slaves also could be freed on account of performing meritorious service if the General Assembly approved.

All of these laws were on the books in February 1794 when testator Ezekiel Lane of Mathews County freed the slaves on his home tract: Tom, Ruth, Kate, Guy, Henry, Isaac, Abram, Princess, and Nanny and all of her children. He asked his executors to give Tom and the children he had had with Ruth five barrels of corn, a hundred pounds of pork, a cow, and a calf. The slave named Nanny and her children stood to receive five barrels of corn, and Abram was to get one barrel. Lane did not free Bob, a slave living on his Point of Woods tract at Gwynn's Island, nor did he free Ben, who was living at New Point Comfort.[49] A woman called Sall (Sally), freed under the will of someone named Callis, began paying taxes on 25 acres in 1798. In 1801, she was joined by a woman named Alice, who also had been part of the Callis estate. By 1806 the two women were credited with 35 acres. Tax records for 1821 indicate that their land, which was on Bandy Ridge, about two miles southeast of the courthouse, lacked structural improvements; however, their building or buildings may have been so insubstantial that the assessor considered them uninhabitable.

Thanks to passage of the emancipation laws, during the 1780s and 90s an estimated 20,000 Virginia slaves were freed. At first, many people seemed to favor giving slave owners the right to free their slaves, even though it ran contrary to tradition. However, in time there was a backlash of public opinion, for those uninterested in emancipating their slaves were convinced that newly freed blacks were a disruptive influence. In 1788, the General Assembly enacted legislation prohibiting the importation of slaves. The abolition of primogeniture and entail in 1785 was intended to increase younger heirs' property rights and to give a testator the right to bequeath his real and personal property to his heirs of choice. Although the new inheritance laws broke up Virginia's largest landed estates, they led to further disruption of slave families whose members were distributed to various heirs. For example, on February 1, 1798, when Edmund (Edmond) Borum made his will, he bequeathed his slaves to his widow, son, and daughters, and named his grandchildren as residual heirs. In a way, making slave ownership more diffuse broadened public support for slavery.

In 1791, Mathews County tax officials began listing the names of free black and racially mixed household heads who were of tithable age and had paid their personal property taxes.[50] Some people's names appeared inconsistently, probably because they were unable to pay what they owed, a circumstance that put them at risk of being re-enslaved. Richard Cook (Cooke), Robert Peters, and three members of the Driver family (Emanuel, John, and William) were identified as free blacks in 1792. Emanuel Driver had been freed on account of his service during the Revolutionary War. The names of Edmund and Sukey Driver, perhaps his kin, appeared for the first time in 1795. Cook may have been able to make some economic progress, for he paid taxes on a horse. As time went on, tax officials began noting by whom a former slave had been freed and whether the manumission was the result of a bequest. For example, in 1798 the assessor noted that Kitt had been freed on account of Callis's will. By 1803, Joe, who had been part of the Tabb estate, had been freed, and slaves named Primus and Tom were freed under the terms of Ezekiel Lane's will. In 1805, William Anderton, William Buckhannon, Francis and Richard Cooke, Edward and John Driver, Charles King, John Manly (Manley), Robert Peters, David Ware, and a man named Ephraim were identified as free blacks or mulattoes, as were Abraham (Abram) and Primus. William Buckhannon, a mulatto, paid taxes on a horse and one slave who was age 16 or older. While he could technically be classified as a slaveholder, the slave attributed to his household most likely was a family member he had purchased but had no legal right to free.[51]

In early June 1792, a group of Mathews County citizens sent a petition to the governor, asking for weapons that could be used as a show of force or to suppress a rebellion among local slaves. The petitioners claimed that they were defenseless and that "the late insurrection on the Eastern Shore" had alarmed most of the counties, especially those with large numbers of slaves.[52] On account of the rumors of unrest, when the General Assembly met later in the year, new restrictions were imposed on ex-slaves. For example, all free blacks and mulattoes were obliged to register with officials of the county or city in which they lived and had to specify when and by whom they had been emancipated or whether they were born free. A certificate of registration, valid for three years, was to be given to each free black, who had to obtain a new copy from the clerk of court every year for a fee of 25 cents. Free blacks were required to have their certificates of registration with them at all times, and anyone hiring a free black without one was subject to a fine. The county clerk of court was supposed to record descriptive information about every free black he registered, and no free people of African descent were to enter the state of Virginia unless they were employed as servants or were working aboard naval vessels. As time went on, anti-manumission sentiments grew, and in December 1796, the legislature passed an act specifying that if a master took a slave to a state where slavery was illegal and then brought the same individual back to Virginia, that person still would be considered enslaved.[53]

The Formation of Mathews County

On November 11, 1790, a group of 123 white men in Kingston Parish sent a petition to the House of Delegates, asking that Gloucester County be divided. They said that most of the parish's inhabitants lived nearly 40 miles from the county courthouse. Because the majority did not own horses, they had to walk to the county seat or "resque [*sic*] their Lives often over a wide & dangerous Bay in cannoes." Moreover, in the wintertime, "their roads are rendered almost Impassable oweing to the Lowness of their Lands." The petitioners added that Gloucester County's justices had so many cases to process that they could "scarce go half over their docket," even though they sat in court for six days each quarter. They proposed that the new county's boundaries be coterminous with Kingston Parish and proffered that "this Division is the ardent prayer of Numbers" and lacked opponents. Just over a month later, the General Assembly endorsed the petitioners' recommendation, and agreed that separation would become effective on May 1, 1791. However, instead of using colonial Kingston Parish's westernmost boundary line, i.e., the North River's *easternmost* branch and Wadinger Creek, to separate the new county from Gloucester, they chose the river's *westernmost* branch (Burke Mill Stream) and Muddy Creek, now a nameless stream just west of Holland Point. They named Mathews County after Thomas Mathews of Norfolk, Virginia, Speaker of the House of Delegates and a key sponsor of the legislation that had led to the new county's formation.[54]

Mathews County's monthly court was scheduled to meet on the second Monday of each month and quarterly courts were to be held in March, May, August, and November of each year. The first group of county justices or commissioners of the peace, appointed by the governor, were told to convene on the first court day after Mathews County came into existence—that is, on Monday, May 9, 1791. They were to meet at the home of Thomas Williams, one of the newly appointed justices, who lived near the East River warehouse. At that first court meeting, each justice was required to take an oath of office and post a bond, guaranteeing that he would fulfill his duties. The justices were authorized to appoint a qualified clerk of court, but the governor, with his council's advice, was to select the county's first sheriff, who was to hold office for one year. Afterward, the sheriffry was to rotate among the justices. During Mathews County's first year of existence, Gloucester County's sheriff was supposed to collect taxes, just as he usually would, and Gloucester's justices were to complete all of the legal cases associated with the new jurisdiction's territory. Mathews County was kept in the same judicial and senatorial districts as Gloucester County.

One of Mathews County's justices' first—and most important—duties was to select a site as the new county's seat of government, but they were to defer that decision until a majority of the justices were present. Because the courthouse was supposed to be close to Mathews County's geographic center, the justices chose a site at the head of Put In Creek that was accessible by water, but also close to the intersection of two major roads, the forerunners of Routes 198 and 14. This centralized location gave county residents ready access to the courthouse and other public buildings. A fragmentary plat reveals that during the late 1760s, Wilkerson (Wilkinson) Hunley had some entailed land that straddled the head of Put In Creek.[55] Although primogeniture lost legal status in 1785, Hunley's descendants still owned property in 1791.[56] To the south of the Hunley acreage and also on the east side of Put In Creek were the holdings of the Davis, Respess, and Plummer families.[57] On the east side of the main road (Main Street) were tracts that belonged to the James, Davis, and Soper (Soaper) families.

Until a county courthouse was built, Mathews County's justices had the right to convene as a monthly court wherever they saw fit. Although records associated with those first meetings are almost nonexistent, on April 18, 1793, the justices, convening as a court of claims, decided to pay Edward James £25 for the use of his house; this suggests that the first court sessions were held in his home. Simultaneously, William Plummer, a licensed tavern-keeper from at least 1791 to 1797, was paid £1 for victualing a prisoner who was being detained, an indication that his business establishment was in the immediate vicinity of the newly chosen county seat.[58]

In October 1792, when the General Assembly convened, its members made changes to the laws regulating the functions of county government and specified the types of public facilities counties were to have. Each county was to have a sturdily constructed courthouse that was fabricated of stone, brick, or timber and kept in good repair at all times. There also had to be a common jail (or debtors prison) and a prison for criminals that was "well secured with iron bars, bolts and locks."[59] County justices were ordered to purchase two acres on which all of these public buildings were to be situated, and they had to erect a whipping post, stocks, and a pillory. County justices could have a ducking stool built, if they so desired. In accordance with the 1792 law, Mathews County's original courthouse green would have encompassed two acres. Property transfers that occurred during the early-to-mid nineteenth century reveal that the two-acre courthouse lot enveloped the green as it is currently defined but it also extended further east, abutting the west side of Main Street.[60]

The First Courthouse

On October 8, 1792, Richard Billups, who appears to have been acting as a general contractor, received £80 as part of the funds levied for building the county courthouse. A month later, the sheriff was authorized to pay Billups an additional £65 toward courthouse construction. These payments came shortly after the General Assembly specified the types of buildings each county seat was to have. In November 1793 Billups returned £20, part of the funds he had received, probably because his work was incomplete. Construction seems to have continued during 1794, and in May 1795 Billups paid John Steder (Stedder), a Kingston Parish resident and probable subcontractor, a total of £2.5. Specifically, Steder received £1.1 for applying plaster to the courthouse's interior walls, nine shillings more for whitewashing the interior, and another six shillings for his work in lathing and in laying bricks. The first meeting known to have been held in the Mathews County courthouse occurred on April 2, 1795.

A study undertaken by architectural historians and the College of William and Mary's Center for Archaeological Research determined, on the basis of architectural and archaeological evidence, that Mathews County's first courthouse (the one built in the 1790s) no longer exists, and that it was replaced by the structure currently known as the "old courthouse." In fact, a text that appeared in the Congressional Record for March 24, 1834, makes reference to a meeting that was held on February 10 in Mathews County's "new and spacious court-house" which was "crowded to excess." Joseph Martin's *Gazetteer*, published in 1836, also made reference to "the new C.H.," indicating that the building was recently built. The Mathews County Courthouse Square is on the National Register of Historic Places.[61]

Mathews County's Earliest Public Officials and Their Duties

From the close of the American Revolution until the mid-nineteenth century, the responsibilities of Virginia's county court justices differed little from their colonial counterparts. They heard civil suits, held preliminary hearings in criminal cases scheduled for trial in the circuit court, issued tavern licenses, naturalized aliens, and decided whether freed slaves should be allowed to remain in the county. They also had overall responsibility for seeing that local roads were kept in usable condition and that the poor received some assistance in the form of public welfare. Although relatively few of Mathews County's antebellum court records survive, executor's bonds and fragmentary documents scattered among collections of private papers provide us with some information about Mathews' first public officials. For example, it is certain that in 1791, when the county became a functional entity, Thomas Williams and Thomas Tabb were among the several men that Governor Beverley Randolph designated justices of the monthly court, with Tabb being appointed as Mathews County's first sheriff. The justices themselves chose John Cary as the clerk of court, a position he held until 1794, and Cary's deputy clerk was C. (Christopher) Pryor. In accordance with the law, the office of sheriff rotated among the justices. Therefore, in 1792, the sheriffry passed from Thomas Tabb to Thomas Smith, and George Guthrie, a tavern-keeper, became the deputy sheriff. Richard Billups, who oversaw construction of the county's first courthouse, served as a justice in 1792, 1793, and 1794; and he may have also held office in 1791.[62] In 1793, Richard Jones became deputy clerk of court, and Thomas Tabb was returned to office as sheriff. By 1795, John Patterson, a Revolutionary War veteran, had replaced John Cary as clerk of court and served until at least 1799.

Surviving chancery documents disclose the names of the men who served as justices of Mathews County's monthly court during 1795: Francis Armistead, William Buckner, Dudley Cary, Hunley Gayle,[63] Mordecai Gregory, Richard Gregory, Houlder Hudgins, Armistead Smith, Thomas Smith Sr., and Thomas Smith Jr. Hunley Gayle maintained an account book in which he noted what he spent for breakfast and grog at a tavern. If he bought food and drink at the county seat, he would have patronized the tavern owned by William Plummer or that of his competitor, Henry Respess. In 1796, Thomas Tabb and John and Dudley Cary were joined by a new justice, James Van Bibber. By 1797, Richard Gregory had become sheriff with Richard Ayres as his deputy. Other Mathews justices included Milton S. Glasscock, John Smith, and James Spark. Glasscock was sheriff during 1798 and was succeeded by William H. Hudgins.

One of the first cases the newly established county's justices tried was that of William Smith and John and Emanuel Driver, Mathews County residents who were charged with burglary. All three men were convicted and were given the death sentence by the judge of the district court, whose seat was in Williamsburg. On November 25, 1791, a Philadelphia newspaper reported that the accused criminals had been executed.

On Thursday, April 2, 1795, when a court of oyer and terminer (which had the right to try capital crimes) convened at the Mathews County courthouse, William Respess's slave, George, was accused of breaking into Leaven Gayle's storehouse on March 7. Justices William Buckner, Dudley Cary, Holder Hudgins, Armistead Smith, and Thomas Smith Jr. heard the case against George and decided his fate. Although he pled not guilty, he was convicted and sentenced to be hanged "at the common gallows" on May 1. His value, the sum his owner was to be paid if he was executed, was set at £80. As it turned out, George's life was spared as "an object of mercy," which meant that he was eligible for a reprieve by the governor.

On April 21, 1795, another slave was put on trial in Mathews County. This time, a court of oyer and terminer was held at the request of Richard Gregory, and the same justices were summoned. A male slave named Currell, who belonged to Benjamin Marable, was accused of breaking into Leaven Gayle's storehouse on the night of March 14. Although Currell, whose value was set at $300, pled not guilty and a slave named Matt was sworn in and testified on his behalf, he was found guilty; and he was sentenced to be hanged on May 22. However, because Currell was known to have been of "good character previous to his committing the aforesaid offence," his case was referred to the governor for a possible pardon.

In 1805, Elizabeth, the pregnant widow of Richard Respess Jr., sued her late husband's executor, Richard Billups, in a particularly acrimonious case that dragged on for more than a decade and ended up in the District Court in Williamsburg. However, most of the court cases brought before Mathews County's justices involved much more mundane matters, for the docket was usually filled with petty disputes and other routine proceedings. For example, in January 1818 John Patterson tried to recover funds from Thomas W. Norman, who lived out-of-state, and named as defendants several local men who were renting Norman's land. The court decided the case in Patterson's favor and authorized trustee Francis Armistead to collect the rent money as it came due and to sell Norman's personal property, which included slaves Minny and Randall, his livestock, a canoe, and an ox cart.[64]

The New County Seat

Relatively little is known about the Mathews County seat's earliest years. However, the public house of William Plummer, who provided food to a prisoner in 1793, was located there and was still entertaining guests in 1798, when it was run by his widow, Sarah E. Plummer, a licensed tavern-keeper. The Plummers' tavern was on the west side of Main Street and the south side of Route 198, near the intersection later known as Hyco Corner. Christopher Tompkins eventually purchased the Plummer lot, which was located just north of his store. Licensed tavern-keeper Henry Respess's ordinary was also at the county seat, probably on his two-acre lot on the east side of Main Street near the 30 acres Respess had acquired from the Sopers. In 1798, officials decided to have the incoming mail delivered to Respess's tavern. After his death around 1809, the executor or administrator of his estate rented the tavern to one or more tenants. In 1818, Thomas Edwards, who married Respess's daughter, Lucy Ann, and became guardian of his underage sister-in-law, Mary Respess, sought the General Assembly's permission to sell the decedent's property, which consisted of his tavern and 30 acres of adjoining land. Edwards acknowledged that there should be a public house at the county seat, but contended that the Respess property's only real value lay in its improvements: a large, "dilapidated and ruinous" frame house "originally built of bad materials." He claimed that the structure wasn't worth repairing and that the rent the tavern generated, the Respess orphans' only source of income, was on the decline. A group of Mathews County citizens endorsed Edwards's request to sell the property. However, the legislature did not agree, and seems to have ordered Edwards to improve the Respess heirs' land, which in 1820 had $800 worth of buildings. By 1820, Thomas Edwards had begun purchasing licenses for the tavern he kept at Mathews Courthouse, probably in a refurbished or newly constructed building erected on his late father-in-law's property. As late as 1828, the land and its improvements associated with Henry Respess's estate were still attributed to his heirs.[65]

In 1785, the General Assembly began requiring tavern-keepers to procure a license from the county court and it became illegal "to sell by retail, wine, beer, cyder, or rum, brandy, or other spirituous liquor, or a mixture thereof" in "any booth, arbour or stall." County courts could grant annual licenses to those thought "able to provide for the accommodation of travellers, and in such places as are most convenient for them." Gambling was not permitted; and the prices tavern-keepers could charge for room and board, alcoholic beverages, stabling, and pasturing were set by the county court. Those fees were to be posted in plain view in a public room "not more than six feet above the floor." Perhaps to discourage habitual drunkenness, tavern-keepers were prohibited from selling more than 25 shillings' worth of liquor a year to anyone who lived within a 20-mile radius of the tavern. Moreover, tavern-keepers weren't allowed to pay workers, in whole or in part, with alcoholic beverages. These new rules may have been linked to some of the religious movements that gained popularity in Virginia around the time of the American Revolution, for some denominations believed in abstinence and were convinced that gambling was immoral.

Virginia's rural county seats usually bustled with commercial and social activity, and on the days the monthly court was in session, people flocked to the courthouse community, often with their families in tow. There, they would conduct business, exchange news, buy and sell produce, or purchase the goods and services they needed. Sometimes, they attended auctions of real estate, slaves, livestock, and other personal property and they gossiped and socialized with friends and neighbors. Slaves and real estate were offered for sale in the county seat, usually at auctions held in front of the courthouse. In 1810, when Richard Billups, perhaps as county sheriff, announced the sale of the late Dr. Frederick W. Hearn's 220-acre farm on the North River, he said that the property had a good dwelling, several outbuildings, and a commanding view of Mobjack Bay and indicated that Hearn had purchased his plantation from John Hayes.

Militia musters, held at the county seat every two months except between December and March, provided the public with entertainment and occasional levity. Sometimes, militia commanders, attired in a dress uniform, offered prizes such as pistols and swords to competitors in wrestling, battling with cudgels, or foot-racing. Traveling musicians, magicians, and other entertainers performed at local taverns, which were popular gathering places. Some taverns had billiard tables; bowling, backgammon, chess, or draughts (checkers) also were popular and socially acceptable pastimes. Betting and games of chance, such as faro, were prohibited by law because disagreements between winners and losers sometimes erupted in violent disputes. Private lotteries were an acceptable form of private fundraising during the eighteenth century, but when gambling was prohibited, raffles became illegal.

In accordance with state law, every four years, qualified voters gathered at the county courthouse on the first Monday of November to vote for members of the General Assembly. When the first elections were held in Mathews County, Houlder Hudgins and Thomas Smith Jr. were chosen delegates to the General Assembly, which convened from October 1 to December 28, 1792. Matthew Anderson was elected state senator for a district that included Mathews, Gloucester, and Middlesex Counties. In the elections held in 1793, 1794, and 1795, all three men were returned to office. In Virginia, there was a longstanding tradition of allowing political candidates to make liquor available while voting was underway, and in most counties, at least one tavern was near the courthouse green. Congressional and presidential elections also were held at the county seat. In 1792, Deputy George Guthrie certified that on February 14, 1792, Mathews County's electors were qualified to vote for Francis Corbin, a candidate for the U.S. House of Representatives. The members of Mathews' standing committee for elections were Joseph Billups, James Spark, Henley Gayle, Thomas Brooks, and Joshua Brown. In June 1824, voters gathered at the courthouse to voice their support of John Quincy Adams as President of the United States and General Andrew Jackson as Vice President. At the citizens' meeting, Hunley Gayle served as chair and James H. Roy as secretary.[66]

Local Bridges and Ferries and Other "Internal Improvements"

In 1792, there were two licensed ferries across the Piankatank River, both of which were in Gloucester County. One was at Seaton's, at the mouth of Ferry Creek, and the other was Turk's Ferry, which was located further west. The rates that ferry-keepers could charge were set by state law, but county court justices could decide how many boats and hands were to be used at each ferry, within certain parameters. In December 1806, a small group of Mathews County citizens signed a petition opposing the establishment of a new ferry that would run from the Mathews County land of William Fitchett to the property of the late Thomas E. Churchill of Middlesex County. The petition, initiated by Elizabeth E. Churchill's guardian, was submitted in opposition to Fitchett's proposal that a ferry be established on his property. The General Assembly approved Fitchett's proposal, which had been published in the Richmond *Enquirer* in September 1806, and authorized the establishment of a ferry from his land to Churchill Point, the promontory now known as Wilton Point.

One foreign visitor commented that eastern Virginia was crisscrossed by roads that were "mere tracks large enough for wagons, occasionally bridged across ditches, streams or mud holes by small tree trunks placed close together." He said that travelers could expect to see coaches, wagons, and ox carts moving along laboriously, and often people on horseback. As the economy of the new nation began to take hold, Virginians became increasingly interested in the development of transportation infrastructure or "internal improvements" such as canals and turnpikes, and they also wanted better public roads. The General Assembly established the Board of Public Works and encouraged private companies to build turnpikes and bridges with the state as a co-investor. The development and improvement of inland transportation linked the rural countryside with urban markets, fueling the expansion of agricultural productivity and specialization. The Board of Public Works, which managed the state's Fund for Internal Improvements, interacted with a number of joint-stock companies that promised to build canals and turnpikes and to improve the state's navigable waterways.

In November 1795, the General Assembly authorized a group of investors[67] to extend the Piankatank River's navigation by clearing the upper part of the river where it led into Dragon Swamp. Their goal was to make the Piankatank and its headwaters passable for boats, bateaus, or canoes capable of carrying four hogsheads of tobacco. The General Assembly accepted the proposal and authorized the trustees of the Piankatank Canal Company to sell shares of their company at the county courthouses of Gloucester, King and Queen, Middlesex, and Essex Counties. Canal company trustees had the right to purchase land through which the canal would pass and to buy acreage on which to erect a toll house. However, the assembly established the tolls that could be charged for shipping various commodities.

Notes

1 Members of county militias had to supply their own weaponry.

2 Purdie, *Virginia Gazette*, August 4, 1775; October 13, 1775; Dixon and Hunter, *Virginia Gazette,* April 20, 1776; August 24, 1776; Michael Cecere, *Captain Thomas Posey and the 7th Virginia Regiment* (Westminster, Maryland, 2005), 12, 15; Mary Lou Clifford and Candice Clifford, *The New Point Comfort Lighthouse:Its History and Preservation* (Petersburg, 2014), 44.

3 Purdie, *Virginia Gazette*, March 8, 1776; May 30, 1776; Dixon and Hunter, *Virginia Gazette*, August 31, 1776; Elizabeth Fenn, *Pox Americana: The Great Smallpox Epidemic of 1775–1782* (New York 2001), 58; Phillip Ranlet, "The British, Slaves, and Smallpox in Revolutionary Virginia," *Journal of Negro History* 84 (1999):218; BPRO CO 5/1373; William B. Clark and William J. Morgan, *Naval Documents of the American Revolutions* (Washington, D.C., 1964–1981), V, 321, 669, 757–758, 840.

4 William Barry, a mariner, testified about his experience as a detainee aboard the *Roebuck*. Maryland governor Robert Eden, who asked Lord Dunmore to evacuate him to safety, arrived at Gwynn's Island on June 29 (Clark and Morgan, *Naval Documents*, V, 485, 820, 840, 1149).

5 Lord Dunmore, who was convinced that the Americans couldn't overtake his fortified position on Gwynn's Island, dismissively dubbed them "crickets." Fort Cricket Hill is on the National Register of Historic Places (Fort Cricket Hill, National Register of Historic Places File 057–0014).

6 Three Americans, detained aboard the *Roebuck*, managed to jump ship and reach the mainland. One of them, John Emmes, reported that Lord Dunmore had found an ample

supply of livestock on Gwynn's Island where most of the wells yielded very bad water (Clark and Morgan, *Naval Documents*, V, 485, 669).

7 At the end of May, diarist Landon Carter, who lived on the Rappahannock River, noted hearing that Lord Dunmore's fleet had gone to Gwynn's Island. Carter recalled that the island was small with "not more than half a dozen hutts [sic]" on it and probably was "inhabited by the family of that name in Kingston Parish." Carter said that he didn't believe that anyone would "land a force unless it was to steal a few sheep" (Landon Carter, Jack P. Green, ed., *The Diary of Landon Carter* (Charlottesville, 1962), II, 1045–1046).

8 In June 1779 Virginia's governing officials decided to move the state's capital to Richmond, considered a location less vulnerable to attack. The transition had occurred by April 24, 1780.

9 Clark and Morgan., *Naval Documents*, V, 669, 1094, 1150; VI, 172–173, 294, 741; Purdie, *Virginia Gazette*, July 19, 1776. Young Alexander was taken to Williamsburg and Mrs. Lecke was sent to New York.

10 Thomas Jefferson, [Untitled map of Gwynn's Island], [1776] in Barbara Oberg and J. Jefferson Looney, eds., *The Papers of Thomas Jefferson, 1778–January 4, 1780* (Charlottesville, 2009), III, 345; Clark and Morgan, *Naval Documents*, VI, 86–88, 366–367, 1242, 1312.

11 Purdie, *Virginia Gazette*, July 12, 1776; July 19, 1776; August 16, 1776; August 21, 1778; Dixon, *Virginia Gazette*, June 1, 1776; June 15, 1776; July 13, 1776; Selby, *Revolution,* 6, 60; Clark and Morgan, *Naval Documents*, V, 1022–1023, 1068–1069, 1078, 1079, 1150; VI, 86–88, 366–367, 727–729, 743, 849, 1242, 1312; Charles, *Newspapers,* 35–36; Gloucester Legislative Petitions, November 7, 1776; Mathews Archives Box 25.

12 Mathews Legislative Petitions, December 12, 1798.

13 In May 1780 the state legislature decided to eliminate vestries' taxing authority and created county Overseers of the Poor, elected every three years (Hening, *Statutes*, X, 288).

14 Clark and Morgan, *Naval Documents*, VI, 199, 366, 1016–1017, 1206; Randolph W. Church, *Virginia Legislative Petitions* (Richmond, 1984), 61, 221; Dixon and Nicholson, *Virginia Gazette*, November 27, 1779; Purdie, *Virginia Gazette*, November 14, 1777; March 6, 1778; Hunter, January 17, 1777; Hening, *Statutes, IX*, 378–379; Palmer, *Calendar*, II:174.

15 James C. Neagles and Lila L. Neagles, *Locating Your Revolutionary War Ancestor: A Guide to the Military Records* (Logan, Utah, 1983), 36–37; Hening, *Statutes*, IX, 14, 64–65, 91, 345, 456, 566, 589; X, 21, 24, 262; XI, 146, 316, 362, 446–447; XII, 246–247; www.revwarapps.org/revwar-pension-acts.

16 That is, New Point Comfort.

17 Neagles and Neagles, *Revolutionary War Ancestor,* 34–36; Revolutionary War Pension Roll 1360, National Archives, VA 23365 Book C Vol. 6½ page 7; Revolutionary War Pension Claim W 19836; Mathews County Legislative Petitions, December 6, 1798; December 4, 1800; December 17, 1801; Mathews County Census 1850; Gloucester County Legislative Petitions, December 24, 1825; Bobby G. Moss and Michael Scoggins, *African American Pa-*

triots in the Southern Campaign of the American Revolution (Blacksburg, South Carolina, 2004), 80, 119–120; Elizabeth Dutton Lewis, comp., *Revolutionary War Roster, Gloucester County, Virginia* (Gloucester, Virginia, 1976), n.p.; Constance V. Brooks, *Names on Record: A Journal Featuring Virginians of African Descent* (no place of publication, 1998), I, 120.

18 Moss and Scoggins, *African American Loyalists*, 36–37, 45, 82–83, 115–116, 333–334; Graham R. Hodges and Susan H. Cook, *The Black Loyalist Directory: African Americans in Exile After the American Revolution* (New York, 1996), 64, 196, 200; Clark and Morgan, *Naval Documents*, V, 485; Dixon and Hunter, *Virginia Gazette*, January 31, 1777.

19 Vestry members included Gabriel and Edward Hughes, William Armistead, Sir John Peyton, Major Thomas Smith, and Captains John Billups and John Dixon. Thomas Smith Jr. and his brother, Armistead, the sons of Thomas Smith Jr., were among the original founders of Phi Beta Kappa, established at the College of William and Mary on December 5, 1776 (Lyon GF. Tyler, ed., Formation of a Charter Party, *William and Mary Quarterly* 1st Ser. 4 [1896]:245).

20 In November 1777 Kingston Parish churchwardens John Dixon and Edward Hughes placed an advertisement in the *Virginia Gazette*, seeking a qualified Anglican clergyman, and indicating that the parish glebe was in good order and had two valuable slaves. A couple weeks later, the Rev. Thomas Feilde notified the public that his livestock, household and kitchen furniture, riding chair, a bateau, and other possessions were to be auctioned off at the glebe on December 30, 1777. He also had for sale a set of iron kettles and pots for boiling salt (Purdie, *Virginia Gazette*, November 21, 1777; Hunter and Dixon, *Virginia Gazette*, December 12, 1777).

21 Peter W. Coldham, comp., *American Migrations 1765–1799* (Baltimore, 1980), 554; Chamberlayne, *Kingston Parish*, 108; Peter Wilson Coldham and Sally L. M. Haigh, comp., *American Loyalist Claims Abstracted from the Public Records Office* (Washington, D.C., 1980), 151–152; SR 3077; ADM 12/54 f 166; 12/101 f 5; 12/106 f 40; 12/109 f 140; 13/28 ff 388–391; 13/29 ff 610–633.

22 Bristow's property extended in a westerly direction and abutted Diggs Creek.

23 In 1752 Francis Willis placed an advertisement in the *Virginia Gazette*, trying to recover a runaway slave. Fifteen years later 40 of Robert Bristow's slaves, who were in Chesterfield County, were offered for sale at the Rocky Ridge warehouse (Hunter, *Virginia Gazette*, January 10, 1752; Purdie and Dixon, *Virginia Gazette*, October 8, 1767).

24 Inquisition of escheat on Robert Bristow's estate, Executive Papers of Governor Thomas Jefferson: Governor's Office Letters Received; Coldham, *American Migrations*, 536–538; Coldham and Haigh, *American Loyalist Claims*, 54; SR 2244, 2645; ADM 12/109 f 86; 13/28 ff 1–69; 13/84 ff 7–228, Folder B; 13/102 ff 49–50; Dixon and Nicholson, *Virginia Gazette*, October 9, 1779; Walsh, *Motives*, 477; Gloucester County Legislative Petitions, November 4, 1793.

25 John Randolph Grymes' uncle, Benjamin, rose to his defense (Purdie, *Virginia Gazette*, July 5, 1776).

26 Grymes probably exaggerated the size of his plantation on Gwynn's Island, for in 1776 Thomas Jefferson estimated that the entire island consisted of only around 2,200 acres. Jefferson's map, which is highly schematic, suggests that the Grymes plantation comprised a relatively small part of the island.

27 The *Virginia Gazette* reported that Grymes lost 35 slaves and some horses, cattle, and furniture (Clark and Morgan, *Naval Documents*, V, 1150). Coldham, *American Migrations*, 563–564; Coldham and Haigh, *American Loyalist Claims*, 205; ADM 12/54 f 388; 12/99 f 18; 12/109 f 150; 13/29 ff 736–755, Folder G; VCRP SR 2245; Purdie, *Virginia Gazette*, July 5, 1776; Philip A. Bruce, ed., "Virginia Families," *Virginia Magazine of History and Biography*, 3(1896):605–607; Middlesex County Will Book E (1760–1772):134–136; J.A.C. Chandler and E.G. Swem, eds., "Petition of American Loyalists, 1778," *William and Mary Quarterly* 2nd Ser. 1 (1921):70–71; Thomas Jefferson, [Untitled map of Gwynn's Island],[1776].

28 Coldham, *American Migrations*, 587; ADM 12/101 f 63; 12/112 f 1; 13/32 ff 221–228; 13/90 ff 420–424; SR 2248, 3042; Mathews Personal Property Tax Lists 1791–1796; Billups Papers, Swem, Box 2 folder 5.

29 William G. Stanard, ed., "Virginia Legislative Petitions," *Virginia Magazine of History and Biography* 15 (1908): 292–295; Purdie, *Virginia Gazette*, May 24, 1776; Coldham, *American Migrations*, 606; ADM 12/102 f 203; 13/25 f 529; 13/32 ff 695–698; 13/137 f 656; SR 2649.

30 ADM 13/79 Folder WII; 13/87 ff 295–298, Claims W; Coldham, *American Migrations*, 607; High Court of Admiralty (HCA) 32/285 folder 12; SR 2640, 2648, 3162, 5455.

31 Coldham, *American Migrations*, 3–4, 122, 168, 268, 344–345.

32 The *Orozimbo* reportedly visited many foreign ports and was still in service in 1862 (Mathews County Historical Society, *History and Progress: Mathews County, Virginia, Reprints from 1949 and 1979 Special Editions, Gloucester–Mathews Gazette-Journal* [Marceline, Missouri, 1982],114).

33 The runaway apprentice was a young lad around five feet nine inches tall, fair skinned, and had "a pleasant countenance." When he fled from his employer, he was wearing a striped Holland short coat and a brown linen frock and trousers; he also took along a striped jeans jacket and a short coat made of black homespun cloth (*American Gazette and Norfolk and Portsmouth Public Advertiser*, September 1, 1795).

34 Dixon, *Virginia Gazette*, September 12, 1777; Dixon and Hunter, *Virginia Gazette*, July 10, 1778; October 16, 1778; Dixon and Nicholson, *Virginia Gazette*, April 2, 1779; Purdie, *Virginia Gazette*, March 6, 1778; Charles, *Newspapers*, 41–42; Mason, *Gloucester*, II, 71; *The Maryland Journal and Baltimore Advertiser*, December 27, 1794; *American Gazette and Norfolk and Portsmouth Public Advertiser*, September 1, 1795; *American and Commercial Daily Advertiser*, September 11, 1807; *American Beacon and Commercial Diary*, October 2, 1816; Billups Papers, Swem, Box 2 folder 5; SR 5901.

35 The name "Sluts Creek" had come into use by the mid–eighteenth century and persisted for at least a century. According to the Oxford English Dictionary, the word "slut" is synonymous with "dirty" or "unclean."

36 Jane Carson, *Travelers in Tidewater Virginia, 1700–1800* (Williamsburg, 1965), 116; Selby, *Revolution,* 310, 312; Henry P. Johnston, *The Yorktown Campaign and the Surrender of Cornwallis, 1781*, 108, 128–130; Charles, *Newspapers*, 41; Mathews Archives Box 25; McIlwaine, *Council of State*, II, 403; *Executive Journals*, III, 122; Hening, *Statutes*, XIII, 324; Palmer, *Calendar*, III, 43; IX, 588–589; Rice et al., *American Campaigns*, I, 65; II, 170–171; Janice L. Abercrombie and Richard Slatten, *Virginia Public Claims* (Athens, Georgia, 1992), Certificates redeemed at Gloucester County court between February 1780 and December 1781, n.p.

37 Hening, *Statutes,* X, 9–11, 243, 502–503; XI, 140–145.

38 Hening, *Statutes*, IX, 65; X, 165–167, 279–285, 490, 502; XI, 67, 93, 113, 418; XII, 431; Palmer, *Calendar*, IV, 77, 275, 467–468, 470–471, 530; Gloucester County Legislative Petitions, April 17, 1787; November 15, 1787; Personal Property Tax Lists [Kingston Parish] 1783; Berlin and Morgan, *Cultivation and Culture*, 187.

39 Palmer, *Calendar*, IV, 52; McIlwaine, *Council of State*, IV, 21.

40 Palmer, *Calendar*, VI, 394, 469–470, 473; VII, 165, 184; VIII, 271, 311–312, 321–322, 461; IX, 219, 522, 574.

41 Tindall, *America*, 118–119, 247; Christopher Colles, *A Survey of the Roads of the United States of America, 1789*; Edith F. Axelton, *Virginia Postmasters and Post Offices, 1789–1832* (Athens, Georgia, 1991), 121–122; Martin, *Gazetteer,* 226–229; Mason, *Gloucester*, II, 48, 81–82; Charles, *Newspapers*, 49.

42 The reconstructed 1790 census indicates that Gloucester County had 13,498 people, 7,063 of whom were enslaved. There also were 210 free non-white people (http://mapserver.lib.virginia.edu/index.html).

43 As William Hugh Grove noted in 1732, many Virginia plantations had numerous outbuildings and resembled "little villages."

44 U.S. Bureau, *Heads of Families*, 68; Billups House (Milford), National Register of Historic Places, File 057-0023; Mason, *Gloucester*, II, 73–74, 80. Mrs. Marie A. Baldwin of Gloucester, Virginia, wrote a letter in September 1948, stating that one of her forebears, Dr. John S. Bohannon, owned a Chippendale-style secretary desk that was made by Kingston Parish cabinetmaker Jesse Hudgins. Mrs. Baldwin, who was in the process of selling her secretary desk to Preservation Virginia's predecessor, indicated that its bottom drawer contained a piece of paper signed by John S. Bohannon, which stated that "This desk was made by Jesse Hudgins, Mathews, Va., in the year of 1778." Another letter in Preservation Virginia's files indicates that the secretary desk the organization procured from Mrs. Baldwin was lost (www.oldsalemonline.org). Unfortunately, cabinetmaker Jesse Hudgins' presence in Kingston Parish during the eighteenth century isn't substantiated by historical records. Also, experts at the Museum of Early Southern Arts date the piece of furniture, which was intact when examined, to 1810–1820 (personal communication, Kim May,

January 6, 2015). The 1850 census for Mathews County includes a farmer named Jesse Hudgins, who was age 75 (Mathews County Census 1850). According to his descendants, he was a cabinetmaker.

45 During this period, many of Virginia's Anglican churches came into the hands of other denominations or simply fell into disrepair.

46 During Mr. Hopkinson's ministry, Kingston Parish churchwardens Samuel Williams and Armistead Smith bound out Moses Hudgins' son, William, as an apprentice to John Billups Jr. so that William could learn the mariner's trade.

47 Meade, *Old Churches*, II, 325; Hening, *Statutes*, XI, 532; XII, 266–267; Samuel Shepherd, *The Statutes At Large of Virginia* (New York, 1980), I, 114–119, 142–145, 192–193; Chamberlayne, *Kingston Parish*, 119, 123–125, 127; Gloucester County Legislative Petitions, July 1786; Mason, *Gloucester*, II, p 72; Billups Papers, Swem Box 2 folder 5; Tompkins Family Papers, Virginia Historical Society, Mss1 T5996.

48 Ludlum, *Hurricanes*, 29–30; Palmer, *Calendar*, IV, 467–468.

49 He indicated that he had bought his Gwynn's Island acreage from John Callis and his New Point Comfort parcel from James Davis.

50 From the beginning, free tithable male whites and mulattoes were taxed at the same rate, but free tithable blacks of both sexes were taxed at a higher rate. During the 1850s tithable white males were taxed at 40 cents each but the tax rate for free tithable blacks was $1.00 each.

51 Hening, *Statutes*, X, 115, 211, 372; XI, 39–40, 308–309; John H. Russell, *The Free Negro in Virginia* (New York, 1969), 72–73; Katz, *Negro in Virginia*, 140–141; Edmund Morgan, *American Slavery, American Freedom: The Ordeal of Colonial Virginia* (New York, 1975), 59; Shepherd, *Statutes*, II, 19–20; III, 290; Thad W. Tate, *The Negro in Eighteenth Century Williamsburg* (Williamsburg, 1965), 120–126; Mathews County Personal Property Tax Lists 1791–1895.

52 Palmer, *Calendar*, V, 585. The event to which the Mathews County residents referred occurred in Northampton County, where a few slaves talked about making a break for freedom. County magistrates had some of the men flogged and three were transported to Cuba (Taylor, *Internal Enemy*, 89–90).

53 Ezekiel Lane, February 3, 1794, will, proved April 15, 1794; Mathews Archives Box 39 R; Edmund Borum, February 1, 1798, will; Mathews County Land Tax Lists 1797–1821; Hening, *Statutes*, IX, 471–472; XI, 140–145; Alan Taylor, *Slavery and War in Virginia, 1772–1832: The Internal Enemy* (New York, 2013), 6; Palmer, *Calendar*, V, 58; Shepherd, *Statutes*, I, 238–239.

54 Mathews was a distinguished military officer during the American Revolution and served as a representative to the state convention that ratified the U. S. constitution.

55 When Hunley made his will on February 27, 1747, he divided his property among his sons, Charles, George, Joshua, and John. The same year that his land was surveyed, he signed a document promising not to break the entail on the acreage on which he was then

living (Mason, *Gloucester*, II, 60; Billups Papers, Swem, Box 10 folder 1; Gloucester County Surveyors Book A [1733–1810]:41).

56 Members of the Hunley family had been in possession of land along the east side of Put In Creek's head since 1651 (Patent Book II, 330; VII, 522).

57 In 1791 the land of Joseph Davis, whose property bordered the east side of Put In Creek, included the acreage on which Palace Green eventually was built.

58 According to real estate tax rolls, James and Plummer owned land at Mathews Courthouse (Mathews County Land Tax Lists 1814).

59 Prisoners who weren't accused of a felony or treason, were to be given access to an area in which they could exercise.

60 Hening, *Statutes*, XIII, 162–163; XIII, 422, 427–428, 449–455; Gloucester Legislative Petitions, November 11, 1790; Salmon and Campbell, *Hornbook*, 267; Mason, *Gloucester*, II, 77–79; Mathews County Personal Property Tax Lists 1791–1797. A plat on which the courthouse green is delimited indicates that in 1916 it encompassed 1.6 acres (Mathews County Land Book 1:468). When the lots between Court and Main Streets are included, which in 1851 encompassed the site of the "old jail," the total is just over 2 acres.

61 Hening, Statutes, XII, 162–163; Mason, *Gloucester*, I, 117; II, 77–79; Palmer, *Calendar*, VII, 462; William and Mary Center for Archaeological Research (WMCAR), *Integrated Management Plan, Mathews County Courthouse Square Historic District (057-0022; 44MT0073), Mathews, Virginia* (Richmond, Virginia, 2007), 12–13; *Congressional Record, 23rd Congress, 1st Session*, House of Representatives Document No. 218:1–2; Billups Papers, Swem, Box 2 folder 5; Becky Foster Barnhardt, personal communication; Mathews County Courthouse Square, National Register of Historic Places File 057-0022.

62 In 1794 he signed a receipt, certifying that Robert Green had paid his taxes for 1793–1794 (Billups Papers, Swem, Box 2 folder 1).

63 In October 1833 all of the late Hunley Gayle's personal property was offered for sale by his executors, Christopher Tompkins and John D. Jarvis, two local merchants (Billups Papers, Swem, Box 1 folder 29; Charles, *Newspapers*, 77).

64 Mason, Gloucester, I:122; II:78, 82–83, 122; Billups Papers, Swem, Box 2, folder 1; Box 10, folder 2; Jane B. Goodsell, *Mathews County, Virginia, Records* (Athens, Georgia, 2000), 39–43; Charles, Newspapers, 42, 55, 66; Moss and Scoggins, *African-American Patriots*, 80; Palmer, *Calendar*, V, 390; VII, 462, 467–468.

65 Thomas Edwards owned other property in Mathews County and after his death, his farm on Gwynn's Island and two parcels just west of Mathews Courthouse were offered for sale at a public auction held in 1857 (Charles, *Newspapers*, 100).

66 Gloucester County Surveyors Plat Book A (1733–1810):12–13, 23; Mathews County Land Tax Lists 1791–1829; Personal Property Tax Lists 1791–1829; Legislative Petitions, December 11, 1818; Mason, *Gloucester*, II:81–82; Charles, *Newspapers*, 49, 66; Rhys Isaacs, *The Transformation of Virginia, 1740–1790* (Chapel Hill, 1982), 168–169, 247–250;

Shepherd, *Acts of the General Assembly of Virginia, Passed at the Session of 1843–1844*, 26–27; Leonard, *General Assembly*, 188, 190, 192, 193–194, 196, 198; Palmer, *Calendar*, V, 448; IX, 79, 85, 124. John Hayes owned the Ransones' Isle of Wight Plantation.

67 Shepherd, *Statutes*, I, 154,158, 399–402; Fry and Jefferson, "Virginia and Maryland," 1754; Mathews County Legislative Petitions, December 10, 1806; Shepherd, *Statutes*, III, 333; Charles, *Newspapers*, 47. Most of the investors were from Middlesex and King and Queen Counties, although two or three were from Gloucester. Shepherd, *Statutes*, I, 399–402.

7

So Wondrous Free
1796–1835

Shipbuilding Comes Into Its Own

Shipbuilding played an important role in Kingston Parish's economy throughout the eighteenth century but truly gained primacy after the American Revolution. Between 1790 and 1835 Mathews County had at least 50 shipbuilders, most of whom were engaged in other types of moneymaking activities. Mathews shipbuilders produced vessels known for their fine workmanship and speed. In August 1794, shipbuilder and county clerk John Patterson, who resided at Miss Young's in Mathews Courthouse, informed the Baltimore *Daily Intelligencer*'s readers that he had for sale two vessels designed for fast sailing. In 1800, he threatened legal action against two Baltimore men who failed to pay him for a new schooner. In 1809, John Dudley, a Mathews County shipwright, hired two teenage apprentices, John Dudley Jr. and Robert Longist (Longest), agreeing to teach them the "craft, mistery [*sic*], and occupation of a ship carpenter." Both youths, who had to work for Dudley until age 21, were sent to him by lower Middlesex County's Overseers of the Poor. In 1812, William Fitchett, a Mathews County shipbuilder and ferry-owner, placed an advertisement in a Norfolk newspaper trying to recover John Moore, a runaway slave accustomed to working in ship carpentry. Fitchett described Moore as "very fond of spirits of any kind" and said that he fancied himself "much of a doctor."

When the *Argus*, built in Mathews in 1811, was sold at auction in Baltimore, its hull was described as copper-protected.[1] John Billups of Milford

Haven informed the public that he was almost ready to sell a vessel capable of stowing about 220 tons of tobacco or flour; nearly three years later, several other new schooners and brigs, built in Mathews County by David Milhado and other craftsmen, were offered for sale in the major shipping hubs of Norfolk, Alexandria, Philadelphia, New York City, and Baltimore. Many of the advertisements for Mathews-built vessels indicated that they were made from white oak and were sheathed with copper. According to contemporary news sources, the *Ferrata*, America's very first three-masted schooner, was built in Mathews County in 1827. Its owner and builder, Captain Isaac Foster, sailed her to Baltimore, where she was extensively outfitted with iron and used in the Rio trade. Later the *Ferrata* was used in transatlantic commerce.[2]

Exceptional Entrepreneurs

During the late eighteenth and early nineteenth centuries, several Mathews County residents obtained licenses as tavern-keepers.[3] Among them were Joseph Billups Jr., Jasper S. Clayton, Terry Connelley, William Dudley, John Elliott Sr., James Gibson, Duncan Glen, George Guthrie, John Hudgins, Charles Jones, John Litchfield, Benjamin Marable, William and Sarah E. Plummer, and Henry Respess and his heirs. Hudgins and Dudley successively kept a tavern at The Battery, near the head of Blackwater Creek, and the Plummer and Respess taverns were at the county seat. The establishments operated by George Guthrie and John Litchfield were equipped with billiard tables, which were taxable. Litchfield and his brother, Francis, whose property was on the East River at Put In Creek, also were shipbuilders, and Thomas Litchfield, perhaps a kinsman, was a licensed storekeeper. In 1802, William Dudley paid taxes on a "wagon stage," a four-wheeled vehicle in which he could transport passengers and freight from his tavern to the stage line at Gloucester Courthouse. Between 1820 and 1824, Thomas Edwards obtained a license to keep a tavern at the county seat, succeeding his late father-in-law, Henry Respess. Mathews County usually had between four and six taverns; at least two were at the county seat. The others would have been on well-traveled thoroughfares or near landings. Some tavern-keepers and storeowners earned money by owning stud horses that were for hire.

Taverns, mills, stores, and the workshops of tradesmen traditionally were at the core of rural life. For that reason, auctions often were held there or at the county seat. For example, in 1817 Robert Callis's slave, Peter, was sold at auction in front of the courthouse by constable William H. Billups in order to settle some of Callis's debts, and in 1819 three slaves were auctioned off in front of Mr. Atkinson's tavern to settle a suit against the late Jacob Williamson's estate. On the other hand, in 1845 the late Robert Armistead's 300-acre farm, Fair Prospect, which overlooked Mobjack Bay, was sold at auction in front of the courthouse to settle a chancery suit. Storekeepers extended credit to farmers, who borrowed against future crop earnings or posted their land as collateral. It was through this means that some of Mathews Courthouse's merchants came to own land throughout the rural countryside. During the mid-1830s John H. Miller mortgaged his personal property when obtaining a loan from Shepherd G. Miller, and Andrew A. Van Bibber borrowed money from Philip E. Tabb and mortgaged his North End tract and the North River Mill. Often, borrowers or their heirs faced the consequence of their indebtedness, often to local merchants.

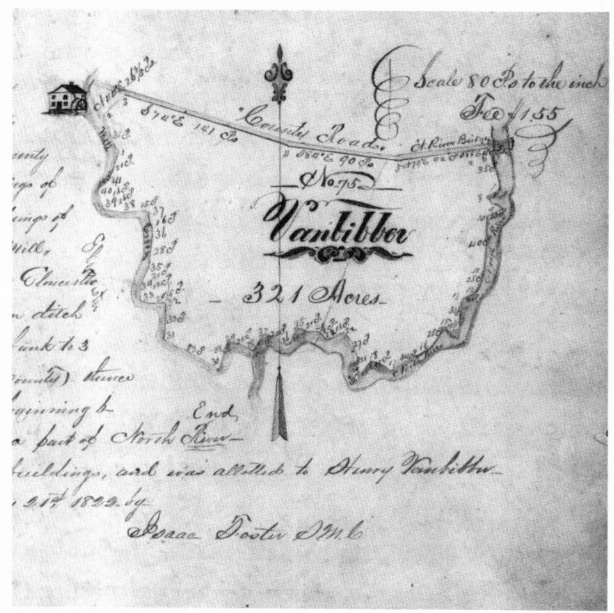

North River mill in 1822.
Mathews County Land Book 1, p. 37

Around 1813, the state began licensing millers, and in 1814, for the first and last time, Mathews County tax officials noted whether local mills were powered by wind or by water. Most of Mathews County's mills were worth between $100 and $300, although John Borum's was worth only $30 and those of John Billups Sr., William Callis, and Thomas Lilly were valued at $50 each. The mills of Joseph Billups, John Brownley, Henry Diggs, John L. Hudgins, and Thomas Tabb were worth between $100 and $150, whereas the mills owned by Miles King and William Lane were valued at $300. The "watermills," or tide mills, owned by Henry Diggs and Miles King in 1814 were located on the East River.[4] The windmills owned by John L. Billups, William Lane, and Joseph Billups Jr. were on Milford Haven, whereas John Brownley's windmill was at the mouth of Stutts Creek. William Callis's and John L. Hudgins's windmills were on Queens Creek, and Thomas Tabb's windmill was probably located on Stutts Creek. Alden G. Cushman, a merchant and shipbuilder, when offering his half-interest in a steam-powered sawmill on Queens Creek to the highest bidder, said that it produced lumber that was saleable in Baltimore, Norfolk, Alexandria, Washington, and Georgetown. In 1820, Benjamin Hursey and Company had a steam-powered sawmill and grist mill in the eastern part of Mathews County that produced more than 200,000 feet of plank each year. The shops of artisans like tailor William Anderton and weaver William James would have been located where they were readily accessible to the public.

In 1798, the state began requiring those who sold imported goods to obtain special trading licenses. Mathews County tax records reveal that over the years, the county had an abundance of licensed retail establishments. This is despite the fact that farmers could sell goods they brought home from market without the need for a license.[5] The county had 16 licensed stores in 1798, but by 1807 there were 35. In 1811, the county had one licensed peddler, Barney Duff. In the run-up to the 1819 recession, more than half of Mathews County licensed merchants went out of business. After an economic recovery took hold, the number of merchants increased, and during the 1820s and 1830s the county usually had 20 to 30 stores.

Nearly half of Mathews County's retail establishments were owned by shipbuilders and were situated on navigable waterways, where mariners could purchase supplies and other customers would have access by boat.

For example, shipbuilder Lewis Hudgins had a store, and William Fitchett had one near the public ferry that he operated between Wadinger Creek and Churchill Point.[6] From 1825 on, mariners who sold goods from their ships were classified as peddlers and had to purchase licenses. Francis Armistead and his son had a store at the county seat and William Bohannon and his son had one nearby. Joseph G. Brown went into business with his brother, but sometimes seemingly unrelated people formed partnerships. During the 1820s, Mary Cully, Ann Hudgins, Nancy Hudgins, and Peggy Knight were licensed storekeepers, and during the mid-1830s Ann Callis operated a store. Most, if not all, of these women probably took over mercantile establishments formerly owned by male family members.

Some of the men who combined storekeeping and shipbuilding also operated mills or taverns. Shipbuilders John Anderson and John L. Hudgins, who owned property on Queens Creek, obtained merchant's licenses and had stores close to their landings; Hudgins also had a windmill. Merchant Joseph Billups Jr., who owned property on Milford Haven and Bandy Ridge, combined storekeeping with the operation of a windmill and a tavern, whereas Richard Billups, who regularly obtained a merchant's license and had land on Milford Haven and Garden Creek, earned money building houses and ships. John Brownley, a licensed storekeeper from 1807 through 1826, operated a windmill located at Fanneys Point, on the upper side of Stutts Creek's mouth. During the late eighteenth century, either Brownley or his father was a shipbuilder. Also located on Stutts Creek were shipbuilders and storeowners Thomas Hudgins and George Gayle. Andrew, Benjamin, and George Owen were storekeepers, and Andrew supplemented his income with shipbuilding and carpentry. George Owen was paid for making a coffin for William Lilly of Lilly's Neck and supplying brandy for Lilly's funeral. Storekeepers and shipbuilders William Brooks, John Hudgins, Robert Hunley, and John Foster were located on Winter Harbor, whereas William Callis of Queens Creek combined milling and shipbuilding. Langley B. Eddins (Eddens), whose property was on Milford Haven, combined storekeeping with shipbuilding, and members of the Billups family also had stores there, too. Shipbuilders and storeowners John Thomas and Peter and Thomas Smith were located on Horn Harbor, as was Thomas Armistead, whose store was near Horn Harbor's head.[7] Francis Jarvis, whose land bor-

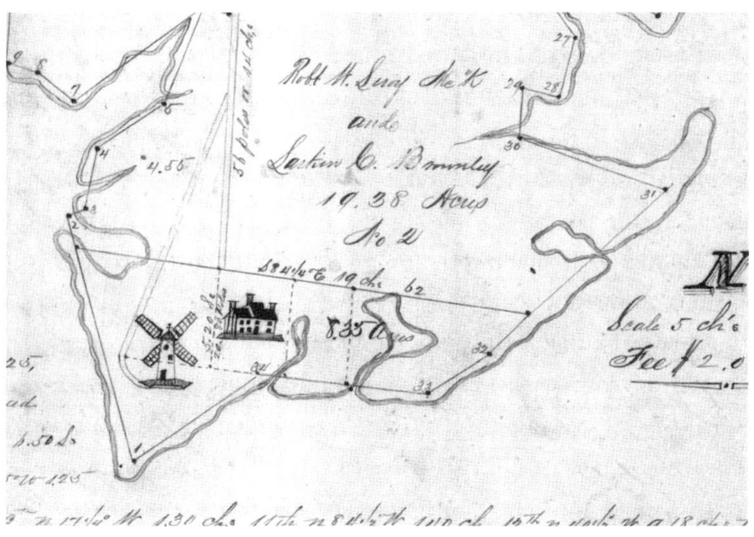

John Brownley's windmill at the mouth of Stutts Creek, 1835. Mathews County Land Book 1, p. 151.

dered Pepper Creek and Horn Harbor, also combined shipbuilding and storekeeping. From at least 1798 to the 1830s, James Gwyn and his family had a store on Gwynn's Island, where Humphrey Keeble, whose plantation overlooked the mouth of the Piankatank River, was a licensed merchant and shipbuilder. There seems to have been relatively little commercial activity on the North River, although merchant Hunley Gayle of Blackwater Creek built ships there between 1795 and 1826. Thomas Ransone and James H. Roy, who was living at Green Plains by 1814, were also merchants and shipbuilders.

The East River was the home of numerous other men who combined store ownership with shipbuilding. They included Alden G. Cushman, Edward and James Davis, Henry Diggs, Mathew Gayle, Richard Hunley, and John Patterson, who had stores and built ships near Williams Wharf. Miles King, a mariner who lived at Woodstock, between Tabbs (Cullys) and Weston Creeks, was known for building exceptionally fine ships and he also had a store and a mill. King's plantation was adjacent to Poplar Grove, then owned by John Patterson, another very successful entrepreneur. James R.J. Hunley, whose land bordered Put In Creek, and John D. Williams, who owned acreage near Williams Wharf, were involved in storekeeping and shipbuilding during the years that there was an operational customs facility at the wharf. Storeowner William Hudgins owned land on Dyers Creek and the East River and also built ships. Likewise, Houlder Hudgins, who lived on Queens Creek, combined both professions. Perhaps on account of their regular contact with the public, storekeepers were often elected to political positions.

There are remarkably complete details about some Mathews County storekeepers and their businesses. In 1814, Christopher Tompkins, a savvy entrepreneur who resided on Horn Harbor but eventually moved to Poplar Grove, purchased a retail license and did so annually until at least 1834. On February 12, 1816, Tompkins insured his store and its storage building, which were located side-by-side on a 1½-acre lot at the county seat. Both were one-story frame buildings that had brick foundations, faced east, and were situated on the west side of the main road, the forerunner of today's Main Street. Tompkins's store, which was valued at $700, was twice as long as it was wide, and on the rear of the building there was an attached shed with a brick chimney. A portico extended across the front of the store, providing customers with a covered entrance. Tompkins' lumber-house, a storehouse that in 1816 had an estimated worth of $300, was 33 feet from his store's south side and also paralleled the main road. Insurance agent Thomas Jones noted that the replacement value of both buildings was $1,150. He deducted $150 for decay, which suggests that neither structure was new. This raises the possibility that John Patterson, the licensed merchant from whom Tompkins had purchased the property in 1814, had also used the buildings for retail purposes.[8] According to Tompkins' insurance policy, tavern-keeper William Plummer's land was contiguous to the north, Henry Diggs's and Thomas James's property lay to the south, and William Hunley's acreage was to the west.[9] When Christopher Tompkins insured his store in 1816, John D. Jarvis, who owned an unoccupied building and lot on the east side of the main road, and tavern owner Henry Diggs, whose land later became the site of the Lane Hotel, served as witnesses.

Christopher Tompkins's store ledger reveals that he sold groceries, whiskey, chamber pots, and tobacco, as well as dry goods, shoes, stockings, suspenders, and readymade clothing. One customer, cordwainer James Davis, bought shoe thread. Tompkins's store also carried supplies regularly used by seafarers and shipbuilders. For example, mariners purchased supplies like rope, canvas, oakum, iron, paint, and anchors for the schooners *Thomas Hall*, *Sarah Ann*, *Ann Maria*, *Thomas Hunley*, *Elizabeth*, and *Jesse Digges*. Tompkins's store ledger suggests that some of his customers were free blacks. For instance, "Free Kit (the ditcher)," "Ruben (the ditcher)," "Old Sam," and "Amos (the sawyer)" bought tobacco, coffee, salt, and large quantities of whiskey and rum, and Ruben reportedly paid his bill by "cutting 225 yards of ditch." Between 1820 and 1822, Mathews County's School Commissioners bought spelling books, an English reader, and paper for their students. John Hudgins of Garden Creek purchased whiskey, rum, molasses, coffee, sugar, and a pair of compasses, whereas Mathew Gayle invested in a vest pattern and some cloth. Whenever Tompkins's customers paid their debts, he crossed them off in his ledger. Occasionally he made note of customers' family relationships or commented on their appearance. For instance, he identified his customer John Digges as having a "cut nose," presumably to distinguish him from another John Digges, whose nose was intact. By the late 1830s, Christopher Tompkins, Francis Armistead, and Albert Diggs had formed a business partnership that enabled all three men to maximize their investments in the county seat.

According to Martin's *Virginia Gazetteer*, the county seat, which had a population of 150, had four stores in 1835.[10] Tax records indicate that they belonged to Christopher Tompkins, Walter G. Lane, business partners John D. Jarvis and Elijah Barnum, and Thomas James. James began purchasing an annual merchant's license in 1808 and did so repeatedly over the years. His store, located on the east side of Main Street, occupied a building that is dated by dendrochronology (the study of tree-ring growth) to 1820, making it one of the oldest surviving stores in the South.[11] Receipts for items people purchased from James' store during 1816 reveal that they bought and sold goods that ranged from sugar and coffee to gunpowder, stamps, yard goods, and iron.[12] The James family retained their store until around 1847, when it was bought by merchants John D. Jarvis and Elijah Barnum. In 1821, Thomas James and Thomas James Jr. individually purchased merchant's licenses.[13] In 1830, while Thomas Jr. was Mathews County's sheriff, he bought a merchant's license and signed his own receipt. Historic James Store is now on the National Register of Historic Places and Virginia Landmarks Register.[14]

The Mutual Assurance Society

During the early nineteenth century, at least a dozen Mathews County property owners purchased policies from the Mutual Assurance Society of Virginia.[15] These policies, comparable to today's homeowner's insurance policies, contain detailed information about the insured structures, list the names of neighboring property owners, and usually contain primitive sketches of the buildings being insured. For example, the policies that Jasper S. Clayton purchased in 1802 and 1806 when insuring his home, Windsor, indicate that the main house, which measured 24 feet by 16 feet, had an English basement and a wing on each end. During 1802, Philip Mayo insured Fair Prospect, James H. Roy bought a policy for Hazelwood, and Armistead Smith insured Belleview, later renewing his insurance policy in 1806 and 1813. Mayo's property included a large workshop, and Smith's, located on Pepper Creek, included the usual outbuildings, such as a kitchen, smokehouse, slave quarters, barns, and a dairy, along with a schoolhouse. In 1803, Lyne Shackleford, a resident of Mathews County and a justice of the Williamsburg Chancery Court, insured Springfield, a frame dwelling with a brick cellar.

John D. Jarvis, a merchant, purchased a policy for the buildings on his plantation, The Haven, in 1813, the same year that Christopher Tompkins insured the home he called Horn Harbor (later known as Beachland). Both men later insured their buildings at the county seat. The house Jarvis owned in Mathews Courthouse in January 1816 faced the east side of Main Street and was unoccupied. It was a large frame building that consisted of two disproportionate sections that were probably constructed during different building campaigns. The smaller component had a Dutch roof and a central chimney, whereas the larger one had a plain roof, a shed on the back, and a half-piazza and shed on the front. Jarvis noted that John Soper's (Soaper's) estate bordered his property on the north and east and that Henry Respess's acreage lay to the south. Since tax records indicate that John B. Roberts sold his half-acre lot to Jarvis in 1815, and since both men were merchants, the insured structure may have seen use as a store.

James H. Roy, who insured Hazelwood in 1802, purchased policies for the buildings at Green Plains in 1814 and 1816. He insured his elegant two-story Georgian mansion for $5,250, and then bought a policy for the plantation's seven outbuildings, which were worth $1,950 and included his office. In 1815, Roy insured a dwelling on the west side of the East River, abutting William Brownley's property, and William White bought a policy on his large brick home in Whites Neck. White also insured a smaller dwelling and a weaving house. Isaac Brownley insured his dwelling in 1815, and a year later John Patterson bought a policy for his buildings at Poplar Grove. The structures Patterson insured were a dwelling with two wings, a kitchen, a dairy, a laundry, and a barn, all older buildings with some evidence of decay. Whenever Mathews County landowners purchased insurance policies from the Mutual Assurance Society, local appraisers certified the value of the buildings.[16]

Unrest and Restrictions

Gabriel's Insurrection, which occurred in 1800 and was well organized, involved large numbers of armed slaves who vowed to overcome all opposition. That incident, though quelled, confirmed slaveholders' worst fears and left no doubts about the potential for a slave revolt. Legislative backlash restricted slaves' nighttime religious meetings, imposed stronger penalties for wrongdoing, and further limited the mobility and activities of the enslaved. Two black men from Mathews County, Frank and James, were convicted of committing a crime and sentenced to "transportation." On October 16, 1802, Governor James Monroe ordered Mathews officials to send both men to the state penitentiary in Richmond, where they would be detained until they could be sent away. By 1806, the laws controlling manumission had tightened further. Although newly-freed slaves had to leave Virginia, some neighboring states wouldn't allow them to settle there.

Occasionally, slaves attacked and killed an overseer on account of his cruelty. In 1809, Miles King of Mathews County hired overseer John Mathews, whose reputation for brutality preceded him. On May 31, Frank, Jack, James, and Edmund, who were field hands, seized Mathews and crushed his skull with their iron hoes. Then, they hid his corpse in a ditch until nightfall, when they loaded it into a canoe hidden in a small tributary of the East River. At that point, King's foreman, Joe, and a plowman named

Peter tied a stone-filled bushel basket to the dead man's ankles, took him to Cully's Point, and lowered him into the deepest water. Mathews' body eventually floated to the water's surface, and on the night of June 9, it became entangled in the oars of a white man's boat and was hauled ashore. Miles King, upon learning that his slaves had decided to kill Mathews "the moment they understood I had engaged him," had them arrested and trussed up. Making use of the superstitious belief that a corpse would bleed in the presence of its murderer, King forced each of his slaves to touch the dead body. Old Billy, when ordered to put his hand on Mathews, fearfully described the murder. Afterward, six of King's slaves were jailed by local authorities and tried. The four men directly involved in the killing were sentenced to hang, and two others (Joe and Peter, considered accessories to murder) were branded in the hand with a hot iron and given 39 lashes apiece. In a particularly gruesome display of brutality, the county justices had the executed men's severed heads hoisted onto poles and put on display at the courthouse "as a warning to others." However, fear wasn't always a deterrent to violence. In late December 1828, Captain John Pritchett's slave, Dick, and a hired man named Henry entered the Pritchett family's home at New Point Comfort and demanded money from his wife, Ann, who was between 45 and 50 years old. When she claimed that she couldn't pay them until her husband returned, the two men suffocated her and then strangled her to make sure that she was dead. They threw her body into a nearby well and rummaged through the house, searching for money. A few days later, when Mrs. Pritchett's remains were discovered, the perpetrators confessed to the crime. Newspapers from as far away as New Jersey reported on the incident.

Even after slaves were freed, they faced new challenges. In 1812, Peter Burwell, an emancipated slave from Gloucester County, asked the General Assembly for permission to continue living in Virginia. He said that although his late master had freed him on account of his faithful service, being forced to leave the state, as the law required, would be almost as much of a hardship as slavery itself. Burwell's petition was denied. In 1829, Phil (Phill) Cooler, another former slave from Gloucester, submitted a petition in which he stated that he was married to Eliza Morris, a free black woman who had purchased his freedom. He said that he and Morris had several children and that he would like to remain in the state, where he and his wife owned some real and personal property. Although 18 white men endorsed Cooler's petition and asked that he be allowed to stay in Virginia, his request was denied.[17]

Freedom as a Birthright

One of Mathews County's most unusual legal cases involved a lawsuit initiated in 1806 by Jackey Wright, a slave, who sued her owner, Houlder Hudgins. She claimed that because she was of Native American descent, she should be free. Court testimony reveals that Wright sued Hudgins because he had sold her and her three children to a slave trader who was planning to take them south to another state. Wright claimed that she was the great-granddaughter of an Indian woman named Frances Mingo of Prince George County, the granddaughter of Betty Mingo, and the daughter of Phoebe Wilson. She also said that she and her mother, Phoebe, had been sold to Sir John Peyton and that after his death, Houlder Hudgins had purchased Jackey and her children from his estate. Renowned jurist George Wythe, then Chancellor of the Chancery Court, ruled in Jackey Wright's favor, noting that Virginia's bill of rights declared that "freedom is the birth-right of every human being." Wythe's decision infuriated Hudgins, who filed an appeal with the forerunner of the Virginia Supreme Court. He hired Edmund Randolph as his attorney, who when making his case noted that "the grounds of the decree are subversive to slavery." Hudgins insisted that Jackey Wright had always been a slave, and that in 1794 he had legally bought her from Peyton's estate for £55. He said that he had been present when Peyton purchased Jackey's mother and that her mother was the daughter of an Indian *man*, not an Indian *woman*. This was a critical issue, because under Virginia law, a child assumed the status of its mother. On that basis, Hudgins contended that Jackey Wright and her children were not entitled to freedom. William Dudley, Peter Foster, Martha Gunther, James H. Roy, and Philip Tabb came into court to substantiate Hudgins' claim that Phoebe Wilson was a slave, but they did not address her ancestry. Ultimately, St. George Tucker and his fellow Supreme Court justices ruled that Hudgins had not provided sufficient evidence to refute Jackey Wright's claim to being of Indian descent through her maternal line. In support of their decision, they noted that Jackey Wright was fair-skinned and had long, straight hair.

Some white Virginians had antislavery sentiments but did not favor manumission. The American Colonization Society (ACS) was established in late 1816 for the purpose of transporting America's free and newly freed blacks to Liberia, in West Africa, where they could establish a colony. Among the ACS's proponents were James Madison, Thomas Jefferson, John Hartwell Cocke II, and Henry Clay, who considered it a practical alternative to emancipation. During the 1840s, members of Mathews County's Tompkins family supported the ACS's work financially. Although the organization tried to convince the public that colonization was a good solution to a vexing problem, it was an issue on which whites and blacks were divided along philosophical lines. Ultimately, less than 7,000 freed slaves were transported to Liberia and over time, and support for the ACS waned.

A newspaper article published in New York City in August 1817 reveals that the Virginia's General Assembly occasionally enacted laws that conflicted with the Constitution of the United States. For example, Mathews County's court justices were obliged to deal with a case involving a free black woman from Rhode Island, who had settled in Mathews. Because a state law prohibited free blacks from other states from moving to Virginia, some local citizens wanted the newcomer, termed an "intruder," to be removed. However, her attorney laid a petition before the circuit court, asking for a writ of *habeas corpus* on the grounds that the woman was a United States citizen who was enrolled in her home state's militia and "was entitled to all the privileges and immunities of Citizens in the several States." The same issue reportedly surfaced in Louisiana and other states.[18]

Overland Transportation and Communication

During the first half of the nineteenth century stage coaches made regular runs through Gloucester County using the Old Stage Road, the forerunner of the modern Route 17. Mail intended for Mathews County was transferred to a post rider who brought it overland. In 1800, post offices were established in three locations: Belle Isle (Hudgins), with Thomas Lumpkin as postmaster; Mathews Courthouse, with Henry Respess as postmaster; and North End, with Andrew Van Bibber as postmaster. Over the years, a succession of local businessmen served as Mathews Courthouse's postmaster. In April 1806, tavern-keeper Henry Respess was replaced by Edmund J. Briggs, who was followed by Seth Briggs in October 1808. Thomas James became the community's postmaster in October 1809 and almost certainly used his store as the post office. In January 1818, he was replaced by Alden G. Cushman, another storeowner, who served until January 1824, when merchant Benjamin Bramhall took over. Finally, in November 1835 Elijah Barnum, a Mathews Courthouse merchant, became postmaster. All of the men who served as the postmaster of Mathews Courthouse owned property on the main roads that passed through the county seat. Some mail probably arrived by water carriage, perhaps at nearby Williams Wharf, and then was brought overland. Andrew Van Bibber served as North End's postmaster until January 1809 when he was replaced by Jasper S. Clayton. William Blake took over in December 1813 and served until January 1819, when Henry P. Van Bibber became postmaster. Philip Sale succeeded him in July 1828, but Van Bibber returned to office just a few months later, in December 1828.

A schematic map made by President James Madison's cousin, Bishop James Madison, in 1807 and updated in 1818 reveals that much of Virginia was served by well-established public roads and lesser byways. In 1807 the forerunners of Routes 14 and 198 and were identified as important transportation corridors. Madison labeled Gwynn's Island, Milford Haven, and Winter Harbor. He identified Mathews Courthouse, the New Point Lighthouse, Belle View (Armistead Smith's home), and areas he associated with Major Tabb, John Patterson, and the Clayton family. He indicated that there was a mill at the head of Stutts Creek, but he omitted most of the other man-made features in Mathews County.

In 1819, the General Assembly enacted legislation requiring Virginia's court justices to commission maps of their counties, drawings that were to be used in preparing a detailed map of the state. Cartographer John Wood was hired by the Commonwealth of Virginia, and on February 4, 1820, he informed the General Assembly that he had surveyed ten counties and presented two copies of each map. Although some of Wood's county maps have survived, if he made a map of Mathews County, it has not come to light. However, Wood's drawing of the Piankatank River basin, prepared in 1817, before he was hired by state officials, identifies by name the sites of several points of land on which he may have set up his surveying equipment. They were Cow, Burtons, Iron, Rowens, and Holland Points, Tomson's (Thompson's) house just west of Burtons Point, and Dickson's (probably Dixon's) house, just east of Iron Point. John Wood died before he finished mapping Virginia and was replaced by Herman Böye. Böye's map of the state, made in 1825 and published a year later, probably includes much of the topographic information Wood compiled, but it is less detailed and contains less information about the built environment.

Virginia officials hoped to foster economic development by publishing Böye's map, which depicted the state's relatively elaborate network of public roads that would accommodate commerce and trade. On the Böye map, the forerunners of Routes 14 and 198 were shown prominently and were linked by the forerunner of County Route 602, now known as Burkes Pond Road. A mill was located where Route 14 crossed Burke Mill Stream and another mill was shown at Burke Pond. At Blackwater Creek's head, Böye placed a symbol, identifying a public house of worship, the site at which Kingston Parish's Upper Church stood. He also labeled the location traditionally known as The Battery. The forerunners of County Routes 617, 618, and 660 extended into Whites Neck, which Böye identified by name. He identified Mathews Courthouse as the county seat and showed Route 198's junction with County Route 223, which headed toward Cricket Hill and Gwynn's Island. The forerunners of County Routes 639 and 640 extended into Crab Neck and County Route 644's forerunner led toward Billups Creek. Böye indicated that there was a house of worship on the lower side of Put In Creek, where Kingston Parish's Lower Church was located, and he showed another church at the intersection of Routes 198 and County Route 223, now the site of Mathews Baptist Church. A church also was located near the intersection of Route 14 and County Route 608, which headed toward Horn Harbor. Along the way, County Route 608 intersected with County Route 609, which met up with County Routes 611 and 613. Interestingly, Williams Wharf, an official port and customs facility, was not identified, nor were Mathews County's wharves and ferries.[19]

The New Point Comfort Lighthouse

On March 3, 1801, Congress agreed to erect a lighthouse at New Point Comfort, where the Chesapeake and Mobjack Bays converge, and appropriated $5,000 for the project. They also called upon Virginia's governor to secure land in the area and to then cede it to the United States government.[20] Shortly thereafter, William Davies, superintendent of the lighthouses in the Port Norfolk region, was ordered to select a suitable site on which the New Point Comfort lighthouse could be built, taking into account the land's elevation. After that had been accomplished, he was supposed to hire a contractor and procure building materials. Customs duties were to provide the funds needed for lighthouse construction. In May 1801, James Patterson surveyed New Point Comfort Island, selected what he considered a firm and elevated site, and recommended that one and a half or two acres be purchased. However, property owner Philip Tabb of Gloucester County wanted more than the land was worth. Ultimately, though, Tabb sold the entire island at the tip of the New Point Comfort peninsula to his neighbor, Elzy Burroughs, and recommended that Burroughs be chosen to construct the lighthouse. Afterward, Burroughs, who had erected the Old Point Comfort and Smith's Point lighthouses, sold two acres to the government for $150.

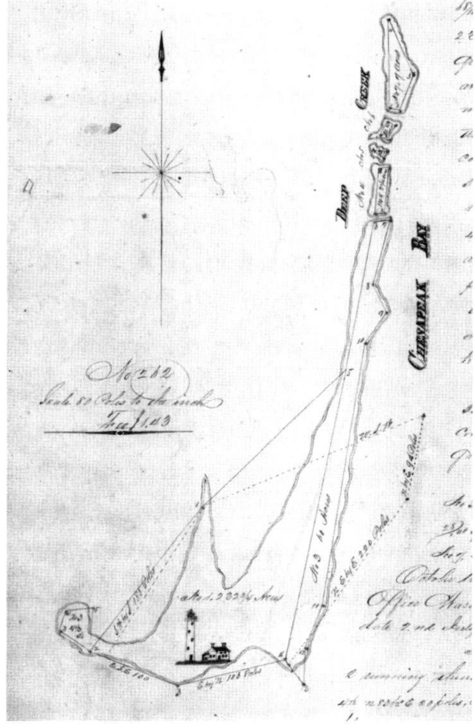

New Point Comfort Lighthouse and environs in 1833. Mathews County Land Book 1, p. 154.

On January 15, 1802, Virginia's General Assembly authorized the governor to transfer the lighthouse acreage to the United States government, but stipulated that if it wasn't built within seven years, or was abandoned for seven years, the property would revert to the state. When bids were sought for construction of the New Point Comfort lighthouse, no one applied. However, Congress appropriated an additional $3,500 in March 1803, and Elzy Burroughs, whose work was highly regarded, submitted the successful proposal. The octagonal lighthouse, constructed with hewn sandstone and lined with rubble stone, was to be 58 feet high and close to a brick oil vault, a two-story brick dwelling, and a brick kitchen that was to be no more than six feet from the house. Francis Armistead was assigned to oversee construction. Work on the lighthouse commenced in spring 1804 and proceeded at a brisk pace, but the contractor hired to build the lighthouse keeper's dwelling became ill and failed to complete it. Burroughs, who had erected a home on the island and moved his family there, sought—and received—permission to act as the lighthouse's keeper.[21] On January 17, 1805, the New Point Comfort lighthouse's lantern was lit for the first time, and the lighthouse project was completed by April 15, 1806.

Seasonal hurricanes and nor'easters impacted coastal Virginia from time to time, almost always wreaking havoc, and at least two of these storms occurred while the New Point Comfort lighthouse was under construction. During an October 1802 storm, as many as 11 square-rigged vessels reportedly gathered at New Point Comfort. British and French ships often paused there to take on water, as did other ocean-going vessels that came up the coast. Although there is little information about the hurricane that hit the East Coast in September 1804, it is known to have struck South Carolina, and then moved in a northerly direction along the Virginia coast, bringing high winds and unusually high tides to localities bordering the Chesapeake Bay. In late December 1804 a French frigate, *Le President*, paused at New Point Comfort to wait out a winter storm. Aboard were Napoleon Bonaparte's youngest brother, Jerome, and his pregnant wife, the former Elizabeth (Betsy) Patterson of Baltimore.[22]

A large hurricane moved up the coast in late August 1806. After crossing eastern North Carolina and passing just east of Norfolk, it roared up the bay. It appears that there was little damage to shipping, but buildings, fences, and trees were blown down. Over the years, many vessels whose crews experienced distress at sea on account of severe weather sought refuge at New Point Comfort. Sometimes, turbulent weather proved overwhelming. A shipwreck occurred in the vicinity of New Point Comfort in early December 1812, when the schooner *Fox* was cast away during a severe storm. Because the calamity occurred about 200 yards offshore, the crew made it to land safely, but the *Fox's* cargo was lost. In early September 1821, a truly memorable storm swept up the East Coast. According to newspaper accounts, on the morning of September 3 heavy rain commenced to fall. It was followed by gale-force winds that toppled chimneys and trees, broke windows, and ripped ships from their moorings. One mariner who passed by New Point Comfort shortly after the storm reported seeing numerous cattle, sheep, and horses that had been drowned. Low-lying communities on both sides of the Chesapeake Bay suffered greatly and crops were destroyed. Only four years later, another destructive hurricane hit eastern Virginia during the first week of September, and it brought rain, violent winds, and high tides. The storm lingered for 27 hours, and the tide reportedly rose 18 inches higher than it had within the last 40 years. In August 1830, gale force winds swept through Mathews County, knocking down trees and destroying field crops. According to one account, the storm lasted for five hours.[23]

The Wolf Trap's Navigational Aids

The shoals known as the Wolf Trap, located midway between New Point Comfort and Gwynn's Island, continued to pose problems for ships in the Chesapeake Bay, and in early March 1819 Congress authorized the construction of a lighthouse on Windmill Point *or* the placement of "a light vessel or boat on the Wolf Trap shoals." A decision was made to mark the Wolf Trap and, in 1821 a 180-ton lightship, one of the first in the nation, was placed at the shoals. Congress's appropriations for 1823 included $500 for the lightship's keeper's salary. Despite the presence of a lightship, in 1824 the *Draper* of Boston ran aground on the Wolf Trap. In 1835, Joseph Martin made note of the New Point Comfort lighthouse and said that the Wolf Trap shoals were marked by a light boat stationed offshore.[24]

Williams Wharf

Samuel Williams, who during the early 1770s had purchased the plantation that surrounded the East River warehouse, paid taxes on 580 acres in 1782. His property, which abutted the lower side of Put In Creek's mouth, extended down the East River for approximately two miles. When the state enumeration was compiled in 1783, he headed a household that included 10 white people and 25 enslaved blacks. A more comprehensive enumeration taken in 1784 reveals that the Williams plantation had one dwelling and ten other buildings. During 1786, Samuel Williams bought a neighboring parcel from James Pead (Peed), and a year later, he purchased some adjoining land from Richard Callis. Both of these parcels, delimited on a plat made during the 1790s, were located close to the mouth of Put In Creek. By November 1783, Williams had been named to the Kingston Parish vestry, and in January 1784 he became a churchwarden. He and a fellow vestryman, Armistead Smith, signed a document, making Moses Hudgins's son, William, an apprentice to John Billups Jr., who agreed to teach him the mariner's trade. In 1787, Williams and Smith, as churchwardens, were ordered to report on the revenues derived from rental of the parish glebe and its slaves.

Samuel Williams made his will on February 19, 1788, and died on May 19, 1789. He was interred in a family cemetery overlooking a small tributary of Put In Creek. An inventory of his personal effects made on October 4, 1790, reflects his affluence and diverse interests. His home was well furnished, and his family had use of several silver tablespoons, an abundance of ceramic vessels for serving and consuming food and beverages, and fine glassware. He was probably clean-shaven, for razors and razor straps were listed in his inventory, and he owned a silver watch. He had an assortment of books, an indication that he was literate. Williams (or a member of his family) had an interest in music, for a violin and a flute were among his possessions. He owned many valuable slaves and large herds of sheep, cattle, hogs, and horses, along with utilitarian items, such as scales for counting currency, a loom, a spinning wheel, and a substantial quantity of agricultural tools. He also had a whaling vessel.

Shortly after Samuel Williams's death, his land was distributed among his heirs, and when Mathews County's first tax commissioners compiled their records in 1791, Williams's youngest son, Thomas, was paying taxes on parcels that consisted of 340 acres and 35 acres. In 1793, the assessor began putting the initials "WH" by Thomas Williams' name, implying that he was in possession of the warehouse property. His holdings then extended in an easterly direction as far as Weston Creek. On May 5, 1791, Thomas Williams paid Mathew Floyd and Daniel Dunston for building a mill.[25] The late Samuel Williams' second oldest son, William, was credited with 105 acres "at the church," whereas his widow Margaret had use of 212 acres, her dower third. By 1795, William Williams had come into sole possession of 317 acres in the immediate vicinity of the church. A plat shows that it consisted of the 105 acres he had inherited in 1791 plus the acreage previously attributed to his stepmother, Margaret. One corner of his property, identified as "CC," was next to Kingston Parish's Lower Church.[26] William Williams died in 1798, and John Patterson acquired 317½ acres from his estate. That land was located on the lower side of County Route 614, and in 1770 had been part of a 341-acre tract that Francis Tomkies surveyed for Caleb Hunley. Patterson, who represented Mathews County in the General Assembly and served as a county justice and clerk of court, eventually acquired some additional land in the same vicinity. At the time of his death in August 1824 at age 63, he was in possession of the 600-acre plantation known as Poplar Grove and an adjoining 245-acre tract that was contiguous and further upstream. His administrator and son-in-law Christopher Tompkins offered Patterson's land and slaves for sale at public auction and then purchased the property himself.[27]

The East River Custom House

In February 1802, a group of Mathews County citizens began urging their federal representatives to establish a port or customs office in the county. Their lobbying proved successful, and a new port of entry, the District of East River, opened for business on June 30, 1803. The new district was supposed to serve the North and East Rivers, Mobjack Bay, and all of the other navigable waterways within Mathews County. The President of

Custom House at Williams Wharf.
Courtesy of the Virginia Department of Historic Resources.

the United States was authorized to appoint a collector and surveyor or inspector of the customs for the newly created district. The East River District's principal customs official was to have an office at the port and receive an annual salary of $200 a year plus the other fees and emoluments to which he was entitled under the law.

On July 8, 1802, William Nelson Jr., a federal judge, sent a letter to President James Madison, recommending that his nephew, Thomas Nelson Jr., be appointed collector of the newly-established East River District customs office. He said that Thomas, who was almost 22 years old, was college-educated, had some legal training, and had for a time lived in a counting house. Despite Judge Nelson's recommendation, merchant Francis Armistead of Mathews County received the appointment. The custom house, an agency of the United States Treasury Department, was located on land that Thomas Williams had inherited from his late father, Samuel Williams, the tract on which the Easternmost or East River warehouse had stood. Over the years, Thomas Williams retained ownership of the custom house property and rented it to the United States government. When he died in 1823, his acreage descended to his heirs. An October 1828 survey depicts the 180-acre parcel of cleared land on which the custom house stood, acreage that had been allocated to William Williams, Thomas's son. Although very little information is available about the East River custom house's earliest years, some insight can be gleaned from a newspaper article published in 1818. When a small schooner suspected of piratical activities entered local waters, the Collector of Customs dispatched the revenue cutter to investigate. Although Captain Ham took the cutter into nearby waterways, he couldn't gather meaningful intelligence. However, a local pilot named Williams reportedly saw the schooner enter the North River and then hide just out of the cutter's view. Mathews County residents, rallying to the threat posed by pirates, overpowered the schooner's crew and the Collector of the East River custom house took possession of their vessel. The suspected pirates were promptly arrested and jailed but later slipped away to Baltimore. Several months later, Captain Ham had to deal with the captain and crew of a Spanish ship captured by an American privateer in the Gulf of Mexico and brought up the coast. The privateer's crew mutinied; when they reached Mobjack Bay, they put the Spaniards ashore, leaving them to fend for themselves. Virginia officials, upon conferring with the Spanish consul, transferred the men to a ship that was bound for Baltimore. In January 1819, the presence of a British frigate and two brigs at New Point Comfort caused some uneasiness, but a deserter reported that their objective was to winter over in Mobjack Bay.

Occasionally, mariners tried to elude customs officials. In March 1823, the revenue cutter *James Monroe* encountered two vessels that had come to the aid of the *Dash*, a schooner that had run aground on New Point Comfort during a strong gale. The rescue ships offloaded the *Dash's* cargo, enabling it to get afloat, but Captain John C. Jones of the *James Monroe* discovered that the *Dash* had spent five days in Mobjack Bay without making contact with customs officials. Therefore, he took custody of the ship and its cargo and delivered it to the Collector of Customs.

Besides enforcing the law, the men who operated revenue cutters tried to assist mariners in peril at sea. For example, when the New York schooner *Prompt* ran aground at New Point Comfort, not far from the lighthouse, in

1826, a revenue cutter and some other vessels came to her aid and helped in recovering her cargo. Sometimes, watercraft that already had been inspected by customs agents congregated at New Point Comfort.

An account book that was maintained by Collector of the Customs John B. Roberts, a merchant, contains information that spans the years 1819 to 1852.[28] For example, Roberts noted that in October 1819 Leaven Gayle, Richard Billups, John Patterson, Christopher Tompkins, Miles King, and Humphrey Gwyn posted bonds on which they paid interest, funds covering the customs duties they owed on their vessels and on imported goods.[29] Humphrey Gwyn, as customs inspector, made sure that all goods were examined and weighed. Roberts, as customs collector, paid the office rent and bought stationary and other supplies out of the duties received on goods imported in American vessels. He also made regular disbursements toward the operation of lighthouses, the American marine hospital, and the revenue cutter. On December 31, 1826, when Roberts took an inventory of the government property at the East River custom house, he indicated that besides a revenue boat, there were 11 volumes of United States law books, copies of certain Acts of Congress, and a volume listing the tariffs charged as duties. A thermometer, a hydrometer, a beam, a gauging rod, and a vantage rod also were on hand. Roberts indicated that as Collector of Customs, he was responsible for the revenue cutter and the volumes of legal records, whereas the customs inspector was responsible for the various instruments used in performing inspections. During 1826, customs duties were paid by Samuel W. Brown, James and Edward Davis, Isaac Foster, Alex Galt, John L. Hudgins, Barzillar Kirwan, and John Thomas, who were licensed merchants.

William White and Francis Armistead became Surveyors of the Customs in 1827, and John B. Roberts and Humphrey Gwyn continued serving in their former capacities. In 1831, Roberts informed his superiors that no sick or disabled seamen in his district were being paid out of the hospital fund. He died shortly thereafter and in July his executrix, Frances Roberts, presented his accounts as collector of customs. A report filed in September 1834 indicates that there were four registered vessels then operating in the East River District: a ship, a brigantine, and two schooners. A total of 52 schooners, five sloops, and five vessels had passed through the East River

District, where a total of 120 seamen were usually employed. During 1830 and 1831 four seamen received funds under the Act for the Relief and Protection of American Seamen. Two were from Fredericksburg, while James McBride and Michael Robins were Mathews County natives. McBride was reportedly 39 years old and 5 feet 9 inches tall, whereas Robins was age 19 and 5 feet 6 inches tall. Both men had a dark complexion. According to Joseph Martin's *Gazetteer*, a total of 1,700 tons of shipping passed through the East River customs facility in 1835. He said that the vessels based there included a ship, a brig, a number of schooners, and some smaller watercraft, and that some of the vessels had made voyages to almost every part of the commercial world.

In March 1839, Surveyor of the Customs Francis Armistead reported that he had presented an account of the custom house's activities to Thomas Nelson, Esq. and prepared a report for the Treasury Department. Armistead, a poor record-keeper, left a seven-year gap in the records. He died, and in September 1839 was replaced by Thomas Williams's son, William, who had inherited the land on which the custom house stood. In 1840, William Williams reported that he had expended $2.50 a year in office rent and another $2.00 on stationary. He said that he had measured a new square-sterned schooner, the *Mary Ann*, which had been built in Mathews County by Elijah and George Hudgins and was 52 feet long. Three years later, he filed a report stating that the custom house's only revenue boat, in service since 1827, was leaky and wasn't worth repairing. He indicated that the vessel lacked a deck, was 20 feet long, had three sails, and two attached oars. By June 1844, the port of East River had been made part of the District of York and had ceased being independent. William Williams was still serving as collector in 1846 when his annual salary, $200, was approved by William Nelson, Esq., the collector at Yorktown. An account book that dates to the 1850s and early 1860s reveals that Williams Wharf still was an important customs facility and that Joseph Bohannon was postmaster at the wharf.[30]

The War of 1812

On June 10, 1798, shortly before the French Revolution drew to a close, a group of Mathews County citizens voiced their concerns about America's deteriorating relationship with France, its closest ally. The men, with Rev. Armistead Smith as chairman and John Patterson as clerk, drafted a series of resolutions that they forwarded to Thomas Evans, their Congressional delegate, who presented them to President John Adams. At a time when America's political elite were split along pro-French and pro-British lines, Mathews citizens urged the president to maintain a policy of neutrality. The Mathews men's petition came at a sensitive time, for the British had begun harassing neutral American merchant ships, and the French government's consul to the United States flaunted his opposition to American neutrality. Great Britain and France continued to engage in conflicts that threatened American interests on the high seas. Men from British ships boarded American vessels and impressed seamen into the Royal Navy, whereas French privateers preyed upon American merchant ships.[31] Newspapers along the Atlantic Seaboard recounted instances of American ships being waylaid by British and French vessels. Presidents Thomas Jefferson and James Madison successively applied economic pressure in an attempt to enforce American neutrality, but their strategies were unpopular because they put thousands out of work. In late 1811, when conflict appeared imminent, President Madison and Congress applied a new set of trade restrictions. They proved unsuccessful, and on June 18, 1812, the United States declared war on Great Britain. The British responded by blockading the Chesapeake Bay and the Delaware River. Although American ships occasionally slipped through the British blockade, it severely impacted the nation's economy and deprived the government of revenue normally derived from trade.

America's small fleet of naval vessels, gunboats, and revenue cutters was the force that had to face the Royal Navy's 600 ships. Heavily-armed American privateers and warships engaged British ships on the high seas, but revenue cutters, navy gunboats, and a few American warships tried to defend the East Coast from the combined might of the Royal Navy and British privateers. Although Virginians expected the federal government to defend their state against invasion, President James Monroe informed

Governor James Barbour that it was instead up to him to do so. Therefore, if British raiding parties were to land, the local militia commander would have to summon the county's white men between the ages of 16 and 45, most of whom were unaccustomed to obeying orders and whose only training was attending musters at the county seat. The 61st Regiment's muster rolls for Mathews County included: Quartermasters John P. James and A.G. Cushman, Quartermaster Sergeant William Bohannon, Sergeant Major Joseph C. Maigne (?), and Sergeant Mates Bartholomew Gayle and William Taliaferro. On the other hand, Captains John Billups, Langley B. Eddins, Peter Foster, Gabriel Hughes, Thomas James, Francis Jarvis, Christopher T. Lewis, Henry W. Soles, Christopher Tompkins, and Frederick Weedon, and Lieutenant Thomas T. Tabb led companies of men. Most of the soldiers were privates, who served between 10 and 25 days. Some companies had a fifer and a drummer, and Lieutenant Tabb's company had a musician, Humphrey Hunley. A significant number of the men in Captains Hughes's and Soles's companies were detached from other units.

Because Virginia's governor was keenly aware of Tidewater's vulnerability, he ordered 12,000 men to be prepared for mobilization. Meanwhile, the construction of navy gunboats got underway in Norfolk, Hampton, and Mathews County. The newly designed watercraft were intended to be faster than the ones they replaced, but still capable of entering shallow water. State officials knew that the British were likely to invade by means of the Chesapeake Bay and realized that its numerous navigable tributaries made Mathews and Gloucester Counties especially vulnerable. Those fears became a reality on February 4, 1813, when five British warships entered the Chesapeake Bay, seized and burned merchant ships, landed a small force at New Point Comfort, and came ashore on Gwynn's Island. By March 6, there were 17 British warships in the bay, more vessels than the entire American Navy had at sea.

On March 14, 1813, Major Mann Page informed the governor that for the past week he and the 61st Regiment's 2nd Battalion had been at the mouth of the Severn River, where they had "a full view of the British Ships and tenders off New Point Comfort ... the best harbour for Privateers and Ships that draw no more than 3½ fathoms of water." Page said that some enemy vessels had moved into East River and expressed his hope that the British might "receive some aid" from the field pieces in Mathews. He added that "Among the vessels that run into these waters are many of a very suspicious character" and said that he was sure that they were furnishing the British fleet with provisions and intelligence. He said that on Friday, a large ship dropped anchor near New Point Comfort, a brig that had slipped in after dark.

Governor Barbour and his council voiced their concerns about the Mathews militia, for the county clerk had derided Colonel Leaven Gayle by declaring that he was "the most uninformed man upon earth" who possessed "no military talent whatsoever." Criticism was also leveled at Major John Billups, who was described as an elderly drunk who rarely showed up for duty. Thanks to pressure from the governor's council, Billups was relegated to a figurehead and was replaced by Christopher Tompkins, a well-connected merchant and mariner whose experience extended beyond Mathews County. However, Tompkins's detractors said that the majority of Mathews militiamen despised him and would defy his orders. Significantly, when the Council chose Tompkins, they disregarded Langley B. Eddins, who had been nominated by the justices of the county court and had the support of Houlder Hudgins. Eddins caused problems when he told local militiamen that "they were not bound to obey any officer except Colonel Gayle." Although Eddins wasn't arrested for mutiny, he eventually resigned his captain's commission. As time went on, at least two prominent local citizens proffered that the militiamen were so tired and dispirited that they were likely to abandon the county to the mercy of an invading foe.

Some Mathews County slaves, who seem to have assumed that the British would prevail, seized the opportunity to commit a robbery. According to communiques sent to Governor James Barbour, on the night of March 2, 1813, nine slaves (eight adult males and a 16-year-old boy named Sci Gillett)[32] assembled near the Rev. Armistead Smith's gate. Then, they walked to John Ripley's store and broke in. The would-be burglars awakened Ripley, who reached for his musket, which misfired. The slaves, who identified themselves as Englishmen, brandished a sword, threatened Ripley's life, and claimed that in the past he had refused to let them have water or fresh provisions. After they stole $1,900 in gold and silver coins from Ripley's money box, they left. Later, each man took $6, and a slave named Humphrey reportedly buried the rest of the coins. John Patterson of Poplar Grove became suspicious when his slave, Harry, began spending more money than "he could have acquired by honest means" and had his overseer interrogate Sci Gillett, who confessed. After the perpetrators were rounded up and put in jail, Humphrey was induced to lead local magistrates to the site where Ripley's coins were buried. On March 18, 1813, all eight adult slaves were tried for burglary and sentenced to hang. Because the men had been convicted of a capital offense, transcripts of their trial were forwarded to the governor and his council for confirmation of the verdict. On April 17, Council members decided that Humphrey and Harry would be hanged in Mathews County. The other men were to witness the execution and then be sold to a slave trader, who would transport them out of Virginia. Sci Gillett, though spared harsh punishment, eventually fled to the British. News of the slaves' robbery of Ripley's store and their subsequent punishment spread as far as Providence, Rhode Island.

Newspapers in Philadelphia, Boston, and New Hampshire reported that by March 11, the British had taken control of Mobjack Bay and that one of their launches and two tenders had chased a pilot boat into the mouth of the East River. A little fleet of sharp vessels that had been anchored in the Severn River moved into the East River and sailed upstream as far as they could. Two large Baltimore schooners also took refuge in the East River, which was defended by an artillery company that had two field pieces and three companies of infantry. Captain Sinclair and his flotilla, which controlled the Piankatank River's mouth, confronted the *Lottery*, a large British schooner that lay at anchor; the *Lottery* was heavily damaged and later sank off Gwynn's Island. Despite the Americans' success, the British captured between eight and ten vessels near Gwynn's Island and New Point Comfort, and by March 12 they had regained control of the Chesapeake Bay. However, they were thwarted in an attempt to reach the mainland, thanks to a March 17 confrontation with Captain Weedon's men, who were camped near New Point Comfort.

British barges were able to enter Virginia waters at will, capturing vessels one or two at a time, and rumors spread that the British were encouraging Virginia slaves to revolt. In mid-March, Lieutenant Colonel Leaven Gayle informed his superiors that the county's waterways were controlled by the enemy and that waterborne communication was impossible. He said

British soldiers relaxing at a sutler's booth.
Courtesy of the Anne A.K. Brown Collection, Brown University and www.warof1812.com.

that three gunboats were sent to the mouth of the Piankatank River because some unfamiliar schooners were sighted and that several richly-laden merchantmen en route to France had taken shelter in the East River. Gayle said that two British tenders and three barges, supported by a large gun brig lying in Mobjack Bay, entered the mouth of the East River but were driven back by two schooners from his little fleet and 200 men from his regiment. Nathaniel Burwell of Gloucester County informed the governor that a large British fleet came within four miles of Gwynn's Island and that the enemy was capable of landing anywhere in the region within two hours. Moreover, his men's arms and ammunition and their two cannon had been sent down to Norfolk.[33]

In mid-June 1813, a British barge captured a pilot boat anchored in Pepper Creek, and later in the month, 900 enemy troops landed on the James-York Peninsula and began advancing west toward Richmond. In July and August, Sergeant William A. Billups and his men were stationed at the Garden Patch; Captain Weedon, Sergeant Christopher Billups, and some men from other companies were based on Gwynn's Island; and men from Peter Foster's company were at John Winder's point. Local citizens were ordered to send their canoes to Queens and Stutts Creeks, where they would be protected by armed guards. Naval action continued, and in early December, five British barges chased the *Friends Adventure*, which was carrying a cargo of tar when it ran aground at New Point Comfort. Later in the month, a significant engagement at the mouth of the Piankatank River resulted in the sinking of a British schooner. Captain Joseph Tarbell, who was proceeding up the Chesapeake Bay with nine gunboats and two tenders, reached the mouth of the East River just as some fog was lifting. There, he found several British vessels that were previously anchored in the Piankatank. When a British frigate's crew spied the American vessels and signaled to the brigs, they headed for the New Point Comfort lighthouse and dropped anchor. The next day, Tarbell and the vessels under his command left Mathews County, thanks to a strong northwesterly wind, although they had hoped to intercept two British brigs that were interfering with coastal trade. On December 29, the British landed at New Point Comfort, destroyed the lighthouse's oil vault, damaged the keeper's dwelling, broke the lantern's panes of glass, and raised the British flag over the lighthouse.

In late January 1814, a man whose regiment had been at New Point Comfort for three or four days informed a friend that the British had brought three brigs as close to the point as they dared, ostensibly so that they could replenish their drinking water. However, two slaves and a British sailor, who had deserted from one of the ships, claimed that the vessels were short of provisions. The Americans, upon realizing that the British might send some foraging parties ashore, threw up a small earthwork on the mainland and commenced firing a six-pounder. As soon as one of the British barges was hit, the fleet hurriedly left. At the beginning of March, Major Christopher Tompkins informed the governor that the British had returned to New Point Comfort and were using the lighthouse as a watchtower from which they could see everything within a three-mile radius. Tompkins urged the governor to send at least 170 men from the state militia to Mathews County to relieve the local militiamen of their duties, as their families depended on them for support. Tompkins said that a guard of twelve local men could be placed in the county's most exposed locations and that a "flying camp" or rapid response force of 250 state militiamen would be less costly and more effective. He added that one company of mounted riflemen, one of light artillery, and two of infantry would provide great relief to the region. He said that although the lieutenant colonel had the authority to call upon adjacent counties' militias, the enemy could enter Mathews's waters without warning. Indeed, the British returned to New Point Comfort in mid-March and attempted to reach the mainland. Captain Weedon had his men fire on them, and although a British barge with 12-pound cannon came into position, it was driven back by the Americans' cannon fire.

Lieutenant Thomas R. Yeatman of Isleham on Blackwater Creek informed Major Christopher Tompkins that he had visited British Commodore Robert Barrie's ship, the *Dragon,* under a flag of truce and learned that 13 slaves had come aboard two nights earlier: four from Milford Haven, four from the East River, and five from the Blackwater Creek area. Yeatman asked Barrie what was being done with slaves who absconded to the British, and learned that some were taken to the King's Dockyard in Bermuda, where they entered the King's Service, received a man-of-war's allowance, and a shilling a day. Other slaves were sold by the British government for £30 a person and became indentured servants. Yeatman asserted that the British were deluding slaves with promises of a better life. In fact, the Rev. Armistead Smith claimed that runaways would often have returned home, had they not been persuaded that they would be better off on a British warship.[34] Barrie urged Yeatman to dispose of the ship he was having built or to be prepared to defend it, as Admiral George Cockburn was determined to burn every sailing vessel he encountered. When Tompkins passed Yeatman's information along to the governor, he said that Barrie claimed to be very familiar with the Americans' defensive forces and boasted that he could overwhelm them whenever he wanted to. In response to a new law that required privately-owned boats to be kept under the watchful eyes of armed sentinels, Tompkins noted that there were a thousand or more canoes in Mathews County and that almost every white person and most blacks had one.

During the spring and summer of 1814, the British fleet returned to the Chesapeake Bay, strengthened by units made available at the end of the Napoleonic Wars. In May, Christopher Tompkins informed the governor that thanks to an artillery piece, John Patterson had captured an enemy schooner in the East River loaded with more than a thousand barrels of flour. In June, the Richmond *Enquirer,* which had gained access to a letter Lieutenant Colonel Leaven Gayle sent to his adjutant general, reported that the British had taken control of Tangier Island and were using it as their base of operations. From there, they could cruise close to the Chesapeake's shoreline and venture unseen into the Rappahannock, Piankatank, East, and North Rivers at nighttime. The *Enquirer* noted that at least six large barges with 30 to 40 men apiece had reached the head of each river and taken soundings. When the British entered the East River, they captured the Baltimore schooner *Grecian* and seized its cargo. A Boston newspaper reported that in early June the British landed a barge in Mathews County and burned a new ship still on the stocks. When the British returned a few days later, they met with resistance from the local militia. In late June, several British barges near New Point Comfort were attacked. Although the barges were driven off, five militiamen were killed and six others were wounded.

The war dragged on, and in October 1814 some Mathews County citizens and people from neighboring counties asked the General Assembly not to allow militia officers to press men, horses, mules, oxen, wagons, and carts into service, or to remove boats or other watercraft to purportedly secure locations. According to the petitioners, if they were deprived of their canoes and other light watercraft, they would be unable to make a living. They also said that because the confiscated vessels were inadequately guarded, slaves were able to slip away to reach British ships. A month later, Mathews County residents sent their own petition to the assembly. Again, they stressed the need to prevent slaves from running away.

On Christmas Eve 1814, the Treaty of Ghent was signed, technically bringing the war to an end. Some war-weary men, eager to return home, left the army before they were officially released and were considered deserters. For example, 24-year-old John Williams, a Mathews County farmer, left his unit at Greenleaf's Point, in Washington. The army placed an advertisement in a Washington, D.C. newspaper, offering a reward to anyone who would deliver him to a military post in the United States. Nonetheless, overall the War of 1812 had a noticeable impact on the development of the United States, for it fostered nationalism and stimulated pride in the young nation's military.[35]

The Fate of Local Slaves Who Fled to the British

Thanks to the presence of British ships during 1812, 1813, and 1814, a significant number of Mathews County slaves seized the opportunity to escape to freedom. Houlder Hudgins reportedly lost ten slaves to the British and feared that he might lose the rest, fretting that he would be "left in his old age destitute of that support." The Rev. Armistead Smith sent two of his slaves, Bob and Robin, to the Richmond area so that they would "be out of the way of the Enemy." In April 1814, he reported that a protracted court martial hearing was held to debate the fate of two black men who had been spying for the British. Sometimes, runaway slaves were captured, whipped, and then jailed. Toward the end of the war, Mathews County's clerk of court reported that the county jail then held nine runaways who had been captured aboard a British schooner. The slaves' owners were urged to pay the jailor's fees and to reward the militiamen who apprehended them, or they else would be sold at auction.

Sci Gillett, the young slave whose life was spared because he had identified the men who had robbed John Ripley's store, fled to the British in March 1814. In June 1816, when John Patterson sailed to Bermuda aboard his schooner, *Maid of the Isles*, he recognized at least 15 ex-slaves from Mathews County who had joined the Colonial Marines. Three of them had formerly belonged to Patterson: Sci Gillett, Ned, and Hull, who had become a drummer. While Patterson's schooner was tied up in Bermuda, some ex-slaves from Mathews County, attired in their natty red, white, and black Colonial Marines uniforms,[36] went aboard to visit with the crew, men they had grown up with. According to the *Maid of the Isles*'s captain, William Dixon, when Hull came aboard, he saluted Patterson, saying that "he did not elope from him in consequence [of] ill treatment ... but that he preferred having his freedom." Scholars estimate that approximately 4,000 enslaved African Americans (primarily from the Chesapeake region and coastal Georgia) escaped from slavery during the War of 1812. Approximately half sailed to Nova Scotia and the remainder settled in Trinidad and other British colonies. Black refugees in Nova Scotia encountered an unwelcoming society and a government that repeatedly tried to remove them. An economic depression that followed the War of 1812 made jobs scarce, but the majority of black refugees who settled in Nova Scotia refused to leave. As late as December 1814, there were reports of slaves fleeing to the British.[37]

Providing for Military Veterans

Congress expanded the scope of military veterans' benefits in 1806 to include disabled men who had served in state troops and militia units. By 1816, there were 2,200 qualified pensioners on the federal roll, which included veterans from the War of 1812. In 1818, Congress decided to provide lifetime pensions to poverty-stricken Revolutionary War veterans of the Continental Line and the U.S. Navy, so long as they had served at least nine months. So many men submitted applications that in 1820 the government began requiring applicants to document their assets and income. For instance, when George Forrest of Mathews County, a 63-year-old disabled Revolutionary War veteran with four children, applied for a pension in August 1820, he acknowledged that he owned 42 acres of land; some cattle, sheep, and hogs; and an assortment of household and kitchen furniture. His claim was rejected. In 1828, Congress eliminated the requirement that veterans be permanently disabled or poverty-stricken. In June 1832, Congress passed a new pension act that allowed any officer or enlisted man who had served at least two years in the Continental Line, a state troop, a volunteer unit, a militia, or in any naval or marine forces to receive full pay for life. Those serving at least six months but less than two years could receive a smaller pension based upon their length of service. This relieved the state of Virginia of its obligation to provide veterans' pensions. In June 1836, Congress decided that the widows of Revolutionary War veterans could apply for a pension if they had married a veteran before January 1, 1794, and had not remarried. This policy remained in effect for many years.[38]

Collateral Damage

During 1814, when the British fleet's presence in the Chesapeake Bay made an invasion likely, Virginia's governor sent a detachment of Caroline County soldiers, who were under the command of a Captain Sizer, to Mathews County, where they were stationed for six months. These reinforcements were probably sent in response to Major Christopher Tompkins's request for state militia troops. Captain Leaven Gayle authorized the Caroline County men to use Kingston Parish's "Old Church" as their quarters—that is, the old house of worship near Williams Wharf. While the Caroline County soldiers stayed there, they destroyed the church's wooden flooring, most of the pews, and the communion table.[39]After the war, when the state gave Kingston Parish $205 in compensatory damages, the funds were given to Anthony Hudgins, who had custody of the church property. In December 1822, the General Assembly authorized Mathews County's Overseers of the Poor to sue Hudgins for refusing to relinquish Kingston Parish's $205. With the Lower Church destroyed and the Upper Church crumbling into ruins, worship services were most likely held in private homes. According to a newspaper article published in 1941, Mrs. Euphan Washington Roy of Green Plains, who was born in 1823, eventually saw that a wooden house of worship was built close to the site of Kingston Parish's old Upper Church, but it was destroyed by fire.[40]

The Kingston Parish Glebe

On December 8, 1809, the Rev. Armistead Smith of Kingston Parish submitted a petition to the General Assembly proposing that the glebe be sold and its proceeds invested.[41] He said that the glebe's buildings were ruinous and that neighbors often stole timber from the property. Smith suggested that his annual salary consist of the interest earned on the funds yielded by sale of the glebe, and said that his parishioners had no objections to his proposal. Smith's petition was approved and plans for the sale moved forward. A survey done in early 1810 determined that the glebe contained 500 acres, 33 acres less than the 1712 survey indicated. After the property's newly-defined boundaries were marked, it was carved into eleven large parcels. A dwelling overlooking Woodas Creek, the glebe's westernmost boundary line, was shown prominently on the 1810 plat, but the site on Put In Creek, occupied by a glebe house in 1712, was vacant. Court-appointed commissioners[42] placed an advertisement in the February 16, 1810, edition of the Richmond *Enquirer* announcing that the glebe would be auctioned off at the county courthouse on March 12 and that purchasers could buy the land on up to three years' credit. When the sale was held, John Patterson, Henry Digges, and Edward White bought three parcels apiece; William

Hurst bought two; and the remaining piece was purchased by Zachariah Adams. Because Adams died shortly thereafter, his 200-acre tract was carved into four 50-acre lots and resold, with John Patterson as purchaser. As soon as sale monies were in hand, the commissioners paid local men for assisting the surveyor, writing deeds, drawing up mortgages and bonds, advertising the auction, and cutting the glebe's saleable timber. Auctioneer Gabriel Hughes was also paid.[43]

After the glebe was sold, John Lewis, who owned some property near the head of Put In Creek, initiated a lawsuit alleging that the commissioners had sold 89 acres that belonged to him. Several witnesses' sworn statements provide useful insights into the glebe's history. Mathew Gayle, who was 73, recalled that the Rev. Blacknall had occupied the glebe around 61 or 62 years earlier and had lived at James's Point, near the head of Put In Creek, and a Mrs. Dixon, who was 64,[44] said that Kingston Parish clergy had always had possession of the disputed acreage. She recalled that 37 or 38 years ago, Rev. John Dixon had rented part of the glebe to a man named Green, who also rented Dixon's blacksmith shop and built sailing vessels there.[45] John Gayle, another witness for the defendants, said that around 43 years ago, Mr. Dixon had authorized him to cut timber from the acreage Lewis was trying to claim. The Rev. Armistead Smith testified that in February 1809 he had sent some of his people to the glebe with a Mr. Foxwell to cut some heart pine logs for shingles and that the disputed acreage belonged to the parish. John Miller's son, Frank, who lived near the boundary line between Lewis and the glebe, said that he had never heard any complaints about encroachment. Miller's statement was corroborated by Gabriel Hughes, who claimed that he had lived on or close to the glebe for his entire life. Ultimately, plaintiff John Lewis lost his suit and was ordered to pay $2,000 for long-term use of the 89 acres he tried to claim.

When real estate tax rolls were compiled in 1814, three men were credited with portions of the glebe: Edward White had 44 acres; Thomas Hall had 25 acres; and William Hurst had 55 acres. The tax commissioner noted that their land had been transferred by the "commissioners for the sale of the glebe." The following year, tax officials credited George Lewis's estate 50 acres of the glebe and Seth Shepherd, with another 50 acres. John Patterson then had 164 acres of the glebe, which included the late Zachariah

Adams's land. All of these parcels were two miles from the courthouse. The remainder of the glebe's acreage was omitted from the tax records, probably because its purchasers hadn't finished paying for it.[46]

Providing for the Poor

The Rev. Armistead Smith died in late 1817, and two years later a group of local citizens asked the General Assembly to give the county's School Commissioners and Overseers of the Poor the funds generated by the sale of Kingston Parish's glebe and silver plate.[47] The petitioners noted that the county's poor were receiving food and shelter, but were not being educated, and recommended that a poorhouse and free school be built with the proceeds of the sale. In a separate petition, another group of Mathews County citizens noted that most poor children, especially orphans, were placed in families that required them to perform menial tasks and didn't allow them to attend the schools for the poor underwritten by the state's Literary Fund. They claimed that poor orphans were often placed in the homes of the lowest bidders, indigent families who used the children's stipends for their own support. The petitioners asked the General Assembly to merge the county's School Commissioners and Overseers of the Poor into one annually elected entity that would ensure that poor children received proper care and were taught to read and write.

Although the state legislature failed to adopt the petitioners' proposal, within a relatively short time Mathews County's Overseers of the Poor began making plans to operate a poorhouse. Between 1821 and 1822 they purchased 80 acres on the East River from the executors of the late Francis Litchfield (a shipbuilder), who had acquired his land in 1806. When the poorhouse property was surveyed in 1822, it was found to contain 85 acres rather than 80. The poorhouse tract bordered the East River and the upper side of Put In Creek's mouth and on the south, it was contiguous to Thomas Williams's land, which included the site of Kingston Parish's old Lower Church. The north side of the poorhouse land abutted the New Town tract's southern boundary and it extended east as far as Route 14's forerunner. By 1823, the Overseers of the Poor had erected $170 worth of buildings on their 85 acres, which were tax exempt. During 1826, they acquired 25 acres of adjoining land from Larkin Litchfield, some vacant property that was shown on the 1822 plat. Tax records suggest that the buildings on the poorhouse tract were in existence until around 1839.[48]

Steamboats and Packets Ply the Chesapeake Bay

From 1813 on, a multitude of steam-powered vessels from Baltimore provided passenger and freight service to Norfolk, Hampton, and Washington, D.C. Steamboats connected farmers and merchants to urban markets, industrial and cultural centers, and overseas outlets. Same-day steamers provided service to river landings, giving their passengers a pleasant daytime excursion, whereas other steamers furnished a fast shuttle service. The largest class of steamboats that operated on the Chesapeake was the overnight packet, which visited landings throughout Tidewater Virginia and Maryland. However, travel by steamboat was not without risks for vessels sometimes caught fire and collisions, groundings, and wrecks occurred from time to time. Steamboats also were at the mercy of the hurricanes and storm-force winds that swept up the bay, demolishing landings and ruining cargo. Ice sometimes blocked the bay's shipping channels and clogged the rivers for lengthy periods of time. Rate wars, economic depressions, and ruthless competition also characterized the steamboat era. However, for many years steam-powered vessels played a vitally important role in the economy of Tidewater Virginia. By the time the Maryland and Virginia Steam Boat Company was formed in 1838, steamboats were not a novelty on the Chesapeake Bay, for steam packets had been providing regular service for passengers, mail, and some freight for more than two decades. The new company, a consolidation of several much smaller competitors, advertised their vessels' days of departure and sailed whether or not their cargo holds were filled. The predictability of the packets' arrivals and departures were appreciated by the public and the business community. Steamboats frequently ran summer excursions between their regular runs. In 1839 the Baltimore Steam Packet Company emerged from the Maryland and Virginia Steam Boat Company.[49]

The Path to Religious Diversity

Although the first Great Awakening focused on people who already belonged to a faith community, the second Great Awakening, which began about 1800, extended to the unchurched. During revivals, evangelical preachers sought to include everyone in conversion. In the Tidewater and Low Country, Baptist and Methodist preachers converted whites and large numbers of blacks, both enslaved and free. Many whites took blacks' religious experiences seriously and welcomed them into their churches. The message of spiritual equality appealed to slaves and for the first time large numbers of blacks accepted Christianity. Sometimes, they slipped away to meet for worship in "hush harbors" or "brush arbors" that were hidden away in the woods.

Even before the Disestablishment, religious dissenters saw—and seized—the opportunity for evangelism. Late nineteenth-century Bishop William Meade of the Protestant Episcopal Church took a dim view of other denominations, noting that after the Disestablishment, the Lower Church of Middlesex County's Christ Church Parish was modified by "New Lights": evangelists intent on destroying "every vestige of Episcopal taste and usage." He said that "the high pulpit and sounding-board have been removed, and the reading-desk placed within the chancel." Sometimes a platform was erected to accommodate an evangelical preacher and pews were replaced with rough-cut and backless wooden benches. These changes were welcomed by those who had deeply resented the Anglican Church's status under colonial law and longed for a less formal, more emotional style of worship.

Francis Asbury, an ordained preacher, was one of five missionaries Anglican Methodist John Wesley sent to America in 1771. Wesley, arguably the moving force behind American Methodism, promoted the circuit riding system and traveled more than 100,000 miles in his mission.[50] Asbury's ordination as a bishop in 1784 marked the beginning of the Methodist Episcopal (or M.E.) Church, which was the first expression of Methodism in the United States. By the early nineteenth century it was the country's largest Protestant denomination. On January 3, 1788, Bishop Asbury, who had been riding a circuit in the Northern Neck, crossed the Rappahannock River, entered the M.E. Church's Gloucester Circuit and paused at "Brother Billups's in Kingston parish, Gloucester County," where he conducted "religious exercises." "Brother Billups" was most likely Humphrey Billups of Mathews County, who joined the M.E. Church as a young adult and was licensed to preach on September 30, 1812.[51] In time, the congregation of the Billups Meeting House, near Moon, built what became known at first as Salem Methodist Church, and eventually as Salem United Methodist Church. Other Methodist congregations who trace their beginnings to an early date include the Mathews Chapel Methodist Church, located east of Cobbs Creek,[52]and the St. Paul and Beulah Methodist Churches, both of which are descendants of the Point Comfort Church at Susan. The congregation of what became known as Bethel Methodist Church was formed by 1805.

In September 1819, the Revs. Samuel Garrard and Miles King of the M.E. Church placed an announcement in the Norfolk *American Beacon*, inviting the public to attend religious services that were to be held at the New Point Comfort Meeting-House on the 30th of the month. They said that their campground was located within 300 yards of Horn Harbor but was within a mile of Pea Creek and the East River. A year later, camp meetings were held at New Point Comfort and on Tangier Island. Captain L. Holden of the steamboat *Powhatan* offered to provide daily transportation to both meetings and to carry baggage, provisions and camping equipment free of charge. During the late 1820s and the into 1830s, the Rev. W.A. Billups performed weddings for couples who had procured a marriage license from Thomas R. Yeatman, clerk of the county court. Temperance became an increasingly important issue in the M.E. Church, and when a quarterly conference was held at Bethel in 1833, a resolution was passed against the sale or use of alcohol and congregations discussed forming temperance societies. In 1837, Humphrey Billups became a circuit rider on behalf of the Virginia Conference, and in 1839 the Mathews Circuit was formed from part of the Gloucester Circuit.

The Baptist faith in Mathews County dates to the last quarter of the eighteenth century and probably was introduced by Pastor Iverson Lewis of King and Queen County, who started churches in Gloucester County. The congregation of Mathews's first Baptist meeting house endorsed the Primitive Church's strict principles, which frowned upon intemperance, dancing, and fiddle-playing. The congregation, originally known as Kingston Baptist Church, eventually changed its name to Mathews Baptist Church. In time, it gave rise to ten other Baptist congregations in Mathews County. During the 1820s, Elder Peter Anslie, pastor of Mathews Baptist Church, and some other church leaders accepted the teachings of the Rev. Alexander Campbell, leader of the Disciples of Christ movement. By 1832, the Dover Baptist Association, which included Mathews Baptist Church, had severed its relationship with Campbell's followers. Some of Mathews Baptist's members, proponents of Campbell's teachings, left three years later, and by 1837 had established the Ephesus Meeting House near Hyco Corner. In October 1837, representatives from more than 50 of the Dover Baptist Association's churches convened at the Mathews Meeting House and drafted a petition they submitted to the state legislature in January 1838. At issue was the tendency of vendors to converge upon religious meetings, trying to sell cakes, sweets, and intoxicating beverages. Although the petitioners acknowledged the vendors' right to sell their goods, they claimed that such sales disrupted public worship and asked that they be prohibited.[53]

Mathews County Episcopalians, despite the growth of other Protestant denominations, continued to hold regular worship services. However, after the Rev. Armistead Smith's death in 1817, support seems to have waned. The parish's Lower Church, occupied by Caroline County troops during 1814, was never restored to use, and the Upper Church, if usable before Smith's death, gradually crumbled into ruins. Only a few pages of Kingston Parish's early nineteenth-century records survive. They indicate that during 1826 and 1827 three of Thomas James's slaves were baptized and that two parishioners died.

In 1835, Joseph Martin reported that Methodism was the predominant denomination in Mathews County and that there were seven meetinghouses, two of which belonged to reformed Methodists, and two Baptist meeting-houses whose congregations were small. He indicated that Mathews County had a few Episcopalians, whose churches had "fallen into dilapidation and decay" and that there were some Universalists who never had had a church. Martin indicated that almost every house-of-worship in Mathews County had a Sunday School.[54]

The Genesis of Public Education

Thomas Jefferson, unlike many of his contemporaries, was a proponent of public education, for he believed that an enlightened electorate was the best protection for rights of the free. In 1779, he proposed building public grammar schools in Virginia's counties where children of both sexes could be educated *gratis* for a three-year period, or longer if tuition were paid. Although the General Assembly rejected Jefferson's ideas, a 1796 law authorized (but did not require) Virginia counties to establish public schools. This was the true beginning of publicly-sponsored education in Virginia. Locally elected officials could hire and fire teachers, build and maintain schoolhouses, and evaluate teachers' and students' performance. But because the basic cost of public schools was borne by local taxpayers, many communities chose not to have schools, and people who could afford to hire a teacher for their children simply did so. For instance, Captain Thomas Roberts paid John Read for offering instruction to his children and furnishing them with books, paper, and other essentials in 1792 and 1793.[55]

In 1810 the General Assembly established the Literary Fund, whose principal was derived from fines, forfeitures, confiscations, escheats, and war debts recovered after the American Revolution. The fund's earnings, supplemented by local revenues, were intended to underwrite the cost of providing instruction to poor white children and could be used to pay teachers, build schools, and purchase books. Money from the Literary Fund was loaned to the federal government during the War of 1812 but was later repaid. In 1816, the General Assembly decided that as soon as the Literary Fund produced an annual income of $45,000 or more a year, those earnings would be distributed to Virginia's counties. Five school commissioners, appointed by local court justices, were authorized to disburse their county's share of Literary Fund income to teachers who kept attendance records documenting the number of the poor children they taught. Teachers were paid a penny a week for each pupil to whom they offered instruction. In 1820, the law was amended to allow up to ten percent of a county's Literary Fund allotment to be used for schoolhouse construction, as long as the locality paid three-fifths of the cost. An additional five percent could be used toward the purchase of books and each county could spend $100 on teachers' salaries as long as local citizens supplied matching funds. Mathews County's School Commissioners purchased school supplies from storekeeper Christopher Tompkins, and from 1820 to 1822 they bought writing paper for William Callis and books for Thomas James, T.J. Banks, and Thomas Hudgins. Only the poor were eligible for public school tuition, but other children could attend classes by paying fees teachers and parents found mutually agreeable. Many families who couldn't afford to send their youngsters to school refused to accept the Literary Fund's tuition subsidy because it would mean publicly acknowledging that they were poor. As time went on, state officials diverted the Literary Fund's earnings into projects that had nothing to do with education. In 1835, there were thirteen "common" or public schools in Mathews County, but no academies—that is, institutions of higher education. According to records maintained by the state auditor's office, in 1832 there were 92 poor children in Mathews County, 60 of whom had attended school. The average number of days each poor child attended school was 112 at a cost of three cents a day.[56]

Insights from Mathews County's Tax Rolls

When Mathews County moved into the nineteenth century, the number of small farmers increased, and the position of the large landowner gained stability, trends that were accompanied by growth in personal wealth. Because the War of 1812 left the state of Virginia with a substantial amount of debt that General Assembly's members were eager to retire, in 1814 they modified the tax code, making it more comprehensive. Those who owned houses worth $500 or more were supposed to pay a special tax. Mathews County's tax commissioner, Francis Armistead, decided to expand his records to include all houses that were worth $200 or more. Thanks to his efforts, we know that in 1815 there were at least 38 houses that he considered upscale, dwellings that would have belonged to the upper middle class or the elite. Seth Shepherd's house was worth $200. Richard Billups, John Brownley, George Brooks, James Carter's estate, Hunley Gayle, Thomas James, Thomas Ransone Jr., John B. Roberts and Thomas R. Yeatman owned dwellings with an estimated worth of $300 each. Thomas Hudgins and William Respess had homes valued at $400. Francis Armistead Jr., Joseph Ashberry, John C. Booker, William P. Foster, Leaven Gayle, John L. Hudgins, Houlder Hudgins, Thomas W. Norman, Sands Smith, and James Vaughan Jr. owned houses valued at $500. James Sparks' residence was worth $700.

Taxpayers whose houses were even more expensive included Isaac Brownley, Daniel D. Fitchett, William Lane, Thomas Tabb, and clerk William White, all of whom owned houses worth $1,000. In 1815 Brownley was unique, for he owned two houses, each of which was worth $1,000. Armistead Smith's dwelling was valued at $1,300, whereas John D. Jarvis had a house worth $1,500. John Patterson owned two homes that were valued at $1,500 apiece. James Blake's dwelling was worth $2,000, and William Fitchett's and Miles King's houses were worth an estimated $2,500 apiece. Mathews County's most valuable dwellings belonged to Christopher Tompkins, whose house on Horn Harbor was worth $3,000, and James H. Roy, whose home, Green Plains, was valued at $4,500. Two Mathews County homeowners had ice houses that were for private use.[57]

Besides the usual taxes on slaves, livestock, and wheeled vehicles, certain types of personal property, classified as luxury items, were taxable in 1815. Those who owned mahogany or walnut furniture, silver or gold flatware and serving vessels, mirrors or picture frames of a certain size, pianos or harps, or fine timepieces had to pay a special tax, as did the owners of thoroughbred horses used as studs. Personal property tax lists for 1815 provide insight into the material culture of Mathews County's wealthier residents. For instance, we know that a relatively large number of homes had mahogany or walnut furniture and one household had a settee or sofa decorated with gold or silver leaf.[58] Many of these wealthier individuals also had chairs that were made of fine wood and embellished with metallic leaf. Seven households owned carpets, and a total of 67 homes had window curtains that were made of fine fabric, and were therefore taxable. Some people had oil paintings and other elegantly-framed artwork and there was an abundance of large mirrors. Three households had large musical instruments—such as pianos, harpsichords, organs or harps—that were worth less than $300. One Mathews County homeowner had a lighting fixture (possibly a cut-glass candlestick, lamp, chandelier, epergne, or giraridole [sconce]) that was classified as a luxury item. Many people had silver drinking vessels and quite a few households had glass or silver decanters, pitchers, bottles, goblets, and wash basins. There were two silver urns or coffee pots, three silver teapots, and six silver pitchers and wasters in the county, along with 18 silver-plated candlesticks. Many well-to-do households owned valuable clocks and fine watches made of gold or other precious metals. James H. Roy was in possession of nine pieces of mahogany furniture, three pieces of walnut furniture, more than a dozen chairs decorated with silver or gold, two expensive carpets, a large quantity of gold or silver vessels for food or beverage consumption, a cane ornamented with silver or gold, and a fine gold watch. Roy, who farmed with slave labor, paid taxes on a large herd of cattle and ten horses. The homes of Miles King and Andrew Van Bibber were also elegantly equipped, and Van Bibber had portraits in oil and pastels, mirrors, a musical instrument, and fine furniture. By 1816, the General Assembly had eliminated the comprehensive luxury tax of 1815, probably because it was extremely unpopular and affected Virginia's wealthiest and most influential citizens, many of whom were in the legislature. However, taxes were still levied on slaves, livestock, wheeled vehicles, and a very limited number of personal items.[59]

The 1819 Recession and Changes in Tax Policy

Around 1815–16, the nation's economy had entered a period of stagnation which culminated in the Panic of 1819, America's first great depression. The population of nearly half of Virginia's counties east of the Blue Ridge dwindled, thanks to a general outmigration. In Tidewater, where very little attention had been paid to soil replenishment, farmland was now relatively unproductive and had declined in value. Also, many large estates were broken up and redistributed when members of old, well-established families moved west in search of better land. Members of the lower and middle classes also moved on, for they foresaw opportunities to improve their lot. All of these changes occurred amidst wildly fluctuating agricultural prices and relatively unstable economic conditions. Virginia's influence on the national political scene diminished as other states became more populous.

At its 1818–19 session, General Assembly members enacted legislation that was intended to generate additional tax revenue. Under the new law, which took effect on February 1, 1820, county tax commissioners were to determine the assessed value of newly constructed buildings, adding their estimated worth to the assessed value of the land on which they stood. Tax officials were told not to assess any new building that was uninhabitable or worth less than $100 and to make sure that their estimates were applied fairly and uniformly throughout their districts. Unfortunately, when assembly members crafted the new tax law, they failed to specify how county tax commissioners were supposed to deal with older buildings—that is, structures that had been erected *prior* to February 1, 1820. As a result, some tax assessors ignored the older structures, regardless of their value, and focused exclusively upon new construction. This omission, which deprived the state of revenue, was discovered when the State Auditor's Office received the records compiled during the 1820 assessment.[60] Therefore, when the General Assembly convened in its 1820–21 session, its members explicitly instructed "the commissioners of the revenue to value all old buildings within their respective districts, which may have been omitted in the last assessment, in the same manner in which they are now directed by law to value new buildings." That is, assessors were to include all *habitable* buildings, whether old or new, with the exception of new buildings worth less than $100.

Mathews County's sole tax commissioner, Francis Armistead, was among those who imperfectly understood the changes to the tax code that had occurred in 1819. When he conducted the annual assessment in 1820, he revised each parcel's value per acre, perhaps taking into account the value of any buildings that were present; however, if he did so, he failed to disclose what he thought those structures were worth. It is unclear whether Armistead's error was discovered by Mathews County's principal assessors, who were supposed to certify the accuracy of his work, or by someone in the State Auditor's Office. At any rate, in 1821 the principal assessors had Armistead transcribe the information he had gathered in 1819 and then *revise* it in accord with the refined law that had taken effect in 1820. Perhaps as a means of making their point, they had Armistead draw a vertical line through the column in which he had listed each parcel's value per acre, the old way assessments were compiled. Then, they had him add two new columns: one in which he recorded each property's value per acre *including* buildings, and another in which he listed the collective value of those buildings. Thanks to the principal assessors' teaching exercise, the tax records that Francis Armistead collected in 1821 were compiled correctly. They make it possible to identify properties with old but *habitable* buildings that were worth less than $100, and new, habitable buildings that in 1821 were worth $100 or more. However, Armistead's records do *not* differentiate between old and new buildings that in 1821 were worth $100 or more. [61]

In 1821, a significant number of Mathews County taxpayers had buildings that were worth less than $100. In fact, ten people owned buildings that were worth only $10 to $15, an indication that they were at the lower end of the socioeconomic spectrum. The majority of the county's landowners had buildings whose assessed value was $50 to $100, an indication that they were members of the middle class. A much smaller group owned buildings that were worth $100 to $300, sums usually associated with the upper middle class. Mathews County also had its share of the elite. There were nine landowners whose buildings were worth $500 to $999 and eleven whose structural improvements were worth between $1,000 and $1,999. A total of eight people had homes that were valued at $2,000 or more. By 1822 John D. Jarvis had replaced Francis Armistead as Mathews County's tax commissioner for reasons that are unclear.[62]

Representation in the General Assembly

During the late eighteenth century and the early-to-mid nineteenth century, almost all of Mathews County's delegates to the General Assembly served for one or two terms, and from 1791 to 1830 the county was represented by two delegates per legislative session. Successively, they included Thomas Smith Jr., Houlder Hudgins, William Buckner, William Lane, Joseph Billups Jr., Zadock Litchfield, Lyne Shackleford, Houlder Hudgins, John Peyton, Richard Billups, Perrin Smith, Christopher Tompkins, Thomas Hudgins, Langley B. Eddins, Joseph Billups Jr., Thomas Hudgins, Richard Billups, William H. Ransome, Thomas James Jr., James H. Roy, and John Patterson. Patterson was elected to the House of Delegates' 1819–20 session, but he became a state senator when Senator Severn E. Parker was elected to Congress; Thomas James Jr. took Patterson's seat as delegate. During the 1820s, Thomas Hudgins, Thomas James Jr., Murtius S. Sparks, ex-state senator John Patterson, Samuel Diggs, Thomas James, and Seth Shepherd served successively in the assembly. In 1826, Humphrey Billups was elected to the House, but he was disqualified because he was a licensed Methodist-Episcopal preacher (and therefore prohibited from holding public office), so Thomas James was returned to office. When elections were held in 1828, former state senators Houlder Hudgins and Carter M. Braxton became Mathews County's delegates. In 1829, local voters tried to send Humphrey Billups to the assembly, but once again, he was disqualified because he was a clergyman; Dr. Augustine H. Garnett served in his place.

Residents of the western part of Virginia, which was experiencing rapid population growth, grew dissatisfied with the old state constitution which allowed each county to have two delegates regardless of the county's population. Westerners felt underrepresented and believed that a disproportionate amount of power was controlled by slave-owning elitists who lived in the Tidewater and Piedmont. Westerners, as taxpayers, also resented the old state constitution's landowning requirement because it disenfranchised approximately half of the state's potential electorate, most of whom paid personal property taxes. Their persistence paid off, and plans were made to hold a state constitutional convention. In March 1829, a large group of Mathews County voters met at the courthouse and selected five delegates who would nominate four men to represent their senatorial district at the state convention. Those delegates, who were collectively entitled to one vote, were William Bohannon, Thomas Hudgins, John D. Jarvis, William H. Roy, and Christopher Tompkins. Later, a joint delegation made up of representatives from Accomack, Gloucester, Mathews, Middlesex, and Northampton Counties convened in Mathews and ratified each county's delegates. The state convention, held from October 5, 1829, to January 15, 1830, was dominated by issues of representation and suffrage. Ultimately, the western counties received more equitable representation and the vote was extended to white male landowners, leaseholders, and householders as long as they were at least 21 years old and met residency requirements.

In 1829, Christopher Tompkins of Mathews County informed the governor that according to a local widow, "it was expected generally among the slaves that they were to be free in a few weeks." He added that two white men reported overhearing similar talk among slaves at a local blacksmith shop. Tompkins went on to say that some slaves were convinced that the state constitutional convention was being held "exclusively for its object the liberation of blacks" and some believed that their masters were deliberately withholding their freedom papers. Rumors continued to send ripples of fear through Tidewater counties, and once again, local militia commanders asked the governor for arms and ammunition. A Richmond man told the governor that there were growing concerns that blacks in Gloucester, Isle of Wight, Mathews, and adjoining counties were going to revolt. He said that county jails were crowded with blacks and that militiamen from New Kent County had been sent to Mathews and local volunteer companies were patrolling the area. Quoting Francis Foster, he added that according to the man who carried the mail from Richmond to Mathews, the jail there was full and closely guarded. This raises the possibility that blacks were being preemptively imprisoned out of fear of revolt.

From 1830 through 1892, Mathews and Middlesex Counties were jointly represented by one delegate. When an election was held in 1830, preacher Humphrey Billups was chosen, but again he was barred from serving. Although he relinquished his ministry license and enrolled in a militia company, the Committee of Privileges and Elections still considered him ineligible. When a new election was held, Houlder Hudgins was chosen and served two terms. He was succeeded by William H. Roy, William Shepherd, and William Todd. State Senator Matthew Anderson represented Mathews, Gloucester and Middlesex Counties during the early 1790s, but he was replaced by Warner Lewis, who held office until 1798. He was succeeded by Houlder Hudgins, Richard Baynham, Christopher Garland, Richard Jones, and John Patterson. Redistricting had occurred by the time of the 1821–22 session when Carter M. Braxton commenced representing Accomack, Gloucester, Mathews, Middlesex, and Northampton Counties. He was still holding office in 1825, but was followed by William Jones, John G. Joynes, and William Armistead, whose realigned district embraced Gloucester, King and Queen, King William, Mathews, and Middlesex Counties. Armistead served until 1833, when he was unseated by Philip Aylett who was himself replaced by Archibald R. Harwood.

In June 1831, a group of Mathews County men publicly expressed their regret that the legislature had replaced General Court and Circuit Court Judge James Semple Jr. with William Browne. After their opinion was published in a Richmond newspaper, Semple responded by saying that he appreciated the petitioners' sentiments but looked forward to his retirement. When a Commercial Convention was held in Norfolk to discuss foreign trade, a delegation of twelve men attended on behalf of Mathews County. In 1835, members of the Republican Party gathered at the Mathews County Courthouse and prepared a text, urging fellow voters to hold a national convention. They also voiced opposition to a proposal allowing the United States Congress to choose the president.[63]

The Mathews County Seat

In 1814, Virginia's tax commissioners began estimating the distance and direction of each landowner's property from the county courthouse and they also listed the names of those who owned property in the county seat. The smallest parcels in Mathews Courthouse were the half-acre lots that belonged to merchants John B. Roberts and Thomas Ransone and to Machen Parrott's estate. Roberts's lot was on the east side of Main Street's forerunner, then known as the main road, and Parrott's lot was northwest of the courthouse green, probably on the forerunner of Route 198, now Buckley Hall Road. The store belonging to Christopher Tompkins, located on the west side of Main Street and northeast of the courthouse green, and the retail establishment of the firm Litchfield and Lewis occupied somewhat larger lots, as did the taverns owned by the heirs of Henry Respess and William Plummer. George Owen and the estate of George Lewis were credited with lots at the county seat, and significantly larger parcels "at the courthouse" belonged to Catherine James, Dorothy Ransone, Thomas James Jr., and the estate of John Soper. Mutual Assurance Society policies and tax rolls reveal that the James and Soper holdings lay along the east side of Main Street (as did the land of John D. Jarvis), and that Soper's property extended in an easterly direction along Buckley Hall Road. John and William Hunley owned land that abutted Put In Creek, to the west of the courthouse, whereas Nehemiah Hunley's estate extended to the north and northwest, perhaps along Buckley Hall Road, where Zadock Litchfield's property was also located. Elias Pugh owned twenty acres on Put In Creek, approximately half a mile north of the courthouse. To the south of the county seat and only half-a-mile away was the 187-acre plantation of Joseph Davis, on whose land Palace Green eventually was built.[64] By 1816, John D. Jarvis acquired storeowner John B. Roberts's half-acre lot, which contained a large frame dwelling that Jarvis insured. William Bohannon and Francis Litchfield bought some of the Pickett family's land at the county seat, whereas John Minter purchased some of the Hunleys' land northwest of the courthouse. James Minter acquired seven acres from John D. Jarvis, who later sold merchant Benjamin Bramhall a half-acre lot[65] and a twenty-acre parcel on the east side of Main Street, just north of County Route 611 (modern Tabernacle Road).[66]

At the heart of the county seat was the courthouse green—public land that contained the courthouse, the clerk's office, and two jails: one for criminals and slaves and one for debtors. One of the jails burned in February 1827, when a female slave who was incarcerated set it ablaze and then escaped. The records compiled by Mathews County's tax commissioner in the early 1820s reveal that the county seat was sparsely developed and that its buildings' value ranged from $15 to $800. The improvements on tavern-keeper Henry Respess's estate, worth $800, were the community's most valuable buildings and Thomas James's 74 acres at Mathews Courthouse had buildings worth $666. The store and storehouse on Christopher Tompkins's one-and-a-half-acre lot were collectively worth $350, but the Litchfield and Lewis store was worth $400. Tompkins owned a six-and-a-half-acre vacant lot located between his store lot and the uppermost branches of Put In Creek, which had already begun to accumulate silt. It abutted west on Larkin Litchfield's acreage, north on merchant John P. March's property, and northeast on Buckley Hall Road. Henry Diggs owned three acres that abutted the north side of the courthouse green and had buildings that were worth $400; this was the acreage on which the White Dog Inn was later built. During 1828, Walter G. Lane acquired Diggs's property and its improvements and purchased an adjoining seven-acre tract from Christopher Tompkins, probably his purported six-and-a-half acres. Catherine James's 18 acres had $216 worth of improvements, but those on James Minter's property were worth only $69. In 1821, the late William Plummer's one-acre tavern lot had a building worth only $20, and the fifteen acres in which Frances Pickett had a life interest contained $15 worth of structural improvements. Samuel Lewis, William Bohannon, Sarah and Lucy Hunley, Francis Litchfield, James Minter, Elizabeth Pickett, and Seth Shepherd owned vacant parcels in the county seat or on the community's outskirts. By 1822, merchant Benjamin Bramhall had constructed $800 worth of buildings on his twenty-acre tract on the east side of Main Street, the land that he had bought from John D. Jarvis. Bramhall also had a half-acre parcel with structures worth $250. Christopher Tompkins bought the one-acre lot on which William Plummer's tavern had stood, just north of his store, and promptly added $150 worth of buildings to the property. In 1829, Edmund P. Benson acquired some acreage on Put In Creek that had only $49.50 worth of improvements and was half-a-mile northwest of the courthouse, probably near Buckley Hall Road. A year later, he bought an undeveloped parcel from George Lewis's heirs, land that was half-a-mile west of town, perhaps on the forerunner of Church Street, a road that seems to have come into existence during the second quarter of the nineteenth century as development spread to the west of the courthouse green.

Around 1829, Christopher Q. Tompkins, Christopher Tompkins's eldest son, purchased a three-quarter-acre lot and its $600 worth of improvements from Dr. Augustine H. Garnett, who by 1832 had bought 70 acres of land at the county seat from William Bohannon and Benjamin Bramhall. Christopher Q., like his father, seems to have speculated in real estate. Around 1833, he had sold his lot to John H. Diggs. He, in turn, promptly conveyed it to John D. Jarvis and Elijah Barnum, who had acquired a small parcel on Put In Creek in 1832 (Richard Billups's land). During the early 1830s, Jarvis and Barnum enhanced the value of the improvements on their three-quarter-acre lot. John Bohannon and Larkin Litchfield bought some undeveloped acreage near licensed merchant John P. March's land on Put In Creek, close to the county seat. During 1832, Henry G. Murray, a shoemaker, bought a one-acre lot and its $200 worth of improvements from John Minor. Throughout the 1830s, many other pieces of land in the immediate vicinity of the county seat changed hands. Often, merchants acquired and quickly resold these parcels. By 1839, Thomas Edwards had commenced paying taxes on fourteen acres at the courthouse, land that had $616 worth of improvements; that acreage, formerly part of Dr. Augustine H. Garnett's estate, had descended to Edwards' third wife, Louisa (the late physician's widow) as her dower share. Concurrently, Dr. Garnett's son, James, inherited 93 acres of undeveloped land at the courthouse.

According to Joseph Martin's *Gazetteer*, Mathews County's seat of government, Mathews Courthouse (or Westville), was a thriving community with a population of 150.[67] In 1835, the county seat had mail service, around 30 houses, four mercantile establishments, a tan yard, three factories or shops for making boots and shoes, a tailor, two blacksmiths, a saddler, a carriage-maker, and a tavern. Martin added that Mathews Courthouse was a port of entry served by two packet boats that made weekly trips to Norfolk and another ship that went to Baltimore. He described the county's public buildings as "very neat" and "well-built of brick." He said that there was a new court house,[68] two jails, and a clerk's office. Martin indicated that Mathews County justices convened on the second Monday of every month and that the quarter court met in March, May, August, and November. Sessions of the Circuit Superior Court of Law and Chancery, with Judge Semple presiding, were held in April and October. Perhaps around the time a new courthouse was built, one or both of the county jails was replaced, for by 1841 the public property on which the "old jail" stood had been conveyed into private hands. When architectural historians analyzed the structural attributes of the oldest buildings on the historic courthouse green in 2007, they concluded that the two-story brick building situated in the southwestern corner was erected during the second half of the nineteenth century and was a larger jail intended for criminals.[69]

Edmund Ruffin's Influence upon Virginia Agriculture

Although eastern Virginia farmers experienced hard times during the early nineteenth century, economic conditions improved once they learned that marl could be used to restore the fertility of soil acidified by the long-term production of tobacco. This important discovery is usually attributed to Edmund Ruffin, who tested soil samples and discovered that abandoned fields covered with second-growth pine could be made productive if marl or "calcareous earth" were applied. Once the soil's acidity was neutralized, manure and vegetable waste could be added as fertilizer. Ruffin also studied crop rotation, drained overly moist fields, and penned his livestock in order to obtain a supply of manure. His essays on scientific farming were published in the *Farmer's Register*. Some farmers sent letters to newspapers, sharing the results of their own agricultural experiments, and in 1818 a Mathews County man invented a threshing machine, which he patented. James H. Roy of Green Plains sent a lengthy letter to the Norfolk newspaper, *American Beacon*, in June 1820, stating that agriculture in Gloucester, Mathews, and Middlesex Counties was much improved thanks to crop rotation, deep plowing, and the use of manure. He said that barley, wheat, corn, and Indian peas were grown for market and that the cultivation of tobacco had been abandoned almost entirely. He added that most of the farmers in his neighborhood planted oats or corn and used a three-crop rotation system. Roy shared his views on feeding cattle, sheep, and horses and indicated that the son of Norton, a blacksmith who lived on Queens Creek, could make all types of agricultural implements, including the Cary and Barshear plows. He said that his plantation consisted of 650 acres of arable land as well as 100 acres of timber, used as a source of fence rails and firewood. John R. Lumpkin of Mount Carmel in Mathews County sent a letter to the Richmond *Enquirer*, describing the success he had had with two barrels of Italian spring wheat. He said that he achieved a bountiful harvest although his land was not rich and that part of his crop was affected by insect damage and a blight or "rust."

In 1810, Mathews County's agricultural economy largely depended upon slave labor. The county was home to 4,227 people, 2,068 of whom were enslaved and 41 of whom were free blacks. By 1820, the county's population had risen to 6,920, 3,616 of whom were whites. There were 118 free African Americans and 3,186 slaves. Mathews County had 2,262 residents engaged in agriculture in 1820, 110 involved in commerce, and another 200 in manufacturing or trades. A substantial percentage of the white population was landless, but owned slaves and livestock and may have farmed land owned by other family members. Approximately half of all Mathews County taxpayers owned slaves, but around 80 percent of the county's slaveholders had no more than five slaves. (These trends still held true in the 1850s.) In 1830, Mathews County had a population of 7,667 people, 3,481 of whom were enslaved. There were 189 free blacks, approximately half of whom were females. There also was one non-naturalized alien.[70]

Notes

1 Copper sheathing protected the hulls of wooden ships from the ravages of the naval shipworm, *Teredo navalis*.

2 Middlesex County Deed Book 13 [1810–1817]:117–118, 141–142; *Norfolk Gazette and Public Ledger*, July 1, 1812; Charles, *Newspapers*, 42–44, 46, 53–54, 56, 58–60, 63–64, 67–69, 73–74, 94, 132–134.

3 From 1819 on, butchers, bakers, brewers, distillers, and others producing and selling consumable goods could be punished if they sold an unwholesome product. For example, if a butcher sold meat that came from a diseased animal, he could be forgiven, but he would be pilloried for his second offence, sent to prison and fined for his third offense, and sentenced to six months of hard labor for his fourth offence (Thomas Ritchie, ed., *The Revised Code of the Laws of Virginia, Being a Collection of All Such Acts of the General Assembly* [Richmond, 1819], I, 551).

4 King then owned the plantation that became known as Woodstock. The mill that Thomas Williams had built in 1791 on the property that became known as Poplar Grove was gone.

5 Mathews County Miscellaneous Deeds, 1814, 1835–1908. In 1805 clerk of court John Patterson admitted that he hadn't issued licenses to hawkers, peddlers, and tavern-keepers during 1805–1806, although the sheriff had collected the license fees, in accord with the law. William Lane, sheriff in 1809–1810, collected some of the taxes local citizens owed, but the General Assembly gave him another 12 months to collect arrearages (Mathews County Executioners Bond Book 1795–1825; Mathews Archives Box 82 R).

6 Much later, this became the site of Twiggs Ferry and the modern bridge over which Route 3 passes.

7 There may have been a connection between Thomas Armistead of Mathews and William A. Armistead of Norfolk, who in 1807 sold the *Courtney Norton*, which was outfitted and sent to New York (Billups Papers, Swem, Box 3, folder 9).

8 Real estate tax lists indicate that Patterson bought the 1½ acre lot from the Respess estate during 1810 (Mathews County Land Tax Lists 1810–1811).

9 Thus, Tompkins's store was not located in the early nineteenth century building known as the Tompkins Cottage, situated on the south side of the historic courthouse green. Instead, land records and Tompkins's insurance policy suggest strongly that the store, whose dimensions and architectural attributes were different than the cottage, was situated between the Foster-Faulkner Funeral Home and Moughons Hardware Store, a site with

convenient access to the forerunners of Routes 14 and 198. A compass rose on Tompkins's 1816 insurance policy, and maps made in the 1870s and 1880s, indicate that the main road that passed by Tompkins's store then ran on a northeast-southwest axis, an indication that the upper part of Main Street has shifted in a westerly direction.

10 According to Joseph Martin's *Gazetteer*, the courthouse community had three physicians. They were Drs. William T. Thurston, William Shultice, and Augustine H. Garnett.

11 Local tax records indicate that Thomas James purchased a merchants license in 1808, 1809, 1814, 1816, 1820, 1822–1824, 1826–1833, and 1836–1843; Thomas James Jr. purchased one in 1821 (Mathews County Personal Property Tax Lists 1808–1843).

12 The elder Thomas James became Kingston Parish's vestry clerk in 1783 and served through 1796. Over the years, he had 14 of his slaves baptized as infants. Two had surnames: Daniel Parker and Peyton Collier (Chamberlayne, *Kingston Parish*, 114, 130; McCartney, *Kingston Parish Slave Register*, 15, 63).

13 Storeowner Thomas James and Thomas James Jr., who became county sheriff and eventually served in the General Assembly, were not father and son. Thomas James, the owner of historic James Store, was the son of Matthias and Elizabeth James and was born in 1777. Mathews County had a third Thomas James: Thomas Degge Davis James, the son of Thomas and Betsy James, who was born in 1792 and became a shipbuilder (Matheny and Yates, *Kingston Parish Register*, 73).

14 Shepherd, Statutes, ed., *Supplement to The revised code of Virginia: being a collection of all the acts of the General Assembly, of a public and permanent nature, passed since the year 1819 ... To which are prefixed, the acts organizing a convention, the Declaration of Rights, and the amended Constitution of Virginia*, I, 108–110, 192–193, 204–205; III, 324, 334; Mutual Assurance Society Vol. 46 policy 505; Charles, *Newspapers*, 59–60, 64–65. 86–87, 93; Robert Callis, Receipt, December 23, 1817, www.unknownnolonger.vahistorical.org; Mathews County Census of Manufacturers for 1820; Personal Property Tax Lists 1791–1835; Land Tax Lists 1791–1848; Land Book 1:6, 151; Martin, *Gazetteer*, 226–229; Christopher Tompkins Account Book 1819–1821; Billups Papers, VHS, Mss1 B4977a; McCartney, *Kingston Parish Slave Register*, 3, 5, 11, 15, 18, 27, 39, 48, 51, 58, 63, 89; Armistead and Diggs Ledger, Mathews Archives Box 90 R. An advertisement that appeared in a Norfolk newspaper in 1817 reveals that a Thomas James of Mathews County sold a slave named Frank, who fled from the home of his new owner in Currituck County, North Carolina (Charles, *Newspapers*, 54).

15 An almost complete collection of the policies the Society issued from 1796 to 1867 (31,138 policies) is preserved at the Library of Virginia. A few additional policies are on file at the Huntington Library in San Marino, California.

16 Mutual Assurance Society Vol. 16, policies 785, 787, 788, 789; Vol. 27, policy 2297; Vol. 40, policies 1128, 1150; Vol. 42, policy 1311; Vol. 46, policies 503, 505, 506; Vol. 48, policies 454, 457, 477; *The Virginia Argus*, Richmond, December 31, 1803. The Patterson and White insurance policies are preserved at the Huntington Library but facsimiles are in the Mathews Archives, Box 7 folder 11.

17 Gloucester County Legislative Petitions, December 12, 1812; December 17, 1829; Executive Papers, John Tyler, Miles King to Christopher Tompkins, June 30, 1809; Mathews County court trial transcript, June 15, 1809; Charles, *Newspapers*, 69; *Norfolk Beacon*, January 8, 1829; http://infoweb.newsbank.com; Taylor, *Internal Enemy*, 68–69; Palmer, *Calendar*, IX, 327. In 1834 John Pritchett (Pritchard), who owned 298 acres of land on New Point Comfort, received a patent for almost 75 acres of additional land (Virginia Land Office Grants No. 83:391–396). This previously unowned acreage may have been created by shifting sand and shoreline changes.

18 William W. Hening and William Mumford, comp., *Reports of Cases Argued and Determined in the Supreme Court of Appeals of Virginia* (New York, 1809–1811), 134–137, 142; Tucker-Coleman Papers, 1752–1827, Swem Library Department of Special Collections, November 11, 1806; Taylor, *Internal Enemy*, 106; Warner T. Jones Papers, Box 7, folders 381 and 382; Charles, *Newspapers*, 54–55. When Houlder Hudgins made his will on February 20, 1815, he owned a large number of slaves whom he distributed among his next of kin. A transcription of his will, proved in 1816, was entered in Mathews County's records in 1868. At the time of his death Hudgins owned Chesterville and another farm in Elizabeth City County and two plantations in Mathews County: Isle of Wight, which he had bought from William Hayes, and the 500 acre plantation on which he lived. Hudgins' will was proved on February 16, 1816 (Mathews County Will Book 1:24–28).

19 Bishop James Madison, "A Map of Virginia Formed from Actual Surveys, and the Latest as well as the most accurate observations," 1807; John Wood, "Chart of the Piankatank," 1817; Herman Böye, "A Map of the State of Virginia," 1826, 1859; Edith F. Axelson, comp., *Virginia Postmasters and Post Offices, 1789–1832* (Athens, Georgia, 1991), 121–122; Marguerite Sadler, "Post Offices, Postmasters, and Postmarks of Mathews County, 1798–1991," Mathews Archives Box 21 R.

20 A lighthouse was also to be built on Smith's Point in Northumberland County.

21 In 1808, the justices of York County's monthly court hired Burroughs to build a clerk's office on the public square in Yorktown. Burroughs, the low bidder, had completed his work by September 19, 1808, and was paid $540 (York County Judgments and Orders Book 8 [1803–1815]:266, 280–281, 297).

22 In the fall of 1804, Jerome and Betsy attempted to reach France in time for his brother's coronation, but they were delayed. When they finally arrived, she was denied permission to set foot in continental Europe by order of Napoleon, who wanted the marriage annulled. Betsy gave birth to a son in London on July 7, 1805, and then returned to Baltimore. Her husband, who yielded to his brother's demands, returned to the French Navy and at Napoleon's insistence, wed a German princess although his first marriage had yet to be dissolved. Betsy eventually obtained a divorce (en.wikipedia.org/wiki/Jerome_Napoleon_Bonaparte).

23 Ludlum, *Hurricanes,* 39, 55, 81–83, 87–90, 98–99, 128–129, 173; Mathews Archives Box 18 R, Box 83 R; Lighthouse-Board, *Laws of the United States Relating to the Establishment, Support, and Management of Light-Houses, Light-Vessels, Monuments, Beacons, Spindles, Buoys, and Public Piers of the United States from August 7, 1789, to March 3, 1855,* 18–19, 22, 31; National

Archive Records Group 26, Entries 17A, 18, 122; Clifford and Clifford, *New Point Comfort*, 6–17; Charles, *Newspapers*, 41–42, 44–48, 50–51, 60, 64, 68, 73, 95.

24 Mathews Archives Box 18 R; Maine, *Weekly Eastern Argus*, September 17, 1824; Boston, *Commercial Gazette*, December 27, 1824; Boston, *Independent Chronicle*, December 29, 1824; Martin, *Gazetteer*, p. 226.

25 This structure predates the existing tide mill at Poplar Grove (Carl Lounsbury, personal communication, July 16, 2014).

26 This raises the possibility that by 1797 Kingston Parish's Lower Church had become known as Christ Church, the name it bears today.

27 Chamberlayne, *Kingston Parish*, 114–118,123–125; Matheny and Yates, *Register*, 115; Mason, *Colonial Gloucester*, II, 72; Rind, *Virginia Gazette*, October 11, 1770; Purdie and Dixon, *Virginia Gazette*, October 18, 1770; Gloucester County Land Tax Lists 1782–1790; Mathews County Land Tax Lists 1791–1798; Land Book 1:243; U.S. Bureau, *Heads of Families*, 53; Williams Family Papers May 5, 1791, receipt; Anonymous, "Plat of 375 acres of land belonging to Mr. Thomas Williams," n.d.; Samuel Williams, February 19, 1799, will; October 4, 1790, appraisal; Sheridan and Ernst, *Tombstones*, 156; Richmond *Enquirer*, August 13, 1824, and October 19, 1824.

28 When Harriet G. Miller, a WPA worker interviewed Milton Murray Sr. (whose grandfather had been the custom house's inspector and surveyor from 1839 to 1852) in 1939, she was shown this account book. The custom house, which Mr. Murray assumed was the original one, was a two-story unpainted building that was weather-beaten and was losing the shingles on its roof. The structure had heavy doors and exterior blinds that opened outward and were fortified with iron bars. According to Mr. Murray, the building's upstairs room served as the custom house and the lower one as a store. He said that the building was eventually used by Miss Betty Williams as a millinery and dressmaking establishment (Miller, "Interviews," Box 10).

29 In 1820, when King, who was eager to raise some cash to cover his debts, announced that he intended to sell several slaves at a public auction in Mathews Courthouse, he noted that two of them were experienced weavers (Charles, *Newspapers*, 60).

30 Mattern et al., eds., *The Papers of James Madison, Secretary of State Series* (Charlottesville, 1995), *vol. 3, 1 March–6 October 1802,* 384–385; Mathews County Land Book 1: 85; Land Tax Lists 1791–1821; Charles, *Newspapers*, 45, 55–59, 65, 67, 73; Martin, *Gazetteer*, 228; Account book of Custom House, East River District, 1826:1, 101, 104, 106, 118–119, 126, 130–131, 171; MCHS, *History and Progress: Mathews County, Virginia, Reprints from 1949 and 1979 Special Editions, Gloucester-Mathews Gazette-Journal,* 41.

31 Scholars believe that more than 400 American ships and cargoes were seized by the British between 1807 and 1812 and that between 1803 and 1812, approximately 6,000 American citizens were impressed into the British navy (Ralph E. Eshelman et al., *The War of 1812 in the Chesapeake: A Reference Guide to Historic Sites in Maryland, Virginia, and the District of Columbia* [Baltimore 2010], 2).

32 Harry, Abram, Humphrey, Yeoro, James, Billy Goodchild, Wharton, Hugh, and Sci Gillett belonged to various owners (Taylor, *Internal Enemy*, 155).

33 On account of the shortage of cannon, one man, convinced that the militia was useless against British ships' firepower, proposed that heavy battery cannon be mounted on well-constructed traveling carriages that could be moved from place to place, as needed (Executive Papers, John Clark to Governor James Barbour, March 26, 1813).

34 Smith's writings reveal his personal bias. He gave a young slave named Nancy to his daughter, Harriett. As time went on, Harriet and her husband died with the result that Nancy descended to their daughter, Sally. In early 1814 when Nancy decided to sue for her freedom, citing a discrepancy in her late owner's' will, Smith denounced her "diabolical plan" and vowed to see "that the vile Strumpet may at last be defeated in her views & Justice be done." Clearly, he could see no merit in a slave's desire for freedom (Taylor, *Internal Enemy*, 47).

35 Charles, *Newspapers*, 43–44; George B. Tindall, *America, A Narrative History*, 338–343; William H. Theisen, *United States Coast Guard: War of 1812, Rescue Cutter Operations and the Core Coast Guard Missions* (Washington, D.C., 2012), 2–3; Eshelman et al., *The War of 1812,* 1–5; Taylor, *Internal Enemy*, 149–150, 155–160, 166–171, 266–267, 475, footnote 37; Charles, *Newspapers*, 48–54; Palmer, *Calendar*, X, 187, 193, 202–203, 244–245, 305–310, 328; Executive Papers, John Patterson to Governor James Barbour, June 14, 1813, and February 5, 1814, letters; Leaven Gayle to Governor James Barbour, March 13, 1813, letter; Governor James Barbour, March 18, 1813, correspondence; Nathaniel Burwell to Governor James Barbour, April 8, 1813, letter; Billups Papers, Swem, Box 9 folder 27; Mathews Archives Box 22 R; Palmer, *Calendar*, X, 328; W. F. Ritchie, *Muster Rolls of the Virginia Militia in the War of 1812*, 23, 640; Virginia State Library, *A Hornbook of Virginia History*, 80–81; Charles, *Newspapers,* 51–54; *Poulson's American Daily Advertiser*, Philadelphia, Pennsylvania, March 25, 1813; *Virginia Patriot*, Richmond, March 30, 1814; *New Hampshire Sentinel*, Keene, New Hampshire, April 3, 1813 *War Journal*, Portsmouth, New Hampshire, June 25, 1813; *Mercantile Advertiser*, New York, New York, December 6, 1813; *Daily National Intelligencer*, Washington, D.C., December 21, 1813; *Carolina Gazette*, Charleston, South Carolina, December 25, 1813; *The Reporter*, Brattleboro, Vermont, January 29, 1814; *Richmond Enquirer*, Richmond, Virginia, January 27, 1814; June 4, 1814; *New York Commercial Advertiser*, New York, New York, March 28, 1814; *Federal Republican*, Washington, D.C., June 8, 1814; *Boston Daily Advertiser*, Boston, Massachusetts, June 15, 1814; *Norwich Courier*, Norwich, Connecticut, July 6, 1814; Mathews County Legislative Petitions, October 22, 1814; Clifford and Clifford, *New Point Comfort*, 21–22.

36 The Colonial Marines were attired in red coats, white jackets and pantaloons, black gaiters and stocks, and they wore narrow-brimmed black hats trimmed with white feathers.

37 Charles, *Newspapers*, p. 52; *Newburyport Herald*, Newburyport, Massachusetts, April 15, 1814; Taylor, *Internal Enemy*, 268–271, 344–345; www.novascotia.ca/nsarm/virtual/africans/ns; www. infoweb.newsbank.com.

38 www.revwarapps.org/revwar-pension-acts.

39 They may have used the wood for their campfires.

40 Mathews County Petitions, December 18, 1822; Census 1860, 1870; Palmer, *Calendar*, X, 305–306; Ellen Roy Goldsborough obituary, *Gloucester Journal*, March 13, 1941; Thomas Ritchie, ed., *Acts Passed at a General Assembly of the Commonwealth of Virginia, 1822* (Richmond, 1823), 90.

41 It is unclear why the glebe wasn't sold at the end of the Rev. James McBride's time at Kingston.

42 Richard Billups, Anthony and Houlder Hudgins, Gabriel Miller Sr., and Perrin and Sands Smith II served as special commissioners for sale of the glebe.

43 In February 1822, Hughes was paid for selling off the late Richard Billups Sr.'s slaves (Billups Papers, Virginia Historical Society, Mss1 B4977a).

44 She may have been the late Rev. John Dixon's daughter-in-law.

45 Green may have rented part of Dixon's land near Williams Wharf.

46 Kingston Parish Vestry Book 1774–1798; Chamberlayne, *Kingston Parish*, 122–127; Mathews County Legislative Petitions, December 8, 1809; Land Tax Lists 1814–1815; Deed Book 1:651; 2, 1–2; Billups Papers, Swem, Box 9, folder 27; Charles, *Newspapers*, 51–52; Thomas Ritchie, comp., *Acts Passed at a General Assembly of the Commonwealth of Virginia, 1809* (Richmond, 1810), 59.

47 On October 24, 1814, the General Assembly authorized the Overseers of the Poor for Mathews, Middlesex, and Warwick Counties to recover and sell the communion silver, bells, and other ornaments that had belonged to the former State Church (Thomas Ritchie, comp., *Acts Passed at a General Assembly of the Commonwealth of Virginia, 1814* [Richmond, 1815], 3).

48 Mathews County Legislative Petitions, December 8, 1809; August 30, 1819; Land Tax Lists 1821–1839; Land Book 1, 31, 263, 470.

49 David C. Holly, *Tidewater by Steamboat: A Saga of the Chesapeake Bay* (Baltimore, 1991), xv–xvii; Alexander C. Brown, *Steam Packets on the Chesapeake: A History of the Old Bay Line Since 1840* (Cambridge, Maryland, 1961), 1–2, 8–9, 12, 14.

50 When Asbury arrived in Maryland, he resolved to work for the freedom of all slaves. However, most evangelical abolitionists, who included Methodists, Baptists, and Presbyterians, encountered strong resistance. Eventually, enlarging a church's membership took precedence over expelling slaveholders (David Brion Davis, *Slavery in the Colonial Chesapeake* [Williamsburg, 1986], 38–39).

51 As noted above, he was elected to the House of Delegates twice and was disqualified both times on account of his ministerial calling.

52 According to local tradition, Mathews Chapel's founding members originally met in a private chapel that was associated with Hesse, the Armistead family's plantation. The brick mansion now known as Hesse, a replacement for the original dwelling which was

destroyed by fire in ca. 1790, is on the National Register of Historic Places (Hesse [Pond Point House] National Register Nomination, HABS File 057-0007).

53 In 1939 when Harriet G. Miller, a WPA worker, visited the home of a Billups family on Billups Creek, one of the occupants showed her some old books and papers. One was entitled *General History of the Baptist Denomination in America and Other Parts of the World*, a volume that was published in 1813. Sponsors of the book included John Spencer, a Baptist minister and the father of John Spence, one-time postmaster at the North End (Miller, "Interviews," Box 6).

54 Meade, *Old Churches*, I, 242, 372; II, p. 47; Isaac, Transformation, 299, 315; Billups Papers, Swem, Box 4 Folder 5; W. D. Keene Jr., *Memoirs—200 Years!" Soldiers of the Cross, 1785–1987* (Decorah, Iowa, 1988), 140–141; Francis Asbury, *The Journal of the Rev. Francis Asbury, Bishop of the Methodist Episcopal Church from August 7, 1771, to December 7, 1815* (Baltimore, 2010), II, 24–25; Kingston Parish Register, 1746–1827; Robert L. Brown, *Old Kingston Parish, 1652–1976* (Mathews, 2002), 24–25; Charles, *Newspapers*, 59–60, 63; Mathews County Marriage Records and Licenses, 1827–1835, 1839–1850; Legislative Petitions, October 7, 8, 9, 1837; Martin, *Gazetteer*, p. 228; Mathews Archives Box 1 R; Box 18 R; Perdue, *The Negro*, 113, 121.

55 Likewise, between 1768 and 1772, the late George Hunley's executor paid John Forrest Jr. for providing the decedent's children with schooling.

56 Mason, *Gloucester*, II, p. 69; John Read receipts 1792–1793, Billups Papers Box 1 Folder 29, Swem Library; A.J. Morrison, *The Beginning of Public Education in Virginia, 1776–1815* (Richmond, 1917), 17, 22–25; Thomas Jefferson, *Notes on the State of Virginia* (Chapel Hill, 1954), 146–151; Christopher Thompkins Store Ledger; Martin, *Gazetteer*, 78–79, 228.

57 In 1816 when John Patterson insured Poplar Grove, he estimated that it was worth $5,000.

58 Antebellum household inventories reveal that relatively few people had sofas and settees. Those who could afford chairs usually had large numbers of them.

59 Mathews County Personal Property Tax Lists 1815–1816.

60 It is unclear how many of Virginia's county tax officials omitted older buildings from their 1820 assessments, prompting the General Assembly to take action.

61 For example, because we know that only habitable buildings could be taxed and that newly constructed buildings had to be habitable *and* worth at least $100, it is safe to assume that Hugh G. Adams' $30 worth of improvements on Milford Haven were erected before 1820. On the other hand, because the improvements on Richard Armistead's property on Dyers Creek were worth $108, the tax rolls do not allow us to determine whether his buildings were old or new, only that one or more habitable buildings were present.

62 Palmer, *Calendar*, X, 406; Virginia State Library, *Hornbook*, 82–83; Tindall, *Narrative History*, 365; Thomas Ritchie, comp., *The Revised Code of the Laws of the Commonwealth, Being a Collection of All such Acts of the General Assembly 1819* (Richmond, 1819), I, 174; II, 17–25; *Supplement to the Revised Code of the Laws of Virginia: Being A Collection of All The Acts of the Gen-*

eral Assembly of a Public and Permanent Nature, Passed Since the Year 1819 (Richmond, 1833), 319–320; Mathews County Land Tax Lists 1817–1822.

63 Leonard, *General Assembly*, 200, 202, 204, 206, 208, 210, 212, 214, 216, 218, 220, 222, 224, 226, 228, 230, 232, 234, 236, 238, 240, 242, 244, 246, 248, 250, 252, 254, 257, 259, 261, 263, 266, 268, 270, 272, 274, 276, 278, 280, 282, 284, 286, 288, 290, 292, 294, 296, 299, 302, 304, 307, 309, 312, 314, 317, 319, 322, 324, 327, 329, 332, 334, 337, 339, 344, 347, 349, 352–354, 356, 358, 360, 362, 364, 368, 370, 372, 374; Charles, *Newspapers*, 69–71, 73, 75–76, 82–85, 88–89; Palmer, *Calendar*, X, 568–569.

64 Joseph Davis's land descended to his sons, William, James, and Edward. In 1817 William Davis sold 16 ½ acres to Alden G. Cushman. Around 1842, Francis Armistead (the second of that name) acquired Cushman's property and built the home known as Palace Green. According to a notation on a September 1834 plat, when Mrs. Cushman received a dower third of her late husband's estate, R. S. Davis owned the property that was contiguous and to the southeast (Mathews County Land Book 1, 140).

65 Perhaps the half-acre lot with the building Jarvis insured in 1816.

66 Mathews County Land Tax Lists 1814–1822.

67 The origin of the name "Westville" is uncertain. However, in 1861 Mathews County's tax assessor identified Thomas M. Hunley's 107-acre plantation as Westville, raising the possibility that the county seat's name was derived from a Hunley family tradition (Mathews County Land Tax Lists 1861).

68 The "new courthouse" to which Martin referred is the historic brick courthouse that fronts on Court Street.

69 Mathews County Land Tax Lists 1814–1839; Land Book 1, p. 50; Martin, *Gazetteer,* 226–229; WMCAR, *Integrated Management Plan*, 26.

70 Mathews County Personal Property Tax Lists 1812; Census 1830; Charles, *Newspapers*, 61–63, 87; http://mapserver.lib.virginia.edu/index.html.

8

Fruits of Prosperity, Storms of Life
1836–1860

The Agricultural Revolution's Impact

Thanks to advances in scientific farming, by the 1830s small and middling farmers throughout Virginia had been able to improve their standard of living. Increasing numbers of people switched to a mixed crop system and grains became an important part of the local economy. Most rural households raised sweet and Irish potatoes, peas, and beans; and a substantial number of farmers raised beef and dairy cattle, sheep, hogs, and poultry. These changes—fueled by readily available waterborne transportation—strengthened Mathews County's economy. In 1831, the mowing machine replaced the labor-intensive process of hand-cutting hay, and then during the 1840s the grain reaper came on the market. Edmund Ruffin reported in 1842 that farm income had increased by hundreds of thousands of dollars and that Tidewater land values had risen significantly. He attributed much of that economic progress to advances in agricultural technology, such as improved equipment to till the soil. By the mid-nineteenth century, progressive farmers eagerly embraced improvements as soon as they came along. For example, Philip E. Tabb bought a threshing machine shortly after they became available. William H. Roy of Green Plains publicly endorsed Tabb's purchase and described the equipment's merits in an essay he submitted to the *Richmond Enquirer*.[1]

Around 1835, *Gazetteer* author Joseph Martin noted that Mathews County soil was well suited to the production of corn and oats (but not wheat) and said that the land was so level that it was hard to drain. He commented that oak grew well; he also said that according to ship's carpenters, local oak was as good or better than the live oak, pine, chestnut, and gum that could be found outside of the county. He added that if cultivated land were allowed to lay fallow, it quickly sprouted pine, and noted that the castor oil bean had been cultivated widely until recent times. However, he stated that Mathews County people were preoccupied with shipbuilding and maritime pursuits and that agriculture had been neglected until recent years. He commented—without substantiating his claim—that Mathews had to import corn for home consumption. He said that about twenty years earlier, Mathews County shipbuilders produced around 100 ships a year and that there were around 200 ship's carpenters in the county, many of whom worked in navy yards in the summertime and returned home in winter.

In March 1839, Congress authorized funds for the collection of agricultural statistics, and by 1850 the state of Virginia had begun compiling records called agricultural censuses. This documentation, collected every decade from 1850 through 1880 by the same men who went door to door gathering demographic data, provides the number of acres under the plow and the number of acres that lay fallow or were forested, thereby yielding countywide information on land use patterns. Agricultural census records reveal whether a farmer had made a significant investment in agricultural equipment and whether he and his family were producing crops (such as fruits and vegetables) that could be sold in urban markets. Some farm families produced saleable commodities, such as smoked hams, honey, and manufactured goods. As time went on, the data collection process included dairying, egg production, and wine-making. There also was a modest reduction in farm size. Collectively, these records demonstrate how important advances in farming technology were to a revitalization of the region's agricultural economy.

In 1850, the majority of Mathews County's farmers utilized slave labor, had much of their acreage under the plow, and grew large field crops. Most farmers had a few horses or mules, a small herd of dairy cattle, and perhaps a few other cattle; the more successful had one or two teams of oxen. Less than half of Mathews County farmers raised sheep, largely for wool production, but most had substantial herds of swine. Throughout the county, corn was the main crop raised, although a few local farmers grew wheat. Most farmers raised a few bushels of oats along with sweet potatoes (a staple of the slave diet), Irish potatoes, peas, and beans. They also raised some hay for their livestock and many farmers had apiaries. The 1850s brought the grain drill, and the steam thresher arrived in 1860. These inventions further enhanced the farmer's efficiency and productivity. Mid-nineteenth-century topographic maps depicting the shore line of eastern Virginia's rivers reveal that almost all of Mathews County's waterfront land was being farmed. Houses, mills, and small commercial centers, typically at crossroads or boat landings, were scattered throughout the region, and development was concentrated at the county seat. Shipbuilding and other maritime activities continued to be extremely important to the local economy, but commercial shipping made urban markets readily accessible to farmers and watermen. For example, when Jacob Rammel, a New Jersey native who had moved to Mathews County, offered to sell his 275-acre farm on Mobjack Bay in 1856, he described its new two-story dwelling, outbuildings, and arable land. He said that his property was convenient to markets in Baltimore and Norfolk and that three steamboats passed by his door three times a week.

By 1860, the fair market value of Mathews County's rural properties had risen, partly in response to improvements in the agricultural economy, but also because of an inflationary trend that was in evidence throughout Virginia. Most farmers, regardless of their property's size, had from half to two-thirds of their acreage under the plow. A mixed crop system predominated, and most Mathews County farmers were raising more corn and wheat than they had in 1850 but had fewer acres planted in oats. A few people raised some tobacco, perhaps for their own consumption, and roughly a third of farms had orchards, which during 1859 collectively produced $4,573 worth of fruit. Many rural households had dairy herds that produced substantial quantities of butter, and most farmers sold a modest amount of "homemade manufactures," usually cured meat.

Many Mathews County farmers had invested in modern agricultural equipment by 1860. There were 400 farms in the county, none of which were as large as a thousand acres. Only six farms were between 500 and 999 acres in size, but there were 80 that were between 100 and 499 acres and 74 that were between 50 and 99 acres. There were 133 small farms between 20 and 49 acres in size, 74 that were between 10 and 19 acres, and 33 that consisted of between one and nine acres. In 1860, the average farm-hand, who received room and board from his employer, earned $18 a month, whereas a day-laborer without board earned 87 cents a day (or 62 cents with board).

Census-taker George W. Bohannon reported that Mathews County's soil, when properly drained, was well suited to the cultivation of wheat and corn. He said that there were no rocks larger than pebbles and that the only fertilizer farmers needed to use was the lime they obtained from oyster shells. He noted that pine, oak, and chestnut were the principal types of timber and that they grew more abundantly in the western part of the county.[2]

Plantation Management

Slaveholders with an interest in scientific farming often consulted agricultural literature, seeking the latest information on managing the enslaved, ostensibly for the purpose of maximizing the efficiency of their plantations. Such articles, included in agricultural journals, dealt with everything from food, housing, and clothing to health care, discipline, and religious instruction. Journal articles also discussed hygiene, marriage, and the care slaves required in their old age. Most slaveholders realized that adequate nourishment was essential to their slaves' health and that skimping on food was not only inhumane, but also financially risky. For example, one Virginia planter reported that his slaves' breakfasts usually consisted of bread and milk or salted herring and at midday they had bacon and vegetables. The writer said that his slaves dined on meat at suppertime and that he allowed them to raise hogs and poultry. Another Virginian reported that his slaves had an inexhaustible supply of vegetables during the summertime and that in the winter they could supplement their diet with stored root crops such as potatoes, beans, pumpkins, and turnips. A third Virginia slaveholder said that potatoes, cabbage, turnips, and peas, when boiled with beef or bacon, would provide slaves with a wholesome breakfast or lunch. The ideal slave diet was thought to include meat, cornmeal, vegetables, and fruit. Housing was considered a matter of great importance, and slaveholders generally agreed that the ideal slave cabin was a one-story weatherproof building that was elevated two or three feet from the ground to provide adequate ventilation and ease of cleaning. It was to have a brick chimney, a shingled roof, a plank floor, and windows to provide fresh air and light. There was general agreement that durable clothing should be issued to slaves and that in the interest of economy, much of it should be made on the plantation.

It is undeniable that some slaveholders and overseers were inhumane and sadistic, but during the nineteenth century, most enlightened farmers agreed that corporal punishment should be minimized and never administered during a moment of anger. Extra work, confinement, and loss of privileges were considered good substitutes for whipping, but most slave owners agreed that use of the lash was warranted for certain types of offenses. Plantation owners, though largely motivated by economics, generally agreed that maintaining the health of their slaves was extremely important. Pregnant and lying-in women were to be provided with preventive medicine and assigned lighter tasks. One Virginia planter said that he allowed his overseer to visit the sick twice a day. However, elderly slaves were usually expected to continue working. For example, an old woman might be expected to provide care to her owner's children. Because older slaves' productivity was limited, they ceased being classified as taxable personal property.

Letters written in 1847 by Adam Foster, Dr. Henry Wythe Tabb's houseguest, provide insight into the lives of the servants and slaves at his plantation, Auburn. Foster said that Dr. Tabb employed two "upper servants," who were white. One was a Mr. Saunders, an overseer or farm manager, who received a salary of $150 a year and a generous ration of meat and meal, and was provided with a house, a large garden, a cow, and a horse.[3] He oversaw the agricultural operations at Auburn and managed the field hands. The other "upper servant" was Miss Betsy Thomas, who was responsible for housekeeping operations. Foster added that she was a good seamstress and that she was a trusted employee who carried a small white basket with keys to closets, storerooms, the cellar, and other areas that needed to be secured.[4] Thomas oversaw the duties of four household slaves: two men who served as waiters, brought firewood into the house, and performed other heavy tasks, and two women, who were housemaids. Foster said that Auburn had a hundred slaves, always referred to as "servants," who were decently clothed and lived comfortably. He indicated that most of Dr. Tabb's slaves were worth about $400 apiece, but that he probably wouldn't part with his carpenter, bricklayer, coachman, or butcher for $1,500 each. The slaves' clothing was made on the plantation by old men and women, who spun and wove the fabric. According to Foster, each slave received a half-pound of bacon and a half-pint of molasses or whiskey each day, as well as about a peck of meal each week. There was a garden near every slave cabin and slaves were allowed to keep as much poultry as they wished. They were also allowed to provide themselves with fish and oysters and often sold seafood to small schooners that entered local waters. Foster added that the slaves' sale of oysters oftentimes violated a state law specifying that no vessel could take aboard more than 30 bushels. He said that Dr. Tabb sometimes sold his property's white oak timber and that recently, some was bought by a shipbuilder from Maine.

"Slave Schedules," largely statistical tabulations compiled by census-takers in 1850 and 1860, include the ages, sexes, and racial composition of the slaves that belonged to specific individuals. In 1860, census-takers noted the number of houses or cabins that each slaveholder provided to his slaves. Most of the Mathews County's slaveholders provided their slaves with separate accommodations, but men and women with only one or two slaves usually expected them to live in the loft of an outbuilding, perhaps above the plantation's detached kitchen or laundry. People who owned large numbers of slaves almost always had several cabins on their property, small dwellings that appear to have housed eight to ten individuals of various ages. For example, Thomas Smith, who owned 54 slaves, provided them with five cabins and Sands Smith, the owner of 39 slaves, had four cabins. An exception was Thomas J. White, who provided only one house for his 20 slaves, perhaps a barracks-like structure. Many slaveholders had one or two slaves who were age 60 or older and one man owned a slave who was 92.[5]

The Great Rebuilding

Throughout the first half of the nineteenth century, Mathews County had a significant number of large and prosperous plantations whose owners were at the upper end of the economic spectrum. One example is Poplar Grove, the home of John Patterson, a Revolutionary War veteran. His plantation, situated on a tributary of the East River, included part of the extensive holdings of the late Samuel Williams and land that had belonged to Dr. Victor Augustus Fulwell. Architectural historians have dated the oldest part of the existing house to the late eighteenth century. An insurance policy that Patterson purchased in 1816 for the main buildings at Poplar Grove, none of which were new, provided coverage for a house with two wings and four outbuildings: a kitchen, a dairy, a laundry, and a barn. Captain Christopher Tompkins, who married Patterson's daughter, Maria (Mariah) in 1815, acquired Poplar Grove in 1826.

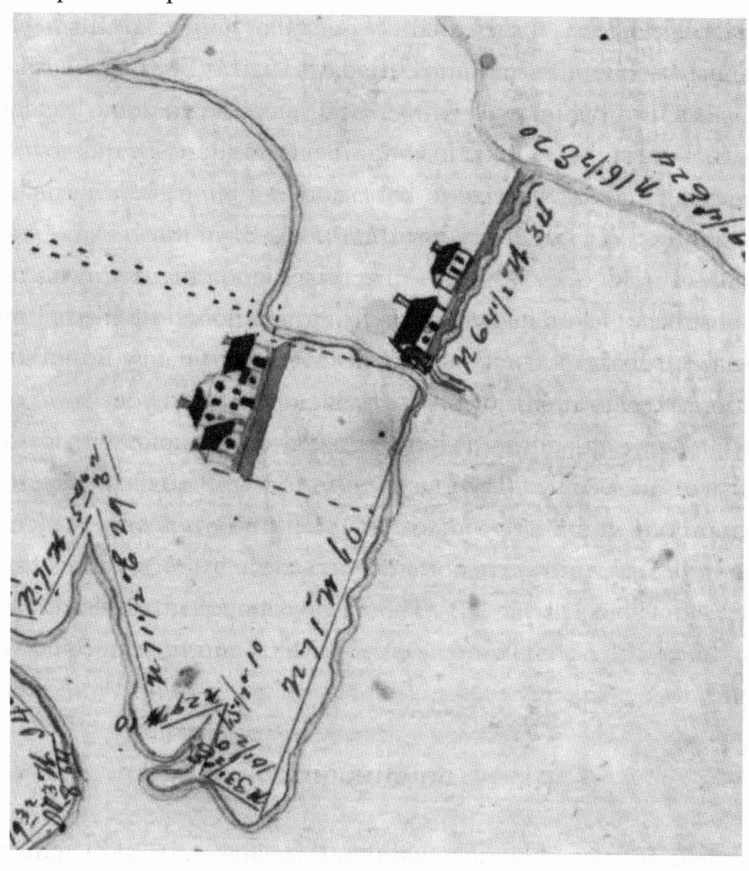

Poplar Grove house and tide mill, 1825. Mathews County Land Book 1, page 243.

Springdale is situated approximately one mile south of Mathews Courthouse and is on the National Register of Historic Places. According to architectural historians, it contains elements of construction that predate 1800, a period during which William Respess owned the property.[6] In 1823 Respess's widow, Joice, heir to part of her late husband's landholdings, conveyed his acreage on Put In Creek to her son-in-law, Richard Billups. Around 1824 Billups constructed a home on the property, perhaps incorporating portions of the old (presumably uninhabitable) Respess house into his dwelling. Similarly, when Benjamin Owen built the house known as Magnolia, he may have utilized part of a dwelling that was on the property he bought from Mathew Bailey's estate, improvements that predated 1820 and were then worth only $94.50.

When Isaac Foster prepared a plat of William White's property on the west side of the East River's mouth around 1830, he showed two old houses and a barn that were situated near two creeks. By October 1838, when another survey was made of the White property, one of the old frame houses had been replaced by a large, elegant brick home. Around 1837, William Todd purchased some land from John W. Jarvis and William Hunley and built a fine home he called Hyco, located only a quarter mile north of the county courthouse. Hyco's assessed value was $1,500, an indication that it was a fine residence that was suitable for an upper middle class household. Todd, who had served in the House of Delegates, went on to serve in the state senate. Oakland, a frame dwelling on the North River, was built around 1840 by Charles H. Blake, a professionally-trained engineer. It was the home of Delegate Samuel Digges and his wife, Mary Frances. In 1847, Digges, who represented Mathews County in the General Assembly for two terms and was a local tax official, also owned Windsor, the home once occupied by botanist John Clayton and his descendants.[7]

Christopher Tompkins: A Savvy Investor

One of Mathews County's most enterprising citizens was Christopher Tompkins, whose lucrative entrepreneurial activities included speculating in real estate. Although he took possession of twenty or more tracts of rural land, scattered throughout the county, he executed another fourteen transactions that involved parcels in or close to the county seat. Tompkins seems to have placed much of his land in the hands of tenants who paid whatever taxes were owed. Over the years, he retained possession of his ½-acre store lot in Mathews Courthouse, the acreage he acquired from John Patterson in 1814, and in 1829 he purchased a neighboring parcel, the one-acre lot on which William Plummer's tavern had stood. In 1832, Tompkins, who was in his late 50s, bought from hotelier and storekeeper Walter G. Lane a 1¾-acre vacant lot that was a quarter-mile west of the county courthouse, and he acquired two more undeveloped parcels in the same vicinity in 1836. That same year, Tompkins formed a partnership with fellow merchants Francis Armistead and Albert Diggs. Together, the three men acquired three parcels in Glebe Neck that Richard Hunley had mortgaged.[8] In 1837, Tompkins gained possession of an eleven-acre parcel located a quarter mile south of the county seat and constructed buildings that were worth $880. He acquired a one-acre lot at the county seat (which he bought from shoemaker Henry G. Murray) that contained a building worth $200. He also acquired a quarter-acre lot with a tailor shop that had an assessed value of $100, property that fronted on the south side of the courthouse green and contained the building eventually known as the Tompkins Cottage.

Archival records reveal that Christopher Tompkins died on August 16, 1838, from a respiratory infection.[9] Prior to that, he and his business partners gained possession of the easternmost part of the courthouse green, a three-quarter-acre parcel of public land containing the county's "old jail." It was probably around this time that Court Street's forerunner (perhaps a well-worn path) came into existence. Sometime prior to November 15, 1838, Dr. Henry W. Tabb of Auburn, the late Christopher Tompkins's executor and son-in-law, transferred Tompkins's one-and-a-half acre store lot and its improvements to his business partners, Armistead and Diggs, who by March 1840 had commenced trading as Armistead, Diggs, and Company.[10] The reorganized firm also bought Tompkins's blacksmith shop, and on June 3, 1840, they began making payments on both properties and the merchandise in his store. The ledgers and journals maintained by the mercantile firm Tompkins, Armistead, and Diggs, and its successor Armistead, Diggs and Company reveal that their store sold general merchandise that ranged from loaf sugar, mustard, apple brandy, yard goods, buttons, stockings, and shoes to paper, nails, tablespoons, varnish, saw files, candles, soap, furniture, plates, and eyeglasses. The store's proprietors procured many of their saleable goods from Norfolk, Richmond, and Baltimore. Most customers made their purchases on credit and paid their bills when they could. Sometimes, they used their land as collateral when securing store credit or borrowing money; if they failed to repay their debts, the merchants gained possession of their property through foreclosure. It was most likely through this means that Christopher Tompkins and his fellow investors were able to gain possession of land throughout Mathews County and in the county seat. The real estate transactions of Tompkins's executor reveal the extent of Tompkins's success in acquiring real estate.[11]

Armistead and Diggs not only bought the late Christopher Tompkins' store and blacksmith shop at the county seat, they also acquired his legal interest in the three-quarter-acre parcel that originally had been part of the courthouse green. In 1841, the county tax assessor indicated that Armistead and Diggs' three-quarters of an acre had been carved into three small lots, each of which contained buildings. The northernmost lot, directly across from the county courthouse, encompassed a half-acre, on which there were improvements worth $1,000. Next door and to the south was a quarter-acre lot that had $100 worth of buildings; and below that was an eighth-acre lot that had $400 worth of improvements. In 1851, the county tax assessor again attributed all three lots to Armistead, Diggs, and Company, just as he had done a decade earlier, and the buildings' assessed value was the same. However, the assessor identified the half-acre parcel as the "store lot," noted that the quarter-acre lot contained the "old jail," and indicated that the eighth-acre lot was occupied by an "office." An entry in the Armistead, Diggs, and Company ledger reveals that by 1849 a tavern had been erected on the half-acre store lot whose improvements were still worth $1,000,[12]and that from 1849 to 1852 that parcel was rented to John N. Armistead, an innkeeper.[13] In 1853, Armistead and Diggs sold their store/hotel lot to Sheriff John H. Dunlavy (Dunlevy), who finished paying for it on August 30, 1862. Four months later, Dunlavy bought Armistead and Diggs's blacksmith shop. It is unclear how the quarter-acre lot containing the old jail was used during the 1840s; however, by 1849 Armistead, Diggs, and Company had begun renting their eighth-acre lot and office, on the northernmost corner of Main and Brickbat, to tailor William F. Pugh. During 1861 and 1862, Dr. Silas C. White, a physician, rented the office lot and the adjoining parcel that contained the old jail, then worth only $30; he purchased the office lot for $450 in 1863. Meanwhile, in 1861 Benjamin Williams bought the quarter-acre parcel with the old jail and sold it to John H. Dunlavy a year later. A detailed topographic map that was made in 1853 reveals that all of these structures paralleled Main Street and Court Street, which intersected Church Street and Brickbat Road. On the east side of Main Street was a row of irregularly spaced buildings. In 1853, Church Street crossed Put In Creek's headwaters by means of a bridge, skirted the north side of the courthouse green, and then terminated at Main Street.

Executor Henry W. Tabb continued to dispose of Christopher Tompkins's land. During 1839, he conveyed to William S. Thurston, a physician, a one-third acre lot that abutted Brickbat Road and fronted on the south side of the courthouse green. The parcel had $800 worth of improvements and was just west of a half-acre corner lot that abutted the main road and later contained a store. Around 1845, Tabb transferred to Tompkins's youngest son, Benjamin G. Tompkins, the elder Tompkins's quarter-acre lot that contained a tailor's shop worth $100. It was located on the south side of the courthouse green, next door and just west of Dr. Thurston's property. Tabb also transferred to Benjamin G. a one-acre lot that contained $100 worth of improvements, the parcel that formerly belonged to shoemaker Henry G. Murray.[14]

A Fleeting Glimpse of the County Seat

During the 1840s, Mathews Courthouse was a small but thriving village that consisted of small lots interspersed with larger partially wooded parcels. At the core of the community was the courthouse green with its public buildings. Between the east side of the green and the west side of the main road (Main Street) were three small lots that contained a store, and by 1849 a tavern; the old jail; and an office. The late Christopher Tompkins had held a legal interest in these properties, which his executor transferred to Armistead, Diggs, and Company around 1840. The forerunner of Brickbat Road, which ran from Main Street toward Put In Creek, defined the south side of the courthouse green. On the corner, abutting east on Main Street and north on Brickbat Road, was the Armistead and Jarvis store. To the west, fronting on Brickbat Road and the courthouse green, was Dr. William S. Thurston's medical office. Next door and to the west of the Thurston property was the tailor shop that Benjamin G. Tompkins had inherited from his father. On the north side of the courthouse green was Walter G. Lane's hotel. Between 1839 and 1840 the assessed value of the buildings on Lane's property rose from $400 to $2,000, reflecting the construction of his hotel. Lane also owned a store, and he had a tannery that was located an eighth of a mile west of the courthouse, on the far side of Put In Creek.[15]

By 1837, William Todd's home, Hyco, stood at the northern terminus of Main Street, close to its intersection with Buckley Hall Road. Nearby was the Ephesus Meeting House, precursor of the Westville Christian Church, a place of worship utilized by the Rev. Alexander Campbell's followers. Development extended in a northwesterly direction along Buckley Hall Road, where there were tracts owned by merchant Alexander Marchant, John Parrott Jr., and the estates of Mary and Charles Hodges. To the east of Hyco Corner, probably on Buckley Hall Road, was a three-quarter acre lot with $1,000 worth of buildings that merchants John D. Jarvis and Elijah Barnum bought from John L. Diggs around 1837. Approximately ten years later, Jarvis and Barnum came into possession of the one-acre lot and store that had belonged to the late Thomas James; by 1861 the property belonged solely to Barnum, who had outlived his business partner. Blacksmith John White purchased a quarter-acre lot from John L. Diggs in 1841, and in 1861 he bought the one-acre lot that had belonged to (in succession) shoemaker Henry G. Murray, Christopher Tompkins, and Benjamin G. Tompkins.

By 1839, Edmund P. Benson had come into possession of 32 acres at the county seat, land that was on the east side of Main Street and south of Buckley Hall Road. He erected what was called Benson's Hotel, which was adjacent to a large undeveloped tract he probably used for farming and as a source of firewood. Benson's Hotel, whose assessed value was $800 during the 1840s and 50s, was acquired by the Jarvis and Barnum firm around 1848. By 1860, Francis T. White, the county jailor, had come into possession of the 32-acre hotel tract and its improvements, whose value had risen to $1,000. Like his predecessors, White operated a modest-sized hostelry.

He also owned a neighboring parcel the tax assessor identified as "the hotel woods." When a census-taker visited the hotel in 1860, White, his wife, and their four young children were living there, as were Dr. William S. Thurston (a physician), John B. Donovan (an attorney), Alexander Marchant (a merchant), and William E. Williams (the hotel's clerk). Besides his duties as a hotelkeeper and jailor, White farmed the land associated with his hotel and probably provided food to the county jail's prisoners. He had five adult slaves, some of whom probably did chores in his hotel. By the close of the Civil War, White's hotel had come into the hands of Yancey Sleet, who commenced calling it Sleet's Hotel. It was one of two hotels Yancey Sleet owned and one of three the Sleet family operated in the succeeding years.

To the south of Benson's Hotel and also on the east side of Main Street was the Mathews Academy, sometimes called the Mathews Seminary, erected around 1838–39 by a group of investors. To the south and just above the intersection formed by Main Street and County Route 611 (Tabernacle Road), which in 1821 was identified as a "new road," was a 20-acre parcel owned and occupied by merchant Benjamin Bramhall, whose landholdings included acreage on nearby Reed Swamp and on the Piankatank River. On the west side of Main Street and closer to Mathews Courthouse was a plantation owned successively by Alden G. Cushman and Shephard G. Miller. Around the time Miller sold his land to Francis Armistead, the stately home known as Palace Green was built. Further south and extending along both sides of Route 14 were farms of various sizes and the county poorhouse.

Palace Green. Courtesy of the Mathews County Historical Society.

A surviving account book from one of Mathews Courthouse's hotels indicates that during the 1840s, many people came to town whenever court was in session. Some had probably traveled for a considerable distance and needed overnight accommodations, food and drink, and feed for their horses. Others, who lived close to the county seat, stopped at the hotel to enjoy a meal, smoke a cigar, or sip a glass of wine, sangaree, or brandy. For example, Miss Polly Hodges, the only woman listed in the unidentified hotelkeeper's account book, paid for a half-pint of wine. On one occasion, Thomas F. Lewis, a regular customer, had four drinks in one visit; he may have become rambunctious, for he had to pay for the two window panes he broke. Another hotel guest was Circuit Court Judge Joseph Christian, who had ridden in from Middlesex County.

Mathews County in 1840

Demographic records compiled in 1840 indicate that Mathews County had a population of 7,442 people, 3,309 (or 44.5 percent) of whom were enslaved. Of the non-enslaved, there were 3,969 free whites and 164 free blacks. A total of 1,852 Mathews County residents were engaged in agriculture, 35 in commerce, and 392 in manufacturing and trade. There also were 19 "learned professionals and engineers" plus 136 people engaged in "navigation of canals" and 42 others employed in "navigating the ocean." Mathews County had two academies and grammar schools, which had 92 students, and another 257 children were enrolled in private schools or in "common" (public) schools. A total of 69 students were attending school at public expense, perhaps because their families were indigent. In 1840, Mathews County had 368 whites who were age 20 or older and illiterate; none of the county's free blacks (and probably few or none of the enslaved) could read or write.[16]

Virginia Laws Affecting Mathews County

By the mid-1830s members of Virginia's General Assembly had become concerned about the destruction of the fish and shellfish on which many citizens depended for their livelihood. At their 1836–37 session, assembly members placed restrictions on the quantities of oysters and terrapins that could be harvested from the upper part of the North River and Blackwater Creek. They also restricted the length of seines (floating fishing nets) and the hauling of seines in certain places and between May and October; no one was allowed to harvest more than two bushels of oysters a day for his family. Slaves who violated this law were to be whipped; others were to be fined. In April 1839, the regulations were expanded to include oystering in all of the waters of Mathews, Elizabeth City, and Warwick Counties. That prompted Mathews County watermen, whose livelihood depended upon the seafood industry, to submit petitions to the General Assembly. One group opposed the restrictions placed on harvesting oysters from Milford Haven and the Piankatank, North, and East Rivers during a five- or six-month period and proposed that the limits be applied for only two or three months. The General Assembly responded by making it legal for the inhabitants of Mathews and Middlesex Counties to harvest oysters in April, May, and September within their own waters. The other group of watermen protested a new law that prohibited fishermen from hauling their seines ashore on privately-owned beaches on the Mobjack and Chesapeake Bays.

Mathews County citizens were keenly interested in what went on at the federal level, and on February 10, 1834, a large group of men met at the county's "new and spacious court-house" to discuss whether public deposits should be withdrawn from the Bank of the United States and whether the bank should be re-chartered. William H. Roy favored funding and re-chartering the bank, but Dr. William Shultice took the opposing view. After a heated debate, the group reconvened on February 15 and formulated a series of resolutions that were published in newspapers in Richmond and Norfolk.[17]

The Wolf Trap Light and the New Point Comfort Lighthouse

In 1841, a new lightship with two lights was moored on the Wolf Trap shoals. On June 21, 1851, a seaman who passed the Wolf Trap lightship at 7 PM reported that it was not illuminated. He added that the vessel, whose keeper was an old sea captain, had been set adrift several times and noted that there was a buoy in front of the lightship. The Lighthouse Board's officers published a report in 1852, describing the New Point Comfort lighthouse and its keeper's dwelling. They said that Isaac Foster, a retired sea captain, had become the principal keeper in January 1847 and received $400 a year for his services; his female slave assisted him in maintaining the light. Board members expressed frustration with Foster, who turned on the light at dark and extinguished it at dawn, claiming that "the light is not considered bad in the bay." They also said that Foster considered the lighthouse's curtains useless so he didn't bother to use them. He admitted that he didn't bother to keep watch, but always woke up "at the right time."

Congress decided to place a buoy at New Point Comfort in 1854, the same year that Edward S. White was appointed lighthouse keeper, and in 1855 the United States Coast Survey announced the discovery of a new hazard to mariners, the New Point shoal, which was located southeast of the lighthouse and covered by 16 feet of water. When the lighthouse's light was refitted in 1855, it was made visible for 13 nautical miles. Despite these enhanced aids to navigation, shipwrecks occurred from time to time, and in July 1856 Robert E. Hudgins accepted a gubernatorial appointment as Commissioner of Wrecks for Mathews County. In 1860, Hudgins was told that if neither a vessel's captain nor its crew survived a shipwreck, he—as wreck-master—could take charge. Despite the presence of the New Point Comfort lighthouse, mariners continued to have problems. A schooner ran aground at New Point Comfort in 1859 but was able to get off after her load was lightened.[18]

Absconding to Freedom

Runaway slaves often tried to slip aboard a vessel while it was at anchor. By 1804, this had become so problematic that a law was passed specifying that mariners found guilty of enabling slaves to escape were subject to a fine of $100 to $500 and two to four years in the state penitentiary in Richmond. In April 1843, David Ripley, a Mathews County seaman, who ran afoul of this law, was found guilty of "negro stealing," and was sentenced to time in the state penitentiary. According to deputy sheriff John Spencer, Ripley, a "large and strong man," had "many friends of great savage fierceness and strength" who had tried to wrest him from the sheriff's custody and were unruly at the court hearing. Therefore, Spencer asked the county court to allow Larkin Miller and Baldwin Foster to serve as guards when Ripley was taken to Richmond. Afterward, a number of local citizens signed a petition, supporting Spencer's request, and stated that Ripley's father and others had asked when the prisoner was to be transported to prison. By 1850, David Ripley, a married man, had been released from jail and was living in Portsmouth. Sometime prior to 1860, he returned to Mathews County, where he was still employed as a seaman.

Sometimes, apprentices ran away, frustrating their parents' or guardians' attempts to have them educated in a useful trade. In July 1819, two Mathews County boys, Ralph Tomblin and William Grunwell, who had been apprenticed to the same Norfolk shipbuilder, ran away; the shipbuilder, in turn, offered a reward for their recovery. In 1839, Chadwick Hudgins of Mathews Courthouse, who was sent to Samuel Bickley at age 19 to learn the trade of a shoemaker and boot maker, fled from his master. Bickley placed an advertisement in a Baltimore newspaper, offering a reward for his apprentice's return. A 16-year-old Mathews County boy named Josephus Wiatt, who was apprenticed to a coach-maker in Baltimore, also ran away. It is likely that some of these youths became homesick or had received harsh treatment from their masters.

There is no question that some slaveholders also lacked compassion. An elderly ex-slave, Mrs. Elizabeth Sparks, who had lived in Mathews County all of her life, recalled how her young mistress, whom she described as a good woman, used to slap or beat her once in a while. She also recollected seeing her mistress's father, Shepard G. Miller of Spring Hill, have slaves beaten to death, usually for not getting their work done. She added that he tended to hire cruel overseers and that she had seen Miller beat both men and women. She said that he would have them stripped naked, beaten, and then washed down with brine. Sometimes, slaves fled into the woods after a beating. Other slaves would slip them food and usually one of the black foremen would try to coax the runaway to return home. If slaves ventured out at night, they could be caught by patrollers, patrolmen on horseback responsible for enforcing the slave code. There could be dire consequences for slaves caught out at night without a pass. Mrs. Sparks said that Miller's wife was bad tempered and would beat slaves with a broom, a leather strap, a switch, or anything else she had handy. The Millers' slaves worked six days a week, sunup to sundown, with a brief break for lunch. Their foreman would sound a horn to signal when it was time to start or stop work. Another former slave from Mathews County, Lisa McCoy, who was born in 1844, said that she was one of Warner Boran's slaves.[19] She claimed that he would whip her whenever he could catch her and that Bob (Robert) Billups, her father's master, sold him to someone in Georgia. Billups also sold her Aunt Charlotte, purportedly because she had conceived a white-skinned child with her young master's son.[20]

Mathews County's Free Blacks

Historian Luther P. Jackson, who made abundant use of Virginia's local court records, concluded that most of the state's free blacks were the offspring of slaves freed between the close of the American Revolution and 1806, when the laws regulating manumission became more stringent. In 1807, when Mathews County tax assessors listed free people of color, they noted that some were from Lilly's and Callis's estates; three years later, they compiled lists, separating free black and mulatto taxpayers from free whites. In 1810, all of the former slaves in the 1805 list were included again, but they were joined by Allen, John, and Richard Cooke; Edmund and William Driver; Joe Field; and John Lemmon. Also among the former slaves were Joe and Kitt, freed by Lilley's estate; Guy and Tom, freed under Lane's will; George, freed by Line Shackleford's executors; James, freed by the Hayes estate; Kitt and Toney, freed by Callis's estate; Ralph, freed by Churchill's estate; and Toby, freed by the Van Bibber estate. The name of Gary, freed by Ezekiel Lane's executors, appeared in the tax rolls for the first time in 1812, probably because he had turned 16. Ex-slave Richard Cooke seems to have made some economic progress, for he was credited with a horse, as were Frank Whiting and Joe Field, who also paid personal property taxes on slaves of their own. In 1814, John Berry and William Beaufort joined the ranks of the free; however, it is unclear whether they were newly freed or had just attained tithable age. Demographic records reveal that in 1830 and 1840 many of Mathews County's free blacks resided in white households, although black female heads of household were fairly common and sometimes, women headed households that included one or more men of tithable age. In 1840 two people in Mary Manley's household were engaged in manufacturing or trades. Harry Brown, Rose Gordon, Thomas and James Gregory, Warner Hern, Thornton Johnson, Armistead Street, John Lemmon, Ann and Nancy Morse, and Jenny, Judith, and William Lane were among Mathews County's free black household heads.

Virginia had a total of 30,570 free blacks in 1830, most of whom were in the eastern part of the state. By that time, the number of free black landowners had grown significantly, and it doubled between 1830 and 1860. But nearly half of all free black landowners had 25 acres or less. Most of eastern Virginia's free blacks lived in a rural setting; less than a fifth lived in towns and cities. The typical free black family tilled a few acres but also sought employment with white landowners. Farm hands and laborers always outnumbered mechanics and other types of skilled artisans. Many women found work as washerwomen or farm hands. Corn was usually the free black farmer's biggest cash crop but the majority also raised hogs and other livestock. Tenant farming was common and most free black farmers paid their rent in agricultural commodities; watermen also paid their rent with the fruit of their labor. Real estate tax rolls reveal that Henry Cake owned three acres near Cricket Hill, whereas in 1845 Nancy Morse (Moss), who had 17¾ acres in Cow Neck, had a building or buildings worth $140, a value indicative of middle class housing. Sally and Alice, freed by the Callis estate in the mid-1790s, were identified as household heads Sally and Alice Callis in 1840 and were between 55 and 100 years old. Landowner and household head Nancy Morse was in the same age group, as was Susan Manley (Mantley).

In 1851, Mathews County's tax commissioners recorded the names of all of the free black men between the ages of 21 and 65: James T. Carter; William Casey; Charles, John, Lewis, Walter, and William Callis; Ezekiel Foster; Charles W., Henry, Richard, and William Cooke; William W. Crawford; Carter, James, and William Hayes; John S. and Warner Horner; Lewis, Philip, Richard, Walter, and William Lane; John G. Lemon (Lemmon); Ebenezer Machen; John Mantly; Francis, George, and John Morse; Joshua and Shadrack Peyton; Joseph Pen; and Joshua Pratt. A year later, the tax assessor included the ages and occupations of free black taxpayers.

They included six sailors (William Casey, Henry Cooke, Philip and Richard Lane, Francis Mantly, and Shadrack Peyton), a house carpenter (Ezekiel Foster), and three shoemakers (Francis, George, and John Morse). Most of the free black males in the tax lists were identified as laborers, although Richard Ruff was a house carpenter. Census records suggest that many of the county's free black men were unemployed. Nonetheless, one or more household members must have managed to generate enough income to pay the personal property taxes that kept them from being re-enslaved. Census records compiled in 1850 indicate that Mathews County's free black population consisted of 67 males and 80 females. Of those 147 individuals, none could read and write. Only four free black household heads reportedly owned real estate: Elizabeth Cooke, Henry Cooke, Philip Lane, and Nancy Morse. A total of 18 households were headed by men and 17 by women, and many households were multigenerational. When personal property tax records were compiled in 1858, the names of free black men who were age 21 or older were listed at the end of the tax book. They were: Joseph Benn; John and William Casey; Charles, Henry, James, Richard H., and Robert Cook; W. Crawford; John Dudley; Ezekiel Foster; Carter and John Hayes; Ephraim, Jacob, John S., and Warner Hearn; John, Philip, Richard, Walter and William Lane; William G. Lemon; Ebenezer Machen; John Manly; Francis, George, John, and Thomas Morse.

One of Mathews County's most interesting free black households was headed by John Hearn (Hern, Herne), perhaps a descendant of Ephraim Hearn, who was freed on account of his service during the Revolutionary War.[21] In 1840 John Hearn's household included seven people: a man and a woman who were between 24 and 35, probably John and his wife; a boy and two girls who were less than 10 years old; and a young male and a young female who were between 10 and 23. Two members of the Hearn household were employed in manufacturing or trade, which would have provided the family with a livelihood. By 1849, John Hearn had bought an 11.1-acre tract "near the Battery" from Benjamin D. Metcalf of Maine, who had purchased the 381-acre North End tract from John Horn's widow. Hearn's land was vacant when he bought it, but by 1861 he had managed to add improvements worth $50. Hearn's acreage buildings were still in his possession in 1868.[22]

Mathews County's Military Veterans and their Dependents

As stated earlier, legislation enacted by Congress in July 1832 provided pensions for veterans and qualified widows and relieved the state of Virginia of that obligation. During 1833 and 1834, federal officials were flooded with veterans' pension applications. Among the Mathews County men whose requests were approved were privates William Armistead, George Callis, John Christian, Thomas Davis, William Diggs, William Evans, Simon Green, Anthony Hudgins, Gabriel Hudgins, Hugh Hudgins, Richard Hurst, John Morgan, William Morgan, Josiah Pugh, Richard Ripley, Isaac Smith, James Thomas, and John White. All of these men, who had been in the Virginia militia, were in their 70s when they commenced receiving a veteran's pension from the federal government. In 1835, the pension applications of Purnell Houston and William Hull, who were both age 80, were approved. When census-takers compiled records on Mathews County in 1840, they listed the names of military veterans and veterans' widows then receiving pensions. The list of Revolutionary War veterans included George Callis (age 78), Thomas Davis (78), Mathias Gayle (78), Thomas Hall (75), Hugh Hudgins (76), and Josiah Pugh (78). Veterans' widows included Bathsheba Brooks (75), Mary Davis (86), Joice Gayle (79), Mary Martin (76), Nancy Morgan (74), Avarilla Owen (74), Johanna Watson (84), Dorothy White (78), and Elizabeth White (67). William D. White (48) was also included in the list, presumably as a veteran of the War of 1812. Most, but not all, of these people were living in their own homes.[23]

Changes in Tax Policy Yield New Insights

By 1842, pianos, clocks, and gold and silver watches were considered taxable luxury items, and in 1845 medical professionals, such as physicians, surgeons, and dentists, and lawyers, were taxed on the fees they earned. Also taxed were those who received income from investments, office-holding, public ferries and bridges, or from owning newspapers or printing presses. These tax records provide a glimpse into the professional and socioeconomic makeup of the county.

In 1845, Mathews County had five physicians and surgeons: Drs. William H. Farrar, William Shultice, William A. Spence, Henry W. Tabb, and William S. Thurston. By 1850, Drs. Farrar and Spence were gone but Drs. John H. Garrett, George M. Hicks, Samuel Hudgins, Thomas Vaughan, and John H. White had begun practicing medicine in Mathews, giving the county a total of eight physicians and surgeons, seven of whom were licensed. In 1850 the county had four licensed attorneys: William H. Roy, John W. Jarvis, Daniel H. Foster, and H.W. Daingerfield. A year later Woodson Moody began practicing law in Mathews County and Drs. John Bohannan Sr., James W. Garrett, Augustine Hicks, and Albert G. Hudgins had begun practicing medicine. When William Thomson's *Medical and Professional Directory* was published in 1851, Mathews County reportedly had four physicians: Dr. James H. Garrett (Garnett), who was at the courthouse, and Drs. Augustus M. Hicks, William Shultice, and William S. Thurston (Thruston).

Personal property tax rolls for 1858 reveal that Walter G. Lane and Francis T. White purchased licenses as tavern-keepers, whereas Daniel H. Foster, Edward E. Orvis (Ovis), and William H. Roy were licensed attorneys. The county's licensed physicians were Drs. John Bohannon, John G. Bohannon, Thomas H. Dunn, James H. Garnett, A.M. Hicks, W. Shultice, W.S. Thornton, and Silas C. White.

Merchant's licenses were bought by John N. Dixon, William P. Hudgins and Brother, Francis Armistead and Company, Napoleon B. Anderson, Elijah Barnum, Thomas D. Borum, Franklin S. Billups, Andrew J. Davis, Chaplin B. Diggs, Thomas J. Hudgins, Leonidas James, Francis P. Jarvis, John N. Jarvis, Walter G. Lane, M.H. Perkins, M.A. Richardson, T.R. Ransone, A.D. Saunders, and M.H. Oliver. Most of the county's merchants sold wines and obtained a special license permitting them to do so. In 1859, a person identified as L. Hamie, who was identified as an "exhibitor of paintings," bought a license that authorized him to display—and presumably sell—artwork for one night.[24]

Insights from Fiduciary Records

The accounts kept by those who settled Mathews County residents' estates reveal that the bulk of most slaveholders' wealth was invested in their slaves. Such was the case with lighthouse keeper Isaac Foster, Collector of Customs John Daingerfield, and others for whom court records are available. The same was true of William T. Hodges, a mariner and tenant farmer of relatively modest means. Fiduciary records suggest that supporting his household (which included a wife, eight children, and eight slaves) left him with relatively little disposable income. When Hodges died in 1855 at age 50, his household furnishings included four bedsteads with straw mattresses, a mahogany table, a cupboard, four mirrors, and eleven chairs, five of which had rush seats. The family's culinary equipment consisted of basic cookware: a kettle and spider (a metal pot stand), an oven (probably a Dutch oven), a grindstone, and tubs for salting meat. The bulk of Hodges's money was invested in his eight slaves and his livestock, which included a pair of oxen, a cow, four swine, and a young ox. He also had three plows, hoes, axes, a fork, a harrow, and an ox cart. He was credited with a canoe, four pair of oyster tongs, a stack of fodder, and supplies of corn and peas. Mrs. Ellender Hodges's dower share of her late husband's personal property may have been excluded from his inventory.

Mathias Hunley, an unmarried boat-builder who died in 1855 at age 52, was relatively prosperous in comparison to Hodges. Although he owned no real estate, his household furnishings included a brass candlestick, an abundance of plates, cups and saucers, four small bowls, a tea pot, sugar dishes, a dozen spoons, three coffeepots and a coffee grinder, two large dishes, a pitcher, some bottles, and a substantial quantity of knives and forks. He also had the usual culinary equipment, such as iron cook pots, a frying pan, and a spit, plus a spinning wheel, two tables, a safe, fourteen chairs, a bedstead, a floor mat, and a clock. The bulk of Hunley's investment was in the tools of his trade: an adze, a wooden maul, two chisels, a compass, a hatchet, scales, a lye strainer, two iron wedges, a smoothing plane, two blacking brushes, a hand saw, and a lot of plank. He wasn't a slaveholder but at the time of his death he had a hired man who was black. Hunley's livestock included a steer and two fat hogs and he had on hand eleven barrels of corn.

Although very little documentation on local burial practices has come to light, in March 1857 when William R. Smart's aunt, Julia Gibbons, made her will, she asked that her body be allowed to remain in her house for two days ("a proper length of time") and requested that her grave be lined with bricks or plank before she was buried. She also wanted her grave to be properly enclosed and left funds to accommodate her requests.[25]

The Expansion of Waterborne Commerce: An Economic Stimulus

The role that steamboats played in transportation and communication reached its zenith during the second and third quarters of the nineteenth century. Wharves that accommodated passengers and freight were strategically located on Mathews County's waterways. According to the late Milton Murray Jr.'s writings, three steamers served the Mobjack Bay area six days a week for almost 50 years. The arrival and departure of a steamboat, heralded by a whistle's blasts, generated a certain amount of excitement. The steamer *Coffee*, which operated out of Norfolk and Portsmouth, made two weekly trips to Williams Wharf throughout the 1850s, transporting passengers and freight to and from its home ports and Mathews County. Mathews also was served by the steamers *Gladiator*, *Planter*, and *Starr* during the late 1850s and in the very early 1860s by the steamers *Mattano*, *Mattawan*, *Seabird*, and *Monmouth*. One of Mathews County's most popular landings was Fitchett's Wharf, which was located on the lower side of Stutts Creek, close to Billups Creek's mouth. It was an important center of commercial activity from 1845 until the 1930s and served as a major port of call for vessels navigating the Chesapeake Bay. Lewis Hudgins operated a shipyard at Fitchett's Wharf

Steamboat on the East River near Poplar Grove, 1825. Mathews County Land Book 1, page 243.

and built several brig and schooner class commercial ships there. The shipyard was burned in 1864 by Union forces.[26]

Post Offices

During the third decade of the nineteenth century, the post offices at Mathews Courthouse and North End continued to serve the public, but the one at Belle Isle was discontinued. In 1852, the Postmaster General signed a contract with Charles H. Shield of Norfolk, who agreed to transport mail from Norfolk to Mathews Courthouse and back twice a week by steamboat. The mail was to leave Norfolk at 8 AM on Wednesdays and Saturdays and reach Mathews Courthouse by 4 PM Likewise, it was to leave Mathews at 8 A.M. on Wednesdays and Saturdays and reach Norfolk by 7 PM A post office was established at Cobbs Creek in 1853 with Alfred Billups as postmaster. The new facility, located in a growing community, was to receive mail service twice a week. Billups was replaced by Henry L. Matthews in 1858 and assistant postmaster Benjamin G. Blake resigned. In 1859 William A. Richardson became postmaster at North End but assistant postmaster A.D. Saunders resigned. [27]

Henry Howe's Observations

According to Henry Howe's *Historical Collections of Virginia,* published in 1852, Mathews County was "a peninsula, extending into the Chesapeake Bay." Howe added that about 60,000 acres of the county's land was of medium fertility and that marl could be found in some parts of the county. He said that "formerly shipbuilding was carried on to such an extent that agriculture was almost entirely neglected." He noted that windmills and tide mills supplied the county with meal and that because the land was almost flat, no streams of fresh water ran through it. He commented that during long, dry seasons, the waterholes for livestock dried up, leaving the cattle thirsty. Howe stated that Mathews Courthouse or Westville was near the center of the county and situated on a small tributary of the East River. Echoing Joseph Martin's *Gazetteer*, he said that the county seat was a port of entry and contained around thirty dwellings.[28]

Crime and Punishment

In September 1850, a murder occurred in Mathews County that attracted national attention. According to newspaper accounts, brothers Sidney (Sydney) and William Lane, who worked in a Mathews County shipyard, clashed over Sidney's abuse of a black woman who was gathering woodchips. Sidney, who seems to have had a mercurial personality, suddenly redirected his rage at his brother. He shot and killed William and then fled in a canoe. After Sidney Lane was apprehended, he was put into the Mathews County jail, where he was detained with John Edwards, accused of murdering two men in 1848. Both men were transferred to the Norfolk jail because the Mathews jail was considered "unsafe." Later, Lane was tried, convicted, and sentenced to two years and six months in the state penitentiary; Edwards's fate is uncertain.

In 1854, William L. Hawkins of Mathews County, who had been convicted of second-degree murder for killing a seaman on a steamer, was pardoned on account of insanity. Three years later, Marcus J. Tarr and Robert Howlett of Mathews County were attacked and beaten in a Baltimore bar and barely escaped death.[29] These episodes of violence, though uncommon, disturbed Mathews County's tranquility.

Strong Winds and Winter Weather

The hurricane seasons of the 1830s and 40s seem to have been relatively quiet, although tropical storms passed up the Atlantic coast in late August 1839 and in 1842, affecting the communities in their path. A tornado touched down in Mathews County in January 1847 and destroyed one house, ripped the roofs off several others, and blew down fences and trees. Moving along the East River, it damaged the vessels in its path and overturned numerous small buildings. John Dangerfield, the Collector of Customs for the East River District, was riding in a gig and was killed instantly when his frightened horse bolted at the sight of the tornado.

In 1842, a newspaper correspondent from the *Norfolk Herald* who lived in Mathews County claimed that it had rained on court day for the past 18 years. A journalist from the *Richmond Compiler* followed up, surmising that "There must be something very remarkable in the course of Justice in Mathews, when it causes the heavens to weep thus." Both reporters' comments were republished in a newspaper in Gettysburg, Pennsylvania.

The 1850s were not as quiet as the previous decades and several hurricanes affected eastern Virginia. In late August 1850, the countryside along the lower Chesapeake Bay was hit by a storm that was considered the worst in 30 years. According to news accounts, a powerful gust of wind stripped the wheelhouse from the deck of the steam-powered *Osceola*, which was plying the bay, and blew it overboard. As the storm continued up the bay, buildings and crops were laid low. Two hurricanes passed through the region in August 1856. Although the first one didn't do much damage, the second one produced high, damaging winds.

Winter weather, though rarely severe, could be devastating to the area as well. In mid-January 1857, people living in Virginia and much of North Carolina were affected by a blizzard termed the worst ever to hit the state. Temperatures hovered around zero, and in some places, howling gale-force winds produced drifts of snow up to the eaves of buildings. This bout of extreme weather was dubbed "Cox's Snow" because Dr. Philip Cox, a Chesterfield County physician, froze to death while making a house call in his buggy. His death was not the only one attributable to the snowstorm, which created massive drifts that derailed at least two railroad trains in central Virginia. Snow accumulated to a depth of 15 to 16 inches in parts of Tidewater. Relief finally came on January 28 when it began to rain. Afterward, the *Richmond Enquirer* reported that the wind's violence during the storm had "caused serious loss of life and property on the sea-coast." [30]

Education and Literacy

During the first half of the nineteenth century, the privately-supported "old field school," an updated version of the plantation school, could be found in many rural communities. One teacher, who had attended an old field school in his youth, recalled that these little schoolhouses usually were constructed of boards or logs and stood in old, abandoned agricultural fields. Sloping shelves attached to the school room's interior walls served as desks and pupils sat upon hard, backless benches. He said that some of those who taught in old field schools were stiff, formal pedagogues who "were a terror to their pupils." Students usually learned by rote and had to recite their lessons in front of the teacher and fellow classmates. Punishment, often inflicted with a ruler, horsewhip or leather strap, was administered for misbehavior but also for failure to learn. For instance, Dr. Henry Wythe Tabb, who was reared at Toddsbury in Gloucester County and lived at Auburn, said that in 1799 and 1800 he received instruction from a private teacher named White, "a severe and cruel man." One nineteenth-century educator commented that "most young ones go to the school when they must, escape when they can, and finally leave it with stubborn resolution to have as little to do with books as possible." Some neighborhoods had Sunday Schools where religious and secular education were intermingled. The sequel to the old field school was the academy which provided secondary education. There, pupils could learn Latin, Greek, modern languages, higher mathematics, and sciences such as physics, chemistry, and botany. Most Virginia counties had one or two academies that were chartered by the state but received no public support. Students sometimes boarded with their teacher. For example, in 1841 John W.H. Lane agreed to provide some weeks of instruction to Robert Dee Miller for $10 and to provide him with room and board for an additional $25.[31]

In 1840, the census-taker noted that Mathews County had a dozen primary and common schools and that 69 pupils had attended school at public expense. Of the county's whites who were age 20 or older, 368 were unable to read or write. Between 1843 and 1846, Leroy Dixon, a school teacher in his early 40s, began providing instruction to 26 Mathews County children who were identified as poor. They attended a "common" or ungraded primary school in which children of all ages were taught by teachers, usually with little or no training in their profession. Dixon received compensation of 4 cents per day per pupil. The attendance records he compiled, which documented the number of pupils he had, reveal that he usually taught reading and writing to 20 children, arithmetic to two, and spelling to four. Most of the students attending Dixon's school were between the ages of 7 and 14. Some attended class for only seven days, but others were enrolled for approximately 150 days. In 1843, Dixon offered instruction to Thomas, Robert, Daniel and Sarah Callis; Kitty and James Clark; Nancy Forrest;

Dorinda and Philip H. Hunley; Anladelin and Elizabeth Jarvis; John B. and William Jarvis; Charles and Patsy Kelly, Christopher and Mary Marchant; Betsy, Mary S., and John Morgan; and Mary S., Robert, and Lewis Powell. Several months later, those enrollees were joined by Jesse Oliver. Attendance records compiled in January 1845 indicate that George H. and Thomas Hall had commenced attending Leroy Dixon's school.[32]

In December 1858, school commissioner George K. Brooks compiled a report on the number of poor children who had attended school during the past year at a cost of 6¼ cents per day per pupil. The report included the names of the seventeen boys and girls who had received instruction from W.M. Brownley, the names of each child's parents or guardian, and how many days each pupil had attended school. Most received between 135 and 140 days of instruction, but some had received less than 50. Most of the children were between 11 and 14 and were taught reading, writing, arithmetic, and orthography (spelling); however, three also studied history and philosophy. Richard H. Respess, who owned land near Cricket Hill and had a home on Gwynn's Island, was determined to see that his children were educated. On February 7, 1851, when he made his will, he specified that his land "near Cricket Hill be set apart for the Schooling of my young children." In making this provision, he failed to say whether he wanted a schoolhouse to be built on his land or whether funds derived from renting his acreage were to be used to hire a tutor or pay tuition. When a census-taker visited Mathews in 1860, there were 25 common schools in the county

Newspapers Tell the Story

Those fortunate enough to be literate could read books and newspapers, which typically arrived by stagecoach, mail cart, or steamer. The press offered news of a local, national, and international nature, printed advertisements and legal notices, and published informative articles on everything from farming and political complaints to physical ills. For example, during 1836 and 1837 Charles Atkinson and John Pritchett of Mathews County publicly endorsed R.S. Bernard's patent medicine, which was supposed to cure *cholera morbus*, a type of acute gastroenteritis often associated with the summer months. Atkinson claimed that he had been stricken while visiting

Norfolk and had been cured within four hours of taking Bernard's remedy. On the other hand, John Spencer, the storekeeper and postmaster at North End, recommended Moffat's Vegetable Life Pills and Phoenix Bitters, which could cure a variety of digestive upsets as well as rheumatism, bilious and liver affections, asthma, and the "sickness incident to Females in delicate health."

In July 1819 a newspaper in Springfield, Massachusetts reported that a giant turtle that was eight feet long, three feet thick, and weighed 627 pounds had been caught in Put In Creek. (The accuracy of the story is open to conjecture.) During the late 1850s Mathews Courthouse storekeeper Elijah Barnum sued Ebenezer Bohannon because he had failed to pay for two years' worth of subscriptions to the *Intelligencer* and the *Harbinger.* Mathews County's first known published author was Elizabeth Ellen Hill of Gwynn's Island, who wrote for *The Repository,* a literary journal. Mrs. Hill and her family, who were New Englanders, reportedly moved to Buckchase Plantation during the 1850s. She used the *nom de plume* May Evergreen when writing about Gwynn's Island and the Virginia plantations she had visited.

Besides the weather, other types of natural phenomena made it into the newspapers, which often "borrowed" stories from one another. In 1840 an African-American woman living in Mathews County reportedly gave birth to triplets, two of whom were Siamese twins. The *Baltimore Sun* said that according to a Mathews County physician, the twins failed to survive. The *Sun*, which seems to have savored sensational stories, also reported that two exceptionally tall Mathews County couples had wed: both grooms were six feet six inches tall and their brides were six feet tall. [33]

The Mathews Academy

In April 1839, the General Assembly authorized the incorporation of the Mathews Academy and designated its first group of trustees: John R. Billups, Samuel Diggs, John Foster, Thomas Hudgins, William G. Lane, Wade Moseby, John N. Sale, William Shultice, and William Todd. The trustees, who could hold office for a maximum of two years, were allowed to purchase up to $20,000 worth of land, goods, and chattels, and a majority could authorize the sale or mortgage of any real estate the academy owned. They were encouraged to draft a set of bylaws and rules for the academy and one man was supposed to serve as the Board of Trustees' treasurer. Shortly after the academy received its state charter, the trustees acquired an eleven-acre parcel that was located a quarter of a mile south of the courthouse, perhaps the same eleven acres that Christopher Tompkins purchased during 1836, to which he added $880 worth of improvements.[34] In 1844 the General Assembly allowed the Mathews Academy's trustees to borrow $700 from the state's Literary Fund. They secured their loan by using the school's land and buildings as collateral, and agreed to repay the $700 in semi-annual installments. However, in 1846 the trustees requested some additional funds, which raises the possibility that the school was still experiencing financial difficulties. The academy closed in 1847 and in 1848 the school's buildings, which were worth $1,000, and its eleven-acre lot reverted from public to private property that was credited to W.G. Lane, Thomas E. Edwards, and the school's other trustees. By the time of the tax assessor's visit in 1849, Edwards had purchased the Mathews Academy lot and its improvements. He died in 1857, having instructed his executor, Francis Armistead, to sell his real estate. However, Edwards' estate was still credited with the Academy property in 1863, at which time it was occupied by Dr. John G. Bohannon and his family.[35] Today, the house is known as Edwards Hall or Hurricane Hall II.

New Restrictions on African Americans

During the late eighteenth and early nineteenth centuries, Methodists, Quakers, and some slaveholders took an interest in teaching African-American slaves to read, write, and count. However, after Gabriel's Insurrection, Virginia legislators imposed strict penalties upon anyone who tried to educate blacks, and in the wake of the 1831 Nat Turner revolt, all forms of slave education were prohibited by law. Free blacks sometimes managed to send their children out of state to be educated, but after 1838 those who left were not allowed to return. In 1842, it became illegal for blacks to assemble "for the purpose of instruction in reading and writing or in the night time for any purpose." Although some whites believed that slaves should receive basic religious instruction and be taught to read, many feared that literacy would promote disobedience and rebellion. Schools for black Virginians were considered unlawful assemblies and county officials were ordered to close them. Pupils found at such schools were subjected to whipping, and whites operating a school for free blacks could be fined. Despite these obstacles, some blacks managed to acquire a rudimentary education, thanks to their own inventiveness. Through stories and songs, cultural values and folklore were transmitted from generation to generation, a time-honored tradition within the African-American community. The owners of slaves sometimes taught them crafts in order to enhance their usefulness, unwittingly conveying other forms of knowledge. Probate records and advertisements for runaways reveal that slaves became highly skilled in a variety of trades and often could read and write a little. If they were able to escape to an urban area or flee aboard a ship, sometimes they could pass for free.[36]

In 1848, some Mathews County citizens sent a petition to the General Assembly, asking that virtually all blacks be prohibited from owning or breeding dogs or taking them along when traveling from place to place. They justified their position by pointing out that dogs often killed valuable livestock. They recommended that slaveholders be fined for allowing their slaves to disobey the law and that free blacks, if unable to pay their fine, should be hired out by the day or the month until their obligation was met.

Slaves were sometimes subjected to brutal corporal punishment. Dr. Augustus M. Hicks, a 50-year-old physician from Mathews County, submitted a sworn document to the General Assembly in 1850. He testified that on April 11, 1849, he had been summoned to examine a runaway slave named Dempse who had received "a high punishment" at the hands of William Lane "for his insolence and audacity." Hicks said that he had recommended that Lane confiscate Dempse's clothes and shoes every night to keep him from returning to the home of Walter G. Hudgins, to whom he belonged. He added that Lane didn't heed his advice and that Dempse ran away on the night of April 15. He went on to describe Lane, a neighbor, as an "Honorable young Gentleman" of the "old Virginia School." Hicks' testimony suggests that Dempse's final punishment proved fatal.[37]

By the mid-1850s, some members of the General Assembly encouraged the passage of legislation that would force Virginia's 50,000 or so free blacks to leave the state. However, the legislation's proponents faced opposition from people living in the eastern part of the state, where extra farm labor was needed at harvest time and in the Piedmont where tobacco was an important crop. In fact, the editors of three Richmond newspapers said that if the state were to "suddenly expel from her borders fifty thousand of her laboring population … when the very demand for labor and increased wages are operating to improve the condition of those whom it is proposed to expel," it would ruin farmers in the areas with the largest number of free blacks.

In 1857, a cluster of laws passed by the General Assembly placed additional restrictions on the rights of free blacks. One had a severe impact on family life, for free blacks were prohibited from owning slaves other than their own children, a restriction that would have prevented a free black man or woman from purchasing an enslaved spouse. Free blacks couldn't purchase wine or liquor without the consent of three local court justices and the beverages had to be bought from a licensed tavern. Thanks to the prohibitions on educating blacks, relatively few were literate. Nonetheless, census records for 1860 reveal that there were 50 free black people in Mathews County who were capable of reading and/or writing. They were employed as seamen, laborers, washerwomen, and house servants. A map made in 1860 depicting the distribution of slaves throughout the state of Virginia reveals that the Tidewater Virginia counties that lay closest to the Atlantic coast had fewer slaves than the counties that adjoined them on the west. In 1860, 43.4 percent of Mathews County's population was enslaved, but the percentage of slaves in Mathews' nearest neighbors was significantly larger, for Gloucester County had 55.9 percent and Middlesex County had 56 percent. The eastern Piedmont's percentages were especially high, but the numbers dropped off dramatically further west, and very few slaves lived in the counties west of the Blue Ridge.[38]

Courtesy of the Library of Congress.

Mathews County's Elected Officials

Like their predecessors, almost all of Mathews County's delegates to the assembly served for only one or two terms. In 1836, John R. Taylor represented Mathews and Middlesex Counties in the House of Delegates and Archibald R. Harwood was the district's state senator. A year later, Harwood was opposed—unsuccessfully—by Dr. William Shultice, whose candidacy was announced in the *Richmond Enquirer.* Delegate Taylor was replaced by Houlder Hudgins and Corbin Braxton succeeded Senator Harwood. During the 1838 session, members of the General Assembly decided that state senators and members of the house could receive a travel allowance of 20 cents a mile for making the journey to and from Richmond. The distance involved in a round trip was established by law and a delegate from Mathews County was eligible for compensation for a 100-mile trip. Delegate John R. Taylor was returned to office in 1839, but was ousted by Samuel Diggs, and William Tod (Todd) became the state senator for Gloucester, King and Queen, King William, Mathews, and Middlesex Counties. Three years later, George L. Nicholson replaced Diggs as delegate. Nicholson, like his predecessors, served briefly and was succeeded by John R. Billups, John R. Taylor, Alexander K. Shepard, and Christopher T. Brown. In 1843, a group of Democrats from the Middle Peninsula proposed that their party hold a national convention. A year later, Mathews County voters of both parties rallied in support of John Tyler's candidacy for the presidency. By 1848, Samuel M. Harwood became the district's state senator.

During the mid-1840s, Virginians had begun complaining about the method by which county justices were chosen. Some people contended that allowing county justices to appoint their successors and select sheriffs, deputy-sheriffs, and other county officers was inconsistent with the principles of a republican form of government. Also, because the General Assembly elected the governor, the lieutenant governor, and the United States senators, citizens in the western part of Virginia felt they had little influence on the state's leadership. However, westerners' attempts to win electoral reform proved futile. Some of them began openly discussing the abolition of slavery or secession from the state. Ultimately, this wave of discontent culminated in a statewide referendum and a constitutional convention.

In 1847, the General Assembly established a circuit or rotating Superior Court of Law and Chancery that was intended to serve Essex, Gloucester, Mathews, and Middlesex Counties. Court sessions were to be held in Mathews on the second Monday of every April and October. In January 1848, a group of local citizens sent a petition to the General Assembly, asking that additional polling places be established in the county. They said that many of Mathews County's eligible voters failed to vote because they lived too far from the county seat, the only polling place, and were unwilling or unable to make the commute. The petitioners noted that several neighboring counties had at least two polling places and proposed that Mathews citizens be allowed to vote at George W. Simmons's store in the vicinity of the Piankatank and at John Hudgins's store near New Point Comfort.

On October 14, 1850, delegates from all of Virginia's counties convened in Richmond at the Constitutional Convention of 1850–51, which lasted until August 1, 1851. Muscoe R.H. Garnett, Muscoe Garnett, and James Smith collectively represented Essex, King and Queen, Mathews, and Middlesex Counties. While the Constitutional Convention was in session, Robert L. Montague served as Mathews and Middlesex Counties' delegate to the General Assembly, and John W.C. Catlett was state senator. Virginia's new state constitution, ratified in 1851, brought about numerous changes in the structure of government. For the first time, the governor, lieutenant governor, and attorney general were to be elected by popular vote, not chosen by members of the General Assembly. Moreover, county justices, sheriffs, and other local officials were also subject to election.

Perhaps the 1851 constitution's most significant change was the establishment of universal white male suffrage. The Constitution of 1851, a landmark document that was in effect until after the Civil War, also authorized the establishment of circuit courts. In May 1852, when Virginia counties held their first local elections under the new constitution, many former justices were returned to office, which suggests that most voters found fault with the old *method* of choosing local officials, rather than the officeholders themselves. George L. Nicholson replaced Robert L. Montague in the House of Delegates. He served only one term and in the 1853–54 session was replaced by John H. Blake. Nicholson regained his assembly seat in 1855, but was ousted by Mathews County hotelier Walter G. Lane in

1857–58. When the House of Delegates convened at its 1859–60 session and reconvened between January and April 1861, Andrew B. Evans represented Mathews and Middlesex Counties and Joseph Christian replaced longtime State Senator John W.C. Catlett. These were Mathews County's representatives shortly before Virginia seceded from the Union.[39]

Providing for the Poor

A devastating fire seems to have occurred at the county poorhouse between the time the tax assessor visited in 1839 and returned in 1840, for the $170 worth of structural improvements associated with the 110 acres were gone.[40] The poorhouse tract stood vacant until 1850, by which time $1,000 worth of buildings had been erected and the farm had been enlarged to encompass 140.1 acres. The improvements retained their value through 1859, but before the tax records were compiled in 1860, 101 acres of the poor farm and its $1,000 worth of buildings were transferred to Seth G. Miller. This left the Overseers of the Poor with 39.1 acres that had $200 worth of improvements. The county poorhouse and its dependencies are identified on a topographically sensitive map that dates to 1853. The map also reveals that all of the buildings were located on the 25 acres of vacant land that the Overseers had acquired from Larkin Litchfield in 1826. Over the years, the Overseers were credited with several pieces of undeveloped land in various parts of the county, perhaps because their owners had used them as collateral when securing a loan, or the county had seized them for unpaid taxes. When a census was taken of Mathews County's inhabitants in 1850, James Pead, a local farmer, was identified as the poorhouse's steward. The poorhouse provided accommodations to 21 paupers of all ages and both sexes. All of these individuals were white; one was blind and two others were mentally disabled. However, the county had 75 people who were classified as paupers. By 1860, Thomas Davis had begun serving as steward for the poor and there were twelve people living in the poorhouse. One was a mulatto infant named Steavens Hurst. According to demographic records, the county had a total of 85 paupers, all of whom were native-born. In 1860, the county spent $1,531 on support for the poor.[41]

Public Health

As advances in medical science gave rise to increasingly sophisticated methods of treatment, American doctors began questioning the quality of health care their colleagues were providing to patients. In 1847, the fledgling American Medical Association conducted a survey of the country's doctors in an attempt to learn how many had attended medical school. The statistics compiled for Virginia reveal that only two-thirds of the state's 972 doctors had had any formal medical training, and some of them had attended only one or two courses of lectures. More than a fourth of Virginia's physicians practiced without any formal qualifications whatsoever. Although the AMA collected information on most of Virginia's counties, it failed to provide data on Mathews County's practicing physicians.

When there was a yellow fever outbreak in Portsmouth during the summer of 1855, local residents were advised to leave the town for a safer location. According to a Columbus, Ohio, newspaper, a large number of people from Portsmouth went to Mathews County, where they were doing well.

The account book Dr. George Tyler maintained between 1857 and 1864, which is included among Mathews County's court papers, indicates that his practice included both white people and their slaves. From time to time he performed blood-letting and cupping procedures, and he applied blisters. He also pulled teeth and on one occasion provided a male patient with a truss. He charged a slaveholder for clipping the tongues of two slave children, who were tongue-tied, and on at least two occasions, when Dr. Tyler's patients didn't respond to treatment, he consulted with a Dr. M. Pendleton.

In 1860, census-taker George W. Bohannon put a notation at the end of his record book, stating that until around 1850, ague and bilious fevers were prevalent in Mathews County during the summer and fall months. He added that "since that time a system of limeing [*sic*] and draining throughout the county has brought about an extraordinary change." He said that as a result, Mathews County residents were among the healthiest in the state and only occasionally was there a case of typhoid fever. He indicated that most people drew potable water from wells that were eight or ten feet deep and said that although the water was "not very clear, it has a pleasant taste." He added that there were "many springs of delightful water" and mentioned the abundance of fish, oysters, and wild fowl that were available.[42]

Religion and Churches

The number of people who joined the Methodist-Episcopal church continued to grow, with the result that some local congregations outgrew their houses of worship. In 1835, the members of Mathews Chapel built a new church on some land donated by John Lumpkin. The congregation continued to grow, and they built a new church in 1893. In 1855, members of the Billups Meeting House erected a one-room building they called the Salem Meeting House, which forms the core of the current building. The Bethel and Point Comfort Churches also attracted more members and both congregations constructed buildings that would accommodate larger numbers of the faithful. In 1849, the Providence Methodist Church was built in Whites Neck. Around 30 years later, Providence's members decided to build a new church, a structure they used until they erected a large brick church in 1932. Congregations sometimes hosted camp meetings, a popular form of worship.

Mathews Baptist Church, originally known as the Mathews Meeting House, grew steadily and by 1858 had 795 members, 445 of whom were black. Almost all—if not all—of the church's African-American members were slaves; census records for 1850 and 1860 reveal that there were less than 150 free blacks in Mathews County. When the founding members of the Westville Disciples of Christ, who met in the old Temperance Hall, built a church in 1859, they included a gallery for slaves. The Disciples, who built the Ephesus Meeting House around 1837, also probably worshiped with the enslaved.

Demographic records for 1850 reveal that Mathews County had nine churches: five Methodist-Episcopal, one Methodist, one Episcopal, one Baptist, and one Campbellite—that is, the Disciples of Christ. Each of the county's churches reportedly was large enough to accommodate a hundred or more people at a time. In 1860, the census-taker failed to list the number of churches in Mathews County, but he indicated that the denominations represented were Baptist, the Disciples of Christ, Episcopal, Methodist, and Methodist-Episcopal. He also indicated that collectively, the county's churches would accommodate 4,000 worshipers. Evangelical camp meetings were popular and often resulted in professions of faith. For example, Eunice Gertrude Smith, when only 13 years old, underwent a conversion experience at a camp meeting held in 1859 by Brother J.B. Laurens. When Miss Smith died of typhoid fever in 1864, her obituary mentioned her 1859 profession of faith and the Rev. William Brownley preached her funeral sermon.

The Episcopal Church in Mathews County seems to have lacked an ordained leader after the Rev. Armistead Smith's death in 1817, and during the 1820s services may not have been held on a regular basis, if they were held at all. According to Bishop William Meade, whose church history was published in 1857, Miss Elizabeth Tompkins, the eldest daughter of Christopher Tompkins of Poplar Grove, was determined to see that a new house of worship was built on the grounds of colonial Kingston Parish's old Lower Church. That building, fabricated of brick, was completed prior to Miss Tompkins's death in 1842. At her urging, the Rev. W.Y. Rooker, who had been serving small congregations in Middlesex County, was hired by Kingston Parish, a mission church. In 1844, when a plat was made of the 3.26-acre lot on which the Upper Church had been located, the outline of a building was shown in the northeast corner of the property, most likely the ruins of the colonial church. Mr. Rooker's ministry was followed by that of the Rev. George S. Caraway (Carraway), who came to Kingston Parish in 1846 and stayed until 1857. During his time in the ministry in Mathews County, the size of the congregation grew dramatically and a new church was built on the lot once occupied by the parish's old Upper Church. The new building, a frame structure, was completed in 1854 and became known as Trinity Church.[43]

Shipbuilding

In March 1848, the General Assembly enacted legislation that was designed to limit the amount of land that the Rappahannock Ship Timber, Lath, and Stave Manufacturing Company could own in counties in the Northern Neck and the Middle Peninsula. Mathews, Middlesex, Gloucester, Westmoreland, Richmond, Lancaster, and Northumberland Counties were all affected. The company, which manufactured ship's timbers and other lumber products, was prohibited from owning more than 2,000 acres in any of those localities, perhaps because it was causing timber shortages that affected local residents. Shipbuilding continued to play an important role in Mathews County's economy. However, it was not without its risks, and in 1848 a young man named Brooks, who was from Mathews County, fell from a scaffold in Norfolk's Gosport Dry Dock and sustained severe injuries. In 1859, a large schooner built by Gabriel F. Miller, which had staterooms for officers and passengers, was offered for sale in Baltimore.[44]

Mathews County in 1850

By the time the 1850 census was compiled, Mathews County had lost approximately 10 percent of its population and had only 6,714 people. Of those, 2,923 were enslaved. One Mathews County native was in the state penitentiary. A total of 400 pupils were enrolled in the county's twenty public schools, each of which had its own teacher, and literacy was on the rise; however, there were 426 illiterate white adults in the county and none of the 147 free blacks were able to read and write. The county's public schools received only $375 in revenue from the state's Literary Fund, and had no support from local tax revenue or endowments. There were two libraries in the county, neither of which was public or affiliated with churches or schools, but 35 households had private libraries or collections of books. Mathews County had 293 farms, which included 24,521 acres of improved land and 18,573 acres that were unimproved or fallow. Local farmers had invested a total of $15,106 in farm implements and machinery, an indication that Mathews had its fair share of "enlightened farmers" who availed themselves of the latest advances in agriculture. On average, an acre could be expected to produce fifteen bushels of corn or eight bushels of wheat or seven bushels of oats. An aggregate of $10,500 had been invested in manufacturing establishments, which provided employment to a total of 34 people, and the income from "homemade manufactures" was $5,097. The average amount of yearly wages paid to a farmhand receiving room and board was $50, although a carpenter could earn as much as $125 without board and the average domestic servant was paid $70.

Census-takers were instructed to make a list of those who had died during the first part of the year. In Mathews County, several people perished suddenly from unknown causes and others succumbed to dropsy (or congestive heart failure). There was at least one case of smallpox and several cases of tuberculosis, along with various types of fevers. The industrial statistics compiled in 1850 included the names of local producers of saleable goods that brought in $500 or more. These included the steam-powered lumber mills owned by William and Seth Love and by Love and Bell. These mills employed a dozen or more workers each and were large-scale operations. Walter G. Lane's tannery, close to the county seat, had three employees and reportedly produced 800 tanned hides each year, yielding an annual income of around $2,000. A decade later, when industrial statistics were compiled, the county had six windmills, whose owners were George Brooks, William M. Brownley, James E. Davis, George and Lewis Hudgins, and William Shultice. The county had two tide mills, one owned by Christopher T. Brown[45] and the other by John and Thomas Green; both tide mills were significantly more productive than the windmills. There was a water-powered mill at North End and the Belle Isle Mills included a sawmill and a gristmill that were steam-powered. Steam-powered mills seem to have required more employees than the mills that relied on wind or water.[46]

Prosperity in Mathews County

Some Mathews County homes were elaborately furnished, a reflection of their owners' social and financial status. In 1847, a visitor to Dr. Henry W. Tabb's home, Auburn, remarked upon the abundance of fine mahogany furniture, expensive carpets, and works of art. He also commented on seeing ice houses on some of the larger plantations he had visited in Mathews and Gloucester Counties. William H. Roy, Green Plains's owner, had household furnishings worth $1,250—a remarkable sum for the day. Tabb, a physician, and Roy, an attorney, were in professions that enabled them to earn a substantial amount of disposable income. William James Hubard, a skillful artist and resident of Richmond, married into the

Tabb family and painted portraits of his wife's family and friends. Examples of his work have been preserved by the Mathews County Historical Society.

Personal property tax lists for the 1850s reveal that much of Mathews County residents' money was invested in slaves of tithable age, who outnumbered adult white males two to one; a very small percentage of the population was comprised of free blacks. Most slaveholders had between one and five slaves who were age 12 or older, but some individuals had substantially more. Men like Elijah Borum, Christopher Brown, Holder Hudgins, Humphrey Keeble, Walter G. Lane, and Shepherd G. Miller had between ten and twenty slaves. William H. Roy had 56 slaves and Dr. Henry W. Tabb had 51, while William R. Smart, the owner of Smart's Mill, had 22. In contrast, Dr. William T. Thurston had only two slaves, but he owned $9,500 worth of taxable investments, such as stocks and bonds. The county's largest investment portfolio was owned by William R. Smart, whose holdings were worth $24,000. The county had an abundance of livestock. A third of all adult white males owned a pleasure carriage, and many people had watches and clocks.

According to William Thomson, who compiled a list of businesses located in Mathews County, there were four doctors, three attorneys, two hotelkeepers, and sixteen general stores. Shepard G. Miller was the county clerk, and H.W. Daingerfield, John W. Jarvis, and William H. Roy were practicing attorneys. The courthouse community's hoteliers, according to Thomson, included John N. Armistead and Walter G. Lane.[47] Mathews County's general stores, where groceries, dry goods, alcoholic beverages, personal apparel, hardware, and other merchandize could be purchased, included three in North End (shortened to North) and thirteen in Mathews Courthouse. In North End were the business establishments of Robert Billups, Robert Diggs, and William Dral [*sic*], probably William Drisgal (Drisgale), who purchased a merchant's license from 1841 to 1850.[48] In the immediate vicinity of Mathews Courthouse were the stores owned by Francis Armistead and Company; Armistead, Diggs and Company; Thomas Armistead; Winslow Foster; Thomas and A.G. Hudgins; Lewis Hudgins; Hudgins and Jarvis; Jarvis and Barnum; Leonidas James; Walter G. Lane; P.B. Richardson; Alexander W. Sleet (Fleet); William Thomas; and J.A. and W. Williams. The Mathews County Historical Society Archives, the

Colonial Williamsburg Foundation, and the Library of Virginia have ledgers and account books from many of the county's nineteenth-century country stores, including those at Beachland, Belle Isle, Cobbs Creek, Cricket Hill, Diggs, Gwynn's Island, Hookem Fare, Mathews Courthouse, North, and other locations. These store records reveal that most, if not all, merchants sold a wide assortment of merchandise.

Dr. William S. Thurston, who by 1841 had acquired a small lot with $800 worth of improvements, died sometime after the census-taker's visit in 1860. During 1861 Thurston's executors sold his lot and its building or buildings, then worth only $200, to Captain John Foster. Foster's new lot abutted north on the courthouse green, east on a parcel containing the store owned by Francis Armistead and John W. Jarvis, and west on a quarter-acre lot owned by the late Benjamin G. Tompkins's estate, property that contained the tailor shop that later became known as the Tompkins Cottage. Tax records indicate that Foster's and Benjamin G. Tompkins's lots had once been part of Christopher Tompkins's numerous holdings.[49]

Mathews on the Eve of War

From time to time the buildings in the county courthouse complex were in need of refurbishment. In September 1857, the county justices authorized Sheriff John H. Dunlavy to have repairs made to the chimneys of the courthouse and the railing around the public square. The commissioners appointed to oversee construction of a new clerk's office reported in March 1859 that contractor William H. Brown had completed his work except for whitewashing the interior. Although the new building was "fully fire proof & built in a substantial manner," its roof leaked and the wooden floor sagged. Because the contractor agreed to correct those problems within a reasonable amount of time, the commissioners asked the justices to declare Brown's work complete so that he wouldn't be held liable should there be a "fire or any other accident to the building." Approximately three months later, Captain James H. Garnett of the Chesapeake Guards, a volunteer militia company from Mathews County, asked permission for his unit to use the debtor's jail as an armory.

In 1860, Mathews County's population consisted of 7,091 people, 3,865 of whom were white. There were 149 free blacks, 58 of whom were illiterate adults. Mathews County also had 426 illiterate white adults. There were 386 slaveholders who collectively owned 3,008 slaves. Only $50,105 worth of goods were manufactured in the county during 1859. Personal property tax rolls for 1860 reveal that capitation taxes were paid on 804 white males who were age 16 or older; 1,507 slaves who were age 12 or older; and 21 free black males who were age 21 or older. The tax revenues generated by these three groups of people varied widely, for the free white males of taxable age generated $577.60 in taxes; the slaves deemed taxable yielded $1,808.40; and the free black males over 21 produced $16.80 in revenue

The courthouse community was home to men, women, and children of various socioeconomic statuses. There were several merchants, notably Elijah Barnum, Leonidas James, Francis Armistead, and the firm Armistead, Diggs and Company. Drs. Thomas B. Lane, John G. Bohannon, James H. Garnett, and Silas C. White would have provided medical care to members of the community, while Dr. Hugh D. Smith would have provided dental care. Baldwin Foster, a seaman, lived in the county seat and had a store; Rebecca Bailey, a milliner, was a member of his household. Teachers John T. Robinson and Susan E. Parrott resided in the community, as did coachmaker Alexander W. Marchant. William F. Pugh, a tailor, owned a home that he shared with another tailor, James M. Fleming. Warner and William N. Lewis, who were house carpenters, plied their trade, as did John White, a blacksmith. In 1860, some of the predominately white households in Mathews Courthouse included black or mulatto washerwomen and house servants, hired workers who were free.[50] Census records reveal that female domestic servants who were supplied with board earned on average $1.00 a week. Mathews Courthouse's two free black households were headed by Sarah Mantley and Nancy Moore, who were washerwomen and do not seem to have owned the property they occupied.[51]

A relatively large group of people lived in Walter G. Lane's hotel, which housed several members of his own family. They included professor James H. Lane, merchant Oscar Lane, Dr. Thomas B. Lane, merchant's clerks Julius R. Lane and John D. White, teacher John L. Robinson, dentist

Hugh D. Smith, a seamstress named Mary C. Moon, and house carpenter's apprentice Alonzo I. Lane. Also living in the hotel was the proprietor's wife, Mary A.H. Lane, and Susan A. Lane, who may have been Alonzo I. Lane's wife. Walter G. Lane also owned a tan-yard that was located approximately one mile north of the courthouse, probably on the forerunner of Route 198.[52]

A letter that Miss Ellen M. Keeble of Gwynn's Island intended to send to the *Richmond Enquirer* on the eve of the Civil War expressed some local citizens' sentiments. At issue were the fiery abolitionist views expressed by the Rev. Charles Haddon Spurgeon, a British citizen and famous Baptist clergyman, whose sermons had been published and circulated widely in America. Miss Keeble said that shortly after John Brown's raid, Spurgeon had preached an antislavery sermon in Exeter Hall, England, describing Brown as a saint and a martyr. He also proffered that it was "better that every white man, woman, and child be murdered in the South, and a thousand Unions be dissolved, than human slavery be allowed to exist in peace and quietness in the Southern States." The Rev. Humphrey H. Keeble of Mathews County, also a Baptist minister, took great exception to the Rev. Spurgeon's statements and had seven calf-bound volumes of his sermons burned "at Mathews Courthouse on our May court day last." Miss Keeble said that the sermons were set ablaze "on the head of a flour barrel" in the midst of "a large assemblage" that included people from "the surrounding counties of Gloucester and Middlesex." In closing her narrative, she exhorted "pastors of all other religious denominations in the South" to follow the Rev. Keeble's example and burn all documents that were "calculated to disturb our peace." [53] It is unclear how Miss Keeble's remarks were received by the people of Mathews County and the editors of *Richmond Enquirer.*

Notes

1 When William H. Roy's wife, Ann, died in 1834, her obituary, published in the *Richmond Enquirer,* noted that she had written a "powerful and eloquent address to the citizens of the Eastern States, on the Slave question." Her text not only appeared in the *Enquirer* but also in many papers in the North (Charles, *Newspapers*, 81).

2 Kathleen Bruce, *Virginia Agricultural Decline to 1860: A Fallacy, Agricultural History* 6 (1932):12. Anonymous, One Hundred Years of Agriculture, n.d.; USDA, *Abridged List of Federal Laws Applicable to Agriculture*, 1949; Charles W. Turner, Virginia Agricultural Re-

form, 1815–1860, *Agricultural History* 26 (1952):80–81; Thomas Ritchie, comp., *Acts of the General Assembly, Passed at the Session of 1835–1836* (Richmond, 1836), 64–65; Martin, *Gazetteer*, 227–228; Charles, *Newspapers*, 74, 97–98; Mathews County Agricultural Census Records 1850–1860; http://mapserver.lib.virginia.edu/index.html.

3 Census records for 1850 indicate that Jacob Saunders, then age 58, was a landless farmer (Mathews County Census 1850).

4 During the colonial period and the nineteenth century, many women wore a decorative belt or purse called a chatelaine, which had a hook or clasp on which the keys to storage areas and lockable furniture were suspended.

5 James O. Breeden, ed., *Advice Among Masters: The Ideal in Slave Management in the Old South* (Westport, Connecticut, 1980), 89–90, 93–94, 114, 140, 288; Mathews County Slave Schedules 1860. Henry W. Tabb and Euphan W. Roy had the largest numbers of slaves and also the most slave houses on their plantations.

6 In 1815, the Respess home was said to be worth $400 (Mathews County Personal Property Tax Lists 1814).

7 Mathews County Land Tax Lists 1818–1821; Mathews County Historical Society, *Historic Homes and Properties of Mathews County, Virginia, Pre-Civil War* (Virginia Beach, 2013), Vol. II, 17–20, 24–27; Mathews Archives Boxes 1 R, 2 OV; Mathews County Land Tax Lists 1837; Martha W. McCartney, "Oakland," 7–8; *Richmond Enquirer*, October 1, 1847; Mutual Assurance Society Vol. 16 Policy No. 787; Vol. 40 Policy 1150; Springdale, National Register of Historic Places File 057-0018; Poplar Grove, National Register of Historic Places Files 057-0008 and 057-0009.

8 A store ledger that commences in 1836 and a deed dated July 25, 1845, reveal that Christopher Tompkins, Francis Armistead, and Albert Diggs traded as Tompkins, Armistead, and Diggs, and that after Tompkins's death, Armistead and Diggs, as the surviving partners, continued to conduct business. In 1845, the original firm held a deed of trust for three small parcels in Glebe Neck that Richard Hunley had mortgaged (Armistead, Francis Sr. and Albert Diggs. Memorandum of agreement, Francis Armistead Sr. and Albert Diggs with William Shultice, November 15, 1838, Mathews Archives Box 81 R; Armistead, Diggs and Company Cash Book, Mathews Archives Box 90; Tompkins, Armistead, and Diggs Ledger and Armistead-Tompkins Journal, Mathews Archives Box 91 R; Mathews County Land Tax Lists 1812–1845).

9 A letter that Christopher Tompkins' wife, Maria (Mariah), wrote on December 25, 1837, reveals that he was suffering from a bad cold and asthma. She said that Cousin Henry—that is, Dr. Henry W. Tabb—had "bled him but his shortness of breath and cough was not relieved." Another physician, Dr. Dabney, "put a large blister in his side"—i.e., used a procedure called cupping, which was thought to draw out infection. He also gave him flaxseed tea and tartar water to drink. Tompkins's condition did not improve (Mathews Archives Box 83 R).

10 On November 15, 1838, Francis Armistead Sr. and Albert Diggs executed a partnership agreement with Dr. William Shultice, giving him an equal interest in their firm's assets

(Memorandum of agreement, Francis Armistead Sr. and Albert Diggs with William Shultice, November 15, 1838, Mathews Archives Box 81 R). This would have given them access to additional capital.

11 The fee books maintained by Mathews County's clerk list the court charges that Henry W. Tabb paid as Christopher Tompkins's executor. Such fees usually were associated with suits undertaken to collect debts owed to a decedent's estate. Local merchants and tavern-keepers also filed suits. For instance, during the 1850s Walter G. Lane and John N. Armistead tried to recover funds from their businesses' debtors (Mathews County Clerk of Court Fee Book 1840–1841).

12 It is unclear whether the building that once served as a store was converted to use as a tavern or whether a tavern had been erected next door to the store. An 1853 map, which shows four buildings within those three lots, supports the latter hypothesis.

13 Tax lists for 1851 indicate that John N. Armistead owned a six-acre parcel that abutted the southern boundary of the small lots aligned along the south side of Brickbat Road (Mathews County Census 1850; Land Tax Lists 1850). The food crops and livestock Armistead and his slaves raised on his acreage would have provided sustenance to his tavern's guests.

14 Mathews County Census 1850; Land Tax Lists 1825–1861; *Richmond Enquirer*, September 4, 1835; *Baltimore Sun*, September 5, 1838; Mathews Archives Boxes 6 R, 81 R, 90 R, 91 R; John Seib, "From Wolf Trap to Piankatank River, Including the Head of East River," 1853. A suit undertaken by members of the Tompkins family in the mid-to-late 1840s suggests that they vigorously supported Kingston Parish but also believed in the mission of the Colonization Society (Warner T. Jones Papers, Box 7, folders 381 and 382).

15 Tan-yards, which processed raw hides, were usually odiferous.

16 Mathews County Land Tax Lists 1820–1860; Deed Book 6:237–238; Land Book 1:23; Mathews County Unidentified Tavern Journal 1842–1843, Library of Virginia, Richmond; MCHS, *History and Progress*, 14; http://mapserver.lib.virginia.edu/index.html. The county seat had three hotels in the 1840s: Armistead's (across from the courthouse), Benson's (on the east side of Main Street), and Lane's (just north of the courthouse).

17 Thomas Ritchie, comp., *Acts of the General Assembly, Passed at the Session of 1836–March 1837* (Richmond, 19837), 52–57; *Acts of the General Assembly, Passed at the Session of 1839* (Richmond, 1839), 48, 226; Samuel Shepherd, comp., *Acts of the General Assembly, Passed at the Session of 1839–1840* (Richmond, 1840), 108; Mathews Legislative Petitions, January 8, 1840; February 4, 1840; *Congressional Record, 23rd Congress, 1st Session*, House of Representatives Document No. 218, 1–2; Charles, *Newspapers*, 78–80. Isaac Foster chaired the citizens meeting.

18 Charles, *Newspapers*, 96; Mathews Archives Boxes 6 R, 18 R, 83 R; Clifford and Clifford, *New Point Comfort*, 66, 77.

19 That is, she was one of John Warner Borum's slaves (Mathews County Census 1860).

20 Shepherd, *Statutes,* III, 123; Mathews County Legislative Petitions, December 5, 1845; Census 1850, 1860; Charles, *Newspapers*, 59, 88, 93; Charles L. Perdue et al., *Weevils in the*

Wheat: Interviews with Virginia Ex-Slaves (Charlottesville, 1976), 199–201, 273–277. William Brooks, who was born in 1860 and was a descendant of free blacks, was in Mathews Courthouse when he was interviewed by WPA workers in 1937. He described the rations issued to slaves and talked about the ill treatment they received from the hands of patrollers, whom he seems to have confused with members of the Ku Klux Klan (Perdue et al., *Weevils*, 56–58). The interviewee may have been a descendant of the Brooks family who lived in Mathews County.

21 Hearn, a mulatto, was living in Mathews County in 1840 and 1860, but in 1850 he was residing in Gloucester. Other members of the Hearn family lived in Mathews throughout this period, including a young man named Ephraim Hearn (Mathews County Census, 1840, 1860; Gloucester County Census 1850).

22 Luther P. Jackson, "The Virginia Free Negro Farmer and Property Owner," *Journal of Negro History*, 24 (1939):390, 393–395, 398–399, 406; Mathews County Census 1830, 1840, 1850; Land Tax Lists 1830–1868; Personal Property Tax Lists 1805–1815, 1850–1852, 1858.

23 www.revwarapps.org/revwar-pension-acts; Elizabeth Dutton Lewis, *Revolutionary War Roster, Gloucester County, Virginia* (Gloucester, 1976), 26–27; Mathews County Census 1840.

24 Mathews County Personal Property Tax Lists 1791–1841, 1842–1855; William Thomson, *Thomson's Mercantile and Professional Directory* (Baltimore, 1851–1852), 153.

25 Julia Gibbons, March 4, 1857, Library of Virginia, Lost Records Localities, Mathews County; Mathews County Fiduciary Records, Estate Accounts, Appraisements, Sales, 1850–1857.

26 *Gloucester-Mathews Gazette-Journal*, April 16, 1959; MCHS, *History and Progress*, 39. See Chapter 9 for a reference to the Hudgins shipyard's destruction.

27 Tindall, *Narrative History*, 118–119, 247; Martin, *Gazetteer*, 229; Charles, *Newspapers*, 95–96, 102–103; Sadler, "Post Offices."

28 Henry Howe, *Historical Collections of Virginia* (Charleston, South Carolina, 1852), 376.

29 Charles, *Newspapers*, 94–95, 99–100.

30 Ludlum, *Hurricanes*, 39, 55, 81–83, 87–90, 98–99, 112–113, 128–129, 173; Charles, Newspapers, 59, 64, 89, 95; David M. Ludlum, *Early American Winters II, 1821–1870,* 112–113.

31 William A. Maddox, *The Free School Idea in Virginia Before the Civil War* (New York, 1918), 109–110, 114–115; Cornelius J. Heatwole, *A History of Education in Virginia* (New York, 1916), 109, 116; Morrison, *Public Education*, 84; Diary of Dr. Henry Wise Tabb, Mathews Archives Box 24 R; Mrs. Frances Miller, Mathews Archives, Box 107 R.

32 Mathews County Legislative Petitions, October 1843 to January 1845.

33 Mathews County Land Book 1:80; Circuit Court Papers 1856–1858; Census 1840; Mathews Archives Boxes 1 R folder 1 and 16 OV; Charles, *Newspapers,* 59, 89.

34 Tompkins owned the only 11-acre parcel located in the vicinity of Mathews Courthouse and like the Academy tract, it was a quarter of a mile south of the courthouse. An 1821 plat indicates that Christopher Tompkins also purchased a small L-shaped parcel located at the corner of Route 14 and County Route 611, just south of the property owned by Benjamin Bramhall and Thomas James. Bramhall's land extended in a northerly direction toward what became the Academy lot (Mathews County Land Tax Lists 1836–1838; Land Book 1: 23).

35 Samuel Shepherd, comp., *Acts of the General Assembly of Virginia Passed at the Session of 1839* (Richmond, 1839), 122–123; *Acts of the General Assembly of Virginia Passed at the Session of 1844–1845* (Richmond, 1845), 28; Mathews County Land Tax Lists 1836–1863; Legislative Petitions, January 2, 1846; Census 1860; MCHS, *Historic Homes*, Vol. 2, p.11–13; Virginia Lee Hutchinson Davis, "Will of Thomas Edwards, 1857, Mathews County," *Tidewater Virginia Families*, VII (Urbanna, 1989), 97–99.

36 Russell, *Free Negro*, 137–144; Thomas K. Bullock, *Schools and Schooling in Eighteenth Century Virginia* (Durham, 1961), 53–61; Breeden, *Advice Among Masters,* 11–12, 226, 231–233.

37 Mathews County Legislative Petitions, January 10, 1848; January 31, 1849, testimony 1850; Census 1850. Hicks, a Connecticut native, owned two slaves (Mathews County Slave Schedules 1860).

38 William F. Ritchie, comp., *Acts And Joint Resolutions Passed By The General Assembly, 1857–1858* (Richmond, 1859), 39, 46, 51–51, 152; http://mapserver.lib.virginia.edu/index.html; Mathews County 1860 Census; E. Hergesheimer, "Map Showing Distribution of Slave Population from the Census of 1860," 1861; Jackson, "Free Negro," 395; *Richmond Times*, January 17, 1853; February 12, 1853; *Richmond Dispatch*, February 18, 1853; *Richmond Whig*, January 25, 1853; *Richmond Enquirer*, February 17, 1854.

39 Leonard, *General Assembly*, 376, 378, 380, 382, 385, 389, 391, 393, 395, 397, 399, 401, 403, 405, 409, 411, 413, 415, 417, 420, 422, 424, 428, 432, 434, 436, 439–440, 444, 447, 450, 453, 455, 458, 460, 463, 465, 468, 470, 473; Thomas Ritchie, comp., *Acts of the General Assembly, Passed at the Session of 1838* (Richmond, 1838), 42; Taylor, *Internal Enemy*, 410–411; Charles, *Newspapers*, 69–71, 73, 75–76, 82–85, 88–89, 91–93; William J. Van Schreeven, *The Conventions and Constitutions of Virginia, 1776–1996* (Richmond, 1967), 7; Albert O. Porter, *County Government in Virginia: A Legislative History, 1607–1904* (New York, 1947), 109, 163; *New York Herald*, November 13, 1859; *Ohio State Journal*, November 9, 1859; Shepherd, comp., *Acts of the General Assembly, Passed at the Session of 1846–1847* (Richmond, 1847), 62; Mathews County Legislative Petitions, January 10, 1848.

40 Even though property owned by the Overseers of the Poor was not taxed, the county assessor evaluated it regularly.

41 Mathews County Land Tax Lists 1839–1860; Land Book 1:31, 263, 470; Census 1850, 1860; John Seib, "From Wolf Trap to Piankatank River, including Head of East River," 1853.

42 Charles, *Newspapers*, 97; Mathews County Circuit Court Papers 1857; Census 1860.

43 Meade, *Old Churches*, II, 326–327; Brown, *Old Kingston Parish*, 25–27; Kingston Parish Vestry Book 1850–1867, n.p.; Robert L. Brown, Untitled research notes on Kingston Parish's history, n.p.; Robert E. White, *The History of Providence United Methodist Church, 1849–1978* (Mathews, 1978), 9, 13, 28, 46, 72; Mathews County Census 1850; Land Book 1:273; Social Statistics 1850, 1860; Mathews Archives Boxes 1 R and 10 R.

44 Shepherd, *Acts of the General Assembly, Passed at the Session of 1847–1848,* 305–306; Charles, *Newspapers*, 94, 102–103.

45 By this time Brown owned Poplar Grove.

46 http://mapserver.lib.virginia.edu/index.html; Mathews County Census 1850; Social Statistics 1850; Industrial Statistics 1850, 1860.

47 Both establishments were directly across from the county courthouse. John N. Armistead rented a building from Francis Armistead and Albert Diggs that was between Court and Main Streets, directly across from the courthouse, whereas Walter G. Lane's hotel was located on the north side of Church Street, across from the courthouse green's north side.

48 In 1841 there were 16 licensed merchants in Mathews County and a year later, there were 23 (Mathews County Personal Property Tax Lists 1841–1842).

49 Mathews Archives Boxes 2 R, 13 R, 67 R, 68 R, 70 R, 90 R; Adam Foster, January 7, 1847, letter to Mrs. Cynthia Claxton, MCHS Vertical Files; Mathews County Hookem Fare Store Ledger 1855–1866, 1872–1874, Library of Virginia, Richmond; James S. Shipley Account Book 1855–1858, 1865, 1868–1871, Library of Virginia, Richmond; Mathews County Personal Property Tax Lists 1850–1856; Land Tax Lists 1849–1861; Census 1860; Processioners Records for 1867 District 2; Deed Book 7:176; Thomson, *Directory*, 153; Graham Hood, personal communication, July 24, 2015.

50 Slaves would have been included in the demographic records called Slave Schedules, which omitted the names of the enslaved.

51 Mathews County Minute Book G, 87, 191, 203; Land Tax Lists 1829–1860; Personal Property Tax Lists 1860; Census 1860; Land Book 1:593.

52 This should not be confused with the tannery he owned in the 1830s, which was an eighth of a mile west of the courthouse.

53 Mathews Archives Box 1 R.

9

War's Long Shadow
1861–1865

A Widening Rift Brings Secession

Although politicians, North and South, had been engaged in heated debates for several years, no one seemed to realize that war was imminent. When South Carolina seceded from the Union in late December 1860, Virginia officials called a state convention to decide whether the Old Dominion should follow suit. Robert L. Montague represented Mathews County in those deliberations. The moment of truth came quickly, for the first shots were fired at Fort Sumter on April 12, 1861, and two days later President Abraham Lincoln issued a call to arms. Five days later, Virginia seceded from the Union, and in May, Richmond became the new nation's capital. From December 1861 through March 1863 A.B. Evans represented Mathews County in Virginia's House of Delegates. He was succeeded by Robert B. Fauntleroy, whose district also included Middlesex County. Throughout this period, when Virginia was part of the Confederacy, Joseph Christian was Mathews's state senator.

In June 1861, Virginia's Trans-Alleghany counties, which opposed secession, established the Restored Government, with Francis H. Pierpont as governor. Thus, throughout the war, Virginia had two state governments: a Confederate one in Richmond and a Unionist one in Wheeling, West Virginia (and later, in Alexandria).

John Lewis, a Confederate veteran interviewed in 1921, said that as soon as Mathews County residents learned that Virginia had left the Union, "the citizens of Cobbs Creek got together and made a flag." He recalled that his brother, Tom, and N.A. Hatch cut down two slender trees and fastened them together with a piece of iron, making a flagpole. Then, they hoisted a flag that could be seen for many miles. He said that Union soldiers passing through the county in 1863 cut down the pole and burned it. In May 1861 Captain George E. Tabb offered the Mathews Cavalry's services to Virginia's governor, and Walter G. Lane, on behalf of Mathews County's justices, asked for two companies of well-armed state troops to protect the county from enemy attacks. By June 13, 1861, Colonel John G. Bohannon, a physician and experienced military leader, had been placed in command of two volunteer companies that were part of the 61st Regiment.[1]

Early Emancipation

Union Army Major General Benjamin F. Butler, who arrived in Hampton Roads in late May 1861, decided not to return runaway slaves, declaring them "contraband" or illegally traded Confederate property. His policy, which preceded President Abraham Lincoln's Emancipation Proclamation by more than eighteen months, prompted thousands of slaves to flee to Fort Monroe, often with only the clothes on their backs.

Union Naval officers aboard ships in the Chesapeake Bay encountered runaways who had heard about General Butler's policy. In mid-July 1861, O.S. Glisson, the commander of the U.S.S. *Mount Vernon*, asked his superiors what he should do with the blacks who reached his ship and how he should treat the intelligence information they provided. Some of them claimed that Mathews County Confederates had murdered George Wilson, a Union man who lived near Stingray Point, and threatened his family. They also said that the Confederates' ammunition was scarce.[2] Glisson identified the runaway slaves who had come aboard: John, Miles, and Samuel Hunter, who had belonged to Joseph Moore; Peter Hunter, one of S. Crittendon's slaves; Alexander Franklin, owned by Robert R. Carter; and David Harris, Jeremiah Harron's slave. Two days later, the *Mount Vernon* rescued Lewis Ransom, Robert Brookes, and Albert Hutchings (Hudgins), slaves who had belonged to John H. Dunlavy of Mathews County. In mid-August S.H. Stringfellow of the U.S.S. *Minnesota* reported that he had taken aboard five Mathews County slaves: John Smith and Prophet Washington, who belonged to a Dr. Tabb; and Silas Smith, Iris Grevins, and Iris's three-year-old daughter Catherine, who all belonged to a Mrs. Roy.[3] In October, two men suspected of illicit trading were brought aboard the *Minnesota*; one was George Moss, a free black from Mathews County. The Secretary of the Navy, when queried about how to deal with runaway slaves, said that the government shouldn't encourage them to leave home, but pointed out that to return them would be cruel and impolitic and that they might prove useful to the Union Navy.[4]

Preparing for War

When the Confederacy's first recruitment call went out in April 1861, Mathews County's white males between the ages of 18 and 45 were summoned to the county seat, where militia musters were held. A few older men showed up, probably as a matter of conscience. The Mathews County men who joined the Mathews Light Dragoons or Cavalry entered service on July 21, 1861. When the Mathews County Battalion mustered on October 31, 1861, it included the Crab Neck Company. Four men were rejected outright on account of their age or physical condition: James G. Callis (58), James R. Gwyn (40), Edmond Marchant (43), and L. Sidney Simmons (48). Mathews County men also served in Company H of the Mathews Light Artillery, commanded by Captain Andrew Armistead and assigned to Starke's Battery on the Piankatank River.

Captain Robert E. Hudgins was in charge of Company E of the 61st Regiment. In November 1861, when Dr. Silas C. White informed Colonel Bohannon that Privates Brown and Respess were feigning sickness, Bohannon, then at Mathews Courthouse, said that both men had stopped complaining and that he had ordered Captain Hudgins to send all "disagreeable or disobedient" men to the commanding general at Yorktown.

Company E, under Captain Hudgins, was sent to Gloucester Point in December 1861, along with the 26th Virginia Volunteer Infantry. Both units disbanded on May 4, 1862, when the Confederates withdrew from Gloucester Point. Afterward, Hudgins attached a statement to his unit's muster roll, saying that after the withdrawal, his ranks were reduced by transfers, captures, illness, and reassignment. He acknowledged that some men had gone over to the enemy and added that Peter and Noah Foster, John Carney, and James Green went home sick. On January 31, 1862, Company D of the 26th Virginia Volunteer Infantry was ordered to report to Brigadier General Robert E. Rodes's brigade near Richmond. That unit, comprised of Mathews County men, was led by Captain Alexander James, who was accompanied by a hired slave named Frank.[5] General Rodes sent Company D to reinforce General Henry A. Wise at Chaffin's Bluff, in Henrico County, where they joined Stark's Artillery and units from other regiments.

As 1861 drew to a close, Colonel Bohannon stationed four of Captain Hudgins' men at Mathews Courthouse to guard the commissary's stores. He also had all boats and canoes on the Piankatank River placed under the watchful eyes of an armed guard, supported by a picket stationed on Gwynn's Island. Vessels between Muddy Creek and Burtons Point were to be taken to Cobbs Creek; those between Burtons Point and Cricket Hill were sent to Lewis Powell's wharf on Queens Creek; and those on Gwynn's Island and between Cricket Hill and Morses Point were to be taken to Cricket Hill.[6] Nobody could have access to a boat or canoe without a written order. John R. Callis, James A. and Bartlett Davis, Carter B. and Thomas L. Hudgins, Christopher D.(G.) Marchant,[7] Thomas Sadler, John R. Shipley, and John E. Summers were among the men assigned to canoe guard, with William James as captain. James was authorized to allow John R. Winder's man, Harry, to gather oysters as long as he returned his vessel each night.

Mathews County had a Military Board of Exemptions, which had the right to excuse men from military service. It was comprised of court justices George E. Tabb, William M. Brownley, and William H. Hudgins. When they met on March 8, 1862, George Brooks and Augustus W. Callis asked to be relieved of military duty because their mills were essential to the community's wellbeing; two physicians, Drs. P. Goolrich and Silas C. White, also received exemptions. Captain John Foster, a 45-year-old farmer with a permanent disability, was also excused. A month later, the Confederate Congress authorized the conscription of all white males between the ages of 18 and 35, who were obliged to serve for three years unless legally exempt. Men already in the military were also required to serve for three years. A draftee could avoid service by providing an able-bodied substitute who was ineligible for the draft and men whose occupations were considered critically important to their communities could still receive exemptions.

The upper age limit for draftees was raised to 45 in September 1862, whereupon Hezekiah Blaylock; James Brooks; A.P. Davis; Alexander J., John D., Samuel E., and William H. Diggs; John S. and Sands Forrest; J.T. Foster; Isaac, James, Thomas B., and Thomas J. Hudgins; A.P. Miles; Robert C. Miller; Frederick Richardson; James S. Shipley; William T. Smith; Joseph M. and Samuel D. White; and C.C. Williams appeared before the Military Board of Exemptions and testified that they had medical conditions rendering them unsuitable for military service. All but two (Richardson, a seaman missing part of one foot, and Joseph M. White, a ship's carpenter with a disease of the chest) received exemptions. Albert Diggs claimed that he was disabled and that as an overseer to a dependent person, he should be exempt from military service. He also asserted that Colonel Bohannon had deprived him of his rights.[8] Charles H. Raines, a 29-year-old house carpenter summoned for military duty, asked for the right to present his views in court, perhaps because he had been denied an exemption. By 1863, the Confederacy's need for men had become so great that even those with functional heart disease, the loss of an eye or two fingers, slight deafness, or general disability were not exempt from the draft. In February 1864 the age limit for draftees was expanded to include white males between 17 and 50 and later in the year, slaves and free blacks were declared eligible for the draft and could be used in supportive capacities. Finally, on March 13, 1865, the recruitment of slaves was authorized.[9]

Sometimes older or disabled men or those whose family responsibilities were overwhelming became part of the Confederate Army's Home Guard. They provided assistance to the widows or orphans of military men, tracked down Union and Confederate deserters, gathered intelligence about enemy troop movements, and identified local civilians sympathetic to the Union cause. They were also available as a local defense force, and because they were at home, they could farm their land. Although a roster of Mathews County's Home Guard hasn't come to light, William White of Mobjack was identified as a Home Guardsman in a list of the Mathews men who served in the military, and it is likely that other local men who were too old or unhealthy to be drafted also would have joined the Home Guard. This older cohort included Robert F. Adams; Joseph Benn; Henry Cooke; William Blake; Simon H. Burton; Henry and Robert B. Callis; Bartlett Davis; Benjamin B. Dutton Sr.; Hezekiah M. Dutton; William Foster; James Hill; Milton S. Hodges; Carter B. and Houlder Hudgins; Humphrey H. Keeble; Ezekiel Landron; Addison T. Lewis; Edward T. Mallory; James D. and John J. Marchant; William Mason; Mark H. Morgan; Henry W. Pratt; Thomas Rennalds; Parker B. Richardson; John Shipley; John Spencer; Thomas Webb; William D., William H., and William K. White; Edmond Winder (a farmer); and Edmond Winder (a seaman). At least one of these older men (Carter B. Hudgins) was actively involved in blockade running, and it is probable that some of the others were, too.

Mathews County's shipbuilders rallied to the Confederate cause by constructing gunboats and other vessels at the Gosport navy yard and at West Point. On September 21, 1861, Captain William C. Whittle, commander of the York River defenses, informed his superiors that Gabriel F. Miller of Mathews County had offered to build a steam-propelled gunboat with a 150-foot keel at West Point. He recommended that Miller be authorized to visit the Gosport navy yard to see what types of materials were available for building one or more gunboats with two 11-inch shell guns each. When queried by Confederate Navy Department officials in September 1862, Whittle said that Mathews County had many ship's carpenters and added that ordinary house carpenters also might be able to build gunboats if they worked under a shipbuilder's supervision. He proffered that if the Confederate Navy had had gunboats in 1861, they might not have lost control of Fort Monroe. Afterward, Colonel Bohannon asked Captain Hudgins for the names of all carpenters and joiners who would be willing to work on boats.[10]

The Hardships of Soldiering

At the beginning of the war, the men of both armies suffered from a series of disabling epidemics. Often, new recruits received cursory physical examinations and enlisted despite poor health. Many recruits had little immunity to communicable diseases and quickly became infected. Also, inexperienced soldiers often failed to follow safe sanitary practices and contaminated their encampment's water supply through ignorance. Statistics show that a fourth of all Confederate deaths from disease were attributable to typhoid, which occurred in epidemic proportions among Virginia troops in the summer and fall of 1861. Many raw recruits couldn't understand why their own cooking made them sick. One military doctor commented that the typical new soldier "burned his bread and fried his food saturated with grease and suffered from indigestion, colic and diarrhea, but was ignorant of the cause." Another medic said that such ailments "destroyed more soldiers than gunshot wounds." Medicines were in short supply, makeshift hospitals were extremely unsanitary, and the Confederacy's relatively few surgeons and medical personnel were badly overworked.[11]

Mathews Women in Service of the Confederacy

Not to be minimized is the supportive role that the Confederacy's women played throughout the war. They looked after their families, managed their homes and farms, dealt with shortages of food and manufactured goods, and on an almost daily basis experienced fear and grief. They supported the war effort by making bandages and wound dressings and making uniforms with the wool they obtained from mattresses and carpets, which they wove into cloth. They also unraveled wool scraps, mixed the strands with cotton, and made yarn they knitted into socks. Women ran "wayside hospitals" in private homes and provided care to sick soldiers. In 1924, Walter Stokes, a Confederate veteran, said that when he first joined the army, he discovered that his clothing was insufficient. Therefore, he received a month's furlough so that he could return home to Mathews, where his mother "made me a suit out of what material she had and what the neighbors donated." He added that it didn't fit very well or look like a garment from a tailor shop, but he knew that he would truly appreciate it in the long, cold months that lay ahead. Life on the home front was very difficult, and in 1862 the Confederate government enacted legislation intended to provide women and children with public assistance.[12]

From the ranks of Mathews County's most industrious and dedicated women came Sally Louisa Tompkins, who served the Confederate cause with great distinction and saved the lives of numerous sick and wounded soldiers. Miss Tompkins, the daughter of Christopher and Maria (Mariah) Patterson Tompkins of Poplar Grove, lost her father and some of her siblings at an early age. After Poplar Grove was sold, Sally and her widowed mother lived briefly in Norfolk but then moved to Richmond, where they were residing in 1854 when Maria Patterson Tompkins died. Only ten days after the First Battle of Manassas, which occurred on July 21, 1861, 28-year-old Sally opened a hospital in a dwelling at the corner of 3rd and Main Streets, a house provided by Judge John Robertson. There, she and other volunteers, white and black, nursed the sick and wounded brought to Richmond by train. On September 9, 1861, Confederate President Jefferson Davis appointed Sally Louisa Tompkins a captain in the Confederate Army, a designation that enabled her to receive food and supplies for the men in her hospital. Years later, Captain Tompkins made a notation on the bottom of her commission that she didn't allow herself to be placed on the army's payroll. She kept her hospital open until June 13, 1865, when the last wounded man was discharged. A detailed register of the Robertson Hospital's patients reveals that of the 1,333 men who received care, only 73 died. [13]

The Men Who Served

When the service records of Mathews County's military men are compared with the 1860 census, much can be learned about those who went to war. For example, most of the men who reported for the October 31, 1861, muster of the 61st Regiment (which included the Crab Neck Company) were farmers or seamen in their 20s or 30s. However, the regiment also included men with other skills, such as shoemakers Robert B. Bailey and William R. White;[14] canoe builders Thomas W. Hunley and George R. Callis; ship's carpenters William T. Lilley, William H. and James M. Foster; house carpenter John Dunlavy (Dunlevy); bricklayer Leroy Bohannon; merchants William H. Hudgins and Charles F. Richardson; merchant's clerks Walter G. Hudgins and Peter W. Jarvis; and hotel-keeper Walter G. Lane. Seamen John R. Winder and William H. Respess and farmer, John B. Hill were sent to General John Bankhead Magruder in March 1862, shortly before the Peninsular Campaign got underway. Later, James M. Lewis and Charles F.

Richardson were assigned to the Mathews Artillery and Walter G. Hudgins became a member of the 5th Virginia Cavalry. Washington Brown, William J. Callis, Andrew Chapman, John W. Hunley, and William H. Respess were transferred to the Confederate Navy. John C. Brown and Edmund or Edward Maryner (Mariner) deserted the regiment and joined the Union Navy, where Maryner, a seaman from Somerset, Maryland, became a pilot. In March 1862, canoe builder Thomas W. Hunley was sent to West Point to work on gunboats. Washington H. Respess, a seaman, was transferred to the navy, circulated counterfeit money, and then deserted.

Although the majority of the Mathews County men who served in the Mathews Light Cavalry were farmers or seamen, many other occupations were represented. They included coach-maker's apprentice John A. Diggs, machinist apprentice William Ellis Fitchett, merchant's clerks John A. Fleet and Walter G. Hudgins, mechanic Richard Marchant, plasterer Charles W. Parrott, and physician Dr. Thaddeus Fitzhugh. There were also ten carpenters, six of whom were house carpenters. The Mathews Light Dragoons initially had four ship's carpenters (George Augustine Brooks, James Diggs, John William Howlett, and Gabriel Francis Miller Sr.) and a ship joiner, Albert Parrott; records suggest that the only members of the light dragoons sent to the navy yard to work on gunboats were Brooks and Miller. Also sent to the navy yard were seaman Gaius William Billups, bricklayer Leroy Bohannon, farmer George W. Dixon, house carpenter Thomas R. Hudgins, and seaman Thomas J. Minter. Lewis G. Hudgins, a sail-maker, was sent to the navy and John Edward Foster, a blacksmith, was assigned to the artillery. Richard Marchant, who had been a farmer and seaman before the war, served as a scout and took care of the cavalry's horses, whereas Thomas Marrs, who had trained at Camp Lee in Richmond, became a teamster. Wheelwright John R. Richardson was sent to the cavalry. Bailey D. Hudgins, a shoemaker, was transferred from the 5th Virginia Cavalry to the Mathews Light Artillery,[15] while Henry Brown Dutton left the 5th Virginia Cavalry to join the Confederate Secret Service. A young African American named Private Andrew Minter, the son of Lewis and Vinnie Minter, served as the 5th Virginia Cavalry's cook; after the war he returned home to Mathews County and became a farm laborer. John Emerson Miller resigned from the army to take care of his children.

Military service records reveal that during the war, John R. Banks, Cornelius E. Bohannon, George Augustus Brooks, John S. Clark, David Diggs, George T. Diggs, W.J. Diggs, Robert E. Edwards, William M. Fitchett, Samuel B. Gaines, Lewis T. Green, John William Howlett, Thomas A. Jones, Walter Gabriel Jones, Thomas Henry Machen, John Wesley Minter, Charles W. Parrott, Henry E. Taurman, and Christopher T. White were captured; some of these men were sent to Point Lookout, Maryland, and others to Fort Delaware. Although service records often failed to disclose where men were taken prisoner, some members of the 5th Virginia Cavalry were captured at Yellow Tavern, Fair Oaks, Meadow Bridge, Cold Harbor, Fort McHenry, and in King and Queen County. Eight men in the 5th Virginia Cavalry were wounded: Robert T. Brooks, Dr. Thaddeus Fitzhugh, Richard H. Haynes, Lewis R. Jones, William Machen, Seth H. Minter, D.T. Murden, and John A. Weston.

The Mathews Light Artillery, also known as Armistead's Battery, was comprised of nearly 200 men, and it had fewer farmers and seamen than other local military units. The light artillery, organized in July 1861, had thirteen house carpenters: Christopher Columbus Anderton; James Blake; James S. Brooks; William W. Lewis; James K. Minter; John P. and William J. Morgan; Thomas B. and Wesley F. Ripley; George W., Joseph C., and Lewis T. White; and Benjamin Williams. Pension records indicate that Wesley F. Ripley was eventually assigned to the Navy Department and Joseph C. White became a teamster and ambulance driver. Others who served as teamsters were Charles H. Anderton, Robert H. Blake, Thomas F. Bridges, Fletcher C. Davis, Leonard Smithers, and Miles K. Thomas. Also in the Mathews Light Artillery were students Andrew and William C. Borum; bricklayer's apprentice George W. Burroughs; ship's carpenters Benjamin F., Benjamin J., and James A. Diggs; William T. Hicks; and A.D. Hudgins; and ship joiner John Weston. Laban (Labin) Hudgins and Elijah T. Minter were blacksmiths and James Wesley White was a blacksmith's apprentice. Minter eventually became a nurse in military hospitals and Miles K. Thomas (a seaman) became a teamster. The unit also included bricklayer Napoleon B. Weston, who had served in the Fredericksburg Artillery; assistant lighthouse keeper George T. White; shoemakers Bailey D. and Charles D. Hudgins and John G. Williams; merchants John T. Hudgins and Frederick Richardson; and school teacher J.W. Owens. Although most of the men in the Mathews Light Artillery (by January 1863 members of the Company F of the 5th Virginia Cavalry) were in their 20s and 30s when the war began, there were exceptions such as house carpenter-turned-bugler James Blake (age 48), ship's carpenter Benjamin F. Diggs (50), ship's carpenter William T. Hicks (43), blacksmith Laban Hudgins (46), house carpenter Lewis W. Sadler (47), and several others who were in their early 40s. It is likely that these older men were valued for their specialized knowledge or stayed on because of their belief in the Confederate cause. During the war seven men from the Mathews Light Artillery were wounded and W.J. Henley was captured. Pension applications reveal that the Mathews Light Artillery saw action at Chaffin's Farm and at Yellow Tavern, where W.R.B. Hunley was wounded. With certain exceptions, most of the Mathews Light Artillery's men served for the war's duration and many of them were present for the surrender at Appomattox Courthouse.[16]

The 26th Volunteer Virginia Infantry included a few farmers and a large number of seamen, but also shoemakers R.B. Bailey and William R. White, schoolteacher John Lloyd Minter, carpenter James R. Shackleford, and house carpenters Benjamin, Charles H., and John J. Diggs; John Dunlavy; John E. Hudgins; Edward J. Pritchett; and Joseph T. White. The unit had two shipbuilders, Joseph B. Diggs and Thomas Thompson; ship-joiner John W. Diggs, and four ship's carpenters, Elezy and Thomas D. Hudgins, James R. Ripley, and George A. White. Some men were reassigned. Benjamin and John W. Diggs, Edward J. Pritchett, James R. Ripley, and George A. Wright were dispatched to Richmond to work on gunboats whereas Joseph B. Diggs and Elezy and Thomas D. Hudgins were transferred to the Confederate Navy. Bricklayer Leroy Bohannon and many of the other men who had enlisted voluntarily in 1861 stayed on, even though they had expected to serve for only a year. Crusoe Robinson, an African American, served as the 26th Virginia Infantry's cook. Military records reveal that the men of the 26th saw little action at the beginning of the war, but they eventually were involved in combat at Bermuda Hundred, Hatcher's Run, and Petersburg. At least nineteen men were killed or wounded and four or more were captured and taken to Elmira, New York, or Point Lookout. A significant number of the men of the 26th were at Appomattox for the moment of final capitulation.

One Mathews County man who attained great wartime distinction was mathematics professor and tactician James Henry Lane, a graduate of Virginia Military Institute and the University of Virginia. In the spring of 1861, he was commissioned a major and assigned to the 1st North Carolina Regiment. He rose quickly in the ranks and within less than five months, was made a colonel. In 1862, he participated in the Seven Days Battles and the Second Battle of Bull Run and he rose to the command of Branch's brigade at Antietam. He was promoted to brigadier general in November 1862 and commanded his brigade at Fredericksburg, Chancellorsville, Gettysburg, the Wilderness, and Petersburg. He was wounded at Cold Harbor but participated in the Appomattox Campaign and was paroled on the day of surrender. Lane and his brother Oscar were sons of merchant and hotelier Walter G. Lane, as was Dr. Thomas B. Lane, an army surgeon.[17]

Mathews Citizens Who Opposed the War

Although most of Mathews County's white males were willing to defend the Confederate cause, support for the war was not universal. For example, William L. Walker, a 33-year-old farmer from New Hampshire who owned some real estate in Mathews County, sent a letter to President Abraham Lincoln in April 1861, claiming that he "was driven from Gwynn's Island, Virginia, by the rebels" and asking for protection for his family and other Unionists. The president forwarded Walker's letter to the Navy Department, but little seems to have been done. More than a year later, the Secretary of the Navy informed a senior officer of the Potomac Flotilla that during the three weeks the steamer U.S.S. *Anacostia* had been away from Mathews County, "a marauding party of cavalry came there and carried off Union men and committed other acts of violence." Therefore, he ordered the flotilla's commander to send a gunboat to Milford Haven as often as possible. In March 1862, a Richmond newspaper reported that "Seven traitors [that is, Union sympathizers] were brought to this city on Saturday from Matthews [*sic*] County." However, their names weren't mentioned.

Mathews P. Morse, a 39-year-old farmer originally from Massachusetts, who lived at Windmill Point on Milford Haven, sent a letter to the Union Army command in August 1862, asking for protection for himself and "other of the Union citizens of Mathews." He said that for the past two months they had been harassed by guerilla parties of the Confederate cavalry and sometimes had to leave the country for their own safety. Morse, a married man with young children, recommended that a gunboat be stationed permanently in the waters of Mathews County. He said that illegal trade with the Eastern Shore was unimpeded because Mathews men could travel back and forth in canoes. He added that thanks to the lack of a gunboat, waterborne spies also had ready access to Richmond. He claimed that "the county of Mathews is largely Union in sentiment"[18] and said that most of the men of the 61st Virginia Regiment, which was raised in the county, had deserted when the Confederates abandoned Yorktown. According to Morse, since the Union Army left West Point, the Confederate cavalry had raided Mathews County repeatedly, capturing many of these deserters and some Union men. General John A. Dix, who received Morse's request, forwarded it to Rear Admiral L.M. Goldsborough, asking him to send a gunboat to Mathews if he had one to spare. Attached was a list of the depths of seven of Mathews County's waterways. Goldsborough asked the Treasury Department for a revenue cutter of a very light draft to cruise the waters between the Rappahannock and York Rivers, occasionally venturing into Mathews County's waters.

There is evidence that a number of men deserted from the Confederate army in Mathews County throughout the course of the war. Besides Christopher G. Marchant and Edmund (or Edward) W. Maryner, who departed early on, James M. Foster, a 61-year-old ship's carpenter; Dr. Augustus M. Hicks, a 60-year-old native of New Haven, Connecticut; and 22-year-old John W. Morgan, a seaman and Mathews County native, left the army even though they had enlisted in the 61st Regiment in October 1861. Other deserters (who may not have enlisted willingly in the first place) included Jacob H. Bell, John W. Maclerry, Marcus D. Tarr, and Jonathan J. Collins, who were from Delaware; Littleton C. Johnson, Robert J. Venable, Robert D. Walker, Jesse Langford and John S. Simmons, who were from Maryland; Mathew P. Morse, who was from Massachusetts; George A. Hill, who was from New Hampshire; George M. Patterson and Samuel W. Tilton, who were from New Jersey; Francis Beazley and Israel Dunlavy (Dunlevy), who were from New York; and Thomas L. Maryner and Amos Raines, who were from Pennsylvania. On the other hand, at least two Mathews residents, who weren't from southern states, supported the Confederacy. Henry Bell, a native of Kent, Delaware, became a bugler in Armistead's Battery after he enlisted in the 61st Regiment and Newell R. Hatch, a Nebraska native, helped to raise the Confederate flag at Cobbs Creek in 1861. After the war, Samuel E. Richardson and William H. Winder claimed that they had remained loyal to the Union and sought compensatory claims for damaged and lost property.[19]

Defending the Homeland

General Robert E. Lee, who was responsible for the protection of Virginia's expansive coastline, ordered a blackout along the Chesapeake Bay and the lightships normally stationed at the Wolf Trap and the York Spit were removed. The New Point Comfort Lighthouse's beacon was extinguished as were the lights on Cherrystone, Cape Henry, Smith's Island, and Smith's, Windmill, Back River, and Stingray Points. The absence of these important navigational aids was intended to hinder the movements of Union Navy vessels within the Chesapeake Bay.

By mid-August 1861 General Magruder had grown concerned about Mathews County's vulnerability and informed his superiors that he had heard that "the enemy is in the habit of landing in Matthews [*sic*] County, and that from $5,000 to $8,000 worth of negroes are decoyed off from that county per week." He inquired as to whether he was responsible for the troops stationed at the Mathews County courthouse, who were reportedly "inactive"—that is, not combat-ready—and learned that the entire Mathews Battalion was under his command. He ordered Colonel Charles A. Crump, who was based at Gloucester Point, to take charge of Gloucester and Mathews Counties' defenses as far north as the Piankatank. He was to seize every boat on Mobjack Bay's tributaries and to keep them under close guard. He was also to communicate with the commanding officers of Mathews and Gloucester Counties' volunteers and militia. He was authorized to confiscate citizens' personal property if it was needed to defend the coast and to communicate with the commanding officers in Middlesex County.

On November 26, 1861, General Magruder sent word to the governor that he expected Mathews and Gloucester to be attacked very soon. He said that he had heard "the fact stated by the enemy" and from some gentlemen on the Eastern Shore. With great urgency, he asked the governor to send him some cannon that could be deployed on the coasts of Mathews and Gloucester Counties. He said that he had few men to spare and had decided to "order out all the negroes that may be necessary at once to build works" but added that if he didn't receive the cannon he had requested from West Point, he didn't think that it was right "to take the hands from their owners to construct works which without guns would be useless." Magruder closed his letter by asking for the support of artillery companies and at least four regiments of infantry. In December, he received permission to hire blacks to work on the much-needed coastal fortifications. An account of the troops under General Magruder's command, identified as the Department of the Peninsula, included two Mathews County units, the 61st Virginia Militia, and Captain Todd's company of the Virginia Cavalry, then under the immediate command of Colonel John G. Bohannan.[20]

The Union Army Formulates Its Plans

While Confederate military leaders prepared to defend their territory, Union Army leaders were also strategizing. Toward the end of 1861, Union Army General George B. McClellan, who was keenly aware of General Magruder's presence on the James-York Peninsula, began devising a plan that involved taking control of the lower Chesapeake Bay. He proffered that launching a surprise attack from Urbanna would be highly successful because Urbanna could be easily reached by vessels of heavy draft and the Confederates were neither occupying nor watching over that area. He also noted that Urbanna was only one long march from West Point and two long marches from the Confederate capital. Therefore, McClellan was convinced that, "A rapid movement from Urbana [*sic*] would probably cut off Magruder in the Peninsula, & enable us to occupy Richmond before it could be strongly reinforced." He told his superiors that, "Should circumstances render it not advisable to land at Urbana we can use Mob Jack Bay—or—the worst coming to the worst—we can take Fort Monroe as a base, & operate with complete security." As it turned out, by the beginning of 1862, Confederate General Joseph E. Johnston had moved his army from Manassas to a position on the Rappahannock River. This most likely prompted Union military leaders to disregard McClellan's proposal.[21]

Fort Nonsense

Given the porosity of military communications at the time, it is very likely that General Magruder and his superiors were fully aware of General McClellan's proposed strategy and decided to have fortifications built across Route 14's forerunner in lower Mathews County. Until recently, the origin of these massive and well preserved earthworks, dubbed Fort Nonsense, was enigmatic, and archaeological testing, which usually proves informative, failed to provide a definitive answer. However, thanks to the diligence of Mathews Memorial Library researcher Becky Foster Barnhardt, this important local mystery has been solved. Military records on file at the National Archives reveal that Fort Nonsense, officially named Fort Roy, was built between December 1861 and March 1862 by some enlisted men from the Mathews Battalion and 50 African Americans; the group was most likely made up of slaves hired out by their owners and perhaps some free blacks. All of these men were under the direction of the Confederate Army's 22-year-old engineer-in-charge, Captain William Henry Clarke, a graduate of the Virginia Military Institute, who months earlier had overseen the construction of fortifications at Gloucester Point (which were designed by Captain Charles H. Dimmock).[22] William Dawson Soles of Mathews County, a local farmer in his late 30s, was employed as official manager or "overlooker on [the] defensive works at Smarts Mill."[23] Like others in the Mathews Battalion, he was under the command of Colonel Bohannan. Interestingly, Soles's military records indicate that in July 1861 he enlisted in the Confederate Army as a musician. Fort construction was a labor-intensive process that included the felling of trees, ditch digging, and the fabrication of gabions.[24]

The correspondence that Captain Clarke exchanged with his superiors between early December 1861 and the end of March 1862 reveals that the 50 black men in his work force were provided with fresh beef, bacon, salt, and sometimes dried peas or corn, plus two pounds of meal per day. On March 18, 1862, Captain Clarke asked the commissary for seven pairs of shoes, two flannel shirts, and a jacket for the blacks "employed in the defensive works at this fort" and said that he would deduct the monetary value of the items from the payroll. The latter statement implies that the cost of the shoes and clothing would be deducted from the funds slaveholders stood to receive from hiring out their slaves. Clarke said that the men had no other means of acquiring the items they needed, which were essential to their health and comfort.

It is likely that Fort Nonsense was considered a component in a multifaceted defensive strategy that began to take shape soon after war was declared. The fortifications, which faced east, were presumably intended to thwart—or at least delay—Union forces' plan to attack Gloucester Point from the rear by approaching from the direction of the town of Urbanna or invading by means of the Piankatank, the East, or the North Rivers, all of which had been used by the British during the War of 1812. Fort Nonsense had hardly neared completion when General Magruder put his men to work constructing three lines of earthworks across the James-York peninsula to slow the Union Army's advance from Fort Monroe toward Richmond.

According to an enduring tradition, William Dawson Soles, a Mathews citizen, gave Fort Nonsense the sobriquet that has persisted. He reportedly exclaimed, "My! What a piece of nonsense!" after Union forces approached from a direction totally different than what was expected. Today, the earthworks are owned by Mathews County, which acquired the site from the Mathews County Historical Society. Fort Nonsense has been carefully preserved in a historical park that serves as a gateway to the county. An elevated walkway provides visitors with access behind an artillery position and there is interpretive signage at each strategic point on the viewing platform. A 10-pound Parrott Rifled cannon, donated to the Mathews County Historical Society, overlooks Routes 14 and 3 and draws attention to the roadside park.[25]

Military Action Spreads

On February 4, 1862, the *Philadelphia Inquirer* reported that the Union gunboat *Young Rover* had begun cruising in Mobjack Bay and its tributaries. When it was in the York River, it picked up five runaway slaves who had set out by canoe from Gloucester Point. One, the former butler of a wealthy Mathews County planter, estimated that there were 1,500 Confederates at the Gloucester Point fortifications, a third of whom drilled regularly. At the end of March, the *Baltimore Sun* reported that "Seven traitors were brought to this city on Saturday from Matthews [*sic*] County." The Confederates, keenly aware of their enemy's presence, seized every opportunity to disrupt their operations. On March 14, 1862, President Jefferson Davis, who anticipated a Union Army advance, declared martial law within a region that included the lower part of the James-York Peninsula along with Mathews and Gloucester Counties. Some judicial functions were suspended, but local court justices were allowed to probate wills, oversee the administration of estates, enter decrees and orders for the partition and sale of property, issue road and bridge orders, assess county levies, and order the payment of taxes. However, issuance of a "stay order" meant that nobody could sue to collect debts. Also, the right to issue a writ of *habeas corpus* was suspended. The circuit court, which had been convening in Mathews in April and October since ratification of the 1851 constitution, continued to meet at the courthouse. Summaries of circuit court decisions made in April and October 1862, and April 1863 have survived as have rulings made by county court Judge John M. Gregory in May and October 1862, April 1863, and October 1865.

In obedience to President Davis's orders, on March 19, 1862, General Magruder announced the imposition of martial law within the several counties under his command. A nightly curfew was imposed and no alcoholic beverages could be manufactured or sold. Magruder had the right to have military police enforce his orders and anyone who failed to obey the law was subject to court-martial, which could result in a maximum sentence of one month at hard labor. It was probably around this time that most of Mathews County's legal records were removed from the courthouse and taken to Richmond, the Confederacy's capital, for safekeeping. Although it remains to be discovered precisely when and by whom the records were moved, one early twentieth-century writer claimed that several Tidewater Virginia counties' records were transported by wagon to Richmond at the orders of Confederate General Henry A. Wise, a former governor. These records were stored in the General Court Building, which stood on the southeast corner of Capitol Square and were lost when the building was burned on April 3, 1865.[26]

In May 1862, the Confederates' star-shaped earthworks at Gloucester Point were captured by Federal forces and Confederate troops on the James-York Peninsula were obliged to withdraw toward Richmond. Confederate officials, uneasy about how slowly the capital city's lines of defense were being raised, decided to require all free black males between 18 and 50 to participate in public works projects. They had to furnish their names and addresses to the court of the city or county in which they lived and could be required to serve up to 180 days at a time. In exchange for their labor, free black conscripts were supposed to receive food, lodging, and medical care plus pay commensurate with the work they performed. Through this means the Confederate government mustered the manpower it needed to construct Richmond's defenses. Again, Captains Charles H. Dimmock and William Henry Clarke played a pivotal role.[27]

Early Action in Mathews County

On April 29, 1862, Union Lieutenant R.H. Wyman, who was aboard the U.S.S. *Freeborn*, said that after he had sailed about twenty miles up the Piankatank River and discovered three scuttled schooners, his ship and two others drew fire from a light artillery battery situated on a bluff overlooking the river. He indicated that his men's rifles had prevented the Confederate artillerymen from reloading and discharging their weapons rapidly. Many years later, John Lewis of Cobbs Creek, a Confederate veteran, described this incident, which occurred on April 27, and said that "Two Yankee gunboats came up the Piankatank River, bombarding both sides. At Iron Point, they were answered by some of our guns stationed there; this is often spoken of as the first battle in Mathews County." Lewis reported that one of the Union Navy's gunboats was damaged and all three withdrew.

According to Wyman, some Mathews County citizens claimed that two-thirds of their county's population was loyal to the Union. His informants claimed that all but 18 of the 500 militia men who had been drafted into the Confederate Army had deserted and gone home. He said that Mathews' s Union loyalists asked for protection and that he had told them that if they relinquished their arms and assisted him in gaining control of any government property in the county, he would help them. In his communiqué, he passed along a piece of intelligence he had received from a local loyalist. In June 1862, Wyman informed his superiors that the *Anacostia* had captured the sloop *Monitor*, a Baltimore vessel, while she was leaving the Piankatank. A few days later, he reported that some of the *Anacostia's* men had managed to recover the reflectors that belonged to one of the Chesapeake Bay's light boats, having found them several miles inland, in Mathews County. Wyman indicated that he was enclosing a notice posted by the *Anacostia's* commander, ordering the arrest of certain residents of Mathews known to be in possession of arms and military equipment that could be used to oppose the United States military. Near the end of July, Wyman sent word that he had arrested three blockade runners off Horn Harbor and had captured some salt. He added that the *Reliance* had salvaged a dozen Enfield rifles from the wrecks of two barges that had been plundered by Mathews County inhabitants.[28]

Material Support for the Confederacy

The Confederacy's Secretary of War authorized the crews of a schooner and a sloop, then in Mathews County, to trade with ports where they would be able to procure arms, munitions, and other military stores. This was official acknowledgement of the county's role in the smuggling that went on throughout the war. From the beginning, mariners and watermen on the Middle Peninsula had been able to slip large quantities of contraband goods through Federal lines using canoes, bugeyes, and schooners. One Union Army colonel said that "It was strongly suspected that the enemy had a mail route from the head of Mobjack Bay through a region of the country known as Guinea, and thence through Gloucester Courthouse to Richmond." He said that when his men visited one home in the Mobjack Bay area, they found a basketful of cakes, jellies, and other delicacies, as well as a valise packed with new shirts and other clothing intended for an officer in General Wise's legion. He added that the countryside was well suited to illicit trade, for boats could land in quiet waters, where their cargoes could be offloaded onto wagons and hastily dispatched to the interior. He said that there was a market of sorts on the picket line around Gloucester Point, where blacks sometimes passed clothing to friends.

Union military leaders became increasingly aware of the blockade runners' activities and resolved to stop them. Carter B. Hudgins of Mathews County was suspected of guerilla activities, and on June 27, 1862, Union General Dix sent some of his men to Mathews Courthouse to arrest him and take him to Fort Monroe, where he was to be incarcerated at the Rip Raps. Dix also instructed his men to post a public notice at Mathews Courthouse, announcing that if there were "any further disturbance of the public peace by guerillas" or any violence done to Unionists, those involved would be held accountable. Dix also made plans to have hospitals built on New Point Comfort, but never followed through.

In early July 1862, two hundred men from the 5th Pennsylvania Cavalry landed at Gloucester Point, intent on making a reconnaissance of Gloucester, Mathews, and King and Queen Counties. Later in the month, two groups of Confederate troops made a sweep through the area to round up deserters and assert their presence. Captain Fitzhugh and his men confronted a group of Union Army soldiers in Mathews County and captured five of them; one, an officer from Maine, was sent to Libby Prison. Then, in early September 1862, a Union steamer that was towing 15 barges up the Chesapeake Bay encountered a strong gale. Seven barges broke their towlines and came ashore in Mathews and Middlesex Counties, where local citizens quickly seized them. The barges contained large quantities of ammunition, wagons, harnesses, military clothing, knapsacks, and other types of supplies that were of considerable value to the Confederacy.

In October 1862, a New Orleans newspaper recounted an engagement in which 30 armed men from the Union gunboat *Resolute* and a mortar boat tried to come ashore in Milford Haven and clashed with Confederate guerilla forces. The encounter occurred because the *Resolute's* officers suspected that some boats hidden there were smuggling goods and passengers from the Maryland shore. The Confederates, upon spotting the intruders, drove them off. However, when some of the *Resolute's* men returned the next day, they found six Union loyalists and their families, who were eager to reach Maryland. At the end of October, Lewis Hudgins of Mathews County, who headed a guerilla party that called themselves "the Arabs," managed to board the New York ship, *Alleghanian*, and set it ablaze. Although two vessels from the Potomac Flotilla managed to extinguish the fire, the *Alleghanian* was badly burned and had to be towed away.

On Saturday, November 22, 1862, some navy men and troops from the 52nd Pennsylvania Infantry and the 11th Maine, led by Brigadier-General Henry M. Naglee, set out for Mathews County, where local inhabitants were purportedly engaged in salt-making and smuggling in goods from Maryland's Eastern Shore. General Naglee later reported that his men destroyed 73 large cast-iron vessels they found in nine locations and disposed of more than 1,000 bushels of salt.[29]According to the Union Navy's report of the incident, the expedition into Mobjack Bay and the East River, which occurred on the night of November 22, involved the steamer *Mehaska (Mahaska)*, the *General Putnam*, and a small tug called the *May Queen*. Commander Foxhall A. Parker, who was aboard the *Mehaska,* said that he went to a "fine wharf" that was three or four miles from the mouth of the East River and exactly two miles from the courthouse. There, presumably at Williams Wharf, the troops disembarked and began to march toward New Point Comfort and Winter Harbor, reinforced by a 12-pounder Dahlgren howitzer manned by 20 seamen. The *General Putnam*, with a detachment of seamen and a howitzer boat, continued up the East River, intending to capture or destroy any vessels that could be used as blockade runners. By 8 PM, both expeditions were over and eleven salt works and 300 to 400 bushels of salt had been destroyed.[30] After the war, Union Army Colonel W.W.H. Davis recounted the same incident, but said that 30 to 40 salt kettles were broken up and 3,000 bushels of salt were destroyed. Acting Master's Mate Nathan W. Black, who was heading toward New Point Comfort and Winter Harbor, reported that one of his men had disappeared suddenly, perhaps having been captured by a group of Confederate cavalrymen trailing their rear. Lieutenant N.H. Farquhar, aboard the *General Putnam*, reported that his men had destroyed one salt works and burned three schooners and a number of scows and boats. They had also captured a lighter and 24 large canoes, some of which could hold two dozen men. Commander Parker's report suggests that the salt works and vessels destroyed were in Woodas Creek.[31]

According to Commander Parker, a local informant provided the Union Navy with a great deal of reliable information and indicated that large canoes(like the ones that were captured) were the main type of vessels used by blockade runners. He also told Parker that a significant amount of contraband trade was carried on between the North River and the Back River (in Poquoson), thanks to Union Army sutlers or civilian merchants. On the morning of November 23, while Black's and Farquhar's men were destroying boats on both sides of the East River, a detachment of soldiers headed for Mathews Courthouse. Commander Parker informed his superiors that shortly before he left the East River, he learned that two sloops had arrived in Horn Harbor with cargoes of goods brought in from Maryland. Therefore, he ordered the *Crusader's* commanding officer to send his cutters to destroy them. Parker sailed about three miles up the North River, where Lieutenant Farquhar destroyed a schooner and another naval officer laid waste to a vessel on the stocks, probably a small gunboat. One officer proposed outfitting one of the captured canoes with a howitzer and putting it to use breaking up the contraband trade.[32]

The Emancipation Proclamation

On January 1, 1863, President Abraham Lincoln issued the Emancipation Proclamation. Henceforth, "all persons held as slaves within any State, or designated part of a State, the people Where of shall then be in rebellion against the United States, shall be then, thenceforward, and forever free." The government of the United States, "including the military and naval authority thereof," was instructed to "recognize and maintain the freedom of such persons … in any efforts they may make for their actual freedom." Moreover, former slaves were to be welcomed into the military "to garrison forts, positions, stations and other places, and to man vessels of all sorts in paid service." Frederick Douglass, an ex-slave, declared, "Better even die free, than to live slaves," and recruitment posters urged blacks to "awake, arise, or be forever fallen." Although 186,000 African Americans enlisted in the Union Army— half of whom came from the seceded states—it is uncertain how many Mathews County men were among them, or for that matter, how many people were even aware of the Emancipation Proclamation. William Bohannon, a Mathews County farmer, who made his will on February 1, 1864, bequeathed two of his slaves (John and Eliza) to his widowed daughter, Esther (Easter) Williams, and gave a young slave named Peter to his grandson. Bohannon's slave, Old Hannah, was to be supported out of his estate and the rest of his slaves could be sold after his daughter's death. It is uncertain whether Bohannon, who was 86 when he made his will, ignored the Emancipation Proclamation or simply didn't know about it.[33]

Slave children formerly belonging to Thomas White of Mathews County and taken to the Society of Friends' Orphans Shelter in Philadelphia. Courtesy of the International Museum of Photography, George Eastman House, Rochester, New York

Mathews County Slaves Who Fled to Freedom

Constance V. Brooks, who undertook extensive research in the National Archives, compiled information on Mathews County's slaves who gained their freedom during the Civil War. Her work, largely based on Civil War pension files, augments the official reports written by Union military officers and provides insight into what happened to some of the slaves who risked their lives in order to be free. For example, Richard, Daniel, and William Brooks, who fled from Mathews County in early March 1862, went aboard the *Young Rover* while it was on blockade duty and were joined by Humphrey Brooks, who also was from Mathews. According to tradition, George Williams was rescued at the Stingray Point lighthouse while waving a flag of truce.[34] The *Young Rover*'s log book indicates that a small white boat arrived with five more Mathews slaves: John and Washington Diggs, who belonged to Walter G. Lane; Aleck Billups, the slave of Frank Olmstead, and Joe (or Joseph) P. Williams, who belonged to Thomas Weston. Daniel Brooks later added that all of the Mathews County slaves aboard the *Young Rover* were taken to Hampton Roads and promptly enlisted in the Union Navy. It is unclear whether they realized that navy regulations specified that former slaves could not enlist at a rank higher than 1st-class boy or land man, although free blacks could enlist as 1st-, 2nd-, and 3rd-class boys, land men, seamen, coal-heavers, and firemen. Former slaves could, however, be advanced by the commanding officer of the vessel on which they served. In April 1862 Secretary of the Navy Gideon Wells noted that taking aboard "contrabands" provided an opportunity to acquire acclimated labor for the summer months.

The Brooks men and George Williams were taken aboard the U.S.S. *Arago* and put to work as coal-passers, perhaps without realizing that their vessel's commander had orders to ram the *Virginia*, an ironclad, and that they were replacements for white sailors who had refused to serve on what had the potential to be a suicide mission. All of the Mathews men aboard the *Arago* worked for seven weeks and earned a total of $26.50 apiece. On May 17, 1862, shortly after the *Merrimack* blew up, the *Arago* headed for New York and the former slaves were put aboard the U.S.S. *Minnesota*. The *Minnesota's* muster roll for January 1, 1863, indicated that Daniel Brooks was age 19, William Brooks was 25, Humphrey Brooks was 27, Richard Brooks was 32, and George Williams was 36. William Brooks' service records provide us with insight into the harsh conditions under which some of these men worked. He said that while he was a coal-heaver on the *Minnesota*, her main shaft needed repair, so he was put to work cleaning the inside of her boilers and picking out salt from the flues and crown sheets. Brooks said that after a week, he was unable to see because of the salt and rust that had gotten into his eyes, which were also painfully sore. When he left the fire room, his commanding officer sent him to the surgeon who gave him an eye wash. Brooks went on to become an oarsman on the 4th cutter, but was eventually transferred to the store ship *Brandywine*. In February 1864, he was sent to the *Commodore Morrison*. His service records reveal that he was 5 feet 4½ inches tall. Three other Mathew County men who served on the *Commodore Morrison* were Frank Billups, who had enlisted at Yorktown on April 23, 1861, at age 30, and was 6 feet 7 inches tall; Caesar Foster, who enlisted at Yorktown on June 15, 1863, at age 27, and was 5 feet 8 inches tall; and James McKenzie, who had enlisted in Norfolk on December 21, 1863, at age 24, and was 5 feet 9 inches tall.[35]

Mathews County: A Smugglers' Haven

On December 29, 1862, Confederate Colonel D.J. Goodwin arrived at King and Queen Courthouse and then toured Mathews and Gloucester Counties. In early January 1863, he informed the Secretary of War that the enemy was making almost daily raids and that the counties' inhabitants were begging for a force to repel them. Therefore, he planned to send Captain Littleton's company to Mathews to prevent enemy raids and reassure the local people. Goodwin surmised that with the two companies under his command, he could gather 150 to 200 conscripts in the two counties. He also wanted to have Littleton's men apprehend some unscrupulous blockade runners and confiscate their goods. He said that flour, pork, meal, and other goods were being taken to the Eastern Shore and Northern Neck and exchanged for Yankee goods that were being run through the lines to Richmond. He declared that these unprincipled traders were "mostly conscripts and outrageous extortioners [*sic*]," and said that if authorized, he felt that he could procure heavy woolens, shoes, blankets, medicines and other army goods for the government. While Colonel Godwin was in the midst of writing his letter, some of Littleton's men brought in five smugglers whom he suspected had taken the oath of allegiance to the United States and were serving as spies.

Union military leaders were also concerned about smugglers and in mid-March put together an Army-Navy task force in an attempt to disrupt their activities. Rear-Admiral S.P. Lee informed his superiors that General Dix had cavalrymen and 60 wagons in Mathews County, hoping to intercept a cargo of merchandize on its way to Richmond. When Dix asked Lee to place a gunboat between the Piankatank River and Mobjack Bay, Lee sent four vessels to the area in hopes of capturing smugglers. When three boats with 36 men from the steamer *Crusader* ventured into Milford Haven, they found—and burned—a 50-ton schooner that recently had run the blockade, although its cargo had been unloaded. In early April, a Vermont newspaper reported that when a Union Navy gunboat ventured into the Ware and North Rivers, its crew took custody of two planters who took the oath of allegiance. Although an estimated 30 Confederate cavalrymen emerged from the woods, they left. During the gunboat's expedition, a dozen runaway slaves came aboard and four fine horses were confiscated. A Confederate veteran later recalled that in mid-March 13, 1863, the men of two enemy steamers that landed at the mouth of Cobbs Creek seized poultry and other consumables. Then, in April 1863 a detachment of Union Army infantrymen ventured into the countryside to search for a large body of Confederate cavalrymen thought to be occupying some local mills.

On May 19, 1863, the men of Major General Erasmus D. Keyes, with the assistance of Colonel Judson Kilpatrick, left Gloucester Point and began their sweep through Gloucester and Mathews Counties. Their expedition's main purpose was to obtain mounts for Keyes's men, but they also wanted to assert the Union military's presence. Keyes's land-based forces, when operating near the North and East Rivers, had the support of the navy. A newspaper correspondent based near Union Army headquarters at Yorktown said that both counties, thanks to smugglers, were able to furnish "a large proportion of men, grain and other materials for the rebels" and were "infested with a set of guerillas, termed the 'Chesapeake Partisans Rangers.'" Parroting what he'd heard from Keyes and his men, he said that neither county had been "visited before, and the only loss they had sustained was the occasional straying away of some of their negroes." The reporter said that when Keyes's men reached the East River, they joined forces with some infantrymen who arrived by gunboat. After they separated into small groups, they began combing the countryside, searching for livestock and forage. By nightfall they had gathered 300 to 400 horses and mules plus some cattle and sheep, which they drove through Mathews Courthouse. Again quoting Keyes's men, the newspaper reporter said that few crops were being raised, thanks to the shortage of male labor, but local citizens were determined to support the Confederacy. A Confederate informant's account, published in a Richmond newspaper, provided a different view. He said that General Keyes's 400 to 500 cavalrymen "pillaged everything within their reach" and left very few horses and mules in Mathews County. They also "burnt several flourishing mills, declaring their determination to stop farming operations, and to prevent the grinding of what wheat might be raised." The writer used as an example Mrs. William H. Smart's mill, which was destroyed.[36] He said that when Keyes's men stopped at the home of one prominent citizen, they seized all of his bacon, carried off his livestock, and stole his gold watch.[37] The Union Army continued to apply pressure to the Middle Peninsula and in early June troops moved through western Gloucester County, crossed the Piankatank River, and reached Urbanna.

The Union Navy was also involved in the operations against Mathews County in May 1863. At the beginning of the month, Acting Commander Samuel B. Gregory of the *Crusader* dispatched two boats in pursuit of a schooner his men sighted on Stutts Creek. At the Richardson plantation, they found the schooner and two other vessels outfitted as blockade runners. They burned all three ships and then stopped at Lewis Hudgins's landing where they found a large scow capable of transporting 70 men or a large amount of goods, plus another boat that could hold 50 or more men and operate in shallow water. When Gregory's men talked with Hudgins's slaves and some of his white neighbors, they learned that he was actively engaged in blockade running and had a large quantity of corn stored in his barn, awaiting transportation to Richmond. They also found out that Hudgins's son, Lewis Hudgins Jr., was an agent and pilot for the blockade runners. When Gregory's men seized the corn in Lewis Hudgins's barn, they discovered sails for a large schooner and a large, almost fully-outfitted boat. The next day, Gregory's men visited Carter Hudgins's farm in Queens Creek and burned a schooner used as a blockade runner. According to Gregory, Hudgins was "known to be the most bitter secessionist in this county" and was responsible for several men's being sent to prison in Richmond on account of their Unionist views. He also was credited with firing upon the *Meheska*'s boats. While Gregory's men were at Carter Hudgins's farm, they burned a vessel they found in a tributary of Queens Creek and took custody of a large-decked boat and another large boat outfitted with oars that recently had run the blockade. On May 6, Gregory's men captured a blockade runner's sloop in Milford Haven. The next day, the men aboard three cutters were sent to the Richardson plantation to search for a boat reportedly being outfitted to burn Union Navy vessels in the Chesapeake Bay.[38] They found Captain John Winder's schooner, which they rendered unfit to run the blockade. When they looked for a boat that had burned a tobacco ship several months earlier, they found it in Milford Haven, on the premises of Archibald Hudgins of Stokes Creek. He admitted that the boat's crew consisted of nine armed men from Richmond, who had stayed at his house for several days. In closing his report, Gregory said that the runaway slaves and free blacks, who had come to his ship or sought refuge with his men, had been turned over to army authorities at Yorktown. He was convinced that his men's attempts to deter blockade runners had been fruitful and noted that "the court of Mathews County passed an act to suppress the running of the blockade."

In another communication, Commander Gregory said that when his men pursued two large sailboats that were heading for Archibald Hudgins's landing on Stokes Creek, the vessels' crews abandoned their cargo and tried to slip away into the woods. However, Gregory's men caught E.C. Everson, a self-proclaimed States Rights man from California, and L.J. Handy, a Marylander in the Confederacy's Quartermaster's Department. On June 25 Gregory's men took the *Crusader* and another vessel into Pepper Creek where they found a boat being outfitted for smuggling. Commander R.F. Coffin reported that the *Crusader*'s crew burned three houses, one of which belonged to a known blockade runner named Kerwan (Kirwin, Kerwen), and said that at one home they found enough dry goods and other merchandize to stock a small country store. After exiting the creek, they landed at two points between New Point Comfort and mouth of the East River, where they "burned several houses and destroyed considerable grain." Coffin added that his men destroyed four more farmhouses and outbuildings, where they found a large quantity of grain, bacon, and other food stuffs.[39] This suggests that the *Crusader's* men went ashore near the mouth of Sloop Creek and perhaps further upstream. Real estate tax rolls for 1872 include the names of several people whose buildings were categorized as "destroyed": Ralph A. Davis on Pepper Creek, Barzilla and John Kirwan on Mobjack Bay, Robert B. White and John W. Thomas in Whites Neck, and Cyrus C. White on the East River. Destruction also occurred at Poplar Grove, then the home of Christopher T. Browne.[40]

On July 2, the U.S. schooner *Samuel Rotan*'s commander informed his superiors that he had seized the schooner *Champion* near the Piankatank River and found aboard Mathew P. Morse (the *Champion*'s captain and part-owner), Washington Brown, and James Foster, all of Mathews County. Morse, a purported Union sympathizer, had asked for Federal protection in August 1862 and claimed that he had destroyed his schooner and sunk it about 30 miles up the Piankatank. Foster indicated that his schooner was sunk there, too, and that the *Champion* was the only one they were able to raise. He said that when they were on the way down the Piankatank, they drew fire from guerillas. The *Samuel Rotan's* commander said that Morse seemed to have some useful information and had said that a barrel of poisoned whiskey was at Mathews Courthouse, awaiting the Union cavalry's next raid. An elderly woman named Owens, a Union loyalist whose son was a government pilot, was evacuated from Mathews County in mid-August and the crew of the gunboat *Commodore Morris* captured Carter Hudgins, "whose name has been a terror to all those in Mathews County who have any Union feeling." The commander of the *Commodore Morris* said that Hudgins was well known for his role in sending contraband goods to Richmond and added that with the exception of his own family, people were grateful that he had been apprehended, for they held him and two or three others responsible for fanning the flames of rebellion in Mathews County.

On the home front, times were hard for women whose husbands had left home to join the military and for those who had been widowed. The average war widow was in her late twenties, had two children, and had been married for only six years when her husband left home. Only a third of these women owned land before the war. Therefore, the death of their husbands left them destitute and with children too young to help support the family. In 1863 the Virginia General Assembly ordered county courts to provide such women and their children with food. Although county officials did their best to fulfill this need, they were greatly hindered by the lack of supplies and rampant inflation.[41]

John Taylor Wood

The daring naval exploits of Lieutenant John Taylor Wood earned him widespread recognition in Mathews County, where some of his exploits occurred. Wood, an 1852 graduate of the United States Naval Academy, was teaching gunnery tactics at his alma mater when the war began. He resigned, joined the Confederate Navy, and was wounded while serving aboard the C.S.S. *Virginia* during its engagement with the U.S.S. *Monitor* in the Battle of Hampton Roads in 1862. Afterward, Wood was sent to Drewry's Bluff, where the Confederate States Marine Corps (a branch of the navy) had its headquarters and main training facilities.[42] He helped in the defense of Drewry's Bluff and in several successful assaults on Union Navy vessels. He became a naval aide to his uncle, President Jefferson Davis, and was made a commander in the navy although he simultaneously held the rank of colonel in the cavalry. Wood's dual rank and his familial connection with the Confederate president would have given him access to broad logistical support.

By early 1863, Union Navy gunboats in the Potomac Flotilla had begun dropping anchor in the mouth of the Rappahannock River, where they were poised to intercept Confederate blockade runners headed for Urbanna, an inland port with ready access to Richmond. The Confederates considered the U.S.S. *Currituck*, which had been particularly successful in attacking blockade runners, an adversary that had to be destroyed. Wood's plan involved capturing a Federal gunboat and then using it to attack the *Currituck*. On August 12, he and his 11 officers and 72 men, who were in Richmond, set out for Saluda with four "boats mounted on wheels," that is, naval barges that had been loaded onto modified wagon frames. When they reached King and Queen County, they were joined by John Yates Beall and his men, who had come in from Mathews County.[43] Wood documented his attempt to attack the *Currituck* in an official report he sent to the Secretary of the Confederate Navy on September 7, 1863.[44] He said that on August 16, he and his men reached the head of the Piankatank—about 25 miles from the river's mouth—and launched their barges. Then, they rowed downstream to the river's mouth and waited for a gunboat to appear. Two were sighted but both were underway, so Wood decided to move his men two miles up the Piankatank, where they could conceal their vessels in a creek until nightfall. Unfortunately, at daybreak, when a Union gunboat came into view, its crew spotted one of Wood's men and commenced firing. Since Wood had lost his chance to execute a surprise attack, on August 19 he moved his men and barges close to the mouth of the Rappahannock River and waited for a gunboat to arrive. On August 24 at 1 AM, they spied the *Satellite* and *Reliance*, which had dropped anchor side-by-side at Windmill Point. Wood had his men approach the gunboats, positioning a barge at each gunboat's bow. Then, they quietly slipped aboard and overpowered the vessels' crews. Afterward, Wood and his men sailed the gunboats to Urbanna with their barges in tow, and offloaded their prisoners and the wounded. Because the coal supply of the *Reliance* and the *Satellite* was low, Wood enlisted the aid of 30 sharpshooters from the 5th Virginia Cavalry, and on August 25 he set out for the Rappahannock River's mouth. Despite rough seas, the men managed to capture three transport schooners, one of which, the *Golden Rod*, was taking a load of coal from Baltimore to Maine. Wood still hoped to overtake the *Currituck*, but bad weather and a large enemy force intervened. He and his men took the captured gunboats and schooners upstream to Port Royal, which had railroad access, and stripped all of the vessels of everything but their boilers. The *Golden Rod* was burned but the other boats were scuttled.[45] Union Navy officials, whose men searched diligently for Wood's boats, were unsuccessful. Commander John Taylor Wood and his men later captured the transport schooner *Elnor* and the ship *Alleghany*, and on February 15, 1864, were commended for their achievements. In March, they attacked and seized the tug *Titan*, two Union steamers, and a telegraph station at Cherrystone Point. The U.S.S. *Crusader* was dispatched to the mouth of the Piankatank, and when some vessels with a shallower draft were sent upstream to search for the *Titan,* their crews discovered that she had been burned. They also found seven canoes concealed in the bushes, vessels that belonged to Wood. Wood went on to serve in North Carolina.[46]

Mathews County's Volunteer Coast Guard

Mathews County's Volunteer Coast Guard, a daring group of partisans, operated in the county's numerous inlets and waterways.[47] Thanks to their skillful seamanship and familiarity with local waters, they were able to smuggle foodstuffs and other supplies from the Eastern Shore so that they could be sent to Richmond and other parts of the Confederacy. From September 1863 to early 1865, this relatively small group of raiders, renowned for their exploits, was led by Acting Master John Yates Beall. Beall, who was from Jefferson County in what became West Virginia, enlisted in the 2nd Virginia Volunteers and was wounded at Harper's Ferry in October 1861.[48] He returned to the Confederate Army but became separated from his unit during the Shenandoah Valley Campaign. By September 1863, he had accepted an appointment as an acting master in the Confederate Navy and began leading a party of waterborne guerillas who operated out of Horn and Winter Harbors.[49] Beall and his men captured two ships—one white and one black, the *Swan* and the *Raven*—and used them to make surreptitious attacks on enemy vessels. W.W. Baker of Chesterfield County, who served under Beall, chronicled some of the Volunteer Coast Guard's hair-raising adventures, the group's capture, and their leader's execution.

The bravado of the men of the Confederate Volunteer Coast Guard quickly attracted the Union Navy's attention. On the night of September 18 they set out from Mathews County in a large yawl and a skiff and crossed the Chesapeake Bay. They captured several schooners on the Eastern Shore, took their crews prisoner, and set all but one of the vessels adrift. Afterward, they brought the *Alliance* to Milford Haven and conveyed their prisoners to Horn Harbor in small boats. When Beall's men were confronted by a blockader, they drove the *Alliance* ashore and then burned it. Two witnesses to the attack said that Beall's men weren't wearing uniforms and that they carried revolvers. The Acting Rear-Admiral of the Union Navy declared that he was going to do everything he could to destroy the "boats on wheels" that were operating out of the Piankatank. However, no evidence of them was found. Union Navy officials, who resolved to capture Captain John Yates Beall and his men as quickly as possible, devised a plan which involved coordinating their efforts with Union Army General Isaac J. Wistar and his land-based forces.[50]

Closing Out 1863

On August 27, 1863, Union General Wistar, who was at Yorktown, informed his commanding officer that three companies of Confederate cavalrymen had arrived in Mathews County, where they were searching for conscripts and causing a great commotion. His information came from six Mathews men who had arrived at Yorktown in canoes and asked to take the oath of allegiance. Four days later, Wistar reported that he had received contradictory intelligence, but had heard that Emerson Miller's three companies of cavalry had rounded up some conscripts in Mathews. Wistar added that Colonel Benjamin F. Onderdonk was going to Mathews Courthouse at daylight, reinforced by a gunboat.

On September 29 General Wistar presented his plans to his superiors. He requested support from the Potomac Flotilla and the North Atlantic Blockading Squadron in order to prevent Beall and his men from escaping by water. He recommended that a regiment of infantrymen be positioned at Gloucester Courthouse and that a battery and 200 cavalry be sent to "the neck or Isthmus of the Matthews County peninsula, arriving there about dark and detailing all persons in the vicinity for the night." He noted that "At this point is an old rebel breastwork across the neck, distance from Gloucester Point about 24 miles, from the infantry position at the Court House, about 8 miles." This, then, was the expeditionary force that Wistar positioned near Fort Nonsense. He said that the cavalry could camp near the breastwork until around 4:30 AM, when half of them would commence patrolling the countryside toward Scuffletown—that is, Harcum—on Route 198, and the other half would conduct a thorough search of the countryside. Wistar recommended positioning the gunboat *Putnam*, which had a shallow draft, at the head of the North River around the same time that the cavalry set out. He noted that "from the southernmost of the two roads which traverse the 'neck,'

An advance of the cavalry skirmish line,
a drawing by Edwin Forbes.
Courtesy of the Library of Congress.

the ground is open and falls sharply to the river." He said that if his cavalrymen had to retreat from Mathews Courthouse and were intercepted there, they could reach a position of safety at Gloucester Courthouse.[51] Wistar, who was determined to capture John Yates Beall and his men, told his superiors that another 200 cavalrymen should be ordered to "scour" Mathews County, "with another gunboat and transport at the courthouse to bring them off, if retreat by land should be intercepted." Wistar admitted having a limited knowledge of the Confederate cavalry's strength and position and said that the man he'd hoped to use as a guide wasn't available. He noted that an alternative plan for his expedition would call for concentrating his men at the entrance to Mathews County, but he admitted that it would make a retreat far more risky.[52] A map included with Wistar's correspondence identified the site of Smart's Mill and indicated that he had placed his men astride Route 14, both east and west of its junction with County Route 602, and at two positions on Route 198.

General Wistar set out for Mathews County on October 5 with troops from the 4th U. S. Colored Infantry,[53] detachments from the 11th Pennsylvania Cavalry, the 1st New York Mounted Rifles, two sections of artillery from the 8th New York Battery, and Battery E of the 8th Pennsylvania Light Artillery. Wistar's men were under the command of Colonel Samuel P. Spear

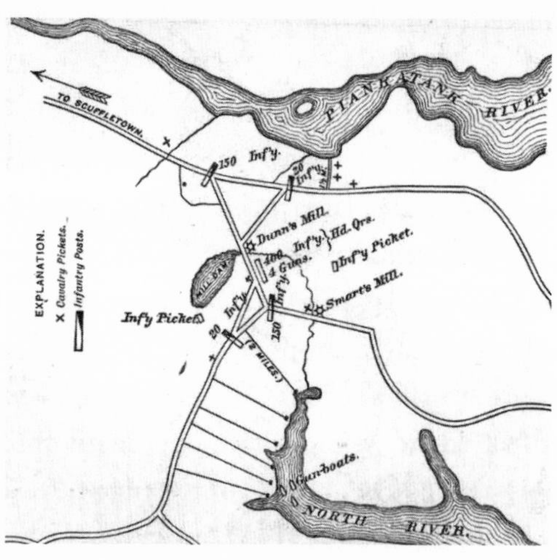

Position of U.S. Forces under General Wistar, October 5 through 9, 1863.
Official Records of the Civil War, *Series 1, Vol. XXIX Chapter 41, 1017.*

and had the support of eight gunboats that were sent into the North and East Rivers, Mobjack Bay, Horn Harbor, and Milford Haven. Meanwhile, two ships were positioned between New Point Comfort and the mouth of the East River.[54] The *General Putnam* sailed inland as far as Williams Wharf, where 12 men, captured by Wistar's cavalry, were taken aboard. Seven more men, taken in the North River, also were put aboard. The prisoners were thought to include four officers and several of Acting Master Beall's men. Lieutenant Commander James H. Gillis of the gunboat *Commodore Jones*, who led the navy task force, commented that it was very difficult to capture rebels because they fled into the woods and used familiar escape routes and hiding places. At the end of the expedition it was reported that 150 boats and schooners and a number of canoes had been destroyed and that 80 head of cattle *en route* to Richmond had been seized.

According to the Union Army's report, the expedition to Mathews County was highly successful, for four Confederate officers were captured, along with 25 other men, and an abundance of livestock and military stores were seized. According to an article in the *Philadelphia Inquirer,* Colonel Spear entered Mathews County at the head of 450 men of the 11th Pennsylvania Cavalry and 600 infantrymen armed with four pieces of artillery, who intended to disrupt "the gangs of guerillas and river pirates" operating in the region. The action that took place between October 5 and October 8 was documented in detailed military communiqués. Three Confederate Army officers, a naval officer, and 16 other men were captured and taken to Yorktown, but most of the sought-after group, the Confederate guerillas, escaped in small boats that put out to sea in a gale and reached the Eastern Shore. Wistar said that his men had arrested more than a hundred people involved in illicit trade, but only some of them were sent to Yorktown. He added that "No marauding or pilfering whatever was allowed," and that no houses were entered except by officers or non-commissioned officers. He admitted, however, that some of the navy gunboat crews landed without his authority "and acted shamefully and disgracefully," noting that "in at least one instance an officer was present and consenting." He praised the deportment of the black troops under his command. An Iowa newspaper reported that around 15 boats and schooners were captured during General Wistar's raid and that one Union cavalryman, a Corporal Hand, was killed by a sniper. This was the man killed by Sands Smith II of Mathews County, who ultimately paid with his own life.

According to the reports filed by Lieutenant Commander Gillis and Major General J.G. Foster, Smith was tried by a drumhead court martial and was hanged at General Wistar's orders. His brother and neighbor, Thomas, was taken into custody because he was found riding along the road at midnight with a pair of pistols in his pockets, purportedly shooting at crows. Gillis noted that Thomas Smith had been actively engaged in blockade running and that his home had been "a regular rendezvous" for Beall's men. He said that when Wistar's men visited Mr. Tabb's home, they found three compasses that had probably been taken from the vessels Beall's men had captured on the Eastern Shore.

Confederate blockade runner depicted in Harper's Weekly, *December 31, 1864. Courtesy of the Library of Congress.*

In 1910, W.W. Baker, a member of the Confederate Volunteer Coast Guard, recounted the group's narrow escape from General Wistar's raiders in early October 1863. He said that Wistar sent out two regiments of cavalry, a regiment of black infantrymen, and an artillery battalion; these troops were supported by three gunboats in the North River, three in the East River, and two in the Piankatank. When Wistar reached Mathews Courthouse, he made Dr. John G. Bohannon's home his headquarters and was unaware that Beall and some of his men were trapped behind his picket lines.[55] Beall, on the other hand, was aware of Wistar's men's presence and knew that lines of pickets had been set up across the main roads between the Piankatank River and Mobjack Bay. Realizing that it would be impossible to pass the Union gunboats, Beall had his men take the *Raven* and the

Swan to Sands Smith II's house, Beachland, at the upper end of Horn Harbor. There, they filled both boats with sand and submerged them below the surface. While Beall's men were hiding their boats, they learned that some of Wistar's men had paused in front of Colonel George Tabb's home, Centerville or Woodstock, and that pickets had been stationed nearby, at the gate of Thomas Smith's home, Willow Grove. At great personal risk, they accepted a dinner invitation from Smith's daughter and enjoyed a hearty meal. When they were ready to leave, one of Beall's men, Edmundson, carefully approached the pickets so that he could retrieve a coat he'd left behind. Then, all of the men slipped through the picket lines and by sunrise had reached safety in the Dragon Swamp. Later, Beall's men learned that General Wistar was infuriated because local citizens had helped them elude their captors.

Despite the close encounter with the Union Army, Beall and his men managed to continue their work. However, Beall later led a failed attempt to free 300 Confederate prisoners who were being detained on Johnson's Island in Sandusky Bay, Ohio. On November 15, 1863, Union forces captured Beall and his men near Tangier Island in Chesapeake Bay. At first they were treated as pirates and taken to Fort McHenry in Baltimore. Later, they were transferred to a ship anchored near Fort Monroe and then to a prisoner-of-war camp at Point Lookout, Maryland. Beall was moved to City Point, near Petersburg, Virginia, and in March 1864 was sent to Richmond in a prisoner exchange. Once freed, he continued his exploits but was recaptured in Niagara, New York, and detained on Governor's Island. He was tried and convicted by a military commission for acting as a spy and violating the rules of war; he was hanged at Governor's Island on February 24, 1865.

Thirty years after the war was over, General Isaac J. Wistar wrote an autobiography and described his expedition into Mathews County in October 1863. He claimed that almost all of the Confederate Volunteer Coast Guard had been captured in the raid, along with a small regiment of cavalry and a few other men. He said that the expedition was so successful that the Secretary of War mentioned it in a report he sent to Congress. Wistar used an incident that had occurred in Mathews County to illustrate how little he could rely on the information he had received from well-intended local blacks. He said that some cavalry officers brought in a storekeeper because some blacks claimed that he had set aside a barrel of poisoned whiskey expressly for the Union Army. Although the blacks continued to insist that the allegations were true, the elderly merchant denied them vehemently and offered to drink a tumbler-full himself. He quickly became intoxicated but otherwise experienced no ill effects. According to Wistar, within ten minutes' time, his men polished off the rest of the whiskey.

Mid-November 1863 brought another invasion of Mathews County, this time by Lieutenant Colonel George M. Guion and 450 men of the 148th New York Infantry, who were also under General Wistar's command. Guion's expedition was deemed highly successful. He and his men arrived in the headwaters of the East River on the gunboat *Morse* and went ashore in small boats. After they marched to Mathews Courthouse, Guion sent two companies down the main road[56] to search the countryside and then meet up with the *Morse* at New Point Comfort. He took the rest of his men, which consisted of seven companies, and set out for Scuffletown (Harcum), searching the countryside along the way and destroying 18 to 20 boats on the Piankatank River.[57] When they were about five miles from their destination, they learned that a party of guerillas was in the vicinity of Gwynn's Island, so they reversed course and camped for the night about two miles from Cricket Hill. At daylight, Guion's men marched to Cricket Hill and learned that a group of Confederates armed with a brass howitzer was on Gwynn's Island. After they crossed over to the island, they captured a Confederate naval officer and 11 of his men, who had thrown their howitzer into the water. After Guion's troops left Gwynn's Island, they destroyed a dozen boats, a sloop, and the barge the navy men had used in privateering. When Guion returned to Mathews Courthouse, he learned that an unarmed guerilla fighter, a blockade runner, and two other Confederates had been captured; the latter had been at home on leave.[58]

Lieutenant Commander Charles A. Babcock, who was in command of the *Morse*, reported that on the morning of November 16, David Ripley,[59] a local informant, claimed that "a party of guerillas were in force, chasing every Union person and committing depredations generally through Mathews County." Babcock, with Wistar's approval, set out from Yorktown with 430 men from the 148th Regiment of New York Volunteers. When he reached the East River's mouth, he slowly sailed upstream as far as the water's depth would permit, while keeping his soldiers out of sight. Then, around 6 PM, he sent his men ashore in boats. Afterward, Babcock dropped back downstream and anchored at what he called the Mathews Courthouse wharf and went to the county seat. Later he and his men set out for New Point Comfort, where two companies of soldiers were encamped.[60]

Sands Smith II's Ordeal

In early October 1863, when General Wistar's men were in Mathews County, in hot pursuit of John Yates Beall and his men, 61-year-old Sands Smith II, a dignified gentleman with a reputation for fearlessness, was brutally slain. According to W.W. Baker, he and the rest of Beall's men learned about Smith's death the day after they had managed to escape from Mathews County. He said that a squadron of Union cavalrymen rode to Beachland, Smith's home, where they confronted him. When Smith, who was almost deaf, received what he interpreted as an insult from a Union soldier, he grabbed a double-barreled shotgun, and shot him dead. He had started to pull another soldier from his saddle when the rest of the squadron arrived. They struck Smith with their sabers, knocked him to the ground, and then tied him up and set him upon the luggage seat of his buggy, claiming that they would take him before their superiors. Baker said that instead, they took him to a site "between Col. Tabb's [Woodstock] and Mathews Courthouse and there hung [him] upon a tree on the roadside." After he was dead, they riddled his body with bullets.

A newspaper article published in Richmond on October 15, 1863, provides us with some additional information. The reporter recounted the arrival of General Wistar's men, the gunboats that commenced shelling the shoreline, and the search for Beall and his "pirates." He said that the last time Union soldiers visited Sands Smith II's home, they had destroyed some of his property and carried off some of his slaves and horses. The writer acknowledged that Smith shot and killed one soldier and had tried to shoot another before being overpowered and taken into custody. He said that while Smith was being taken to Mathews Courthouse, he was brutalized by the soldiers. He asked to speak to Colonel Spear, who instead of reproving his men, reportedly seized a stick and struck Smith over the head. He also refused Smith's request for a drink of water. Afterward, Smith was taken to the home of John J. Burke, on Route 14 about five miles northwest of Mathews Courthouse.[61] Spear had his men to place Smith on horseback with his hands tied behind his back. Then, they tied a rope around his neck and threw the end of it over the limb of a persimmon tree. When the horse was driven from under Smith, he fell to the ground, gasping but still alive. Although he begged for mercy, Spear had his men to shoot Smith and then bury his corpse in a shallow grave. Afterward, they posted a warning that death would be the fate of all bushwhackers. The newspaper columnist went on to say that Thomas Smith was forced to witness his brother's murder. He added that Wistar's men carried off a number of Mathews County citizens, burned a mill, destroyed all the salt works and fishing seines they could find, and drove off a large number of cattle. They also threatened to burn the home of anyone who dared to entertain Beall or his men. The reporter added that the Smith brothers made salt by boiling bay water in kettles, helped their neighbors, and fed and sheltered mariners, blockade runners, and travelers. Thomas Smith, who was taken into custody by Spear's men, was taken to Norfolk and tried by military authorities. However, he was found not guilty and released.[62]

Mathews County in 1864

By 1863, the Confederates had begun placing torpedoes in Virginia waterways that were frequented by the Union Navy. In January 1864, two Northern newspapers reported that the Confederates were known to have placed torpedoes in the York and Pamunkey Rivers and near the mouth of the East River. Five months later, another newspaper published a report by Foxhall A. Parker of the Union Navy's Potomac Flotilla, who stated that "a party of Rebels, somewhere in the vicinity of Urbanna, was engaged in placing torpedoes in the Rappahannock and Piankatank Rivers." The same news item stated that the torpedo party had been found, that 11 Confederates were killed, and 10 were captured. Parker said that four torpedoes were exploded, six removed from the water, and four kegs of powder were detonated.[63]

Sometimes, official communiqués mentioned plans of action that were proposed but not undertaken. For instance, in February 1864 the Union Army's provost marshal at Eastville, on the Eastern Shore, asked his superiors' permission to take 100 cavalrymen to the East River or the Piankatank to capture two companies of Confederate cavalrymen who were reputedly rounding up conscripts. He said that he had learned about their presence from three refugees who offered to serve as guides. However, nothing was done, perhaps because the intelligence was considered unreliable or the plan, unfeasible.

On March 5, 1864, a group of Mathews County men implemented a highly successful surprise attack on a Union position at Cherrystone. According to an article in the *Richmond Examiner*, Captain Thaddeus Fitzhugh of the 5th Virginia Cavalry, a physician, was on furlough in Mathews County when he decided to rally 14 other men and traverse the Chesapeake Bay. Upon reaching their destination, they destroyed the Union Army's telegraph station whose cable provided the only link between Fort Monroe and Washington. They also burned large quantities of commissary and quartermaster's stores, sank a large schooner, and seized two steamers. Fitzhugh's men crossed the Chesapeake in one of the steamers, the tugboat *Titan*, and then beached it in the upper part of the Piankatank River. Then, they stripped it of its machinery and burned it. An official report by Colonel R.L.T. Beale stated that before the tug was burned, a large quantity of sugar, coffee, whiskey, and other items was removed.

In mid-to-late March, a large expeditionary force under the leadership of Union Army General Charles K. Graham approached Mathews County by land and by sea and stayed for two days. A detachment of 400 cavalrymen set out from Gloucester Courthouse. When they reached Cricket Hill, they were joined by a large fleet that included gunboats, a section of artillery, and transports carrying more than a thousand infantrymen, including men from the regiments known as the 4th and 6th U. S. Colored Troops. The latter group had orders to occupy Mathews Courthouse, "seize all suspicious characters, and take such private property as might be useful to contrabands," that is, blockade runners, and to "prevent any plundering by the men." On the way to the courthouse, the 6th U.S. Colored Troops captured a Confederate cavalryman and almost caught another. When they arrived at the courthouse, they discovered that the 11th Pennsylvania Cavalry was already there. Pickets were placed between the heads of the East and the Piankatank Rivers to pick up any Confederates trying to escape and to assist "persons of color or other refugees who might wish to go within our lines." For two days, General Graham's men roamed the countryside, searching for anything that might be of value to the Confederate government. They reportedly encountered little opposition, although they did manage to capture ten soldiers and they discovered the *Titan*, which had been destroyed. Graham reported that the boats cruising up the Piankatank succeeded in capturing a schooner and its two-man crew, who were transporting mail and 66 boxes of tobacco. Graham's men also took custody of 40 runaway slaves. After the expedition was over, superior officers discussed the undisciplined behavior of the small detachments of Colored Troops, who were under the command of noncommissioned officers and "in an enemy's country and for purposes that offered peculiar temptations." At issue was the fact that they had stolen private property. One officer commented that the men "began to consider the expedition a kind of plundering foray" that was impossible to bring under control. When one of the superior officers called for an inspection of the Colored Troops' camp, he found poultry, fresh and cured meat, pieces of culinary equipment, and clothes, linens, and "ornaments of dress" (perhaps jewelry). One man, caught in the act of stealing, was shot in the shoulder as an example, and the resulting fear from that incident reportedly restored discipline to the entire unit. After the Union military left Mathews County, they crossed over to Middlesex.

The Union Navy returned to Mathews County in late September 1864. The U.S.S. *Fuchia,* the *Freeborn,* and the *Mercury* ventured into Stutts Creek in response to a rumor that the Confederates were planning to attack a steamer stationed near the mouth of the Piankatank. The small fleet sailed upstream for about three miles until it reached the farm of a Mr. Hudgins, "a noted rebel," where they found and destroyed several large boats and a fishery. One vessel, a launch, was large enough to carry 80 men. Continuing up the creek, they discovered some smaller boats they rendered inoperable. One naval officer reported that 17 boats were destroyed in this one incident, for a total of 22 vessels during the entire week. As the war drew to a close, the Union Navy continued to enter Mathews County waters from time to time, destroying boats in an attempt to stop smuggling. On one such occasion when they were near the Piankatank, they captured Robert Hudgins of Milford Haven.

Times were hard on the home front, and in February 1864, 12 military men and one soldier's widow applied for public assistance, seeking the relief that was available to indigent Confederate soldiers and their families who lived within enemy lines or neutral territory. Lewis H. Ashberry, John H. Bassett, Jeremiah Callis, William A. Green, William J. Hudgins, Silas Huggett, William M. Lewis, John R. Lilly, Elijah Parker, James Robins, Joel Shackleford, and Joel C. Thomas applied for relief, as did William A. Davis's widow. All of these people headed households that included minor children. A court order dated July 6, 1864, which required the county sheriff to list the names of indigent soldiers and sailors living in the county, included a total of 106 people. There were many widows and some widowers with children. One woman receiving assistance had a young child and a son who was in the army. Mathews County's earliest dated marriage register, which commences in January 1861, reveals that relatively few weddings occurred once the war got underway. Only one marriage was recorded in 1861 (that of Warner L. Hudgins and Laura F. Hudgins), and only four couples wed during 1862. During 1863, seven more couples married and another seven followed suit in 1864. Widows and widowers often remarried and most of the people who wed were in their 20s.[64]

The Local Political Scene

A small, but remarkable, assortment of local records preserved at the Library of Virginia and in the Mathews County courthouse reveal that on May 26, 1864, a full ten months before the surrender at Appomattox, the qualified voters of Mathews County elected four court justices for each of the county's three magisterial districts.[65] This suggests that despite occasional Union raids, local public servants were able to perform some of their official duties. On June 26, 1864, George K. Brooks, William M. Brownley, Winslow Foster, and Lemuel James took their oaths of office as justices for the first magisterial district, whereas Albert Diggs, Thomas M. Hunley, Walter G. Lane, and James B. Thurston became the second district's justices. John H. Blake, Benjamin B. Dutton, Houlder Hudgins, and William H. Hudgins became duly elected justices on behalf of the third district. Each of these men was supposed to hold office until August 1, 1868. No documentary records have come to light that disclose where—or how often—Mathews County's court justices were able to convene while the war was going on; however, because Mathews was not occupied by the Union Army, its justices may have continued meeting in the county seat. A court docket that lists the subpoenas issued between April 1861 and April 1863 includes the names of the plaintiffs, defendants, and witnesses that appeared in court during that period. Surviving legal documents reveal that on January 1, 1865, first district justice William M. Brownley resigned because he had failed to qualify for office. He may have been ill or perhaps lacked the funds he needed to post the bond required of all officeholders.

In accord with tradition, the county's constitutional officers were elected for terms of different lengths. On May 26, 1864, Shepherd G. Miller was elected clerk of court for a term of six years that began on July 1, 1864. When promising to faithfully fulfill his duties, he posted a bond of $1,000 in "lawful money of Virginia." Miller's son, William H. Miller, a former deputy clerk of court, was elected sheriff and was to serve for two years. When he posted a bond, Andrew C. Brown, Thomas M. Hunley, and John H. Dunlavy, and Miller's own father served as his securities. William M. Brownley was elected to a two-year term as Commissioner of the Revenue and was to commence serving on February 1, 1865. George H. Bohannon, who was elected to a six-year term as county surveyor, was to take office on July 1, 1864. On May 26, 1864, three men were elected constable of their respective districts and were supposed to take office on July 1, 1864: John H. Diggs for District 1; Sheriff William H. Miller for District 2; and Carter B. Hudgins for District 3.[66]

Wartime Damage to Local Property

The Union military repeatedly ventured into Mathews County and sometimes destroyed some local buildings. Smart's Mill was burned during General Keyes' May 19, 1863, raid, and when the *Crusader* ventured into Pepper Creek in late June 1863, three houses were burned, including one that belonged to a blockade runner named Kirwan. The *Crusader* then progressed along the east side of Mobjack Bay, between New Point Comfort and the mouth of the East River, and laid waste to several houses plus four farmhouses and their outbuildings. In 1922 when a Confederate veteran was interviewed about the war, he recalled that when Union Army soldiers landed at New Point Comfort, they met with little resistance but set fire to many dwellings. Confederate veteran Walter R. Stokes, who was interviewed in 1924, said that there was a barn "on the Ransone estate at Port Haywood which bears evidence of the war. A cannon ball fired from a boat on the East River, some miles distant, entered the barn." He said that it reportedly "passed through the wheels of a carriage in the building" and came to rest in a pine thicket. Mr. Stokes added that the barn had been repaired many times, but "the board through which the cannon ball passed is intact." The barn and dwelling to which he was referring was owned by Thomas R. Ransone during the 1860s and 70s. The mill at Belle Isle also sustained severe damage. The mill machinery was reportedly hauled away by Union troops, who accidentally dumped the big flywheel in Queens Creek.

Besides capturing the Confederate Volunteer Coast Guard and other blockade runners, the Union military's principal objective was preventing smuggled goods and food stuffs from reaching the Confederate Army, which suffered from constant shortages. As a result, many Mathews County residents sustained the loss of their schooners, skiffs, canoes, and various types of watercraft. There is no real way to determine the monetary value of the numerous vessels that were lost thanks to the Union military's incursions.[67]

The Beginning of the End

On the night of April 1, 1865, the Confederate line near Petersburg crumbled under massive opposition, and within hours President Jefferson Davis and a few government officials boarded a train that took them to Danville. Mobs quickly filled Richmond's streets and looting was widespread. Confederate soldiers, following orders, put the city's warehouses and government stores to the torch, in order to prevent them from being captured. When the wind rose, flames spread wildly, and when dawn came on April 3, the heart of Richmond's commercial district was ablaze. The city's factories were also swept up in the conflagration. At that juncture, General Lee took what remained of his forces and began marching west, hoping to reach the Richmond and Danville Railroad and follow it to Danville, where he could use the hilly terrain as a defensive position.[68] However, the Union cavalry seized control of the railroad, leaving Lee's men to follow unfamiliar roads as they set out for Lynchburg. During an intense fight at Sayler's Creek, more than a third of Lee's men were lost. Simultaneously, hunger, sickness, and fatigue were exacting a deadly toll. When Lee and his exhausted men reached Appomattox Court House, they found lines of Federal troops. There were no realistic alternatives to surrender. On April 9, 1865, General Robert E. Lee decided to meet with General Ulysses S. Grant to negotiate. The two military leaders conferred in the McLean house in Appomattox, where they drafted a document they signed at 4 PM. Afterward, the weary, half-starved, and disheartened Confederates marched through lines of Union infantry and laid down their arms. A significant number of Mathews County men were present. Lee's surrender heralded the end of the war, and at that juncture, one form of suffering yielded to another.[69]

Approximately two weeks after the surrender, the Union Navy's Acting Volunteer Lieutenant-Commander, Edward Hooker, informed his superiors that he had received a note signed by a Mr. Dixon, a Mathews County resident, who invited him to be present on Tuesday, April 25, at a flag-raising ceremony. Dixon said that he had written to him at the request of many citizens. Hooker, upon receiving the message, sailed into the Piankatank and discussed the matter with several local people. He tried to explain that neither he nor his officers could attend the ceremony even though it was a voluntary act on the citizens' part, because if Union Navy men were present, the ceremony could be misconstrued as the response to an order. Hooker went on to say that even if the flag were hoisted, the blockade would not be lifted and trading privileges would not be restored. He recommended holding a public meeting so that opinions could be exchanged freely. He said that if the majority agreed that they wanted to raise a flag, then they should do so, and also sign the oath of allegiance. Hooker later learned that the flag-raising that occurred on April 25 was attended by a few men and a large number of women; however, the majority of Mathews citizens did not participate. Hooker, who seems to have been a perceptive man, said that he felt that if the flag were hoisted without general agreement, it might engender some bitterness, which could be avoided by waiting.[70]

Notes

1 Bruce Catton, *The American Heritage Picture History of the Civil War* (New York, 1960), 59, 62, 75; James I. Robertson, *Civil War Virginia: Battleground for a Nation* (Charlottesville, 1991), 1–13, 109–110; James M. McPherson, *Battle Cry of Freedom: The Civil War Era* (New York, 1988), 234–259; Leonard, *General Assembly,* 475, 481–482, 485, 487, 489–499; Mathews County Census 1860; Mathews Archives, Box 83 R; Palmer, *Calendar*, XI, 132, 143, 185; Mrs. Benjamin Franklin White, *Mathews Men Who Served in the War Between the States* (Norfolk, 1961), 65.

2 The slaves claimed that there were less than two rounds of cartridges among the 500 male Confederate supporters in Mathews County.

3 Dr. Henry W. Tabb lived at Auburn and Mrs. James H. Roy resided at Green Plains.

4 Charles, *Newspapers*, 104; United States War Department (USWD), *The War of the Rebellion: A Compilation of the Official Records of the Union and Confederate Armies* (Washington, D.C., 1891), Series 1, Vol. IV, 649–650, 704, 716; United States Naval War Records Office (USNWRO), *Official Records of the Union and Confederate Navies in the War of the Rebellion* (Washington, D.C., 1894–1923), Series 1 Vol. VI, 8–9, 80–81, 107, 297.

5 In February 1862 when James hired Frank, one of the late John P. Hudgins' slaves, he agreed to see that he was provided with good summer and winter clothing, socks, a hat, a pair of double-soled shoes, and a blanket. He also promised not to take Frank out of the county (Mathews Archives Box 6 R).

6 The boats at Cricket Hill were to be guarded by Private John Davis (Mathews Archives Box 6 R).

7 Marchant, a young seaman, deserted sometime prior to May 4, 1862.

8 On October 11, 1862 the Confederate Congress granted a draft exemption to males owning 20 or more slaves. The "Twenty-Slave Law" was modified on May 1, 1863, to apply only to overseers on plantations that belonged solely to a minor, a single woman, or a person of unsound mind, or to someone away from home on account of military service (www.encyclopediavirginia.org).

9 Mathews County Military and Pension Records, Applications for Exemptions from Military Duty, 1862. The Union Army also had trouble raising the troops they needed (Mark Mayo Boatner, *The Civil War Dictionary* [New York, 1959], 245).

10 http://en.wikipedia.org; Mathews County Census 1860; USNWRO, *Official Records,* Series 1, Vol. IX, 37; Boatner, *Civil War Dictionary*, 172; USWD, *Official Records*, Series 2,

Vol. I, 445–447; Marion Salley, "Behind the Lines: the Achievements and Privations of the Women of the South," *The Confederate Veteran* 32 (1924):56–57; Robertson, *Civil War Virginia*, 104–106; White, *Mathews Men*, 67; Ludwell Lee Montague, *Gloucester County in the Civil War* (Gloucester, 2010), 33; Alex L. Wiatt, *26th Virginia Infantry* (Lynchburg, 1984), 2, 4–5, 7, 10–11, 13, 20, 35; Mathews County Military Board of Exemptions, March 8, 1862; Applications for Exemptions from Military Duty, 1862; Tindall, *America*, 629; Mathews Archives Boxes 6 R, 23 R, 13 OV.

11 Horace H. Cunningham, *Doctors in Gray: The Confederate Military Service* (Baton Rouge, 1958), 33, 45, 74, 87, 93, 163; Wyndham B. Blanton, *Medicine in Virginia in the Nineteenth Century* (Richmond, 1933), 184, 264, 273, 296; Robertson, *Civil War Virginia,* 88–89.

12 In 1939 when Harriet G. Miller, a Works Progress Administration (WPA) worker, interviewed a Mrs. Lewis about life during the Civil War, she recalled her mother's saying that Union soldiers sometimes brought meat and vegetables to their home and demanded that the servants cook it. Her mother complied because she feared what they might do if she refused. Mrs. Lewis said that the soldiers sometimes camped in the lane leading to the Old Office. She said that there was smallpox in the county during the war. In another WPA interview, the informant said that Union soldiers regularly helped themselves to the meal at Burkes Mill and that they often stole poultry (Miller, "Interviews," Boxes 7, 10).

13 There is no doubt that Sally Louisa Tompkins was the first woman to receive a military commission in the Confederate Army. However, she may not have been the only female to receive a commission. In 1862 Mrs. Lucy Mina Otey, who established the Ladies Relief Hospital in Lynchburg, Virginia, reportedly received a captain's commission. In 1937 a copy of that commission, signed by President Davis and the Secretary of War, was reportedly in the possession of Mrs. Otey's granddaughter, Mrs. James A. Scott (WPA, Virginia Historical Inventory, November 23, 1937; Douglas K. Harvey, Lynchburg Museum System, personal communication, December 30 and 31, 2013; James M. Elson, *Lynchburg, Virginia: The First Two Hundred Years, 1786–1986* [Lynchburg, 2004], 154–156).

14 After the unit disbanded, White was detached to make shoes for women and children.

15 Hudgins served until the end of the war and was paroled at Appomattox Courthouse in 1865 (George L. Sherwood, *The Mathews Light Artillery; Penick's Pittsylvania Artillery; Young's Halifax Light Artillery, & Johnson's Jackson Flying Artillery* [Appomattox, 1999], 24).

16 A newspaper clipping describing a November 18, 1863, letter written by Laban Hudgins of Armistead's Light Artillery is on file in the Mathews Archives (Mathews Archives Box 24 R).

17 Mathews County Census 1850, 1860; Mathews Archives Boxes 2 R, 6 R, 13 OV; Boatner, *Civil War Dictionary*, 471; http://lva1.hosted.exlibrisgroup.com; Robert J. Driver Jr., *5th Virginia Cavalry* (Lynchburg, 1997), 45; Sherwood, *Mathews Light Artillery*, 3, 6–7, 9, 21–28. Lieutenant Oscar Lane, General James H. Lane's aide-de-camp and brother, died on July 17, 1864. A lock of his hair is preserved in the Mathews Archives.

18 The 1860 census suggests that Morse greatly exaggerated, for only eight percent of the male household heads in Mathews County were from the North or the border states.

19 Charles, *Newspapers*, 104; USWD, *Official Records*, Series 1, Vol. V, 46, 49, 52–53; USNWRO, *Official Records*, Vol. VII, 636–638; Southern Claims Commission, Claim Nos. 5871 and 8759.

20 Charles, *Newspapers*, 104; USWD, *Official Records*, Series I, Vol. IV, 644–645, 649–650; Vol. IX, 37; Vol. 11 Part 1: 410, 704, 716.

21 Stephen W. Sears, ed., *The Civil War Papers of George B. McClellan: Selected Correspondence 1860–1865* (New York, 1989), 168, 204. In another portion of his communiqué, General McClellan discussed future strategy and addressed the Union Army's moving into the Deep South. Interestingly, he commented that once those states were retaken, the army could "force the slaves to labor for our subsistence instead of that of the rebels" (Sears, *McClellan*, 168). Thus, he does not seem to have eschewed the idea of slave labor.

22 National Park Service historian Robert E.L. Krick, the author of *Staff Officers in Gray: A Biographical Register of the Staff Officers in the Army of Northern Virginia*, noted that early in the war, William H. Clarke, like many other young engineers, was a contractor. As such, he would have reported to a supervisor who was a commissioned officer (David Riggs, personal communication, September 24, 2014; *Richmond Dispatch*, January 1, 1896). At Fort Nonsense, Clarke employed the redan, the redoubt, and the lunette as defensive mechanisms in a continuous line of fieldworks.

23 During the 1860s, the old North End mill was owned by William R. Smart and State Route 3 had not been built. Therefore, those traveling overland would have utilized the forerunner of County Route 602 (Burkes Pond Road) when going to and from State Routes 198 and 14. A topographic quadrangle sheet published in 1917 and a 1969 survey reveals that Fort Nonsense originally sat astride Route 14's forerunner and that the southerly part of the earthworks was impacted when Route 14 became a four-lane highway. Part of Fort Nonsense was also adversely affected by the construction of Route 3 (USGS, "Mathews," 1917; Mathews County Plat Book 6:330).

24 A gabion, a massive basketwork capable of holding earth, was fabricated from vines, saplings and small trees.

25 USWD, *Official Records,* Series 1 Vol. II, 866; Vol. IV, 634; Vol. IX, 49; Mathews County Historical Society, *Mathews County Panorama: A Pictorial History of Mathews County, 1791–1941* (Marceline, Missouri, 1983), 31; White, *Mathews Men*, 66; www.mathewscountyhistoricalsociety.org.

26 Some of Mathews County's antebellum records have survived, probably because public officials hid them or took them home.

27 Charles, *Newspapers*, 104; Palmer, *Calendar*, XI, 140, 166–172; William F. R. Ritchie, comp., *Acts And Joint Resolutions Passed By The General Assembly of the State of Virginia Passed During the Session of 1861–1862* (Richmond, 1862), 61; USWD, *Official Records*, Series 1, Vol. 2, Part 1:97; Part 3:386; Vol. 9:49,61; Vol. 11, Part 3:369; Series 2, Vol. III, 124; Lyon G. Tyler, "Sketches from the Journal of a Confederate Soldier," *Tyler's Quarterly* 6 (1925):32.; Mathews County Order Book 1856–1871.

28 USWD, *Official Records*, Series 1, Vol. V, 45–46, 49, 52–53; USNWRO, *Official Records*, Vol. VII, 636–638; White, *Mathews Men*, 66.

29 Salt was manufactured by boiling brackish water in large iron kettles.

30 On December 4, 1862, the *Philadelphia Enquirer* reported that twelve salt works, five schooners, two sloops, several smaller boats, and 24 large canoes were destroyed (*Philadelphia Enquirer*, December 4, 1862).

31 In 1924 when Walter Stokes, a Confederate veteran, was interviewed about his wartime experiences, he said that "You can still see on the banks of Woody's [Woodas] Creek the remains of two Confederate Supply boats. These boats were burned by the Northern soldiers in 1864." After a lapse of 60 or more years, Mr. Stokes may well have misremembered the date. In 2009 a cannon ball was recovered from some private property on Woodas Creek, not far from the East River (White, *Mathews Men*, 67; *Gloucester-Mathews Gazette-Journal*, July 1, 2009).

32 http://infoweb.newsbank.com; USWD, *Official Records*, Series 1, Vol. V, 139; Vol. XVIII, 462; Vol. 51 (Part 2), 542; Series 2, Vol. IV, 90–91; USNWRO, *Official Records*, Series 1, Vol. VIII, 227–229; Charles, *Newspapers,* 104–105; White, *Mathews Men*, 67; Mathews Archives Box 25 R.

33 Langston Hughes et al., *A Pictorial History of African Americans* (New York, 1983), 171–172, 183; Mathews County Will Book 1:1; Census 1850, 1860.

34 The pension records of James H. Brooks, who served in the Union Navy, reveal that his father, Richard Brooks, a slave who worked as a timber-cutter, set out to visit his wife, Patsy, without a pass and was caught and beaten by a patroller. Afterward, he fled. William Brooks indicated that he belonged to Mrs. Judy Brooks but stayed with his young master, James Brooks. Williams and Brooks family tradition indicates that these men went to Gloucester Point, reached Hampton Roads by March 25, 1862, and promptly enlisted in the navy (Brooks, *Names on Record*, I, 11, 20).

35 Brooks, *Names on Record*, I, 11, 20, 23, 27–28, 35, 48, 71–72, 82; USNWRO, *Official Records*, Series 1, Vol. VII, 294, 324–325.

36 Smart's Mill, which was situated on the headwaters of the North River and close to Route 14, is shown on a Union Army map that was included in General Wistar's report.

37 An undated and unsigned letter in Warner T. Taliaferro's distinctive handwriting, addressed to General Keyes, stated that the people of Gloucester and Mathews Counties had been subjected to thievery and other indignities at the hands of Keyes' men, particularly those in the navy. He said that Mr. Smart's valuable gold watch was stolen and that the home of Mrs. Roy, a respected gentlewoman, had been robbed. Other atrocities reportedly were committed (Ludwell Lee Montague, *Gloucester County in the Civil War*, 170–172).

38 This suggests that the boat was being outfitted as a fire ship.

39 Ludwell Lee Montague reported that the homes destroyed by the *Crusader's* crew belonged to Boswell Kirwin (who was old, blind and bedridden), John Kirwin, Raphael Davis, Chester Minton, Joshua Gale, Mrs. Lucy Gale (a poor widow), Robert White, and Bartlett

White. He also said that the captain of the *Crusader* claimed that Boswell Kirwin was a notorious rebel and blockade runner. Montague offered no documentation to support his statements (Montague, *Civil War*, 62).

40 If these were the buildings burned in 1863, it is unclear why assessors failed to make note of it when they began compiling tax records in 1866 and 1868. Of course, if they didn't visit each property in the county, they may not have known that the buildings had been destroyed.

41 http://infoweb.newsbank.com; USNWRO, *Official Records,* Series 1, Vol. V, 361; Vol. IX, 92, 203, 205, 207–209, 305, 318; www.encyclopediavirginia.org/Civil_War_Widows; White, *Mathews Men*, 66; Charles, *Newspapers*, 106–108; Mathews County Land Tax Lists 1872.

42 Mathews men in the Mathews Light Artillery and the Mathews Light Dragoons were nearby at Chaffin's Bluff (Montague, *Civil War*, 35).

43 According to Ludwell Lee Montague, Wood gave "his now famous 'boats-on-wheels' to Acting Master [John Yates] Beall, who had them carried off to Mathews" (Montague, *Civil War*, pp.73, 75). To date, no documentary sources have come to light that support this statement.

44 He signed all of his correspondence J. Taylor Wood, which suggests that he normally went by his middle name.

45 In 1938, Harry C. Bland, an elderly Confederate veteran, described Wood's expedition to the Rappahannock. His account of the events that transpired and the capture of the *Reliance* and *Satellite* differed significantly from John Taylor Wood's official report. Bland, who attributed the events to 1862 instead of 1863, apologized for his lapses in memory (Smith, Nellie Shackleford, comp., *Reminiscences: Confederate Soldiers of Gloucester County, Virginia* [Gloucester, 2001], 59–60).

46 USNWRO, Series 1, Vol. V, 344–346, 370–371, 398; Vol. IX, 529–530; E.B. Long and Barbara Long, comp., *The Civil War Day By Day* (Garden City, New Jersey, 1981), 400, 472; R.U. Johnson and C. C. Buel, comp., *Battles and Leaders of the Civil War* (New York, 1956), Vol. IV, 598–599, 705, 764, 766. In 1865, after the surrender at Appomattox, Wood went to Georgia as part of President Davis's inner circle. Davis was captured, but Wood escaped and managed to reach Cuba. From there he moved to Halifax, Nova Scotia, where he and his family settled permanently. Wood's wife was President Zachary Taylor's daughter (http://en.wikipedia.org/wiki/john_taylor_wood).

47 These men should not be confused with the so-called Confederate Marine Corps, a branch of the Confederate Navy that trained at Drewry's Bluff.

48 He witnessed John Brown's execution at Harper's Ferry in late 1859.

49 W.W. Baker, one of Beall's men, said that there were 18 in the group, but a report by a Union Navy officer indicated that Beall had 25 men.

50 www.unc-library; Cameron S. Moseley, *Encyclopedia of Virginia Biography* (Richmond, 2006), Vol. I, 417–418; ORCW, Series 1, Vol. 29, Part I, 639–640; Series 2, Vol. VIII, 279–282; USNWRO, *Official Records,* Series 1, Vol. V, 361; Vol. IX, 203, 205, 207–209, 305, 318.

51 Wistar meant that if his cavalrymen had to retreat from Mathews Courthouse, utilizing Route 14, and another group of cavalrymen were stationed at Fort Nonsense to cover their withdrawal, they could safely reach County Route 602 (Burke Pond Road) and escape to Gloucester Courthouse by means of Route 198, or they could move toward the courthouse on Route 14. It was a judicious strategy, for a regiment of Confederate cavalry encamped at Plain View, in Gloucester County, learned about General Wistar's plans and intended to confront him (USNWRO, *Official Records*, Series 1, Vol. IX, 236).

52 An abbreviated version of General Wistar's letter can be found in the Official Records, whereas the original letter, which provides more detail, is preserved in the National Archives.

53 Union Army Major J.G. Foster informed his commanding officer that many of the troops at his disposal were too sick to undertake long marches, although they could carry out expeditions by water. He added that the only men healthy enough to march to Mathews County to "scour" the countryside were his black infantrymen.

54 Four of these gunboats belonged to the navy and four to the army.

55 Bohannon's dwelling, once the site of the Mathews Academy and Thomas Edwards's home, became known as Edwards Hall or Hurricane Hall II (MCHS, *Old Houses*, Vol. II, 11–13).

56 That is, Route 14 east.

57 Guion and his men would have marched west along Route 198.

58 Mary T. Hunley Edwards kept a diary in which she gave a personal account of the Union military raids on Gwynn's Island (Mathews Archives Box 71 R). A transcription of her narrative has been published by the Gwynn's Island Museum.

59 In 1860 David Ripley, a seaman in his 30s, was living in Mathews County with his wife and children (Mathews County Census 1860).

60 Charles, *Newspapers,* 108; USWD, *Official Records*, Series 1, Vol. XVIII, 359–361, 462; Series 4, Vol. II, 301–303; Vol. 29 Part II, 104, 116, 205–207, 236, 267, 653–655; USNWRO, *Official Records*, Series 1, Vol. VIII, 611; Vol. IX, 30–32, 45–46, 103, 154, 207–210, 310–311; National Archives Record Group 393–5063, Letters received, Department of Virginia Headquarters, U. S. Forces, Yorktown, Virginia, September 29, 1863; W.W. Baker, *Memoirs of Service with John Yates Beall* (Richmond, 1910) 17–18, 24–27; Isaac Jones Wistar, *An Autobiography of Isaac Jones Wistar, 1827–1905* (Philadelphia, 1914), 424–425. An account of the 148th New York Infantry's expedition was published in a magazine in December 1874. The writer claimed that as soon as the infantry reached Mathews Courthouse, a band of Confederates hastily departed. He said that he and some of his comrades sought out the courthouse and went to sleep on some of its benches. He said that when he awoke the next morning, he found that he had been using a decapitated chicken for a

pillow. He claimed that some of Colonel Guion's men chatted with a few local citizens and encountered "a portly man in the decline of life, whose stove pipe had suggested the days of Patrick Henry, shad-bellied coat and pants with the time-honored flap in front, all indicated the Old Virginia gentleman." They asked the man whether Jefferson Davis had lice, and then drowned out his response with gales of laughter (Anonymous, *Home Mail*, I [1874], 178).

61 The Burke farm was near the Mathews Convenience Center and should not be confused with the location known as Burkes Mill, which lay several miles further west.

62 Baker, *Memoirs,* 27–28; Mathews Archives Accession No. 37–9; *Richmond Daily Enquirer*, October 15, 1863; www.infoweb.newsbank.com; *Macon Daily Telegraph*, October 21, 1863. In 1922 a Confederate veteran, when referring to Sands Smith II's ordeal, said that "one of Mathews County's sons was dragged for miles along the road and finally hung on a tree at the home of Mr. John Haynes" (White, *Mathews Men*, 66)

63 Although the Union Navy's official records make reference to destroying torpedoes found in the James, York, Pamunkey, and Rappahannock Rivers, no information has come to light suggesting that any were discovered in Mobjack Bay or in the North, East or Piankatank Rivers.

64 Charles, *Newspapers*, 109–110; *Hartford Daily Courant*, Hartford, Connecticut, January 30, 1864; *Evening Union*, Washington, D.C, January 29, 1864; *Philadelphia Inquirer*, Philadelphia, Pennsylvania, May 17, 1864; www.infoweb.newsbank.com; USNWRO, *Official Records,* Series 1, Vol. V, 484–485, 564; Vol. IX, 236; Vol. XXXIII, 208, 247, 253–256, 604, 649, 658, 671; Mathews County Military and Pension Record of Indigent Soldiers in 1864; Marriage Register Book 1.

65 County justices were elected for the first time in May 1852, in accord with the 1851 state constitution, and served four year terms. Therefore, the terms of the Mathews justices elected in 1860 would have expired in 1864, the year that the new elections were held (Mathews County Commissions 1864–1869).

66 Mathews County Commissions 1864–1869; Deed Book 1:6–11; Subpoena Docket 1854–1863; Census 1850, 1860.

67 White, *Mathews Men*, 66–67; MCHS, *Historic Homes and Properties,* Vol. II, 21–23; Mathews Archives Box 21 R.

68 One participant was Major Giles Buckner Cooke, who went on to serve as the rector of Kingston Parish. He kept a diary from June 1864 to April 1865 in which he described the siege of Petersburg and the Battle of the Crater. He died in 1937 and was the surviving member of General Robert E. Lee's staff (Mathews Archives Boxes 21 R, 23 R).

69 Curiously, the coat of Union Army Colonel Ulric Dahlgren, which had been removed from his corpse in March 1864 in King and Queen County, allegedly found its way to Mathews County. When queried about it, Mathews citizens reportedly were indignant. Later, the coat was found in Norfolk (Charles, *Newspapers*, 111–112).

70 Long et al., *Day By Day*, 512–513, 652; Robertson, *Civil War Virginia,* 152–153, 165–167, 171; USNWRO, *Official Records,* Series 1, Vol. V, 361, 561–562; Vol. IX, 92, 203, 205, 207–209, 305, 318; James Henry Lane Letter Book, Matehs Archives Box 25 R).

10

Binding the Wounds
1866–1880

Aftermath

During the Civil War, more than 200 military engagements occurred within the state of Virginia. Throughout the rural countryside, crops and livestock were gone, and countless homes, mills, and other businesses were irreparably damaged or had succumbed to neglect. Some 20,000 to 30,000 Virginia soldiers lost their lives and thousands of others were permanently maimed. Confederate money and bonds were worthless, inflation was at an all-time high, legal tender was almost nonexistent, and the state's economy was ruined. At least 25,000 white Virginians subsisted on army rations for the first six months after the surrender at Appomattox, as did many of the 36,000 ex-slaves who also lacked the basic necessities. As one former bondsman put it, the ex-slave was "free from the old plantation, but he had nothing but the dusty road under his feet. He was free from the old quarter that once gave him shelter, but a slave to the rains of summer and the frosts of winter." Similarly, a former Confederate general proffered that newly freed blacks had "nothing but freedom." Some Northern politicians favored giving freedmen 40-acre homesteads formed out of land confiscated from Southerners whose taxes were in arrears. This gave rise to rumors that freedmen would get "40 acres and a mule." Blacks and whites struggled to redefine their roles in society, often with mixed results.

Throughout the South, real estate values plummeted. Also gone was the slaveholder's monetary investment in slaves—typically the Tidewater farmer's most valuable asset. The damage to Virginia's industrial infrastructure was so massive that the state that didn't attain prewar production levels for several years. The loss of manpower and draft animals, the overgrown agricultural land, and labor shortages impacted the economy on a local and regional level. Undoubtedly, many returning soldiers were confronted with what seemed like an insurmountable array of problems. Neglected farmland had sprouted young pines and dense vegetation that had to be cleared away before plowing could be done. Predators had had a chance to multiply in the underbrush, creating problems for those fortunate enough to own poultry and other livestock. Most farmers' agricultural equipment was worn out or obsolete, and they lacked the disposable income they needed to replace it (if indeed new implements were available). According to an article that appeared in the *Baltimore Sun,* Mathews County farmers, like their counterparts in other parts of Virginia, were finding it difficult to hire freedmen by the year. Local watermen suffered, too, for their boats had been lost or destroyed and their opportunities to sell their catch profitably were very limited. Recovery took time, money, ingenuity, and a tremendous amount of hard work. For many veterans, the battle for economic survival was almost as arduous as the war itself. Virginia's General Assembly enacted legislation that was in effect from 1867 to 1894, providing disabled veterans with prostheses and other benefits. The Board of Commissioners on Artificial Limbs coordinated the program and oversaw the distribution of aid. Applicants had to document their military service, provide a detailed medical history, and describe the nature of their disability, all substantiated by certification from their local court.[1]

The Local Political Scene

In the wake of the surrender at Appomattox, Governor Francis H. Pierpont of Virginia's Restored Government became the state's chief executive. In an official broadside published on August 2, 1865, he informed county court justices that in accordance with the State Constitution of 1864, no one who had supported the Confederacy could vote or hold office unless specifically approved by an act of the General Assembly.[2] Therefore, he required each newly elected officeholder to take a loyalty oath, crafted by the United States Congress in 1862, certifying that he had never "voluntarily borne arms against the United States," engaged in hostility against the United States, or held an office, performed a function, or supported "a pretended government." All duly elected officeholders, including Constitutional Officers, who could not (or did not) sign the oath were excluded from holding office and were subject to replacement. The policies established by Governor Pierpont created insurmountable problems, for it was extremely difficult to find eligible men who were literate and had the basic skills their jobs required.

In May 1864, John H. Blake, Benjamin B. Dutton, Houlder Hudgins, and William H. Hudgins had been elected Mathews County's court justices for the third district; they were supposed to serve from June 27, 1864, to August 1, 1868. However, on account of Governor Pierpont's stance, all four men were disqualified, and they were replaced by Henry Bell, Thomas Davis, John W. Dixon, and William J. Winder, who all signed the loyalty oath on September 1, 1865. The newly elected men's positions, and that of Thomas G. Weston, another Supervisor, were confirmed by Governor Pierpont. Like the men they displaced, their terms expired on August 1, 1868. Bell, a house carpenter from Delaware, went on to become a member of the House of Delegates. Dixon, who became a delegate to the State Constitutional Convention of 1867–68, served briefly as a court justice but resigned, and on August 27, 1866, he was replaced by Edmund Winder.

The First Vote.
Harper's Weekly, *November 16, 1867.*

Second district justices Albert Diggs, Thomas M. Hunley, Walter G. Lane, and Mathew Gayle took the loyalty oath on September 1, 1865, and like Mathews County's other justices, they were authorized to serve until August 1, 1868.[3] Surviving court records show that Gayle replaced former justice James B. Thurston. All of these men's certificates of appointment were endorsed by Governor Pierpont. Thanks to gaps in the records, it is unclear who served as the first district's justices, but George K. Brooks, Winslow Foster, and Humphrey Hudgins seem to have been qualified to serve. During 1866, four blank books were purchased from the Commonwealth of Virginia for use by Mathews County's clerk of court.

John H. Diggs was elected Mathews County's sheriff. He posted a bond on September 1, 1865, and was to serve until January 1, 1867. He replaced William H. Miller, who had been duly elected on May 26, 1864. John Lloyd Minter was elected constable for the second magisterial district on August 3, 1865. Lemuel W. Hudgins became the first district's constable, and Walter G. Hudgins was elected constable for the third district. Each of these men posted bonds and was qualified to sign the loyalty oath that Governor Pierpont required of all officeholders. Shepherd G. Miller was chosen as clerk of court and William M. Brownley as Commissioner of the Revenue, the positions to which they had been elected in 1864, and Booker M. Miller began serving as Mathews County coroner. An undated newspaper clipping found among chancery court documents indicates that in late November or early December 1865 a group of people in Mathews County asked Governor Pierpont to appoint an officer to organize a local militia to deal with the potential threat posed by ex-slaves who were acquiring arms and ammunition.

In autumn 1865, elections were held to choose representatives to the General Assembly. John T. Seawell was sent to the House of Delegates, representing Mathews and Gloucester Counties, and Warner T. Taliaferro Jr. became the state senator for Mathews, Gloucester, Middlesex, King and Queen, King William, and Essex Counties. Both of these men would have been ineligible for public office had they been unwilling to sign the loyalty oath. Delegate Henry F. Bell represented Mathews County in the General Assembly during 1869–71, whereas William K. Perrin served a senatorial district that included Gloucester, Mathews, Middlesex, and King and Queen Counties. Bell was replaced as delegate by Thomas J. Christian, who served during 1871 and 1873. By January 1874, he had been ousted by C.A. Bohannon and Benjamin F. Bland had become state senator. Both men still held office in 1879 but were turned out a year later. In 1880, H.F. Bell became delegate and James G. Cannon was elected state senator. [4]

Adjusting to Change

According to James Henry Lane, a former Confederate general and the son of hotelier Walter G. Lane, a small number of Union troops stayed on in the Mathews County seat after the surrender at Appomattox. He developed a cordial relationship with the provost marshal, Captain A.O. Hitchcock, who had a sergeant and a detachment of troops under his command. Lane said that he clashed with the sergeant from time to time over his allowing his men to let their hungry horses devour his small corn crop. In an October 5, 1865, letter, Lane said that he and the sergeant had had a loud argument that prompted "the Yankees [to come] out of the Court-House to see what was the matter" and added that he seemed to have a penchant for getting into trouble. On one occasion, Lane told Hitchcock that one of his proudest moments was when Stonewall Jackson recommended him as commander of one of his largest brigades. He admitted that he had "taken the oath & applied for pardon because I could see no hope & believed that the Confederacy was dead." When queried by Hitchcock about what he would do if he "could have things [his] own way," Lane said that he "would establish a Southern Confederacy and the North and South should be two separate & independent nations." When Hitchcock asked what he thought conditions would be like under those circumstances, Lane said that he didn't know, "yet I prefer our independence as a nation, separate & distinct from the North." He said that "whatever might be my regrets at the failure of our cause & whatever might be my feelings now," he had taken the oath and as a gentleman "knew what importance to attach to such a step." He went on to say that "Open hostility to the U.S. government now could do no one any good & might result in much harm" and added that although he had done everything he could for the Confederate cause, since "our subjugation, I have been very prudent in expressing my opinions." It is likely that many local citizens shared Lane's views and conducted themselves similarly during the war's aftermath.

Captain W.P. Hudgins, a Mathews County shipbuilder's son, exemplifies the adaptability of the human spirit. Hudgins, a college graduate and teacher, opened a school before the war. However, when Virginia joined the Confederacy, he was among the first to enlist and joined the 40th Virginia

Regiment, convinced that the Southern cause was right. He was severely wounded at Gaines Mill and had to retire from the active military, but he became one of the Confederate government's civil servants. After Sherman's infamous march to the sea cut the Confederacy in two, he was put in charge of the Trans-Mississippi Department's post office and treasury departments. After the war, Hudgins returned to teaching and established another private school. Although he accepted the failure of the cause for which he had fought, he believed that the loss was "the will of God" and "not of men."[5]

Spirit and Pride

Despite four years of war and numerous hardships, in September 1865 a jousting tournament was held at Mathews Courthouse.[6] These equestrian events, popular in the South during the nineteenth century, gave male riders (or "knights") a chance to demonstrate their horsemanship and compete on behalf of young females who would become part of a "court" that included a queen and her attendants. The finely-dressed riders usually wore badges trimmed with ribbons and rosettes. Each horseman carried a ribbon-decorated wooden lance and his horse's bridle had matching streamers. General Lane, who was considered a local hero, was asked to serve as the tournament's chief marshal but declined. However, at the urging of family and friends, he finally agreed to officiate on the field and at a ceremony in which the queen was crowned. After the tournament, light refreshments were served in a nearby orchard. Then, the queen and her attendants boarded a carriage and rode through the village, followed by the knights and chief marshal on horseback. The procession ended at the Odd Fellows Hall, where there was a dance.

A few days after the tournament, a Union Navy steamer unexpectedly appeared at a wharf near Mathews Courthouse and Lane was arrested. Later, he learned that he was accused of making secessionist speeches, purportedly saying that no knight should be able to participate in the tournament unless he had served in the Confederate military. Provost marshal A.O. Hitchcock, who knew Lane, allowed him to stay at his family's hotel until he was taken to Fort Monroe, noting that he would not put Lane in his "dirty & filthy prison" unless specifically ordered to do so. When Lane reached Fort Monroe, he appeared before General Miles, who accused him of expressing "disloyal sentiments" at the tournament. Witnesses, including Dr. James H. Garnett and some Northerners who had attended the tournament, denied that Lane had said anything of the sort and ultimately he was released. According to a Trenton, New Jersey newspaper, Dr. Garnett was then charged with the offence and sent to Richmond to appear before General Terry. Lane, upon reflection, concluded that the Union Army sergeant commanding the soldiers at Mathews Courthouse had leveled the accusations at Dr. Garnett and him and told family members about another man who was arrested. He said a fellow named Smith had whipped a black man, a government agent, with his cane for "ungentlemanly conduct" and that he, too, was taken to Fort Monroe and imprisoned. Lane was convinced that this event had given rise to the arrests that occurred. He said that the provost marshal had invited him to visit his home in Massachusetts if he ever went north. Lane said that according to General Miles, whom he had encountered at Fort Monroe, "We are a noisy & turbulent set of secessionists down here & not disposed to behave ourselves."[7]

Picking Up the Reins of Government

In June 1865, state officials authorized the collection of local real estate and personal property taxes. Mathews County officials seem to have compiled lists of taxpayers and the sums they owed, based on former years' estimates.[8] During 1866 and 1867, a significant number of properties were attributed to male property owners' estates, perhaps because the overwhelming amount of probate work that wartime deaths brought to county courts. Tax records compiled from 1868 through at least 1870 suggest that very little new construction occurred, although Marshall B. White added some taxable improvements to his property on the North River. In 1872, tax officials made note of buildings that had been destroyed, probably late in the war. Some local people had to forfeit their land because their taxes were in arrears; assessors, when identifying real estate that had been mortgaged, noted that its owner of record was "to pay." Without a doubt, times were hard. In 1865, Barzilla Kirwan, Joseph Bohannon, and Joseph Smith went to court to publicly acknowledge their debts and admit that they had used their real estate, livestock, and personal belongings as collateral. Merchants located outside of Mathews County sometimes tried to collect debts incurred by local citizens before or immediately after the war. For example, in 1866 E.H. Stabler and Company of Baltimore brought suit against George W. Simmons in an attempt to recover what he owed the firm for medicinal items, paint brushes, cologne, and black ink. The firm also sued several other people. Lists of local taxpayers included several small properties owned by people identified as "colored," a term that became increasingly common as time went on.[9] Tax records for 1867 indicate that the collective value of all of the county's watercraft—defined as ships, barges, and boats—was $16,710. This sum was comparable to the value of all of the livestock in the county.

From 1867 through 1869 the printed books issued to Virginia's tax officials had a special column for the names of white males age 21 or older. There also were columns in which officials were supposed to list the names of black males age 21 or older, along with the locations in which they were living. Mathews County's tax assessor used the latter column to note whether taxable black males were homeless, had land of their own, or were residing on someone else's land. For instance, Samuel Armistead reputedly had "no particular home," whereas Kit Armistead was "at John H. Armistead's." On the other hand, William R. Armistead was described as "transient." A large number of Mathews County taxpayers of both races were living on land owned by others, suggesting that throughout the county there was a substantial increase in the number of sharecroppers or tenants. Occasionally, the Mathews County assessor noted that a black man lived in a specific location like Cow Neck but had "no particular home." During the postwar period, when Virginia's economy was struggling, large farms were often subdivided into smaller parcels that were sold. This pattern, evident in Mathews County, was replicated throughout Virginia, particularly in the Tidewater region where many farmers had relied on slave labor. The tax code was revised extensively in 1870, and many types of personal property were deemed taxable, just as they had been during the 1850s. This time, however, taxes were imposed on agricultural and machinist's tools, watercraft, and felled timber, along with the usual luxury items, such as musical instruments and gold watches. Tax records reveal that in 1870, nobody in Mathews County had annual income that exceeded $1,500. A total of $29,950 had been invested in businesses that did not require licenses.[10]

Coping with Economic Hardship

Between 1866 and 1869 several Mathews County women went to court to seek an exemption from so-called "stay laws" that placed a moratorium on suits for the collection of debts. For example, John L. Knight's widow and administrator, Elizabeth, asked for the right to collect his debts because she needed the interest they accrued. Mrs. Knight, who seems to have been unaware that the Confederate government's legal code no longer applied, referred to the March 23, 1862, "stay law," passed shortly after Confederate President Jefferson Davis had declared martial law. On the other hand, William E. Thomas's widow, Elizabeth, who sought to recover debts owed to his estate, made reference to a stay law the Confederate government enacted on March 3, 1865. John Sparrow's widow, Charlotte, also wanted the right to recover a $130 debt that William H. Winder owed to her late husband's estate. In all of these instances, Mathews County's court justices, in accord with federal law, authorized the women to take legal action against their debtors.

Fiduciary records, specifically inventories and estate sales of Mathews County residents from 1868 on, shed a great deal of light upon the material culture of the time. For example, a list of the contents of Walter G. Lane Sr.'s Mathews Courthouse hotel provides detailed information on the building's furnishings and some of the amenities provided to guests. Census records for 1870 reveal that many households included one or more unrelated people, perhaps boarders or extended family members who banded together for mutual support. On account of financial hardship, many rural landowners were forced to subdivide their farms and modify their agricultural practices to accommodate the loss of slave labor. These changes are reflected in agricultural census records. For example, at Centreville (Woodstock), the widowed Mary H. Tabb, who was obliged to sell off some of her farmland, had less than half of her acreage under the plow in 1870, and grew only corn as a field crop. She had also sold off most of her livestock. By 1880 Mrs. Tabb's farm had become much more productive and there was more diversity in the crops she raised than there was before the war. She also placed more emphasis on animal husbandry.

When newly freed blacks became farm laborers, they were hired for a specific wage and sometimes occupied the slave cabins on their employer's property. Laborers usually received weekly rations, usually three pounds of bacon, a peck and a half of corn meal, and some vegetables. Many farms were operated by sharecroppers or leaseholders, who built their own cabins and worked for a stake in the crop rather than a specific sum. Often, they had the right to cut firewood and were given a small plot of ground next to their cabin, where they could plant a garden or to raise a cow or pig. Sometimes, blacks chose to remain on or near the plantations on which they'd formerly been slaves.

The state's economy gradually improved, and by the mid-1870s some new construction had begun to occur in Tidewater Virginia. However, many people continued to struggle financially. When the going got tough for Yancey Sleet, the owner of Sleet's Hotel in Mathews Courthouse, he mortgaged his personal property; however, by 1882 he was obliged to sell his real estate, which included his hotel and the 32 acres on which he had a stable and barn. Northern speculators with expendable capital sometimes seized the opportunity to purchase cheap land, often for paying back taxes. Marylanders Benjamin B. Brown and C.S. Malby purchased Mathews County property, as did Benjamin D. Metcalf, who was from Maine, and John Taylor, a New Jersey native. Court records demonstrate that people sometimes invested in large farms they subdivided or quickly resold in hope of turning a quick profit. Occasionally Northern buyers occupied the land they purchased. For example, Byron Sutherland, who had been in a Pennsylvania regiment and was wounded twice, purchased a Mathews County farm known as The Sycamores, near Hicks Wharf, and he was living there in 1915 when he died. A few months after Sutherland's demise, his widow put his Mathews County property on the market.

In 1867, the owner of Oakley Place tried to sell his property. His realtor placed an advertisement in the *American Farmer,* stating that his 578-acre farm had an abundance of arable land and was on the waters of Milford

Haven but within sight of Westville, the county seat. He said that although the farm's main dwelling "was burned during the war," its walls were still standing, making it possible to rebuild economically. There were numerous outbuildings, including two barns and cottages for workers, agricultural equipment, livestock, and a large peach orchard. There also was "a large and substantial steam saw and grist mill, being erected since the war" that was two stories high, had a fireproof roof, and was capable of producing large quantities of lumber. A track ran from the mill to a wharf where vessels could take aboard lumber or grain. A steamboat carrying mail from Norfolk and Old Point Comfort stopped at the wharf, which was 2½ miles away, but a daily boat was expected by summer. The real estate agent stated that "The farm is rented at present to freedmen on shares—vegetable garden, &c., for use of house." A plat that was made in February 1867, when the farm was divided into large plots, reveals that the *American Farmer*'s realtor greatly exaggerated Oakley's proximity to Westville and Milford Haven, for it was located midway up Morris Creek's east side. Throughout the 1860s, 70s, and 80s, numerous real estate ads for Mathews properties appeared in publications in Baltimore, Philadelphia, and New York, documenting local citizens' attempts to attract Northern buyers with money to spend.[11]

Mathews County's Processioners Records

In April 1867, Thomas M. Hunley, a court-appointed special commissioner, was ordered to collect evidence of lost deeds. Because most of Mathews County's legal records were lost or destroyed during the war, it would have been very difficult for local court justices and other officials to carry out their mandated duties. Those functions included making an accurate record of land that was bought or sold, settling boundary disputes, and overseeing the distribution of deceased people's estates. Local officials addressed this problem by having every parcel of land in the county "processioned"—that is, having properties' boundaries walked and then marked—in the presence of those who owned contiguous acreage. This time-honored procedure was first used by parish vestries during the eighteenth century as a means of curbing boundary line disputes.[12] On October 4, 1866, several months before the Reconstruction Acts were imposed upon the state of Virginia, court-appointed processioners commenced work in Mathews County. Three sitting county justices—George K. Brooks, Humphrey Hudgins, and William F. Armistead—were designated Processioners for Militia District Number 1 on November 6, 1866, and were ordered to commence work. Justices Winslow Foster, Thomas G. Weston, and George Brooks were assigned to Militia District Number 2 and commenced visiting the properties within their territory.[13] These respected local citizens, like colonial vestrymen, went from one piece of property to another, making note of each parcel's boundaries and reaffirming them in the presence of the landowner and at least two neighbors. Processioners' records, though less detailed than deeds, would have made it possible for local landowners and public officials to establish agreed-upon property boundaries, thereby forming a basis for future land transfers and the division of estates.[14]

In 1867, the processioners who visited some of the properties in Mathews Courthouse described the boundaries of the three lots across from the courthouse, delimited by Main Street, Court Street, Church Street, and Brickbat Road. In 1867, Yancey Sleet, a farmer-turned-hotelier, was credited with the northernmost lot in this long, narrow block. His half-acre parcel, the "tavern lot," abutted north on Church Street and south upon the quarter-acre lot owned by Benjamin Williams, a house carpenter. Williams's lot was near the center of the block and contained what was left of the old county jail. To the south of Williams' lot and abutting Brickbat Road was a corner lot containing an office occupied by Dr. Silas C. White.

Tax records provide additional information on each of these lots. Sheriff John H. Dunlavy purchased the tavern lot around 1853 and retained it until 1862, when he conveyed it to Yancey Sleet. Sleet already owned the Benson Hotel, which was located on a 32-acre tract on the east side of Main Street and included an adjoining 17 acres known as the hotel woods. Sleet became overextended financially and mortgaged the Benson Hotel property in 1867. Although he sold off some of his holdings in an attempt to repay his debts, he borrowed money from William Lane in 1870, using as collateral what he called Sleet's Hotel and a piece of rural property. Again, he repaid his debts, but within three years' time he had to get a loan from the county's Overseers of the Poor. By 1875, Sleet was totally immersed in debt, and because he had defaulted on his loan, he lost all of the properties he had posted as collateral. Meanwhile, in April 1872, Dr. Silas C. White, the physician who during the 1860s rented and then bought the corner lot that contained an office, purchased the adjoining quarter-acre lot on which the old jail had stood, the property that carpenter Benjamin Williams sold to Sheriff John H. Dunlavy in 1867. Several months later when Dr. White sold both of his lots to William H. and Benjamin B. Dutton, he indicated that the property contained a drugstore.

On the south side of Brickbat Road and extending along Main Street was a half-acre parcel that in 1867 contained a store owned by Francis Armistead and attorney John W. Jarvis. Next door and to the west of the Armistead-Jarvis store lot, and fronting north on the courthouse green and Brickbat Road, was the one-third acre lot that Captain John Foster had acquired from Dr. William S. Thurston's estate in 1862. The Foster lot, which abutted south on John N. Armistead's six acres, contained Dr. Thurston's medical office and was property that Thurston had purchased from Christopher Tompkins's executor in 1840. From 1841 to 1863 the improvements on the lot had an assessed value of $800, a relatively substantial sum. By 1867, John Foster, like many of his contemporaries, had begun to struggle financially. He borrowed money from the Overseers of the Poor, using his farm as collateral, and because he was on the brink of bankruptcy, he transferred all of his personal estate to his aunt and her daughter. Ultimately, he was able to retain his small lot on Brickbat Road and seems to have converted Dr. Thurston's office into a store, which he sold to George E. Sleet in 1882.[15] When Sleet made improvements to Foster's store, he unwittingly encroached upon the courthouse green. He discovered his own error and in November 1883 brought it to the attention of the Mathews County Board of Supervisors, who agreed to sell him the miniscule quantity of land on which he had intruded.[16] A plat made in 1884 depicts the boundaries of the Foster/Thurston lot and the properties that flanked it, along with the sliver of public land Sleet obtained from the county.

To the west of Captain John Foster's lot and also abutting the courthouse green and Brickbat Road was a quarter-acre lot that belonged to John H. Dunlavy, who had purchased it from Benjamin G. Tompkins's estate in late 1861. Dunlavy's lot faced the county jail, extended west as far as Put In

Creek, abutted south on John N. Armistead's property, and contained improvements whose assessed value was $300. In 1845 when Benjamin G. Tompkins, a licensed merchant and Christopher Tompkins' youngest son, received the quarter-acre lot as part of his inheritance, it contained a tailor shop worth $100. From the time of Benjamin G.'s death in 1847 until 1861, the tailor shop and the lot on which it stood were credited to his estate and its value remained constant. By 1867, Dunlavy, like his next-door neighbor John Foster, had fallen on hard times. He sold some of his acreage and personal possessions and in 1868 borrowed money from the Overseers of the Poor, using most of his remaining property as collateral. Dunlavy's creditors sued him, and in 1873 his lot on Brickbat Road, then described as one-half acre, was sold at auction to Napoleon B. Anderson.[17] In 1876, Lemuel James's wife, Maria, as one of Anderson's heirs, acquired the Dunlavy lot and put it into a trust for the benefit of Mary S. Hall and her children. However, in 1904, Mrs. Hall and her children, adults who lived in Norfolk, decided to sell their dwelling and triangular half-acre lot to F. Theodore Miller, whose name is shown on plats made in 1904 and 1916. This is the dwelling that was dubbed the Tompkins Cottage during the 1960s.[18]

No processioners records are currently available for Militia District 3, which ran along the east side of Main Street and the north side of Church Street. However, the historic Thomas James store, which came into the hands of John D. Jarvis and Elijah Barnum around 1847, had become Barnum's solely owned property by 1861. The store and the one-acre lot on which it stood were part of Barnum's estate from 1862 to 1893, at which time the "Barnum Store house lot" was purchased by William N. Trader and John W. Dixon Jr. in a sale resulting from a chancery suit. A topographic map made in 1877, which shows the central part of the courthouse community, indicates that there were relatively few buildings. On the north side of Church Street and to the east of Put In Creek were two structures, one of which was the Sleet (formerly Lane) hotel.[19] Only three structures were shown on the east side of Main Street within the county seat. To the southeast of Brickbat Road but above County Route 611 (Tabernacle Road) was Edwards Hall. Buildings were shown on the courthouse green and on the east side of Court Street, between Court and Main. A row of buildings was aligned on the south side of Brickbat Road and along the west side of Main

Street, below Brickbat. A map made in 1886 suggests that although nearly a decade had passed, relatively little new development had occurred.[20]

Other Mathews County Businesses

Census records for the Westville Township, which encompassed Mathews Courthouse, indicate that in 1860 and 1870 the community was home to a substantial number of people whose occupations were relatively lucrative. There were six physicians: Drs. Thomas G. Billups, John G. Bohannon, Thomas B. Lane, John H. Sears, N.W. Washington, and Silas C. White. Dr. Sears and George E. Sleet were hotelkeepers, G. Taylor Garrett was a practicing attorney, J.A. Cox Garrett was a druggist, and Joseph Owen was a postmaster. There were four blacksmiths (Beverley Dabney, John E. Foster, John R. Rodgers, and John White), and three wheelwrights (William M. Foster, William A. Green, and A.W. Marchant). Boot- and shoemakers included Robert Bailey, Joseph P. Forrest, and Marshall and William S. White. William F. Pugh was a tailor. Among the county officials living close to the seat of government were the clerk of court, the deputy clerk of court, the commissioner of revenue, the county surveyor, and the deputy sheriff. A total of 15 storekeepers selling general merchandize were living in Mathews Courthouse. C.C. Davis was also an agent for the Billups Champion Plow. The courthouse community was home to two clergymen, domestic servants, farmers, house carpenters, laborers, a land agent, oystermen, school teachers, shipbuilders, and washerwomen, plus many housewives and children. At least two local women ran boarding houses. During the late 1860s and early 1870s William A. Ransone repaired saddles, harnesses, reins, and other horse furniture. He sued Robert Sibley, for whom he had made a quilted saddle girth and done several repairs. Ransone was identified as a bricklayer in 1860, but by 1870 he had evidently become a farmer.

Oystering was a big business in Mathews County and many thousands of bushels of oysters were sent to Baltimore each year. Fishing on a commercial basis was also a lucrative pursuit. R.H. Respess and Son had a store on Gwynn's Island from 1874 to 1897 and another store at Pleasant Point. Many of the goods they sold came from Baltimore. In 1875, the *Baltimore*

Sun, which published business and financial news, announced that O.E. Maltby had purchased the fish guano factory that was located at New Point Comfort.[21]

Mathews Union Loyalists Claim Wartime Damages

In 1871, the United States Congress established the Southern Claims Commission (SCC), a federal agency charged with processing the claims of Union loyalists who requested reimbursement for goods confiscated by federal troops or property damage. The claims Mathews County citizens filed with the SCC's regional headquarters in Richmond shed a great deal of light on loyalists' contributions to the cause they supported. At least two Mathews County residents filed damage claims. Detailed documentation was required, and each claim had to be signed by witnesses qualified to attest to its accuracy. For example, in 1875 William H. Winder filed a compensatory claim, asserting that General Kilpatrick's men took one of his horses while it was in Larkin Davis's custody at Dunns Mill in Gloucester County. Winder said that Colonel Draper's men took an ox from his farm, butchered it, and then carried the meat aboard a gunboat at Cricket Hill. Winder's claim was denied, perhaps because he had enlisted in the Crab Neck Company in 1861, and thus was not a loyalist.

Samuel E. Richardson, a native of Anne Arundel County, Maryland, who moved to Mathews County between 1850 and 1860, filed a claim in

Gwynn's Island Viewed from Cricket Hill.
Harper's New Monthly Magazine, *Vol. 57, July 1878.*

1875, attempting to recover funds equivalent to the value of the personal property he lost. He said that General Kilpatrick's men set fire to his woods and swamps when trying to capture John Yates Beall and that he had lost 200 acres of timberlands and chestnut rail fencing. He added that he also had lost his dwelling and some other buildings, a boat, a double-barreled gun, 300 pounds of tobacco, five gallons of whiskey, an ox, a horse, a stallion, two horse harnesses, a lead and bridle, and some corn and bacon. Richardson, in an attempt to document his loyalty to the Union, said that although he had voted for the secessionist candidates to the State Convention, it was because he feared violence. He was drafted into the Confederate Army in 1862, but produced a letter from General Dix, who stated that in 1863 two people had vouched for his loyalty. To further substantiate his loyalty to the Union, Richardson named a witness, a black youth who was 15 when the war began. Richardson's claim was denied by federal officials who indicated that he insufficiently proved his loyalty.[22]

The Bureau of Refugees, Freedmen, and Abandoned Lands

In March 1865, Congress established the Bureau of Refugees, Freedmen and Abandoned Lands, a little-known branch of the War Department. Its purpose was to help ex-slaves become self-supporting and acclimated to a new way of life. The Bureau, which was authorized to exist for one year after hostilities ceased, was supposed to distribute food, clothing, and fuel to ex-slaves. The Freedmen's Bureau also had special courts that processed cases involving African Americans and could impose a maximum fine of $100 or three months in jail. Bureau personnel were authorized to seize private property that had been abandoned by its owners or to confiscate it from landowners whose taxes were in arrears.[23] Bureau officials typically subdivided confiscated acreage into small parcels that were leased to refugees who paid rent in crop-shares. The Bureau of Refugees' agents could negotiate labor contracts for ex-slaves and assure that they were provided with medical care and schooling, often in cooperation with the American Missionary Association and other private agencies. In July 1866, Congress extended the Bureau's mission indefinitely and granted it the authority to establish schools for freed people. The Bureau could provide schoolhouses or furnish materials from which they could be built and it could transport teachers to their teaching posts. However, the Bureau relied heavily on religious and philanthropic societies to recruit and pay teachers and provide them with instructional material.

During the seven years the Bureau was in existence, its officers usually worked with honorable and fair-minded local citizens. However, verbal agreements between blacks and whites, if made without the aid of a Freedmen's Bureau agent, sometimes resulted in labor disputes. Many ex-slaves went to Norfolk, Hampton, Richmond, and other cities hoping to find jobs, but they quickly discovered that urban areas already had a substantial African-American population living in ramshackle huts near the docks and marketplaces. Therefore, many blacks elected to stay in their old neighborhoods and sought employment as hired hands or became sharecroppers because they lacked the necessary funds to purchase land. For example, in 1867 freedmen were reportedly renting parcels at Oakley Place and raising vegetable crops in exchange for a place to live. Former slaves usually let their white employers know that they expected to be paid for the services they performed, making it patently clear that the old social order was gone.

After the war, many African Americans struggled to survive. Harper's Weekly, *May 21, 1870.*

Mathews County was one of the several counties within the Freedmen's Bureau's District Number 9. E.A. Chandler was the assistant superintendent of the Mathews County field office from April 1866 to March 1867. He was succeeded by F.K. Smith, who served from April 1867 to July 1867, with E.R. Williams as sub-assistant commissioner. They were followed by E.A. Chandler, who was in the Mathews County field office during July and August 1867, but was replaced by Thomas Rice, who was sub-assistant commissioner from August 1867 to December 1868. Freedmen's Bureau personnel sometimes referred cases to military authorities because local civil authorities were reluctant to take action when an offence was committed against blacks. Records maintained by the Freedmen's Bureau in Mathews County reveal that on at least one occasion, racial tensions culminated in violence. On March 31, 1866, the Bureau's assistant superintendent reported that a building used as a black church and schoolhouse had been burned. This may have been a reference to an arsonist's purposeful destruction of the buildings in Pugh's Thicket that belonged to the First Baptist Church's founding members. On October 9, 1866, Robert Miles, a black man, was summoned to appear before Mathews County's justices and accused of stealing goods from Chaplin B. Diggs's store. He was found guilty and fined $10.00. Two other black people, Fanny Miles and William Dixon, were found guilty of committing lesser offences and each was fined $5.00. These cases were processed by local authorities without interference from the Freedmen's Bureau, presumably because they were handled fairly.

Although the Bureau confiscated farms in many parts of Hampton Roads where there were large concentrations of former slaves, only one piece of Mathews County property seems to have been seized.[24] On September 22, 1865, the Taliaferro farm on the North River was taken under the orders of Captain C.B. Wilder, who identified it as abandoned property. The 500-acre farm reportedly consisted of 300 acres of cleared land and 200 acres of woodland, and the buildings, quarters, and barns on the property were said to be "in poor condition." However, an addendum to the Freedmen's Bureau records indicates that the Taliaferro property was "taken up by mistake" and was "restored by order of Colonel O. Brown." Real estate tax records indicate that the only Taliaferro who had land in Mathews County during the 1860s was State Senator Warner T. Taliaferro Jr., who owned Isleham, a 489½-acre farm on the west side of Blackwater Creek. Curiously, throughout the 1860s and early 1870s, Isleham's buildings had an assessed value of $900, an indication that they were not dilapidated. Taliaferro sold two small parcels to John H. Dunlavy and Nathan H. Walker in 1866. He moved to Portsmouth and in 1869 sold the rest of Isleham to Benjamin W. McCready for $10,000. The deed the two men exchanged indicated that Taliaferro had lived on the property until he sold it and that he had acquired it from his father, Warner T. Taliaferro Sr., in 1856. When Warner T. Taliaferro Jr. died in January 1881 at age 47, he was living in Norfolk and was described as a real estate agent. His obituary stated that he was a Mathews County native and the brother of General William B. Taliaferro of Gloucester. He had reportedly served in the state legislature for several years, and during the Civil War he was a major in the Army of Northern Virginia, serving as one of General Joseph J. Johnson's officers. As a state senator, Taliaferro had represented a district that included Essex, Gloucester, King and Queen, King William, Mathews, and Middlesex Counties in assembly sessions held between December 1865 and April 1867.[25] As a legitimate officeholder, he would have taken the loyalty oath that Governor Pierpont required, but he had obviously served the Confederacy as well.

Marriages Documented by the Freedmen's Bureau and Other Authorities

One of the Freedmen's Bureau's lesser known functions was validating former slaves' marriages, thereby legitimizing their children. This legal acknowledgement was in keeping with a February 27, 1866, act of the General Assembly. If the Freedmen's Bureau agents assigned to Mathews County compiled a register of slave marriages, it has been lost or destroyed. However, the registers kept by Bureau agents in Hanover and Gloucester Counties include information about ex-slaves from Mathews County who wed people in those areas. Each entry contains the married couple's names, ages, and previous marital status, along with their place of birth and parents' names. Also listed are husband's occupation and the month and year in which each couple wed. Thanks to these remarkable sets of records, we know that in August 1860, 20-year-old Mary Jane Smith of Mathews County, the daughter of Richard and Fanny Smith, married Henry Washington, a 20-year-old farmhand from Hanover County. The bride and groom were identified as slaves and Henry's parents as Arthur Hundlin and Betsey Washington. In 1870, the young couple was still living in Hanover County. In September 1863, Mary Jane Smith Washington's brother, Rave, a 25-year-old widower from Mathews, married Mary, the daughter of Archy and Dinah Onner of Hanover County. The marriage register also reveals that in July 1865, William Taylor, a Mathews County widower and farm laborer, married Ella Harris of Hanover County. Taylor was the son of William Taylor Sr. and Lucy Ann Braxton, whereas Harris was the daughter of John Harris and Mary Washington. In 1870 the Taylors and their four children were living in Hanover County.

The Freedmen's Bureau's marriage register for Gloucester County contains the names of Warner Washington, a 37-year-old house servant, and his wife, 36-year-old Jane Carter, a widow whose parents were Samuel and Molly Carter of Mathews County. By 1870, Jane Carter Washington, who was still living in Gloucester, appears to have been a widow. John Phillips, who was age 63 and was a Gloucester County native, married 54-year-old Pelina (Paulina) Forests, the daughter of James and Lorner Forests of Mathews County; after they wed, they resided in Gloucester. Warner Washington indicated that his father, Newman Cooper, was white and that his mother, Rose Booth, was black. Likewise, John Phillips, who identified Dawson Cook as his father and said that he was white, indicated that his mother, Fanny Phillips, was black. By the time these two couples' marriages were legally recognized, the Washingtons had four children and the Phillipses had eight.

The first African-American couple whose marital information was entered into the official Mathews County Marriage Register was G. Billups, a 22-year-old mariner, and Kitty Smith, who was age 20. The bride and groom were from Mathews and his parents were listed as A. and A.N. Billups and hers as P. and B. Smith. William Thornton performed the wedding ceremony on October 4, 1869. On October 26, 1869, Bailey Knight, a farmer and widower, wed M. Jackson, a spinster. The couple's parents were C. and P. Knight and B. and B. Jackson. During November 1869, three more black couples were married: William Underwood and Milly Hunley; T.H. White and M. Carter; and W.S. Carter and J. Brooks. In each case, information was recorded about the couples' ages and in most instances, their parents' names were mentioned. As time went on, more marriages among blacks were entered into the county's marriage register.[26]

Changes to the State Constitution

John W. Dixon served as Mathews and Gloucester Counties' delegate to the state constitutional convention held in 1867–68. When the so-called Underwood Constitution was put to a referendum in 1869, its disenfranchisement and test oath clauses were defeated, but the rest of the document was approved.[27] The Constitution of 1869 remained law until 1902, when a new state constitution was adopted; it included racial segregation and discriminatory voting restrictions. When Virginia's General Assembly convened in October 1869, it ratified the Fourteenth and Fifteenth Amendments to the U.S. Constitution. Therefore, in January 1870, Military District Number 1, created during Reconstruction, ceased to exist and Virginia was readmitted to the Union with a Gilbert C. Walker (a New Yorker) as governor. The Underwood Constitution wrought major changes in local government, one of which was the establishment of county Boards of Supervisors. An elected body, the Supervisors assumed many of the decision-making duties formerly left to county justices. The Constitution of 1869 created a statewide public school system and it established a different type of local court system. Each county court, which convened monthly, was to have a judge chosen by the General Assembly, and the courts themselves were placed within a judicial circuit that had a district court. In 1871, Mathews County was made part of the ninth judicial circuit, which included Essex, Gloucester, King and Queen, King William, Lancaster, Middlesex, and Northumberland counties; but in 1876 Mathews was made part of the eighth circuit.

The Constitution of 1869 also called for Virginia counties to be subdivided into townships with one elected supervisor apiece. Mathews County was subdivided into three townships or voting precincts: Chesapeake, Piankatank, and Westville. Each township was further subdivided into road districts, and men within each one were responsible for the maintenance of public roads. Those who did not fulfill their obligations could be fined and were subject to a Grand Jury indictment. In 1873, Ezekiel L. Hudgins and John A. Mason were indicted for not maintaining the public roads for which they were responsible, but when they were tried, they were exonerated and released without penalty. The overseers of public roads were elected by popular vote and within each district there were numerous polling places, usually country stores. A Road Book containing records dating from 1875 to 1891 lists the names of the men assigned to specific sections of public roads. In 1874, the magisterial district replaced the township as the basic unit of local government, but local citizens were still responsible for road maintenance. Minutes of meetings held in each district reveal how much money was spent on repairing bridges and maintaining roads. In September 1877, William M. Fitchett was indicted by a Grand Jury for failing to fulfill his obligations as surveyor of public road number one, which extended from the Gloucester County line to "the sign Board in Mathews County," crossing the North River Mill.

The Board of Supervisors appointed election officials and road surveyors and confirmed licenses. Those who failed to perform their mandated duties were summoned to court. Because the Mathews County's Board of Supervisors' earliest dated minutes have been lost or destroyed, it is uncertain when they convened for the first time or who they elected as chair. However, nearby Gloucester County elected its first Board of Supervisors as soon as the 1869 constitution became law and the Board held its first meeting on September 27, 1870. It is probable that Mathews County met in 1870, too. A fragmentary record book, whose first entry commences on page 402 and continues thereafter in uninterrupted sequence, contains the minutes of a Mathews County Board of Supervisors meeting that was held on June 18, 1887. These records reveal that much of the Supervisors' work still concerned the maintenance of public roads and the establishment of new ones at the request of local citizens. However, they also dealt with people who broke the law by dredging for oysters; they were summoned to appear.[28]

Fluidity in Demographics and Agricultural Patterns

Mathews County's earliest dated marriage register reveals that by January 1865 some "May–December" weddings had begun to occur. For example, Ann R. Douglas, who was 30, wed Thomas R. Riley, who was 61, and Eliza Callis (23) married mariner Francis R. Adams (73). The 22-year-old Amanda Callis wed Henry Callis, a 62-year-old farmer, and John M. Billups took as his bride Sophronia Miller, who was less than half his age. Despite these marriages (in which economics may have played a role), most people chose a life partner who was close in age. During the postwar period, many widows found a new spouse and many men sought a wife upon returning from the war. Within several years' time, more than 300 local weddings occurred.

Census records for 1870 reveal that Mathews County had a population of 6,200 people, a little more than half of whom (3,221) were female. Blacks of both sexes comprised a third of county's population. Statistics on illiteracy indicate that nearly 17 percent of the county's residents who were age 15 or older were unable to read or write and that illiterate black adults outnumbered illiterate white adults by a margin of almost three to one. Between 1860 and 1870 there was a dramatic change in the size of local farms. In 1860 Mathews County had six farms that were between 500 and 999 acres in size, but by 1870 there were only two. The number of farms that were between 50 and 499 acres was approximately the same, but there was significant growth in the number of small farms—that is, farms that were 49 acres or less. In 1870, the value of the agricultural implements owned by Mathews County farmers was very low, as was the dollar value of farm productivity. The county had five manufacturing establishments that provided employment for 16 people. Two were the watermills owned by Frank Billups of the Westville township and Christopher T. Browne of the Chesapeake township. Each of these mill owners reported that they had invested $2,000 in their mills, a sum that included the wheel and one stone, and their mills were in operation for six months of the year. Billups reported that his mill annually processed 1,600 bushels of corn that was converted into 1,800 bushels of meal worth $1,800, while Browne's processed 1,200 bushels of corn and wheat into 1,350 bushels of meal that was worth $1,485. Billups had two hired hands who were at least 16 years old and earned $50 a year, whereas Browne said that he had only one hired hand. A tide mill, the last surviving structure of its type in Virginia, is still located on Browne's Poplar Grove property. Circular sawn timber and mature cut nails, used in the tide mill's construction, have led architectural historians to date it to the second half of the nineteenth century.

Farmers used some mechanized farming equipment but relied on draft animals. Mathews County Historical Society.

By 1880, Mathews County's population had grown to a total of 7,501 people, 2,459 of whom were black. The county's inhabitants included a number of out-of-state residents: 109 Marylanders, three people from New Jersey, 26 New Yorkers, and six Pennsylvanians. This influx suggests that the local population was becoming less homogeneous than it had been in the past. Some of these newcomers may have been ex-soldiers who had visited Mathews County during the war and were attracted by its climate, bountiful natural resources, and cheap land.

In 1880 Mathews County had 902 farms. Although the average-size farm was 45 acres, there were 199 farms that were between three and nine acres, and one that was smaller. The value of all farm production was $195,356. At the time, the county had 15 manufacturing establishments that employed 26 men. During 1879 only three sailing vessels were built in Mathews County for a collective worth of $2,400. Most of the county's boat owners were in possession of vessels built in Middlesex, Nansemond, Isle of Wight, and Norfolk Counties. This suggests that the importance of Mathews County's shipbuilding industry diminished significantly after the Civil War. Agricultural census records reveal that in 1880 Mathews County's Westville Township had the largest quantity of acreage under the plow, the Piankatank Township had the second-most, and Chesapeake had the third-most. Twice as much land in the Piankatank Township was forested as in the Chesapeake Township and there was relatively little woodland in the Westville Township. Almost all Mathews County farmers grew crops of Indian corn, and Westville (which had more livestock) was the most productive of the three townships. Many farmers raised crops of oats and the Westville and Piankatank Townships were the most productive areas.[29]

Matters of Life and Death

A small volume called the "Register of Deaths, 1865–1874," preserved in the office of the Mathews County Clerk of Court, reveals that 479 local citizens died during that nine-year period—a relatively significant portion of the county's population. Many of these men, women, and children succumbed to communicable diseases and other illnesses eventually brought under control in the United States, thanks to vaccinations and treatment with antibiotics. For example, 44 people died from tuberculosis, six from measles, and 20 from typhoid fever. Four others died from smallpox, one from scarlet fever, one from erysipelas, and three from diphtheria. Pneumonia was relatively common and several people died of heart and kidney disease. Ten women died during childbirth and nine babies perished. There were ten accidental deaths by drowning and one suicide by hanging. One man died when struck by lightning and two succumbed to gunshot wounds. Other causes of death included dysentery and various gastric complaints. Although 36 people reportedly died of old age, roughly a third of all deaths occurred in children under age one.[30]

The Promise of Rail Transportation

During the 1850s plans were made to extend the newly-chartered Richmond and York River Railroad's tracks from Richmond to a terminal at West Point, at the head of the York River. However, the Civil War intervened and the rail line's tracks were destroyed in 1862 during the Peninsular Campaign. In 1866, investors raised enough money to rebuild the railroad, and by 1867 the Richmond and York River Railroad's tracks once again crossed the Pamunkey River and reached West Point. In June 1870, the General Assembly authorized the railroad company to extend a spur line to a point on the Chesapeake Bay, between the mouths of the Rappahannock and York Rivers. Company officials decided to run the railroad's tracks to the east side of the Piankatank River's mouth in Mathews County, but before the spur line could be built, the railroad company went bankrupt. When the owner of a 500-acre farm at the mouth of the Piankatank River tried to sell his property in 1873, he noted that a proposed extension of the Richmond and York River Railroad terminated on his land and said that the railroad right-of-way already had been surveyed. The landowner placed an advertisement in the *Philadelphia Inquirer*, probably hoping to pique the interest of Northern investors. He said that his farm, which overlooked the Chesapeake Bay, had a good dwelling and outbuildings, spanned three-quarters of a mile of waterfront, and had access to an abundance of fish and shellfish.

Although the proposal for extending the Richmond and York River Railroad to the mouth of the Piankatank River never came to fruition, in February 1880 a bill introduced into the House of Delegates authorized the Chesapeake and Ohio Railroad to build a branch line from a site near Hanover Junction (now Doswell) to a point on the Piankatank River where there would be access to the deep waters of the Chesapeake Bay. However, the C&O, perhaps yielding to Collis Huntington's influence, decided to extend its rail lines to Newport News. As late as 1890, the idea of bringing rail service to Mathews County was still being discussed, this time by means of a spur line from the Northern Neck.[31]

Waterborne Commerce

After the close of the Civil War, the Baltimore Steam Packet Company rebuilt its business. The company contracted for a new iron-paddle steamer, and in 1865 it acquired a small wooden paddler, the *Eolus*, built in New York in 1864. The *Eolus*, a 144-foot-long steamboat, made three trips a week, plying routes that linked Mathews and Gloucester Counties to Yorktown, and Norfolk and Old Point Comfort. On alternate days it went to Cherrystone on the Eastern Shore. In July 1865, the Baltimore Steam Packet Company became known as the Old Bay Line, which grew famous for its fine meals that included Mobjack Bay oysters and other delicacies harvested from the Chesapeake. The Old Bay Line's competitor, the Chesapeake Steamship Company, operated steamers on the York River that went to Old Point Comfort and Norfolk from 1850 through 1854; the independent ship *Monmouth*, whose home port was Baltimore, made trips to the East River. Iron gradually replaced wood in the construction of new ships, producing more durable vessels. In 1871, the Maryland Steamship Company built its first steamer, the iron-hulled *Enoch Pratt*, which in 1881 replaced the *Kent* on its Piankatank River route. The *Avalon* was rebuilt in 1882, and it, too, was placed on the Piankatank route for a short time. However, on September 4, 1882, she burned to the waterline at Freeport.

Mathews County's economy reaped tremendous benefits from steamboat service. Businesses sprung up close to the landings; passengers, freight and mail could flow to and from distant locations on a regular basis; and agricultural products and seafood could be sent to urban markets in exchange for manufactured goods. In early 1867, the Old Dominion Steamship Company of Norfolk took over the services formerly provided by the Atlantic Coast Mail Steamship Company, which operated between Norfolk, Richmond, and New York before it became defunct. The new company also absorbed the New York and Virginia Steamship Company, a potential competitor. An important component of the Old Dominion line's service was coastal trade with the New York market. This made it possible for Tidewater Virginia truck-farmers and watermen to ship their agricultural products, livestock, fish, and oysters to Norfolk for transshipment to New York. Last but not least, the Old Dominion line provided steamboat service to and from Richmond and Norfolk, stopping at landings on Mobjack Bay, the York and James Rivers, and the Eastern Shore. Although the Old Dominion Steamship Company experienced some financial reversals in the 1870s, its contribution to Tidewater Virginia's postwar economic development was immense.[32]

The New Point Comfort and Wolf Trap Lights

Even before the surrender at Appomattox, federal officials discussed the need to restore the southern coastline's navigational aids. In July 1864, Congress appropriated funds to reestablish these lights and to moor a lightship at the Wolf Trap. By July 1865, extensive repairs had gotten underway at the New Point Comfort lighthouse and its keeper's dwelling, work that was completed by the end of September. In 1870, mariners with vessels whose draft was 25 feet or more were warned not to come within half-a-mile of the lighthouse's east side. A fixed white flashing light was placed on the Wolf Trap shoal and the lightship marking it was removed. Despite these improvements, shipwrecks sometimes occurred, and in May 1877 it was announced that a green can buoy with the word "wreck" had been placed off New Point Comfort. A 199-ton schooner laden with lumber ran aground at New Point Comfort during a nor'easter in March 1879, but a tug deployed from Norfolk put it afloat. Then, in late August 1879, a strong storm swept up the Chesapeake Bay, wreaking havoc along the way. The Maryland Steamboat Company's steamer *Ken* was driven ashore near Fitchett's Wharf and an abandoned schooner went ashore on Gwynn's Island. Lashed to the schooner's mast was the body of a woman who was about 35 years old. Meanwhile, the sloop *Morgan*, from Mathews County, was beached at Cape Charles. More violent weather occurred in February 1880, and a three-masted schooner from New Jersey was driven ashore at New Point Comfort.

The New Point Comfort Lighthouse was among the few Chesapeake Bay light stations that had an African-American keeper. J. McHenry Farley, who served from 1871 to 1873, found his assignment very difficult, for he was isolated for months at a time and had difficulty procuring supplies from the mainland. In 1872, he asked the Light-House Board for an assistant keeper with whom he could share his duties or for an alternative arrangement that would enable him to obtain provisions more easily. Farley said that during the winter of 1871–72, he was unable to obtain firewood and as a consequence suffered greatly from the cold. He was a preacher in the Methodist-Episcopal Church and claimed that being unable to attend church was a hardship. In 1873, Farley was replaced by John D. Hudgins and a succession of other men. In 1896, lighthouse keepers were classified as civil service employees. This brought to an end the appointment of political favorites. Edward H. Sibley, the last fulltime keeper at the New Point Comfort lighthouse, retired in 1919 when the light became automated and a laborer began performing regular maintenance.[33]

Bolstering the Local Economy

In September 1865 the United States Postmaster General notified the public that the Mathews Courthouse post office would be reopened with William F. Pugh as postmaster and J. Bohannon as assistant postmaster. Shortly thereafter, the *Baltimore Sun* announced that the fast steamer *Eolus* would be leaving Norfolk every Monday, Wednesday, and Friday at 6:30 AM, taking passengers and mail to Mathews and Gloucester Counties, Yorktown, and the Eastern Shore, with a stop at Cherrystone.

According to a newspaper account published on October 27, 1869, a post office was established at Cobbs Creek in August 1869 and James T. Carter was named postmaster. However, when Anne W. Diggs was interviewed during the 1970s, she indicated that her grandfather, James A. Williams, was Cobbs Creek's first postmaster and that he was succeeded by her mother in 1934. In 1871, post offices were established at Port Haywood and Wolftown, with C.H. Hudgins and James W. Banks, respectively, as postmaster.

During the late 1870s and early 1880s, times were still hard and a number of Mathews County residents put their real estate on the market. For example, a 50-acre farm on the Milford Haven that had a two-story dwelling and outbuildings, good spring water, and ready access to thrice weekly steamboat service was advertised in a Baltimore newspaper. In May 1879, someone at Hicks Wharf sent a letter to the *Baltimore Sun*'s editor, saying that a good crop year was expected and that the fish harvest was uncommonly good. The writer went on to say that Mathews County was well suited to orchard crops and truck farming and had transportation links to all of the principal cities of the North. When the 170-acre farm, Springdale, was offered for sale in 1881, it was said to have a nine-room dwelling that had several outbuildings. The advertisement said that the property was located on Put In Creek, about half-a-mile from Mathews Courthouse, and was convenient to steamers that ran to Baltimore and Norfolk five times a week. The farm called Brighton, whose dwelling was reportedly built in 1879, was also offered for sale. It was only two miles from Williams Wharf, where the Norfolk steamboat (which connected with the Baltimore Bay Line at Old

Point Comfort) provided direct access to Baltimore. Near at hand were two stores, a post office, and churches. Some local landowners were well-to-do, and in 1874, Riverlawn, near Williams Wharf, was built as a vacation home by Baltimore architect Heron Campbell Murray and his wife, the former Cordelia Williams. Before constructing Riverlawn, the couple also helped to build the B. Williams and Company Store in 1870. Both properties are on the National Register of Historic Places. One Mathews County family that hoped to take in boarders during the summertime placed an advertisement in a Baltimore newspaper, promising the comforts of home and "water luxuries"—presumably fishing, boating, and swimming. Likewise, Auburn's owners tried to attract boarders, noting that the location offered good fishing, sailing, shooting, and an abundance of fruit. Also available was ready access to the Norfolk steamer, which ran to Old Point Comfort.[34]

Deriving a Living from the Sea

For many centuries, native people and European colonists relished the abundance of seafood available locally. By the early nineteenth century, people in Tidewater Virginia discovered that they could earn a good living by harvesting and selling fish and shellfish. During February, watermen would lay out nets to catch rockfish and shad. Then, in March and April, when the crabs started coming in, they would use trotlines. Oysters were another popular and saleable seasonal delicacy. During the summer months and into the early fall, fish such as spot, croaker, and flounder could be caught and sold. When steamboats began plying local waters, vast quantities of local seafood were taken to urban markets. This conduit of trade provided Mathews County residents with an important source of income. In time, shucking houses purchased oysters from local watermen and processed them for shipment. Sturgeon and sheepshead flourished in the waters of the Chesapeake Bay until the second half of the nineteenth century. Sturgeon was harvested in float seines or gill nets that rose with the tide. Sometimes they were taken to West Point where they were sold and then transported to Richmond and points north; sturgeon roe was often transformed into caviar. In December 1866, an article in the *Baltimore Sun* described the Piankatank River in glowing terms and emphasized the abundance of fish and oysters. According to the writer, a vessel carrying 1,000 bushels of oysters could be loaded in a day and taken to market. Other species were caught from time to time. According to a Galveston, Texas, newspaper, in 1876 ten whales that were driven onto a sandbar in Mathews County were captured by local fishermen.

In 1939, Harriet G. Miller, a WPA worker assigned to interview people in Mathews County, acknowledged that she had tried in vain to interview fishermen who lived along the shores of the Mobjack Bay. She finally succeeded in chatting with Wilson Brooks, who described the enormous quantities of shad that he and Captain Henry Billups had caught and delivered to a steamer that took them to Baltimore and New York. Brooks and another local man credited two Northerners with introducing the pound net or fish trapping.[35] Brooks also mentioned the large catches of sturgeon that Captain Al Tatterson caught in his pound nets. He said that sometimes tug boats and barges loaded with lumber and coal would run through the pound nets at night without realizing that they had destroyed them. Ms. Miller also interviewed John Hudgins and his son Pete, who lived at Motorun and were experienced fishermen. Both men spoke of the enormous numbers of shad, mackerel, and croaker they had caught at various times and sold to buyers in Baltimore and at Old Point Comfort.[36]

During the second half of the nineteenth century, two methods of harvesting oysters were popular with watermen. "Tongers" (or "tong men") gathered oysters from the floor of the Chesapeake Bay using long-handled metal tongs that terminated with what resembled garden rakes facing in opposing directions. In temperate weather, tongmen, using small canoes or skiffs, could harvest oysters from shallow waters. Therefore, they were protective of the oyster beds that lay within their reach.

Oystermen who operated dredges used an entirely different type of equipment; dredges consisted of iron rings that were linked together to form mesh bags. A dredge's mouth was held open by an iron frame that had iron teeth. Four bars of iron, attached to the frame, converged at a point to which a short chain and long rope were attached. Dredgers would drag the teeth of their dredge across the bottom of the bay, scraping up oysters that would be deposited in the mesh bag. They could bring up oysters from greater depths than tongers and could break up old oyster beds, distributing them more widely. When dredgers ventured into shallow waters, they encroached on the oyster beds used by tongers, thereby diminishing their livelihood.

Ultimately, this led to armed conflict in the years that followed the Civil War, when the oyster industry was extremely important to the region's economy. Mathews County's clerk of court, Shepherd G. Miller, issued oyster licenses and some have been preserved that date to 1866 and 1867. Violations of the oyster laws occurred from time to time and lawbreakers were summoned to court. For example, Andrew Powell was indicted by a Grand Jury and on March 26, 1875, was convicted of "willfully dredging and scraping for oysters ... within the lines prohibited by law." Constant dredging permanently destroyed many oyster beds and reduced the number of oysters available in Virginia waters. In 1879, the General Assembly, concerned about loss of the tax revenues derived from the oyster industry, outlawed dredging on natural rocks and disbanded its so-called "oyster police." However, during the winter of 1879–80, nearly 40 dredging boats set to work in the Rappahannock River. When local tongmen tried to drive them away, the dredges opened fire. The tongers complained to the legislature, which decided to provide them with artillery, rifles, and ammunition. Members of the General Assembly also enacted legislation calculated to protect the state's oyster beds from overuse and exploitation by people outside of Virginia.[37]

Crime and Punishment

In 1868, Robert Jones, a black man, was arrested for stealing money from Thomas J. Powell, the captain of the schooner on which he worked, and was presented to a local grand jury. In 1870, two Mathews County court cases made the news. One involved 40-year-old John B. Donovan, a prominent local lawyer who lived in the Mathews County seat. He got into a quarrel with 33-year-old George B. Maccubin of Baltimore, Maryland, a store clerk and his former partner in a real estate firm. During the disagreement, Donovan became enraged and shot Macubbin in the abdomen. The other case involved a Mathews County woman whose husband went to North Carolina seeking work and stayed gone for two or three years. Later, she learned that while he was there, he had married another woman. The Mathews woman's attorney, faced with proving that the accused man was guilty of bigamy, used a photograph to identify him. According to a Georgia newspaper, this was the first known incidence of photography being used as evidence in a divorce case.

In late May 1879, the residents of Mathews County were shocked to learn that 29-year-old Ellen Gwynn, who was black and lived in the Piankatank District, had been brutally assaulted by 22-year-old Charles Guin of Westville. Guin was thought to have fled to New York, where a reward was offered for his arrest. Another violent crime occurred in 1911 when a young white man attacked Ellen Miller, the daughter of Sheriff Seth A. Miller. Bloodhounds were sent out to search for the assailant, and there was some concern that he would be lynched, if he were caught. He was apprehended in Richmond and brought before a court of law. However, not all crime was violent. A Mathews County man, Philip T. White, was found guilty of committing a white-collar crime. While he was employed as the auditor of a paint company in Brooklyn, New York, he organized a gang of thieves who robbed his employer's bank messengers. When confronted in court, White admitted his guilt and was sentenced to Sing Sing.[38]

Education: A Pathway to Success

During the Civil War, the Literary Fund's revenues were diverted into the Confederate military budget and public education was virtually abandoned. The literacy rate plummeted, and at the end of the war nearly 22 percent of the state's whites and almost all blacks were unable to read and write. Thanks to the 1869 constitution, provisions were made for free public schools to be established in Virginia, with mandatory attendance. Legislators also had the authority to establish teachers colleges and institutions where agricultural science could be taught. State law provided for a Superintendent of Public Instruction and a State Board of Education, which was authorized to see that textbooks were uniform and schoolhouses were furnished with libraries, essential equipment, and furniture. The Literary Fund's earnings were to be supplemented with monies raised from the capitation tax and property taxes. Also, each county and district was authorized to levy taxes to support public education. All school monies, state and local, were to be placed in the hands of the county treasurer. Legislation stipulated that 90 percent of the state school fund had to be assigned to the counties. However, despite state officials' good intentions, between 1870 and 1879 large amounts of money intended for Virginia's public schools were diverted to other uses, as by 1873 the country had entered a lengthy period of economic depression.

Even so, the Constitution of 1869 brought Virginia's governing officials the first unequivocal mandate to provide public education. Public free schools were to be introduced into all of the state's counties no later than 1876, and there were no legal loopholes or permissive clauses that made public education a local option. In 1870, the Rev. William R. Ruffner, who believed that there should be separate schools for blacks and whites, became the state's first Superintendent of Public Instruction. During his twelve years' tenure, significant progress was made. The State Board of Education was supposed to oversee the operation of the free school system, to appoint school district trustees, and to render an annual report to the General Assembly. County school superintendents were to inspect their jurisdiction's schoolhouses, preserve documents associated with operating the schools, and render an annual report to the Superintendent of Public Instruction. County school superintendents were allowed to decide what constituted local school districts. Schools and school property, by law, were vested in local school officials and buildings had to be maintained in "respectable condition." Teachers were required to document their credentials and had to sign a contract. They also had to maintain a daily register of students (ages 5 to 21) entitled to free schooling. Neither teachers nor students could attend school if infected with a contagious disease. Students were required to be clean, well behaved, and vaccinated. They were to be taught reading, writing, arithmetic, orthography (spelling), grammar, and geography, using texts selected by the State Board of Education.

According to Alfred Foster, whose commentary appeared in the *Gloucester-Mathews Gazette-Journal*'s commemorative edition in 1949, the earliest record of a public school in Mathews County was 1871 and G. Taylor Garnett was the first local school superintendent. In 1874 the county's schools had a total of 948 pupils, most of whom attended one-room schools, although there were exceptions. Children received instruction in reading, writing, and arithmetic and the school term was about five months long. They also could study Latin and geometry if they wished. According to Mr. Foster, each schoolroom was heated by a three-legged coal stove, and a bucket and a common cup supplied pupils' drinking water. Students sat on large wooden benches and sometimes as many as three children shared a desk. Teachers were paid between $18 and $22 a month and rarely had the luxury of a desk.

One major obstacle to improving public education was the shortage of trained teachers. Philanthropist George Peabody established a million-dollar fund to promote education in the Southern states. Popular opinion was easily aroused against common free schools during the postwar period, for they were costly and came at a time when the state staggered under massive debt, followed by a recession. Also, some people linked the idea of public education to the Reconstruction period's political controversies and egalitarian theories. Philosophically, many Virginians were opposed to a public free school system, for some believed that it was inappropriate to educate all children (especially blacks). Others were of the opinion that educating the young was a function of the home, and therefore a private, not public, responsibility. Sometimes, local families decided to establish schools of their own. During the 1870s, Miss Elizabeth Ann Soles gave permission for a school to be built on a remote part of her farm which bordered Morgan's Branch. The first schoolhouse was a small Sunday School. Soon, it became the nucleus of a congregation that gathered for weekly prayer meetings, and eventually it gave rise to the Locust Grove Methodist Church.

Newly emancipated blacks were eager to attend school, for many of them viewed education as a means of achieving all that slavery had denied them. Some blacks advocated integrated schools or one common system of free schools for both races, but most whites disagreed. Although massive public debt and sectionalism slowed the development of public education, by 1880 the issue was settled permanently, largely because voters west of the Blue Ridge and newly enfranchised blacks elected state and federal representatives that supported universal education. During the 1880s, while Richard R. Farr was State Superintendent of Public Instruction, Virginia's educational system became firmly established and slowly but surely began earning the respect of the general public. The Rev. Giles Buckner Cooke of

Mathews County founded a church day school for blacks in Petersburg. The school evolved into a theological seminary that became known as the Bishop Payne Theological Seminary. The Rev. Cooke, who died in 1937, felt that his real contribution to history and humanity was the work he initiated in the dark days of Reconstruction.[39]

Public Assistance

Mathews County's Overseers of the Poor assisted the indigent before and after the Civil War. Court records dating to the 1860s reveal that the Overseers loaned money to local citizens, whose interest payments largely funded public assistance. For example, on July 12, 1858, John H. Dunlavy borrowed $500 from the Overseers of the Poor. To secure his debt, he mortgaged his 300 acres between the East River and Queens Creek. He was unable to repay his loan and as a consequence, in October 1866 the Overseers took him to court in an attempt to recover their funds. Despite this chain of events, they later loaned him some additional money. William H. Brown also secured a loan from the Overseers of the Poor, and on April 11, 1859, borrowed $300, using his 206-acre farm as collateral. In October 1867, he acknowledged his debt in court, noting that his original deed of trust had been lost or destroyed. After the close of the war, the Overseers continued to loan money to local people. In June 1869, they let Gabriel F. Miller borrow $1,000, using his land as collateral. John Foster Jr., who mortgaged his 200 acres on Put In Creek, repaid his debt and the Overseers of the Poor provided him with a quitclaim deed, nullifying their lien on his property.

Entries in a merchant's account book suggest that in October 1868 the Overseers of the Poor opened what they called the Poor House store, where they sold general merchandize such as coffee, shoes, fabric, and whiskey to the public. During the late 1870s, the Overseers of the Poor sold off part of the poorhouse tract and some of the real estate that they had accepted as collateral. A plat made between 1878 and 1880 reveals that earlier on, the Overseers had purchased 80 acres "for the poor" from Dr. William Shultice, but that during the late 1870s, they had sold 45 acres to C.W. Forrest and 19 acres to L. Forrest. That left the poorhouse lot, which consisted of just over 16 acres, and abutted the Poorhouse Road, County Route 615, the forerunner of Town Point Road. When the poorhouse lot was surveyed in 1916, it was found to contain 18.36 acres.

Records kept by the Superintendent of the Poor between 1871 and 1889 reveal that each magisterial district had an overseer, who gathered information about his territory's paupers. The Superintendent's record book listed the numbers of blacks and whites receiving support each year, how much was spent on each person, and whether they lived in private homes or at the county poorhouse. In December 1871, the Superintendent of the Poor reported that public assistance had been given to thirteen white people and two black people in the Chesapeake District, almost all of whom were women. In the Westville District, four white women, eight black women, and five black men had obtained support, and six white women had received assistance in the Piankatank District. The Superintendent stated that there were six paupers "at the place of reception"—that is, the poorhouse. Three were described as very old and infirm and a fourth was blind "and unable to move about." All four of these people were cared for by the other two resident paupers who cooked meals, did laundry, and otherwise tended to their needs. The Superintendent noted that this was the first report he had made "under the new Constitution"—that is, the one adopted in 1869.

In 1873, when a statewide depression got underway, the Superintendent of the Poor reported that 43 white people and 41 blacks were receiving public assistance, almost all of whom were living "at home" or with someone else. Seven people of both races were then residing at the poorhouse. Most of them were women and three died during the year. By 1876, the number of paupers had risen to 89; six people—four whites and two blacks—were living at the poorhouse. The need for public welfare was great throughout the 1870s, but by the early 1880s the number of those needing assistance had begun to decline and only a handful of people (all blacks) were living at the poorhouse. In 1883, the Superintendent of the Poor reported that a house was being built for him at a cost of $384 and that during the past year a doctor was paid for tending the sick at the poorhouse, where there was one case of smallpox. He also noted that the Overseers had started the year with a $1,100 deficit, but had begun to recover some of the funds they were owed. In 1886, seven people received care in the county poorhouse. Six blacks (Peter Anderson, Lucie Digs, Charis [Clary] James, Gabriel James, Joice Miller, and Rosa Smith) were unable to work and had lived in the poorhouse for the entire year; William E. Moss, who was white, stayed there for only a month. Walter Ingram, a white man, lived at the poorhouse in 1887, as did the same six blacks who had been there the year before. From 1887 on, the Superintendent began reporting the dollar value of the support each pauper received. By that time, the poorhouse was almost exclusively the home to six or seven indigent blacks.

In June 1887, Mathews County's Board of Supervisors authorized payment of a modest salary to the county's three Overseers of the Poor and approved small sums owed to merchants who had provided food and other supplies to the county's institutionalized poor. The inmates of the poorhouse were supplied with bacon, hog jowls, soda bread, coffee, flour, herring, mackerel, lard, molasses, sweet potatoes, Irish potatoes, rice, salt, pepper, sugar, peas, matches, salt, soap, tobacco, and kerosene oil. Dr. Thomas B. Lane was compensated for providing poorhouse inmates with medicine and medical care during 1887, during which time he treated one pauper for smallpox. The Supervisors used a sealed bidding process and in 1888 merchants C.H. Hudgins and Charles L. Williams were the low bidders, as was Dr. Lane, the only physician who applied.[40]

Local Places of Worship

After the Civil War ended, some of Mathews County's religious denominations were revitalized and a number of new congregations were formed. Some of the Point Comfort Methodist Church's communicants decided that they wanted a more convenient place to worship. At first, they held services in an arbor, but during the 1870s they acquired land and erected the Beulah Methodist Church. Meanwhile, in 1873 Methodists living near the county seat decided that they, too, wanted a church closer to home. Therefore, they secured some land and built the Central Methodist Church. Another group of local Methodists, eager to hold revivals, held tent meetings at a site known as Vaiden's Grove. In 1879, they replaced their campground with a tabernacle. Revival meetings, held during the summertime, attracted evangelists and song leaders from surrounding states. Services that included preaching and large choirs were usually held in August and lasted for two weeks. The original tabernacle was replaced in 1922 by the large structure that still exists. The Mathews Methodist Tabernacle, now privately owned, is on the National Register of Historic Places.

The Mathews Baptist (or Old Baptist) Church, which in 1868 had two Sunday Schools that provided instruction to both blacks and whites, later gave rise to a dozen new churches. In 1864, nearly 300 blacks, who formerly attended Mathews Baptist Church, established a mission in a little log cabin they purchased in Pugh's Thicket, just east of Hyco Corner; it was destroyed by fire. They bought a second building in the same vicinity and it, too, succumbed to arson.[41] In 1865, this group of worshipers received a formal letter of dismissal from Mathews Baptist Church and achieved church status. Two years later they purchased a half-acre lot and erected a small building they called the Second Baptist Church. By 1885, the congregation had grown so large that a new, much larger, church was needed, the house of worship now known as the First Baptist Church. In time, a total of seven churches descended from First Baptist, the "mother church" of Antioch, Ebenezer, Emmaus, Providence,[42] Rising Sun, Wayland, and Zion. Antioch Baptist Church's history is especially well documented. In 1869, John Hudgins, John Turner, John Singleton and Robert Forrest, who lived near the community called Susan, felt that local black children needed a school. Mrs. Lucy Singleton, who was white, donated a quarter-acre site on which a log cabin schoolhouse was built. Women in the community met there for worship and the Rev. Robert Lattimore of Elizabeth City became pastor of what became known as Antioch Baptist Church. During the 1870s the congregation erected a frame building that was much larger than the log cabin in which they originally worshiped.

Mathews Baptist Church's white members went on to form four new churches: Gwynn's Island, Spring Hill, and Westville, which date to 1874; and Macedonia, which was established in 1886. In April 1887, the trustees of Mathews Baptist Church conveyed to the trustees of the Macedonia Baptist Church their legal interest in the one-acre lot on which Macedonia's house of worship was located. The quitclaim deed the two churches' trustees signed acknowledged that their congregations had divided when the Macedonia congregation was formed.

Mathews County's Episcopalians continued to hold regular worship services. Vestry records reveal that the congregations of Trinity Church and Christ Church were small but that both had active Sunday Schools in which both white and black children received instruction. In 1867, after the death of the incumbent rector, a Mr. Lewis, the vestry decided to reunite with Middlesex County's Middlesex Parish and jointly hire a new clergyman. The Rev. George S. May agreed to serve both parishes. Although Kingston Parish was short of funds, its vestry managed to recover some money that had been loaned to Miss Ellen R. Tabb before the war. Parishioners also raised funds. In January 1868, the women of Kingston Parish held a bazaar, hoping to raise money that could be used in repairing both of the parish's churches. Unfortunately, part of the money they took in included counterfeit bills. At the end of the year, the Rev. May and the vestry parted company "owing to the unhappy dissention in the parish" and the inability to raise the funds needed to pay his salary. Although new rectors were hired, they tended to serve briefly. By 1875, the vestry began trying to find enough money to provide their clergy with a rectory. Finally, in 1877 the parish agreed to share the Rev. C.B. Bryan with Ware Parish and gathered the funds they needed to purchase a rectory.[43]

Notes

1 Penelope K. Majeske, "Your Obedient Servant: The United States Army in Virginia During Reconstruction," 29, 56; Robertson, *Civil War*, 174–176; Gloucester County Historical Committee, *Reminiscences*, 4, 56; Tindall, *America*, 671–672; Mathews County Census 1870; Agricultural Census 1870; Land Tax Lists 1867–1870.

2 In 1864, while Pierpont was the Restored Government's governor, a state constitutional convention was held. During the war, it was effective only in those portions of Virginia that the Union Army controlled. After the war Pierpont tried to apply it to the entire state (Sara B. Bearss, "Restored and Vindicated: The Virginia Constitutional Convention of 1864," *Virginia Magazine of History and Biography*, Vol. 122 [2014]:171–175; Charles, *Newspapers*, 111–112).

3 Diggs, Hunley, and Lane had been elected on June 26, 1864.

4 Leonard, *General Assembly*, 501, 503, 509, 511, 518, 520, 522, 524, 526, 528, 532; Mathews County Deed Book 1:11–18; Commissions 1864–1869; Chancery Court Dockets 1842–1843, 1867: unidentified newspaper clipping microfilmed with chancery records.

5 Charles, *Newspapers*, 162–163; Mathews Archives, Box 25 R.

6 During tournaments, competing riders, whose horses ran at top speed, would try to spear small rings suspended several feet above ground. The rider snaring the most rings received a prize and was allowed to select the tournament's queen. In 1871, a tournament held in Gloucester County was intended to bring together Union and Confederate officers and men in a social situation. Delegations were expected from Richmond, Norfolk, Yorktown, Portsmouth, and other parts of the state (Charles, *Newspapers*, p. 115).

7 James Henry Lane Diary, Mathews Archives Box 25 R; Charles, *Newspapers*, 111. James Henry Lane, one of the founders of Virginia Tech, eventually moved to Alabama and taught at Auburn University.

8 A list of taxpayers, compiled in Mathews County during 1865 and 1866, suggests that some people managed to pay what they owed. The local sheriff listed the sums he collected along with fees paid to the clerk of court and other officials (Mathews County Miscellaneous Tax Lists 1865–1868).

9 For instance, in September 1865 when Ellen Armistead bought a pair of shoes, a dress, and a hoop skirt at the Shipley and Howlett store, she was identified as "colored." When one of the proprietors extended a line of credit to her, he noted that she could continue to charge merchandise "so long as she remains with me" (Shipley and Howlett Miscellaneous Accounts 1857–1867, Library of Virginia, Richmond).

10 Mathews County Executions and Miscellaneous Court Cases; Improper Assessment of Land 1845–1869 [Untitled List of Taxes Paid in 1867, 1868, 1871–1875]; Deed Book 1:18–19, 43, 51–54, 57; Land Tax Lists 1868–1872; Personal Property Tax Lists 1865–1870; Circuit Court Papers 1866

11 Mathews County Fiduciary Accounts 1868–1872; Petitions of Widows and Orphans for Support Under the Stay Law of 1866–1869; Pension Records and Applications for 1877–1878, 1883, and 1888; Will Book 1:2, 29; Agricultural Census 1870, 1880; Land Tax Lists 1868–1870; Deed Book 2:36–37; 7:176–177, 366; Land Book 2:61; Charles, *Newspapers*, 112, 164–166; *American Farmer*, December 1867.

12 Although processioners records are relatively rare, this technique was used in nearby Gloucester County after a 1820 courthouse fire destroyed deed books and will books. Processioning would have established a basis for future land transactions.

13 To date, no processioners records have come to light for District 3, the Piankatank District. Based on the properties omitted from the records of Districts 1 and 2, District 3 appears to have bordered the north side of Church Street and the east side of Main Street.

14 Mathews County Processioners Returns for Land Processioned in Militia District No. 1 July 1867; Processioners Returns for Land Processioned in Militia District No. 2 July 1867; Executions and Miscellaneous Court Cases; Improper Assessment of Land 1845–1869 [Untitled List of Taxes Paid in 1867, 1868, 1871–1875]; Deed Book 1:18–19, 43, 51–54, 57; Land Tax Lists 1868–1872; Personal Property Tax Lists 1865–1870; Circuit Court Papers 1866.

15 In 1887, George E. Sleet's wife, Virginia, owned what they called Sleet's Hotel, currently known as the White Dog Inn. Mr. Sleet was identified as a hotelkeeper in the 1880 census (Mathews County Census 1880; Land Tax Lists 1880–1890).

16 The deed prepared by the Board of Supervisors conveyed to Sleet 0.024815/1,000,000 of an acre (Mathews County Deed Book 7:547; Land Book 1:306).

17 For the first time, the quarter-acre lot was listed as one-half acre, raising the possibility that it had been surveyed and found to be larger than assumed. On the other hand, when extending toward Put In Creek, the lot may have taken in some unclaimed or abandoned land.

18 Mathews County Processioners Returns, Militia District No. 1, July 1867; Processioners Returns, Militia District No. 2 July 1867; Mathews County Census 1860; Land Tax Lists 1847–1894; Deed Book 1: 92, 180, 196–197, 225, 276, 301, 547, 601, 645–646, 651, 722, 727–728; 2:450, 611–612; 3:80, 240–241; 4:143, 199–201; 5:11–12; 14:169–160; 10:403–404; Land Book 1:306, 393–394, 468.

19 The hotel, now known as the White Dog Inn, is on the National Register of Historic Places (Lane Hotel, National Register of Historic Places File 057-0070.

20 Mathews County Processioners Returns for Land Processioned in Militia District No. 1 July 1867; Processioners Returns for Land Processioned in Militia District No. 2 July 1867; Mathews County Census 1860, 1870; Land Tax Lists 1847–1894; Deed Book 1:92, 180, 196–197, 225, 276, 301, 547, 601, 645–646, 651, 722, 727–728; 2:450, 611–612; 3:80, 240–241; 4:143, 199–201; 5:11–12; 14:169–160; 10:403–404; Land Book 1:306, 393–394, 468; A. D. Bache, "Coast Chart No. 32, Chesapeake Bay Sheet No 2, Rappahannock Entrance, Mobjack Bay, and Cherrystone Inlet.

21 Mathews County Circuit Court Papers 1866; Census 1860, 1870, 1880; Charles, *Newspapers*, 118; Mathews Archives, Box 34 R.

22 Mathews Archives Box 2 R; Mathews County Census 1860; Southern Claims Commission 1871–1878, claim numbers 5871, 8759. The records of the Southern Claims Commission are available at the National Archives and on www.fold3.com.

23 Sometimes, property seems to have been seized punitively.

24 Only two farms were taken on the Middle Peninsula: one in Gloucester and one in Mathews.

25 Tindall, *America*, 672–673; Freedmen's Bureau, District 9 folio 2; www.freedmensbureau.com; Mathews County Land Tax Lists 1850–1865; Executions 1862–1866; Land Book 2:71; Deed Book 2:6–7; Circuit Court Papers 1866; Commonwealth's Attorney's Notes, October 1866; Norfolk County Census 1870, 1880; Charles, *Newspapers*, p. 120; Leonard, *General Assembly*, p. 503; *American Farmer*, December 1867.

26 Richard Lowe, "The Freedmen's Bureau and Local White Leaders in Virginia," *The Journal of Southern History* 64 (1998):470–471; Mathews County Executive Papers, 1865–1868, March 2, 1867; Census 1870; Marriage Register Book 1; Hanover County Marriage Register of Freedmen Living in Hanover County, http://digitool1.lva.lib.va.us; www.freedmensbureau.com/virginia/gloucester.htm.

27 The Convention of 1867–68 was chaired by John C. Underwood, a New Yorker and judge in Richmond's U.S. Circuit Court, who wielded so much influence that the document the delegates drafted became known as the Underwood Constitution. On the last day of the constitutional convention, General Schofield urged delegates to modify the article that established voting and office-holding criteria, noting that in some counties no more than two or three literate people were able to take the test oath. He was right. When postwar elections were held, more than half of the state's 5,446 offices were left vacant and a substantial number of those elected were disqualified on account of service to the Confederacy.

28 C.A. Schaffter, comp., *Acts and Joint Resolutions Passed by the General Assembly at the Session of 1870–1871* (Richmond, 1871), 56, 417, 426, 432; R. F. Walker, comp., *Acts and Joint Resolutions Passed by the General Assembly at the Session of 1872–1873* (Richmond, 1873), 68, 182, 387, 402; *Acts and Joint Resolutions Passed by the General Assembly at the Session of 1875–1876* (Richmond, 1876), 18, 116; Mathews County Road Commissioners Minutes 1870; Board of Supervisors Minute Book 1887–1900:402, 404, 437, 680; Circuit Court Executions 1858–1895; County Court Papers 1877; Leonard, *General Assembly*, 505.

29 Mathews County Marriage Register Book 1; Agricultural Census 1880; Industrial Statistics 1870; Carl Lounsbury, personal communication, July 16, 2014; http://mapserver.lib.virginia.edu/index.html.

30 Mathews Archives Box 22 R.

31 Richard E. Prince, *Steam Locomotives and Boats, Southern Railway System* (Green River, Wyoming, 1965), 46; Charles, *Newspapers*, 117–120, 137; Fairfax Harrison, *A History of the Legal Development of the Railroad System of Southern Railway Company* (Washington, D.C., 1901), 238–241.

32 Holly, *Steamboat*, 83, 109–110; Robert H. Burgess, and H. Graham Wood, *Steamboats Out of Baltimore*. (Cambridge, Maryland, 1968), 42–43, 148; Prince, *Locomotives*, 46; Brown, *Steam Packets*, 52–53, 62, 71, 147.

33 Clifford and Clifford, *New Point Comfort*, 28–29, 31, 79–80, 82, 88; Charles, *Newspapers*, 104, 114, 118–119; Mathews Archives Boxes 18 R and 83 R.

34 Charles, *Newspapers*, 111, 113, 115, 117–120, 122; Riverlawn, National Register of Historic Places File 057-0036; B. Williams and Company Store, National Register of Historic Places File 057-0035; MCHS, *History and Progress*, 134–135).

35 Wooden stakes were driven into the shore bottom and nets were arranged to corral the fish. Watermen could then gather up the nets and harvest the fish that had become entrapped.

36 A pound-netter working in the Chesapeake Bay's biggest open waters would need a heavy, deep-hulled boat capable of withstanding rough weather. The bay's characteristics led to the creation of an array of indigenous watercraft.

37 Charles, *Newspapers*, 111–112; James Wharton, *The Bounty of the Chesapeake: Fishing in Colonial Virginia* (Charlottesville, 1957), passim; Miller, "Interviews," Boxes 10, 11; Mathews County Circuit Court Executions 1858–1895; Chancery Court Dockets 1842–1843, 1867; Oyster Licenses 1866–1867; Court Docket 1879–1890; www.marinersmuseum.org.

38 Charles, *Newspapers*, 111–114, 119, 163–165; Mathews County Census 1870; Baltimore, Maryland, Census 1870.

39 Heatwole, *Education*, 210, 214, 223, 246; Maddox, *Free Schools*, p. 166; J. L. Buck, *The Development of Public Schools in Virginia, 1607–1952* (Richmond, 1952), 65, 70, 83, 85, 88; MCHC, *History and Progress*, 11–13, 48–49; . *Richmond News Leader*, February 5, 1937.

40 Anonymous Merchants Account Book 1868, Library of Virginia, Richmond; Mathews County Deed Book 1:322, 651; 2:1–2; Land Book 1:263, 470; Superintendent of the Poor Annual Reports 1871–1889; Board of Supervisors Minute Book 1887–1900:404, 410, 413.

41 These fires probably were the ones to which Freedmen's Bureau personnel referred in March 1866.

42 Providence Baptist Church was located on Church Street where the annex to Thomas Hunter School now stands. Its location is shown on a topographic quadrangle sheet that was made in 1917 (U.S.G.S., "Mathews," 1917). This house of worship should not be confused with the Providence Methodist Church in Whites Neck, another church that has disappeared from the cultural landscape.

43 Mathews Archives Boxes 18 R and 19 R; Charles, *Newspapers*, 112–113; MCHC, *History and Progress*, 11, 89; Brown, *Old Kingston Parish*, p. 29; Brown, "Notes," no pagination; Kingston Parish Vestry Minutes 1873–1938:19, 37, 42, 45, 48; Helen and Charles Forrest, Oral History File TMP-044, July 17, 2014; Miscellaneous Records of the Mathews and Macedonia Baptist Church Minutes, 1887, 1897, Mathews Archives, Box 1; www.weareantioch.com/history.html.

11

Defining the Future
1881–1917

Confederate Veterans and Their Widows

Virginia's General Assembly passed Confederate pension acts in 1888, 1900, and 1902, and a series of supplementary acts between 1903 and 1934. The 1888 act provided pensions to disabled Confederate veterans and to the widows of men killed during the war, so long as their annual income was $300 or less, they did not own personal property worth $1,000 or more, and had not remarried. The maximum pension a widow could receive was $30 a year. Subsequent acts expanded coverage to include all veterans, their widows, and their unmarried or widowed daughters. Widows whose husbands died during the war could receive $40 a year, but the widows of veterans who died later stood to receive a survivor's benefit of only $25 per year. At first, applicants were required to be residents of Virginia, but later, coverage was expanded to those living in the District of Columbia. Pension applicants had to document the veteran's service with sworn statements, submit a medical evaluation performed by a doctor, and provide information about his income and property. Widows had to disclose the date and place of their marriages; anyone who wed a Civil War veteran after Dec. 31, 1882, was not entitled to a state military pension. An estimated 4,000 to 6,000 Virginia women lost their husbands during the Civil War. The majority of them were relatively young, had brief marriages, and had children too young to help support the family. Although roughly half of all young widows remarried, many wed men who were significantly older or younger than themselves.[1] Middle-aged widows were less likely to remarry.

On April 18, 1900, Mathews County's Confederate Pension Board convened for the first time and met in the office of the clerk of court. The Board's members, appointed by the incumbent Circuit Court judge, included three Confederate veterans (William E. Fitchett, William Machen, and Sands Smith III) and two sons of Confederate veterans (V.V. Shipley and A.J. Diggs). Fitchett was elected Pension Board chair. Charles H. Atherton, B.F. Bridges, Albert Foster, Neuval A. Hatch, James H. Richardson, and Lewis T. White submitted pension applications, documented their military service, and in March 1900 they were each authorized to receive a $30 pension. The widows of Betheny Cray, Joseph Foster, Hugh K. Hudgins, and John W. Hudgins also qualified for an annual pension of $25. In May 1900, the widows of Richard H. Blake, James F. Brooks, John T. Diggs, John J. Minter, and Albert Williams submitted pension applications. A month later, they were followed by veterans Peter Daniel, Henry T. Diggs, James W. Jarvis, Thomas H. Machen, Leroy T. Owens, R.F. Owens, Richard Summerson, John G. Williams, and the widows of John R. Bennett, Thomas Bridges, John T. Brooks, and R.T. Douglas. All were approved, although some men were authorized to receive only $15 a year, probably on account of their brief military service. Later, applications were submitted by veterans Daniel Downs, Thomas Foster, Thomas Graves, James Robins, Isaac L. Sadler, Robert J. Sadler, Robert T. Thompson, and the widows of W.A. Cox, Bailey Diggs Jr., Frank J. Kemp, A.B. Sadler, Miles K. Thomas, Robert G. Weston, Samuel B. White, and William T. Williams. In May 1901, veteran Thomas Diggs and Silas Huggett's widow applied for pensions. Four widows were asked to document the year in which they wed their husbands, but ultimately, all of these applicants received pensions.

The documentation that Mathews County's Confederate veterans and their widows submitted in support of their pension claims sheds a great deal of light on the men's military service and their physical condition after the war. We know, for example, that when shoemaker Robert B. Bailey of the 61st Regiment applied for a pension, he suffered from rheumatism and general disability. On the other hand, James Green, a farmer, had a hernia and was troubled by an old war wound. Charles Frederick Richardson, a merchant, suffered from apoplexy and Lewis Sadler was disabled on account of poor eyesight. Eleven men who had served in the 5th Virginia Cavalry had what they described as "general disability" and some other medical issues. For example, George Augustus Brooks had heart trouble, whereas George T. Diggs had ongoing problems with an old hip wound, and W.J. Diggs had hemorrhoids. Josiah Brooks, Thomas R. Hudgins, Charles W. Parrott, H.D. Pynes, R.H. Sadler, William Henry White, and Albert H. Williams developed rheumatism and Williams also had lumbago. William Ellis Fitchett, who sustained two wounds, eventually developed stomach cancer. George Augustus Brooks, Charles Edward Hobday, and John William Howlett had heart disease and Isaac T. Hudgins, Robert T. Lewis, and Thomas R. Ransone developed kidney ailments, which most applicants described as "Bright's disease." After Leroy Bohannon, a bricklayer, died of pneumonia, his widow, Mary A., applied for his pension. A total of 12 other widows, whose husbands had served in the 5th Virginia Cavalry, applied for their late husbands' military pensions.

Service records and pension applications filed by men who served in the Mathews Light Artillery suggest that their medical ills differed somewhat from those of the 5th Virginia Cavalry. For instance, Robert H. White, who had been a fisherman before the war, was deafened by a cannon explosion, whereas Wesley F. Ripley had been blinded by a blast. After the war, 24 men reportedly developed rheumatism, which some of them attributed to exposure. Three men had kidney disease, seven had heart disease, and one had liver disease. Benjamin F. Bridges and Joseph R. Diggs contracted typhoid fever and Thomas J. Hudgins developed tuberculosis. Six men had serious problems with their vision. James S. Brooks and Wesley F. Ripley were blind and Lewis H. Ashbury and Thomas F. Bridges each lost an eye. Six men had hernias and two others suffered from skin diseases. After the war, 24 widows of Mathews Light Artillery veterans applied for their late husbands' military pensions.

In March 1921, John Thomas, a 103-year-old Confederate veteran who lived with his daughter, Mrs. Mary E. Treakle, fell into a well near his home and drowned. At the time of his death, he was reportedly " hale and hearty despite four years of hunger and hardship with the Confederate forces." According to the Library of Virginia, which maintains facsimiles of pension applications, claims were submitted by more than 500 African Americans who had assisted the Confederate Army by working as cooks, herdsmen, laborers, servants, or teamsters. Andrew Minter of Mathews County, an ex-slave who had served as a cook for the 5th Virginia Cavalry, does not seem to have applied for a pension.[2]

Governor Cameron's Oyster Wars

Virginia Governor William E. Cameron, a Confederate veteran who held office from 1882 to 1886, decided to lead the state government's efforts to curb unlawful dredging by out-of-state oystermen. On February 17, 1882, he and his staff joined some troops from Norfolk aboard two well-armed steamers that took them to the mouth of the Rappahannock River, where some oyster-dredgers were known to be at work. When the steamers came within firing distance of the dredgers' schooners, Governor Cameron and his men discharged a volley of shot. The oyster-dredgers surrendered immediately, as did two other vessels, but a fourth schooner hoisted its sails and sped away. Governor Cameron's steamer set out in hot pursuit and soon captured it. The other schooners, near the mouth of the Piankatank River, surrendered to the governor's second steamer. On the morning of February 18, the captured vessels and their crews were handed over to Mathews County Sheriff Sands Smith III, son of the man brutally slain by the Union Army in 1863. Sheriff Smith, reinforced by a posse of 50 armed citizens, marched the prisoners to the county seat where they were put into jail. When they stood trial on March 18, they were convicted. Each man was sentenced to a year in the state penitentiary and boat owners had to forfeit their vessels. A seaman named William Larkin escaped from the county jail after setting it ablaze but was recaptured. Although Mathews County's judge and jurors had upheld the law, they disagreed with the decision they felt obliged to make. Therefore, they sent a petition to the governor, asking for the convicted men to be pardoned.

At first, newspapers proclaimed that Governor Cameron's raid on the "oyster pirates" was a huge success. However, when it was determined that only one of the captured vessels was from out-of-state and the rest were from Virginia's Eastern Shore, Cameron became the butt of jokes. After appeals for clemency began to appear in Virginia newspapers, Governor Cameron agreed to pardon all of the watermen, and he commuted the sentences of the dredge-boat captains. He also had to deal with the disgruntled owners of the confiscated dredge-boats, who had been forced to purchase their own vessels at a public auction in Mathews County. They aired their grievances before the State Supreme Court of appeals, which declared that they hadn't been adequately represented in the Mathews County trial and ordered the state to pay them a settlement.

After all this, Governor Cameron was still determined to oust the oyster-dredgers, and at midnight on February 23, 1883, he set out from Norfolk with two steamers and a complement of armed men. This time, they headed for the mouth of the Potomac River, where numerous dredgers were rumored to have been at work for several months. Cameron's vessels encountered bad weather and only one steamer reached its destination. Although the dredgers scattered, some were captured. Their crewmen were taken to Mathews County and turned over to Sheriff Smith, who saw that they were jailed until they could be tried. Then, the governor and his staff adjourned to the Hygeia Hotel to celebrate their victory.[3] A young journalist aboard Governor Cameron's steamer lampooned him in an eyewitness account of the second expedition, and a Norfolk poet commemorated the event with a satirical verse he set to song. Although Governor Cameron's oyster wars made him the object of ridicule, he continued his campaign against the "oyster pirates" and named Captain Lewis M. Hudgins of Mathews County commodore of the oyster navy, which was supposed to protect Virginia's oyster beds from out-of-state oystermen.[4] In 1885 and 1886, the men of the oyster navy continued to pursue Maryland boats caught dredging in Virginia waters, particularly near Gwynn's Island. The oyster navy was still patrolling the Chesapeake during the 1890s, arresting unlicensed oystermen.[5]

Social and Cultural Change

Reconstruction was followed by two decades in which blacks and whites continued struggling to redefine their roles in society. An 1887 law stipulated that county tax books had to be organized into magisterial districts with separate sections for blacks and whites, and in 1890 non-white taxpayers were identified as "colored." During the 1890s, the Conservative Party gained control of the General Assembly. Some of its policies, which evolved into the "Jim Crow" laws, paved the way for sweeping changes, including racial segregation and "separate but equal" facilities. Soon, the principle of segregation permeated every area of Southern life and was applied not only to public facilities but also privately-owned business establishments, such as restaurants, hotels, and hospitals. In 1901–02 when a state constitutional convention was held, G.T. Garnett represented Gloucester and Mathews Counties. The delegates largely focused on how to restrict black voting rights without violating the Fifteenth Amendment to the United States Constitution or disfranchising poor whites. The 1902 Constitution also authorized racial segregation in public schools, which already existed on a *de facto* basis.

Because there was concern over African-American opposition, the proposed constitution was passed by the legislature and was not put to a popular vote. The state constitution that became law in 1902 required voters to pass a difficult literacy test and pay poll taxes. Those changes effectively disfranchised black voters, though many illiterate whites were also unable to meet the new requirements. In 1900 blacks made up nearly 36 percent of Virginia's electorate, but in succeeding elections, relatively few blacks were eligible to vote. The 1902 state constitution was in effect until July 1, 1971, and as late as 1950, fewer than 20 percent of African Americans met the poll tax requirements for voting.

In 1912, the General Assembly legalized neighborhood segregation. Although blacks and whites were traditionally neighbors in the rural countryside, racial restrictions could be—and usually were—applied to planned development. For example, on August 15, 1914, when the Dixie Auction and Realty Company announced that it would be holding an auction at Springdale, which was to be subdivided into lots and small farms and developed as Mathews Park, the *Mathews Journal* noted that "This property will be sold strictly to white people and no bids will be received or accepted from colored people or those of African descent." The auction company's president, Franc L. Ives, went on to say that mercantile and manufacturing industries would be restricted to the east side of the public road. By the late

1920s, *de facto* segregation was the norm in urban areas and there was full-scale segregation of public services. [6]

Confederate Veterans and Their Descendants Remember the War

A reunion was held in Richmond in 1896 at Captain Sally L. Tompkins's Robertson Hospital. Men and women from all parts of Virginia and people from as far away as Georgia and Texas attended. In 1906 an Oklahoma newspaper published an article about "Captain Sally," as she was affectionately known, and described her remarkable military career and personal sacrifices. She was then living in Richmond in the Home for Confederate Women and spent much of her time reading, writing, knitting, and entertaining her numerous visitors. When Captain Sally died in 1916 at age 83, her body was taken to Mathews County, where she was interred in Christ Church's cemetery with full military honors. Her casket was draped with a Confederate flag and carried to its final resting place by six aged veterans. On June 3, 1925, a granite monument was unveiled at her grave.

When the war's most painful memories began to recede, veterans and their families formed organizations that commemorated the past and recognized outstanding military feats. When a reunion of Confederate veterans was held in Dallas, Texas, in April 1902, Mathews men from the Lane-Diggs Camp of the Confederate Veterans attended. The camp's adjutant was Sands Smith III. In 1912, a monument was erected on Mathews County's courthouse green, recognizing those who had served in the Confederacy. The Lane-Diggs Camp of Confederate Veterans and the Sally Tompkins Chapter of the United Daughters of the Confederacy issued invitations to the monument's unveiling. Veterans continued to gather from time to time to reminisce with former comrades-in-arms. After the veterans' ranks were reduced by death, the Lane-Diggs Camp was replaced by the Sons of the Confederate Veterans, which was formed in 1920 under the direction of the Rev. Giles Buckner Cooke. In October 1921, J. Boyd Sears, a Mathews County attorney, went to Chattanooga, Tennessee, to speak at a veterans' reunion.

Elkanah Diggs, Mathews County's last surviving Confederate veteran (born on December 30, 1844) died only two days before his 91st birthday. When interviewed by Nellie Rhea White shortly before his death, Mr. Diggs said that he enlisted in the army as a private in Company D of the 26th Virginia Regiment, commonly known as Wise's Brigade. His military career commenced with brief tours of duty in Charleston, South Carolina, and Jacksonville, Florida and when his unit returned to Virginia, he was stationed outside of Petersburg for nearly a year. When Mr. Diggs applied for a veteran's pension in 1909, he gave his age as 64 and said that he had been a farmer all his life. He indicated that he had been unable to work for the past two years on account of rheumatism and old age. He said that he had entered the army in Charlestown in 1863 and had served for two years. His military service claims were verified by Benjamin D. Williams and Andrew Miller and his statements about his disability were supported by Dr. C.C. White. When Mr. Diggs was interviewed shortly before his death, he recalled that General Lee's men faced continuous pressure from Grant's army and that "Our supply of food was nearly exhausted," especially during the fall and winter. He added that "Lee, with his dwindling army, tried to guard the long lines around Richmond and Petersburg" but ultimately, had to retreat and to surrender. Mr. Diggs, like many other Mathews County soldiers, walked home from Appomattox. He came by way of Richmond and said that when he reached Mathews Courthouse around nightfall, he took shelter on the porch of Frank Armistead's store. He started for home at daybreak and encountered his mother, who had set out to meet him.[7]

Local News Media

In the late nineteenth and early twentieth centuries, Mathews County residents had the option of reading several locally available newspapers. Among them were the *Chesapeake Current* (1870–ca. 1876), the *Gloucester Herald* (1870–ca. 1875), *The Mail* (1884–85), and the *News Reporter* (1912–ca. 1918). The *Gloucester Progress* (1911–ca. 1912), the *Tidewater Liberal* (1881–ca. 1885), and the *Tidewater Virginian* (1886–ca. 1889) also served the area, and at Gloucester Point there was the *Tribune* (1908–11). A book called *Virginia Newspapers* claimed that the *Mathews Journal* first went to press in 1903[8] and that the *Mathews and Gloucester Tribune* was published from 1903 to 1905. The *Mathews Journal* was established by John J. Burke, who sold it to W. Marvin Minter. He, in turn, conveyed it to Paul Titlow and Paul Cline. At first, the *Mathews Journal* was printed in a rented building close to the Westville Christian Church, but the newspaper eventually moved to a lodge hall located on the west side of Main Street. The *Mathews News-Reporter* was published from 1912 to 1914. Like the *Gloucester Gazette*, which was established in January 1919 by Alanson Crosby, it was eclipsed by the *Mathews Journal*. The Great Depression took a toll on the financial health of both papers, and as a result, they merged into a new publication called the *Gloucester-Mathews Gazette-Journal* on October 14, 1937, and the new paper published its first consolidated issue on November 11, 1937. When John Warren Cooke was interviewed in 1992, he said that the Bank of Gloucester and the Farmer's Bank of Mathews had advocated the merger as a business strategy that may have kept both newspapers from failing.

The *Gloucester-Mathews Gazette-Journal* has traditionally played an important role in community life. Before it came on the scene, many local citizens subscribed to the *Norfolk-Virginian Pilot*, which arrived every other day by steamboat. Locals also read the *Richmond Times-Dispatch* which came by mail overland from West Point. Home delivery of the *Richmond Times-Dispatch* and *Richmond New Leader* began in 1929. John Warren Cooke invested in the *Gloucester-Mathews Gazette-Journal* in 1946 and became the newspaper's vice president. Then, when John DuVal died in 1954, Mr. Cooke purchased DuVal's financial interest and became majority shareholder and publisher. Over the years, the *Gloucester-Mathews Gazette-Journal* has fostered an interest in local history and historic preservation through feature articles and special publications. When the George P. Coleman Bridge opened in 1952, forging a link between the Middle and James-York Peninsulas, the *Daily Press* opened a branch office in Gloucester.[9]

The Courthouse Community

Maps, plats and photographic evidence provide insights into the character of the Mathews Courthouse community during the late nineteenth and early twentieth centuries. A photograph taken from Church Hill in

1894 contains some readily recognizable landmarks, such as the old Lane Hotel (White Dog Inn), the historic courthouse, the old and new clerk's offices, the jails for debtors and criminals, a doctor's office, and a handful of other buildings. A rail fence then enclosed the courthouse green. A chimney that protruded above some of the other buildings was identified as the Davis Hotel.[10] When a plat was made to redefine the southeast corner of the courthouse green's boundary line in 1904, Leonard M. Callis was in possession of a lot on the south side of Brickbat Road that abutted east on Main Street. This was the parcel that during the mid-to-late nineteenth century was occupied by the store owned by Francis Armistead and John W. Jarvis. On the north side of Brickbat Road, directly across from Callis's store, was a drugstore that abutted the main road. Next door to the drugstore, and just north of a vacant lot, was the "tavern lot." A 1916 plat indicates that the courthouse green encompassed 1.6 acres and included the courthouse, the clerk's office, jail, and the Confederate monument. By that time, the old debtor's jail depicted in the 1894 photograph was gone. Church Street bore its current name, but what is now known as Brickbat Road was labeled Jail Alley. Between Court Street and Main Street were four lots of somewhat unequal size. On the corner now occupied by the Halcyon Building was Marchant's Store and to the south was a "tavern"—presumably a hotel. The surveyor noted that G.S. Marchant had asserted a claim to some additional acreage that extended in a westerly direction toward the courthouse green.

On the east side of Main Street was the mercantile establishment that belonged to Henry and Francis Joseph Sibley, who in May 1899 bought half of a one-acre store lot that had originally belonged to Thomas James and his descendants, and in the 1840s to John D. Jarvis and Elijah Barnum. Barnum had sole possession of the store lot when he died in 1860, and in 1893 the property was purchased by William N. Trader and John W. Dixon Jr. Trader and Dixon then conveyed half of it to the Sibleys in 1899. Within months of the time the Sibley brothers made their purchase, they erected a two-and-a-half-story general store on their lot. By that time, the old Thomas James store had been moved to the rear of the original store lot. The Sibley brothers operated their business for many years, and when Joseph Sibley's son, Cecil M., returned from World War II in 1945, he became the store's proprietor.

Mathews County's first bank, established in Mathews Courthouse in 1900, was a branch of the L.E. Mumford Banking Company of Cape Charles. The Mumford Bank was situated on the east side of Main Street, just south of Wyatt Wolffe's store. J.P. Nottingham of Mathews was the first cashier of the Mumford Bank. He went on to become cashier of the Gloucester-Mathews Bank, formed in 1910, and president of the Bank of Mathews, established in 1912. In 1933 the Bank of Mathews merged with the Farmers and Fishermen's Bank, established in 1920, to become the Farmers Bank of Mathews. The façade of the Farmers and Fishermen's Bank, with its prominent porch and columns, has been preserved, and the Farmers Bank of Mathews' stone building, beautifully maintained, now houses the Mathews Memorial Library.

A topographic map published by the United States Geological Survey reveals that by 1917 Mathews Courthouse was more densely developed than it had been in the 1870s. The buildings on the courthouse green were shown schematically, as were the structures between Court and Main Streets. Buildings were thinly scattered along both sides of Church Street and there were two churches on the south side of the street: the Central Methodist Church and the Providence Baptist Church.[11] Along the south side of Brickbat Road, buildings occupied the lots then owned by L.M. Callis, George E. Sleet, and F. Theodore Miller.[12] On the east side of Main Street was the Westville Christian Church, built by the Disciples of Christ. To the south of the village, development was sparse and fine old homes bordered Put In Creek. On the east side of Main Street and north of Church Street were eight structures, one of which was the Westville Baptist Church. On the west side of Main Street, above Church Street, development was concentrated in the vicinity of Richardson's Drugstore, although a few buildings extended in a northerly direction toward Route 198. To the northwest of the village, on Route 198, cartographers identified the site of the original Lee-Jackson School. To the east of Hyco Corner was another school that wasn't identified by name, most likely a school for black children.

Photographs of the Confederate monument that was erected in 1912 reveal that the rail fence that had defined the courthouse green in 1894 had been replaced with a more substantial barrier comprised of medal crossbars affixed to sturdy posts. Drainage near the county's public buildings was poor and whenever there was a heavy rain, Court Street flooded. A well and a pump were installed on the courthouse green, thanks to funds donated by Mrs. E.M. Blake and Sheriff John E. Miller; it provided the public with a source of drinking water. Despite the addition of the new fence and a pump, within a few years' time, local citizens began complaining about the condition of the county's buildings and the green on which they stood. In 1912, county officials took action. New doors were installed in the courthouse's main entrance: one for the Treasurer's office and the other for the Commonwealth's Attorney. Additional improvements were made to the courthouse in 1920 and included a new extra door and interior and exterior painting. Three years later, new furniture was purchased for the judge. In time, the Treasurer's office was renovated and the courthouse got a new roof. Today, the historic courthouse complex includes the courthouse, built in the 1830s; the clerk's office erected around 1859; an early jail that most likely dates to the late eighteenth or early nineteenth century; another jail that was built during the second half of the nineteenth century; a privy that was built in 1934; and the original county library, later converted to other uses.

The coming of the automobile dramatically changed life in Mathews County and brought more people to the county seat. F. Theodore Miller, who lived on Brickbat Road, owned a one-cylinder Reo, perhaps the first automobile in the county. Although motorists discovered that travel on unpaved roads was slow, bumpy, tedious, and sometimes precarious, the automobile quickly became the preferred mode of transportation for those who could afford one. Vernon E. Davis, who by 1902 had a livery stable in Mathews Courthouse, responded to the changing times by opening an automobile service center. H.K. Taylor and S.C. Hutson also acknowledged the rising popularity of the automobile and opened the Mathews Garage, where they repaired and performed maintenance on cars and engines. Taylor later decided to become a dealer for Ford vehicles and Dearborn farm equipment. The Model Ts he sold, which came partially disassembled, were brought in from Baltimore, offloaded at Cricket Hill, and then reassembled and sold. When interviewed in 1949, Taylor said that whenever he drove to Gloucester, he always brought along tools and spare parts because he often found vehicles stranded by the side of the road. Photographs taken in the county seat in the early 1920s reveal that the automobile had become an indispensable mode of transportation and that gas pumps and unpaved and deeply rutted streets were a conspicuous part of the local landscape.[13]

Country Stores and Post Offices

During the 1880s and 90s rural post offices proliferated in Mathews County and new facilities were established at Blakes, Bohannon, Cardinal, Cricket Hill, Diggs, Dixie, Fitchetts, Foster, Grimstead, Gwynn, Hicks Wharf, Hudgins, Laban, Mobjack, New Point, North, Penny, Port Haywood, Retz, Shell, Soles, Susan, Warehouse, and Williams Wharf. Most of them were close to wharves at which steamboats docked or near the intersections of well-traveled roads. Before paved roads came to Mathews County, little communities like Cobbs Creek, Hudgins, Laban, Moon, North, Port Haywood (Traders), and Susan had one or more mercantile establishments, and the post office was in a store. As time went on, consolidation occurred. For example, when the post office at Soles closed, its work was taken over by the one at Dutton, and when the Warehouse post office closed, its duties were transferred to the Blakes post office, whose responsibilities were eventually given to Cobbs Creek. Likewise, the business of the post office at Penny was transferred to Laban, and that of the Shell post office was given to the post office at North. At one point, Mobjack's postmaster asked for his facility's name to be changed to Windmill Point and Shell's postmaster wanted his post office to be called Auburn. Business license reports compiled between 1903 and 1931 document the presence of the county's numerous mercantile establishments, and surviving store ledgers reveal that numerous types of items were sold. A newspaper ad that dates to August 1914 indicates that everything from cabbage plants and hay to horses, oxen, fish, and a 35-foot-long canoe were offered for sale at these focal points of community activity. Local business records also include the transactions that occurred between 1898 and 1906 at a boarding facility called Hudgins House, later known as Riverview or River Bend.

In 1883, the *Baltimore Sun* published a lengthy complaint about the delays created by changes that the U.S. Post Office Department had made to the traditional method by which mail was transmitted between Baltimore and Mathews County. In the past, the Old Bay Line's steamers carried the mail from Baltimore to Fort Monroe, where it was transferred to the steamer *Northampton* and then delivered to Mathews County's post offices. This provided tri-weekly mail service from point of origin to destination within 24 hours. Under the post office department's new system, mail was transported from Baltimore to Richmond and then carried overland from post office to post office to Virginia's easternmost counties. As a result, it took three or four days for Baltimore mail to reach Mathews and a like amount of time for the return trip, a delay that business interests considered a significant impediment. The post office department's superintendent quickly came up with a scheme intended to rectify the situation. He indicated that once the Baltimore mail reached Richmond, it could be sent by rail to West Point, which would save 24 hours. He added that the post office department had not renewed its contract with the Old Dominion Steamship Company because it could save $2,000 using its new procedures. He did inform steamship company officials that if they would be willing to carry the mail at a more modest rate, a new contract would be issued. In 1890, W.E. Hicks was appointed postmaster at Hick's Wharf and R.C. Brooks was appointed at Laban.

At the turn of the twentieth century post offices were established at Auburn Wharf, Beaverlett, Hallieford, Miles Store, Moon, Motorun (Bavon), Peary, Pribble, Redart,[14] Ruff, Sarah, and Tabernacle. T. Brooks Ruff and his successor, Mrs. Mary L. Ruff, were the only black postmasters in Mathews County. In time, more consolidation occurred, and Tabernacle's duties were transferred to Mathews, Motorun's to Shadow, Ruff's to Beaverlett, Sarah's to Onemo, and Auburn Wharf's to Cardinal. The responsibilities of the post office at Redart were temporarily transferred to Hudgins in 1916, and other transfers occurred as time went on.[15]

Entrepreneurial Endeavors

By the late 1870s and early 1880s, Mathews County property owners, in the interest of attracting visitors, began placing advertisements in Baltimore newspapers, calling attention to the abundance of recreational pursuits that were available locally. For instance, in August 1893 a lengthy article in the *Baltimore Sun* described the natural beauty of the Hudgins House, which provided a commanding view of the convergence of the Piankatank, Rappahannock, and York Rivers and Gwynn's Island. The writer described the area's healthfulness and then lapsed into a discussion of colonial history. In 1904, some entrepreneurs, who called themselves the New Point Comfort Corporation, hoped to build a local seaside resort. The proposed development lay between Deep Creek and the Chesapeake and Mobjack Bays and included land in what's known as New Point Comfort Island. The acreage was surveyed and laid out into 37 blocks of tiny lots, but little progress was made, and by the 1940s much of the area was inundated by the waters of the Chesapeake Bay.

Producing and selling alcoholic beverages was another way to make money. During the 1880s, anyone who wanted to manufacture or distill alcoholic liquors had to procure a license from the state, but no special qualifications or restrictions seemed to have been involved. However, by May 1888 the majority of Mathews County voters had decided that the county should be "dry," and the Commonwealth's Attorney took steps to revoke the annual licenses of all liquor dealers whose permits had been granted shortly before the vote. Although the county judge upheld that decision, within a month, Mathews liquor dealers hired an attorney who succeeded in getting Judge Jeffries to issue a writ of error. [16]

Matters of Life and Death

Mathews County's vital records dating from the 1880s and 90s provide genealogical information and useful insights into everyday life. The county's Register of Births lists the names of children and their parents along with the child's place of birth. Similarly, the county's Register of Deaths includes the decedents' names along with their race, occupation, place of birth, parents' names, and cause of death. These records reveal that during the 1880s people in Mathews County perished from communicable diseases like typhoid, whooping cough, diphtheria, cholera, pneumonia, and tuberculosis. They also died as a result of childbirth complications, cancer, diarrhea, dysentery, infections, dropsy (congestive heart failure), and paralysis. All of these causes of death were common in the 1850s, 60s, and 70s. One person died from "congestion of the brain"—perhaps encephalitis—and others died of accidental causes, such as injuries or drowning. For example, we know that in July 1887, 18-year-old Charles Pritchett of Horn Harbor, the son of Erastus and Laura Pritchett, died of the burns he received when he was scalded. Larkin Hudgins of Winter Harbor, a 21-year-old blacksmith and the son of John T. and Rosanna Hudgins, died from typhoid fever. Occasionally, newspapers mentioned drownings that occurred in Mathews County waters.

One of the county's medical practitioners was Dr. James Warren Dorsey Haynes, who was born at Cobbs Creek in 1868 and graduated from the University of Maryland in 1891. After practicing medicine for three years, he took a postgraduate course at the University College of Medicine in Richmond. Dr. Haynes lived at Hyco, where his medical office was located. Like his contemporaries, he made house calls in a horse-and-buggy, which he replaced with an automobile in 1910. He carried a portable operating table in his vehicle and readily admitted that he enjoyed doing surgery. He also spoke of a severe snowstorm that had occurred in Mathews County in 1899 and produced drifts that were up to ten feet deep. Dr. Haynes's services would have been in great demand in 1920 when a flu epidemic struck the county. He retired from his remarkably long medical practice in 1953.

Frank Knight and his horse-drawn hearse. Courtesy of the L.W. Wales Center, Antioch Baptist Church.

Robert Forrest established a funeral home in western Mathews County in 1879, and his son Charles Edward Forrest Sr. joined the family business in 1905. Shortly thereafter, the firm changed its name to the R.H. Forrest and Son Funeral Home. The undertaking establishment, whose clientele was white, was located on Route 14, across from Trinity Church. Another undertaker who became established in Mathews County in the early 1900s was Frank Knight, whose clientele was black. Because he had not been trained as an embalmer, whenever a death occurred, he brought in embalmer Charlie Jones, who arrived from

Hampton by steamer. The Knight Funeral Home then transported the decedent in a wagon hearse drawn by two horses.[17]

Steamboat Service

Steamboats continued to be Mathews County residents' primary means of contact with the outside world and were a major source of consumer goods. They brought in large quantities of manufactured ice and picked up cargoes of live poultry, eggs, oysters, clams, crabs, fish, potatoes, and other produce. For many years steamboats docked regularly at landings on the East, North, Ware, and Severn Rivers and Mobjack Bay. The steamer *Mobjack*, part of the Old Dominion Line, provided regular service to Philpotts Wharf, Williams, and Hicks Wharves on the East River, and during the early twentieth century service was extended to Diggs Wharf. The *Mobjack* also stopped at Auburn Wharf and at Dixondale. The steamer *Northampton* was on the Norfolk run from 1880 to 1897; the *Mobjack* from 1899 to 1920; and the *General Mathews* from 1920–30. The Baltimore line provided steamboat service to the Piankatank River and Milford Haven, utilizing the side-wheelers *Maggie, Enoch Pratt, Ida, Trivoli, Joppa, Avalon,* and *Middlesex*, and later, the *Piankatank*. In 1917, the Old Dominion Steamship Company considered withdrawing its vessels from Virginia waters to put them "to a more profitable use."

In 1949, when Elwood Callis was interviewed, he said that his grandfather, William James Callis, had built the first Callis's Wharf. He also indicated that his father, W. Eugene Callis, had erected a greatly improved dock on the same site. Afterward, the Maryland Steamboat Company, which operated out of Baltimore, and the Chesapeake and Atlantic Steamboat Company began stopping at Callis's Wharf. Mr. Callis said that in 1912 he began running his father's seafood business, which had a packing house at the wharf. His work involved purchasing, packaging, and shipping various types of seafood. There was a herring cannery at New Point, where barrels of fish were packed and ready for shipment, and fish were also readied for shipment and sold to buyers at Bayside. In August 1918, the Mathews County Board of Supervisors decided to accept bids for the construction of a public road from Callis's Wharf to the forerunner of Route 198.

Steamboats sometimes provided people with an opportunity to pursue their own dreams. In February 1890 William L. Diggs and Alice A. Hudgins, who planned to elope, took a steamer from Fitchett's Wharf to Baltimore, where they got married. Fitchett's Wharf, like many other steamboat landings, had a store. In October 1903, the proprietors of the Stoakes and Brothers Store, which was located there, published a handbill, announcing their closeout sale which included dry goods, furniture, farm implements, and livestock.

In 1907 Robert R. Miles, who had some land on the upper side of the mouth of Vessel Landing (now West Landing) Creek, conveyed a small parcel to Floyd C. Hurst, who was living on the property and operating a store. In 1911, Hurst sold his acreage to Andrew J. Diggs, who built a pier there, a transportation hub that became known as Diggs Wharf.[18] In March 1913, the *Mathews Journal* announced that Diggs had arranged for steamboat service to his wharf. Later in the year Diggs enhanced the size of his landholdings at Diggs Wharf by purchasing some additional acreage from George P. Hudgins; then, he sold the enlarged parcel to O.R. Gayle. In 1917, Gayle sold the property to Herman Hollerith, who quickly conveyed Diggs Wharf and some adjoining land to O.L. Powell, who lived there and ran a store. In 1921, Powell and his wife sold part of their land to the Standard Oil Company of New Jersey. Diggs Wharf, which had a post office and a freight railway that could be powered by hand or an engine, was a focal point of commercial activity until the devastating 1933 hurricane and its 1954 successor, Hurricane Hazel, which obliterated what remained.

When cartographers from the United States Geological Survey made maps of Mathews County in 1916 and 1917, they identified the routes used by steamboats and the wharves at which they stopped. There was steamboat service to Fitchett's Wharf on Stutts Creek and to Callis's Wharf on Gwynn's Island, and steamboats entered the Piankatank River and stopped at the wharves at Warehouse and Green Points before heading upstream to Freeport. On the east side of Mobjack Bay there was steamboat service to Bayside and Mobjack. Steamboats entered the mouth of the East River and paused at Diggs Wharf, Hicks Wharf, and Williams Wharf, where a steam-powered marine railway was built around 1908. On the North

River, steamboats stopped at the Auburn Wharf and then entered Blackwater Creek, pausing at a wharf between Oakland Creek and Green Mansion Cove.[19]

Other Transportation Conduits

Around 1883, some residents of Gwynn's Island and the mainland decided to build a hand-powered cable ferry that ran between the Narrows and Cricket Hill. William Foster and Charles Hudgins constructed a flat boat capable of carrying two buggies and a road cart, and they extended a cable across the water and fastened it securely. Thomas E. Edwards, a former ferryman who was interviewed in 1952, said that it was the hardest work he had ever done. He explained that the ferryman, positioned at the boat's bow, gripped the cable with a wooden device and then slowly walked toward the boat's stern. He'd then loosen the wooden device, slide it back to the bow, get a grip, and repeat the process. By this means, the ferryboat slowly inched across the water, propelled by the ferryman's strength. Mr. Edwards said that after gasoline-powered boats became available, one was lashed to the side of the ferryboat and propelled the ferry across the water. A larger company eventually began operating the ferry that ran from Callis's Wharf to Green's Wharf or Cricket Hill. It was replaced by a state-run ferry that served the traveling public until a bridge was built in 1939.

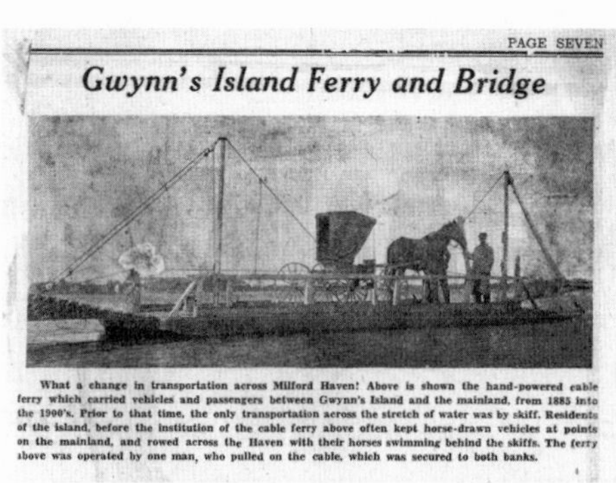

PAGE SEVEN

Gwynn's Island Ferry and Bridge

What a change in transportation across Milford Haven! Above is shown the hand-powered cable ferry which carried vehicles and passengers between Gwynn's Island and the mainland, from 1885 into the 1900's. Prior to that time, the only transportation across the stretch of water was by skiff. Residents of the island, before the institution of the cable ferry above often kept horse-drawn vehicles at points on the mainland, and rowed across the Haven with their horses swimming behind the skiffs. The ferry above was operated by one man, who pulled on the cable, which was secured to both banks.

Hand-powered cable ferry between Gwynn's Island and the mainland. Courtesy of Tidewater Newspapers, Inc.

By 1911, Mathews County residents had use of James Andrew Twigg's ferry which plied the waters of the Piankatank between the Green Point Wharf in Mathews County and Wilton Point in Middlesex. Twigg operated two barge-type ferries, the *Captain John Smith* and the *Miss Washington,* to which he lashed a motorboat. Anyone who needed to cross the river simply signaled him by ringing a bell or raising a flag.[20] When the state highway department took over the ferry in 1939, they added a diesel-powered boat that could carry eleven cars. On September 23, 1953, Twigg's ferryboat crossed the Piankatank for the last time and the James Andrew Twigg Bridge was opened to the traveling public.[21]

Disasters at Sea

The hexagonal lighthouse placed at the Wolf Trap in 1870 survived until it was carried away by ice in January 1893 during an extremely harsh period of winter weather. In fact, it was so cold that portions of the Chesapeake Bay were frozen from shore to shore, rendering the bay almost impassable for small vessels. Dangerous ice floes drifted about, imperiling everything in their path, and pressed against the pilings that kept the hexagonal Wolf Trap light station in place. Assistant keeper John William Thomas, who realized that his light station was doomed, tried in vain to signal for help. Finally, he spied a steamer that was about half-a-mile away and stopped by the thick ice. Thomas, who decided that reaching the steamer was his only hope of survival, set out across the ice while trying to attract the attention of anyone aboard. Fortunately, he succeeded. Thanks to the steady pressure of the ice, on January 22 the Wolf Trap light station was ripped from its pilings and according to an article in the *Baltimore Sun*, its top "can now be seen at the mouth of [the] Rappahannock River." Later, the light station floated down the bay and was found by the revenue cutter *Morrill* about one mile northeast of Thimble Shoals, on its way out to sea. Because the Wolf Trap light was an essential aid to navigation, a lightship was stationed there until it could be replaced.

The Chesapeake Bay froze, bringing maritime commerce to a standstill. Courtesy of the Gwynn's Island Museum.

An article published in the December 12, 1893, edition of the *Baltimore Sun* described the new 52-foot Wolf Trap lighthouse in considerable detail. Its base was a concrete-filled cast iron caisson, surmounted on a wooden crib embedded 18 feet in the sandy bottom. This provided a foundation for an octagonal brick building, capped by a light tower. Work on the lighthouse keeper's dwelling began in July 1894 and the light was first used on September 20, 1894.

Sometimes, navigational aids were not enough to prevent disasters at sea. In February 1890 two three-masted schooners that were headed in opposite directions collided just southeast of New Point Comfort. The *Frank Pratt Lee*, which was loaded with coal, was sunk. Later, it was raised and towed to Baltimore so that it could be repaired.

The winter of 1917–18 was one of record-setting low temperatures, which resulted in its being known as the "great freeze." For 30 days, the Chesapeake Bay was frozen from its mouth to its head. When the thaw finally came, it began in the vicinity of Norfolk. Robert M. Sigman, the steamer *Mobjack's* purser, later recalled that Captain George E. Caffee would steer his ship forward, ramming through the ice until it came to a dead halt. Then, he would back up and move forward again, inching further through the ice. Sigman spoke of the *Mobjack's* engineer's chipping ice off of the side-wheeler's paddles. Another exceptionally harsh winter occurred in 1927.[22]

Pursuing an Education

During the late nineteenth and early twentieth centuries, most youngsters, regardless of race, received all of their instruction from one teacher, who taught several grades in a one-room schoolhouse. Children walked to school unless their families were fortunate enough to have a horse they could use for the commute. The public school curriculum, though varied, was oriented toward reading, writing, and arithmetic. High-ceilinged schoolhouses, built in accordance with state guidelines, had blackboards that could extend up to seven feet above the floor. Teachers were encouraged to acquire wall maps, charts, and other graphics to provide students with visual and intellectual stimulation. A bucket and ladle for drinking water and brooms and brushes for cleaning were part of a schoolhouse's usual equipment, and a privy accommodated nature's needs. During the late nineteenth century, Mrs. Dora Armistead taught at the Williams Wharf Lane School and Mrs. George E. Tabb had a school at Woodstock, then the home of Dr. Thomas B. Lane. During the 1890s, J.D. Harris operated a private school at Palace Green. White children living near North could attend the Battery School and those near Laban could receive instruction at the Woodland School. The Virginia State Board of Education combined Mathews and Middlesex Counties into a school district that had one superintendent. A two-room school for white children was built in Mathews Courthouse around 1880 and was enlarged around 1888 to accommodate higher grades. By 1904, there was growing interest in building a high school in Mathews County. This institution of higher education, nicknamed the Tadpole or Tarpot Academy and located on the west side of Main Street, was created by enlarging a two-room school that had been erected around 1880. Growing attendance resulted in the need for a larger school, which was built by 1910. Later, the old high school was sold to R.W. Foster, an undertaker, who converted it into a funeral home, the forerunner of the Foster-Faulkner Funeral Home. A wind storm that occurred in mid-February 1909 destroyed an old schoolhouse on Gwynn's Island. Later in the year, island residents formed a Citizens Improvement League whose purpose was to build a modern school that would accommodate 200 or more white children.[23]

In 1906, the General Assembly enacted legislation that was intended to establish a system of public high schools. The legislature also made a modest sum available to counties that would provide matching funds. The new law gave rise to a plethora of public high schools in Mathews County. During the first few months of 1910, the *Mathews Journal*'s editor urged citizens to seek a tax increase to support public schools and School Superintendent E.C. Percifull also encouraged the public to provide more support to local schools. On one occasion he sent a letter to the newspaper, recommending that some of the funds usually spent on the poor be applied toward schools. In March 1911, the *Mathews Journal*'s editor renewed his plea for an increase in school funding. Superintendent Percifull asked taxpayers to continue the progress that had been made and in a second letter, he presented information in support of his position. Significant progress was made. By 1911 high schools that included seven or eight grades were built at Cobbs Creek, New Point, and Woodstock, and in Whites Neck (the Peninsula School) and Mathews Courthouse. Simultaneously, some of the county's old public schoolhouses were sold at auction, the usual procedure whenever one neighborhood school was replaced by another, and later when school consolidation occurred. On Gwynn's Island, local residents purchased a building from the Odd Fellows and converted it to use as a school. At Mathews Courthouse, a committee appointed by the Westville School Board selected a suitable site for the construction of a high school, a large lot on the lower side of Route 198, to the northwest of Hyco Corner.[24] Contractor J.M. Shinault built the new high school, a 60-foot-by-80-foot frame structure with eight classrooms and a hipped roof. Unfortunately, on the night of March 4, 1915, the county seat's new high school was destroyed by fire. School trustees, concerned about students missing time from school, arranged for classes to be held temporarily in meeting halls that belonged to the Masons, the Red Men, and the Junior Order, and immediately began planning for the construction of another high school. This time they decided to place the building a little further from the road. At the recommendation of the Sally Tompkins Chapter of the United Daughters of the Confederacy, the name Lee-Jackson High School was chosen. Unfortunately, on the night of February 15, 1922, the new high school, which like its predecessor was of frame construction, was destroyed by fire. Its replacement was a much more substantial brick building.[25]

Teams of surveyors making topographic quadrangle sheets in 1916 and 1917 used a little symbol (a flag) to show where Mathews County schools were located; a few were identified by name. The location of the Lee-Jackson High School on Route 198 was labeled, as was the Cattail School on the upper side of Stutts Creek, south of County Route 639. School B (a schoolhouse for black children) was near Hudgins, on the west side of County Route 223, south of its intersection with County Route 639. The Lawrenceville School was in Whites Neck, close to Miles Store, whereas the Battery School was on Route 14, a short distance west of North. The Westville School was located near the corner of Glebe and Long Roads (County Routes 621 and 622), whereas the Wharf Lane School, on County Route 614, was close to the Wayland Church and Ruff. The Beaverdam School was near the head of Garden Creek and Beaverlett, whereas the Hamburg School was on County Route 608, a short distance east of Port Haywood and near Winter Harbor's head. Woodland School, a two-room schoolhouse, was located at Laban.

In the 1910s schools were located near Laban, Peary and Susan. A school was also situated near the head of Pepper Creek, between New Point and Motorun; perhaps this was the newly-built New Point High School, which opened in October 1911. In 1919 Gwynn's Island residents purchased some land across from the Baptist Church and began raising the funds they needed to build a new school. By October 1920, the Gwynn's Island School League had managed to hire a contractor.

Because the Mathews County Board of Supervisors was concerned with the health and well-being of public school students, in 1916 they instructed their clerk to print cards that could be posted in each classroom, stating that, "All children attending the school shall free themselves from all vermin." If infested, they were to be suspended until the vermin (probably head-lice) were gone. Pupils also were cautioned about "all careless breakage or damaging of school property," which also would result in suspension. Although there were nearly two dozen schools, in 1920 the *Mathews Journal's* editor pointed out that the sum per-capita that Mathews County taxpayers spent on its students was very low in comparison with other Virginia communities. By the beginning of 1930 the newspaper's editor began advocating an increase in the school levy, citing overcrowded classrooms. In rebuttal, one local citizen proposed closing some of the county's schools. Another issue that the newspaper brought to the public's attention was the lack of school buses.

For African-American families who wanted to see that their children were educated, it was much more difficult. Mrs. Emily Gwynn Lumpkin Thomas, who was interviewed in 1986 at age 92, identified herself as the granddaughter of Ellen Billups, a former slave at Magnolia Farm. Mrs. Thomas said that she had attended the Glebe School, a one-room schoolhouse, until she was 14 years old, and qualified for enrollment in the Hampton Normal School. She caught a steamboat at Williams Wharf and when she reached Old Point Comfort, she was met by people from the school, where she became a boarding student. After three years there, she moved to New Jersey. In 1992, Mrs. Mary Pusey Smith, a Hudgins native who had just turned 100, said that during her childhood, she was educated at home by her parents. However, at age 18 she enrolled in St. Augustine College in Raleigh, North Carolina, and graduated in 1917. She said that when she returned home, she taught for four years at the Hookemfair School near Hudgins. It was not until 1927 that a public high school was built for blacks, the Thomas Hunter School at Mathews Courthouse. Today, very few of the one-room schools built for African Americans survive. Although the Jim Crow laws stratified Virginia's public school system, Northern and Midwestern philanthropists established trusts (such as the Slater Fund, the Jeanes Foundation, and the Rosenwald Fund) that provided financial support to black schools.[26]

Mathews Churches Grow in Strength

Mathews County's Methodist churches seem to have experienced a growth spurt during the 1890s. When Emmanuel Methodist Church's building grew too small, some of its members formed Grace Church in Mobjack. They joined with members of Providence Methodist Church to form the Grace Providence Methodist Church. After the pastor of Westville Christian Church (Disciples of Christ) began holding tent meetings at Mobjack, some of Emmanuel Methodist Church's members left to form the Oak Grove Christian Church. Two other Methodist congregations formed during the late nineteenth and early twentieth centuries: Locust Grove (near Windsor) and St. Matthew (in Potato Neck). The congregation of Point Comfort Methodist Church erected a new house of worship in the early 1890s and named it St. Paul's Methodist Church. The congregation of the Mathews Chapel Methodist Church built a new church during the 1890s. Later, the congregation of the Shiloh United Methodist Church on Gwynn's Island merged with that of the Mathews Chapel Methodists. In time, the congregation of Salem Methodist Church grew in strength and expanded its building.

During the mid-1890s the New Point Friends Church was organized in response to a tent meeting held at New Point by Quakers affiliated with the Society of Friends of the Ohio Yearly Meeting. Two local men oversaw the building of the New Point Friends Church at Susan, and Charles H. Diggs served as the congregation's first pastor. The members of the New Point Friends Church were Quakers, but their style of worship differed from that of silent meeting Friends. The Peniel Evangelical Friends Church was formed in 1915 and members held services in a building donated by members of the Mount Calvary Friends Church and brought to Laban (Onemo).[27] Later, the Peniel congregation erected a new church on a lot donated by Andrew J. Diggs in 1920. The Church of the Nazarene at Cricket Hill, organized in 1908, was a Protestant Christian church in the Wesleyan-Holiness tradition.

By the 1890s, historic Kingston Parish, which had struggled financially during the 1870s and 1880s, finally began to make progress. In 1894, the vestry purchased a lot in Mathews Courthouse that had a dwelling suitable as a rectory. A few years later, the congregation decided to build a new church. The new house of worship, built in 1898, was called St. John's and stood just south of the rectory. St. John's Church was used regularly until 1930, but was dismantled in 1954 and was replaced by a parish house two years later. Eventually, that structure was razed and replaced by a much larger parish house set back from the road. Meanwhile, in 1924, Trinity Church was lifted from its foundation and moved further from the public roads that defined two sides of its lot. At that time, a chancel and sanctuary were added to what had been a simple rectangular building. On January 18, 1904, historic Christ Church, the Episcopal house of worship built by Elizabeth Tompkins around 1841, was almost completely destroyed by fire; only its brick walls and large front doors survived. The congregation quickly rebuilt the church, and while construction was underway, services were held in the Williams Store at Williams Wharf. The rebuilt Christ Church, a project furthered by Milton Murray Sr., was fabricated from bricks salvaged from the ruins of the burned building and was slightly larger than the structure it replaced. It was ready for use by November 1904 when the Rev. Giles Buckner Cooke became Kingston Parish's new rector.[28]

During the early twentieth century some Mathews churches began publicizing the date and time of their Sunday services by means of advertisements that appeared in the newspaper. One article from August 15, 1914, noted that Sunday School picnics were to be held by the congregations of the Central and Bethel Methodist Churches. The writer may have said more than the churches intended, for he warned of the dangers of "Summer Constipation" because "the food you eat is often contaminated and is more likely to ferment in your stomach." Revivals were held on Gwynn's Island from time to time and in September 1916 the *Mathews Journal* announced that there had been numerous converts and that 19 baptisms occurred at Cherry Point.[29]

Progressive Farming

The advent of the twentieth century brought a number of significant changes to rural and urban America. Technological advances such as gasoline-powered farm vehicles—which were faster and more efficient than steam- or horse-powered agricultural equipment—were put to use on farms around 1906. A few years later the kerosene tractor became available. This greatly enhanced the American farmer's productivity. For example, in 1830 it took a farmer 61 hours to harvest 20 bushels of grain but in 1900 the same task took less than three hours. The operator of a corn sheller replaced 50 field hands. Modern equipment like mechanized potato planters, manure spreaders, and hay driers contributed to the considerable progress that was made. People who could afford to buy motorized farm equipment were able to increase their productivity, and therefore, their profits, dramatically. On the other hand, the increased costs associated with mechanized farming made it difficult for small operators to compete in the marketplace, and those costs put some farmers out of business. Mechanization also cost a number of hired farm workers their jobs. Some were able to acquire new, more marketable skills, while others became laborers in truck farming operations. Local people also worked in timbering and lumbering.

The twentieth century brought federal legislation that regulated the quality of milk, butter, and meat. Other laws required fungicides, pesticides, and herbicides to be labeled properly. A 1912 quarantine act was intended to curb the spread of plant diseases and insect pests within the United States. The Agricultural Extension (or Smith-Lever) Act authorized land grant colleges to offer public instruction in agricultural and home economics and to distribute information of potential use to rural households. This legislation gave rise to the Cooperative Extension Service. Agricultural Extension agents provided local farmers with practical information about crop production and the use of improved seeds and fertilizers. By the 1920s, Home Demonstration agents, whose goal was to improve the quality of rural life through homemaking and home economics, had become available as part of the statewide Extension Service program. Funding also became available to bring the 4-H program to rural youngsters. The Extension Service changed with the times and today its agents provide information on crop and soil sciences, family and consumer services, agricultural and natural resources, and 4-H youth development.

Despite advances in progressive farming, Mathews residents remained subject to unexpected phenomena. In November 1903, a Michigan newspaper reported that large numbers of Mathews County cattle had drowned on account of the phosphorescent light seen in marshes after a storm. The cattle were feeding in the marshes when the mysterious light commenced flashing and were drowned when the wind-driven tide came in.

When agricultural census data were compiled in 1910 and 1920, there were more than 1,385 farms in Mathews County that encompassed a total of more than 40,000 acres of land. A significant number of Mathews farmers were involved in animal husbandry, but a relatively small number of people were engaged in truck farming. Local farms produced corn, rye, wheat, white potatoes, sweet potatoes, hay, alfalfa, timothy, and small grains. As time went on and improved seeds and fertilizers became widely available, the yield per acre increased.

By 1902, Mathews County had commenced holding an annual fair, an outdoor event that was popular and well attended. Among the events held was harness-racing. The fair would have given local farmers a chance to show off their prizewinning livestock and produce. Although fairs ceased being held in 1911, they resumed in 1925. But like all social events in the early twentieth century, the Mathews County Fair was racially segregated.[30]

Mathews County's Board of Supervisors and Their Duties

The earliest existing minutes of the Mathews County Board of Supervisors, which date to June 1887, reveal that the Board issued orders for their own compensation and for funds paid to other local officials, such as the clerk of court, the county jailer, the Commissioner of Revenue, and the county coroner. In 1887, G.S. Garnett was the circuit court judge, George Hunley was Commonwealth Attorney, and Sands Smith III was the Clerk of Court. J.B. Thurston, Andrew Borum, and S.B. Montague were county supervisors.

Mathews County's Board of Supervisors distributed funds to people who had performed work on the county's behalf, provided monetary support to the indigent, and saw that public buildings were maintained. They also paid local people for cleaning ditches and furnishing the supplies needed for road repair. In 1890, the superintendent of public roads in Virginia's magisterial districts gained the right to require all males between the ages of 18 and 60 to do road work two days a year. Those who refused were fined and those fees were applied toward road repairs. The road repair act, which was highly unpopular, was repealed in 1894. Four years later, the responsibility of repairing and maintaining public roads and bridges was relegated to each county's Board of Supervisors, who could hire contractors or day laborers to perform road repairs. The Board also had the right to purchase teams of draft animals, road machinery, tools, and other implements for use in repairing local roads. A 1916 law permitted the Board to contract with any local person or company willing to maintain public highways, as long as local voters approved.

When the Mathews County Board of Supervisors convened in 1899, its members debated whether to make smallpox vaccinations compulsory for everyone. Local doctors argued for compulsory vaccinations, and the Supervisors decided to procure pure vaccine and to require vaccination.[31] Another important issue that was discussed in 1899 was the need to establish definitive boundary lines for each of the county's three magisterial districts. In 1900 W.N. Trader, who had been hired as census-taker for the Piankatank District, resigned his post without indicating why he did so.[32]

The 1886 and 1897 Earthquakes

When a devastating earthquake struck Charleston, South Carolina, in 1886, strong tremors rumbled up the coast, attracting attention as far north as the state of New York. The Light-House Board noted that shocks and aftershocks were felt "from the mouth to the middle of the Chesapeake Bay" and were reported by lighthouse keepers throughout that region. Charles W. Forrest was then on duty at the New Point Comfort lighthouse.

The 1886 earthquake was one of the most powerful tremors to hit the southeastern United States since the 1811 and 1812 quakes in New Madrid, Missouri. The 1897 earthquake, which occurred on May 31 around 2 P.M., also jarred eastern Virginia and portions of ten other states. In Richmond, buildings swayed violently and a deep rumbling noise was heard, followed by sharp cracking. The earthquake lasted for approximately five minutes and involved movement that traveled from north to south.[33]

The County's Political Representatives

The county was served by a variety of representatives in the state government. Delegate Andrew B. Evans commenced representing Mathews and Middlesex Counties in the General Assembly in 1881, while State Senator Thomas J. Christian served on behalf of a district that included Gloucester, King and Queen, Mathews, and Middlesex Counties. Both men held office until 1885 when Evans was replaced by John C. Bohannon and Christian was ousted by James N. Stubbs, who served until 1897. When elections were held in 1887, L.C. Bristow became Mathews County's delegate, but he was unseated by George Y. Hunley in 1889.

In 1891, R.T. Bland became the delegate for Mathews and Middlesex Counties, but he was replaced in 1893 by John Newstead Tabb, who served Gloucester and Mathews Counties until 1897. Tabb was succeeded by former senator James N. Stubbs and Thomas E. Blakey became the senator for a slightly larger district that included Essex, Gloucester, King and Queen, Mathews, and Middlesex Counties. By 1899, George Y. Hunley had become Mathews County's delegate but Senator Blakey was reelected. When a state constitutional convention was held in 1901–02, G.T. Garnett represented Gloucester and Mathews Counties. Delegate George Y. Hunley served through 1903, the year that J. Boyd Sears became the state senator for a district that included Mathews, King and Queen, Gloucester, Essex, and Middlesex Counties. Both men still held office in 1905. In 1906, G.E.T. Lane became the delegate for Mathews and Middlesex Counties and Senator Sears was reelected. By 1908, W.D. Evans had become Mathews County's delegate and John R. Saunders was state senator; both were reelected and served through 1911. Delegate Julian T. Christian took office in

1912 and Senator Saunders served through 1916. However, by 1914 Christian had been ousted and replaced by J. William Daniel. His time in office was abbreviated and by 1916 he had been unseated by R.H. Stubbs. [34]

On the Cusp of a New Century

Although America's burgeoning population had almost overwhelmed the United States Census Bureau in 1880, Herman Hollerith of Mathews County came to the rescue when he introduced an electrical enumerating machine, a mechanized method of managing the data that had been collected. Hollerith's punch-card system, which was used during the 1890 census, reportedly enabled the average clerk to feed almost 8,000 cards a day through the system. This invention was personally lucrative, too; Hollerith went on to become one of the founders of International Business Machines (IBM). By the time of the 1900 census, demographic records reveal that Mathews County had a population of 8,239 and that of that number, 2,395 were black. The county was home to 579 people age 10 and older who were unable to read and write. Census-takers reported that there were 1,642 dwellings in the county and that there were 924 farms that were owned and occupied by whites, plus an additional 39 farms rented to white sharecroppers. There were 254 black-owned farms and 22 additional farms rented to black sharecroppers. The total income derived from manufacturing in Mathews County was $61,780.

By the time demographic records were compiled in 1910, some modest changes had occurred. The total population had increased to 8,922 people, 2,513 of whom were black. There were 1,831 dwellings in the county and 1,387 farms, less than 17 percent of which were owned by blacks. Around 20 percent of all farms were between three and nine acres in size. Illiteracy was still a serious problem, but almost 1,600 children had attended school in 1909.

The majority of Virginia's African-American farmers were at the lowest end of the economic spectrum and owned less land than they had in 1860. While overall economic trends lay at the heart of this issue, the poverty of many rural blacks was palpable. When motorized farming equipment became available, fewer field hands were needed. Also, a significant number of small farmers (mostly blacks) were put out of business because they could not compete with their better equipped neighbors. Between 1890 and 1920, a substantial number of blacks moved north, seeking work and a greater opportunity to succeed. As John W. Dixon's history of Gwynn's Island demonstrates, in 1910 the island had 811 people of whom 135 were black, but by 1920, the island's total population of 579 included only 19 blacks. On August 24, 1916, an article in the *Mathews Journal* noted that no black teachers had been appointed for Gwynn's Island for the 1916–17 school year. Less than a month later, the newspaper reported that the last black family had moved off the island. A downturn in the oyster business most likely contributed to the exodus of blacks from Gwynn's Island.[35]

The Jamestown Exposition

As 1907 (Virginia's 300th anniversary) approached, Virginians began discussing how to commemorate the event. In early 1901, the state's General Assembly authorized Governor A.J. Montague to invite Virginia localities to submit proposals on how the occasion should be celebrated. Ultimately, Sewell's Point, in Norfolk, a site that would accommodate a large naval display, was chosen as the site at which the celebration would be held. As preparations for the Jamestown Exposition moved forward, the General Assembly appropriated funds for the construction of buildings and displays at Sewell's Point. Exhibits featuring Virginia counties' industrial, agricultural, mineral and commercial resources were to be displayed at the exposition. Items in the Mathews County Historical Society's files suggest that some local residents participated in the Jamestown Exposition.[36]

Early Social, Civic, and Service Organizations

During the late nineteenth and early twentieth centuries, fraternal organizations became extremely popular throughout the United States. Mathews County citizens joined social and civic organizations that provided them with good fellowship but also worked toward the community's betterment. During the 1880s, a men's group known as the Odd Fellows, affiliated with the United Order of Odd Fellows (later the Independent Order of Odd Fellows), acquired property in Mathews Courthouse and held their meetings there. Another meeting unit, the Mobjack Lodge of the Independent Order of Odd Fellows, chartered in 1904, acquired a building on the west side of the East River in 1906. Members met there until 1950, when they purchased the Peninsula School building. At one point there were Odd Fellows lodges at Hudgins, Port Haywood, and Cobbs Creek. There also were two meetings (or "tribes") of Red Men in Mathews County during the early twentieth century. One was the St. Tammany Tribe of Red Men, which was viable in Mathews by 1903, and the other was the Omaha Tribe of Red Men, organized in 1913 and located in North. Yet another fraternal group that was active in Mathews County was the Good Samaritan Lodge, which formed in the 1890s and owned property in the county. In April 1919, the Newport News Council of the Boy Scouts of America purchased a ten-acre tract on Gwynn's Island and established a summer camp, which they immediately put to use.

Atlantic Lodge No. 201 of the Independent Order of Good Templars, whose organization was modeled on Freemasonry, was established sometime prior to 1907 when its members sold their property at Hudgins to the Mathews Baptist Church. The Good Templars also had a meeting hall on Gwynn's Island, reportedly the first facility of its kind in Mathews County. The county's Masonic Lodge, Oriental Lodge No. 20, was established in 1868 and was founded by John B. Donovan, the group's first Worshipful Master. Another member of Oriental Lodge No. 20 was Andrew D. Armistead, who during the Civil War commanded Armistead's Battery of the Virginia Light Artillery. The members of Oriental Lodge No. 20 purchased a building in Mathews Courthouse that had belonged to the Good Templars. By 1961 they had razed the older structure and erected their new Lodge, the building in which they still meet.[37]

Expanding Cultural Awareness

A group of dedicated volunteers whose fervent belief in the importance of expanding knowledge through reading fostered the establishment of the Cardinal Athenaeum, a private library that came into existence around 1909. There, many local citizens had their first exposure to great literature and culturally enriching programs like musical concerts. Miss Bernice Machen was the Cardinal Athenaeum's first librarian. The facility, described as a "library out in the woods," was open on Saturdays from 3 P.M. to 5 P.M. Only card-carrying members of the library were allowed to check out reading materials, but local residents were encouraged to visit the library's reading room and to attend cultural programs. An article that appeared in the *Mathews Journal* on February 8, 1923, noted that Miss Emma Nottingham was the Athenaeum's new librarian and that a wide assortment of books and magazines were available. Around 1927, the board of the Cardinal Athenaeum voted to become a free community library (the West Mathews Library) that was intended to serve the residents of western Mathews County. Five years later, the Cardinal Athenaeum gave its volumes to Mathews County's first public library, the Mathews Memorial Library.[38]

World War I

In 1914, the outbreak of hostilities between the Allies and the Central Powers took many Americans by surprise even though the country generally supported President Woodrow Wilson's policy of neutrality. Mrs. Giles B. Cooke and Miss Mary Randolph Lane already were active in soliciting clothing and provisions for Belgian relief. On August 3, 1916, the *Philadelphia Inquirer* reported that a German submarine, the *Deutschland*, and her convoy, the tug *Thomas F. Timmons*, had spent an afternoon in the deep water near New Point Comfort, awaiting a chance to slip by the Allied warships that were just outside of the three-mile limit off the Virginia coast. Mariners surmised that the *Deutschland* would stay hidden until dark and then make a quick dash for the capes. As it was a cloudy, moonless night and the seas were rough, conditions were ideal for her to slip away, which she did. Later, the authorities learned that the *Deutschland* had gone to Baltimore to procure large quantities of rubber, nickel, and tin.

In March 1917, after German submarines sank five American merchant vessels, President Wilson and his cabinet unanimously endorsed a declaration of war. Congress agreed, and on April 6, 1917, the United States officially went to war with Germany. The headlines of the March 22, 1917, edition of the *Mathews Journal* announced that a Mathews man was in command of a ship sunk in the war zone. In another wartime incident, a German submarine sank the *City of Memphis* off the coast of Cardiff, Wales, but her commander, Captain L.P. Borum of Mathews County, and all of her crew were saved. Later, Captain Borum said that the Germans ordered the crew to leave the ship, which they did in open boats, and then sank the vessel. Coles Franklin Hudgins of Mathews County died in the war zone when a Standard Oil ship leaving Philadelphia was bound for Rotterdam was sunk by a submarine's torpedo off the coast of Holland. The American steamship *Rockingham* was also sunk by a German U-boat in the war zone. Two Gwynn's Island men, Curtis Grimstead and Clarence Irwin Carney, were aboard at the time but managed to survive.

Captain Alexander James, commander of the Lane-Diggs Camp of Confederate Veterans, arranged for a big patriotic rally to be held on the courthouse green on April 21, 1917. The Daughters of the Confederacy and members of the Mathews Civic League made preparations for a luncheon. The buildings on the grounds of the courthouse were decorated with flags and bunting, a stage was erected, and a flag was put on display that had been aboard the steamer *Memphis* when it sank. An array of patriotic speakers addressed a large crowd and pledged support for the war. Detachments of United States Marines and members of a machine gun company held military drills and stirring music was provided by a battleship band.

Over the next two years, the county seat was at the hub of patriotic activities, for there were rallies, honor flag days, Liberty Days, and Chautauqua Week. Mathews County received an honor flag in 1918 for its highly successful Liberty Loan drive and another one for its Victory Loan drive. War Savings Stamps were also a big success, and Mobjack Lodge No. 273 of the International Order of Odd Fellows invested $200 in War Savings Stamps, a remarkable sum at the time.

Mathews County's involvement in the war effort was intensified due to the county's proximity to debarkation points in Hampton Roads and the military installations along the York River. Also, many local men were in the Merchant Marine. By the time war was officially declared, seven men from Mathews were already in the service. When Virginia's governor, Henry C. Stuart, called for recruits for the navy, six Mathews men, all experienced seamen and navigators, enlisted for patrol duty. They became commissioned officers and planted mines and nets and patrolled the coast. Less than four weeks after war had been declared, 33 Mathews County men joined the military. On June 5, 1917, when men between the ages of 21 and 31 registered for military service, a total of 620 men were eligible. When a second registration drive was held in September 1918, another 945 men volunteered to serve. Although Mathews County, on the basis of its population, had been asked to furnish 85 men, it had 275 men in military service. The Mathews-Gloucester Coast Artillery was organized on July 5, 1917, and included 31 men from Mathews County. The Artillery was mustered into service on July 23, 1917, amid much fanfare and afterward set out for Fort Monroe.

The Mathews Chapter of the American Red Cross was organized on May 12, 1917. The organization grew rapidly and had auxiliaries for white members in Cardinal, Gwynn's, and Cobbs Creek, and auxiliaries for black members at Providence, Antioch, and Zion. Many local citizens became involved in the American Red Cross and other service organizations that supported those in uniform. Members of the local Red Cross chapter and the Junior Red Cross produced remarkable quantities of knit sweaters, mufflers, shawls, pairs of socks, gun wipes, and comfort kits. They also darned socks and collected old clothing for refugees. Youngsters joined the Junior Red Cross, which was organized in the county's public schools, and learned about health, hygiene, and food preservation. They also sewed and knitted, made scrapbooks, and collected tin foil, and nut shells. Teachers promoted patriotism, and school children sold war stamps and canvassed their communities for books and magazines that the Red Cross could send to troops. Older students raised funds and collected garments for refugees and donated articles such as pillows for hospitals.

The Rev. B.E. Hudson served as the director of the Junior Red Cross in Mathews. Mathews churches supported the patriotic cause by encouraging members to join the Red Cross. Local women raised poultry and began gardening and preserving food. Farmers were encouraged to use modern techniques to enhance their productivity, and agents of the agricultural extension service helped by disseminating the latest information. Larger potato and wheat crops were planted and there was increased emphasis on the production of vegetables and fruit.

Families whose loved ones went off to war were deeply affected emotionally, but mobilization also entailed great sacrifices on the home front. Wartime agencies were established for the purpose of controlling supplies of food, fuel, and raw materials, and rationing was introduced. Americans were urged to do without wheat and meat at least once a week and pledge cards were sent to homes to encourage "wheatless" and "meatless" days. Households also were encouraged to plant Victory Gardens and to use leftovers. There were limitations on flour, meat, sugar, and ice consumption, and price-fixing became a reality. The Fuel Administration introduced the country to "Heatless Mondays" and Daylight Savings Time in 1918. Other federal agencies regulated railroads, the highway system, and shipping.

The Honorable J. Boyd Sears was chair of the County Food Administration, whereas Joseph E. Healy was in charge of food conservation. The Food Administration asked oystermen to double their efforts to increase the food supply and merchants were required to obtain certificates that enabled them to purchase sugar. Older county residents, who recalled conditions during the Civil War, urged the younger generation to be extremely frugal. Woodstoves gradually replaced coal stoves as the price of coal soared. The Radcliffe Chautauqua held a demonstration at the Mathews County seat, offering instruction on home nursing and food conservation. Some local stores closed. Many blacks reportedly left the county, seeking jobs on the James-York Peninsula, and farm labor costs increased from $1 a day to $2.50 a day.

Letters from overseas, published in local newspapers, kept Mathews County citizens apprised of events on the warfront. George Treakle described being gassed, and Rosser Hudgins wrote about how his unit captured a French town. John T. Borum of the 61st Regiment of Marines sent a letter from Germany, and Currie Hudgins wrote from Verdonette, France, telling of life in the trenches. The Belgian government gave Captain L.P. Borum of the steamship *Memphis* a loving cup in appreciation for rescuing 26 Belgian seamen from an open boat in the North Atlantic in June 1918, whereas Waverly Hudgins of Diggs, chief yeoman of the *Elinor,* was cited by the Secretary of the Navy for rescuing a man who fell overboard. One doctor and three nurses from Mathews County were sent overseas: Dr. E.T. Sanberg and Lucile Douglass, Maude Minter, and Mattie Shackelford.

Finally on November 11, 1918, at five o'clock in the morning, an armistice was signed; six hours later, the guns along the front lines fell silent. According to an article that appeared in the *Mathews Journal* on November 14, 1918, there was a big celebration at Mathews Courthouse, where the sound of pealing church bells intermingled with blaring automobile horns. The occasion included a bonfire, gunfire, an oyster roast, and a rider dressed like Paul Revere, who rode up and down Main Street. Besides the Mathews County men who lost their lives, John Bassett was wounded three times, Oscar Hudgins Jr. was wounded and gassed on the last day of fighting, S.W. Treakle was gassed, and J.H. Blaylock, William Hurst, and Wilton Moore were wounded. In 1925, Mathews Post No. 83 of the American Legion erected a plaque in the courthouse, honoring their comrades who had made the ultimate sacrifice: Stanley E. Brownley, Herbert S. Butts, Raymond Collins, Jenifer Garnett, Harold Hatch, Frank Rosser Hudgins, Howard Hudgins, Elbert L. Morgan, Glenn Rayne, Charles R. Richardson, and Rufus Smith. In 2003, those people's names were also listed on a plaque that was erected in front of the new county courthouse complex at Liberty Square.

In 1979 Mathews County's Extension Agent, Gene Dinwiddie, commented that World War I initiated changes in the agricultural economy that were never reversed. He noted that before the war, half of the county's people lived on farms and that farmers relied on their horses and mules for the power they used in the fields. Most family farms were self-sufficient although potatoes were a money crop that could be barreled and shipped out. Many farmers were part-time fishermen and fishing was a good source of income as well as nourishment. Fishing also produced scrap fish that could be used for fertilizer. Dinwiddie observed that when World War I came along, many people left family farms and moved to urban communities and that although food crops were still needed, major changes occurred in local patterns of consumption.[39] These changes would be exacerbated in the post-war period.

NOTES

1 After the war, the number of women who married men ten or more years older than themselves more than doubled and the share of women marrying men who were five or more years younger than themselves tripled (www.encyclopediavirginia.org/Civil_War_Widows).

2 Mathews Archives Box 6 R; Mathews County Census 1860; Records of the Confederate Pension Board 1900–1901:1–9; www.encyclopediavirginia.org/Civil_War_Widows; http://lva1.hosted.exlibrisgroup.com; Charles, *Newspapers*, 168.

3 Once again, the dredgers were tried, convicted, and sent to the penitentiary, but were pardoned and were able to recover the value of their vessels (Charles, *Newspapers,* 124).

4 Hudgins, whose father was a shipbuilder, was an experienced mariner and had been an agent of the Confederate government (Charles, *Newspapers*, 126).

5 www.marinersmuseum.org; Charles, *Newspapers*, 121–123, 125–128, 139, 141.

6 Leonard, *General Assembly*, 573–574; Katz, *The Negro*, 237–242, 244; Mathews Archives Box 21 R; Tindall, *America*, 722; http://en.wikipedia.org/wiki/constitution_of_virginia; Mathews County Land Tax Lists 1887–1910.

7 Charles, *Newspapers*, 158–159, 169; *Richmond Times-Dispatch*, July 26, 1916; *Richmond News Leader*, July 26, 1916; Mathews County Military Pension Records, Adjutant Sands Smith III's Correspondence, Lane-Diggs Camp in 1902; Census 1860; Mathews Archives Boxes 21 R, 24 R; White, *Mathews Men*, 63–65; Sheridan and Ernst, *Tombstones,* 173; http://lva1.hosted.exlibrisgroup.com; MCHS, *Panorama*, 40.

8 When interviewed in 1992, John Warren Cooke said that he was unaware of any copies of the *Mathews Journal* dating to 1903 and questioned the accuracy of the statement made in the book, *Virginia Newspapers*. That volume's author cited as evidence the January 21, 1927, edition of the *Mathews Journal*, No. 3, "the 25th anniversary issue" (Mathews Archives, Box 23 R; Lester J. Cappon, *Virginia Newspapers, 1821–1935* [New York, 1936], 129).

9 *Gloucester-Mathews Gazette-Journal*, December 30, 1999; Mathews Archives, Box 23 R; MCHS, *History and Progress*, 136–138.

10 In 1894 shoemaker Joseph Davis's estate was credited with 27.19 acres at the courthouse that had $500 worth of improvements and general merchant Charles C. Davis's estate was in control of 48.25 acres at the courthouse that had $600 worth of improvements (Mathews County Land Tax Lists 1894; Census 1880).

11 This church no longer exists.

12 Miller then owned the house that later became known as the Tompkins Cottage.

13 Mathews Memorial Library photo 1894; Mathews County Land Book 1:306, 393–394, 467–468; Land Tax Lists 1815–1894; Deed Book 10:403–404; 12:231–232; Will Book 1:14–16; Mathews Archives Boxes 10 R, 82 R; MCHS, *History and Progress*, 55–59, 67, 70–71, 73–74, 127–128; MCHS, *Mathews County Panorama*, 91–95; WMCAR, *Integrated*

Management Plan, 38, 42, 45, 50; U.S.G.S., "Mathews," 1917; *Mathews Journal*, August 17, 1911; March 14, 1912; June 1, 1916; August 17, 1919; June 10, 1920; September 6, 1923; June 1, 1924; August 14, 1924; April 19, 1928; August 25, 1929; December 10, 1929.

14 That is, Trader spelled backwards.

15 Charles, *Newspapers*, 123–124, 137, 142; Mathews Archives Boxes 10 R, 15 OV, 20 R, 21 R, 23 R, 70 R, 79 R, 85 R; Sadler, "Post Offices."

16 Mathews County Court Rule Papers 1866–1872; Charles, *Newspapers*, 131–132, 140–141; Mathews Archives Box 3 folder 1 and Box 1 OV; MCHS, *Panorama*, 61.

17 Mathews County Vital Statistics 1882–1884, 1887, 1897–1899, 1902–1904; Mortality Schedules 1850–1880; www.foster-faulkner.com/about-us; MCHS, *History and Progress*, 122; Mathews Archives Box 34 R; *Mathews Journal*, February 26, 1920; March 11, 1920.

18 Diggs, who also owned some land on Horn Harbor, in November 1912 announced his plans to build a new pier and by February 1913, construction had gotten underway. He made repairs to his Horn Harbor Wharf in 1916 and it seems to have survived until a major northeaster struck in March 1927 (*Mathews Journal*, December 28, 1916; March 24, 1927).

19 *Gloucester-Mathews Gazette-Journal*, April 16, 1959; Charles, *Newspapers*, 137; MCHS, *History and Progress*, 34–37; *Panorama*, 69, 73, 78–81; Mathews County Deed Book 7:512; 15: 582; 17:143; 18: 297–299; 20: 573–575, 588–590; 22:571–572; Plat Book 1:105; *Mathews Journal*, March 14, 1913; October 23, 1913; August 22, 1918; April 8, 1920; May 21, 1930; *Charlotte Observer*, Charlotte, North Carolina, July 17, 1917; Mathews Archives Boxes 1 OV, 34 R; USGS, "Mathews,"1916; "Kilmarnock," 1917.

20 A topographic quadrangle sheet that dates to 1916 reveals that a small ferry, Shipley's, also ran from the west side of Cobbs Creek's mouth, in Mathews, to Mill Creek Neck in Middlesex (USGS,"Kilmarnock," 1916).

21 USGS,"Kilmarnock," 1916; "Mathews,"1917; MCHS, *History and Progress*, 42, 113; *Daily Press*, September 28, 1952.

22 *Charlotte Observer*, February 4, 1893; *Baltimore Sun*, December 12, 1893; Charles, *Newspapers,* 137–139; Mathews Archives Box 18 R; MCHS, *History and Progress*, 6, 37; Charles F. Brooks, "The 'Old Fashioned' Winter of 1917–1918," *Geographical Review*, 5 (May 1918), 405, 410–411; *Mathews Journal*, January 20, 1927.

23 High winds and high tides occurred again in December 1914 and caused a large washout on Gwynn's Island (*Mathews Journal*, December 10, 1914).

24 Years later, Mathews County's new courthouse complex, Liberty Square, was built on the school property.

25 John Warren Cooke said that after one of the high school fires, he attended classes in the county courthouse (Mathews Archives Box 23 R).

26 *Gloucester-Mathews Gazette-Journal*, October 30, 1986; September 17, 1992; MCHS, *History and Progress*, 7, 48–51, 142–144; *Panorama*, 51, 61, 87, 99–100; USGS, "Mathews," 1916;

"Kilmarnock," 1917; Mathews Archives, Boxes 5 R, 23 R, 24 R, 35 R, 88 R; *Mathews Journal*, February 25, 1909; November 4, 1909; January 27, 1910; February 10, 1910; April 7, 1910; August 18, 1910; March 16, 1911; March 30, 1911; May 15, 1919; August 3, 1916; February 26, 1920; October 28, 1920; March 3, 1930; March 20, 1930; April 3, 1930; April 14, 1930; April 24, 1930; Betty Wrenn Day, Oral History File TMP-029, July 7, 2014; www.wikipedia.com.

27 In 1939 when Harriet G. Miller, a WPA worker, interviewed Mrs. Buena Diggs, a skillful quilter, she identified herself as a member of the Peniel Friends Church (Miller, "Interviews," Box 6).

28 The Rev. Cooke was rector from 1904 to 1915.

29 Mathews Archives Boxes 1 R, 21 R; MCHC, *History and Progress*, 11–14, 143; Charles, *Newspapers*, 139, 146; Kingston Parish Vestry Book 1873–1938:42, 48, 52, 57, 73, 76; Brown, *Old Kingston Parish*, 32–33; *Mathews Journal*, September 21, 1916; Janice C. Vogel, *Then and Now: Mathews County* (Charlestown, South Carolina, 2001), 19, 56.

30 www.co.mathews.va.us/departments-services/extension-office; Charles, *Newspapers*, 153–154; Mathews County Farm Statistics 1910–1954, Mathews Archives Boxes 18 R, 24 R; MCHS, *Panorama*, 111; *Mathews Journal*, September 2, 1910; October 20, 1910; August 6, 1925; October 15, 1925.

31 By 1911 Mathews County school children were required to be vaccinated for smallpox (Mathews Archives Box 35 R).

32 Mathews County Board of Supervisors Minute Book 1887–1900: 402, 404, 437, 680, 696, 702, 704, 712; Circuit Court Executions 1858–1895; J.A. O'Bannon, comp., *Acts and Joint Resolutions Passed by the General Assembly of the State of Virginia Passed During the Session of 1889–1890* (Richmond, 1890), 695; *Acts and Joint Resolutions Passed by the General Assembly of the State of Virginia Passed During the Session of 1893–1894* (Richmond, 1894), 492; *Acts and Joint Resolutions Passed by the General Assembly of the State of Virginia Passed During the Session of 1897–1898* (Richmond, 1898), 504; Davis Bottom, comp., *Acts and Joint Resolutions Passed by the General Assembly of the State of Virginia Passed During the Session of 1916* (Richmond, 1916), 459.

33 Clifford and Clifford, *New Point Comfort*, 81; *Virginia Gazette*, June 4, 1897; www.wikipedia.org.

34 Leonard, *General Assembly*, 534, 536, 538, 540, 542, 544, 546, 548, 550, 552, 554, 556, 558, 560, 562, 564, 566, 568, 570, 572–574, 577, 580, 586, 589, 591, 594, 596, 601, 603, 605, 607, 609.

35 Mathews Archives Box 22 R; Keith Reid-Green, "The History of Census Tabulation," in *Scientific American*, February 1989, 98–103; Geoffrey D. Austrian, *Herman Hollerith: Forgotten Giant of Information Processing* (New York, 1982), 61–73; http://mapserver.lib.virginia.edu/index.html; Jackson, "The Virginia Free Negro," 438; John W. Dixon, *The Black Americans of Gwynn's Island, 1600s Through 1900s* (Mathews, 2005), 16–17; *Mathews Journal*, August 24, 1916; August 24, 1916.

36 J.A. O'Bannon, comp., *Acts and Joint Resolutions Passed by the General Assembly of the State of Virginia Passed During the Session of 1901–1902* (Richmond, 1902), 21; *Acts and Joint Resolutions Passed by the General Assembly of the State of Virginia Passed During the Session of 1902–1904* (Richmond, 1904), 264; Mathews Archives Box 9 R.

37 Mathews County Land Book 1, 327; Book 2, 337, 347, 374, 381, 384; MCHS, *History and Progress*, 52–53, 144; www.grandlodgeofvirginia.org/lodges/20/history.asp; www.wikipedia.org; *Mathews Journal*, April 10, 1919; August 7, 1919; July 29, 1920.

38 Friends of the Mathews Memorial Library, *The Ancestry of the Mathews Memorial Library*, n.p., MCHC Archives Box 38 R.

39 Charles, *Newspapers*, 166–167; www.virginiamemory.com; Mathews Archives, Box 23 R; *Mathews Journal*, April 26, 1917; May 10, 1917; MCHS, *History and Progress*, 118–119; *Panorama*, 89; Bertha B. W. Foote, "Mathews County in War Time: A Community History," *Virginia Communities in War Time*, Arthur Kyle Davis, ed., Vol. 1:235–253, Mathews Archives, Box 23 R folder 87; American Legion Monument, Liberty Square, Mathews, Virginia.

12

Our Flag's Unfurl'd to Ev'ry Breeze
1918–1945

The Transition from War to Peace

When World War I ended and military personnel were released from active duty, Americans commenced the transition to a peacetime economy. Some had been wounded or were partially or permanently disabled. Others were scarred by what they had seen. Despite these obstacles, most returning veterans were grateful to be home and quickly settled into civilian life. American Legion Post No. 83 was organized in September 1919 and a women's auxiliary was formed a few weeks later. A local Boy Scout troop was also organized in 1919. At first, an unforeseen postwar boom eased the economy along. However, the summer of 1919 brought race riots in both North and South, and a growing suspicion of anyone ethnically or culturally "different." Economic conditions were challenging, for building materials were expensive, food prices were greatly inflated, and durable goods were in short supply. In recognition of the war's impact on the state's communities, the Virginia War History Commission appointed local committees whose duties included gathering Red Cross reports, military records, diaries, soldiers' letters, and economic information. A Mathews County committee collected those materials, and afterward, Arthur K. Davis's essay, "Mathews County in War Time: A Community History," was published by the War History Commission. A strike on the Old Dominion Steamship line in December 1919 stymied transportation in Mathews and a great deal of money was lost due to the spoilage of oysters, fowl, eggs, and other perishable food stuffs. The strike ended but the steamship company discontinued service in April 1920. This prompted a group of Mathews and Gloucester citizens to organize a stock company and purchase a steamer. According to Mathews County's Extension Agent, Gene Dinwiddie, after World War I hybrid corn and other improved seed became available to local farmers, who discovered that greater amounts of fertilizer and lime increased yields dramatically and that mechanization greatly improved efficiency. Thanks to these changes, one farmer could produce enough for 30 people, further lessening the need for farms and farm workers. There was a general slump in the economy and farm prices began to drop. Although many farmers and watermen were fortunate enough to find a marketing niche that enabled them to prosper, some experienced serious problems. Toward the end of the decade, a statewide depression suppressed the lumber industry and other businesses that contributed to Mathews County's economic well-being.[1]

World War I produced some lasting changes that affected American society as a whole. Many women who found jobs outside the home or became involved in emergency war work gained a new sense of confidence. When labor-saving devices, such as sewing and washing machines, and packaged and commercially canned food became widely available, women began to accumulate leisure time and some began questioning certain gender-based limitations that were traditionally imposed by society. A significant one was denial of the right to vote. In June 1919, Congress passed the Nineteenth Amendment to the United States Constitution, which became effective in August 1920, and gave women the right to vote. (Remarkably, it wasn't until 1952 that Virginia's General Assembly ratified the Nineteenth Amendment.) On September 2, 1920, an editorial in the *Gloucester Gazette* congratulated local women on achieving suffrage. Increasing numbers of women entered the workforce during the 1920s. The majority were employed in traditional occupations such as secretarial work, teaching, nursing, sewing, and domestic work.

When census records were compiled in 1920, Mathews County had a total population of 8,447 people, 2,363 of whom were black. Some 450 people over the age of 10 were illiterate and two-thirds of them were black. Mathews County had 1,293 owner-operated farms and another 90 farms that were in the hands of tenants. The census-taker noted that there were 1,845 dwellings in the county and 16 manufacturing establishments, although he didn't indicate what those establishments produced. According to the United States Census of Agriculture, between 1910 and 1920 there was a slight increase in the numbers of cattle, hogs, and sheep raised in Mathews County, but a decrease in the number of horses and mules, probably because fewer were needed as draft animals. The number of farmers raising oats, corn, and wheat declined, and more land was left fallow or wooded.

By 1930, Mathews County's population had dwindled slightly and there were only 7,884 people. There were 341 illiterate residents in the county, and once again, the number of illiterate blacks outnumbered illiterate whites by almost two to one. Nearly 300 local people of working age were unemployed. The county had a total of 1,296 farms, 1,101 of which were operated by white farmers. Livestock production increased slightly from 1920 but fewer field crops were raised. There still was a considerable amount of interest in agriculture, and in August 1925 R.W. Foster purchased the old fairgrounds near Ward's Corner and had an exhibition hall built. The fair held there that fall was the first since 1911. One of the fair's most popular events was harness-racing.[2]

Racial Turbulence

On Christmas Eve 1915, an incident occurred on Gwynn's Island that generated a considerable amount of uneasiness. According to John W. Dixon's narrative, an intoxicated black man named James (Jim) Smith entered the Hudgins and Mitchem store and made an antagonistic comment to a local white man. A fight broke out and two white men were wounded during the melee. Smith fled to the Grimstead and Adams store, where Mr. Grimstead held off his pursuers until a law enforcement officer arrived. In mid-January 1916, Smith was charged with maliciously wounding two men, a felony in each instance, and was bound over for trial. A jury found him guilty of assault and battery and sentenced him to 30 days in jail plus fines of $15 and $20. In August 1916, the *Mathews Journal*'s Gwynn's Island correspondent reported that most of the black people on Gwynn's Island had moved to Hampton and that the remaining ones were preparing to leave. On September 16, 1920, the reporter said that the last black family had departed.

Another event that occurred in June 1922 suggests that racial tensions never were very far below the surface. According to a newspaper account, Matt or Mike Tabb, a local black man, assaulted Henry B. James, a white man from Mathews Courthouse. The confrontation reportedly occurred on a Friday night while both men were on a ferryboat, crossing from Middlesex County to Mathews. A crowd of young men from Mathews reportedly seized Tabb and placed a noose around his neck. The crowd was ready to lynch him when some older men intervened. Tabb was turned over to the local authorities and James, who was hospitalized, was expected to recover. An account of the incident appeared in newspapers as far away as Florida and Nebraska.

During the early-to-mid-1920s a local chapter of the Ku Klux Klan was organized in Mathews County, and a cross was reportedly burned at the courthouse in 1925. Peter Allen of Mathews County, an African-American man interviewed in 1998 when he was in his late 90s, recalled being unable to eat in local restaurants and drugstores.[3]

The Courthouse Community

In 1919, Leonard M. Callis moved his general store from the southwest corner of the intersection of Main Street and Brickbat Road to a two-story frame building on the east side of Main. That decision probably saved his business, because on August 3, 1921, a searing blaze raged through the business section of Mathews Courthouse. The fire, discovered around 2 P.M., was thought to have started in the Jarvis and Pugh department store and may have been burning for only a short time. According to a newspaper account, 500 of the village's inhabitants, including women and children, did their best to extinguish the blaze, but they lacked fire-fighting equipment and made little headway. A brisk breeze fanned the flames, and before they could be brought under control, the fire had swept through two blocks of the business district, destroying ten buildings. Fortunately, it did not spread to the north side of Church Street, where Charles Edward Forrest

Sr. and his son Charles Jr. had their funeral home in the old Tarpot Academy school building. Law enforcement officers tried to determine whether the fire, propelled by the wind, was the work of an arsonist but were unable to reach a definitive conclusion.

Photographs taken in the early-to-mid 1920s, after the downtown was rebuilt, show some of the numerous businesses that lined both sides of Main Street, which was unpaved and deeply rutted. The numerous automobiles parked in front of various establishments attest to the vibrancy of the area. In 1921, Dr. Ellis C. Richardson, who owned and operated a large drugstore in Port Haywood, purchased some property on the northwest corner of Main and Church Streets. There, at a site where Captain Robert Lee Sears and Warren Williams had opened a mercantile establishment after the Civil War, he erected a two-story brick drugstore and office building, a first for the Mathews Courthouse community. Dr. Richardson's drugstore at Mathews Courthouse descended to members of his family and today is a popular restaurant.

Main Street as it appeared in ca. 1924.
Courtesy of Tidewater Newspapers, Inc.

Another building that was an important fixture in the county seat was the Mathews Ice Company's main plant, which opened in 1924 and was situated on the lower side of Route 198, a short distance northwest of Hyco Corner. It provided ice to local households and to fishermen and farmers who formerly relied on ice brought in by steamship. The ice company's plant not only manufactured and stored ice, but also sold ice cream and groceries.[4] The Mathews Ice Company had a second ice plant at Bayside, near Bavon, where it provided ice that could be used for packing shipments of fish.

Fires at the county seat were not infrequent, and in 1934 Leonard M. Callis's two-story building burned. He replaced it with a modern brick structure on the east side of Main Street, just south of the Westville Christian Church. According to John Warren Cooke, Callis sold groceries, meat, and ice, as well as seed, feed, and farm machinery. As time went on, many business owners replaced their frame buildings with brick structures.

Another longtime business establishment in Mathews Courthouse was Hudgins Drug Store, founded in 1922 and initially called the C. Bernard Hudgins Drug Store. It was situated on the northwest corner of the intersection formed by Brickbat Road and Main Street, at a site that had been occupied by a drugstore since the early 1870s. Brothers Bernard and Bailey Hudgins formed a partnership in 1928. Their drugstore eventually moved into the building that formerly housed the Farmers and Fishermen's Bank. When the Hudginses ordered medications, they procured them from Baltimore by means of a boat that arrived daily. Similarly, the Hudgins Drug Store's soda fountain sold ice cream brought in from Norfolk. In 1992, John Warren Cooke recalled that the Jarvis and Pugh department store, a blacksmith's establishment, Joe Healy's law office, the post office, and several small shops were at the south end of Main Street. He said that there were some small buildings along Brickbat Road or Jail Alley. He noted that the old Twigg and Davis Chevrolet dealership eventually became Christie's, and that new stores were built from there to the corner.

In December 1930, G.S. Marchant, a local businessman, opened the Westville Theatre, the first sound projection movie house in Mathews County. It was located in a long, narrow building that extended through the block defined by Court and Main Streets. Before Mr. Marchant opened his theater, local residents could see silent movies, which were shown at the Lee-Jackson School on Friday and Saturday nights. In 1936, Bob Bertschy and his wife Helen bought the Westville Theatre from Mr. Marchant and renamed it the Be-Jo after their daughters, Betty Lou and JoAnne. According to Mr. Bertschy, who was interviewed in 1973, the Be-Jo Theatre attracted moviegoers from Mathews, Gloucester, and Middlesex Counties. The theater, whose seating capacity was around 300, had upholstered seats in the rear of the auditorium that were reserved for adults, and wooden benches upfront that accommodated young people and children. The Be-Jo, which was racially segregated, served the public until 1949. After each reel was shown, it would be carried to the Thomas Hunter School for viewing by an all-black audience.

Another source of enjoyment for Mathews County's white residents was Bob Bertschy's bowling alley. There also was a skating rink on the third floor of Foster's Department Store, now known as the Halcyon Building. Everyone could partake of the fine ice cream available at the Mathews Dairies, located on the west side of Route 198, next door to the Mathews Ice Company.

A second devastating fire roared through the courthouse community on November 29, 1941. Although there was a fire truck in the village by that time, there was no real fire protection. The blaze—which was so hot that it cracked concrete—spread even further than the 1921 fire did. It destroyed Joe Davis's restaurant, Joe's Place, which was located close to the southwest corner of Brickbat Road and Main Street, as well as Davis's Hotel, which was next door. The blaze also spread north to the next block, reaching the building in which Hudgins Drugstore is now located. Among the other buildings damaged in the 1941 fire were the W.E. Callis and Brother Grocery Store, the French building (which had a sweet shop and pool room), Ripley's Barber Shop, South's Hotel, and Dr. Fleet's office. Dr. Nelm's office on Court Street also burned as did the Sadler Brothers Grocery and Mathews Supply.

According to John Warren Cooke, a lifelong resident, the Mathews Hotel, a large two-story frame building, was located on the west side of Main Street midway between Church Street and Route 198. Nearby was a vacant lot, a favorite site for tent shows and circuses. Frank Hudgins' butcher shop was in the same block, as was Lee Miles's store. Mr. Cooke recalled that there were relatively few businesses at the north end of Main Street, although one or more blacksmith shops and a wheelwright's establishment were close to Hyco Corner. On the east side of Main were some residences, the Westville Baptist Church, and the Lodge Hall that belonged to the St. Tammany's Lodge of the International Order of Red Men. The Lodge Hall, a multi-story frame building, was moved further back from Main Street in 2010 and converted to use as condominiums. Mr. Cooke said that around 1925 Wesley Foster decided to develop a subdivision called Mapleview and proposed that Maple Street be extended in an easterly direction. Although a few lots were sold, they were not developed, and Maple remained a private street.

Northeast of Mathews Courthouse, on Holly Point Road, was a funeral business that catered to members of the black community. After well-known undertaker Frank Knight died in 1932, his widow, Carrie, and their son, Eugene, ran the family funeral business, using the services of a white embalmer. Meanwhile, their youngest son, R. Stanley Knight, continued his education, and in 1935 became the Commonwealth of Virginia's first licensed African-American funeral director and embalmer. When interviewed by the *Gloucester-Mathews Gazette-Journal*, Mr. Knight indicated that all of the people he prepared for burial had their funerals in local churches, usually on a weekend.[5]

Prohibition

Prohibition, which was rooted in the mid-nineteenth century temperance movement, came to Virginia in October 1916 when the General Assembly passed legislation that outlawed the sale and consumption of alcoholic beverages. This came three years ahead of American voters' passage of the Eighteenth Amendment to the United States Constitution, which extended the ban nationwide. Around this time Virginia's Sunday "blue laws" became more stringent. Mathews County was already "dry," for in 1888 the majority of the county's voters opposed the issuance of local liquor licenses.

In 1922, Julian T. Christian, a former member of the House of Delegates and a Mathews Courthouse storekeeper, was convicted of selling "ardent spirits," in violation of the prohibition law. The local circuit court sentenced him to a month in jail and a $100 fine. Although Christian tried to have his conviction overturned by a higher court, he was unsuccessful. Evidence showed that each month he purchased five gallons of what he called "turpentine" from a western source and used it to prepare a drink he called a "high ball" that he sold for 25 cents a glass. The appellate court judges decided that because the beverage produced intoxication and effects that resembled narcotics, it was covered by the state's prohibition statutes. It is unclear whether the judges in the circuit court and the court of appeals sampled Christian's beverage when trying to determine whether it should be classified as ardent spirits. In June 1929 the *Mathews Journal* announced that Mrs. Howard M. Hoge, president of the Women's Christian Temperance Union, was going to visit the county and would be speaking at the Baptist Church and at the Mathews County Methodist Sunday School Association, which was in session at the Methodist Tabernacle.

According to John Watson Ward, quite a few Mathews County residents were involved in bootlegging and made their whiskey from local corn. Clearly many Virginians supported Prohibition, though others steadfastly resisted it. The backlash against Prohibition gradually gained momentum as jails throughout Virginia began to overflow with prohibition violators, and law enforcement officers were kept busy seizing stills and illegal caches of liquor. Finally, in 1933 the Eighteenth Amendment, which legalized Prohibition, was repealed. Afterward, on October 25, 1933, Virginia lawmakers held a state convention whose delegates were elected at large and ratified the Twenty-First Amendment to the U.S. Constitution. Later, the General Assembly limited the sale of liquor to state-run stores.[6]

Modernization and Change

Electric power reached portions of the Middle Peninsula by the turn of the twentieth century. Thanks to the Tidewater Electric and Telephone Company, which provided electric and telephone service, lines extended toward the westernmost part of Mathews County. The East Coast Utilities Company Inc., a provider of electric power and telephone service, purchased and renamed the Tidewater Electric and Telephone Company during the late 1920s. In mid-July 1929, the *Mathews Journal* announced that electric lines had reached several stores in Mathews Courthouse and that W. Frank Hudgins was the first to have electric lights. Then came Philip Levy and the Hudgins Drugstore, which promptly installed two electric fans. The *Mathews Journal*'s reporter noted that "The new lights are much more brilliant than those of the individual [generator] plants" and expressed his hope that the courthouse community would soon have street lights. He added that, "It is well known that people, like moths, like to gather where the lights are bright" and expressed his opinion that streetlights would attract patrons to local businesses. Although electricity reached Mathews Courthouse by 1929, those who lived in the rest of the county had to rely on generators if they wanted to have electric power in their homes. The East Coast Utilities Company Inc. gradually began acquiring rights-of-way that would enable its workers to bring electricity to rural homes in Mathews County.[7] Between March and October 1938, the company received hundreds of landowners' permission to erect the utility poles and string the lines that would provide access to electric power. The process was laborious, because each utility pole had to be set into the ground and many miles of electric lines needed to be strung. During 1942 the Tidewater Electric Service acquired many more deeds for rights-of-way and they were still receiving them between 1943 and 1945.

Telephonic communication reached the Middle Peninsula during 1900. In June, a Petersburg newspaper reported that the mayor of Newport News was going to transmit a message by telephone from his city to Yorktown and Gloucester Courthouse by means of two lines. The writer went on to say that a telephone line already ran from Newport News to Yorktown, where it fed branch lines that provided telephone service to Warwick and York Counties. He indicated that in the immediate future, a telephone cable was going to be laid across the York River, linking Yorktown and Gloucester Point. The new cable was intended to feed lines that ran to Gloucester, Mathews and New Kent Counties.[8]

When the East Coast Utilities Company Inc. purchased the Tidewater Electric and Telephone Company, it also bought the Northern Neck Telephone and Telegraph Company. By the time World War II ended, East Coast Utilities wanted to sell off its telephone business, which was purchased by a group of local residents, who in 1945 formed the Tidewater Telephone Company. One of the new company's early board members was John Warren Cooke of Mathews.

Virginia Hunley Nicodemus was a Mathews County telephone operator from 1928 to 1950, serving subscribers who used hand-crank telephones that generated their own electricity or candlestick desk phones. She said that when she commenced work, there were 200 telephone subscribers in the county; when she retired, there were 400. Early on, only one telephone operator was on duty at a time, but as the number of subscribers increased, there were two operators per shift. Party line subscribers were contacted by means of a combination of long and short rings, but those who had private lines, and were in the courthouse community, were assigned numbers. Even those with numbers were contacted with a certain number of rings.

In 1950, the Tidewater Telephone Company, whose office was in Gloucester Courthouse, converted Mathews County's local telephone exchange to a dial system. Telephone service in rural Mathews County was not widespread until late 1946, at which time the Tidewater Telephone Company began acquiring rights-of-way to numerous rural residences. Telephone service was still being expanded in 1954.

By 1924, local citizens had begun to complain about the unsightliness of the courthouse green, which had very little grass and was delimited by a rusting pipe rail fence. People who came to town in buggies sometimes pastured their horses on the green, which had a ditch running through the middle. An editorial that appeared in the *Mathews Journal* in January 1924 complained about the "strewing of loose paper" and the "dilapidated works of man" that defiled a public space that otherwise "could be made so beautiful." The writer recommended razing the "disreputable vacant buildings," repairing the fence around the courthouse green, and grading its surface. He suggested that the yard in front of the courthouse should be made a place "that commands respect ... rather than something to be ashamed of." A few months later, the newspaper's editor called for tearing down "the old building in the corner," a reference to the old clerk's office that stood close to the southeast corner of the green and was being used to store hay and horse fodder. However, little appears to have been done, and in 1927 the *Mathews Journal*'s editor spoke of the courthouse's grounds having become a "parking garage" with litter scattered about. Near the parked cars were "piles of ashes ... dead trees blown down months ago," road construction debris, and "junk thrown out of the jail."

Three years of appealing to the public's conscience finally paid off, and in 1928 a "thorough clean-up" occurred, perhaps around the time that the old clerk's office and old debtor's jail were razed. Plans were made to have the courthouse green graded and a lockable gate was installed to prevent motorists from parking on the lawn. A large flagpole was erected near the courthouse in 1928, and a year later, the Daughters of the American Revolution put up a monument to commemorate the Battle of Cricket Hill and the American Continental Soldiers who served in Mathews. By 1930 a local citizens group was formed for the purpose of beautifying the courthouse green and removing litter and plans were made for some additional grading. In 1933, the old jail was renovated so that it could be used as the sheriff's office. According to John Warren Cooke, the beautification of the courthouse green and its buildings was done at the insistence of Circuit Court Judge J. Boyd Sears.

Mathews County's first sewage treatment plant was built in the 1930s by a very small quasi-private organization. The facility was designed to relieve the septic tanks that formerly served the courthouse community. Eventually the sewage treatment plant became public property and was part of Sanitary District No. 1. Clarence Minters, who attended the Thomas Hunter School and then went on to Virginia State, started working at the Mathews Sewage Treatment Plant in 1976. He said that in 1999 it was replaced by a pump station operated by the Hampton Roads Sanitation District.[9]

Local Curiosities

In 1924, J.D. Phillips, whose home was on the west side of Put In Creek, sunk a well, striking a heavy flow of natural gas at a depth of 110 feet. The gas the well emitted burned furiously for about a week before the well caved in. A year later, when a magnitude 6.2 earthquake struck eastern Canada, water wells in Mathews County that were sunk to a depth of 75 feet or more started emitting gas, and the water was rendered unpalatable. By July 1929, the Phillips property had changed hands, and its new owners, W.M. Minter and Dr. Marchant, were eager to determine whether there was oil on the property. Davis Elkins of West Virginia hired the Arkansas Drilling Company to drill an oil well 14 inches in diameter. Ninety tons of heavy equip-

The oil rig on Put In Creek. Courtesy of the Mathews County Historical Society.

ment were brought to Williams Wharf and transported to the proposed well site, and a 114-foot-tall oil derrick was erected. The drillers decided to sink the well shaft to a depth of 3,500 feet unless granite (bedrock) was encountered. The men's efforts were unproductive, and they quit when the well reached a depth of 1,000 feet. A photo of this, Mathews County's first and only oil well, appeared on a postcard published by E.C. Richardson. According to a newspaper report, the local economy was stimulated by an influx of visitors, for drilling company workers filled up hotels and boarding houses and curiosity-seekers arrived. According to a 1929 newspaper article, a group of Boy Scouts from Camp Powhatan on Gwynn's Island had hiked to Mathews Courthouse to see the well.

Perhaps even more surprising than the prospect of striking oil in Mathews County was a writer's claim that during the eighteen century, some Kingston Parish settlers acquired just over seven acres of land on Manhattan Island. According to an article that appeared in the *Mathews Journal* between 1925 and 1935, Robert Edwards assigned the acreage to John and George Cruger for 99 years in exchange for £1,000 and a peppercorn. The article, which named Edwards' heirs, went on to say that Wall Street and an assortment of skyscrapers and corporate headquarters currently were situated on the land.[10] No archival evidence has come to light giving credence to this story.

Transportation Improvements

Although steamboats continued serving the Chesapeake Bay and its tributaries, by 1926 fewer Mathews County wharves offered freight and passenger service. Steamboats continued to visit Fitchetts and Callis's Wharves, passing through The Narrows. Then they stopped at Cricket Hill before sailing up the Piankatank, pausing at Warehouse and Green Points before heading inland to Bland and Freeport in Gloucester County. However, the advent of paved roads in the late 1920s brought to an end the steamboat companies' flourishing trade. Although some held on until the Great Depression, they eventually were done in by competition from the rapidly expanding trucking industry and perhaps by motor packet boats.

According to John Warren Cooke, the county's first paved road was the section of Route 14 connecting Gloucester and Mathews Counties. The pavement for this "oiled road" was laid in 1927–28 and around 1930 paving was extended from Mathews Courthouse to New Point Comfort. In general, the county's roads were bad and prior to the time they were paved, local residents struggled with dust in the summer and mud in the winter. According to one local resident, many of Mathews County's smaller rural roads weren't paved until around 1940. Mr. Cooke recalled that on Route 14 in Gloucester County there was a high spot at James Store that was very difficult for motorists to negotiate, a steep incline that was eventually leveled out. He said that a steamer, which came to Williams Wharf daily, provided service to Norfolk and Baltimore, and that a bus line ran from Mathew and Gloucester to Lee Hall, where there was train service. He remember hearing that at one time, Put In Creek was deep enough to accommodate vessels with a four- to five-foot draft, but he added that eventually, the accumulation of silt had made the creek impassable.

Significant improvements to the state's highway system led to an increase in automobile and truck traffic. This change in transportation patterns decreased county residents' reliance on steamboats, and Richmond gradually replaced Baltimore and Norfolk as the urban market on which local people relied. The seafood industry became more specialized, and fewer Mathews County residents were earning a living from truck farming. In March 1932, the Baltimore and Virginia Steamship Company, which had served the region for many years, went into receivership and a year later, the Norfolk and Mobjack Bay Steamship Company, successor to the Old Dominion Line, gave up. A new company was organized that provided freight and limited passenger service, but its diesel-powered *Munnatawket,* the last of the passenger-and-freight boats that made regular runs to Mobjack Bay, burned at Hicks Wharf on September 5, 1935. Thanks to the heroic efforts of Bernard Anderton, William Raines, and Walter and Ernest Hugate, who managed to cast off the vessel's lines and push her away from the pier, Hicks Wharf was spared.

Although a smaller power boat was tried in place of the *Munnatawket*, the venture proved unsuccessful. The Baltimore, Chesapeake, and Atlantic Line, once owned by the Pennsylvania Railroad, folded around 1932, and the Western Shore Freight Line was started but proved to be short-lived. The last steamer from Baltimore to Milford Haven was the *Maryland,* a Cape Charles boat, which came to Callis's Wharf on Gwynn's Island in summer 1937. In essence, by 1936 steamboat service from Mathews to Norfolk had come to an end after more than a century. The Old Bay Line tried to make a comeback after World War II, but its efforts proved unsuccessful.

In 1923, the Gwynn's Island School and Community League recommended deepening the channel at the Hole in the Wall or Sandy Point, and proposed that a free ferry or drawbridge be put in place to span the Narrows. They also suggested that an ice plant with cold storage facilities be built on the island and contended that a centrally located electricity-generating plant would be of great benefit to the county. A few months later, the existing owners of the Gwynn's Island ferry asked the Board of Supervisors to consider having the county take over their ferrying operations. However, little, if any, progress was made. In 1926, representatives of the Milford Haven Community Ferry Company appeared before the Circuit Court where they debated with investors in the "Old Ferry Company" over whether the ferry should be moved or stay in its traditional location. Finally, in early 1931 the Virginia State Highway Commission decided to take over operation of the Gwynn's Island ferry, which was to be toll-free. By February 1935 the state highway department had decided to build a bridge to connect Gwynn's Island with the mainland. The new bridge was officially opened on December 1, 1939, amid great fanfare.[11]

Economic Progress on Gwynn's Island

In June 1924, the *Mathews Journal* reported that the Gwynn's Island Fish and Oyster Company had produced a remarkable 108,000 cans of herring plus 2,000 barrels of tightly-packed herring, along with barrels of fish scraps and scales. The newspaper's reporter added that 1.5 million herring, 800,000 pounds of salt, 35 tons of coal, and $3,000 worth of cans had been needed to produce those products. By June 1930 a group of investors had decided to establish the Mathews Sea Food Products Company on Gwynn's Island, a large factory where fish were packed and crabs, fish roe, and vegetables were canned. J. Newton Foster and Son also had a cannery at Grimstead, where local tomatoes and roe were packed and shipped to Baltimore. Besides these entrepreneurial ventures, there was interest in building a fish refrigeration plant and quick freezer on Gwynn's Island. One of the project's proponents was H.P. Etheridge, who already had a large fish-packing facility at Bayside. The new enterprise was expected to provide employment to significant numbers of local people. In December 1932, the *Mathews Journal* announced that the Gwynn's Island Operating Company at Callis's Wharf, a seafood-processing facility, was ready to open. The Great Atlantic and Pacific Tea Company built a plant on Gwynn's Island, where shellfish were purchased and packed for A&P stores throughout the United States. Captains Howard and Randolph Hudgins were hired to operate dredge boats that were expected to supply around 75 barrels of crabs per day. However, by June 1933, the A&P's leadership had decided that it could supply its stores more cheaply by purchasing seafood directly from packers instead of operating its own plant. In July 1934, during the Great Depression, officials from the Federal Emergency Relief Administration considered using A&P's former facilities on Gwynn's Island to establish a canning and packing plant.[12]

The Great Depression

In 1929, the stock market crashed and America sank into a lengthy period of economic depression. Businesses and banks closed and the production and sales of goods and services was severely reduced. Men and women who had gone to the cities to find work returned home in need of food and shelter. Although money and work were in short supply, many Middle Peninsula residents already lived on family-owned farms and could provide themselves with sustenance; some, however, eked out a more marginal existence. In 2007, Catherine C. Brooks, who grew up in the Fitchetts neighborhood, recalled rural life during the Great Depression. She said that although she didn't pay much attention to the grownups' conversations about politics, she remembered hearing that President Hoover had said, "Eat every bean and pea on your plate."

In 1933, President Franklin D. Roosevelt inaugurated the Federal Emergency Relief Administration (FERA), which was intended to provide work to employable people who were on public relief. FERA instituted the Civil Works Administration (CWA) as a short-term measure to put people to work. Although the CWA program ended in March 1934, it was replaced by FERA's Emergency Work Relief Program, which continued and expanded many of the construction projects the CWA had begun. In Mathews County, J. Eddie Callis, a local contractor, became the CWA's local administrator. The most ambitious of the CWA's local projects was having its workers excavate a six-foot wide canal at the head of Put In Creek, creating a turning basin for recreational watercraft. The objective was to make the county seat more accessible to visitors. A 1935 photograph of the turning basin reveals that it was close to the western boundary of the courthouse green. According to the recollections of John Warren Cooke, little was done to stabilize the lower or south end of the canal, which quickly filled up with silt and defeated the purpose of the project. Soil removed during excavation of the canal was placed along the westernmost side of the courthouse green, creating a gentle slope. One of the CWA workers' most labor intensive projects was opening a canal that ran from Garden Creek to Winter Harbor and the Chesapeake Bay. Local residents also favored the construction of a 40-foot-wide canal that would run from the Chesapeake Bay to the upper end of Milford Haven, to allow boats to pass from the bay to the harbor; however, no funding was available. During 1934 CWA workers built a brick privy on the courthouse green.

The canal and turning basin at the head of Put In Creek in 1935.
Courtesy of Tidewater Newspapers, Inc.

The Works Progress Administration (WPA) was the largest and most diffuse of President Roosevelt's New Deal agencies. It was responsible for the construction of public buildings and roads, but it also employed artists, writers, musicians, and thespians. One WPA program was the Virginia Writers' Project, whose employees interviewed numerous Virginians and compiled "life histories." These biographical sketches, now available for a substantial number of Mathews County residents, provide us with insights into what life was like during the Great Depression. Because many of the people interviewed were elderly, their narratives also shed light on earlier times. WPA worker Claude W. Anderson spoke with at least two former slaves, Mrs. Elizabeth Sparks and Lisa McCoy, who were interviewed in 1937 as part of the Virginia Negro Studies Project. Another WPA worker, Harriet G. Miller, interviewed nearly a dozen white people in 1939 and gathered information on topics that ranged from handicrafts, poetry, and fishing to belief in supernatural phenomena.

WPA workers who visited Mathews Courthouse reported that the community's population was then 450. They commented upon the T-shaped courthouse, noting that it was erected in the nineteenth century, and stated that "Nearby is the old square jail, now used as the sheriff's office." They added that "The cultivation of narcissus bulbs on a commercial scale makes the county in early spring a veritable flower garden."[13] WPA workers remarked on Christ Church and Captain Sally Tompkins's grave, and mentioned that she had been commissioned by Confederate President Jefferson

Davis. Poplar Grove was described as "a large rambling frame house with a tall portico and many other additions," and WPA workers took note of the functional tide mill. They said there was a mile-long pier at Bayside, to the east of Davis Creek, where fishermen landed their catches, and that offshore was New Point Comfort, an island with a three-mile-long sandy beach.

In the early- to mid-1930s, the Virginia State Commission on Conservation and Development received funds from the WPA's Federal Art Project to hire five artists to create drawings for a publication on Virginia's historic shrines. Like other WPA-funded projects, the artists applied for work through local emergency relief offices before being assigned to the Federal Art Project. Under the direction of Hamilton J. Eckenrode, in 1932 the commission's Division of History and Archaeology began making a record of historic buildings in Virginia. Field assistant and artist Rex M. Allyn took photographs of buildings while on assignment to the Division's Historic Highway Marker project. From 1932 to 1937, Allyn and four other artists—Edward A. Darby, Dorothea A. Farrington, E. Neville Harnsberger, and Elsie J. Mistie—created numerous pen-and-ink and pencil drawings from the photographs. WPA artist Edward A. Darby made detailed pen-and-ink drawings of Auburn, Hesse, and the tide mill at Poplar Grove.[14] According to one local source, there was a functional tide mill at Bohannon that belonged to I.K. Ward and continued to grind meal as late as the 1930s.[15]

A pen-and-ink sketch of the Poplar Grove tide mill, made by Edward A. Darby, a WPA worker. Courtesy of the Library of Virginia.

The Hurricanes of 1933

On August 23, 1933, a hurricane of catastrophic proportions swept through much of coastal Virginia and caused more than $27 million worth of damage and more than a dozen fatalities. Elderly Mathews County residents remember the devastation caused by the Wednesday storm and recall torrential rain, strong wind, and a storm surge that was around 12 feet above a normal high tide. The floodwaters reached their crest between 10 and 11 AM and inundated more than half of the county, soaking fertile farmland with brackish water. Buildings were torn apart or lost their roofs, livestock and other domestic animals were drowned, and local residents were driven from their homes by the angry seas. Many people used boats to escape the rising tide, while others tried to swim, wearing life preservers.

On August 24, the *Mathews Journal*'s editor, Paul Titlow, described the storm in considerable detail. He said that he had waded through waist-deep water to reach his office and had worked by the light of oil lanterns. By nighttime, electric power was restored in Mathews Courthouse and he was able to go to press. Some of the local residents Mr. Titlow interviewed told him that devastation was particularly widespread in the New Point, Potato Neck, Garden Creek, and Milford Haven areas. Crops were destroyed, along with food that had been stored to feed Mathews families and livestock during the coming winter. Warehouses and wharves, including the county's sturdily-built steamboat landings, were destroyed or severely damaged, as were numerous local businesses. Automobiles were ruined, and boats were swept away or deposited inland, far from their moorings. In Mathews Courthouse, water in the streets reached a height of at least four feet and flooded buildings, damaging office equipment, business records, and merchandize. Gasoline and oil, which had leaked into the water, created new dangers. When the floodwaters receded, they left in their wake an awful stench that emanated from rotting fish, dead livestock and game animals, decomposing vegetation, and perishable goods. Debris was strewn everywhere. Because there was no electric power outside of the courthouse community, radios were inoperable and telephone service was very limited. Therefore, it was extremely difficult to communicate with the outside world.

The wholesale grocers at Williams Wharf, the Mathews Supply Company, whose large warehouse was built out over the water, sustained significant damage. Losses were also great at Mobjack, where George A. Philpotts had a steamboat wharf, feed mill, crab-packing plant, marine railway, and distributorship for petroleum products. The pipelines that carried gasoline from storage tanks to the wharf ruptured, releasing thousands of gallons of toxic fluid into the water. Stanley Walker's store and other buildings along Mobjack's waterfront were flooded, as were private homes. The area along the North River was flooded and some residents narrowly escaped with their lives. On Mobjack Bay, damage was severe at the Bayside Wharf, where the tracks of its narrow gauge railway were left twisted and useless. At nearby Davis Creek, the wharf was swept away and nothing was left of the New Point wharf except a few pilings. At Diggs Wharf, destruction was widespread. The warehouse at Fitchett's Wharf blew into Milford Haven. Nothing was left of the Sand Bank Wharf and the wharf and ferry landing at Cricket Hill were ruined. Because the James-Adams Floating Theater had been moved to the Cricket Hill Wharf, it was spared from destruction. Gwynn's Island was flooded and the damage there was widespread.

A second hurricane struck the Mid-Atlantic states less than a month after the August 23 storm. A weather log maintained by the Red Cross's Disaster Relief Headquarters reveals that on September 16 at 2:55 AM, the tide, accompanied by heavy rain, rose rapidly at Gwynn's Island and by 4:30 AM floodwaters had gone inland at Cricket Hill for an estimated 300 yards. At 5:50 AM, the tidal surge at Milford Haven had reached a point 500 yards inland.

At the time of the 1933 hurricanes, Mathews County, like the rest of the country, was still grappling with the economic effects of the Great Depression. State Senator W.M. Minter, who was Mathews County's Commonwealth's Attorney, and Judge J. Boyd Sears sought—and received—the support of Congressman S.O. Bland and Senator Harry F. Byrd I for relief efforts. Thanks to their influence, crews of men from Civilian Conservation Corps (CCC) camps in West Point and Yorktown were brought to Mathews County and deployed to the areas of greatest devastation. Arrangements were also made for commercial fishermen and small farmers in Mathews and Gloucester Counties to receive the loans they needed to pursue their livelihoods.

Thanks to the efforts of Miss Sadie James, a special representative of the National Red Cross, relief funds became available to Mathews residents; local public and private agencies also rendered much needed assistance. The state's Department of Public Welfare, assisted by the Governor's Commission, studied the area's needs and helped by funding emergency relief and rehabilitation. The Mathews Chapter of the American Red Cross, under the leadership of the Rev. C.E. Otey, was at the forefront of local emergency relief efforts and received assistance from trained disaster workers sent to the area by the National Red Cross headquarters. The Rev. W.C. Diggs of Onemo headed a special Red Cross disaster relief committee, which accepted and distributed clothing, bedding, household goods, and furniture to families who were unable to fulfill their basic needs. They also provided people with temporary shelter and supplied building materials that enabled them to repair or restore their homes to habitable condition. Records maintained by the Mathews Chapter of the American Red Cross include the names of the men, women, and children who received assistance, the types of help they received, and who authorized it. The race of the recipient families was also noted in the records that were maintained.[16]

The Mathews Memorial Library

The Cardinal Athenaeum is considered the ancestor of the Mathews Memorial Library, but Mrs. Ethel White Legg, a sometime-Mathews resident later known as Polly Cary Mason, provided the impetus for the establishment of the county's first truly public library. In July 1926, she sent a letter to the editor of the *Mathews Journal*, inquiring why there wasn't a public library at the county seat. Within two weeks' time the local Chamber of Commerce's Committee on Education and Public Health commenced calling for the establishment of a public library. By October, substantial progress had been made, and in April 1927 the state, which had mobile libraries it loaned to localities, provided 50 volumes. At first, the books, which were suitable for adults and young readers, were housed in the office of the *Mathews Journal*. The Chamber of Commerce's committee quickly discovered that the lending library was extremely popular and asked for books to be donated. The Chamber also noted that the free library's popularity was a reflection of the community's need. Fundraising progressed slowly despite diligent efforts on the part of local citizens and Mrs. Legg, who continued her support. The new library, which was to be located on Church Street, within the boundaries of the courthouse green, was to be fabricated of brick and have a slate roof. In 1929, just as the Great Depression had gotten underway, J. Eddie Callis, a local builder, won the contract as low bidder; however, due to a shortage of funds, construction was delayed. Even after the library building was completed, there was no money to cover the cost of shelving for books, office furniture, and essential equipment like plumbing fixtures and a furnace. The Cardinal Athenaeum decided to donate its entire collection of books (some 1,700 volumes) to the county's new library. Unfortunately, during the 1933 hurricane, the library building was flooded and several hundred books that were stacked on the floor, waiting to be shelved, were damaged. Miss Scotia Ballard, who oversaw public works projects in Mathews, requested permission to use part of the new, but unoccupied, library building through March 1934. In return, she offered to apply for funds that could be used to repair flood damage, purchase furniture, and install a new floor, plumbing fixtures, and a heating plant. The Civil Works Administration also provided funds that could be used for the repair of the library's water-damaged books, which a group of dedicated volunteers began cleaning, rebinding, and cataloging. The Mathews Memorial Library opened to the public on August 1, 1935, and on November 11, 1937, Armistice Day, it was officially dedicated. In more recent times, the library moved into the building formerly occupied by the Farmer's Bank of Mathews.[17]

Acquiring an Education

In 1920, the State Department of Education began furnishing architectural plans to communities that intended to build new schools. From then until 1946 Virginia's schools became increasingly standardized in accordance with the basic specifications used for construction. For example, the plans provided by the state called for a combination auditorium/gymnasium that could serve as a community center in which local activities and programs could be held. In keeping with that policy, when the Lee-Jackson High School was destroyed by fire in 1922, it was replaced by a two-story brick building with a multifunctional gymnasium. The new Lee-Jackson High School served white children in the courthouse community until November 4, 1932, when another fire occurred. While the new Lee-Jackson High School was being rebuilt, children attended class off-campus, just as they had done when the school's predecessors burned. On January 19, 1939, a contract was let for the construction of the Mathews High School. With the assistance of WPA workers, it was built in accordance with one of the State Department of Education's standardized architectural plans. The new school opened for use on September 14, 1939, and its first seniors, who had completed the eleventh grade, graduated as the class of 1940. As soon as Mathews High School was ready to receive students, Lee-Jackson High School was converted to use as the Lee-Jackson Elementary School, which accommodated white children in grades one through seven.

During the early twentieth century, neighboring families sometimes arranged for their children to ride to school together in a horse-drawn wagon, usually driven by a parent or an older student. When some neighborhood schools were consolidated, county officials established routes along which school wagons picked up children. John Watson Ward, who lived in the Cobbs Creek area, recalled that he commuted to school in a makeshift school bus: a Model-T truck with a wooden body mounted on the back, with curtains on the sides. He said that the first real bus he rode was owned and driven by Bryant Edwards, who was hired by the Mathews County School Board. In 1925, the School Board announced that it was trying out a new school truck in the Piankatank District. There seems to have been little control over drivers' qualifications, for in May 1932 a school girl drove a bus into a ditch while transporting students from Cricket Hill to Cobbs Creek; several of the bus's passengers were injured.

According to Morris and Altha Thompson, John Murray Brooks, who later became principal of the Thomas Hunter School, purchased a bus he used to transport black children to school. In time, the county contributed half of the funds that were needed to purchase a bus for black students. Sometimes, a vehicle formerly used by white children was passed along to black students. The Thompsons recalled that different text books were issued to black pupils than were provided to white students.

School consolidation in the 1920s affected Mathews County's black children, most of whom had been receiving a rudimentary education in local churches or in one of the tiny schoolhouses scattered throughout the county. Local residents recall that black children often had to walk several miles to reach their school and if a family wanted their children to receive an education beyond the sixth- or seventh-grade level, they had to go to Hampton, Norfolk, or another urban community. On April 15, 1923, members of the local black community established the Mathews Educational League, which sought to improve the quality and quantity of education African-American children received. Within three years' time, the League managed to raise the $9,900 they needed to build a school. That sum was comprised of $8,000 contributed by the black community, $800 in public funds, and $1,100 from the Rosenwald Fund. When donations were solicited, George E.T. Lane of Woodstock, who gave $25, stipulated that the new school would be named after the late Thomas Hunter, one of his family's former slaves and a longtime employee. As soon as enough money was in hand, the Mathews Educational League's trustees purchased 3.6 acres of land on Church Street, and on September 6, 1926, they laid the cornerstone of the Thomas Hunter Agricultural Training School. The first Thomas Hunter School, which opened in October 1927, was an H-shaped unheated frame building that was closer to the street than today's school. At first, it accommodated four teachers, who taught black children in grades one through seven; in 1928 an eighth grade was added. All of Mathews County's black students eventually attended Thomas Hunter, which had grades one through eleven, and eventually a twelfth grade. John Murray Brooks, who was principal from 1933 to 1961, saw that the school received accreditation. In 1953, while Virginia schools were still segregated, a brick building was erected behind the original Thomas Hunter School, which was moved further from the street and put to use as a cafeteria and vocational shop. The frame building was torn down in 1965 to accommodate an addition to the brick school.

The Rev. L.W. Wales Jr., who during the early twentieth century became the pastor of Antioch Baptist Church in Susan, did what he could to further black children's educational opportunities. He secured money from the Rosenwald Fund and gathered additional support from the local community. The funding for the Antioch School, which cost $4,900, consisted of $3,700 raised from the black community, $500 in public money, and $700 from the Rosenwald Funds. Thanks to the Rev. Wales's efforts, in 1926–27 a three-room school that was supposed to accommodate two teachers was built close to the Antioch Church. In 1938, the Rev. Wales and Miss Ella Hudgins were honored for their contributions to the Antioch School. Today, the school building, now known as the Wales Center, houses a library and an apartment that is used as a parsonage. Besides the Thomas Hunter and Antioch Schools, the Rosenwald Fund also contributed funds toward another local school for black children. In 1923–24 a two-teacher type schoolhouse that cost $3,500 was built near Hudgins with $1,600 provided by the black community, $1,200 in public funds, and $700 from the Rosenwald Fund. This schoolhouse was in the immediate vicinity of the building identified as "School B" on a topographic quadrangle sheet made in 1917 and updated in 1965. Besides monetary support, the Rosenwald Fund provided architectural plans for schoolhouses of various sizes, teachers' houses, and privies.

Dr. Lyman Beacher Brooks.
Courtesy of Tidewater Newspapers, Inc.

Despite the numerous challenges faced by black children whose families wanted them to obtain a good education, some were highly successful. For example, Dr. Lyman Beacher Brooks, who was born in Mathews County at Blakes, graduated from the Virginia Union University in Richmond and got his master's degree and doctorate from the University of Michigan. Dr. Brooks, a distinguished educator, went on to become the president of Norfolk State University.[18]

Mainstays of the Local Economy

For generations, men and boys from Mathews County were able to derive a good living from the sea. Although it was not an easy life, most watermen found it satisfying. Their days were regulated by the cycle of changing tides, and pound fishermen rose early, went out into the Chesapeake Bay, and set their pound nets. When fish weren't available, they harvested oysters; when neither fish nor shellfish were available, they farmed. It was a way of life that involved skills passed down from father to son. Local people interviewed as part of a 2014 oral history project indicated that most watermen tended to work within territory they traditionally used and that they often looked out for each other without heed to ethnicity. Boat-building continued to be an important part of the local economy and knowledge of the craft descended through families.

In 1941, when L.M. Walker, Mathews County's Commissioner of Agriculture, reported on the local farm economy, he listed the quantities of various types of livestock owned by local farmers. He also used his record book to make note of those who owned automobiles, boats, nets, and furniture. Statistics compiled by the United States Department of Agriculture reveal that by 1940 the number of farms in Mathews County had begun to decline. However, there was an uptick in the amount of dairy and poultry products produced, along with increased quantities of oats, hay, corn, soybeans, and wheat. Undoubtedly, when the United States went to war in 1941, local farmers gave their full support.[19]

The Changing Political Spectrum

In 1918 and 1919 Delegate R.H. Stubbs represented Mathews and Gloucester Counties in the General Assembly and State Senator J. Douglas Mitchell served a district that included Mathews, Gloucester, Middlesex, King and Queen, and Essex Counties. Mitchell was returned to office and served through 1923, but Stubbs was replaced by Gilbert L. Diggs, who held office from 1920 through 1923. By 1924 Delegate Zachery T. Gray represented Gloucester and Mathews Counties and former delegate Stubbs had become the state senator for an enlarged district that included Mathews,

Gloucester, Middlesex, King and Queen, Essex and York Counties. Senator Stubbs held onto his seat through 1930, but there was turnover among those serving as Gloucester and Mathews Counties' delegate. Gilbert L. Diggs served as delegate during 1926 and 1927 but in 1928 was replaced by John Tabb DuVal. From 1930 through 1933 Emma Lee Smith White, a Mathews County physician's wife, represented both counties in the House of Delegates. Although she sought reelection in 1935, she was unseated by John Tabb DuVal, who held office through 1937. Senator R.H. Stubbs was ousted from office by William A. Wright, who held office through part of 1942, when he resigned. Meanwhile, in 1938 James Bland Martin replaced Delegate John Tabb DuVal and held office through 1940.

One of Mathews County's most highly respected citizens and distinguished politician was John Warren Cooke, who was elected to the General Assembly in 1941 at age 26 and in January 1942 commenced representing Gloucester and Mathews Counties. When interviewed in 1992, he said that until redistricting occurred, there had been a long-standing informal agreement that a person from Gloucester County would serve two terms and then vacate office so that someone from Mathews County could serve. Mr. Cooke said that during the 1942 session of the assembly, Middlesex County was added to his district. He served in the assembly sessions held in 1944 and 1945. When a state constitutional convention was held in April and May 1945, former delegate John Tabb DuVal represented Mathews, Gloucester, Middlesex, Essex, York, and King and Queen Counties. At issue was amending the constitution to accommodate voting by qualified military personnel.[20]

Cultural Events and Community Betterment

The James Adams Floating Theater, built by vaudevillian James Adams around 1914, visited small communities throughout the Chesapeake during the summer months of the 1920s and 30s. The theater usually made a weeklong visit to Mathews County and docked at Williams Wharf or Cricket Hill. The theater's cast typically performed six nights each week in its 800-seat auditorium, but would also have a Saturday matinee. Large numbers of rural residents, hungry for entertainment, commuted to the

Courtesy of the State Archives of North Carolina.

shows by boat or automobile. Novelist Edna Ferber was reportedly living on the James Adams Floating Theater when she wrote *Show Boat*, which Jerome Kern and Oscar Hammerstein II made into a famous Broadway musical. During the early twentieth century local churches, schools, and social clubs sometimes staged theatrical productions. In 1946 professional actors and actresses, part of the famous Barter Theatre's troupe, came to the Middle Peninsula.

Another set of events that local people enjoyed from the 1920s to the early 50s were the annual May Day celebrations that were held at Mathews County schools. The day's activities usually included students dancing around a Maypole, the presentation of a king and queen, a baseball game, and an evening meal. By the 1950s, however, many Americans began to associate the words "May Day" with Communism, so the celebrations were discontinued.

During the early- to mid-twentieth century, several new social and service organizations were formed. Through their good works, they have enriched the lives of Mathews County residents and contributed to the community's betterment. In 1928 the Mathews Chapter of the Order of the Eastern Star, Oriental Chapter Number 30, held its first meeting. Two years later, the Garden Club of Mathews County was organized. When Garden Club members were asked to assist in improving the appearance of the courthouse green, they responded energetically. Over the years, the Garden Club has held contests in local schools, fostering interest in the area's birds and native plant materials, and members hold annual flower shows.[21] After World War II was over, the Garden Club of Mathews and the Mathews Woman's Club worked with the highway department to beautify Route 14 as a memorial to those who had lost their lives. Two other organizations that have contributed to the quality of life in Mathews County are the Mathews Woman's Club and the Mathews Junior Woman's Club. The Mathews Woman's Club, founded by Mrs. Mabel Billups, became affiliated with the Virginia Federation of Women's Clubs (now the General Federation of Woman's Clubs) in 1936. The GFWC's goal is the improvement of the lives of others through volunteer service.

Over the years, the Mathews and Piankatank Ruritan Clubs have contributed greatly to the betterment of Mathews County, as have American Legion Post 83 and the Mathews Rotary Club. Among the American Legion's good works is public recognition of the military's role in preserving America's freedom. The Mathews Chamber of Commerce, comprised of the county's business and civic leaders, has played an important role in the county's well-being. The Mathews County Lions Club, formed more recently, has worked diligently to raise funds for organizations such as the Mathews Volunteer Fire Department, the Mathews Volunteer Rescue Squad, and the William H. Hatten Scholarship Fund. The Lions also have provided support for community projects such as the prevention of blindness and eye care. The Mathews Chapter of the National Association for the Advancement of Colored People (NAACP), formed during the early 1940s, has been dedicated to improving the lives of Mathews County's African-American citizens. During the 1940s, members of the local NAACP asked local businesses to hire more blacks in positions for which they were qualified. They also tried to recruit more teachers for black schools and to encourage blacks to vote. Mrs. Beatrice Lee Bobo, a local school teacher, was instrumental in seeing that the NAACP was revitalized in 1971.[22] Separately and collectively, all of these organizations have made important contributions to community life.

World War II

In 1937, Americans became increasingly uneasy as Hitler's tyranny in Europe began to unfold and Italy and Japan became part of the "Axis." The United States looked toward strengthening its own defenses and local Selective Service Boards started sending out draft notices. When the Japanese attacked Pearl Harbor on December 7, 1941, the American government abandoned its policy of neutrality and declared war on Japan. Germany and Italy retaliated by declaring war on the United States.

Mathews County men in the merchant marine risked their lives whenever they plied routes along the Atlantic Coast or sailed to the Caribbean, for their ships were unarmed and there were no convoys to protect them from German submarines' deadly torpedoes. Thanks to the merchant marine, oil was brought in from Aruba and Curacao and bauxite, the main ore used in the manufacture of aluminum war planes, was procured from Trinidad. The first Mathews County man to lose his life aboard a merchant marine ship was Captain Earnest Thompson, who was on the tanker *Rochester* when it was sunk. A total of fifteen Mathews men aboard merchant marine vessels lost their lives during 1942. Protective convoys were not available until June 1943, by which time fifteen ships had been lost within 60 days. William Hammond, whose ship was sunk in May 1943, was adrift for two days before being picked up. The next time he went to sea, he was less fortunate, for his ship was torpedoed and he did not survive. Likewise, Genious (Genius) T. Hudgins Jr. survived one such deadly attack only to lose his life in another. Other Mathews men lost their lives when the merchant marine ships they were aboard came under attack in the North Atlantic. Charles Edwards lived to describe his harrowing experiences under fire at Murmansk. In time, the Allies' antisubmarine defenses became more effective.

Mobilizing for war required industrial conversion and America's entrepreneurs rose to the occasion. Automobile and home appliance manufacturers began producing tanks and munitions, and clothing manufacturers switched to the production of military uniforms, tents, bedrolls, and mosquito netting. During World War II it took steady pressure to broaden black participation in the defense industries. The war effort changed the status of

American women forever, for the draft created severe labor shortages. By 1944, over 6 million women had entered the work force (an overall increase of 50 percent), and nearly 200,000 women joined the armed forces. For the first time in history, more married women than single were employed outside the home.

On the home front, local citizens salvaged rubber, scrap paper, and other used materials, and fats were saved to make explosives for the military. When shortages developed and inflation threatened, price controls and rationing were implemented. Wartime spending caused the national debt to soar; income taxes were levied to cover part of the expense. War bond drives and rallies were also held to encourage the public to invest in America's defense. Congress passed a law creating Daylight Saving Time, as setting clocks forward one hour lengthened the workday.

The Civilian Airplane Defense Observation Corps was organized in Mathews County. One of its most important duties was providing an early warning of an enemy attack. Observation or surveillance posts in various parts of the county were manned by airplane-spotters, who served in shifts and provided 24-hour coverage. They recorded information about all of the planes they saw and were on the alert for enemy aircraft. Among the civilian volunteers who manned local observation posts was John W. Brownley of Port Haywood. Catherine C. Brooks recalled that all localities were supposed to hold blackouts and air raid drills and said that her parents, like everyone else, purchased blackout shades that covered their windows.[23] Church bells were to be rung to signal the onset of a blackout.

Mathews County citizens rallied in support of the war effort in many other important ways, for they contributed to organizations such as the American Red Cross, the United Service Organization, and Civil Defense, while also buying up war bonds and war savings stamps. Girls and women knitted scarves, caps, and other items that could be use by service men, just as they had during World War I. Home Nursing classes were held in the community and in high school shop classes, boys and girls received instruction and acquired many useful skills. The local agricultural extension agent, E.L. Phillips, urged everyone to plant Victory Gardens, and throughout Virginia, home demonstration agents provided women with information on food preservation and other economic strategies. There was relatively little business activity, thanks to a shortage of saleable goods and a limited amount of disposable income. Local households dealt with the rationing of gasoline, sugar, meat, and canned goods, while merchants and the owners of rental property were obliged to accept price controls. Farmers were allocated gasoline stamps according to the amount of acreage they tilled.

The U.S.S. *Mathews*, named in honor of Mathews County's mariners and shipbuilders, was an attack cargo ship. The *Mathews* was launched and turned over to the navy in March 1945. Although the war ended while she was en route to Guam, she saw service in the Korean War.

After Hitler's death and Italy's unconditional surrender, the war in Europe finally ended on May 8, 1945, when Germany officially capitulated. Then, in early August a new weapon, the atomic bomb, was dropped on the Japanese city of Hiroshima, a prime military target, and shortly thereafter, the Japanese surrendered.[24]

Honoring The War Dead

An elaborate commemorative event known as Mathews Day was held at Hudgins Bay Shore on September 28 and 29, 1946, while the U.S.S. *Mathews* was anchored off Gwynn's Island. It included a memorial service that honored the Mathews County mariners who lost their lives while serving in the Merchant Marine, the Coast Guard, and the Navy. Congressman S. Otis Bland of Newport News was the principal speaker at the gathering, which was attended by an array of public officials, local clergy, the captain of the *Mathews,* and 500 to 700 other people.

The members and auxiliary of American Legion Post 83 erected a plaque in front of the Lee-Jackson School in 1953, honoring the 40 local men known to have made the ultimate sacrifice during World War II. When a new plaque was cast and erected at Liberty Square in 2003, some additional names were added. Those currently listed are: Wallace M. Albertson, Boyd Lee Armistead Jr., Robert F. Belvin, Charles O. Billups, William T. Bohannon, Carl Weldon Brooks, Homer V. Callis, Lewis Wesley Callis, Robert M. Callis, Perrie Boyd Collier, Stewart B. Cullen, Eugene R. Davis Jr., Vernon Emmitt Davis, Andrew Dennis, Sam Jones Diggs, Wilson T. Forrest, Nat. D. Foster Jr., William Burton Gay, William Franklin Hale,

William F. Hammond, George E. Harrison, William Jennings Heywood, George Dewey Hodges, Leslie H. Hodges, Wendell R. Hudgins, Genious T. Hudgins Jr., Robert H. Humphrey, John Clifford Jackson, George A. Jarvis, Herbert Johnson Jr., Thomas E. Johnson Jr., Lemuel A. Marchant, Levi Marchant Morgan, Howard D. Morris, Thomas B. Owens, John W. Peterson, Walter B. Pierson, Alfred Martin Raines, Luther A. Ranier, Mellin E. Respess, William C. Ripley Jr., Harry Lewis Sadler, Luther Smith, Wilton Vernon Smith, Alvin Cornwell Soles, Frederick M. Spears, Earnest Thompson, James R. Thornton, Harold Treakle, James Edward White, and Merritt Franklin White. Mr. Albertson, who died in 1942, was Mathews County's first naval casualty.[25]

Notes

1 Records of the Mathews Chapter of the American Red Cross, spanning the years 1933–34 and 1950–70, are preserved at the Library of Virginia.

2 Tindall, *America*, 979, 998–1001; Salmon et al., *Hornbook*, 65–66; Mathews Archives, Boxes 18 R, 23 R, 24 R; http://mapserver.lib.virginia.edu/index.html; MCHS, *History and Progress*, 118–119; *Panorama*, 111; *Mathews Journal*, August 6, 1925; September 17, 1925; October 15, 1925.

3 Mathews County Common Law Order Book 4:631–632; Dixon, *Gwynn's Island*, 19–20; Elsa Cooke Verbyla, *Gwynn's Island Times, Items from the Mathews Journal, 1905–1937, the Gloucester-Mathews Gazette-Journal, 1937–1950* (Gloucester, 1998), 13–14, 23; Charles, *Newspapers*, 170; *Mathews Journal*, August 31, 1916; September 16, 1920; http://infoweb.newsbank.com; *Daily Press*, February 8, 1998.

4 Katherine Hendrick, when interviewed in 2014, recalled that her grandmother had an ice box that accommodated a big block of ice (Katherine Hendrick, Oral History File TMP-027, June 28, 2014).

5 Charles, *Newspapers*, 169; MCHS, *History and Progress*, 56–59, 67, 70–71, 122, 125–126; Mathews Archives, Box 23 R; Katherine Hendrick, Oral History File TMP-027, June 28, 2014; Allen Moughan, Oral History File TMP-036; www.foster-faulkner.com/about-us; *Mathews Journal*, February 1, 1923; Vogel, *Then and Now*, 60, 64.

6 Charles, *Newspapers*, 131–132, 169; Tindall, *America*, 992–995; Leonard, *General Assembly*, 652; *Mathews Journal*, June 27, 1929; John Watson Ward, Oral History File TMP-045, July 29, 2014; Methodist Tabernacle, National Register of Historic Places File 057-0030.

7 On May 20, 1936, Congress passed the Rural Electrification Act (REA), one of the most important pieces of legislation in President Franklin D. Roosevelt's New Deal. This law allowed the federal government to make low-cost loans to groups of farmers who created non-profit cooperatives to bring electricity to rural America. REA cooperatives used a

6900-volt distribution network, which could support much longer runs of up to about 40 miles. Although more expensive transformers were required at each home, the overall system's cost was manageable (www.wikipedia.com).

8 In June 1888 the *Baltimore Sun* reported that "Contracts have been made with various parties for furnishing the poles for the telephone from this place to Mathews Court House, Gloucester Court House, and Saluda, and the enterprise seems an assured success" (Charles, *Newspapers*, 132).

9 Charles, *Newspapers*, 147; MCHS, *History and Progress*, 132–134; Mathews County Deed Books 34, 37, 38, 41, 52, *passim*; Mathews Archives, Box 23 R; *Mathews Journal*, January 24, 1924; May 8, 1924; January 13, 1927; March 10, 1927; March 22, 1928; April 19, 1928; January 24, 1929; May 16, 1929; July 18, 1929; July 25, 1929; September 4, 1930; April 23, 1931; February 9, 1933; March 29, 1934; Clarence Minters, Oral History File TMP-048, July 31, 2014. The Tidewater Telephone Company was succeeded by the Continental Telephone System in 1972.

10 Mathews Archives, Boxes 10 R, 34 R, 42 R; MCHS, *Panorama*, 95; *Mathews Journal*, August 7, 1926; June 27, 1929; July 11, 1929; Verbyla, *Gwynn's Island Times*, 48; http://earthquake.usgs.gov.

11 Mathews Archives, Box 23 R; MCHS, *History and Progress*, 6, 35, 102–105; United States Corps of Engineers, "Transportation Lines of Chesapeake Bay serving the Port of Baltimore, Maryland," 1926; *Mathews Journal*, February 1, 1923; July 19, 1923; February 25, 1925; May 13, 1926; February 5, 1931; March 3, 1932; February 28, 1935; *Gloucester-Mathews Gazette-Journal*, November 25, 1937; February 23, 1939; November 16, 1939; April 16, 1959; Catherine Brooks, Oral History File TMP-0034, July 13, 2014; Vogel, *Then and Now*, 87.

12 *Mathews Journal*, June 5, 1924; June 19, 1930; July 31, 1930; December 1, 1932; December 8, 1932; July 19, 1934.

13 Mathews Archives, Box 47 R. Daffodils, thought to have grown wild on the Middle Peninsula since colonial times, also were a source of income. Charles Heath, a New Yorker who visited the area during the early 1900s when the daffodils were in bloom, moved to Auburn and ordered Holland bulbs from a New York firm. In 1926 when a blight struck Holland's bulb crop, the firm from which Heath had ordered bulbs remembered his claims of his success and purchased bulbs from him. In 1938 the Heaths established the Daffodil Mart, which included the Gloucester-Mathews Narcissus Tour (Fred C. Biggs and Chris Plummer, *Gloucester County, Virginia, A Bicentennial Perspective* [Gloucester, 1976], 10).

14 Edward Darby operated his own advertising and commercial illustration business in Atlanta, Georgia, and Baltimore, Maryland, before joining the WPA's state-sponsored Virginia Writers' Project. In 1940, thirteen of Darby's illustrations were published in *Virginia: A Guide to the Old Dominion*, compiled by WPA workers.

15 *Mathews Journal*, March 8, 1934; June 14, 1934; May 7, 1931; January 4, 1934; March 1, 1934; MCHS, *Panorama*, 76, 106 and errata; Miller, "Interviews," Boxes 6 and 10; Works Progress Administration, *Virginia: A Guide to the Old Dominion Compiled by Workers of the Writers' Program of the Works Progress Administration in the State of Virginia*, 456–457; www.vir-

giniamemory.com; Charlotte C. Brooks, *Didn't Know We Were Poor* (West Conshohocken, 2007), 102; www.gazette-journal.com/ancest/business.php; Kevin Godsey, Oral History File TMP-032, July 11, 2014; Mathews Archives, Box 23 R; Vogel, *Then and Now*, 29.

16 www.virginiamemory.com; MCHS, *History and Progress*, 25–30; *Panorama*, 72; Mathews Archives, Box 34 R; Catherine C. Brooks, *War Brought Trials and Anxiety at Home and Overseas* (West Conshohocken, 2009), 94; Gwynn's Island Museum, *Gwynn's Island and the Great Storm of 1933* (Gwynn's Island, 2002), 2, 4–5, 14–16.

17 Mathews Archives, Boxes 23 R, 38 R; Friends of the Mathews Memorial Library, *The Ancestry of the Mathews Memorial Library* (Mathews, 1997), n.p; *Mathews Journal*, January 24, 1929; July 25, 1929; MCHS, *History and Progress*, 91.

18 James H. Hershman Jr., "Public School Bonds and Virginia's Massive Resistance," *The Journal of Negro Education* 52 (1983), 398–409; MCHS, *Mathews County Panorama*, 98, 138; Mathews Archives Boxes 23 R, 32 R, 34 R, 35 R; Brooks, *Didn't Know*, 218; *Gloucester-Mathews Gazette-Journal,* December 15, 1938; November 11, 1982; February 26, 1987; Becky Foster Barnhardt, "Thomas Hunter School, An African American Communities Vision," n. p.; Amy Hauser, February 3, 2014, presentation; Mathews County School Board Records; Elsa Verbyla, Oral History File TMP-030, July 7, 1914; Catherine Brooks, Oral History File TMP-034, July 13, 2014; John Watson Ward, Oral History File TMP-O45, July 29, 2014; Allen Moughan, Oral History File TMP-036, July 14, 2014; Morris and Altha Thompson, Oral History File TMP-042, July 17, 2014; USGS, "Mathews," 1917; http://www2.vcdh.virginia.edu/schools; *Mathews Journal*, May 26, 1932.

19 Mathews County Report of Livestock 1941; Mathews County Farm Statistics 1910–1954, Mathews Archives, Box 18 R; Mary Jo Robinson, Oral History File-025, June 28, 2014; Don Bowman, Oral History File-031, July 11, 2014; Kevin Godsey, Oral History File-032, July 11, 2014; Gilbert Hall, Oral History File-038, July 13, 2014; Robert Hudgins, Oral History File-039, July 14, 2014; A.J. Hurst, Oral History File-035, July 13, 2014; MCHS, *History and Progress*, 115.

20 Mathews Archives, Box 23 R; Leonard, *General Assembly*, 613, 616, 618, 621, 623, 626, 628, 631, 633, 636, 638, 641, 643, 646, 648, 651, 652, 654, 657, 659, 662, 664, 667, 669, 672, 674, 679, 683–684.

21 At one point there were four garden clubs in Mathews County.

22 MCHC, *History and Progress*, 24, 53–54, 145; Mathews Archives Boxes 18 R, 22 R, 23 R, 33 R; Brooks, *Didn't Know*, 217; Betty Wrenn Day, Oral History File TMP-029, July 7, 2014; *Gloucester-Mathews Gazette-Journal*, March 3, 1983; November 5, 2014; Verbyla, *Gwynn's Island Times*, 48; http://civilliberty.about.com; http://centennial.legion.org/virginia/post83; Gwynn's Island, *Great Storm*, 4–5, 14.

23 On the other hand, Betty Wrenn Day, when interviewed, said that Mathews County residents did not have air raid drills (Betty Wrenn Day, Oral History File TMP-029, July 7, 2014).

24 Mathews Archives, Boxes 10 R and 21 R; MCHS, *History and Progress*, 21–23; Tindall, *America*, 1135–1139, 1141–1144; Brooks, *War Brought Trials,* 26, 78–79, 82; Edward and Louise Diggs, Oral History File TMP-026, June 28, 2014; Betty Wrenn Day, Oral History File TMP-029, July 7, 2014.

25 American Legion Monument, Liberty Square, 2003; *Gloucester-Mathews Gazette-Journal*, April 9, 1942; September 19, 1946; October 3, 1946.

13

Looking to the Future, Remembering the Past

1946-present

Postwar Mathews County

At the end of World War II, returning veterans were eager to settle into civilian life. For those that needed retraining before they could join the workforce or wanted to broaden their opportunities through education, Mathews County's Selective Service Board, located in Mathews Courthouse, served as an official Veterans Information Center and the local headquarters of the Retraining and Employment Administration.[1] There, veterans were able to learn about the medical, educational, and financial benefits to which they were entitled, and they could receive assistance in asserting their reemployment rights. Some World War II veterans enrolled in college with funding from the GI Bill of Rights. A reenlistment program offered special benefits to qualified veterans interested in joining the new volunteer peacetime army. There were special vocational training programs for those interested in farm employment, forestry, and other lines of work, and also a program that enabled qualified veterans to receive financial assistance when purchasing farm machinery. Many of the same programs and benefits that were available to World War II veterans later were offered to those who served in the Korean conflict, which claimed the life of William L. Joyner of Mathews County.

After the war, the number of farms in the county began to dwindle, as did the number of people employed in agriculture. Although there were 427 farm workers in Mathews in 1950, by 1960 there were only 140, and in 1980, only 90. The agricultural pursuits that did remain included field crops, especially soybeans and corn; commercially grown daffodils and other florist plants; and animal husbandry. Photographs taken during the mid-twentieth century depict enormous fields of daffodils that were being cultivated as money crops; workers in Mathews and Gloucester picked the flowers, which were packed and shipped to urban centers.

As time went on, an increasing number of Mathews County citizens left home, seeking employment elsewhere. A substantial number of people found jobs in shipbuilding or military installations in Hampton Roads. Those who found jobs locally were usually employed in boat-building and repair, seafood processing, or the lumber industry. Although boat-building waned in importance as time went on, when master craftsman Edward Diggs was interviewed in 1979, he was still fabricating wooden boats in his workshop and was one of a handful of men who did so. He did indicate that when he had started building boats, he used timber grown locally and processed at local sawmills, but in more recent years, he had had to use factory lumber or procure the right type of wood from other parts of the United States. Mr. Diggs surmised that wooden boats eventually would be replaced by mass-produced fiberglass vessels, a prediction that largely came true.

Local agriculture also changed. By 1979, some Mathews County farmers were using no-till corn and soybean plants, which enabled them to reduce labor costs and lessen their need for farm machinery. Some local farms began producing specialized agricultural products, such as "pick your own" berries, greenhouse plants, nurseries, and truck gardens.[2]

In 1946, S.E. Sutton and C.E. Kline opened a business in Mathews Courthouse, where they sold farm supplies. Both men had practical experience in the field of agriculture, as Sutton had been in the trucking business and Kline had been an agricultural instructor at Mathews High School and a Farm Security Administration supervisor. At first, Sutton and Kline's retail establishment was located in part of a wooden building adjacent to the Mathews Ice Company's plant (which also housed an automobile repair shop). In March 1947, a fire that started in the repair shop quickly spread to Sutton and Kline's store and consumed much of their inventory. Undaunted, the two men salvaged what they could and immediately resumed sales. Soon after, they erected a modern cinderblock building and expanded their business to include products provided by Southern States Cooperative, which included hardware and home appliances. In 1972, Kline, as the surviving owner, sold the business to Allen Moughon, an experienced professional educator, who shared responsibilities with his wife, an English teacher and the store's bookkeeper.

Another successful business that was located in Mathews Courthouse during the 1940s was Foster's Department Store, situated on the southwest corner of Church and Main Streets, in what is now called the Halcyon Building. On the east side of Main Street was the Tatterson Brothers Department Store, which was just south of Maple Avenue and Sibley's General Store. At the rear of Tatterson's was a dry-cleaning plant. There were automobile dealerships in Mathews Courthouse and the community got its first shopping center in 1958. In 1954 James A. Faulkner and Norton Hurd of Deltaville formed a partnership and opened Hurd's Appliances in a building that formerly had been the Odd Fellows Lodge Hall.

The Forrest Funeral Home, owned by Charles Edward Forrest Sr., was located on the west side of Main Street, to the north of Richardsons Drugstore and Hurd's Appliances. After Mr. Forrest's death in 1946, Charles W. Faulkner Sr. and Kenneth Evans joined the business and eventually purchased it. In 1962, Mr. Faulkner (then the Faulkner Funeral Home's sole proprietor) joined Wilber T. Foster and his wife, Marjorie (owners of the Foster Funeral Home) in consolidating their businesses, and they took Charles M. Bristow Jr. (whose funeral establishment was in Saluda) as their partner. This was the genesis of today's Foster-Faulkner Funeral Home. The Knight Funeral Home on Holly Point Road also continued its proud tradition of service to the community. R. Stanley Knight became the first African-American member of the Virginia Board of Funeral Directors and the first black member of the Mathews County School Board.

Another successful local business that was started right after World War II was the establishment of P.G. Dillehay and R.T. Whitney, located at the corner of Route 198 and County Route 223 in Hudgins. The men called their business "Chimney Corner Inc." because it was located close to the site of Mrs. Nell Dixon's Chimney Corner Tea Room, a popular eatery during the early twentieth century. When the men first opened their business, they sold gas appliances, tires and automotive supplies, and bottled gas. Within two years' time they expanded to include a Pontiac automobile dealership, a franchise previously held by Fred Joslyn of Cobbs Creek. The establishment's other moneymaking enterprises included outboard motor sales and repairs, a service station, tire sales, and an automobile repair shop.

Another business that was located in Hudgins was Hudgins Home Appliances, which was next door to Donk's Theatre, built by W.C. ("Donk") Dunton during 1946–47. Donk's was the second movie projection theater in Mathews County, and it remained in use until 1970. The theater, which opened its doors to the public on June 9, 1947, had more than 500 upholstered seats and was cooled by two enormous fans. The Duntons added a storefront addition to their theater when their son Bud returned from the military after the Korean War. There, he sold guns and ammunition and operated a pool hall. Although Donk's Theatre closed in 1970, it was re-opened by the Smith family in 1975 as a Grand Ole Opry-style country music concert hall, still a popular source of entertainment. Also located in Hudgins during the 1940s was the Foster Garage, operated by Allen and Roland L. Foster, Jr., who sold Dodge and Plymouth automobiles and repaired all makes and models of cars. Buck's Service Station, U.G. Dillehay's grocery store, and E.L. Billups's shoe repair and awning shop were also close by.[3]

The Seafood Industry's Gradual Decline

Although successive generations of Mathews County watermen were able to derive a living from the sea, after World War II, there was a downturn in the seafood industry. Over time, market forces took their toll. According to a collaborative study undertaken by the Virginia Institute of Marine Science and the College of William and Mary's Business School, the price of seafood soared to unprecedented heights during World War II and reached an all-time high in 1945. This unusually high demand for various types of seafood may have been a result of meat rationing. These high prices attracted men to the fishing industry, but soon they created a glut on the market and a corresponding decline in prices. A decline in the catch of important food fish, which occurred shortly thereafter, did not improve the situation. Although the price of croakers and trout rose briefly due to their scarcity, prices fell sharply when the population recovered and they were once again found in abundance. Researchers concluded that these dramatic fluctuations in the price of fish, rapid growth of the frozen fish industry, and a lessened demand for fresh fish severely impacted Chesapeake watermen.

A similar, but not quite so disastrous, situation occurred in the oyster industry, where harvests diminished but the price failed to rise significantly. According to fisheries biologists, the blue crab fishery has responded over the years to changing biological and economic conditions much like the oyster and food fish industries. Blue crab prices rose during the war, reaching a high in 1945, and then began fluctuating upon a return to a peacetime economy. Other factors, such as the rising cost of labor, contributed to the declining profitability of the seafood industry. An outbreak of the MSX disease in 1960 dealt the oyster industry a crippling blow. Statistics compiled by the Commonwealth of Virginia reveal that between 1960 and 1968 there was a 4.8 percent decline in the number of people employed in the fisheries industry, and between 1968 and 1980, the number of fisheries workers declined by an additional two percent. According to John W. Dixon, the bay was over-fished and the fishing and farm products packaging facilities on Gwynn's Island were unable to maintain a high level of output. He said that in time, Baltimore, Norfolk, and other localities took over a greater share of the seafood market. World events exerted an impact, too, for the expansion of the United States Navy's fleet created jobs in the shipbuilding industry. Jobs were plentiful in large industrial centers in Hampton Roads and attracted workers from rural areas.[4]

Severe Weather

By the end of World War II, meteorologists' ability to track severe weather, particularly tropical storms, had become more sophisticated. Although improved communications and weather scanning systems substantially improved public safety and preparedness, in June 1951 a twister moved down the Piankatank and cut across Gwynn's Island, damaging the homes in its path. Despite forecasters' warnings, in mid-October 1954 nobody was truly prepared for the devastation caused by Hurricane Hazel, which came ashore in the Carolinas and then moved north, wreaking havoc in Mathews County. The wind, which began to blow around noon on Friday, October 15, had reached gale force by 4 PM and continued for several hours, producing significant property damage but no loss of life. The One-mo-Laban section of the county sustained severe damage as did the Cobbs Creek area. The Bayside and Diggs Wharves were demolished. There was widespread destruction on Gwynn's Island, particularly on the Milford Haven side, and throughout the county electric power and telephone lines were affected, leaving many homes without service for several days. Oyster beds were also destroyed. Officials realized that Hazel's damage would have been much worse, had the storm's high winds coincided with high tide.

Mathews County was affected by severe winter weather on March 6 and 7, 1962, when an abnormally high tide, swelled by melting snow, caused water to rise to dangerous levels. The Chesapeake Bay shoreline was breached in a number of places, allowing seawater to surge inland, and the bay side of Gwynn's Island was damaged. The impact to utilities was extensive. Afterward, the 1962 flood was thought to have produced damage that rivaled the August 1933 storm. In October 1997, Hurricane Josephine came ashore at the southeastern end of Gwynn's Island and felled a large number of oak trees. More recently, the storm surge and high winds that accompanied Hurricane Isabel struck southeastern Virginia in early September 2003 and did a great deal of damage in Mathews County.[5]

Political Representation

Delegate John Warren Cooke, who was elected to his first term in the House of Delegates in 1942, was returned to office in 1944 and served through 1980. From 1942 through 1965 he represented Mathews, Gloucester, and Middlesex Counties. Thanks to redistricting, in 1966 Mr. Cooke began representing a much larger jurisdiction, one that included the Middle Peninsula counties within his original district, plus New Kent and Charles City Counties. When redistricting occurred again in 1972, New Kent and Charles City Counties were added to a district in the Southside, whereas King William, King and Queen, and Essex Counties were added to Mr. Cooke's district. One of Virginia's most distinguished statesmen, he became the House of Delegates' majority leader in 1956 and Speaker in 1968. After Mr. Cooke retired in 1980, Delegate Harvey B. Morgan began representing Mathews, as well as Gloucester, Middlesex, Essex, King and Queen, and King William Counties. However, from 1992 through 2001, Mathews was represented by Robert S. Bloxom and was in a district that included Accomack, Northampton, and part of Gloucester County. Redistricting occurred again, and from 2002 through 2011 Mathews County was represented by Harvey B. Morgan, who served a district that included Essex, Gloucester, King and Queen, King William, and Middlesex Counties. More recently, Mathews has been represented by M. Keith Hodges. Among those who have served as Mathews County's representative in the State Senate are Elmo G. Cross Jr. (1976–79), Ralph S. Northam (2008–12), and Lynwood Lewis (2014–16).[6]

The Civil Rights Movement and School Integration

When the United States Supreme Court rendered its decision in *Brown vs. Board of Education* in 1954, it forced state governments to address the issue of racially segregated schools. At the same time, counties and cities throughout Virginia faced rising school enrollment and sought to build more educational facilities. Officials stated that they intended to improve black schools, in hope of preserving the concept of "separate but equal" facilities.[7] In March 1956, a state constitutional convention was held for the purpose of enabling Virginia's legal system to resist the United States Supreme Court's 1954 decision barring public school segregation. In that convention, Charles E. Ford represented Mathews and five other counties, plus the city of Williamsburg. The 1956 amendment to the state constitution gave the General Assembly the authority to appropriate funds for the education of students in public and nonsectarian private schools and other institutions of learning.

In September 1957, President Dwight Eisenhower signed into law the first civil rights legislation since Reconstruction. It empowered the U.S. Attorney General to seek court injunctions in order to protect blacks' voting rights in federal elections. Eisenhower also ordered federal troops to enforce the integration of an all-white high school in Little Rock, Arkansas.

Although some Virginians, especially on the south side of the James River, mounted what they called the "Massive Resistance" campaign, the Virginia Supreme Court of Appeals ruled that the state had to keep its public schools open.[8] State legislators responded by rescinding Virginia's mandatory school attendance law, making enrollment a local option, and some communities exercised their right to close their public schools. In 1959, Governor J. Lindsay Almond Jr. called a special session of the General Assembly for the purpose of doing away with the Massive Resistance laws. Although he had previously supported the concept, ultimately he concluded that a program of limited desegregation was preferable to closing public schools. Although this viewpoint prevailed, the next few years proved to be contentious.

Pressure applied by the Civil Rights Movement, the Civil Rights Act of 1964, and the Voting Rights Act of 1965 resulted in new state legislation that overturned the most controversial aspects of Virginia's 1902 Constitution. Specifically, new laws eliminated voting restrictions and mandated school integration. To make funds available for the construction of new schools, Governor Mills Godwin, who was elected in 1965, strongly advocated the loosening of the strict constitutional restrictions on state-issued bonds and borrowing, and he used his power and popularity to push for a new constitution. In 1968, a joint resolution of Virginia's General Assembly approved a new commission, chaired by former Governor Albertis Harrison, charged with revising the state constitution. The Commission on Constitutional Revision presented its report and recommendations to Governor Godwin and the General Assembly in January 1969, and eventually drafted a version based on consensus. In a referendum, the proposed constitution was overwhelmingly approved by Virginia's voters, who included newly enfranchised African-Americans. The new state constitution took effect on July 1, 1971.[9]

During the late 1960s, the Mathews County School Board approved a desegregation plan. This decision came more than a decade after the U.S. Supreme Court had reaffirmed the principle of public education without racial discrimination. In July 1969, the Board of Supervisors noted that the Gloucester-Mathews School Division, created in 1949, was to be dissolved, making Mathews County a separate school division. Because more funds were needed for teachers and educational facilities, Mathews officials decided to ask the State Board of Education to consider uniting Mathews' school division with that of another county. In 1971 Mathews County's School Superintendent received the Board of Supervisors' approval for a Mathews High School improvement project that involved an infusion of federal funds.

One Mathews resident, a high school student when segregation ended, said that a few students from the all-black Thomas Hunter School decided to attend Mathews High School. She recalled that the transition had occurred smoothly and said that she admired those young people's bravery. Mary Jo Robinson, who was teaching at the Lee-Jackson School when integration occurred, said that there were no real problems and that in her opinion, older folks had a more difficult time accepting the change than younger ones did. Allen Moughan, a faculty member of Mathews High School, remembered that out-of-state monitors were placed in the schools to make sure that racial integration occurred and that students readily accepted the change. School consolidation accompanied integration, and by 1970 the county had three schools: Lee-Jackson Elementary School, Mathews Middle School, and Mathews High School. In 1990 the county's intermediate school was renamed the Thomas Hunter Middle School. The Lee-Jackson Elementary School building, erected in the 1930s as a high school, was razed during the early 1990s so that a new county courthouse complex known as Liberty Square could be built on the site. Meanwhile, a new elementary school, called the Lee-Jackson Elementary School (like its predecessor) was built adjacent to the Thomas Hunter Middle School in 1996.

Katherine Nathan of Moon, who retired in 1991 from employment as secretary/treasurer of the Thomas Hunter School and later, the Mathews Middle School, witnessed the end of segregated schools in Mathews County. Lois Robinson of Blakes, a graduate of North Carolina Central University who retired in 1991 after 31 years of teaching, was also at Thomas Hunter and Mathews High School when integration occurred. The same was true of Georgienne Laws and Martha Thomas, graduates of Hampton University, who taught in Mathews County's black schools and were on staff when the county's two school systems were combined. Another person who was a faculty member when Mathews County schools were integrated was Sally Spriggs Foster of Cardinal. After she graduated from the Thomas Hunter School, she earned associate's and bachelor's degrees from Virginia State College, now known as Norfolk State University. Later, she went on to earn two master's degrees from Hampton University's fore-runner, Hampton Institute. Mrs. Spriggs taught science and mathematics at Thomas Hunter (before school integration) and afterward, at Mathews High School. Virtually all of these women, like other African-Americans of their generation, received their college degrees in segregated institutions of higher education. Funeral director R. Stanley Knight, who was on the Mathews County School Board for eleven years, was reportedly a "positive and calming influence" during the years of integration.[10]

The Kennedy and Johnson Years

During President Lyndon B. Johnson's administration, new social programs were developed as part of the War on Poverty. Johnson proposed federal aid to education and advocated a medical care program for the elderly (Medicare) supported by the Social Security system. The Civil Rights struggle and the Vietnam War (1961–75) forced many Americans to take a long, hard look at the country's foreign and domestic policies. The Vietnam War claimed the lives of three Mathews County men: Terry Hudgins Brooks, James Harold Callis, and Alvin Garvie Morris. On July 20, 1969, when the first manned spacecraft landed on the moon, the little fourth-class post office at Moon was flooded with an estimated 2,500 requests for postmarks to commemorate the event. Mrs. Shirley M. Snow later recalled that she spent the entire day stamping postmarks. Another flood of requests for postmarks came in autumn 1969 when there was another moon landing.[11]

Racial Tensions

On Saturday, August 23, 1980, a racially-charged incident occurred in Mathews County that could have had dire consequences. A 23-year-old African-American man, Michael Saunders Johnson, stopped on suspicion of drunk driving, got into an altercation with John Thornes, a deputy sheriff who was twice his age and new to his job.[12] When the confrontation became physical and Thornes was knocked to the ground, he drew his gun and fired what proved to be a fatal shot. The incident, which many people considered a senseless killing, generated anger and fear in the community along with the potential for additional violence. Large crowds of people gathered in the ABC store parking lot, where the shooting occurred, and on the courthouse green. Sheriff Kenneth H. Jordan Jr. summoned the state police and law enforcement personnel from Gloucester and Middlesex Counties, who showed up in riot gear. He also telephoned Mrs. Beatrice Lee Bobo of North, then president of the Mathews Chapter of the NAACP. When she arrived, she persuaded the crowd to stay calm and to instead hold a peaceful protest march. Thanks to Mrs. Bobo's efforts, the next morning approximately 300 protesters, both black and white, walked in orderly fashion from the courthouse to First Baptist Church. Leading the march, which occurred without incident, were Mrs. Bobo; the Rev. Alvan James, pastor of First Baptist Church; and Virginia NAACP Executive Director Jack Graveley. Deputy Thornes, who resigned, was arrested and charged with unlawful homicide. Although he was not indicted, the Johnson family filed a civil suit, alleging that Deputy Thornes "had a history of intemperate behavior, rude manners, and injury by firearm of persons in his authority while making an arrest."[13]

Highway Improvements and Bridge Construction

For many years, the Gloucester-Yorktown Ferry, Inc., a private corporation, operated a ferry that plied the waters of the York River. However, as automobile traffic increased, so did interest in building a bridge. In 1927 the Eastern Bridge Company was authorized to construct a span, but never followed through. Three other groups also received permission to undertake construction but failed to do so, probably on account of the cost involved. Finally, in 1940 the General Assembly decided to underwrite bridge construction. Although World War II sidetracked the project, it came to fruition in 1952 when the George Preston Coleman Memorial Bridge was opened to traffic. The new span, which has been widened, permanently linked the Middle and James-York Peninsulas, strengthening the economy of both areas.[14]

Modernizing County Government

Today, Mathews, like the majority of Virginia's other counties, operates under what is known as the traditional form of county government, one in which an elected Board of Supervisors is responsible for the legislative and administrative affairs of their county. The Supervisors establish local public policy, raise revenue for the support of local public programs, and oversee the conduct of county business. During the twentieth century, an increasing number of Virginia's county Boards of Supervisors began hiring County Administrators to assist them in implementing Board policies and decisions and in carrying out the day-to-day administration of county business. On August 27, 1994, the Mathews County Board of Supervisors voted to hire its first County Administrator and three days later they appointed Charles H. (Sonny) Richardson to that position. Today, virtually all of Virginia's Boards of Supervisors that operate under the traditional form of county government employ a County Administrator.

Mathews County government has other important officials who are responsible for the conduct and administration of county business: the Commissioner of the Revenue, the Treasurer, the Clerk of Court, the Commonwealth's Attorney, and the Sheriff. These individuals, who are elected, are generally known as Constitutional Officers because their positions are identified by name in the state constitution. A number of appointed officials, boards, commissions, and advisory agencies also serve the county. For example, the Mathews County Planning, Zoning and Wetlands Office addresses the county's changing needs. Its responsibilities include long-range land use planning and enforcing the various ordinances that the Board of Supervisors has approved, such as those pertaining to the control of erosion and sediment, wetlands preservation, and zoning. The county has a five-member Board of Zoning Appeals and a seven-member Planning Commission that advises the Board of Supervisors on land use issues. All Virginia counties are assisted by the employees of various state agencies. For example, game wardens, foresters, health department workers, highway department employees, and agricultural extension agents serve the counties within a specific district. Mildred Hudgins, who became Mathews County's home demonstration agent in 1973, provided homemakers with information on food preservation and other economic strategies. Some state agencies serve the Commonwealth as a whole but all of them work with local officials.[15]

Those Who Serve and Protect

The Mathews County sheriff, a Constitutional Officer, is assisted by deputies and other professional personnel in upholding law and order and preserving the peace. The Sheriff's Office performs many other types of services that benefit residents of the community. For example, a School Resource Officer serves students at the Thomas Hunter Middle School and the Mathews High School. The Sheriff's Office has 911 and 627 emergency assistance links that connect citizens to the fire department and rescue squad. Other services that are provided by the Sheriff's Office include the Drug Abuse Resistance Education program (or DARE); Project Lifesaver, an electronic tracking program that assists in locating people with Alzheimer's disease, dementia and other impairments; and Applicant Fingerprinting. Deputy Sheriffs make security checks of local residents' homes and businesses and assist in setting up Neighborhood Watch programs, and the Triad Program provides several other important services to the public.

Many other members of the community strive to keep Mathews County and its citizens safe. The Mathews Volunteer Fire Department was reportedly formed in 1949, with substations at Bohannon, Gwynn's Island, and Cobbs Creek. Today there are fire stations at Bohannon, Cobbs Creek, Gwynn's Island, Mathews Courthouse, and New Point. The most common type of call that all three stations receive involve woods and brush fires.

The Mathews County Emergency Services office is responsible for handling all responses in the event of a natural disaster and or terrorist threat. Throughout the year, the Emergency Services Coordinator receives specialized training in order to be well prepared for all types of emergencies.

Members of the Mathews Volunteer Rescue Squad, organized in 1968, have been serving the community ever since.[16] The squad's first rescue vehicle, acquired in 1968, was eventually replaced by three ambulances and a rescue boat. The group's first board of directors included Robert W. Orrell, Edward C. Kobylinski, Wallace B. Twigg, Mrs. Stanley E. Payne, and

Richard T. Whitney. Members of the rescue squad attended first aid classes conducted by the American Red Cross. In November 1968 the squad purchased a lot next to the Mathews Laundromat and within months broke ground for its first building. The group moved into a newer and much larger structure on Cricket Hill Road in 2006. Today, many of the squad's members have become certified Emergency Medical Technicians (or EMTs) and a certified EMT has to be present on each rescue squad run. Another group that helps to keep Mathews County citizens safe is the United States Coast Guard, which established Station Milford Haven at Cricket Hill. The men and women of the Coast Guard perform search and rescue operations, uphold safe boating standards, enforce marine environmental law in the Chesapeake Bay and its tributaries, and play a role in law enforcement. The Coast Guard's Auxiliary Flotilla, an all-volunteer group, also makes a strong contribution to its parent organization's mission, particularly when it comes to boating safety.[17]

Social and Cultural Activities

The Gwynn's Island Civic League, organized in 1948, began meeting regularly in the Gwynn's Island School. At first, the League tried to secure a public telephone for the island and to see that the community had a building that could be used for recreation and special events. Over the years, the League achieved many of its objectives, which included persuading the highway department to pave the roads on Gwynn's Island, building a firehouse and a parking lot for the cemetery, and encouraging local residents to vote in general elections. The Gwynn's Island Civic League also fostered the establishment of the Gwynn's Island Garden Club, organized in the 1950s, and a Girl Scout troop.

As early as 1938, Mathews County citizens began hosting an annual daffodil tour. The county started participating in the annual Historic Garden Week in Virginia, a program sponsored by the Garden Club of Virginia, and in 1950 the first annual Mathews House and Garden Tour was held. In 1951, Mathews County, at the initiative of the Mathews County Junior Woman's Club, began holding an annual spring festival. The popular three-day event featured a parade, a beauty pageant, boat races, and visiting celebrities and state dignitaries. All of these events showcased Mathews County's natural beauty and rich history. By the mid-1950s, a committee comprised of representatives from the Junior and Senior Woman's Clubs, the Ruritan Club, the Lions Club, and the Chamber of Commerce took over management of the Spring Festival, which boosted the local economy and promoted tourism. The festival held in 1957 (Virginia's 350th anniversary) featured a pageant about the formation of Mathews County. By 1961 the Mathews Spring Festival's organizing committee decided to purchase eight acres of waterfront property on the Chesapeake Bay that could be opened as a public beach: the Milford Haven Festival Beach. Maintaining the property may have proved to be too much, for in April 1973 representatives of Mathews Spring Festival Inc. offered to give its beach property to county government. The Board of Supervisors' response was delayed until 1976, when it accepted the beach property on behalf of the county. Afterward, the Lions Club, which obtained a one-year lease, began a much-needed cleanup of the property. In 1974 the county held its first Mathews Market Days, a highly successful event that quickly became an annual tradition.

In 1976, Mathews, like other Virginia counties, celebrated the bicentennial of American Independence. In honor of the occasion, the Gwynn's Island Civic League held a four-day festival. One highlight of the event was production of a musical called "Crickets on a Hill," centering on the historic Revolutionary War battle of Gwynn's Island. A celebration was also held in Mathews Courthouse, where a parade marked the occasion. Several special publications that commemorated Mathews County's history included a bicentennial poster with sketches of fifteen local landmarks, histories of local churches, and set of biographies of important Virginia leaders. In 1991 when Mathews County celebrated its own bicentennial, special events were held, and the *Gloucester-Mathews Gazette-Journal* published a collector's edition recognizing the county's 200th anniversary.[18]

Preserving and Celebrating Local History

Local organizations such as the Mathews County Historical Society, the Mathews Maritime Foundation, the Mathews Land Conservancy, and the Gwynn's Island Museum, along with the Middle Peninsula chapter of the Archeological Society of Virginia, have worked diligently to identify and preserve the sites at which cultural features, such as standing historic structures and archaeological sites, are located. Those groups, along with the *Gloucester-Mathews Gazette-Journal's* publication of commemorative editions and its production of historic newspaper databases, have promoted public interest in Mathews County's cultural heritage. Studies sponsored by the Virginia Department of Historic Resources, through the agency's landmarks register and review-and-compliance programs, strive to document and preserve Mathews County's abundantly rich cultural heritage, which is unique but representative of rural America. Grant funding from federal and state agencies has furthered these important initiatives. The Mathews County Historical Society, a nonprofit organization established on January 16, 1964, not only serves as an advocate for historic preservation, but has published a number of books that promote an appreciation of local history. The historical society also sponsors public lectures, participates in events that foster an awareness of the county's heritage, and maintains its archives at the Mathews Memorial Library.

In 1994, the Mathews Land Conservancy, with a combination of grant funding and private support, purchased approximately four acres at Williams Wharf, a natural and historic landmark that provides a site offering environmentally friendly waterfront activities for Mathews County citizens and visitors. Williams Wharf serves as the Mathews Land Conservancy's headquarters and it is also home to the Mathews High School Crew Team, the Mobjack Rowing Association, and the Mathews YMCA's Sailing Camp. Each of these groups use the facilities at the wharf for training purposes and special events. A picnic pavilion, a reviewing stand, and boat launching ramps also are available at Williams Wharf. Also located there is the historic B. Williams and Company Store, the remains of old docks and a marine railway, and an assortment of historic outbuildings.

The Mathews Maritime Foundation, whose mission is to preserve Mathews County's maritime heritage and present it to the public, was incorporated in 1999. The Foundation's public outreach activities include the Mathews Maritime Museum and the Gwynn's Island Boat Shop. Also furthering the public's interest in Mathews County's nautical heritage is the Mathews Maritime Heritage Trail, a component of the Chesapeake

Bay Gateways Network. The initial phase of the Mathews Maritime Heritage Trail focused upon the East River's cultural resources such as historic wharves, fish and crab packing houses, historic shipyards, marinas, and sites that are environmentally significant.

By 1976, the annual "Homecoming Day," sponsored by the Gwynn's Island Civil League since 1949, had evolved into the Gwynn's Island Festival, a popular annual event that features arts and crafts, music, and food. The Gwynn's Island Museum, first known as the Gwynn's Island Cultural Center, initially was housed in the former Shiloh United Methodist Church and included a private artifact collection. Over time, the Cultural Center's collections grew so large that more space was needed. Thanks to the generosity of the Allen family, a building located at the corner of Route 33 and Rose Lane was donated to the Civic League. The century-old structure, which originally served as the Odd Fellows Lodge and then as the island's first public school, was restored during the early 1990s and converted to use as the Gwynn's Island Museum. During the warmer months, Gwynn's Island's population increases, thanks to an influx of visitors who enjoy their vacation homes or one of the local campgrounds. Haven Beach near Diggs and the Bethel Beach Natural Area Preserve, northeast of Onemo, also attract numerous visitors, as do the county's twenty public access boat landings.

The Mathews County Historical Society has lovingly preserved an early nineteenth century building that is located on the south side of Brickbat Road in Mathews Courthouse. This structure, which has seen many uses, was designated the Tompkins Cottage in the late 1960s. It was purchased by the Mathews County government in 1964 and has been leased to the historical society since 1969. Currently, it serves as the organization's headquarters and interpretive center. Another historic building that the Mathews County Histori-

Tompkins Cottage today. Photo by Becky Foster Barnhardt, Mathews County Historical Society.

cal Society uses as an interpretive facility is the Thomas James Store, which dates to 1820. The original fabric of this remarkably well preserved building, which encompasses approximately 375 square feet, has overhead attic space and two shed-roofed additions. Although the Thomas James Store has undergone some alterations over the years and has been moved from its original location, it is one of the South's best preserved stores and is on the National Register of Historic Places and the Virginia Landmarks Register as part of the Mathews Courthouse Historic District. Near the Thomas James Store and also on the National Register is historic Sibley's Store, which was built by Thomas James's grandchildren, Henry and Francis Joseph Sibley, around 1899. Sibley family descendants owned and operated the store until 1989. The first floor of Sibley's Store currently serves as Mathews County's tourism center and its second floor is being developed as a museum by the Mathews County Historical Society.

Thanks to the Mathews County Historical Society's diligent efforts, the site of Fort Nonsense has been turned into a county park and interpretive center. The same is true of the New Point Comfort Lighthouse, which the Mathews County government acquired from the state in 1976.[19] Local volunteers raised funds for critical repairs and restoration work and the county has provided maintenance. Riprap was added around the light tower and a new door, a lightning rod cable, and an iron ladder were installed. The Virginia Department of Conservation and Natural Resources provided some of the funding for maintenance and repairs. Additional repairs were undertaken in 1988, and in 2001 the New Point Comfort Lighthouse Preservation Task Force, a committee of the Mathews County government, was formed. By that time, coastal erosion had eaten away much of the land on which the lighthouse is situated, leaving it surrounded by water. The Virginia Chapter of the Nature Conservancy purchased a 95-acre tract they called the New

Courtesy of Becky Foster Barnhardt, Mathews County Historical Society.

New Point Comfort lighthouse and the keeper's house.
Courtesy of the Mathews Archives.

Point Comfort Preserve for the purpose of preserving a significant natural area and later, a land development firm donated an additional thirteen acres. An interpretive overlook and informational signage were installed, which have made the lighthouse a popular tourist attraction. In 2003 the U.S. Army Corps of Engineers commenced a three-year shoreline reconnaissance study, but ultimately concluded that there was relatively little impact on wildlife habitat and that protecting the lighthouse was unfeasible. In 2007 the Mathews County Board of Supervisors executed an agreement with the Virginia Institute of Marine Science, whereby the lighthouse would be safeguarded. Two years later the Virginia Department of Transportation provided funds for the construction of a granite revetment around the lighthouse, and to raise the ground, to construct a new entranceway, to provide a pedestrian path around the light house, and to build a new pier. The New Point Comfort Lighthouse is on the Virginia Landmarks Register and the National Register of Historic Places, as is the Wolf Trap Light Station.[20]

Today, Mathews County's numerous tourist attractions are flourishing and are enjoyed by locals and visitors alike. Seasonal events such as the Tour de Chesapeake for cyclists, Mathews Market Days, the Mathews Farmer's Market, the Gwynn's Island Festival, and Historic Garden Week bring visitors to the county as do a broad variety of cultural events held at the Mathews Memorial Library, Donk's Theater, the Bay School Community

Arts Center, and the Halcyon Theater. Also widely available are opportunities for beach-going, camping, boating and kayaking, boat tours, birding and wildlife trails, cycling, and passive recreational pursuits. A popular vacation destination with lodging and dining facilities, Mathews is heralded as one of the pearls of the Chesapeake.

Notes

1 According to John Warren Cooke, the Selective Service office occupied space in the county library (Mathews Archives, Box 23 R).

2 When interviewed in 2014, Ron and Nancy Rowe, when reminiscing about Mathews County boat-builders, said that the art of building wooden boats is largely gone and that the surviving builders are elderly. They also noted that pound-net fishing has disappeared (Ron and Nancy Rowe, Oral History File-037, July 14, 2013).

3 MCHS, *History and Progress*, 60–69, 115–116, 118–119, 122–123; Allen Moughon, Oral History File TMP-036, July 14, 2014; Mathews Archives, Boxes 18 R and 23 R; Donk's Theatre, National Register of Historic Places, DHR 057-0069; www.foster-faulkner.com/about-us; *Gloucester-Mathews Gazette-Journal*, June 5, 1947; Vogel, *Then and Now,* 40, 43–44, 59, 90.

4 Dixon, *Black Americans*, 16; J.L. McHugh and Robert S. Bailey, "History of Virginia's Commercial Fisheries," *Virginia Journal of Science*, Vol. 8 (January 1957), 42–64; MCHS, *History and Progress*, 108–111; Mathews County Board of Supervisors Minute Book 6:61; Mathews County Farm Statistics 1910–1954, Mathews Archives, Box 18 R.

5 MCHS, *History and Progress*, 100–101; http://en.wikipedia.org; MCHS, *Panorama*, 88; David Callis, Oral History File TMP-040, July 16, 2014; Gwynn's Island, *Great Storm*, preface.

6 Mathews Archives Box 23 R; Leonard, *General Assembly*, 686, 691, 696, 701, 706, 712, 716–717, 719, 725, 730, 736, 741, 747, 753, 760, 766, 773, 777.

7 James H. Hershman Jr., "Public School Bonds and Virginia's Massive Resistance," *The Journal of Negro Education* 52 (1983), 398–409.

8 Speaker John Warren Cooke credited the late Harry F. Byrd Jr.'s organization with the concept of "Massive Resistance" to public school integration. He said that the majority of the General Assembly's delegates and senators were from rural areas and strongly opposed to integration (Mathews Archives Box 23 R).

9 http://en.wikipedia.org/wiki/constitution_of_virginia; Mathews Archives Box 23 R.

10 Verbyla, Oral History File TMP-030, July 7, 2014; Mary Jo Robinson, Oral History File TMP-023, June 28, 2014; Allen Moughan, Oral History File TMP-036, July 14, 2014;

www.encyclopediavirginia.org/desegregation; Mathews Archives, Box 23 R; Tindall, *America*, 1242–1245; *Gloucester-Mathews Gazette-Journal*, January 13, 1990; January 10, 1991; June 6, 1991; June 13, 1991; June 20, 1991; June 27, 1991; Mathews County Board of Supervisors Minute Book 6: 30, 178. Peter Allen of Mathews County, who was interviewed in 1998 when he was in his late 90s, recalled not being able to eat in local restaurants or drugstores, but said that he was able to purchase items there. He said that integration occurred peacefully in Mathews County, with the exception of Gwynn's Island, and noted that many area blacks moved to Hampton (*Daily Press*, February 8, 1998).

11 Virginius Dabney, *Virginia: The New Dominion* (Charlottesville, 1971), 568; MCHS, *History and Progress*, 135–136.

12 Johnson was a member of the Mathews High School class of 1975 and belonged to Antioch Church. When autopsied, alcohol was found in his bloodstream (*Gloucester-Mathews Gazette-Journal*, August 28, 1980).

13 *Gloucester-Mathews Gazette-Journal*, August 28, 1980; September 4, 1980; October 16, 1980; March 3, 1983; Verbyla, Oral History File TMP-030.

14 *Gloucester-Mathews Gazette-Journal*, December 30, 1999.

15 Reed Lawson, personal communication, March 10, 2015; Commonwealth of Virginia, *Virginia Government in Brief, 2014–2018*, 54–55; www.co.mathews.va.us/government; Mathews County Board of Supervisors Minute Book 6:418, 420.

16 According to Wallace Twigg Sr., who was interviewed by the *Gloucester-Mathews Gazette-Journal* in 1979, the Rescue Squad initially used carryalls as ambulances. Eventually, they were replaced by a module that consisted of an ambulance body mounted on the back of a truck (MCHS, *History and Progress*, 140).

17 www.mathewsvrs.org; www.uscg.mil/ds/stationmilfordhaven; MCHS, *History and Progress*, 112–113, 140, 142–143; www.co.mathews.va.us/departments-services/sheriff.

18 MCHS, *History and Progress*, 142–143; MCHC Archives, Boxes 6 R, 19 R, 22 R, 24 R, 28 R, 30 R, 31 47 R, 83 R, 16 OV; *Gloucester-Mathews Gazette-Journal*, October 28, 1948; November 11, 1948; June 16, 1949; June 30, 1949; July 7, 1949; May 24, 1951; March 2, 1961; August 12, 1976; September 10, 2009; *Richmond Times-Dispatch*, June 20, 1965; Mathews County Board of Supervisors Minute Book 5:268; Book 6:81.

19 On April 22, 1969, the Board of Supervisors was informed by the Virginia Commission of Outdoor Recreation that the county could obtain a lease for the New Point Comfort Lighthouse (Mathews County Board of Supervisors Minute Book 6:39).

20 www.gwynnsislandmuseum.org; MCHS, *History and Progress*, 142–143; Jean Tanner, Oral History File TMP-043, July 17, 2014; Mathews County Processioners Records 1866; Land Tax Lists 1815–1900; Deed Book 10: 403–404; 12: 231–232; MCHS, *Panorama,* 116; Sibley's and James Store Historic District, National Register of Historic Places, HABS Files 057-5027, 057-5049; www.mathewslandconservancy.com, New Point Comfort Lighthouse, National Register of Historic Places, HABS File 057-0064; Wolf Trap Light Station, National Register of Historic Places, HABS File 057-0065; Clifford and Clifford, *New Point Comfort*, 93–95.

BIBLIOGRAPHY

Abercrombie, Janice L., and Richard Slatten, comp. *Virginia Public Claims.* Athens, Georgia: Iberian Publishing Company, 1992.

Admiralty Office Papers (A.O.). British Public Records Office, Kew, England. Survey Reports and microfilms, Rockefeller Library, Colonial Williamsburg Foundation, Williamsburg.

American Medical Association. "Report on the Number of Practitioners of Medicine in Virginia," *Transactions of the American Medical Association* 1 (1847), 359–365.

Andrews, Charles, comp. *Narratives of the Insurrections, 1665–1690.* New York: Charles Scribner's Sons, 1967.

Anonymous. "A Plat of the land bought by John Dixon and adjoining the land he [Williams] bought of Davis and Hunley at East warehouse," no date. Library of Virginia, Richmond.

____________. Untitled article. *Home Mail* 1 (1874):clipping. Phelps, New York: Home Mail Publishing Company. Mathews Archives, Mathws Memorial Library, Mathews. Unaccessioned item.

____________. "York River and Mobajack [*sic*] Bay, Virginia," [1861–1865]. Library of Congress, Washington, D.C.

____________. "One Hundred Years of Agriculture." Undated twentieth century clipping from unidentified newspaper on file at James City County Historical Commission, Toano.

Asbury, Francis. *The Journal of The Rev. Francis Asbury, Bishop of the Methodist Episcopal Church from August 7, 1771, to December 7, 1815.* 3 vols. New York: Abraham Paul, Printer, 1821.

Auditor of Public Accounts, comp. *Muster Rolls of the Virginia Militia in the War of 1812*. Richmond: W. F. Ritchie, Public Printer, 1852.

Austrian, Geoffrey D. *Herman Hollerith: Forgotten Giant of Information Processing*. New York: Columbia University Press, 1982.

Axelson, Edith F., comp. *Virginia Postmasters and Post Offices, 1789–1832*. Athens, Georgia: Iberian Publishing Company, 1991.

Bache, A.D. "Coast Chart No. 32, Chesapeake Bay No. 2, Rappahannock Entrance, Mobjack Bay, Cherrystone Inlet." 1877. National Oceanic and Atmospheric Administration, Washington, D.C.

Baker, W.W. *Memoirs of Service with John Yates Beall*. Richmond: The Richmond Press, 1910.

Baltimore, Maryland. City of Baltimore Census 1870. Library of Virginia, Richmond.

Barnhardt, Becky Foster. "Thomas Hunter School, An African American Communities Vision," 2006. Manuscript. Mathews Memorial Library, Mathews.

Bearss, Sara B. "Restored and Vindicated: The Virginia Constitutional Convention of 1864," *Virginia Magazine of History and Biography* 122 (2014):157–181.

Berkeley, Edmund and Dorothy S. Berkeley. *John Clayton, Pioneer of American Botany*. Chapel Hill: University of North Carolina, 1963.

Berlin, Ira. *Many Thousands Gone: The First Two Centuries of Slavery in North America*. Cambridge: Belknap Press, 1998.

Berlin, Ira and Philip D. Morgan. *Cultivation and Culture: Labor and the Shaping of Slave Life in the Americas*. Charlottesville and London: University Press of Virginia, 1993.

Beverley, Robert. *History of the Present State of Virginia (1705)*, L.B. Wright, ed. Chapel Hill: University of North Carolina Press, 1947.

Biggs, Fred C., and Chris Plummer. *Gloucester County, Virginia, A Bicentennial Perspective*. Gloucester: Gloucester '76 Celebration, Inc., 1976.

Billings, Warren M. "Some Acts Not in Hening's Statutes: The Acts of Assembly April 1652, November 1652, and July 1653." *Virginia Magazine of History and Biography* 83 (1975):22–76.

Billings, Warren M., ed. *The Papers of Francis Howard, Baron Howard of Effingham, 1643–1695*. Richmond: Virginia State Library, 1989.

Billings, Warren M. et al. *Colonial Virginia: A History.* White Plains, N.Y.: KTO Press, 1986.

Billups Papers. Richard Billups Papers, 1705–1857. Swem Library Department of Special Collections, College of William and Mary, Williamsburg.

Billups Papers. Billups Papers: Kingston Parish Tithables 1774–1775. Library of Virginia, Richmond.

Billups Papers. Richard Billups Papers, 1809–1832. Virginia Historical Society, Richmond.

Blanton, Dennis B. "The Climate Factor in Late Prehistoric and Post-Contact Human Affairs." In *Indian and European Contact in Context: The Mid-Atlantic Region*, edited by Dennis B. Blanton and Julia A. King, 6–21. Gainesville: University Press of Florida, 2004.

Blanton, Wyndham B. *Medicine in Virginia in the Nineteenth Century.* Richmond: Garrett and Massie, 1933.

Boatner, Mark Mayo III. *The Civil War Dictionary.* New York: David McKay Company, Inc., 1959.

Bond, Edward L. *Spreading the Gospel in Colonial Virginia: Sermons and Devotional Writings.* Lanham, Maryland: Lexington Books, 2004.

Borum, Edmond. Will dated February 1, 1798. Lost Records Localities Collections, Library of Virginia, Richmond, Virginia.

Bottom, Davis, comp. *Acts and Joint Resolutions Passed By the General Assembly of the State of Virginia Passed During the Session of 1914.* Richmond: Commonwealth of Virginia, 1914.

______________. *Acts and Joint Resolutions Passed by the General Assembly of the State of Virginia Passed During the Session of 1916*. Richmond: Commonwealth of Virginia, 1916.

______________. *Register of the General Assembly of Virginia, 1776–1918*. Fourteenth Annual Report of the Library Board of the Virginia State Library. Richmond: Commonwealth of Virginia, 1917.

Böye, Herman. "Map of the State of Virginia," 1826, 1858. Library of Virginia, Richmond.

Breeden, James O., ed. *Advice Among Masters: The Ideal in Slave Management in the Old South*. Westport, Connecticut: Greenwood Press, 1980.

Breen, T.H., and Stephen Innes. *Myne Owne Grounde*. New York: Oxford University Press, 1980.

Bristow, Robert. Account Book 1688–1750; Letter Book 1747–1770. Microfilms, Rockefeller Library, Colonial Williamsburg Foundation, Williamsburg.

Brooks, Charles F. "The 'Old Fashioned' Winter of 1917–1918." *Geographical Review* 5 (1918):405, 410–411.

Brooks, Catherine C. *Didn't Know We Were Poor*. West Conshohocken: Infinity Publishing Company, 2007.

______________. *War Brought Trials and Anxiety at Home and Overseas*. West Conshohocken: Infinity Publishing Company, 2009.

Brooks, Constance V. *Names on Record: A Journal Featuring Virginians of African Descent*. vol. 1. No place of publication: privately published, 1998.

Brown, Alexander C. "Wolf Trap: The Baptism of a Chesapeake Bay Shoal." *Virginia Magazine of History and Biography* 59 (1951):176–183.

______________. *Steam Packets on the Chesapeake: A History of the Old Bay Line Since 1840*. Cambridge, Maryland: Cornell Maritime Press Inc., 1961.

Brown, Kathleen M. *Good Wives, Nasty Wenches, and Anxious Patriarch: Gender, Race, and Power in Colonial Virginia*. Chapel Hill: University of North Carolina Press, 1996.

Brown, Robert L. Untitled notes on Kingston Parish's history, n.d. Kingston Parish Church Office, Mathews.

____________. *Old Kingston Parish, 1652–1976*. Gloucester, Virginia: Gloucester-Mathews Gazette-Journal, 2002.

Bruce, Kathleen. "Virginian Agricultural Decline to 1860: A Fallacy," *Agricultural History* 6 (1932), 3–13.

Bruce, Philip A. ed., "Virginia Families," *Virginia Magazine of History and Biography,* 3(1896):605–607.

Brydon, George M. *Virginia's Mother Church and The Political Conditions Under Which It Grew.* Richmond: Virginia Historical Society, 1947.

Buck, J.L. *The Development of Public Schools in Virginia, 1607–1952.* Richmond: Virginia State Board of Education, 1952.

Bullock, Thomas K. *Schools and Schooling in Eighteenth Century Virginia.* Durham: Duke University, 1961.

Bureau of Refugees. List of Confiscated Lands, 1862–1866. Microfilm, Rockefeller Library, Colonial Williamsburg Foundation, Williamsburg, and National Archives, Washington, D. C.

____________. Freedmen's Bureau Records, 1865–1867. Microfilm, National Archives, Washington, D.C.

Burgess, Robert H., and H. Graham Wood. *Steamboats Out of Baltimore.* Cambridge, Maryland: Tidewater Publishers, 1968.

Callis, Robert. Receipt to William H. Billups, constable, December 23, 1817. Virginia Historical Society, Richmond, Virginia.

Cappon, Lester J. *Virginia Newspapers, 1821–1935*. New York: Appleton-Century Company, 1936.

Carrier, Lyman. *Agriculture in Virginia, 1607–1699.* Charlottesville: University Press of Virginia, 1957.

Carr, Lois G. et al. *Colonial Chesapeake Society.* Chapel Hill: University of North Carolina Press, 1988.

Carson, Cary et. al. "Impermanent Architecture in the Southern American Colonies. *Winterthur Portfolio*," 16 (Summer–Autumn, 1981):135–196.

Carson, Jane. *Travelers in Tidewater Virginia, 1700–1800*. Williamsburg: Colonial Williamsburg Foundation, 1965.

Carter, Landon. *The Diary of Landon Carter*. Jack P. Green, ed. 2 vols. Charlottesville: University Press of Virginia, 1962.

Catton, Bruce. *The American Heritage Picture History of the Civil War*. New York: American Heritage Publishing Co., 1960.

Cecere, Michael, ed. *Captain Thomas Posey and the 7th Virginia Regiment*. Westminster, Maryland: Heritage Books, Inc., 2005.

Chamberlayne, Charles G. *The Parish Register of Christ Church, Middlesex County, Virginia, from 1653–1812*. Easley, South Carolina: Southern Historical Society, 1988.

____________. *The Vestry Book of Kingston Parish, Mathews County, Virginia, 1679–1796*. Bowie, Maryland: Heritage Books, 1999.

Chandler, J.A.C., and E.G. Swem, eds., "Letters Written by Mr. Moray, A Minister, to Sr. R. Moray, from Ware River in Mockjack Bay, Virginia, Feb. 1, 1665." *William and Mary Quarterly* 2nd Ser., 2 (1893–1894):157–161.

____________. "Petition of American Loyalists, 1778." *William and Mary Quarterly* 2nd Ser., 1 (1920):70–71.

Chapman, Blanch A. *Wills and Administrations of Elizabeth City County, Virginia, 1688–1800*. Baltimore: Clearfield Company, 2008.

Charles, Joan, comp. *Gloucester and Mathews Newspaper Articles, 1770–1922*. Gloucester: Gloucester Historical Society, 2014.

Church, Randolph W. *Virginia Legislative Petitions*. Richmond: Virginia State Library Board, 1984.

Churchman, John. "This Map of the Peninsula Between Delaware and Chesapeak[e] Bays." 1778. Library of Congress, Washington, D.C.

Clark, William B., and William J. Morgan. *Naval Documents of the American Revolution*. 11 vols. Washington, D.C.: United States Government Printing Office, 1964–1981.

Clayton, John. Map of Jamestown and May 12, 1688, letter to Robert Boyle. Boyle Papers 39, Item 3, ff 160–162. Archives of the Royal Society of London, London.

Clifford, Mary Lou and Candice Clifford. *The New Point Comfort Lighthouse: Its History and Preservation*. Petersburg: Dietz Press, 2014.

Cocke, Charles F. *Parish Lines of the Diocese of Southern Virginia*. Richmond: Library of Virginia, 1964.

____________. *Parish Lines of the Diocese of Virginia*. Richmond: Library of Virginia, 1967.

Coldham, Peter Wilson, comp. *American Migrations 1765–1799*. Baltimore: Genealogical Publishing Company, 2000.

____________. *British Emigrants in Bondage, 1614–1788*. Baltimore: Genealogical Publishing Company, 2005.

____________. *The King's Passengers to Maryland and Virginia*. Westminster, Maryland: Heritage Books Inc., 2006

Coldham, Peter Wilson and Sally L. M. Haigh, comp. *American Loyalist Claims Abstracted from the Public Records Office*. Washington, D. C.: National Genealogical Society, 1980.

Colles, Christopher. *A Survey of the Roads of the United States of America, 1789*. Walter W. Ristow, ed. Cambridge: Belknap Press of Harvard University Press, 1961.

Colonial Office Papers (C.O.). British Public Records Office, Kew, England. Survey Reports and microfilms, Rockefeller Library, Colonial Williamsburg Foundation, Williamsburg.

Confederate Citizens or Business Claims. Confederate Papers Relating to Citizens or Business Firms, 1862–1864. Microfilm, National Archives, Washington, D.C.

Confederate Rosters. Digital data base. Library of Virginia, Richmond.

Confederate Veterans and Widows Pension Files. Digital files. Library of Virginia, Richmond.

Commonwealth of Virginia. *Virginia Government in Brief, 2014–2018*. Richmond: Office of the Governor, 2014.

Craven, Wesley F. *The Virginia Company of London, 1606–1624*. Charlottesville: University Press of Virginia, 1957.

Cunningham, Horace H. *Doctors in Gray: The Confederate Medical Service*. Baton Rouge: Louisiana State University Press, 1958.

Dabney, Virginius. *Virginia: The New Dominion*. Charlottesville: University Press of Virginia, 1971.

Darlington, William, comp. *Memorials of John Bartram and Humphry Marshall with Notices of Their Botanical Contemporaries*. Philadelphia: Lindsay and Blakiston, 1849.

Davidson, Thomas E. "The People of Tsenacommachah: Powhatan Indians in the Williamsburg Area." In *Williamsburg, Virginia: A City Before the State,* edited by Robert P. Maccubbin, 7–14. Charlottesville: University Press of Virginia, 2000.

Davis, David Brion. *Slavery in the Colonial Chesapeake*. Williamsburg: Colonial Williamsburg Foundation, 1986.

Davis, Virginia Lee Hutchinson, comp. *Tidewater Virginia Families*. 12 vols. Urbanna: privately published, 2004.

Des Cognet, Louis Jr., ed. *English Duplicates Of Lost Virginia Records*. Baltimore: Genealogical Publishing Company, 1981.

Dixon, John W. *The Black Americans of Gwynn's Island, 1600s Through 1900s*. Mathews: Gwynn's Island Museum, 2005.

Donnan, Elizabeth, comp. *Documents Illustrative of the History of the Slave Trade to America*. 4 vols. New York: Octagon Books, Inc., 1965.

Dorman, John F., ed. *Adventurers of Purse and Person, Virginia 1607–1624/25*. 3 vols. Baltimore: Genealogical Publishing Company, 2004–2007.

Driver, Robert J. Jr. *5th Virginia Cavalry*. Lynchburg: H.E. Howard, Inc., 1997.

Dauphine, Durand de. *A Huguenot Exile in Virginia: A Brief Description of America With a Longer One of Virginia and Maryland*, Gilbert Chinard, trans. Press of the Pioneers: New York, 1934.

Efloff, Keith T. et al. *First People: The Early Indians of Virginia*. Richmond: Virginia Department of Historic Resources, 1992.

Elizabeth City County. Personal Property Tax Lists 1782–1791. Library of Virginia, Richmond.

Elliott, Richard V. *Last of the Steamboats*. Cambridge, Maryland: Tidewater Publishers, 1970.

Elson, James M. *Lynchburg, Virginia: The First Two Hundred Years, 1786–1986*. Lynchburg: Warwick House Publishers, 2004.

Eshelman, Ralph E., Scott S. Sheads, and Donald R. Hickey, eds. *The War of 1812 in the Chesapeake: A Reference Guide to Historic Sites in Maryland, Virginia, and the District of Columbia*. Baltimore: Johns Hopkins University Press, 2010.

Executive Papers (Office of the Governor). Letterbook of Governor James Barbour, January 4, 1812, to December 11, 1814. Library of Virginia, Richmond.

Feest, Christian F. "Virginia Algonquins." In *Handbook of North American Indians: Northeast*, Vol. 15., Bruce G. Trigger, ed., 253–270. Washington, D. C.: Smithsonian Institution, 1978.

Feilde, Thomas. February 16, 1771, letter to Dr. Mackenzie. Brock Box 117 f 1, Huntington Library, San Marino, California.

Fenn, Elizabeth. *Pox Americana: The Great Smallpox Epidemic of 1775–1782*. New York: Hill and Wang, 2001.

Ferrar Papers. 1590–1790 Ferrar Papers, Pepys Library, Magdalen College, Cambridge University, Cambridge, England. Microfilms, Rockefeller Library, Colonial Williamsburg Foundation, Williamsburg.

Fithian, Philip V. *Journal and Letters of Philip Vickers Fithian, 1773–1774.* Hunter D. Farish, ed. Williamsburg: Colonial Williamsburg Foundation, 1965.

Fitzpatrick, John C., ed. *The Writings of George Washington from the Original Manuscript Sources, 1745–1799*, Volume 34, October 11, 1794–March 29, 1796. Washington, D. C.: U. S. Government Printing Office, 1942.

Fleet, Beverley, comp. *Virginia Colonial Abstracts.* 3 vols. Baltimore: Genealogical Publishing Company, 1988.

Force, Peter, comp. *Tracts and Other Papers, Relating to the Origin, Settlement and Progress of the Colonies in North America.* 4 vols. Gloucester, Massachusetts: Peter Smith, 1963.

Frederick County. Chancery Causes, 1843. Library of Virginia, Richmond.

Fry, Joshua and Peter Jefferson. "A Map of the Most Inhabited Part of Virginia," 1754–1775. Virginia Department of Historic Resources, Richmond.

Foster, Adam. January 9, 1847, letter to Mrs. Cynthia Claxton; January 12, 1847, letter to Mrs. Cynthia Claxton. Transcriptions by Susie V. Tabb Sanders. Virginia Historical Society, Richmond.

Genovese, Eugene D. *Roll, Jordan, Roll: The World The Slaves Made.* New York: First Vintage Books, 1976.

Gloucester County. Surveyors Plat Book A (1733–1810); Land Tax Lists, Personal Property Tax Lists, Minute Books, legislative petitions. Gloucester County Courthouse, Gloucester, and Library of Virginia, Richmond.

Gloucester County Clerk of Court. Court Order to Edward Gwyn, February 27, 1680. Facsimile, Gloucester 350th Celebration, Gloucester.

Gloucester-Mathews Gazette-Journal. Gloucester-Mathews Gazette-Journal. Gloucester: Tidewater Newspapers, Inc., Gloucester.

Goodsell, Jane B., ed. *Mathews County, Virginia, Records.* Athens, Georgia: Iberian Publishing Company, 2000.

Graham, Willie et al. "Adaptation and Innovation: Archaeological and Architectural Perspectives on the Seventeenth Century Chesapeake." *William and Mary Quarterly* Ser. 3, 64 (2007):451–522.

Gronovius, Johann F. "Virginia," 1762. Library of Virginia, Richmond.

Gwyn, Edward. Deed to the Justices of Gloucester County, February 26, 1680. Facsimile, Gloucester 350th Celebration, Gloucester.

Gwynn's Island Museum. *Gwynn's Island and the Great Storm of 1933*. Gwynn's Island: Privately Printed, 2002.

Hanover County. Freedmen's Marriage Register, 1866. Library of Virginia, Richmond.

Harrison, Fairfax. *A History of the Legal Development of the Railroad System of Southern Railway Company*. Washington, D.C.: Privately Printed, 1901.

Harrower, John. *The Journal of John Harrower, An Indentured Servant in the Colony of Virginia, 1773–1776*. Edward M. Riley, ed. Williamsburg: Colonial Williamsburg Foundation, 1963.

Hartwell, Henry et al. *The Present State of Virginia and the College [1697] by Henry Hartwell, James Blair and Edward Chilton*. Princeton: Princeton University, 1940.

Heatwole, Cornelius J. *A History of Education in Virginia*. New York: Macmillan Company, 1916.

Hening, William W., ed. *The Statutes At Large: Being a Collection of all the Laws of Virginia*. 13 vols. Richmond: Samuel Pleasants, 1809–1823.

Hening, William W., and William Mumford, eds. *Reports of cases argued and determined in the Supreme Court of Appeals of Virginia*. New York: I Riley, 1809–1811.

Henry, John. "A New and Accurate Map of Virginia," 1770. Virginia Department of Historic Resources, Richmond.

Hergesheimer, E. "Map Showing Distribution of Slave Population from the Census of 1860." 1861. National Archives, College Park, Maryland.

Herrman, Augustine. "Virginia and Maryland in 1670," 1673. Virginia Department of Historic Resources, Richmond.

Hershman, James H. Jr. "Public School Bonds and Virginia's Massive Resistance," *The Journal of Negro Education* 52 (1983), 398–409.

High Court of the Admiralty Office Papers (HCA). British Public Records Office, Kew, England. Survey Reports and microfilms, Rockefeller Library, Colonial Williamsburg Foundation, Williamsburg.

Hodges, Graham R., and Susan H. Cook. *The Black loyalist directory : African Americans in Exile after the American Revolution*. New York: Garland Publishing Company, 1996.

Holly, David C. *Tidewater by Steamboat: A Saga of the Chesapeake*. Baltimore: Johns Hopkins University Press, 1991.

Howe, Henry. *Historical Collections of Virginia*. Charleston, South Carolina: W.R. Babcock, 1856.

Hoxton, Walter. "This Map of the Peninsula between Delaware & Chesapeak[e] Bays," 1735. Rockefeller Library, Colonial Williamsburg Foundation, Williamsburg.

Hudgins, Dennis. *Cavaliers and Pioneers: Abstracts of Virginia Land Patents and Grants*. 5 Vols. Richmond: Virginia Genealogical Society, 1994–2005.

Hudgins, Houlder. Houlder Hudgins vs. Jackey Wright et al., appeal from the Richmond Chancery District Court, November 11, 1806. Tucker-Coleman Papers, 1752–1827, Swem Library Department of Special Collections, College of William and Mary, Williamsburg, Virginia.

Hughes, Langston. *A Pictorial History of African Americans*. New York: Crown Publishing, 1983.

Hummel, Ray O. Jr. *A List of Places Included in 19th Century Virginia Directories*. Richmond: Virginia State Library, 1960.

Isaac, Rhys. *The Transformation of Virginia, 1740–1790*. Chapel Hill: University of North Carolina Press, 1982.

Jackson, Luther P. "The Virginia Free Negro Farmer and Property Owner, 1830–1860" *Journal of Negro History*, 24 (1939), 390–421.

Jamison, J. Franklin, ed. *Narratives of New Netherland, 1609–1642*. New York: Charles Schribner's Sons, 1909.

Jefferson, Thomas. [Untitled map of Gwynn's Island], [1776]. Library of Congress, Washington, D.C.

____________. "A Map of the Country between Albemarle Sound and Lake Erie," 1787. Library of Virginia, Richmond.

____________. *Notes on the State of Virginia*, William Peden, ed. Chapel Hill: University of North Carolina Press, 1954.

Johnson, Gerald et al. *Geological Development and Environmental Reconstruction of Jamestown Island.* Williamsburg: National Park Service, Colonial Williamsburg Foundation, College of William and Mary, 2001.

Johnston, Henry P. *The Yorktown Campaign and The Surrender Of Cornwallis, 1781*. New York: Harper and Brothers, 1881.

Johnson, R.U., and C.C. Buel, comp. *Battles and Leaders of the Civil War*. 4 vols. New York: Castle Books, 1956.

Johnston, Angus J. "Virginia Railroads in 1861," *The Journal of Southern History* 23 (1957), 307–330.

Jones, Hugh. *The Present State of Virginia*. Chapel Hill: University of North Carolina Press, 1956.

Jones, Warner T. Inventory of the Warner T. Jones Papers, 1819–1891. Department of Special Collections, Swem Library, College of William and Mary, Williamsburg.

Jordan, Winthrop D. *White Over Black: American Attitudes Toward the Negro, 1550–1812*. Chapel Hill: University of North Carolina Press, 1968.

Katz, William L. *The Negro in Virginia*. New York: Arno Press and the *New York Times,* 1969.

Keene, W.D. Jr. *"Memoirs – 200 Years!" Soldiers of the Cross, 1785–1987*. Decorah, Iowa: Amundsen Publishing, 1988.

Kimber, Edward. "Observations in Several Voyages and Travels in America, 1736," *William and Mary Quarterly*, 1st Ser., 15 (1907), 143–159, 215–252.

Kingsbury, Susan M., comp. *Records of the Virginia Company of London*. 4 vols. Washington, D.C.: U.S. Government Printing Office, 1906–1935.

Kingston Parish. Vestry Minute Book, 1850–1868. Original on file at the Diocese of Virginia, Richmond, Virginia.

___________. Vestry Minute Book, 1873–1938. Original on file at the Diocese of Virginia, Richmond, Virginia.

___________. Vestry Minute Book, 1938–1964. Original on file at the Diocese of Virginia, Richmond, Virginia.

Kulikoff, Allan. *Tobacco and Slaves: The Development of Southern Cultures in the Chesapeake, 1680–1800*. Chapel Hill: University of North Carolina Press, 1986.

Kuroda, Tadahisa. "The County Court System of Virginia from the Revolution to the Civil War," 1972. Dissertation, Columbia University, New York.

Lancaster County. Deed Book 1 (1652–1657). Library of Virginia, Richmond.

Latrobe, Benjamin H. *The Journal of Latrobe*. D. Appleton and Company, New York: New York, 1905.

Leonard, Cynthia M., comp. *The General Assembly of Virginia, July 30, 1619–January 11, 1978, A Bicentennial Register of Members*. Richmond: Virginia State Library Board, 1978.

Lewis, Clifford M. et al. *The Spanish Jesuit Mission*. Chapel Hill: University of North Carolina Press, 1953.

Lewis, Elizabeth Dutton. *Revolutionary War Roster, Gloucester County, Virginia*. Gloucester, Virginia: Gloucester County Historical and Bicentennial Committee, 1976.

Lewis, Sara E. *Images of America: Mathews County* (Arcadia Publishing Company, Charleston, South Carolina, 2007.

Light-House Board. *Laws of the United States Relating to the Establishment, Support, and Management of Light-Houses, Light-Vessels, Monuments, Beacons, Spindles, Buoys, and Public Piers of the United States from August 7, 1789, to March 3, 1855,* compiled by Order of the Light-House Board, June 39, 1855. Washington, D.C.: A.P.O. Nicholson, Public Printer, 1855.

Lindenkohl, A. "Military Map of Southeastern Virginia," 1862. Library of Congress, Washington, D.C.

Long, E.B., and Barbara Long. *The Civil War Day by Day.* Garden City, N.J.: Doubleday and Company, 1981.

Lossing, Benson J. *The Pictorial Field-Book of the Revolution.* 2 vols. New Rochelle, New York: Caratzas Brothers, Publishers, 1974.

Loth, Calder. *The Virginia Landmarks Register.* Charlottesville: University Press of Virginia, 1999.

Lowe, Richard. The Freedmen's Bureau and Local White Leaders in Virginia." *The Journal of Southern History* 64 (1998), 455–472.

Lowery, Darrin L. *Archaeological Survey of the Coastal Shorelines Associated with Mathews County, Virginia: An Erosion Threat Study*. Easton, Maryland: Chesapeake Watershed Archaeological Research Foundation, 2008.

Ludlum, David M. *Early American Hurricanes, 1492–1870.* American Meteorological Society, Boston, Mass., 1963.

_____________. *Early American Winters II, 1821–1870.* American Meteorological Society, Boston, Mass., 1968.

Maddox, William A. *The Free School Idea in Virginia Before the Civil War.* New York: Columbia University Press, 1918.

Madison, Bishop James. "Map of Virginia Formed from Actual Surveys," 1807, 1818. Library of Virginia, Richmond.

Majeski, Penelope K. "Your Obedient Servant: The United States Army in Virginia During Reconstruction," 1980. Dissertation, Wayne State University, Detroit, Michigan.

Martin, Joseph. A *New and Comprehensive Gazetteer of Virginia and the District of Columbia.* Charlottesville, Virginia: Moseley and Tompkins, Publishers, 1836.

Mason, Polly Cary, comp. *Records of Colonial Gloucester County.* 2 vols. Newport News: privately published, 1946 and 1948.

Matheny, Emma R., and Helen Yates, comp. *Kingston Parish Register, Gloucester and Mathews Counties, 1749–1827.* Richmond: privately published, 1963.

Mathews County. Agricultural Census Records 1850–1880; Board of Supervisors Minute Book 1887–1900; Census of Population 1810–1920; Census of Manufacturers 1820; Chancery Dockets 1805–1835, 1842–1843, 1867; Circuit Court Papers 1856–1859, 1866; Circuit Court Executions 1858–1895; Clerk of Court Day Book 1842–1843; Clerk of Court Fee Book 1840–1841; Commissions 1864–1869; Common Law Order Books; Commonwealth's Attorney's Notes, October 1866; Court Docket 1879–1890; Court Papers 1877; Court Rule Papers 1866–1872; Deed Books 1865–2015; Executioners Bond Book 1795–1825; Executions and Miscellaneous Court Cases; Executions 1862–1866; Executive Papers, 1865–1868, March 2, 1867; Fiduciary Records, Estate Accounts, Appraisements, Sales, 1850–1857; Fiduciary Records, Estate Accounts, Appraisements, Sales, 1850–1857; Fiduciary Accounts 1868–1872; Fiduciary Records 1882–1892; Guardian Accounts 1860–1869; Improper Assessment of Land 1845–1869 [Untitled List of Taxes Paid in 1867, 1868, 1871–1875]; Industrial Statistics 1850, 1860; Land Books; List of Oyster Licenses 1866–1867; Legislative Petitions; Marriage Records and Licenses, 1827–1835, 1839–1850; Marriage Register Book 1; Military and Pension Record of Indigent Soldiers in 1864; Military Board of Exemptions, March 8, 1862; Military Board of Exemptions, Applications for Exemptions from Military Duty, 1862; Minute Books; Miscellaneous Tax Lists 1865–1868; Mortality Schedules 1850–1880; Order Books 1856–

1871; Oyster Licenses 1866–1867; Pension Records and Applications for 1877–1878, 1883, and 1888; Petitions of Widows and Orphans for Support Under the Stay Law of 1866–1869; Proceedings in County Court 1882–1886; Processioners Reports from Militia Districts 1 and 2, 1866–1867; Records of the Confederate Pension Board 1900–1901; Miscellaneous Deeds, 1814, 1835–1908; Military Pension Records, Adjutant Sands Smith III's Correspondence, Lane-Diggs Camp in 1902; Report of Livestock 1941; Road Book 1875–1891; Road Commissioners Minutes 1870; Road Orders 1866–1872; Slave Schedules 1850–1860; Social Statistics 1850; Subpoena Docket 1854–1863; Superintendent of the Poor Annual Reports 1871–1889; Superior Court Docket 1809–1830; Vital Statistics 1882–1884, 1887, 1897–1899, 1902–1904; Will Books 1865–2015. 1791–2015. Originals, Mathews Courthouse, Mathews, and microfilm, Library of Virginia, Richmond.

Mathews Archives. Mathews Archives, Mathews Memorial Library, Mathews.

Mathews County Historical Society (MCHS). *History and Progress: Mathews County, Virginia, Reprints from 1949 and 1979 Special Editions, Gloucester-Mathews Gazette-Journal*. Marceline, Missouri: Walsworth Company, 1982.

____________. *Mathews County Panorama: A Pictorial History of Mathews County, 1791–1941*. Marceline, Missouri: Walsworth Company, 1983. Reprinted: 2000.

____________. *Historic Homes and Properties of Mathews County, Virginia, Pre-Civil War*. Volume 1. Virginia Beach: Donning Publishing Company, 2009.

____________. *Historic Homes and Properties of Mathews County, Virginia, Pre-Civil War*. Volume 2. Virginia Beach: Donning Publishing Company, 2013.

Mattern, David B. et al., eds., *The Papers of James Madison, Secretary of State Series, 1 March–6 October 1802*. vol. 3, Charlottesville: University Press of Virginia, 1995.

Maxwell, William, ed. "Early Land Grants," *Virginia Historical Register* II (1849), 190–193.

McCartney, Martha W. *With Reverence for the Past: Gloucester County, Virginia.* Richmond: Dietz Publishing Company, 2001.

____________. "Last Refuge: Tribal Preserves in Eastern Virginia." In *Indian and European Contact in Context: The Mid-Atlantic Region* (Gainesville: University Press of Florida, 2004.

____________. "Cocacoeske, Queen of Pamunkey: Diplomat and Suzeraine." In *Powhatan's Mantle: Indians in the Colonial Southeast.* Peter H. Wood et al., eds. Lincoln, Nebraska: University of Nebraska Press, 2006.

____________. *Virginia Immigrants and Adventurers, 1607–1635*. Baltimore: Genealogical Publishing Company, 2007.

____________. *Jamestown People to 1800: Landowners, Public Officials, Minorities, and Native Leaders.* Baltimore: Genealogical Publishing Company, 2012.

____________. *Kingston Parish Register: Mathews, Gloucester, and Middlesex Counties, Virginia, Slaves and Slaveholders, 1746–1827.* Baltimore: Genealogical Publishing Company, 2014.

McCartney, Martha W. with Lorena S. Walsh. *A Study of the Africans and African Americans on Jamestown Island and at Green Spring, 1619–1803.* Yorktown: Colonial National Historical Park, 2003.

McGhan, Judith, comp. *Virginia Will Records*. Baltimore: Genealogical Publishing Company, 1993.

McHugh, J.L., and Robert S. Bailey, "History of Virginia's Commercial Fisheries," *Virginia Journal of Science,* 8 (January 1957):42–64.

McIlwaine, H.R., ed. *Legislative Journals of the Council of Colonial Virginia*. 3 vols. Richmond: Virginia State Library, 1918.

____________. "Justices of Colonial Virginia." *Virginia State Library Bulletin No. 14*. Richmond: Virginia State Library, 1922.

_____________. *Executive Journals of the Council of Colonial Virginia.* 5 vols. Richmond: Virginia State Library, 1925–1945.

_____________. *Journal of the Council of the State of Virginia, 1776–1777.* Richmond: Virginia State Library, 1931.

_____________. *Minutes of the Council and General Court of Colonial Virginia.* Richmond: The Library Board, 1934.

McIlwaine, H.R. et al, eds. *Journals of the House of Burgesses, 1619–1776.* 13 vols. Richmond: Virginia State Library, 1905–1915.

McPherson, James M. *Battle Cry of Freedom: The Civil War Era.* Oxford and New York: Oxford University Press, 1988.

Meade, Bishop William. *Old Churches, Ministers And Families of Virginia.* 2 vols. Baltimore: Genealogical Publishing Company, 1966.

Melish, John. *Travels in the United States of America in 1806.* 2 vols. New York: Thomas and George Palmer, 1810.

Middlesex County. Deed Book 13 (1810–1817); Order Book 1673–1680, 1732–1737; Surveys 1735–1807; Will Book E (1760–1772). Library of Virginia, Richmond.

Middleton, Arthur P. *Tobacco Coast: A Maritime History of the Chesapeake Bay in the Colonial Era.* Newport News: Mariners Museum, 1953.

Miller, Harriet G. Works Progress Administration (WPA). Virginia Writers Project Life Histories: Mathews County, 1939. University of Virginia, Alderman Library, Albert and Shirley Small Special Collections Library.

Minchinton, Walter et al., eds. *Virginia Slave-Trade Statistics, 1698–1775.* Richmond: Virginia State Library, 1984.

Montague, Ludwell Lee. *Gloucester County in the Civil War.* Gloucester County, Virginia: Privately printed, 2010.

Morgan, Edmund. *American Slavery, American Freedom: The Ordeal of Colonial Virginia.* New York: W.W. Norton, 1975.

Morrison, A.J. *The Beginning of Public Education in Virginia, 1776–1815*. Richmond: Superintendent of Public Printing, 1917.

____________. "Virginia Patents." *William and Mary Quarterly* 2nd Ser., 2 (1922):149–156.

Moseley, Cameron S. Beall, John Yates. In *Dictionary of Virginia Biography*, Vol. 1, John T. Kneebone et al. eds. Richmond: Library of Virginia, 2006.

Moss, Bobby G., and Michael Scroggins. *African American Loyalists in the Southern Campaign of the American Revolution.* Blacksburg, S.C. : Scotia-Hibernia Press, 2004.

Mumford, William, ed. *Reports of Cases Argued and Determined in the Supreme Court of Appeals of Virginia*. 6 vols. Richmond: N. Pollard Printer, 1921.

Mutual Assurance Society. Policies, 1796–1867. Rockefeller Library, Colonial Williamsburg Foundation, Williamsburg, Library of Virginia, Richmond, and Huntington Library, San Marino, California. Facsimiles: Mathews Archives, Mathews Memorial Library, Mathews.

Nash, Gary B. *Red, White and Black: The Peoples of Early America.* Englewood, New Jersey: Prentis-Hall, 1974.

Neagles, James C., and Lila L. Neagles. *Locating Your Revolutionary War Ancestor : A Guide to the Military Records*. Logan, Utah: The Everton Publishers Inc., 1983.

Neville, John D. *Bacon's Rebellion, Abstracts of Materials in the Colonial Records Project*. Williamsburg: The Jamestown Foundation, 1976.

Norfolk County. Deed Book 4 (1675–1686); Census 1870, 1880. Library of Virginia, Richmond.

Northampton County. Wills, Etc. Book 29; Deed Book 26 (1790–1798). Library of Virginia, Richmond.

Norton, John and Sons. John Norton and Sons Papers, August 22, 1750, to October 16, 1816. Manuscripts. Rockefeller Library, Colonial Williamsburg Foundation, Williamsburg.

Nugent, Nell M. *Cavaliers and Pioneers: Abstracts of Virginia Land Patents and Grants.* 3 vols. Richmond and Baltimore: Dietz Press, and Genealogical Publishing Company, 1969–1979.

O'Bannon, J.A., comp. *Acts and Joint Resolutions Passed by the General Assembly of the State of Virginia Passed During the Session of 1889–1890.* Richmond: Commonwealth of Virginia, 1890.

____________. *Acts and Joint Resolutions Passed by the General Assembly of the State of Virginia Passed During the Session of 1893–1894.* Richmond: Commonwealth of Virginia, 1894.

____________. *Acts and Joint Resolutions Passed by the General Assembly of the State of Virginia Passed During the Session of 1897–1898.* Richmond: Commonwealth of Virginia, 1898.

____________. *Acts and Joint Resolutions Passed by the General Assembly of the State of Virginia Passed During the Session of 1901–1902.* Richmond: Commonwealth of Virginia, 1902.

____________. *Acts and Joint Resolutions Passed by the General Assembly of the State of Virginia Passed During the Session of 1902–1904.* Richmond: Commonwealth of Virginia, 1904.

Oberg, Barbara and J. Jefferson Looney, eds. *The Papers of Thomas Jefferson.* Charlottesville: University Press of Virginia, 2009.

Old Rappahannock County. Deed Book 8 (1688–1692). Library of Virginia, Richmond.

Page, Richard C.M. *Genealogy of the Page family in Virginia. Also, a condensed account of the Nelson, Walker, Pendleton, and Randolph families, with references to the Bland, Burwell, Byrd, Carter, Cary, Duke, Gilmer, Harrison, Rives, Thornton, Welford, Washington, and other distinguished families in Virginia.* New York: Publishers Printing Company, 1893.

Palmer, William P., comp. *Calendar of Virginia State Papers.* 11 vols. New York: Kraus Reprint, 1968.

Parks, William. *Virginia Gazette* (Williamsburg), 1738–1750. Rockefeller Library, Colonial Williamsburg Foundation, Williamsburg, Virginia.

Perdue, Charles L. Jr. *The Negro in Virginia.* Winston-Salem, North Carolina: John F. Blair, Publisher, 1994.

Perdue, Charles L. et al. *Weevils in the Wheat: Interviews with Virginia Ex-Slaves.* Charlottesville: University Press of Virginia, 1992.

Perry, William S., comp. *Historical Collections Relating to the American Colonial Church.* Vol. I, Virginia. New York: AMS Press, 1969.

Pinckney, John. *Virginia Gazette* (Williamsburg), 1774–1776. Rockefeller Library, Colonial Williamsburg Foundation, Williamsburg, Virginia.

Potter, Stephen R. "Early English Effects on Virginia Algonquian Exchange and Tribute in the Tidewater Potomac." In *Powhatan's Mantle: Indians in the Colonial Southeast*, edited by Peter H. Wood et al., 151–171. Lincoln, Nebraska: University of Nebraska Press, 1989.

Prince, Richard E. *Steam Locomotives and Boats, Southern Railway System.*, Green River, Wyoming: privately published, 1965.

Privy Council (P.C.). British Public Records Office, Kew, England. Survey Reports and microfilms, Rockefeller Library, Colonial Williamsburg Foundation, Williamsburg.

Porter, Albert O. *County Government in Virginia: A Legislative History, 1607–1904.* New York: Columbia University Press, 1947.

Purdie, Alexander. *Virginia Gazette* (Williamsburg), 1775–1779. Rockefeller Library, Colonial Williamsburg Foundation, Williamsburg, Virginia.

Purdie, Alexander and John Dixon. *Virginia Gazette* (Williamsburg), 1766–1775. Rockefeller Library, Colonial Williamsburg Foundation, Williamsburg, Virginia.

Quinn, David B. *North America from Earliest Discovery to First Settlement, The Norse Voyages to 1612.* New York: Hakluyt Society, 1977.

Ranlet, Phillip. "The British, Slaves, and Smallpox in Revolutionary Virginia." *Journal of Negro History* 84 (1999):218.

Reid-Green, Keith. "The History of Census Tabulation," *Scientific American* (February 1989):98–103.

Reps, John W. *Tidewater Towns in Colonial Virginia*. Princeton: Princeton University, 1972.

Rice, Howard C. et al. *The American Campaigns of Rochambeau's Army*. 2 vols. Princeton: Princeton University, 1972.

Ritchie, Thomas, comp. *Acts Passed at a General Assembly of the Commonwealth of Virginia, 1809*. Richmond: Commonwealth of Virginia, 1810.

____________. *Acts Passed at a General Assembly of the Commonwealth of Virginia, 1814*. Richmond: Thomas Richie, Printer to the Commonwealth, 1814.

____________. *Acts Passed At A General Assembly of the Commonwealth of Virginia, October 1815*. Richmond: Commonwealth of Virginia, 1815.

____________. *Acts Passed at a General Assembly of the Commonwealth of Virginia, 1819*. Richmond: Commonwealth of Virginia, 1818–1819.

____________. *The Revised Code of the Laws of Virginia, Being a Collection of All Such Acts of the General Assembly, 1819*. Richmond: Commonwealth of Virginia, 1819.

____________. *Acts Passed at a General Assembly of the Commonwealth of Virginia, 1822*. Richmond: Commonwealth of Virginia, 1823.

____________. *Supplement to the Revised Code of the Laws of Virginia: Being A Collection of All the Acts of the General Assembly of a Public and Permanent Nature, Passed Since the Year 1819*. Richmond: Commonwealth of Virginia, 1833.

____________. *Acts of the General Assembly, Passed at the Session of 1835–1836*. Richmond: Commonwealth of Virginia, 1836.

____________. *Acts of the General Assembly, Passed at the Session of 1836–March 1837*. Richmond: Commonwealth of Virginia, 1837.

____________. *Acts of the General Assembly, Passed at the Session of 1838*. Richmond: Commonwealth of Virginia, 1838.

____________. *Acts of the General Assembly, Passed at the Session of 1839*. Richmond: Commonwealth of Virginia, 1839.

Ritchie, William F. comp. *Acts and Joint Resolutions Passed by the General Assembly, 1857–1858*. Richmond: Commonwealth of Virginia, 1859.

_____________. *Acts and Joint Resolutions Passed By the General Assembly of the State of Virginia Passed During the Session of 1861–1862*. Richmond: Commonwealth of Virginia, 1862.

_____________. *Muster Rolls of the Virginia Militia in the War of 1812, Being A Supplement to the Pay Rolls Printed and Distributed in 1851. Copied From Rolls In the Auditor's Office at Richmond*. Richmond: W. F. Ritchie, Printer, 1852.

Robertson, James I. *Civil War Virginia: Battleground for a Nation*. Charlottesville: University Press of Virginia, 1991.

Robinson, W. Stitt, Jr. *Mother Earth, Land Grants in Virginia, 1607–1699*. Charlottesville: University Press of Virginia, 1957.

Rountree, Helen C. *Pocahontas's People: The Powhatan Indians of Virginia*. Norman, Oklahoma: University of Oklahoma Press, 1989.

Russell, John H. *The Free Negro in Virginia*. New York: Dover Publications, Inc., 1969.

Rutman, Darrett B., and Anita H. Rutman. *Place in Time, Middlesex County, Virginia, 1650–1750*. New York and London: W.W. Norton, 1984.

_____________. *A Place in Time: Explicatus*. New York and London: W.W. Norton, 1984.

Sainsbury, William Noel et al., comp. *Calendar of State Papers, Colonial Series, America and the West Indies*. 22 vols. Vaduz: Kraus Reprint, 1964.

Salley, Marion. "Behind the Lines: the Achievements and Privations of the Women of the South," *The Confederate Veteran*. 32 (February 1924):56–57.

Salmon, Emily J., and Edward D.C. Campbell. *The Hornbook of Virginia History*. Richmond: Library of Virginia, 1994.

Salmon, John S. *The Official Virginia Civil War Battlefield Guide*. Mechanicsburg, Pennsylvania: Stackpole Books, 2001.

Sams, Conway. *The Conquest of Virginia, The Second Attempt*. Norfolk: Keyser-Doherty Company, 1929.

Schaffter, C.A. *Acts and Joint Resolutions Passed by the General Assembly at the Session of 1870–1871*. Richmond: Commonwealth of Virginia, 1871.

Sears, Stephen W. Sears, ed. *The Civil War Papers of George B. McClellan: Selected Correspondence 1860–1865*. New York: Da Capo Press, 1989.

Seib, John. "New Point Comfort to Wolf Trap, Including Mobjack." 1853. Rockefeller Library, Colonial Williamsburg Foundation, Williamsburg.

____________. "From Wolf Trap to Piankatank River, Including the Head of East River." 1853. Rockefeller Library, Colonial Williamsburg Foundation, Williamsburg.

Selby, John. *Chronology of Virginia and the War of Independence.* Charlottesville: University Press of Virginia, 1973.

____________. *Revolution in Virginia: 1775–1783*. Charlottesville: University Press of Virginia, 1988.

Shea, William L. *The Virginia Militia in the Seventeenth Century*. Baton Rouge: Louisiana State University Press, 1983.

Shepherd, Samuel, comp. *The Statutes at Large of Virginia, From October Session 1792 to December Session 1806 [1807].* 3 vols. New York, New York: AMS Press, 1970.

____________. *Supplement to the revised code of Virginia : being a collection of all the acts of the General Assembly, of a public and permanent nature, passed since the year 1819 ... To which are prefixed, the acts organizing a convention, the Declaration of Rights, and the amended Constitution of Virginia*. Richmond: Samuel Shepherd, Printer, 1833.

____________. *Acts of the General Assembly of Virginia Passed at the Session of 1839*. Richmond: Samuel Shepherd, Printer, 1839.

____________. *Acts of the General Assembly, Passed at the Session of 1839–1840*. Richmond: Samuel Shepherd, Printer, 1840.

_____________. *Acts of the General Assembly of Virginia, Passed at the Session of 1843–1844.* Richmond: Samuel Shepherd, Printer,1844.

_____________. *Acts of the General Assembly of Virginia Passed, at the Session of 1844–1845.* Richmond: Samuel Shepherd, Printer, 1845.

_____________. *Acts of the General Assembly, Passed at the Session of 1846–1847.* Richmond: Samuel Shepherd, Printer, 1847.

_____________. *Acts of the General Assembly, Passed at the Session of 1847–1848.* Richmond: Samuel Shepherd, Printer, 1848.

Sheridan, Christine L., and Elsie W. Ernst, comp., *Tombstones of Mathews County, Virginia, 1711–1986*. Mathews County: Mathews County Historical Society, 1988.

Sherwood, George L. Sherwood. *The Mathews Light Artillery; Penick's Pittsylvania Artillery; Young's Halifax Light Artillery, & Johnson's Jackson Flying Artillery.* Appomattox: H.E. Howard, Inc., 1999.

Sluiter, Engel. "New Light on the '20 and Odd Negroes' Arriving in Virginia," *William and Mary Quarterly* 3rd Ser., 54 (1997), 395–398.

Smith, John. "Virginia Discovered and Discribed [sic]," 1610. Virginia Department of Historic Resources, Richmond.

_____________. *Travels and Works of Captain John Smith, President of Virginia and Admiral of New England, 1580–1631*, Edward Arber, ed. 2 vols. Edinburgh: John Grant, 1910.

Smith, Nellie Shackleford, comp. *Reminiscences: Confederate Soldiers of Gloucester County, Virginia: Late 19th Century Local History 1865–1930.* Gloucester: Gloucester's 350th Celebration Committee, 2001.

Sorbel, Michael. *The World They Made Together: Black and White Values in Eighteenth Century Virginia.* Princeton: Princeton University Press, 1987.

Southern Claims Commission. Claims filed with the Southern Claims Commission by Samuel E. Richardson and William H. Winder, 1871–1878. Manuscripts, National Archives, Washington, D.C.

Stahle, David W. et al. "The Lost Colony and Jamestown Droughts," *Science* (April 1998) 280, 564–567.

Stanard, William G., ed. "Virginia Assembly of 1641: A List of Members and Some of the Acts." *Virginia Magazine of History and Biography* 9 (1902):50–59.

____________. "Virginia Militia in the Revolution," *Virginia Magazine of History and Biography* 2 (1894–1895): 68–80.

____________. "Notes from Council and General Court Records." *Virginia Magazine of History and Biography* 13 (1906):389–401.

____________. "Historical and Genealogical Note and Queries." *Virginia Magazine of History and Biography* 14 (1906):202–208.

____________. "Virginia Legislative Petitions." *Virginia Magazine of History and Biography* 15 (1908):288–296.

____________. "Mann Page Will." *Virginia Magazine of History and Biography* 32 (1924):39–43.

____________. "John Page Will." *Virginia Magazine of History and Biography* 34 (1926):276–277.

____________. "Genealogy.," *Virginia Magazine of History and Biography* 36 (1928): 100.

Stanard, William et al. *The Colonial Virginia Register*. Baltimore: Genealogical Publishing Company, 1965.

State Papers (S.P.). British Public Records Office, Kew, England. Survey Reports and microfilms, Rockefeller Library, Colonial Williamsburg Foundation, Williamsburg.

Survey Reports (SR). Virginia Colonial Records Project Survey Reports. Microfilm, Library of Virginia, Richmond.

Tate, Thad W. *The Negro in Eighteenth Century Williamsburg*. Williamsburg: Colonial Williamsburg Foundation, 1965.

Tate, Thad and David Ammerman, eds. *The Chesapeake in the Seventeenth Century*. University of North Carolina Press, Chapel Hill, 1979.

Taylor, Alan. *Slavery and War in Virginia, 1772–1832: The Internal Enemy.* New York: W.W. Norton and Company, 2013.

Taylor, Jessica, comp. Oral History Files. Tidewater Management Project, Samuel Proctor Oral History Program, University of Florida in Gainesville, Florida. Manuscripts on file in the Mathews Archives, Mathews Memorial Library, Mathews.

Theisen, William H. *United States Coast Guard: War of 1812, Rescue Cutter Operations and the Core Coast Guard Missions.* Washington, D.C.: United States Coast Guard, 2012.

Thomson, William. *Thomson's Mercantile and Professional Directory to Which is Appended an Advertising Register.* Baltimore: William Thomson, 1851–1852.

Thornton, John. "A New Map of Virginia, Maryland, Pennsilvania [sic], New Jersey, Part of New York and Carolina,: [ca. 1700]. Rockefeller Library, Colonial Williamsburg Foundation, Williamsburg.

Thornton, John. "The African Experience of the '20 and Odd Negroes' Arriving in Virginia," *William and Mary Quarterly* 3rd Ser., 55 (1998): 421–434.

Throckmorton, John [untitled plat of the prison bounds], June 31, 1754. Original, Surveyors Book A 1733–1810. Gloucester County Courthouse, Gloucester.

Tindall, George B. *America: A Narrative History.* New York: W. W. Norton and Company, 1984.

Tindall, Robert. "Draughte of Virginia," 1608. Rockefeller Library, Colonial Williamsburg Foundation, Williamsburg.

Tinling, Marion, ed. *The Correspondence of the Three William Byrds of Westover, 1684–1776.* 2 vols. Charlottesville: University Press of Virginia, 1977.

Tomkies, Francis "Town of Botetourt," 1774. Original, Surveyors Book A 1733–1810. Gloucester County Courthouse, Gloucester.

[Tomkies, Francis]. "Pt. of an Acre of land of Land on which Gloucester Courthouse now stands," August 9, 1769. Original, Surveyors Book A 1733–1810. Gloucester County Courthouse, Gloucester.

Tompkins Family. Tompkins Family Papers, 1800–1877. Virginia Historical Society, Richmond, Virginia.

Tucker-Coleman Papers. Tucker-Coleman Papers, 1752–1827, Swem Library Department of Special Collections, College of William and Mary, Williamsburg.

Turner, Charles W. "Virginia Agricultural Reform, 1815–1860," *Agricultural History* 26 (1952): 80–89.

Tyler, Lyon G., comp. *Narratives of Early Virginia*. New York: Barnes and Noble, 1907.

Tyler, Lyon G., ed. "Old Tombstones in Mathews County." *William and Mary Quarterly* 1st Ser., 3 (1895):256–257.

____________. "Formation of a Charter Party." *William and Mary Quarterly* 1st Ser., 4 (1896):242–254.

____________. "Education in Colonial Virginia: Part IV, Higher Education." *William and Mary Quarterly* 1st Ser., 7 (1898):171–187.

____________. "Seawell Family." *William and Mary Quarterly* 1st Ser., 5 (1899–1900):54–62.

____________. "Ransone Family." *William and Mary Quarterly*, 1st Ser., 10 (1902):264–267.

____________. "Virginia Colonial Records," *William and Mary Quarterly* 1st Ser., 15 (1907):39–43.

____________. "Sketches from the Journal of a Confederate Soldier," *Tyler's Quarterly* 6 (1925):29–37.

United States Bureau of the Census (USBC). *Heads of Families at the First Census of the United States, Taken in the Year 1790: Virginia*. Baltimore: Clearfield Company, Inc., 2002.

United States Corps of Engineers. "Transportation Lines of Chesapeake Bay, Serving the Port of Baltimore, Maryland," 1926. Library of Congress, College Park, Maryland.

U.S. Department of Agriculture (USDA). "Status of Virginia Agriculture in 1870," *Report of the Commissioner of Agriculture, 1870*. Washington, D.C.: U.S. Government Printing Office, 1870.

____________. *Abridged List of Federal Laws Applicable to Agriculture, 1949.* James City County Historical Commission, EOC Building, Toano.

____________. *Soil Survey, Mathews County, Virginia*. Richmond: United States Department of Agriculture, Soil Conservation Service, 1958–1962.

United States Geological Survey (USGS). "Mathews" quadrangle, 1916. Rockefeller Library, Colonial Williamsburg Foundation, Williamsburg.

____________. "Kilmarnock" quadrangle, 1917. Rockefeller Library, Colonial Williamsburg Foundation, Williamsburg.

United States Naval War Records Office (USNWRO). *Official Records of the Union and Confederate Navies in the War of the Rebellion.* Washington, D. C.: United States Government Printing Office, 1894–1922.

United States War Department (USWD). *The War of the Rebellion: A Compilation of the Official Records of the Union and Confederate Armies.* Robert N. Scott et al., comp. 128 vols. Washington, D. C.: United States Government Printing Office, 1880–1901.

Van Schreeven, William J. *The Conventions and Constitutions of Virginia, 1776–1966*. Richmond: Virginia State Library, 1967.

Van Schreeven, William J. et al. *Revolutionary Virginia: The Road To Independence.* 8 vols. Charlottesville: University Press of Virginia, 1973–1979.

Verbyla, Elsa Cooke. *Gwynn's Island Times, Items from the Mathews Journal, 1905–1937, the Gloucester-Mathews Gazette-Journal, 1937–1950.* Gloucester: Tidewater Newspapers, Inc., 1998.

Virginia Department of Agriculture and Immigration. *Handbook of Virginia.* Richmond: Department of Agriculture and Immigration, 1923.

Virginia Department of Historic Resources (VDHR). National Register Nomination Forms (various dates); Historic American Buildings Survey Forms; Archaeological Site Survey Forms. Virginia Department of Historic Resources, Richmond.

Virginia Land Office. Patent Books, 1623–1782; Land Grants, 1779–1993. Microfilm on file at Library of Virginia, Richmond, and Rockefeller Library, Colonial Williamsburg Foundation, Williamsburg.

Virginia State Library. *A Hornbook of Virginia History.* Richmond: Library of Virginia, 1965.

Vogel, Janice C. *Then and Now: Mathews County.* Charleston, South Carolina: Arcadia Publishing, 2011.

Walker, R.F., ed. *Acts and Joint Resolutions Passed by the General Assembly at the Session of 1872–1873.* Richmond: Commonwealth of Virginia, 1873.

_____________. *Acts and Joint Resolutions Passed by the General Assembly at the Session of 1874.* Richmond: Commonwealth of Virginia, 1874.

_____________. *Acts and Joint Resolutions Passed by the General Assembly at the Session of 1875–1876.* Richmond: Commonwealth of Virginia, 1876.

Walsh, Lorena S. *From Calabar to Carter's Grove: The History of a Virginia Slave Community.* Charlottesville: University Press of Virginia, 1977.

_____________. *Motives of Honor, Pleasure, & Profit: Plantation Management in the Colonial Chesapeake, 1607–1763.* Chapel Hill: University of North Carolina Press, 2010.

Wharton, James. *The Bounty of the Chesapeake: Fishing in Colonial Virginia.* Charlottesville: University Press of Virginia, 1957.

Washburn, Wilcomb E. *The Governor and the Rebel: A History of Bacon's Rebellion in Virginia.* New York: W. W. Norton, 1972.

White, Mrs. Benjamin Franklin. *Mathews Men Who Served in the War Between the States.* Norfolk: Teagle and Little, Printers, 1961.

White, Robert E. *The History of Providence United Methodist Church, 1849–1978*. Mathews, privately published, 1978.

Wiatt, Alex L. *26th Virginia Infantry*. Lynchburg: H. E. Howard, Inc., 1984.

William and Mary Center for Archaeological Research (WMCAR). *Integrated Management Plan, Mathews County Courthouse Square Historic District (057-0022; 44MT0073), Mathews, Virginia*. Richmond, Virginia: Virginia Department of Historic Resources, 2007.

Williams, Clarence R. "Dr. John Dunn as a Virginia Botanist." *William and Mary Quarterly* 2nd Ser., 15 (1935):109–117.

Williams Family Papers. Williams Family Papers, 1770–1851. Library of Virginia, Richmond.

Williams, John M., comp. *Index to Enrolled Bills of the General Assembly of Virginia, 1776 to 1862*. Richmond: Davis Bottom Superintendent of Public Printing, 1908.

Winfree, Waverley K. *The Laws of Virginia Being a Supplement to Hening's The Statutes at Large*, 1700–1750. Richmond: Virginia State Library, 1971.

Wiseman, Samuel. Samuel Wiseman's Book of Record, 1676–1677. Microfilm, Rockefeller Library, Colonial Williamsburg Foundation, Williamsburg.

Wistar, Isaac Jones. *Autobiography of Isaac Jones Wistar, 1827–1905*. 2 vols. Philadelphia: The Wistar Institute of Anatomy and Biology, 1914.

Withington, Lothrop. *Virginia Gleanings in England*. Baltimore: Genealogical Publishing Company, 1980.

Wood, John. "Chart of the Piankatank." 1817. Library of Virginia, Richmond.

Wood, Peter H. et al. *Powhatan's Mantle: Indians in the Colonial Southeast*. Lincoln, Nebraska: University of Nebraska Press, 1989.

Works Progress Administration (WPA). *Virginia: A Guide to the Old Dominion Compiled by Workers of the Writers Program of the Works Progress Administration in the State of Virginia*. Oxford, England: Oxford University Press, 1940.

Wrike, Peter J. "Mathews County Shipbuilding Patterns, 1780–1860." Master's thesis, Old Dominion University, Norfolk, Virginia, 1990. Facsimile: Mathews Archives, Mathews Memorial Library, Mathews.

York County. Deeds, Orders, Wills, 1672–1691; Judgments and Orders, 1803–1815. York County Courthouse, Yorktown, and Library of Virginia, Richmond. Microfilms, Rockefeller Library, Colonial Williamsburg Foundation, Williamsburg.

Young, Joanne. "The Clerk of Gloucester," *Colonial Williamsburg Journal* Vol. 20 No. 4 (1998): 57–59.

Index

SS→H. Clay